Professional XML for .NET Developers

Dinar Dalvi

Joe Gray

Bipin Joshi

Fredrik Normén

Francis Norton

Andy Olsen

J. Michael Palermo IV

Darshan Singh

John Slater

Kevin Williams

Wrox Press Ltd. ®

Professional XML for .NET Developers

First Published   December 2001

Published by Wrox Press Ltd,
Arden House, 1102 Warwick Road, Acocks Green,
Birmingham. B27 6BH. UK
Printed in the United States
ISBN 1-861005-31-8

Trademark Acknowledgements

Credits

Authors
Dinar Dalvi
Joe Gray
Bipin Joshi
Fredrik Normén
Francis Norton
Andy Olsen
J. Michael Palermo IV
Darshan Singh
John Slater
Kevin Williams

Technical Architect
Amanda Kay

Technical Editors
Phillip Jackson
M.K.L. Lau
Nick Manning
Shivanand Nadkarni

Category Managers
Simon Cox
Dave Galloway

Project Administrator
Beckie Stones

Author Agent
Trish Weir

Indexer
Andrew Criddle

Proof Reader
Chris Smith

Technical Reviewers
Terry Allen
Danny Ayers
Dave Beauchemin
Martin Beaulieu
Maxime Bombardier
Michael Corning
Chris Crane
Doug Dion
Dean Dvorak
Paul Houle
Juan T. Llibre
Anthony Naylor
Johan Normén
Mark Oswald
Jonathan Pinnock
Phil Powers-DeGeorge
J. Andrew Schafer
David Schultz
Andrew Stopford
Adwait Ullal

Production Manager
Liz Toy

Production Co-ordinator
Emma Eato

Illustrations
Emma Eato
Natalie O'Donnell

Cover
Chris Morris

About the Authors

Dinar Dalvi

Dinar was introduced to computers at an early age by his father (Kedar Dalvi) who used to work as a Hardware Engineer. Dinar started off writing code for Unix using C (a pretty interesting project), and then moved to writing Windows applications using VC++, VB, and other Microsoft technologies.

His real interests are in Software Development and applying different methods to enhance the performance of the application. Dinar works as a Senior Software Engineer in the Bay Area, and is responsible for prototyping and developing scalable Internet/Client-Server applications using Microsoft Technologies. About a year and a half ago he was introduced to the .NET Framework, and has been hanging around .NET ever since.

In his spare time (if only there were more than 24 hours a day) he writes and reviews articles for www.asptoday.com and www.csharptoday.com.

> *I would like to thank my wife Pallavi for her patience and encouragement during the writing of the chapters. I would also like to thank the folks at Wrox, for all their help in getting this project done. They are one of the best teams to work with.*

Dinar Dalvi contributed Chapters 1 and 12

Joe Gray

Joe Gray is currently a consultant for Cunningham Consulting, specializing in web-based solutions. Current projects include working on web-based applications written in ASP.NET and C#. He has been a presenter on VB .NET for the MSDN Professional Developers' Chapter Meeting. He has also taught SQL Server, Visual Basic, and XML at a local technical training center. He is an MCSE, MCDBA, MCSD, and CCA. In his personal time, he engages in volunteer educational work along with his wife, Traci, and many of his close friends. He loves to take in a game of golf when time permits.

> *Special thanks to my awesome wife of over 10 years, Traci. Having your support while engaging in projects such as writing is invaluable. Thanks mom and dad for always saying: "You can do it". Thanks Jerry for the homebrew, and thanks Digdug for hanging out with me while writing.*

Joe Gray contributed Chapter 16

Bipin Joshi

Bipin Joshi is a software developer from Mumbai, having skills in Microsoft technologies. Currently he works on .NET technologies with Mastek Ltd. – a global applications outsourcing company having offshore software development centers in India. He runs his personal web site at www.bipinjoshi.com, which provides lots of articles, tutorials, and sourcecode on variety of .NET topics; he can also be reached here. He also contributes regularly to other popular web sites. When away from computers he spends time in deep meditation exploring the Divine.

This work is dedicated to my Buba, Aai, and Bhau (father, mother, and brother). Without their wonderful support and encouragement this would not have been possible.

Bipin Joshi contributed Chapter 11

Fredrik Normén

Fredrik Normén works as a software developer for Density, a Swedish company specializing in Microsoft software solutions. Density's main business area is developing intranet systems for various companies – their intranet solutions being built on its own system platform. Fredrik is one of a team that developed the architecture for this platform and during this time also held .NET seminars for the rest of the company.

Previously, he worked with business-to-business solutions using XML and EDI to exchange business documents.

Fredrik's first experience with computers was in 1986 when he started programming Basic and Assembly. This interest later "converted" from Assembly to C/C++ in early 1993 when he began building Windows applications. In 1997, Fredrik started developing Microsoft DNA solutions, and he is now a Microsoft certified solution developer. The programming languages he uses today are Visual Basic and C#. Fredrik has been studying the Microsoft .NET Framework since August 2000.

Most of his spare time is spent with his girlfriend and his friends. His interests include Hi-Fi and home cinema and he also enjoys spending time in the kitchen.

Fredrik Normén contributed Appendices A and B

Francis Norton

Francis Norton works at iE (http://www.ie.com/) as a senior consultant where he has a special interest in the application of XML technologies to the many challenges of cross-platform retail finance applications. His other interests include running, cooking, travel, and rather too much reading.

I'd like to thank my colleagues and employers at iE for giving me the space and opportunities to pursue my technical interests, especially those who've helped with questions, ideas, and reviews.

I'd also like to thank the Wrox team and technical reviewers for their patience and professionalism.

Francis Norton contributed Chapter 9

Andy Olsen

Andy is a freelance consultant engaged in training, consultancy, and development work in Microsoft .NET and related technologies. Andy studied Physics at Southampton University in England, and began his professional life as a C developer. As the 1990s came and went, Andy migrated into C++, Java, and OO Analysis and Design using UML. Andy has been using Microsoft development tools and technologies since 1987, and has fond memories and many tall stories to tell of times gone by.

Andy now lives by the sea in Swansea, with his wife Jayne, and their children Emily and Thomas. Andy is a keen football and rugby supporter, and enjoys running and skiing (badly).

Andy Olsen contributed Chapters 6 and 7

J. Michael Palermo IV

J. Michael Palermo IV is currently a consultant for Cunningham Consulting – a Microsoft GOLD Certified Partner. His passions for technology are XML, SQL Server, and "*everything* .NET". He is an MCT, MCSE, MCDBA, and MCSD. In his spare time he enjoys teaching OOP concepts to his daughters (five and six years old) and maintaining coral reef aquariums.

> *Once again I want to thank the Wrox team for giving me the opportunity to contribute to such a fabulous title. I also want to express my deep appreciation for Toshia, Izabella, and Sicily for all of their support during this project.*

J. Michael Palermo IV contributed Chapters 8 and 10

Darshan Singh

Darshan Singh is a Senior Developer at InstallShield Software Corporation. He has more than five years of experience as a software developer, and during this period he has worked for Microsoft, Talisma, Persistent Systems Pvt. Ltd. (Pune, India), and Spectrum (India), with major focus on databases and component technologies.

Darshan also manages the XML community web site: www.PerfectXML.com and can be reached at darshan@PerfectXML.com.

> *I would like to thank all the folks at InstallShield, especially Sunny Bajaj for being so supportive and also great fun to work with. My heartfelt thanks go to my sister, Simran and also to my beloved wife, Satwant. Big thanks to the wonderful team at Wrox: Trish Weir, Amanda Kay, Beckie Stones, and Nicholas Manning.*

Darshan Singh contributed Chapter 2 and Appendix C

John Slater

John Slater is a project manager at Management Reports International in Cleveland, OH. At MRI he is currently developing applications for the property management industry. He is currently working on several projects using .NET development tools and .NET Enterprise servers. He can be reached at jr_slater@hotmail.com.

In his free time John enjoys outdoor activities and playing with his children Rachel and Nathan.

I want to thank my wife Beth, for being so supportive of the extra time this project required.

John Slater contributed Chapters 13, 14, and 15

Kevin Williams

Kevin's first experience with computers was at the age of 10 (in 1980) when he took a BASIC class at a local community college on their PDP-9, and by the time he was 12, he stayed up for four days straight, hand-assembling 6502 code on his Atari 400. His professional career has been focused on Windows development – first client-server, then on to Internet work. He's done a little bit of everything, from VB to PowerBuilder to Delphi to C/C++ to MASM to ISAPI, CGI, ASP, HTML, XML, and any other acronym you might care to name, but these days, he's focusing on XML work. Kevin is a Senior System Architect for Equient, an information management company located in Northern Virginia. He may be reached for comment at kevin@realworldxml.com.

Kevin Williams contributed Chapters 3, 4, and 5

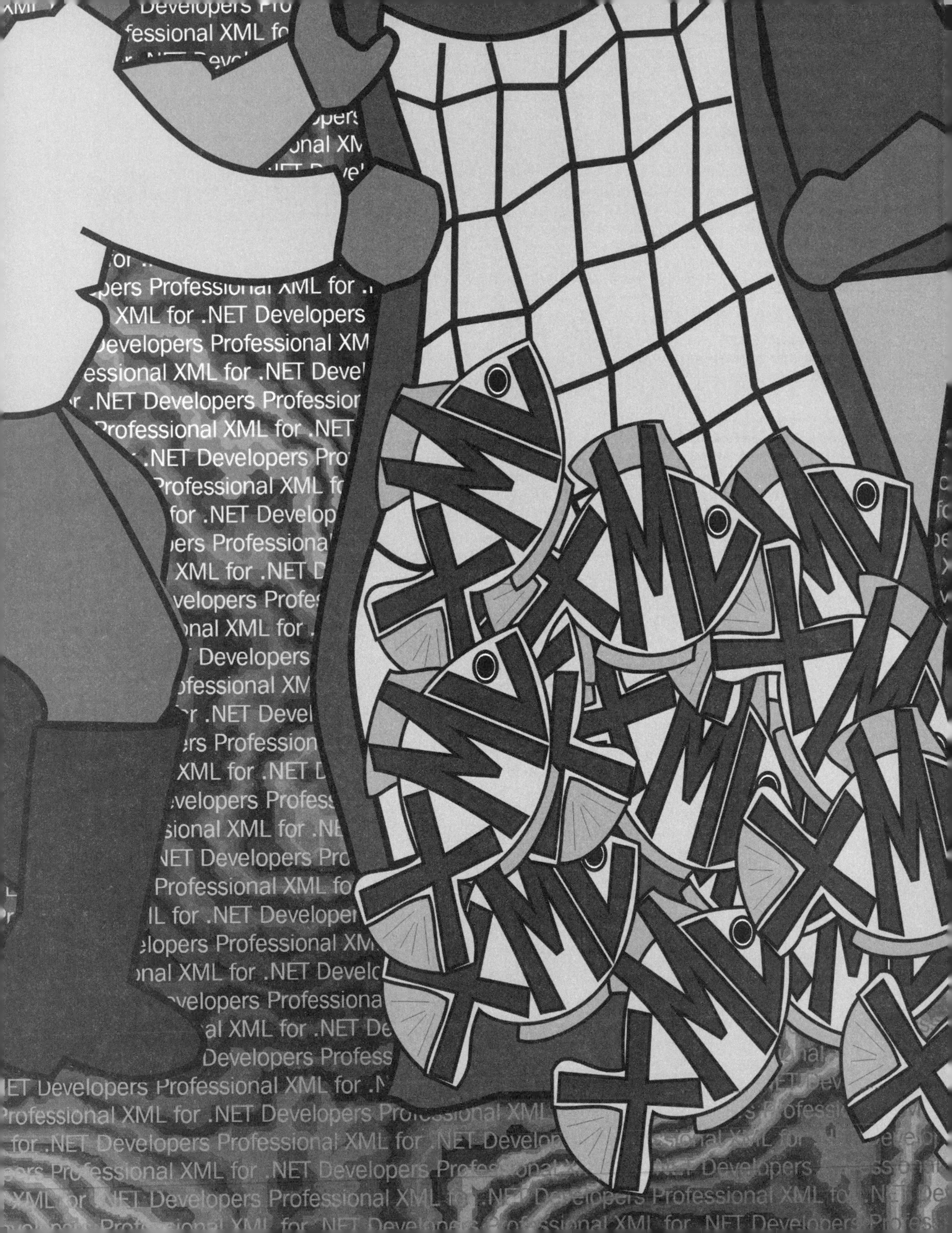
Professional XML for .NET Developers

Table of Contents

Table of Contents

Table of Contents

Table of Contents

Table of Contents

Table of Contents

Table of Contents

Table of Contents

XML for .NET Developers
.NET Developers Professional XML for .NET Developers Professional XML for

Introduction

This book will cover the intersection between two great technologies: .NET and XML.

XML has been a hot topic for some time. The massive industry acceptance of this W3C Recommendation, which allows data communication and information storage in a platform-agnostic manner, has been astounding. XML is seen and used everywhere – from the display of data on various browsers using the transformation language XSLT, to the transport of messages between Web Services using SOAP.

.NET is Microsoft's revolutionary and much vaunted new vision. It allows programming of applications in a language-independent manner, the sharing of code between languages, self-describing classes, and self-documenting program code to name but a few of its capabilities. .NET has been specifically designed with Web Services and ease of development in mind.

To achieve this exciting new programming environment, Microsoft has made extensive use of XML. In fact no other technology is so tightly bound with .NET as XML. It is used as the universal data format for everything from configuration files to metadata, RPC, and object serialization. All the XML capabilities that were formerly available to the programmer through the MSXML parser are now encapsulated in the `System.Xml` namespace of classes, together with added performance, and new and exciting functionality. Connected to this is the new support for XML that ADO.NET has. For example, the programmer now has the ability to access and update data in both hierarchical (XML) and relational (database) form at the same time.

Who Is This Book For?

This book is aimed at intermediate or experienced programmers who have started on their journey towards .NET development and who are already familiar with XML.

While we do introduce the reader to many .NET concepts in Chapter 1, this book is not aimed as a first port of call for the developer looking at .NET, since there are already many books and articles covering this area. Instead we cut straight to the heart of using XML within the .NET Framework. To get the most out of the book, you will have some basic knowledge of, or be learning, either C# or VB .NET. Examples will be given in both languages either within the text or in the code download, wherever possible.

In a similar vein, there are many books and articles that cover the XML technologies that you'll need to use this book. We assume a general knowledge of XML, Namespaces, and XSLT, and a basic knowledge of XML Schemas.

For further information on C#, VB .NET, and XML technologies, check the resources listed in Appendix D.

What Does This Book Cover?

This book looks at how the .NET framework uses XML, and how the developer can utilize the full power of XML within the .NET Framework, and has two main aims:

❑ To give the reader an understanding of the classes within the .NET Framework library that can be used to manipulate XML. For example, reading and writing, validation, and DOM manipulation.

❑ To explain how XML is used by the .NET Framework itself. This includes XML-based configuration files, the use of XML in Remoting and Web Services, and the integration of XML within ADO.NET that allows us extra functionality when dealing with databases.

The following is a more detailed breakdown of the chapters and appendices:

Chapters

1: .NET Framework Overview

In Chapter 1 we aim to give the reader an overview or reminder (depending on their level of existing knowledge) of what the .NET Framework is all about.

We'll look into the .NET Framework, the Common Language Runtime and Common Language Specification. We ask, "What is an Assembly?" and go on to talk about Application Domains and Framework Security. Later on we look at Application Deployment and the .NET languages, C# and VB .NET, before discussing ASP.NET and the various controls available: HTML, Web, Validation, and Mobile controls. Finally we look at the new ADO.NET for database access.

2: XML in the .NET Framework

In Chapter 2, we take a brisk walk through all the XML integration features in the .NET Framework, which we'll look at in more detail throughout the rest of the book.

Microsoft has introduced several new applications of XML in .NET and has also done some innovative work to improve the core XML API. We start with a discussion on the use of XML in configuration files, and look at Startup, Runtime, and Remoting settings. We see how XML, in conjunction with some new ADO.NET features, fixes some of the problems that ADO has. We look at ASP.NET and examine streaming and DOM-based XML classes, before introducing the System.Xml namespace of classes, including the abstract classes XmlReader, and XmlWriter. We take a quick look at DOM, XPath, XSLT, and MSXML in .NET, along with the new C# XML code documentation feature. Finally, we discuss the Framework's support for producing and consuming XML documents.

3: *Reading and Writing XML*

Chapter 3 starts a section of chapters (3 through 7) that look at the functionality contained within the System.Xml namespace in more detail.

In particular, here we look at the fast, forward-only mechanisms provided by the .NET Framework for reading and writing XML documents, namely the XmlReader and XmlWriter abstract classes. We explore the XmlTextReader and XmlTextWriter classes, which are derived from these abstract classes. We go on to discuss node order, whitespace, entity and namespace handling, and other namespace support.

4: *DOM Navigation of XML*

In Chapter 4 we look at the DOM functionality in the .NET framework provided within the System.Xml namespace of classes. We look at opening documents from URLs, files, or strings in memory, and searching and accessing the contents of these documents, before serializing them back out to XML strings. We also take a look at the differences between the XmlDocument object and the XmlReader and XmlWriter abstract classes, and where using each is more appropriate. Finally, we create a class derived from the XmlDocument class, to show how easy it is to add functionality to the classes in the .NET framework.

5: *XSL Transformations of XML*

The .NET framework provides robust support for XSLT and XPath processing. In Chapter 5 we look at the technologies used for XSL transformations in the .NET Framework, namely the System.Xml.Xsl and System.Xml.XPath namespaces, as well as the XslTransform class. The .NET Framework fully supports the XSLT and XPath specifications as defined by the W3C, but also provides many helpful extensions to these specifications, which enhance the usability of stylesheets within .NET applications. We look at using embedded scripting with <msxsl:script> for transforming XML documents and how to extend stylesheets with extension objects. We also discuss XPathDocument objects. Towards the end of the chapter we look at tuning XSL transformations for performance, smart pipelining, and finally other XPath functions.

6: *Validating XML*

In Chapter 6 we take look at the different options for the XML validation grammars: DTDs, XDR schemas, and XSD schemas. We go on to look at all the ways we can create an XSD Schema in Visual Studio .NET: using the XML Designer, from a Database, using the XSD Generator, from an XML Document, from an XDR Schema, or from an Assembly. We discuss the Schema Object and see how we can link XML documents to DTDs, XDR schemas, and XSD schemas, and how to then perform validation using the XmlValidatingReader object from the System.Xml namespace. We look at using XmlSchemaCollection to keep a cache of schemas in memory, to optimize performance, and also deal with unqualified/namespace-qualified content in XML documents.

7: *Serializing XML*

In Chapter 7 we look at serializing objects as XML data using the XmlSerializer class from the System.Xml.Serialization namespace. More specifically we create serializers, and then serialize and deserialize complex objects, properties, enumeration values, arrays, and composite objects. We look at serializing and deserializing with inheritance, followed by formatting XML elements, XML attributes, and text content. Towards the end of the chapter we look at using XSD schemas with serialization and mapping XSD types to Common Language Runtime types. Finally we investigate serializing complex object graphs.

8: MSXML

By Chapter 8 we will already have explored most of the classes provided within the `System.Xml` namespace of the .NET Framework library. So, in Chapter 8, we explore the pre-.NET Microsoft XML API provided in MSXML. We look at this from various standpoints before discussing how some MSXML objects compare to related objects in .NET. We look at MSXML's `DOMDocument` and `FreeThreadedDOMDocument`, and then compare the methods of MSXML's `DOMDocument` to .NET's `XmlDocument`. We demonstrate how to use the classes in the .NET `System.Net` namespace that perform similarly to the MSXML `XMLHTTP` object. Similarly we compare MSXML's `XSLTemplate` (using it in JavaScript), to .NET's `XslTransform`. We compare SAX (which, although available in MSXML, is not directly available within .NET) to DOM and `XmlReader`. Finally we cover using Runtime Callable Wrappers for when we need to use MSXML from within .NET code.

9: Extending XmlReader and XmlWriter

In Chapter 9 we look at extending the `XmlReader` and `XmlWriter` abstract classes we first looked at in detail in Chapter 3, to communicate the grammar specified in a schema. More specifically, we use the extended classes and Runtime Callable Wrappers to enable an application to translate between an XML document, a Microsoft Visio diagram, and a table in a Microsoft Word document.

10: ADO.NET

In Chapter 10 we start to move away from the realm of the `System.Xml` namespace of classes, to explore the broader picture of how XML is used in .NET.

Chapter 10 looks at the role of XML in ADO.NET, and compares ADO.NET with ADO. We cover the capabilities of the new `DataSet` class, including reading and writing XML, and programmatically accessing or changing its XML representation. We highlight how to synchronize `DataSets` with `XmlDataDocuments` (derived from the `XmlDocument` class), and why we would do so. We also cover the advantages of strongly typed `DataSets`. Finally we take a glimpse at how to access some of the XML features available with SQL Server 2000.

11: ASP.NET

In Chapter 11 we examine what ASP.NET is, its compatibility with ASP, and how ASP.NET and XML are related to one another. We look at Server-side and Web controls, as well as error handling and tracing. We see how we can use the `XML` control to display XML from either a file or an `XmlDocument` object, and use the `DataGrid` control to display complex XML documents. Other topics we look at are server-side caching, authentication, authorization, configuration, and deployment. We study the location, structure, and different sections of the XML configuration document `web.config`, before finally looking at custom errors, HTTP handlers, and HTTP modules.

12: Case Study: Using ASP.NET and ADO.NET

In this case study we create an online DVD rental system, and demonstrate how the application can be implemented without large chunks of complicated code. In particular, we look at features of ASP.NET and server-side controls, how to open database connections using ADO.NET, reading data in XML format, and how ADO.NET has a built-in support for XML. We look at the design and other technical requirements, before seeing how we can add new sections and edit rows, and then using server-side XSL, make the application browser-independent.

13: Web Services and SOAP

In Chapter 13 we explore the new world of .NET Web Services, and how they use XML technologies. We show how to build a simple Web Service in Visual Studio .NET, and discuss the protocols used by Web Services, namely HTTP GET/POST and SOAP. As an example we create our own "Stock Quote" Web Service. We look at proxy code, Web Service directories, the businessEntity and businessService structures, the XML-based Web Service Description Language (WSDL), and using the Session and Application objects. Finally we look at deployment and design considerations, and the difference between synchronous and asynchronous Web Services.

14: Case Study: Using Web Services

In this Case Study we create a sample Web Service providing calendar features. We walk through the Web Service's conceptual design including use-cases and functional requirements. We then create and discus a simple database to support our calendar application. The focus of this chapter is on coding the Web Service and its constituent methods. Finally we will build a simple ASP.NET client application to consume the Web Service.

15: Remoting Overview

In Chapter 15 we discuss the remoting basics, followed by object activation on both the client and the server. We cover how remote objects are instantiated and activated and our options for controlling that behavior, as well as discussing how .NET accomplishes remoting using local proxies that represent remote objects. We cover the basics of creating a .NET remoting application including building simple client and server applications, before looking at the objRef class, lifetime leases, remoting and registering channels, and the HTTP and TCP channels.

16: C# Code Documentation

In this final chapter, Chapter 16, we look at the advantages of XML code documentation in C#. We look at how to compile commented code at the command line with the /doc:filename option, as well as the compiler warnings and the /incremental option. We then move on to look at compiling commented C# code in Visual Studio .NET, and an in-depth look at the various compiler-supplied elements and attributes. The next part of the chapter looks at making practical use of comments, the best practices for them, and comments for public and non-public types and members. We then look at transformations to turn our XML into a more readable help file, followed by a sample transformation application and the associated XSLT stylesheet. We end by looking at other considerations such as how Visual Studio .NET provides us with web-based documentation based on our use of the XML documentation tags.

Appendices

A: System.Xml

In Appendix A we look at the System.Xml namespace, and take an overview of System.Xml classes. This namespace, the overall namespace for the XML classes, deals with the functionality of accessing, navigating, and maintaining XML data.

B: System.Xml.Xsl and System.Xml.XPath

In Appendix B we look at the commonly used namespaces System.Xml.Xsl and System.Xml.XPath. These namespaces deal with XSL transformations and navigation of XML documents, respectively.

C: .NET Glossary

Appendix C is a useful reference explaining the meaning of many of the .NET terms.

D: Resources

Appendix D is a helpful list of the URLs and titles referenced throughout this book, for further reading, and downloading products and code.

What You Need to Use This Book

To run the examples used in this book, you will need to install the .NET Framework. You can order a copy of the Framework on CD-ROM, or download it from the Microsoft web site.

> *At the time of writing, the .NET Framework was at Beta 2 version, but any amendments will be posted on the Wrox web site http://www.wrox.com/.*

Most code can be written using you favorite text editor and compiled from the command line using the tools provided with the .NET Framework. However, you may also want to use Visual Studio .NET to create and compile your code: this is currently in Beta 2 and can be downloaded from http://msdn.microsoft.com/vstudio/nextgen/beta.asp.

Where chapters require other software, it is mentioned explicitly. In particular:

❑ Some of the code in Chapters 10, 12, and 14 needs SQL Server 2000. A 120-day trial version for this software can be downloaded from http://www.microsoft.com/sql/.

❑ Chapter 9 *Customizing Abstract Classes* uses Microsoft Word and Microsoft Visio. However, the example will work with just Microsoft Word, but with more limited functionality.

The code included in this book can be downloaded from http://www.wrox.com/. More details are given in the *Customer Support* section below.

Conventions

To help you get the most from the text and keep track of what's happening, we've used a number of conventions throughout the book.

For instance:

> **These boxes hold important, not-to-be forgotten information, which is directly relevant to the surrounding text.**

In comparison, this style is used for asides to the current discussion.

As for styles in the text:

- ❑ When we introduce important words, we **highlight** them

- ❑ We show keyboard strokes like this: *Ctrl-Alt-Delete*

- ❑ We show filenames, and code within the text like so: `sample.cs`

- ❑ Text on user interfaces is shown as: File | Save

- ❑ URLs are shown in a similar font, as so: http://www.wrox.com/

- ❑ Namespace URIs, however, are shown like this: `http://www.w3.org/2001/XMLSchema`

- ❑ When referring to chapter sections or titles, we italicize it, as so: *Introduction*

We present code in two different ways. Code that is new or important is shown like this:

```
In our code examples, the code foreground style shows
new, important, and pertinent code
```

Code that is an aside, or has been seen before is shown as so:

```
Code background shows code that's less important in the present context,
or that has been seen before.
```

In addition, when something is to be typed at a command line interface (for example, a DOS/Command prompt), then we use the following style to show what is typed:

> csc.exe /t:exe /out:example.CS.exe example.CS

Customer Support

We always value hearing from our readers, and we want to know what you think about this book: what you liked, what you didn't like, and what you think we can do better next time. You can send us your comments, either by returning the reply card in the back of the book, or by e-mail to feedback@wrox.com. Please be sure to mention the book title in your message.

How to Download the Sample Code for the Book

When you visit the Wrox site, http://www.wrox.com/, simply locate the title through our Search facility or by using one of the title lists. Click on Download in the Code column, or on Download Code on the book's detail page.

The files that are available for download from our site have been archived using WinZip. When you have saved the attachments to a folder on your hard-drive, you need to extract the files using a de-compression program such as WinZip or PKUnzip. When you extract the files, the code is usually extracted into chapter folders. When you start the extraction process, ensure your software (WinZip, PKUnzip, etc.) is set to use folder names.

Errata

We've made every effort to make sure that there are no errors in the text or in the code. However, no one is perfect and mistakes do occur. If you find an error in one of our books, like a spelling mistake or a faulty piece of code, we would be very grateful for feedback. By sending in errata you may save another reader hours of frustration, and of course, you will be helping us provide even higher quality information. Simply e-mail the information to support@wrox.com. Your information will be checked and, if correct, posted to the errata page for that title, or used in subsequent editions of the book.

To find errata on the web site, go to http://www.wrox.com/, and simply locate the title through our Advanced Search or title list. Click on the Book Errata link, which is below the cover graphic on the book's detail page.

E-mail Support

If you wish to directly query a problem in the book with an expert who knows the book in detail then e-mail support@wrox.com, with the title of the book and the last four numbers of the ISBN in the subject field of the e-mail. A typical e-mail should include the following things:

- ❏ The **title of the book**, **last four digits of the ISBN**, and **page number** of the problem in the Subject field.

- ❏ Your **name**, **contact information**, and the **problem** in the body of the message.

We *won't* send you junk mail. We need the details to save your time and ours. When you send an e-mail message, it will go through the following chain of support:

- ❏ Customer Support – Your message is delivered to our customer support staff, who are the first people to read it. They have files on most frequently asked questions and will answer anything general about the book or the web site immediately.

- ❏ Editorial – Deeper queries are forwarded to the technical editor responsible for that book. They have experience with the programming language or particular product, and are able to answer detailed technical questions on the subject.

- ❏ The Authors – Finally, in the unlikely event that the editor cannot answer your problem, they will forward the request to the author. We do try to protect the author from any distractions to their writing; however, we are quite happy to forward specific requests to them. All Wrox authors help with the support on their books. They will e-mail the customer and the editor with their response, and again all readers should benefit.

The Wrox Support process can only offer support to issues that are directly pertinent to the content of our published title. Support for questions that fall outside the scope of normal book support is provided via the community lists of our http://p2p.wrox.com/ forum.

p2p.wrox.com

For author and peer discussion join the P2P mailing lists. Our unique system provides **programmer to programmer™** contact on mailing lists, forums, and newsgroups, all in addition to our one-to-one e-mail support system. If you post a query to P2P, you can be confident that it is being examined by the many Wrox authors and other industry experts who are present on our mailing lists. At p2p.wrox.com you will find a large number of different lists that will help you, not only while you read this book, but also as you develop your own applications. Particularly appropriate to this book are the xml, ado_dotnet, aspx, dotnet_webservices, c_sharp, and vb_dotnet lists.

To subscribe to a mailing list just follow these steps:

1. Go to http://p2p.wrox.com/.

2. Choose the appropriate category from the left menu bar.

3. Click on the mailing list you wish to join.

4. Follow the instructions to subscribe and fill in your e-mail address and password.

5. Reply to the confirmation e-mail you receive.

6. Use the subscription manager to join more lists and set your e-mail preferences.

Why this System Offers the Best Support

When you join a mailing list you can choose to receive individual e-mails as they are posted, to receive a daily digest of messages, or to receive no e-mail at all and to just read/reply via the web site. You can also search our online archives. Junk and spam mails are deleted, so that only relevant content is sent to you. Queries about joining or leaving lists, and any other general queries, should be sent to listsupport@p2p.wrox.com.

1

.NET Framework Overview

In July 2000, Microsoft introduced the .NET initiative, which is a major technology shift for it. With the .NET platform, Microsoft is reinventing itself by moving away from COM-based technology into a more distributed, open, and dynamic environment. Not to worry, .NET supports backward compatibility with COM and COM+. COM and COM + will stay in business for at least a while. This time Microsoft intends to give the programmers the best of all programming technologies, and to make the development of applications much easier.

The initiative for .NET is broad-based and very ambitious. The .NET framework encompasses programming languages and an execution platform, as well as intensive class libraries providing built-in functionality. .NET means changes for everyone who uses Microsoft technologies. VB programmers get the Object-Orientated Programming (OOP) features they have been wanting for years. Many other languages get the drag-and-drop features seen in VB and VC++. Also introduced in .NET is a new language called C# (pronounced C Sharp). New technologies like: Universal Description, Discovery, and Integration (UDDI); Web Services support; and complete built-in support for XML, are also included within .NET.

Before delving into the chapter further, let us quickly define its scope – it is meant as a rapid overview of the .NET Framework for those who are already somewhat familiar with it. Readers who already feel at home with .NET may want to just skim the pages, or to even skip to Chapter 2, which looks in more detail at how XML and .NET go hand-in-hand.

In outline, this chapter includes:

- ❑ An overview of the different components that make up the Framework, including the **Common Language Runtime** (**CLR**), **Common Language Specification** (**CLS**), **Common Type System** (**CTS**), and Framework classes.
- ❑ A brief look at the different languages of the Framework, such as VB .NET and C#.
- ❑ A summary of different technologies, such as ASP.NET and ADO.NET, and how they fit into the Framework.

.NET Framework

The .NET Framework is a new computing platform designed to simplify application development in the highly distributed environment of the Internet. The Framework covers all the layers of software development above the operating system, providing a rich level of integration between different layers, such as presentation technologies, component technologies, and data technologies. The framework is actually a wrapper over the operating system, insulating the developer from the OS specifics, such as memory allocation and file handling. With this, the applications developed on the .NET framework may be portable to multiple platforms and hardware. The catch is that there is a need to develop .NET language compilers for different platforms.

The .NET Framework has two main components: the CLR and the .NET Framework Class libraries. Other associated components include the languages (such as C#) and other technologies, such as ADO.NET and ASP.NET. We'll take a look at each of these components in the rest of this chapter.

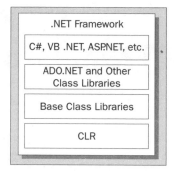

Common Language Runtime

The CLR is the foundation of the .NET Framework. It acts as an agent that:

- ❑ Loads and manages the code at execution time.
- ❑ Provides core services like memory management, thread management, and Remoting.

Code management is the fundamental principle of the Runtime.

When compiling code, the compiler translates the source code into **Microsoft Intermediate Language** (**MSIL**, or just **IL**), which is a CPU-independent set of instructions. MSIL includes instructions for loading, storing, initializing, and calling methods on objects, as well as instructions for arithmetic and logical operations, control flow, direct memory access, exception handling, and other operations.

Before code can be executed, MSIL must be converted to CPU-specific code by a **Just-in-Time** (**JIT**) **Compiler**. As the Runtime supplies one or more JIT compilers for each computer architecture it supports, the same set of MSIL can be JIT-compiled and executed on any supported architecture.

When a compiler produces MSIL, it also produces **meta data**. Meta data describes the types in the code, including the definition of each type, the signatures of each type's members, the members that the code references, and other data that the runtime uses at execution time. The presence of meta data in the file along with the MSIL enables the code to describe itself, which means that there is no need for type libraries or **Interface Definition Language** (**IDL**). The CLR locates and extracts the meta data from the file as needed during execution.

The runtime consists of MSCOREE.DLL and MSCORLIB.DLL, which are the heart of the CLR.

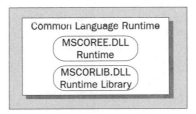

❑   MSCOREE.DLL compiles the MSIL code into machine code before it is executed. MSCOREE.DLL is also responsible for allocating and de-allocating memory objects and security management.

❑   MSCORLIB.DLL contains the core system library, which every CLR based application relies on.

The best way to understand the working of the CLR is to see what happens when the code is compiled. The picture below shows the execution process for a typical .NET program.

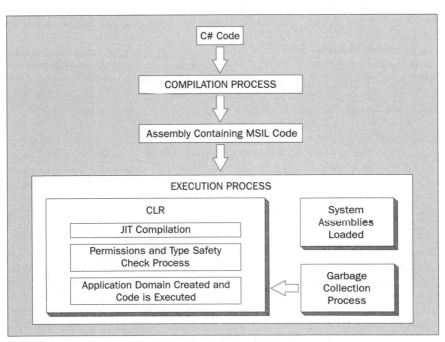

Let us try to understand the execution process in detail. For our example, we write our example code in C#; but before the code is executed it must be compiled. The .NET C# compiler compiles the code into the MSIL language within an assembly – we'll look at assemblies in more detail shortly.

The next steps are to JIT compile the code from MSIL into **machine code** or **assembly language**, check the type safety, create a domain for the code, and execute the code. (Application domains will also be covered in more detail in a later section.) This compilation process happens only once, that is, the first time. Subsequent times, the code is not generally compiled again – but if the JIT compiler finds a mismatch in the hash or the meta data, then the code is compiled again. Once the code is compiled into the assembly language, the entry point addresses are updated with the address of the compiled code. So now the Runtime is all set to execute the application.

Let us see how the execution process works. When the program is executed, the Runtime loads all the Assemblies needed for the execution of our code. Then the Runtime loads our Assembly, which contains the entry code. The hash is verified for any potential tampering. Meta data is read to get the type information and ensures that the Runtime can load the assembly. The permissions for the assembly are checked. This is done to find out if the assembly is trying to access System resources like the Registry, or trying to write a file onto the system. The Runtime checks with the security policy that the account under which the program is going to run is validated for proper permissions. The Runtime then checks if memory allocation can be managed for the assembly. This is very important when creating the Application Domains (which is explained in the following sections). The runtime permits multiple applications to be run under the same process. The Runtime may refuse to run the code if the code is unsafe to run under the Local Security Policy. A process for the code is created with the Application Domain inside the process. If a program needs to run under an existing process, then only a new Application Domain is created.

Now the code execution begins. The Runtime is busy doing the memory management. The memory usage is monitored. If the **Garbage Collection** (**GC**) process is to be initiated to free the unused memory, the Runtime stops the execution and runs the GC. (More information on garbage collection follows in a later section.)

We just saw how the Runtime works – let us now look at some programming features of the Runtime. The Runtime supports a wide range of programming features, but not all the language compilers will support all the programming features supported by the CLR. To make a seamless integration between components compiled using different compilers, a subset of CLR is defined. The subset is called the **Common Language System** (**CLS**) and will be explained in the following sections.

The concept of code management is fundamental to the .NET Runtime. Compilers and tools expose the Runtime's functionality and enable us to write code that benefits from this managed execution environment. Code that targets the Runtime is called **managed code**; code that does not target the Runtime is known as **unmanaged code**. Managed code is explained in the following section.

Managed Code

Managed code benefits from features such as cross-language integration, cross-language exception handling, enhanced security, versioning and deployment support, a simplified model for component interaction, debugging, and profiling services. To use these provided services, the language compilers must generate meta data. Meta data describes the types, members, and references in our code, and is stored with the compiled MSIL code; every loadable common language runtime image contains meta data. The Runtime uses meta data to locate and load classes, lay out instances in memory, resolve method invocations, generate native code, enforce security, and set run-time context boundaries. The Runtime automatically handles object layout and manages references to objects, releasing them when they are no longer being used. Objects whose lifetimes are managed in this way are called **managed data**.

Automatic memory management eliminates memory leaks, as well as some other common programming errors. If the code is managed, then managed data, unmanaged data, or both managed and unmanaged data can be used in the .NET application. As the language compilers supply their own types, such as primitive types, we need not know if the data is managed or not.

Managed code is code written to target the runtime services. In order to use the runtime services the code must provide a minimum level of information in the meta data to the Runtime. Code written in C#, VB .NET and ASP.NET is managed by default, but VC++ .NET code is not. However, the compiler can produce managed code for VC++ .NET by using the command-line switch /CLR.

As we said earlier, managed data is the data that is allocated and unallocated by the CLR's garbage collector. C#, VB .NET, and ASP.NET data is managed by default. VC++ .NET data is not managed by default. When using managed extensions for VC++ .NET, a class can be marked as managed by using the _gc keyword.

> **Note: Managed classes can only inherit from one base class.**

Common Language Specification (CLS)

The CLR supports a wide range of programming features. But not all language compilers will expose all the features supported by the CLR. To make a seamless integration, a subset of the CLR is defined called **Common Language Specification** (**CLS**). As the name suggests, the compilers or the programming language must expose the types within the CLS in order to run on the CLR.

In simple terms, it means that all the public types and their methods are CLS compliant. The private types and their methods may not be CLS compliant, as they are not exposed to the CLR. The attribute that ensures all the public types follow CLS rules is [assembly:System.CLSCompliant]. For example, we can apply a CLSCompliant attribute to the entire assembly:

```
using System;
[assembly:CLSCompliant(true)]
```

> **Note that when building the assembly, if the CLSCompliant Attribute is not used, then the assembly is not CLS compliant by default.**

As it is a multi-language execution environment, the Runtime supports a wide variety of data types and language features. The language compiler determines which features are available and we can design and write code using those available features. The code syntax is determined by the compiler and not by the Runtime. If a component must be completely reusable by other components written in other languages, then the component must expose the features provided in the CLS. The CLR makes the design of components and applications easy. Objects written in different languages can communicate with each other, and their behaviors can be tightly integrated. This is called **cross-language integration**.

For example, we may define a class in C# and use VB. NET to derive a class from the original C# class, or call method(s) on the original class.

For inter-portability purposes, the CLR has a **Common Type System** (**CTS**), which follows the Runtime's rules for defining new types, as well as for creating, using, persisting, and binding to types. The CTS deserves a separate section, which we'll see shortly.

The meta data for managed components carries information about the components and resources they were built against. This information is used by the Runtime to ensure that the component or the application has the specified versions of everything it needs to run. Language compilers and tools expose the Runtime's functionality in ways that are intended to be useful and intuitive to their developers. The experience of the Runtime depends on the language or the tool used.

Let us take an example. Variables named `Myvar` and `MyVar` are different in C# and C++ as they are case-sensitive languages. But as VB. NET is not a case-sensitive language, these variables mean the same in that language. Now the CLS has a workaround here. The specifications say that CLS compliant code should not expose the names of variables if they differ only in their case.

> **We can write applications that are not CLS compliant. However, the compiled MSIL code is not guaranteed to be language independent.**

All the rules that apply to the common type system apply to the CLS; there are some stricter rules that are defined in the CLS. The CLS helps enhance and ensure language interoperability by defining a set of features that developers can rely on being available in a wide variety of languages. If our component uses only CLS features in the API that it exposes to other code (including derived classes), the component is guaranteed to be accessible from any programming language that supports the CLS. Components that are written using the CLS rules and use only the features included in the CLS are said to be **CLS-compliant components**.

MSIL shares the byte code concept with Java. Java byte code provides platform independence. The file containing byte code can be placed on any platform, for example UNIX or Windows. At run time the code is compiled by a compiler running on a particular platform. In the case of .NET, the code gets compiled into the native machine code. MSIL wants the code to be language *and* platform independent. There is an opportunity for different vendors to develop .NET compilers for a variety of platforms. The idea is to be able to write and compile code in any language that supports MSIL syntax, and that the code should work with any code compiled through other language compilers.

CLR provides support for language interoperability called **Cross Language Interportability** (**CLI**). This means that code written in one language can be used by an application written in a different language. To fully interact with other objects, regardless of the language they were implemented in, objects must expose to callers only those features that are common to all the languages. Let us see with an example how CLI works.

Say we write an assembly in C# that overrides the `ToString()` method. Then we write a calling program in C# and VB .NET that uses the C# assembly. The overridable method is exposed to these languages. However, our task is to make this assembly work with *any* language, so we choose VB 6.0 as our calling application. We make a `.TLB` using `Regasm.exe`. Then we write a VB 6.0 calling program. We include the `.TLB` in our VB 6.0 program and try to use the overridable `ToString()` function. This function is not available to the VB 6.0 application, as the VB 6.0 runtime does not support the `override` property for `ToString()`.

Writing CLS Compliant Code

To extend the benefits provided by the Runtime, one must choose from the compilers that target the Runtime. The CLR can be a target platform for languages ranging from COBOL and Fortran, to OO Languages like C#, VB .NET, Visual C++ .NET, and from these to scripting languages like JScript .NET, Perl, Python, etc.

Writing a CLS compliant program without the tool is difficult, as we might not have access to all the CLS features exposed.

Common Type System (CTS)

The CTS defines how types are declared, used, and managed in the Runtime, and is an important part of the Runtime's support for cross-language integration. Different languages use different keywords to use the CTS types. For example, in VB Integer will be converted to System.Int32 at compile time, and in C# int will be converted to System.Int32 at compile time. A seamless inter-portability between VB .NET and C# is possible because both comply with the CLS standards. (We need not declare the type as int or Integer, but can use the System.Int32 namespace.)

Let us look at the CTS Type specification:

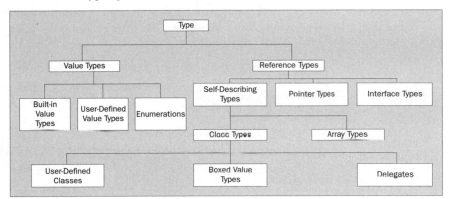

❑   Value types can be built-in types (for example: Integer), user-defined types, or enumerations.

❑   Reference types consist of Classes, self-describing types, pointer types, and interface types. They are further split into arrays and class types. Class types are user-defined classes, boxed value types, and delegates. All delegates inherit from System.Delegate. Classes have the following characteristics: sealed, implements, abstract, inherits. Arrays are derived from System.Array object. They are also called vectors (Java resemblance). Zero dimensional arrays are not permitted. Pointers supported in .NET are managed pointers, unmanaged pointers, and unmanaged function pointers.

Garbage Collection

The garbage collector is .NET's answer to memory management, in particular to reclaiming the memory that is no longer used by any applications. Before .NET, the methods used were manual memory management or having the objects maintain reference counts themselves.

Periodically the program will be paused to do a garbage collection. The namespace used is System.GC. When the garbage collector is run, the system looks through the global variables and stack to determine which objects are currently being referenced. The system also checks whether the objects themselves are correctly referenced to account for linked lists and other linked data structures. The objects that are not in use are freed (if they don't need finalization) or put in a list for finalization. This extra step for finalization is the biggest reason to avoid writing finalizers we do not need. After the objects are finalized, they are freed in some future garbage collection. The Finalize() method is called automatically when the Runtime determines that the object is no longer needed.

Class instances may control resources that are not managed by the CLR, like Windows handles and database connections. As the CLR garbage collector does not manage these resources, running low on these resources will not trigger the garbage collector to run, and so recover the resources. To make it possible for these resources to be recovered as soon as possible, these objects should implement the `IDisposable` interface. `IDisposable` has one method, `Dispose()`, which should be called when we have finished using the object. Implementing `Dispose()` will then free whatever resources are held by objects that are not managed by the Runtime.

What is an Assembly?

Assemblies are the building blocks of .NET Framework applications; they form the fundamental unit of deployment, version control, reuse, and security permissions. They are self-describing through metadata called a manifest, and contain the code that the Runtime executes.

An assembly is a collection of types and resources that are built to work together and form a logical unit of functionality. It provides the common language runtime with the information it needs to be aware of type implementations. Each assembly can have only one entry point.

In traditional Windows programming, we wrote reusable code in the form of a DLL or a COM component. However, when C# code is compiled, the compiler does not emit assembly language, but Intermediate Language. In fact, the compiler does more; it emits IL packaged into an Assembly. The same thing happens when we compile the code into a library. Therefore, the assembly can be a DLL, EXE file, or combination of both. An assembly can be a single file or a number of files.

Assembly Manifest

The Assembly Manifest consists of the assembly name, version number, culture, and strong-name information making up the assembly's identity. To view the contents of an assembly manifest programmatically use the `System.Reflection` namespace. The Assembly manifest consists of the following:

Assembly Information	Description
Assembly name	Assembly identity or text detailing the assembly's name.
Version number	A major and minor version number, and a revision and build number. These numbers are used by the Runtime to enforce the version policy.
Culture	Information on the language the assembly supports. This information must be used to designate an assembly as a satellite assembly containing culture- or language-specific information. Note: An assembly containing culture information is automatically considered as a satellite assembly.
Strong-name information	If the assembly is signed with a strong name the manifest contains the public key from the creator.

Assembly Information	Description
List of all files in the assembly	A hash and the filename for each file contained in the assembly. This happens if an assembly consists of more than one file. Note that all files, which make up the assembly, must be in the same directory as the file containing the assembly manifest.
Type reference information	Information used by the Runtime to map a type reference to the file that contains its declaration and implementation. This is used for types that are exported from the assembly.
Information on referenced assemblies	Names and hashes of the other assemblies that this assembly in turn needs to reference.

There are many ways to create assemblies. We can use development tools, like Visual Studio .NET. We can use tools provided in the .NET Framework SDK to create assemblies with modules created in other development environments. CLR APIs, such as `Reflection.Emit`, can be used to create dynamic assemblies.

Because Assemblies are self-describing, XCOPY deployment makes a zero impact.

The following screenshot displays the Xcopy Syntax:

```
C:\WINNT\System32\cmd.exe                                              _ □ X

D:\>Xcopy /?
Copies files and directory trees.

XCOPY source [destination] [/A | /M] [/D[:date]] [/P] [/S [/E]] [/V] [/W]
                           [/C] [/I] [/Q] [/F] [/L] [/H] [/R] [/T] [/U]
                           [/K] [/N] [/O] [/X] [/Y] [/-Y] [/Z]
                           [/EXCLUDE:file1[+file2][+file3]...]

  source       Specifies the file(s) to copy.
  destination  Specifies the location and/or name of new files.
  /A           Copies only files with the archive attribute set,
               doesn't change the attribute.
  /M           Copies only files with the archive attribute set,
               turns off the archive attribute.
  /D:m-d-y     Copies files changed on or after the specified date.
               If no date is given, copies only those files whose
               source time is newer than the destination time.
  /EXCLUDE:file1[+file2][+file3]...
               Specifies a list of files containing strings.  When any of the
               strings match any part of the absolute path of the file to be
               copied, that file will be excluded from being copied.  For
               example, specifying a string like \obj\ or .obj will exclude
               all files underneath the directory obj or all files with the
               .obj extension respectively.
  /P           Prompts you before creating each destination file.
  /S           Copies directories and subdirectories except empty ones.
  /E           Copies directories and subdirectories, including empty ones.
               Same as /S /E. May be used to modify /T.
  /V           Verifies each new file.
  /W           Prompts you to press a key before copying.
  /C           Continues copying even if errors occur.
  /I           If destination does not exist and copying more than one file,
               assumes that destination must be a directory.
  /Q           Does not display file names while copying.
  /F           Displays full source and destination file names while copying.
  /L           Displays files that would be copied.
  /H           Copies hidden and system files also.
  /R           Overwrites read-only files.
  /T           Creates directory structure, but does not copy files. Does not
               include empty directories or subdirectories. /T /E includes
               empty directories and subdirectories.
  /U           Copies only files that already exist in destination.
  /K           Copies attributes. Normal Xcopy will reset read-only attributes.
  /N           Copies using the generated short names.
  /O           Copies file ownership and ACL information.
  /X           Copies file audit settings (implies /O).
  /Y           Suppresses prompting to confirm you want to overwrite an
               existing destination file.
  /-Y          Causes prompting to confirm you want to overwrite an
               existing destination file.
  /Z           Copies networked files in restartable mode.

The switch /Y may be preset in the COPYCMD environment variable.
This may be overridden with /-Y on the command line.

D:\>
```

Private Assembly

By default, when we compile a C# or a VB .NET program, the assembly produced will be a private assembly. This suggests that it is going to be used by one application. Note that the private assembly must be placed in the same folder on the Windows file system as the calling application or in a subfolder. This assembly is not visible to any other application on the file system. If there is an application that uses many private assemblies, then all those assemblies will have to be distributed with the application. Creating a private assembly is easy since there is no worry over the naming problem. The only point to remember is that the name must be unique in your application.

Shared Assembly

A shared assembly is one that is used by multiple applications. Shared assemblies have some additional requirements to solve the sharing problem. Why do we need a shared assembly? Say we have written a generic library or perhaps some Windows Forms WebForms controls which you want to sell for generic use. If the assembly needs to be shared, then the naming requirements are stricter. The name must be unique across the entire system.

Shared assemblies are typically deployed in the Global Assembly Cache also known as GAC. The global assembly cache is a machine-wide store for shared assembly, which is found on the `WINNT\assembly` (or equivalent) folder on the drive.

Assembly Versioning

Each assembly has a four-part version number (for example1.0.0.0) as part of its identity. Developers and administrators must understand how the version numbers work, as it is the key to how the CLR enforces version dependencies. The version number is represented in the following format:

```
<major version>.<minor version>.<build number>.<revision>
```

Any changes made to the major and minor versions are considered incompatible changes. For example, if we remove some types or functions altogether from the assembly we would change at least the minor version number. On other hand, bug fixes and the like are considered as compatible versions and we would change the build or revision number.

The CLR determines which version of the dependent assembly to load. By default, the assembly that is loaded to resolve the reference must have the same major and minor numbers as were recorded in the reference. If the numbers do not match, then the assembly is considered as incompatible and is not loaded by default. The CLR will pick the assembly with the highest build or revision number.

For example, say our assembly referenced another assembly called `myRefAssembly`. If our assembly, `MyAssembly`, was built with version 1.1.0.0 of `myRefAssembly`, but version 1.1.0.1 was found at run time for `myRefAssembly`, then version 1.1.0.1 will be loaded and not version 1.1.0.0.

Here is a list of things a developer must know about the assemblies:

- ❑ An Assembly can be considered as a logical DLL.
- ❑ An Assembly contains the code that will be executed by the Runtime; there can be only one entry point for the Assembly.
- ❑ The Assembly contains the permissions that are requested and granted for the application to run.
- ❑ The manifest has the rules that are used to resolve the types and resources needed. The manifest also identifies any other dependent assemblies.
- ❑ An application when executed calls only the needed assemblies.
- ❑ Multiple assemblies with same name can be executed side-by-side.

Application Domains

What is an application domain? It is a virtual boundary to isolate an application. In other words, all objects created within the application scope are created within the application domain, for better memory management.

They are designed to ease the overhead involved in running applications that need to be isolated from each other, but also need to communicate with each other. In COM days, programmers let the instances share a process with a risk of performance overhead.

Now the question arises, "Can there be one or more application domains?" Absolutely yes, and one or more applications can run in a single application domain.

Let's look at the following diagram:

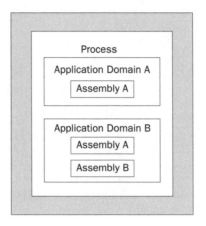

Each application is loaded into a separate memory process, which isolates it from another process. Code from one application cannot directly access code or resources from another application. CLR makes sure that the isolation is enforced to prevent direct calls between objects in different domains.

Every time the CLR initializes a process, the process is run under a domain called a Default Domain. This domain cannot be unloaded by making any system calls. The Domain is destroyed only after the process is unloaded. It is not wise to run code in the default Domain for two obvious reasons:

❑   The domain cannot be destroyed

❑   For security reasons, the code should be run outside this domain

If the default Application Domain is used and for some reason the code crashes the Application Domain, then there is a risk of bringing the whole server down with the application. That is why it is advised not to use the Default Application Domain for programming or running the code directly.

To make calls across domains possible, the objects must be copied or accessed by using a proxy connection. The copied object is local to that domain. The meta data for the referenced object must be available to both application domains. A System.IO exception is generated if the meta data is not available or not accessible to the Runtime.

Can we access objects and data across application domains? Enter Remoting, which is explained in Chapter 15.

To program application domains we use the System.Appdomain Class. The following code displays an isolated environment, which cannot be inherited, in both VB .NET and C#:

```
'VB .NET

Imports System.AppDomain

Public Interface _AppDomain

End Interface
Public Interface IEvidenceFactory

End Interface
Public NotInheritable Class AppDomain
    Inherits MarshalByRefObject
    Implements _AppDomain, IEvidenceFactory
End Class
```

```
// C#

using System;
public sealed class AppDomain : MarshallByRefObject, _AppDomain, IEvidenceFactory
{
}
```

The AppDomain class provides methods that let common language runtime hosts perform the tasks mentioned below:

- ❑ Enumerate the assemblies and threads in a domain.
- ❑ Define dynamic assemblies in a domain.
- ❑ Specify assembly loading and domain termination events.
- ❑ Load assemblies and types into the domain.
- ❑ Terminate the domain.

MarshallByRefObject is the base class for Remoting objects that need to be marshaled by reference. This uses the Singleton factory method for WebService objects.

The AppDomain class implements the _AppDomain interface. The System._AppDomain interface is meant for use by unmanaged code that needs access to the members of the System.AppDomain class. Unmanaged code can obtain a pointer to the _AppDomain interface by calling the QueryInterface on the Default Domain.

Framework Security

The .NET framework provides several mechanisms to protect code resources from unauthorized access.

- ❑ **Web Application Security**: this provides a way to control access to a site by comparing authenticated credentials (or representations of them) to Microsoft Windows NT file system permissions, or to an XML file that lists authorized users, authorized roles, or authorized HTTP verbs.

- ❑ **Code Based Security**: the CLR allows code to do those operations that the code has permission to perform. Code access security uses permissions to control the access code and to protect resources and operations.

```
// C#

[MyPermission(SecurityAction.Demand, Unrestricted = true)]
public class MyClass
{
    public MyClass()
    {
        //The constructor is protected by the security call.
    }
        // Write your functions methods here and they are protected by
        // the security call.
}
```

```
' VB .NET

<MyPermission(SecurityAction.Demand, Unrestructed = True)> Public Class MyClass1

    Public Sub New()
        'The constructor is protected by the security call.
    End Sub
        ' Write your functions and methods here and they are protedted by
        ' the security call
End Class
```

The CLR allows code to perform only those operations that the code has permission to perform. The Runtime uses objects called permissions to implement its mechanism for enforcing restrictions on managed code. The following are the primary uses of permissions:

❑ Code can request the permissions it either needs or could use. The .NET Framework security system determines whether such requests are honored. The code never receives more permission than the current security settings allow based upon a request.

❑ The Runtime can grant permissions to code based on characteristics of the code's identity, on the permissions that are requested, and on how much the code is trusted (as determined by the security policy set by an administrator).

❑ The code can demand that its callers have specific permissions. If such a demand is placed for certain permission on our code, all code that uses our code must have that permission to run.

One more way of using code access security is:

```
// C#

public void MyMethod()
{
    MyPermission Perm = new MyPermission();
    Perm.Demand();
        //protected by the security call.
}
```

Role-based security provides information needed to make decisions about what a user is allowed to do.

Let us take an example: An application may give a Sales Rep. the basic authorization to change the information on leads. Managers for the Sales Rep. may have more access over the same system while the Vice-Presidents may have higher limit for authority (or no limit at all).

These decisions can be based on either the user's identity or role membership or both. Let us write code to create an instance of a `WindowsIdentity` object and a `WindowsPrincipal` object, and display the information on the console. We can use this code to get the value of `WindowsIdentity` and `WindowsPrincipal` on the network environment.

The `WindowsIdentity` object stores data about Windows accounts. The `WindowsIdentity` object can be used if authorization decisions have to be made based on a user's Windows account information. For example, using `WindowsIdentity` and `WindowsPrincipal` objects, we can write an application that requires all users to be currently validated by a Windows 2000 domain.

```csharp
// C#

using System;
using System.Threading;
using System.Security.Principal;

public class ClsSecurity
{
  public static int Main(string[] args)
  {
        //Get the current identity and put it into an identity object.
    WindowsIdentity oIdentity = WindowsIdentity.GetCurrent();
        //Put the previous identity into a principal object.
    WindowsPrincipal MyPrincipal = new WindowsPrincipal(oIdentity);
        //principal values
    string sName = MyPrincipal.Identity.Name;
    string sAuthenticationType = MyPrincipal.Identity.AuthenticationType;
    string sAuthenticatied =
                        MyPrincipal.Identity.IsAuthenticated.ToString();
        //identity values
    string sIdentityName = oIdentity.Name;
    string sIdentityType = oIdentity.AuthenticationType;
    string sIdentityIsAuthenticated =
                              oIdentity.IsAuthenticated.ToString();
    string sItentityIsAnonymous = oIdentity.IsAnonymous.ToString();
    string sIdentityIsGuest  = oIdentity.IsGuest.ToString();
    string sIdentityIsSystem = oIdentity.IsSystem.ToString();
    string sIdentityToken = oIdentity.Token.ToString();

    Console.WriteLine("Principal Values Current thread:");
    Console.WriteLine("\n\nName: {0}", sName);
    Console.WriteLine("Type: {0}", sAuthenticationType);
    Console.WriteLine("IsAuthenticated: {0}", sAuthenticatied);

    Console.WriteLine("\n\nIdentity Values");
    Console.WriteLine("Name: {0}", sIdentityName);
    Console.WriteLine("Type: {0}", sIdentityType);
    Console.WriteLine("IsAuthenticated: {0}", sIdentityIsAuthenticated);
    Console.WriteLine("\n\n Anonymous Identity Values");
    Console.WriteLine("IsAnonymous: {0}", sItentityIsAnonymous);
    Console.WriteLine("IsGuest: {0}", sIdentityIsGuest);
    Console.WriteLine("IsSystem: {0}",sIdentityIsSystem);
    Console.WriteLine("Token: {0}", sIdentityToken);
    return 0;
  }
}
```

Open a text editor and copy the code in the new window. Then save the code as Code.cs (or your preference) on the drive. In our case we have saved the code on d:\

Open the Command Prompt and go to the folder where you have saved the code, and then type:

>csc Code.cs

This will compile the code and generate the executable called Code.exe in the same folder. csc is the command-line C# compiler. Now run Code.exe by typing:

>Code

to generate the following output:

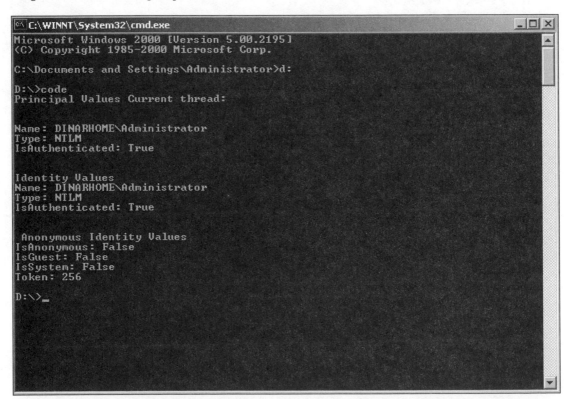

Application Deployment

In the Windows DNA environment, replacing a DLL on the production machine is a nightmare, known in the industry as DLL Hell. We need to stop IIS/the production server, release the DLL, and then copy the new DLL. After copying, it usually doesn't work directly. We need to register it using the Regsvr32 command-line utility or install the DLL under MTS. Then the real nightmares start. The DLL crashes many other applications; because someone forgot to keep the binary compatibility or the registry entries for the old DLL were conflicting with the new entries. Then we often have to run Regclean.exe to clean the Registry and maybe reboot the server.

However, with .NET, deploying applications to the computers with the CLR is a piece of cake. Copy the application on the machine with CLR installed. Then just run the application from the machine, (although advanced programs may need security permissions for some functionality). This means no files are copied onto the workstation, no registry entries are made, and in other words, the workstation is not touched at all. As the workstation is not touched, there is no cleanup, so no uninstall. Since there is nothing to uninstall, we cannot break any other application. This will certainly send shivers down the spine at the companies that specialize in install programs.

If we do not want to run the application across the network, we can simply copy the application using the console window command Xcopy. To uninstall the application, just delete the application and that is it. Assemblies can be copied into the system\folder\add\del><assembly folder by dragging and dropping.

> **However, it is recommended that neither Xcopy nor drag and drop be used for production deployment.**

Windows Installers

Windows Installer 1.5 and above supports installing Microsoft .NET Assemblics, merge module setups, etc.

Create Cabinet Files

Cabinet or CAB files can be created with Visual Studio. NET deployment, or by using the Win32 SDK compression tool. We can compress one file or a complete directory for deployment or download. As the CAB file is in a compressed format, it is faster to download the CAB file rather than the uncompressed files.

.NET supports side-by-side running of different versions of the same application components on the same machine or same process. This is not easily possible with Windows DNA. We have to have two copies of applications using the different DLLs. Windows XP may yet improve in this area, but at the time of writing this is still to be seen.

Configuring Applications

All configuration files in .NET are XML files, which can be changed and parsed as and when needed. Configuration files allow developers to change the settings without recompiling the application. The config files gives administrators the lever to set policies that affect how the applications will run on the network.

The root element of all configurations is <configuration>, and the topic is explained in detail in Chapter 2 *XML in the .NET Framework*. For now, we will briefly mention that configurations fall under the following three categories:

- ❑ Machine Configuration Files
- ❑ Application Configuration Files
- ❑ Security Configuration Files

and we will look at these next.

Machine Configuration Files

```
Path= "%runtime install path%\Config\Machine.config."
```

Application Configuration Files

These are divided into:

❑ EXE-Hosted Applications. The configuration files for EXE-Hosted application are placed under the same directory as the application. For example, if we have an application called ourApplication.exe, it can be associated with a configuration file called ourApplication.exe.config.

❑ ASP.NET-Hosted Applications. The configuration file is called web.config.

For example, given the URL www.wrox.com/myApp1/dotNet/ where www.wrox.com/myApp1/ is the Web application, the configuration file that is associated with the application is located at www.wrox.com/myApp1/. ASP.NET pages that are in the subdirectory /dotNet/ will use both the settings that are in the configuration file at the application level and the settings in the configuration file that is in /dotNet/. More on the ASP.NET configuration is explained in the ASP.NET chapter, Chapter 11.

❑ Internet Explorer-Hosted Applications. The location of the file is specified in the <link> tag:

```
<link rel="Configuration" HREF="[location]">
```

Security Configuration Files

Use tools like the Configuration tool (Mscorcfg.msc) or Code Access Security Policy tool (Caspol.exe) to modify security policy so the configuration files are not corrupted. The tools can be found under the System/Microsoft.Net/Framework/v1.0.2914 folder on your machine if you are using Beta 2.

COM Interoperability

We all know that .NET is going to "kick ass", but many companies will be hesitant about moving to .NET. Companies cannot just scrap their existing code and start from scratch in the new environment. Companies will want (and need) to keep using their existing code and the components that have been developed after spending a lot of money.

Well, .NET components and COM components conform to different compilation standards. COM components use the COM binary standard while .NET components use the CLR specification. Is there a way to coexist, and if so how? We can use some programming techniques and some utility tools given by Microsoft to make COM and .NET coexist.

❑ tlbimp.exe: This lets us import a COM library into a proxy .NET assembly that .NET clients can reference using early binding. (To see this in use, see Chapter 8.)

❑ regasm.exe: This enters the .NET assembly into the Registry so it can be accessed by the COM services.

❑ tlbexp.exe: As the name suggests, this exports a .NET assembly into a Type lib, which is accessed by the COM component using early binding.

❑ aximp.exe: This generates a Windows Forms Control that wraps ActiveX controls defined in the given OCX Name.

Framework Classes

We've taken quite a long look at the CLR and related issues – we'll turn our attention now to the other main component of the .NET framework, namely the Framework class library.

This class library is a library of classes, interfaces, and value types that are included in the Microsoft .NET Framework SDK. It provides access to system functionality and is designed to be the foundation on which .NET applications, components, and controls are built. Remember that in VC++ we had the MFC library, which was a precompiled class library. In Java, we have Swing classes etc.

For example, in Visual Studio 6.0 there is a function COS to get the cosine value. It is a math function. In .NET, all math related functions are encapsulated in the Math class in the System namespace. Therefore, to use the cosine function we would use the System.Math class, and then declare:

```
Public Shared Function Cos(ByVal d As Double ) As Double
```

The System namespace is the root namespace for fundamental types in the .NET Framework. It is important to emphasize that all the languages based on the .NET framework can use the same namespace. We can create our own core classes and make them globally available as pre-compiled functions.

For example, we have our own set of classes called Wrox.Core. To use all the classes in this namespace we call Wrox.Core.<class name>.

We can have our own class, which is extended from a core class to do some special function. Here is an example using the System namespace.

```
' VB .NET

Imports System
Imports Wrox.Core
Public Class Form1
  Inherits Wrox.Core.WinForm
    'Write code to extend the class.
End Class
```

```
// C#

using System;
using Wrox.Core;
public class Form1 : Wrox.Core.WinForm
  {// Write code to extend the class}
```

The System namespace is the root namespace for fundamental types in the .NET Framework. This namespace includes classes that represent the base data types used by all applications: Object (the root of the inheritance hierarchy), Byte, Char, Array, Int32, String, and so on. Many XML-related namespaces, like System.Xml, System.Xml.Xsl, etc., are explained in detail in this book in different chapters. A list of XML-related Framework classes with their descriptions, is explained in detail in Appendix A.

Traditionally, we would use MSXML 3.0 or MSXML 3.0 SP1 to access XML data, however, that may soon change, as at the time of writing MSXML 4.0 is at the beta stage.

.NET has separate series of namespaces to work with XML data. These are based on the namespace `System.Xml`. Here is the list of the different namespaces:

- ❏ `System.Xml`
- ❏ `System.Xml.Schema`
- ❏ `System.Xml.Serialization`
- ❏ `System.Xml.Xpath`
- ❏ `System.Xml.Xsl`

.NET Languages

There are a number of .NET languages. Here we'll look at C# and VB. NET. Throughout the book we will give examples in both C# and VB. NET wherever possible, as we assume that the reader has some familiarity with at least one of these languages. For longer examples, the code in the alternative language will mostly be given in the code download for the book, available at http://www.wrox.com/.

Introducing C#

C# is the new object-orientated programming language and is targeted for the .NET Runtime. The compiler will only produce managed code.

C# is a simple, but powerful programming language intended for writing enterprise applications. It is an evolution of C and C++, and uses many C++ features in the areas of statements, expressions, and operators. It introduces type safety, versioning, events, and garbage collection.

C# code does indeed also resemble Java in many ways. Both languages promote one-stop coding: grouping of classes, programming interfaces, and implementation together in one file, so that we, the developers, can edit the code easily. C# and Java use the objects in a very similar way, by reference rather than by pointers for example.

The C# compiler has the option to produce XML-formatted code documentation using a special syntax, which is explained in Chapter 16. C# provides access to the common API styles: .NET Framework, COM, Automation, and C-style APIs. It also supports unsafe mode, where we can use pointers to manipulate memory that is not under the control of the garbage collector.

C# Syntax

For VB. NET readers, let's take a brief look at the basics of C# code. First, the comments:

```
// this is a comment.
/* this is a comment also*/
```

A C# program must contain a `Main()` method, in which control starts and ends.

```
static void Main()
{
    ...
}
```

Main() can, for instance, return an int:

```
static int Main()
{
    ...
    return 0;
}
```

Main() can also take arguments:

```
static int Main(string[] args)
{
    ...
    return 0;
}
```

The parameter of the Main() method above is a string array that represents the command-line arguments used to invoke the program. Notice that, unlike C++, this array does not include the name of the executable (.exe) file.

To print on screen at the command prompt we can use:

```
System.Console.WriteLine("Hello World!");
```

To compile a C# program at the command line, we can use the command-line compiler csc.exe:

>**csc Hello.cs**

If using an IDE then we can just press *Ctrl + Shift + B* to build the application, and *F5* to start running the application in debug mode, or *Ctrl + F5* to run the application without the debug mode.

Below is a simple C# "Hello World" program:

```
using System;

namespace HelloWorld
{
    class Class1
    {
        static void Main(string[] args)
        {
            Console.WriteLine ("Hello World");
        }
    }
}
```

Save it as helloworld.cs to the drive, and compile the program:

```
C:\WINNT\System32\cmd.exe

D:\>csc helloworld.cs
Microsoft (R) Visual C# Compiler Version 7.00.9254 [CLR version v1.0.2914]
Copyright (C) Microsoft Corp 2000-2001. All rights reserved.

D:\>
```

Now we have the executable compiled, let's run it:

```
C:\WINNT\System32\cmd.exe

D:\>helloworld
Hello World

D:\>
```

For more information on C# please refer to the book *Professional C#* ISBN 1-861004-99-0, also published by Wrox Press.

VB .NET Overview

Visual Basic .NET (or VB .NET) has many new and improved language features, such as inheritance, interfaces, and overloading, which make it a powerful object-oriented programming language. Additionally, Visual Basic .NET applications can perform multiple tasks simultaneously using multithreading (or free threading), a process in which individual tasks execute on separate threads. This helps to improve the performance and responsiveness of the applications.

Other new language features in Visual Basic .NET are structured exception handling, custom attributes, and Common Language Specification (CLS)-compliance. Therefore any other CLS-compliant language can use the classes, objects, and components created in Visual Basic .NET. The CLS features used in Visual Basic .NET programs are assemblies, namespaces, and attributes.

For more details on VB .NET please refer the book *Professional VB .NET,* ISBN 1-861004-97-4, also published by Wrox press.

VB. NET syntax

This is the VB .NET code needed to print Hello World on the console:

```
Imports System
Module Module1

    Sub Main()
        Console.WriteLine("Hello World")
    End Sub

End Module
```

Let's compile the application now in a very similar manner to the previous C# example:

```
C:\WINNT\System32\cmd.exe                                    _ □ ×

D:\>vbc helloworld.vb
Microsoft (R) Visual Basic.NET Compiler version 7.00.9254
for Microsoft (R) .NET CLR version 1.00.2914.16
Copyright (C) Microsoft Corp 2001. All rights reserved.

D:\>
```

Once we have compiled the application we can run the executable. The VB .NET code compiles to exactly the same MSIL as the C# code previously. Hence we run the executable in exactly the same manner as previously, with exactly the same outcome:

```
C:\WINNT\System32\cmd.exe                                    _ □ ×

D:\>helloworld
Hello World

D:\>
```

Let's take a brief look at the basics of VB. NET code:

```
Public Class Form1
    Inherits System.Windows.Forms.Form
    ' Add your code here.
End Class
```

The comment syntax is:

```
' this is a comment
REM this is a comment too
```

To declare a variable, we can still use the traditional VB method, or the new VB .NET method:

```
Dim a As System.Int32
Dim aa As Integer
```

The above declaration is valid for dimensioning an integer.

The following syntax creates a class and creates an object from that class:

```
Class newClass
    Public newVar As Integer
End Class

    Dim oObj As New newClass()
```

33

C# vs. VB.NET

Is there anything C# can do, but that VB .NET can't? Well, almost nothing. However, VB.NET cannot allow for embedded blocks of C++ with code.

Just because VB .NET is powerful does not make it easy to use. We want to emphasize that the addition of new features to VB have made the grammar and syntax of VB .NET different. Learning VB .NET is a challenge for a pure VB programmer unfamiliar with the OOP concept and programming.

In reality, it really does not matter if we choose VB .NET or C#, the idea is to use the language that suits our preference

ASP.NET

ASP.NET is not just a new version of ASP, but also a whole new vision of programming for the Web. The new features were not added over the top of ASP – a new version was written from scratch. ASP and ASP.NET can co-exist, however, as the new extension for ASP.NET is aspx. ASP.NET pages are structured and each page is a class, which inherits from the .NET webPage class.

The Active Server Pages framework, also known as Web Forms, allows the creation of programmable web pages for web applications. We can program Web Services, and Mobile Web Applications including HTTP Handlers using ASP.NET. The choice of language is entirely left to the developer. Web Forms simplify the development of web applications, and provide an event-based programming model on the server.

Web Forms allow complete separation of HTML markup from application logic. The code is compiled for performance, and can be written in VB .NET, C#, C++ (managed), JScript .NET, or any other .NET language, or even any combination of two or more of the above languages. Web Forms, combined with VisualStudio .Net, enable a rich design-time experience, introducing server controls that are used to create the user interface for our web application.

The two types of server controls within the ASP.NET framework are **HTML controls** and **Web controls**. Both render HTML for use by web browsers, and we can create composite controls based on these controls.

HTML Controls

HTML controls exist within the System.Web.UI.HtmlControls namespace, and derive (directly or indirectly) from the HtmlControl base class.

HTML controls are instantiated for any HTML element containing the runat="server" attribute. For example, the following HTML creates an instance of HtmlInputText named "textBox1" with the default value some text:

```
<input type="text" runat="server" id="textBox1" value="some text">
```

The Screenshot below displays the text HTML control:

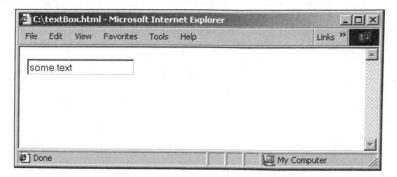

Here is another example:

```
<INPUT style="Z-INDEX: 101; LEFT: 137px; POSITION: absolute; TOP: 197px"
       type="submit" value="Submit">
<DIV style="DISPLAY: inline; Z-INDEX: 102; LEFT: 69px; WIDTH: 70px;
            POSITION: absolute; TOP: 63px; HEIGHT: 15px"
     ms_positioning="FlowLayout">
   Label
</DIV>
<INPUT style="Z-INDEX: 103; LEFT: 69px; POSITION: absolute;
              TOP: 196px" type="reset" value="Reset">
<INPUT style="Z-INDEX: 104; LEFT: 69px; POSITION: absolute;
              TOP: 104px" type="text">
<TEXTAREA style="Z-INDEX: 105; LEFT: 69px; POSITION: absolute;
                 TOP: 141px" rows="2" cols="20">
</TEXTAREA>
```

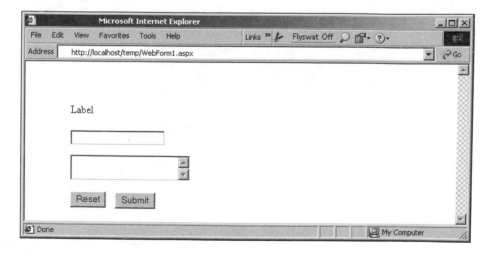

Web Controls

Web controls exist within the System.Web.UI.WebControls namespace, and derive (directly or indirectly) from the WebControl base class.

Web controls include traditional form controls such as the TextBox and Button controls, as well as other higher-level abstractions such as the Calendar and DataGrid controls. They provide several features that simplify our development efforts, including a rich and consistent object model. The WebControl base class implements a number of properties that are common to all controls. These include ForeColor, BackColor, Font, Enabled, etc. The property and method names have been chosen to promote consistency across the framework and the suite of controls. The strongly typed object model implemented by these components helps reduce programming errors.

Web controls automatically detect the capabilities of the client browser and can customize their rendering to make best use of those capabilities.

```
<asp:ImageButton id="ImageButton1" style="Z-INDEX: 102; LEFT: 34px;
                                      POSITION: absolute; TOP: 38px"
               runat="server" Width="242px" Height="164px"
               ImageUrl="file:///C:\WINNT\Zapotec.bmp">
</asp:ImageButton>
<asp:Calendar id="Calendar1" style="Z-INDEX: 103; LEFT: 37px;
                                POSITION: absolute; TOP: 227px"
          runat="server">
</asp:Calendar>
```

The following screenshot shows the above web control code (webform1.aspx), rendered using a web browser. This example uses image and calendar controls.

Validation Controls

Validation Controls are a set of special controls that are designed to make our life easy in validating the input entered on the web page. At present with ASP we need to write JavaScript or VBScript code to validate the user-entered input. Here is an example of some simple validation controls:

```
<asp:RequiredFieldValidator id="RequiredFieldValidator1"
                            style="Z-INDEX: 102; LEFT: 110px;
                                   POSITION: absolute; TOP: 140px"
                            runat="server"
                            ErrorMessage="RequiredFieldValidator"
                            ControlToValidate="TextBox1">
</asp:RequiredFieldValidator>
```

Data binding

In addition, there are several Web controls that can be used to render the contents of a data source.

Web controls appear in the HTML markup as namespaced elements – that is, elements with a namespace prefix. The prefix is used to map the tag to the namespace of the run-time component. The remainder of the tag is the name of the run-time class itself. Like HTML controls, these tags must also contain a `runat="server"` attribute. An example declaration is as follows:

```
<asp:TextBox id="textBox1" runat="server" Text="[Entry Keywords]">
</asp:TextBox>
```

Mobile Controls

Mobile controls are the controls that provide the same functionality as Web or HTML controls, but for small screen devices. Unlike Web controls, Mobile controls use the `System.Web.UI.MobileControls` namespace. These controls can create output in WML or any other language acceptable to the mobile devices. The following HTML, uses calendar, combo, and text controls, and a code-behind: `MobileWebForm1.aspx.vb` (available in the download):

```
<%@ Page Language="vb" AutoEventWireup="false"
        Codebehind="MobileWebForm1.aspx.vb"
        Inherits="MobileWebApplication1.MobileWebForm1" %>
<%@ Register TagPrefix="mobile" Namespace="System.Web.UI.MobileControls"
             Assembly="System.Web.Mobile" %>

<meta content="Microsoft Visual Studio.NET 7.0" name=GENERATOR>
<meta content="Visual Basic 7.0" name=CODE_LANGUAGE>
<meta content="Mobile Web Page" name=vs_targetSchema>
<BODY>
    <mobile:Form runat="server" ID="Form2" >
        <mobile:TextBox id=NameEdit runat="server"></mobile:TextBox>
        <mobile:Command id=Command1 runat="server"> OK </mobile:Command>
        <mobile:SelectionList id=SelectionList1 runat="server">
            <Item Text="www.Wrox.com"></Item>
            <Item Text="www.AspToday.com"></Item>
            <Item Text="www.CSharpToday.com"></Item>
        </mobile:SelectionList>
        <mobile:Calendar id=Calendar1 runat="server"></mobile:Calendar>
    </mobile:Form>
</BODY>
```

When we run the code in IE, we see the output in the following screenshot:

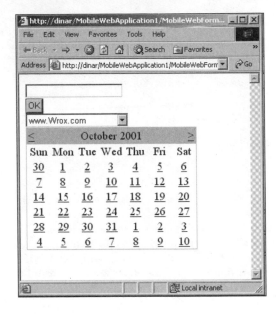

At Release Candidate stage is the Microsoft Mobile Internet Toolkit for .NET. This can be downloaded from:

http://msdn.microsoft.com/downloads/default.asp?url=/code/sample.asp?url=/msdn-files/027/001/516/msdncompositedoc.xml&frame=true

Web Services

Let's say for example, that we are sending orders across the Internet to a server, which processes them and enters the data in an Enterprise Database. We could achieve this concept programmatically by developing Web Services.

Web Services are programmable business logic components. Web Services are based on the application of XML via **SOAP** (**Simple Object Access Protocol**). SOAP defines a standardized way of exchanging payloads between two entities that is truly platform-independent.

More information on SOAP can be found at: http://www.w3c.org/TR/SOAP/ and http://www.develop.com/soap/.

A core part of the .NET Framework design is the handling of Web Services. Using ASP.NET we can easily expose Web Services from our web server to other parties. The developer has to do little more than write a class to expose a Web Service. For example:

```
' VB .NET

Imports System.Web.Services

Public Class Service1
    Inherits System.Web.Services.WebService
```

```
<WebMethod()> Public Function BookName() As String
        BookName = " Professional .NET XML "
    End Function

End Class
```

```csharp
// C#

using System;
using System.Web.Services;

namespace WebService1
{
    public class Service1 : System.Web.Services.WebService
    {
        [WebMethod]
        public string BookName ()
        {
            return " Professional .NET XML ";
        }
    }
}
```

In the example above, we declared a function called BookName() as a WebMethod. Let's see how .NET exposes the function BookName() as a Web Service.

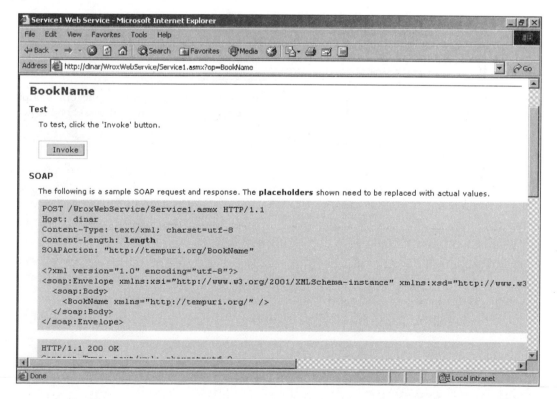

After the Web Service is invoked, an XML file is output, shown in the screenshot below:

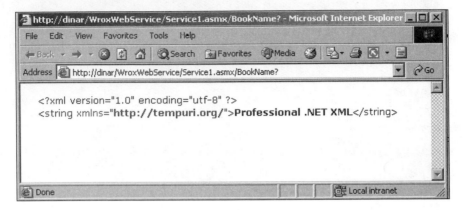

global.asax

The global.asax works mostly in the same manner as the good old global.asa, but with some additions. In this section we will look at these new additions.

Note that global.asax *and* global.asa *are not case-sensitive, so* Global.asax *and* Global.asa *are equally valid.*

Application Directives

Application directives specify optional settings used by the ASP.NET page and application compilers when processing ASP.NET files. Application directives are located at the top of the global.asax file.

```
<%@ directive attribute=value [attribute=value ... ]%>
```

The following three directives are supported:

❑   **@Application**: This defines application-specific attributes used by the ASP.NET application compiler.

```
<%@ Application Inherits="objWrox.Object" Description="Our Wrox APP " %>
```

❑   **@Import**: This explicitly imports a namespace into an application.

```
<%@ Import Namespace="System.IO" %>
<%@ Import Namespace="Wrox.Core" %>
```

❑   **@Assembly**: This links an assembly to the application at parse time.

```
<%@ Assembly Name="MyAssembly.dll" %>
```

Server-Side Object Tags

These are used to declare and create new application and session variables using a declarative, tag-based syntax. For example:

```
<object id="id" runat=server class="Class Name">
```

```
<object id="items" class=" System.Xml.Schema" runat="server"/>
```

Server-Side Includes

These are used to insert the contents of a specified file anywhere in an ASP.NET application. For example:

```
<!-- #include File = "WroxHeader.inc" -->
```

This adds `WroxHeader.inc` in a Web Forms page. The included file is processed first.

ADO.NET

ADO.NET is the substrate that forms the foundation of data-aware .NET applications. Unlike ADO, ADO.NET was purposely designed in observance of more general, and less database-oriented, guidelines. ADO.NET is a combination of classes that allow data handling.

ADO.NET is quite different from ADO. It is a new data access-programming model that requires full understanding, commitment, and a different mindset.

Data Access

Access to data sources is ruled via managed providers. A managed provider is much like an OLE DB provider with two important differences. First, they work in the .NET environment and retrieve and expose data by implementing .NET interfaces like `SqlDataReader`, `OleDbDataReader`, and `DataTable`. Secondly they work with the .NET Data Providers to provide fast data access.

The architecture for these classes is simpler as it is optimized for .NET. Currently, ADO.NET provides two flavors of managed providers: one for SQL Server 7.0 and higher, and one for all the other OLE DB providers we may have installed.

ADO vs. ADO.NET

An ADO.NET application that needs to read some data out of a data source should start by creating a connection object. It can be `SQLConnection` or `ADOConnection` depending on the target provider. All the ADO.NET classes are in the namespace `System.Data`.

ADO.NET OLE DB classes can be used to connect to a SQL Server database. The drawback is that the call passes through an unnecessary extra layer of code. The code calls into the managed provider of the ADO, which in turn calls the SQL Server OLE DB provider. A better way is to use the SQL Server managed provider, which goes directly to the data.

One of the major differences between ADO and ADO.NET connection objects lies in the fact that the ADO.NET connection doesn't support the `CursorLocation` property. This is not a bug, but a design issue.

In ADO, XML support was not built in, so we had to go through the MSXML libraries and access the XML DOM. ADO.NET has solved that problem by having built-in support for XML.

In ADO, we had to use cursors to pull records out of a database. We had a choice of client- or server-side cursors. ADO.NET abstracts from the data source and provides a new programming interface for reading and analyzing data.

In ADO, we create a `RecordSet` object by specifying a connection and a command text. The `RecordSet` has certain policies for cursor location and type. In ADO, we have static, read-only, and dynamic cursors to read the data. ADO.NET makes available two objects to manipulate data pulled out of a data source. They are the `DataSet` and the `DataReader` objects. The `DataSet` is an in-memory cache of records that can be visited in any direction and modified as and when we want.

In ADO.NET there's no support for server-side cursors. To use the server-side cursor you need to import the ADO type library in .NET. Once this is done you can start using native ADO objects in your applications.

ADO.NET unifies the programming interface for data container classes. We can use ADO.NET to handle data in any kind of application – Windows Form, Web Form, or Web Service.

Irrespective of what the data source is – SQL Server database, OLE DB provider, XML file, or an array – we can use the same methods and properties from ADO.NET to scroll and handle the data content.

XML and ADO.NET

ADO.NET uses the power of XML to provide disconnected access to data. XML support is built into ADO.NET at a very fundamental level. Both ADO.NET and the .NET XML Framework classes are components of a single architecture.

Using ADO.NET, we can fill a `DataSet` from an XML stream or document. We can use the XML stream or document to supply the `DataSet` with data, schema information, or both. The information received from the XML stream or document can be merged with existing data or Schema information already in the `DataSet`.

ADO.NET also allows us to create an XML representation of a `DataSet`, with or without its schema, in order to transport the `DataSet` across HTTP for use by another application or XML-enabled platform. As the native serialization format of the `DataSet` is XML, it is an excellent medium for moving data between tiers making the `DataSet` an optimal choice for remoting data and schema context to and from a Web Service.

ADO.Net is explained in greater detail in Chapter 10.

Summary

The .NET Framework and CLR fortunately do not force any particular language on us. However, C# is the most popular choice for a CLS-compliant language. C# has it's own syntax, but was derived from C, C++, and Java, taking the good things from these languages. Let's hope that different vendors will build C# compilers for different platforms.

In this chapter, we have briefly looked into the .NET Framework, ADO.NET, and introduced different .NET tools like C#, VB .NET, and ADO.NET. We have seen how the self-describing assemblies of .NET assist with enduring, robust code and prevent versioning problems.

In the following chapters, we will look into using the .NET architecture to build applications and also learn how XML is the core of the .NET framework.

2

XML in the .NET Framework

It's a fact that Microsoft worked behind closed doors for about three years, before announcing the surprise release of .NET Framework at PDC in July 2000. Nevertheless, behind those closed doors Microsoft engineers kept a sharp eye on rapidly evolving XML technologies. The .NET Framework and class library is designed to make use of XML for enterprise data exchange and "internet-ready" distributed applications.

In this chapter, we'll see how "XML is everywhere in .NET", and also learn how the Framework allows us to make use of XML in our applications. Think of this chapter as a précis for the rest of the book. Specifically, we will look at:

- ❑ .NET Configuration Files
- ❑ XML Documentation
- ❑ ADO.NET, Data, and XML
- ❑ Use of XML with ASP.NET
- ❑ Web Services
- ❑ XML Serialization
- ❑ Streaming and DOM-based XML Classes

Let's get started and first see how the Framework makes use of XML.

.INI Files, then Registry Now?

Microsoft Windows 3.1 introduced the concept of .INI files to store the application configuration information, used to describe an application's behaviors and hold its settings. These .INI files were soon replaced with the use of a "centralized" Registry, a binary file that could only be modified using specific tools. COM components make intensive use of the Registry to configure components. COM+ introduced the concept of a COM+ catalog.

The .NET Framework takes a different, decentralized approach and introduces a simple, but powerful, XML-based configuration system. The applications, systems, and security configuration settings are stored as standard text files with file extension of .config and are written using XML syntax. For each configuration area, the Framework defines an XML schema for configuration files, allowing various tags and attributes to be used to store configuration settings.

Benefits of using XML Configuration Files

Using XML files to hold the application and system configuration settings has many benefits including:

❑ The configuration information is stored in XML-based configuration files that are both human-readable and human-writable. Administrators and developers can use any standard text editor, XML parser, etc. to interpret and update configuration settings. In addition to this, the .NET Framework also provides a set of APIs to read and extend the configuration files.

❑ Prior to .NET, the Internet Information Server (IIS) metabase was being used to hold the Web Application settings and IIS Microsoft Management Console (MMC) Internet Service Manager was used to update the settings. Hence it was not possible to replicate the settings easily onto a different server. But with .NET, these configuration settings are nothing but simple XML files, so the settings can now be easily replicated by just copying these configuration XML files.

However, it is important to remember that there are still a few things that need to be done either using scripts that accesses IIS metabase, or by using the IIS Internet Service Manager MMC snap-in, and cannot be achieved by just using configuration files. Examples of such settings include: creating IIS Web Application/virtual directories, mapping custom file extensions under application settings for IIS, etc. In other words, web server administration still needs to be done using the IIS Service Manager; the configuration files are mostly introduced to ease development and deployment of Web Applications.

❑ With ASP.NET applications, the configuration information is applied hierarchically according to the virtual directory structure. Subdirectories inherit or override configuration settings from the parent directories. This allows different settings for different applications or different parts of a single application.

❑ Avoiding the use of the Registry, and storing the settings in the configuration files, is one of the factors enabling XCOPY deployment.

❑ Finally, as configuration files use the XML syntax, they are "extensible". We can either use the application settings section to store the key-value pairs representing our configuration settings, or create our own sections in the configuration files, and then write a custom configuration handler.

Types of Configuration Files

The configuration settings can be given in three types of configuration files:

❑ Application Configuration Files

❑ Machine or Server Configuration Files

❑ Security Configuration Files

Application Configuration Files

These represent the settings specific for an individual application, such as binding information to assemblies, configuration for remote objects, and so on. If an application is a standard .exe application, then the name of the configuration file is the name of the application with a .config extension, and it resides in the same directory as the application. For instance, an application helloWorld.exe can be associated with a configuration file helloWorld.exe.config. For ASP.NET Web Applications, the configuration details are stored into files named web.config. A server can have multiple web.config files, each existing in application roots or under subdirectories. Configuration files for these ASP.NET applications inherit the settings of configuration files in the URL path.

> It is important to note that the Framework protects configuration files from outside access by configuring IIS to prevent direct browser access to configuration files. HTTP access error 403 (forbidden) is returned to any browser attempting to directly request a .config file.

Machine or Server Configuration File

This is an XML file named machine.config, and is used for system-wide configuration. This file is located under: %SystemRoot%\Microsoft.NET\Framework\v[ver]\CONFIG, where [ver] is the build number of .NET installed. The configuration system first looks in the machine configuration file for API and ASP.NET settings. During a binding process, the machine configuration file is consulted before the application configuration file. The application configuration file can override the settings from the machine configuration. The application configuration file should be the preferred place for application-specific settings so that the machine.config file stays smaller and more manageable. However, for components that both client and server applications use, it is preferable to put the settings for that component in machine.config file.

Security Configuration Files

These are used by the Framework security system to determine what permissions an assembly receives. There are three configurable policy levels: Enterprise, Machine, and User. On Windows 2000 machine, these files are stored as:

```
%SystemRoot%\Microsoft.NET\Framework\v[ver]\CONFIG\enterprisesec.config

%SystemRoot%\Microsoft.NET\Framework\v[ver]\CONFIG\security.config

%USERPROFILE%\Application Data\Microsoft\CLR Security Config\v[ver]
                                                    \security.config
```

respectively. The .NET Framework provides a command-line utility (Code Access Security Policy tool, `Caspol.exe`) and a MMC snap-in (.NET Framework Configuration tool, `Mscorecfg.msc`) to modify the above security policy files. Security configuration files and ASP.NET security in general are discussed in Chapter 11.

Configuration File XML Structure

Having looked at the types and benefits of configuration files, let's now look at what these configuration files actually look like.

Remember that since configuration files use XML syntax, the element and attribute names in these XML configuration files are case-sensitive, and the files themselves are well-formed XML documents.

All configuration information resides between the `<configuration>` and `</configuration>` root XML tags.

.exe Application Configuration Files

The `.exe` application configuration files (for example, `helloWorld.exe.config`) group the configuration into following three categories:

- ❑ Startup Settings
- ❑ Runtime Settings
- ❑ Remoting Settings

Startup Settings

This section of the file is used to specify the version of the common language runtime that should run the application. It's possible that different versions of the runtime could be installed on the same system. With the `<startup>` element, the version of the runtime can be specified. The `<startup>` element contains a `<requiredRuntime>` tag, which actually specifies the version of the common language runtime that should run the application:

```
<configuration>
   <startup>
      <requiredRuntime version="v1.0.2914"/>
   </startup>
</configuration>
```

The value of `version` attribute must match the installation folder name for that version of the runtime. This string is not interpreted. If the runtime startup code does not find a matching folder, the runtime is not loaded; the startup code shows a simple error dialog and exits.

To easily test this, create a simple "Hello World" Console Application (as was shown in Chapter 1), start Notepad, enter the above configuration XML text, and save it as *yourAppName*`.exe.config` in the same directory as the `.exe` title. Note that the above XML configuration code specifies `v1.0.2914` as the version string, which is also the folder name where .NET Framework Beta 2 is installed. If Beta 2 of the .NET Framework is installed, the console application will run without any problems. Now change the version string in the `.config` file to some different value (for example: `v1.9.9999`), and run the console application again, this error message will be shown:

The `<requiredRuntime>` element also has an optional attribute named `safeMode`, which defaults to `false`, telling the startup code to search the Registry to determine the runtime version. We can set the `safeMode` attribute to `true` to prevent the startup code from checking the Registry.

Runtime Settings

This section of the file contains information about assembly binding and the behavior of garbage collection. We can also use this section to specify the location of a shared assembly, if it is not installed on the local computer (`codeBase`).

How a client finds an assembly (also called binding), depends upon whether the assembly is private or shared. Private assemblies must be in the directory of the application or a subdirectory thereof. To extend the search further, we can use the `<probing>` element within the runtime section of application configuration files. Shared assemblies are searched in the global assembly cache. To extend the search further, the `<codeBase>` element can be used to specify a directory, a network share, or a web site URL, where the shared assembly may be present. The global assembly cache and codebases specified in the configuration files are checked, followed by the application directories, and probing rules are then applied to search for the shared assemblies.

The easiest way to deal with runtime configuration settings is to use the Applications hive on the .NET Admin Tool that can be started by running the following from the DOS command prompt:

>mmc.exe %SystemRoot%\Microsoft.NET\Framework\v[ver]\mscorcfg.msc

For instance, on a machine running Windows 2000, and .NET Framework Beta 2:

>mmc.exe c:\winnt\Microsoft.NET\Framework\v1.0.2914\mscorcfg.msc

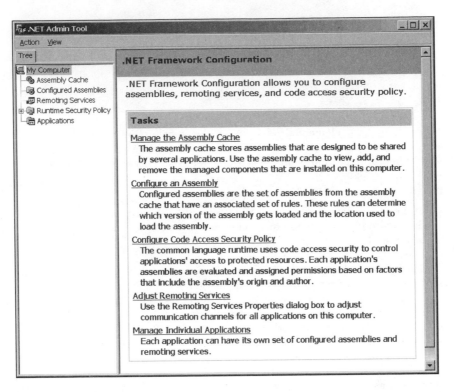

Remoting Settings

These are used to configure applications using .NET Remoting. The .NET Remoting infrastructure is an abstract approach to interprocess communication and can be used to enable different applications to communicate with one another, whether those applications reside on the same computer, or on different computers. Developers publishing or consuming .NET remoting objects can specify the settings either programmatically or by specifying the remote objects in configuration files. Specifying the remoting objects in configuration files enjoys the benefits discussed earlier in the chapter. The .NET Admin tool (also known as .NET Framework Configuration tool) can be used here to adjust the Remoting Services configuration settings. Remoting is discussed in greater detail in Chapter 15, *Remoting*.

Example EXE Application Configuration File

Below is a sample .exe application configuration file:

```xml
<?xml version="1.0" encoding="UTF-8" ?>
<configuration>
    <startup>
        <requiredRuntime version="v1.0.2914"/>
    </startup>
    <runtime>
        <gcConcurrent enabled="false"/>
        <assemblyBinding xmlns="urn:schemas-microsoft-com:asm.v1">
            <probing privatePath="bin;otherbins"/>
            <dependentAssembly>
                <assemblyIdentity name="RASapiAssembly"
                                  publicKeyToken="a1690a5ea44bab32"
```

```
                        culture="en-us"/>
            <codeBase version="6.0.0.0"
                      href="http://somesite.com/RASapiAssembly.dll"/>
        </dependentAssembly>
      </assemblyBinding>
    </runtime>
  </configuration>
```

As per configuration file schema, the top-level tag in the above configuration file for an EXE application is <configuration>, which in turn contains two sub-elements <startup> and <runtime>. The <startup> element above simply specifies that the application should run with version 1.0.2914 of the common language runtime.

The <runtime> section starts with a <gcConcurrent> tag, asking the runtime to disable running the garbage collector on a separate concurrent thread. By default, the runtime runs the garbage collector concurrently on a separate thread – this is good for single-threaded heavy user-interface applications, but for a multithreaded server application, turning off the concurrent execution of garbage collector on a different thread, can actually result in improved performance. In this case, the garbage collector runs in the same thread as the server application.

The next section, under the <runtime> heading in the above sample configuration file, is <assemblyBinding>, which is used to specify the assembly binding information, including how the runtime should locate the assembly, with the help of <codeBase> and <probing> sub-elements.

ASP.NET Applications Configuration Files

For ASP.NET applications, a union of machine.config and any web.config files is applied. The file machine.config is at the machine level and all ASP.NET virtual root directories and sub-directories inherit its settings.

The machine.config file settings can be overridden by individual web.config titles placed in the application directory. Apart from the application virtual root directory, its subdirectories may also contain web.config files. ASP.NET applies configuration settings to resources in a hierarchical manner. Web.config files supply configuration information to the directory in which they are located and all child directories.

It is, however, important to note that configuration settings for virtual directories are independent of physical directory structure. To give an example, let's say we have a page named test.aspx under the e:\d1\d2 subdirectory. Let's assume that e:\d1 is configured as virtual root named d1Vroot, and e:\d1\d2 is also configured as virtual root and is named d2Vroot. Furthermore both e:\d1 and e:\d1\d2 each have web.config files. Now, if we access test.aspx using d1Vroot through http://*serverName*/d1Vroot/d2/test.aspx, the page resource inherits the configuration settings from d1Vroot. However, if the same page is accessed directly using d2Vroot through http://*serverName*/d2Vroot/test.aspx, it does not inherit the configuration settings from d1Vroot.

Both machine.config and web.config files follow a similar XML schema containing a nested hierarchy of XML tags and sub-tags with attributes that specify the configuration settings. The elements, sub-elements, and attributes are all case-sensitive, and the root element of the configuration file is always <configuration>. Within <configuration> there are two important areas: the **configuration section handler declaration** area and the **configuration section settings** area.

Let's see an example `web.config` file:

```xml
<?xml version="1.0" encoding="UTF-8" ?>
<configuration>
   <configSections>
      <sectionGroup name="system.web">
         <section name="dsnstore"
                  type="System.Configuration.NameValueSectionHandler,System" />
      </sectionGroup>
   </configSections>
   <system.web>
      <compilation debug="true" />
      <dsnstore>
         <add key="NWind" value="server=.;database=Nwind;
              User Id=sa;pwd=;" />
         <add key="pubs" value="server=.;database=pb;
              Trusted_Connection=yes" />
      </dsnstore>
   </system.web>
</configuration>
```

Configuration section handler declarations appear at the top of the configuration file between `<configSections>` and `</configSections>` tags. Each declaration, contained in a `<section>` tag, defines a class used to interpret the meaning of configuration data. As the XML configuration files are "extensible" and can contain custom sections, the ASP.NET Framework simply delegates the processing of this data to what are know as configuration section handler classes. In the above example, we are using the built-in handler, however it is easily possible to write our own handlers to process custom configuration data.

It is important to note that configuration section handlers only need to be declared once. We can place them in the `machine.config` file or in a `Web.config` file in the virtual directory containing the Web Application files. All ASP.NET applications inherit the settings from `machine.config` and configuration files in subdirectories automatically inherit configuration handlers declared in parent directories' `web.config` files.

After the `<configSections>` handler declarations come the actual configuration settings; these are referred to as configuration section settings and are generally grouped under section-grouping tags. These section-grouping tags typically represent the class namespace to which the configuration settings apply. For example, the `<system.web>` tag represents all the ASP.NET class settings.

To summarize, the configuration section settings area contains the actual configuration details, and the configuration section handler declaration area contains the information about the class that can process the actual configuration section data. We can use the predefined configuration section handlers that are supplied with the .NET Framework, or we can create our own handlers to process custom configuration types.

Let's look at the predefined ASP.NET configuration sections:

Configuration Section	Description
`<appSettings>`	Key-value combination that allow us to store data within the configuration system and access it within our application, for example database connection strings, log file names, and paths, etc.
`<authentication>`	Configures ASP.NET authentication support. The `mode` attribute has four acceptable values: `Windows`, `Forms`, `Passport`, and `None`.

Configuration Section	Description
`<authorization>`	Allows us to define access control permissions, defined as `<allow>` and `<deny>` settings.
`<browserCaps>`	Configures the settings of the browser capabilities component.
`<compilation>`	Allows us to control some of the compilation behaviors of ASP.NET, such as changing the default language from VB. NET to C#, enabling/disabling debugging, etc.
`<customErrors>`	Configuration details about handling custom errors, as well as common HTTP errors.
`<globalization>`	Application-level options for the request/response character encoding.
`<httpHandlers>`	Maps incoming requests to appropriate HTTP handlers. Custom handlers can be added within this section or existing handlers can be removed.
`<httpModules>`	HTTP modules are like ISAPI filters. They filter each request/response in an ASP.NET application. This section is used to add or remove HTTP modules within an application.
`<httpRuntime>`	Configures ASP.NET HTTP run-time settings, like execution timeout, max request length, etc.

`<identity>`	Allows us to impersonate the user that ASP.NET acts on the behalf of. For instance,
	
	`<identity impersonate="true"`
	`    name="Wrox\UserX" password="pwd" />`
	
	 enables the application to run as `Wrox\UserX`, irrespective of the identity of the request.

`<machineKey>`	A key used for encryption or hashing of some values, such as the data in the Cookie used for Forms authentication. In a Web Farm environment, all the servers must share a common machine key.
`<pages>`	Identifies page-specific configuration settings, for example page buffering, session state, etc.
`<processModel>`	By default, ASP.NET (`aspnet_isapi.dll`) runs out-of-process from IIS and has the capability to recycle by itself. The settings in this section allow us granular control over the behavior of the worker process.
`<securityPolicy>`	Defines mappings of named security levels to policy files.
`<sessionState>`	Options for Session state, such as where the session data is stored, timeout, and support for cookie-less state management.
`<trace>`	Configures the ASP.NET trace service.
`<trust>`	Configures the set of code access security permissions applied to a particular application.
`<webServices>`	Controls the settings of ASP.NET Web Services.

A complete discussion on the above configuration tags can be found in the book: *Professional ASP.NET* (ISBN: 1-861004-88-5) also published by Wrox Press.

Example ASP.NET Application web.config File

Below is a sample web.config file:

```xml
<?xml version="1.0" encoding="utf-8" ?>
<configuration>
   <appSettings>
      <add key="appName" value="My first Web Service" />
      <add key="appVersion" value="1.0.0.0" />
   </appSettings>
   <system.web>
      <compilation defaultLanguage="c#" debug="true" />
      <customErrors defaultRedirect="stdError.aspx" mode="RemoteOnly">
         <error statusCode="500" redirect="serverError.aspx"/>
      </customErrors>
      <authentication mode="None" />
      <trace enabled="false" requestLimit="10" pageOutput="false"
             traceMode="SortByTime" localOnly="true" />
      <sessionState mode="InProc"
                    stateConnectionString="tcpip=127.0.0.1:42424"
                    sqlConnectionString="data source=127.0.0.1;user id=sa;
                    password=" cookieless="false" timeout="20" />
      <httpHandlers>
         <add verb="*" path="*.cs"
              type="System.Web.HttpNotFoundHandler,System.Web" />
         <add verb="*" path="*.csproj"
              type="System.Web.HttpNotFoundHandler,System.Web" />
      </httpHandlers>
      <globalization requestEncoding="utf-8" responseEncoding="utf-8" />
   </system.web>
</configuration>
```

The above web.config file:

- ❑ Uses two application-specific key-value pairs (appName and appVersion).

- ❑ Enables debugging and specifies C# as the default language for the application.

- ❑ Specifies that the custom errors are shown only to remote clients and also provides the custom error and HTTP error page handler file names.

- ❑ Has authentication mode set to None, allowing anonymous access.

- ❑ Has application tracing disabled.

- ❑ Indicates that the session state is stored locally with timeout of 20 minutes.

- ❑ Specifies the default HttpNotFoundHandler handlers for .cs and .csproj files.

- ❑ Finally, the globalization element indicates utf-8 encoding is to be used for the default request and response for the application.

XML Code Documentation

The C++ language provides two styles of comments: single line comments (//) and multi-line comments (/*...*/). C# supports both these styles and also introduces a very neat feature with respect to generating the source code documentation in XML format from inline code comments. These comments are single line comments, but begin with three slashes (///), instead of the usual two. Within these comments, we can place XML tags and descriptive text. The XML tags allow us to mark up the descriptive text to better define the semantics of the type or member and also to incorporate cross-references.

The C# compiler can then extract the XML elements from the special comments and use them to generate an XML file. The compiler validates the comments for internal consistency, expands cross-references into fully qualified type IDs, and outputs a well-formed XML file. The compiler will throw an error if the XML comments don't result in a well-formed XML document.

Let's see an example of how this works. We'll write a C# class to process employee salaries, and save it as Employee.cs:

```csharp
// C#

using System;

namespace FinanceDept
{
    /// <summary>
    /// The implementation of Employee class
    /// </summary>
    public class Employee
    {
        /// <summary>
        /// Employee Name Private Member
        /// </summary>
        private string EmpName;

        /// <summary>
        /// Employee's monthly salary: Private Member
        /// </summary>
        private double EmpSalary;

        /// <summary>
        /// The hourly rate constant class member
        /// </summary>
        private const double PerHourRate = 30;

        /// <summary>
        /// The class constructor
        /// </summary>
        /// <param name="Name">Input parameter: name of the employee</param>
        /// <param name="Salary">
        /// Input parameter: salary of the employee
        /// </param>
        public Employee(string Name, double Salary)
        {
            EmpName = Name;
            EmpSalary = Salary;
        }
```

```
        /// <summary>
        /// Given the number of hours worked, this method returns the salary
        /// and also sets the EmpSalary member variable
        /// </summary>
        /// <param name="HoursWorked">
        /// The number of hours worked, input
        /// </param>
        /// <returns>Employee Salary, output</returns>
        public double CalculateSalary(double HoursWorked)
        {
            EmpSalary = HoursWorked * PerHourRate;
            return EmpSalary;
        }
    }
}
```

Let's now run this file against the compiler and we'll specify the /doc switch to tell the complier to process XML tags inside special documentation comments and generate an XML file. Type the following command on the DOS command prompt:

>**csc /t:library /doc:Employee.xml Employee.cs**

This will generate an XML file named Employee.xml, which when opened in Internet Explorer looks like:

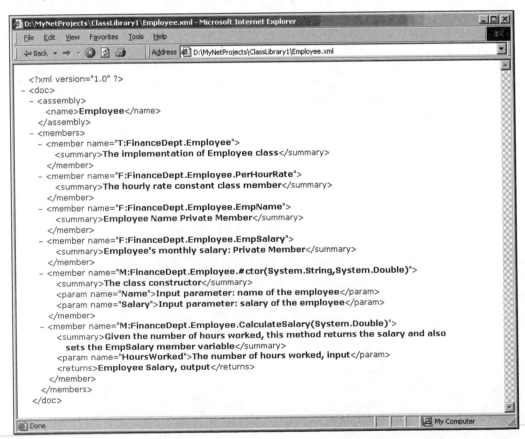

Visual Studio .NET and XML Documentation

Visual Studio .NET greatly simplifies writing XML documentation and also offers the ability to generate HTML format files from the XML documentation comments.

With Visual Studio .NET, all we have to do is type in actual description. As soon as we type three slashes (///) above the type or member declaration, Visual Studio .NET automatically inserts the proper XML tags including the <summary>, <param>, <returns>, and so on. To generate the XML documentation file when the project is compiled, select Project | Properties and specify the XML file name under Configuration Properties | Build | XML Documentation File setting; and to generate HTML-formatted documentation from the XML comments, select Tools | Build Comment Web Pages... from the menu. Here is what the HTML-formatted documentation looks like:

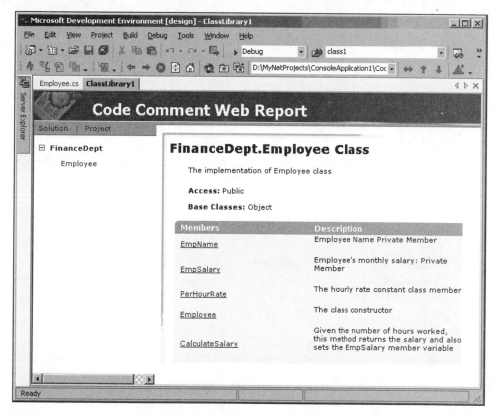

Unfortunately, this XML code documentation facility is currently available for C# only. It is explained fully in Chapter 16, *XML Code Documentation*.

ADO.NET, Data, and XML

In this section, we'll see how the data access mechanism is enhanced in .NET Framework using the XML integration.

ADO Limitations

The traditional data access with ADO has the following limitations, especially for n-tier web database applications:

- ❑ The data access revolves around the fundamental data storage object – the `RecordSet`, which is used for both connected as well as disconnected data access. Hence, there is no "clean" and efficient way to work with disconnected data. It requires dealing with options like client-side and server-side cursors.

- ❑ The ADO `RecordSet` is a proprietary data format. Data transferred or persisted, as an ADO `RecordSet` needs to be MIME-encoded; hence, it is not suited for cross-platform data transfer. COM marshaling was required to transmit a disconnected recordset, which limited the data types to just those defined by the COM standard, and also it cannot penetrate firewalls.

- ❑ There is very limited support for XML in ADO.

- ❑ Since ADO is COM-based, it is not best suited for .NET database applications.

- ❑ It represents a single table of records. If this table comes as the result of one or more `JOIN`s, it can be difficult to update the original data sources.

Enter ADO.NET

Microsoft recognized that an entirely new programming model for data access was needed, one that is built upon the .NET Framework, one that provides highly integrated support for XML, and one that is best suited for both 2-tier (mostly connected) and n-tier (mostly disconnected) applications. ADO.NET (formerly called ADO+), an evolutionary improvement to ADO, was designed keeping these goals in mind.

Data access in .NET is broadly divided into two levels:

- ❑ The connected layer, which consists of managed providers in conjunction with high-performance, stream-based, forward-only `DataReader` classes (`SqlDataReader` or `OleDbDataReader`)

- ❑ The disconnected layer, which involves use of `DataSet`

The `DataSet` provides the basis for disconnected storage and manipulation of relational data. A `DataSet` is a self-contained in-memory database. We can create a `DataSet` from existing data in the database, or fill it directly using code. A `DataSet` also has methods to both read and write XML. As opposed to an ADO `RecordSet`, which can only consume and produce a single XML format based on a single schema, the `DataSet` can read and write XML corresponding to any schema.

XML has two big advantages when it comes to storing and transferring data – it's an accepted industry standard, and it is just plain text. This is the reason ADO.NET was designed to use XML for the `DataSet`'s native serialization format. When a `DataSet` is streamed across the wire, the .NET Framework automatically converts the `DataSet` to XML serialized format, containing data as well as metadata.

Typed `DataSet` is yet another example of where XML technologies are used in the .NET Framework. With a typed `DataSet`, tables and columns that are part of the `DataSet` can be accessed using user-friendly names and strongly typed variables (for example, `EmpDS.Salary` instead of `EmpDS["Salary"]`).

Finally, the Framework provides a class known as XmlDataDocument, which can be used to load either relational data or XML data, and manipulate it using the W3C DOM. XmlDataDocument is composite of an XmlDocument (it inherits from XmlDocument) and a DataSet (it contains a DataSet as a member).

ADO.NET and XML concepts are discussed in greater depth in Chapters 10 and 12.

ASP.NET and XML

As we saw in Chapter 1, ASP.NET is an integral part of the .NET Framework. It introduces a whole new way of programming Web Applications. Programming with ASP.NET is a lot different from traditional ASP web programming, but be assured that all the changes are for the good. ASP.NET has been written from the ground up to provide the best possible web development framework. The most important change to notice is that the ASP.NET is a compiled environment; in general, this means that the first request after a source file change will trigger a "build", and that all subsequent requests will execute from the cached .dll. Another important nice change is that you can use any .NET compatible language, including VB .NET, C#, JScript .NET, or even C++ (managed) to build Web Applications.

XML is pervasive within ASP.NET. The ASP.NET Web Application configuration system is completely based on XML-formatted configuration files. We saw earlier in this chapter the role of web.config and machine.config files with respect to configuring ASP.NET Web Applications.

The ASP.NET Web Services, discussed later, make intensive use of XML at various places. ASP.NET Server Controls use XML vocabulary, which is translated to code at compilation. One of these Server Controls is available to do XML processing on the server side, the **XML Web Server Control**, and can be used to load, process, and also transform XML documents on the server.

There is lot more to ASP.NET than this: for a complete guide to ASP.NET, refer to *Professional ASP.NET* (ISBN: 1-861004-88-5) also published by Wrox Press. The XML features in ASP.NET are covered in this book in Chapter 11, *ASP.NET*.

Web Services

The notion of Web Services enables "internet-ready" and "firewall-friendly" peer-to-peer and distributed application development. A Web Service, in it simplest form, is a new way to perform a remote method call over HTTP using XML and SOAP. Web Services extend the distributed-application example from the enterprise to the Internet.

> *SOAP, or Simple Object Access Protocol, is a W3C Specification (http://www.w3.org/TR/SOAP/), and provides a standard remote object invocation protocol built on Internet standards, using HTTP as the transport and XML for data encoding. Web Services is just a fancy term for SOAP-based RPC access.*

A Web Service can be characterized by following prerequisites:

- ❑ Messages are encoded using a industry-standard text formatting, which can traverse through firewalls, and follows some type system (XML with XSD).
- ❑ It uses an open transport/messaging protocol (HTTP/SOAP).
- ❑ There has to be a standard way to describe and discover Web Services (WSDL, UDDI/DISCO).

XML plays a very important role with Web Services. XML is used for messaging (SOAP request and response payloads), data representation, along with type information, and to describe Web Services. **Web Services Description Language** (**WSDL**) is a W3C Specification, used to describe Web Services. A `.wsdl` file is an XML document written using WSDL XML vocabulary, and defines how a Web Service behaves and instructs clients as to how to interact with the service.

.NET has excellent support for building and consuming Web Services, and it greatly simplifies working with Web Services.

> *The Framework hides the "XML-related" details when working with ASP.NET Web Services, so it is not a requirement to know XML well to work with Web Services in .NET. However, the knowledge of XML, XML Namespaces, and Schemas is a plus point.*

The simplest way to write a Web Service with .NET is to use Visual Studio .NET and choose "**ASP.NET Web Service**" project type. The difficult, but flexible, way is to write your own class that implements the `IHttpHandler` interface.

Writing a Web Services client simply involves right-clicking on the project and selecting **Add Web Reference**. Visual Studio .NET then allows us to point to a WSDL document for the Web Service we are writing the client for. Visual Studio .NET then uses `wsdl.exe` (Web Services Description Language Tool) to generate the client proxy class. The client proxy class for the Web Service is, by default, created in C#, but we can specify VB .NET or JScript .NET as the language argument.

We can call Web Services from any platform and from any language. It simply involves posting an XML payload that describes which method we wish to call on the remote server, and its method parameters. The server then processes that request by looking at the request XML payload, if it does not recognize the method or parameters; it simply sends a fault response payload. Otherwise, the server-side processing is executed and a response is sent, again in XML format. The client can now look at response XML and use the results. The Web Services client can be either a thin client (browser), or an application. In fact, Internet Explorer 5.0 onward supports a DHTML behavior, known as **WebService Behavior**, which can be used to make SOAP calls and write an in-browser Web Service client.

To learn more about Web Services, refer to Chapters 13 and 14.

XML Serialization

Let's say we are writing a Web Service in .NET, and the service has just one method, `GetAllEmployees()`. The method takes no input parameters and should return XML-formatted employee details picked up from some server database. In our implementation, we simply connect to the data store, generate an ADO.NET `DataSet` class object containing employee data, and simply return this `DataSet` class object. On the client side, we automatically received employee data as XML. How does this "object-to-XML" happen and what did it? The answer is: the .NET Framework internally *serialized* the object to XML before sending it to the client. Web Services is just one example where serialization is used, and there are many other places where XML Serialization is used in .NET.

Serialization is the process of taking an object graph and turning it into an XML document, either to persist it or to transmit it. To turn an object into a block of XML, we simply instantiate an instance of `XmlSerializer` class, give it the object to be serialized, and call the `Serialize()` method on it. Likewise, to turn a block of XML into an object, again we use `XmlSerializer` class, but this time we give it a block of XML, as opposed to an object and call `Deserialized()`.

Let's look at an example of this. Let's say we have a class called `Project` that looks like:

```
// C#

public class Project
{
    public string m_Name;
    public string m_Desc;
    public double m_TeamStrength;
}
```

Let's now instantiate an object of this class, initialize it, and then serialize the object to an XML document that we'll save on our local disk.

```
// C#

Project aPro = new Project ();
aPro.m_Name = "My Project";
aPro.m_Desc = "Some Description";
aPro.m_TeamStrength = 5;

FileStream OutputFS = new FileStream (@"c:\1.xml", FileMode.Create);

XmlSerializer ProjSerializer = new XmlSerializer (aPro.GetType());

ProjSerializer.Serialize (OutputFS, aPro);

OutputFS.Close ();
```

The above lines of code simply instantiate and initialize an object of class `Project`, open a `FileStream`, create an `XmlSerializer` object, pass it the `Project` object, and finally call the `Serialize()` method of `XmlSerializer` object, which transforms the object's graph into XML format and saves that into the `FileStream` object, which points to the file `c:\1.xml`.

Deserialization code looks similar to the above code. The .NET Framework makes use of this technique in many places including with Web Services, Remoting, SOAP, MSMQ, .NET sockets, etc. The Framework also provides a tool, `XSD.exe`, that can be used to generate XML schemas from classes in a run-time assembly, or to generate common language runtime classes from XDR, XML, or XSD files. Serialization is discussed in greater depth in Chapter 7.

Streaming and DOM-based XML Classes

By now, you might have realized that most aspects of the .NET Framework take advantage of XML in one way or another. Microsoft spent a significant amount of time and energy improving the core suite of XML APIs in .NET, and at the same time made sure to support key industry standards, such as DOM Level 2 Core, XPath 1.0, XSLT 1.0, XML Schemas (XSD), and SOAP 1.1. In this section, we'll review the XML processing APIs available in .NET.

Introducing System.Xml

The .NET Framework XML classes are partitioned over several namespaces. The core types are available through the System.Xml namespace. The XPath/XSLT-specific classes are contained in the System.Xml.XPath and System.Xml.Xsl namespaces, respectively. XML Schemas-related classes are available in System.Xml.Schema namespace. All these namespaces are packaged in the System.Xml.dll assembly.

> *When processing XML with .NET, we should use the .NET Framework XML classes present in* System.Xml *assembly, instead of using MSXML through COM interop.*

XmlReader and XmlWriter

System.Xml uses a streaming I/O model. At the core of the .NET Framework XML classes are two abstract classes: XmlReader and XmlWriter. XmlReader provides a set of abstract methods and properties for scanning across a stream of XML information items. It provides a fast, forward-only, read-only cursor for processing an XML document stream. XmlWriter provides an interface for producing XML documents. To summarize, XmlReader is used to *process* XML documents, while XmlWriter is used to *produce* XML documents. XmlReader and XmlWriter form an excellent alternative to the classic DOM approach, as these classes use a streaming model and don't require an expensive in-memory cache.

Remember that both XmlReader and XmlWriter are abstract base classes, and merely define the functionality that derived classes must support. This design allows us to develop custom readers and writers and to extend the built-in functionality of the classes. There are three concrete implementations of XmlReader class:

XmlReader derived Class	Description
XmlTextReader	If you need to read XML data in a forward-only manner at a very high speed, and do not need DTD/Schema support, use XmlTextReader class.
XmlNodeReader	The XmlNodeReader is a concrete class that uses an XmlNode as its input source has the ability to read an XML DOM subtree.
XmlValidatingReader	XmlValidatingReader sits on top of any XmlReader implementation and supports validation against XML Schema, XDR, and DTD while reading.

Similarly for XmlWriter, the .NET Framework currently provides just one concrete implementation, XmlTextWriter.

The XmlReader class provides the best of today's XML APIs: SAX (streaming model) and DOM (simplicity). Prior to .NET, the most popular streaming interface suite was the Simple API for XML (SAX). SAX-based parsers delivered the stream of data items by invoking the methods on an object provided by the consumer. Hence it is an event-based push model API. Though the parser implementation was pretty straightforward (simply read the stream and call event methods), it was on the consumer side, where it was harder to design and program, mostly because of state-management issues.

The XmlReader follows a streaming model like SAX, but unlike SAX, it uses a pull model. It allows consumers to pull records (XML data) one at a time and skip records of no interest. The XmlReader provides several methods for iterating through the logical stream of nodes. The most basic and generic iteration is the method Read(), which blindly iterates to the next element node and returns true until it reaches the end of element node stream, when it returns false.

Let's look at a very simple XML processing example that uses XmlReader (actually XmlTextReader, as XmlReader is an abstract class):

```
// C#

using System;
using System.Xml;

class Class1
{
    static void Main(string[] args)
    {
        XmlTextReader reader = null;
        int iCount = 0;
        try
        {
            reader = new XmlTextReader(@"c:\1.xml");
            while (reader.Read())
            {
                if (reader.NodeType == XmlNodeType.Element)
                iCount++;
            }
            Console.Write("Total {0} Elements found!", iCount);
        }
        finally
        {
            if (reader != null)
            reader.Close();
        }
    }
}
```

The above code is for a Console Application that reads an XML stream from a file called c:\1.xml, counts the number of element nodes, and finally spits out the count to the console. We simply create an instance of XmlTextReader class, pass it the file name, and then call the Read() method of XmlTextReader in a while loop, which moves to the next node in the tree till it has reached end of the tree. If the current node is an element node, we increment the count variable.

XmlTextWriter, on the other hand, provides methods and properties to generate XML documents and write them to a stream, file, or TextWriter object. Like XmlTextReader it does it in a forward-only, non-cached manner. Let's look at a simple example of XmlTextWriter:

```
// C#

using System;
using System.Xml;

class Class1
{
```

```
    static void Main(string[] args)
    {
        XmlTextWriter writer = new XmlTextWriter(Console.Out);
        writer.Formatting = Formatting.Indented;

        writer.WriteStartDocument();

        writer.WriteStartElement("Person");
        writer.WriteAttributeString("Sex", "Male");
        writer.WriteAttributeString("FirstName", "Sunny");
        writer.WriteAttributeString("LastName", "Bajaj");
        writer.WriteElementString("Phone", "111-111-1111");
        writer.WriteElementString("Phone", "222-222-2222");
        writer.WriteEndElement();

        writer.WriteEndDocument();

        writer.Flush();
        writer.Close();
    }
}
```

The above code is also for a Console Application, and illustrates producing well-formed XML documents using XmlTextWriter class. We simply create an instance of XmlTextWriter class and pass it a stream (Console.Out in this case) where it should stream out the XML document. Next, we set the Formatting property to get the pretty and indented XML output. Finally, we make sequence of calls like WriteStartDocument(), WriteStartElement(), WriteAttributeString(), and so on, to actually create elements and attributes. Here is what the output looks like:

```
d:\MyNetProjects\XmlWriterTester\bin\Debug\XmlWriterTester.exe
<?xml version="1.0" encoding="IBM437"?>
<Person Sex="Male" FirstName="Sunny" LastName="Bajaj">
  <Phone>111-111-1111</Phone>
  <Phone>222-222-2222</Phone>
</Person>
```

Streaming XML classes are discussed in detail in Chapter 3.

DOM, XPath, and XSLT

In the previous section, we looked at a new stream-based method of working with XML. In this section, we will look at how .NET supports the traditional DOM programming model.

DOM

If you have worked with the MSXML DOM object model, the .NET Framework's XmlDocument class will look familiar. The XmlDocument class implements the W3C Document Object Model (DOM) Level 1 and the DOM Level 2 Core. With DOM API, the entire XML document is loaded into memory (cache), and the API allows navigation and editing on the in-memory XML document. We can use DOM to create an XML document, and then save it to a file, or send it to a stream, etc. In .NET, DOM loading is built on top of the XmlReader class, while DOM serialization is built on XmlWriter class.

The XmlDocument class is equivalent to the MSXML DOMDocument coclass; it has Load() and LoadXML() methods for building in-memory XML DOM trees. Generating XML document's using the .NET XmlDocument class is very similar to doing so in MSXML.

XmlDocument and other DOM classes are discussed in Chapter 4.

XPath

In .NET, XPath namespace classes support XML document navigation. XPath is built to do fast, read-only, iterations and selections on the XML document in a cursory fashion. The XPath functionality is exposed via the XPathNavigator class. Here is a list of the XPath classes:

XPath Class	Description
XPathDocument	This class is optimized to get a view of the entire XML document, for XSLT processing and the XPath data model.
XPathNavigator	This provides the navigation capabilities to an XPathDocument.
XPathNodeIterator	XPathNodeIterator is an abstract class for iteration over selected node-sets.
XPathExpression	XPathExpression class can be used to compile an XPath expression to select a node-set from an XML file.

Let's look at a simple XPath example. For this example we'll use the XML file from the output generated by our previous XmlTextWriter example. Here our sample XML file:

```
<?xml version="1.0" encoding="IBM437"?>
<Person Sex="Male" FirstName="Sunny" LastName="Bajaj">
    <Phone>111-111-1111</Phone>
    <Phone>222-222-2222</Phone>
</Person>
```

The above XML document is saved as c:\1.xml. Let's now create a C# Console Application, with the goal being to navigate to all the Phone nodes within the Person node in above XML document:

```
// C#

using System;
using System.Xml.XPath;
class Class1
{
    static void Main(string[] args)
    {
        XPathDocument doc = new XPathDocument(@"c:\1.xml");
        XPathNavigator nav = doc.CreateNavigator();
        XPathNodeIterator iter = nav.Select("/Person/Phone");

        while (iter.MoveNext())
        {
            Console.WriteLine("Phone: {0}", iter.Current.Value);
        }
    }
}
```

We start by creating an instance of the XPathDocument class and passing it the XML document file to load. Next, we create an XPathNavigator on this document and call the Select() method on it. The Select() call returns an XPathNodeIterator for matching nodes. We then iterate over XPathNodeIterator object members and print their values. Here is what the output should look like:

XPath classes are discussed in Chapter 5.

Transformations

XSLT is an XML-based programming language that facilitates document transformations. Transforming XML from one format to another using XSLT alleviates schema incompatibilities. To work with XSLT in .NET, we can use the XSL classes from the System.Xml.Xsl namespace. The important class here is XslTransform, which supports XSLT 1.0.

The first step is to create an instance of XslTransform class, and then call the Load() method on it specifying the desired XSLT document. The next method to call is Transform(), passing in the XPathNavigator sitting on top of the data source. The Transform() method can output to a Stream, TextWriter, XmlWriter, or an XmlReader instance.

Let's transform the Person sample XML document to a different format. Here is our transformation file, which we save as c:\1.xsl:

```
<xsl:stylesheet version="1.0" xmlns:xsl="http://www.w3.org/1999/XSL/Transform">

    <xsl:output indent="yes" method="xml" />
    <xsl:template match="Person">
        <Person>
            <Sex><xsl:value-of select="@Sex" /></Sex>
            <FName><xsl:value-of select="@FirstName" /></FName>
            <LName><xsl:value-of select="@LastName" /></LName>
        </Person>
    </xsl:template>

    <xsl:template match="/">
        <xsl:apply-templates />
    </xsl:template>

</xsl:stylesheet>
```

The above transformation is simply changing the Person attributes to elements and omitting the Phone elements from the source XML. Our final XML, after transformation is applied, should look like:

```
d:\MyNetProjects\XSLTDemo\bin\Debug\XSLTDemo.exe
<?xml version="1.0" encoding="IBM437"?>
<Person>
  <Sex>Male</Sex>
  <FName>Sunny</FName>
  <LName>Bajaj</LName>
</Person>
```

Here is the code, which uses the `XslTransform` class to apply the transformation:

```csharp
// C#

using System;
using System.Xml;
using System.Xml.XPath;
using System.Xml.Xsl;

class Class1
{
    static void Main(string[] args)
    {
        //load input document
        XmlDocument doc = new XmlDataDocument();
        doc.Load(@"c:\1.xml");
        XPathNavigator nav = doc.CreateNavigator();

        //Load XSLT document
        XslTransform docXSL = new XslTransform();
        docXSL.Load(@"c:\1.xsl");

        //Apply transformation and send output to console
        docXSL.Transform(nav, null, Console.Out);
    }
}
```

The above code simply loads the XML document (`c:\1.xml`), then loads the XSL file (`c:\1.xsl`) using `XslTransform`, and calls the `Transform()` method on it, finally sending the output to console.

> *If you are writing an ASP.NET Web Application and need to display an XML document or transform an XML document using XSL stylesheet server side, you may use the XML Web Server control (`<asp:Xml...>`).*

MSXML in .NET

Let's assume that the latest version of MSXML provides some functionality that is not supported by .NET XML Managed classes (`System.Xml` assembly). As MSXML is shipped as a set of COM components, we can use it from our .NET applications through the mechanism of COM interop.

If we working with Visual Studio .NET, then using MSXML simply involves adding a reference to `MSXMLx.dll` (where *x* is the version of DLL, 3 for MSXML 3 and 4 for MSXML 4 preview and full release), and adding the `using` (C#) or `imports` (VB. NET) statement. We can then start using MSXML classes. For command-line compilation, we first use the `tlbimp.exe` utility to import the MSXML namespace and then while compiling use the `/reference` (`/r` for short) switch.

Let's look at a small example. Start Visual Studio .NET and create a new C# Console Application project. Select **Project | Add Reference...**, select the **COM** tab, and choose **Microsoft XML Parser MSXML 3.0** from the list. Our console application code looks like:

```
// C#

using System;
using MSXML2;

class Class1
{
    static void Main(string[] args)
    {
        DOMDocument30 doc = new DOMDocument30();
        doc.load(@"c:\books.xml");
        Console.Write(doc.xml);
    }
}
```

Note that above program uses the MSXML 2 namespace, which was made available when we added the DLL reference. The above program simply creates an MSXML DOM document, loads an XML document and spits out the document XML text onto the console.

It's very unlikely that we would want to use MSXML, because the .NET XML API (XmlReader, XmlWriter, XmlDocument, etc.) is better suited for processing XML in .NET applications. Only if we already have a lot of code written in MSXML and wanted to quickly migrate to .NET, would we use the COM interop solution with MSXML. MSXML is discussed in greater detail in Chapter 8, *MSXML*.

Summary

XML is truly the core technology substrate in .NET. Most aspects of .NET take advantage of XML in one way or another. In this chapter, we've taken a brisk walk through the XML integration features in the .NET Framework. Microsoft has introduced several new applications of XML in .NET and has also done some good innovative work to improve the core XML API.

We started with a discussion on use of XML in configuration files. We'll see XML configuration files being used a lot with respect to ASP.NET Web Applications and Web Services. We looked at the benefits and types of configuration files and their formats.

Another interesting feature we discussed was C# XML code documentation, where XML tags inside special comment tag (///) can be converted to XML or HTML code documentation.

As XML is about data, it is obvious that ADO.NET uses XML heavily. We saw how XML, in conjunction with some new ADO.NET features, fixes the problems that ADO has. We then talked about the use of XML in ASP.NET and in Web Services. XML Serialization is another interesting topic that we just introduced here.

Finally, we discussed the Framework's support for producing and consuming XML documents. The new streaming pull model (XmlReader) brings many benefits to XML processing and we'll continue talking about it the next chapter, *Reading and Writing XML*.

3

Reading and Writing XML

In this and the next two chapters, we'll take a look at the XML support in the .NET framework and the assemblies that provide access to XML functionality. This chapter deals with serialized access to XML documents using classes derived from the `XmlReader` and `XmlWriter` abstract classes. Some of the subjects we'll be taking a look at are:

- ❑ Using classes derived from `XmlReader` to access XML documents
- ❑ The similarities and differences between `Xml Readers` and the Simple API for XML (SAX)
- ❑ Deriving from `XmlTextReader`
- ❑ Using `XmlTextWriter` to create XML documents node-by-node
- ❑ Filtering documents using an `XmlReader` and an `XmlWriter`

Technologies Used

This chapter will present its examples using the C# and VB .NET programming languages. If you're a C++ programmer, it should be a simple matter to port the examples over – most of what we'll be doing is leveraging objects found in the .NET framework. Sample code will be provided in the form of Console Applications to keep the samples simple and easy to understand. You should be able to compile the samples either using the command-line .NET framework compilers or by inserting the code into a Visual Studio .NET Console Application project.

The System.Xml Assembly

The objects we will be using in this chapter may all be found in the System.Xml assembly in the .NET framework. Note that if you are using Visual Studio .NET to create your code, the System.Xml assembly will automatically be part of your project – so you won't need to manually add it to your references. This assembly contains objects that operate directly on XML documents, including both forward-only, non-cached access objects (similar to the SAX) and random-access objects that load entire documents into memory (similar to the Document Object Model). This assembly also includes some helper classes, such as name table classes, that are used to improve the performance of Microsoft's XML parser. This chapter focuses on the forward-only XML document objects, as well as the document serializer XmlTextWriter.

Reading XML Documents

First, let's take a look at the support Microsoft has provided for reading and parsing XML documents.

The XmlReader Abstract Class

Microsoft has created a general forward-only reader class, called XmlReader. This class defines the properties and methods common to all forward-only XML readers. It provides methods that can be used to navigate through the document (primarily node-by-node, although some helper methods are provided to speed navigation). It also provides methods that allow information about the current node to be read. If we want to implement our own XmlReader class, we can certainly do so (see Chapter 9, *Extending Xml Reader and Writer*). However, this requires overriding pretty much every property and method (as they are all declared as virtual). However, the System.Xml assembly contains three readers that inherit from XmlReader and will likely be the only readers we will need: XmlTextReader, XmlNodeReader, and XmlValidatingReader. We begin this chapter with an introduction to both the abstract XmlReader class and the XmlTextReader implementation of that class, as well as some examples of working with XML data.

How Does XmlReader Compare to SAX?

The forward-only XML document reader classes provided in the .NET framework are similar to the Simple API for XML, or SAX. Both move through the document one step at a time (the term node here is a little imprecise, because certain parts of an XML document – like element start and end tags – that are normally considered part of the same node from a DOM perspective are really read as two steps by both XmlReader and SAX). Both require only a small footprint in memory, as they move a parse window over an XML document rather than reading the entire document into memory at once. However, there is a key difference between the two models – SAX uses a push model, while XmlReader uses a pull model. In other words, SAX returns the XML document contents by raising events – "pushing" them to the code using the SAX parser – while XmlReader returns the XML document as it is asked for, or "pulled", by the code.

The pull model allows the developer much better control over the flow of information from the document, and facilitates more complex programming (such as managing complex state or merging two input XML streams). However, for those already familiar with SAX, the move to using an XmlReader should not prove overly difficult.

The XmlTextReader Class

The most useful version of `XmlReader` is the `XmlTextReader` class. This class is designed to manipulate string information – whether from an Internet URL, a stream, or a string in memory – and parse it into XML elements, attributes, and so on. Let's take a look at some sample code for this class.

Constructing an Instance of XmlTextReader

The constructor for the `XmlTextReader` class is extremely overloaded – there are twelve different public constructors, or twelve different ways that we can create an `XmlTextReader`. Rather than going through each one, let's take a look at the different types of streams, strings, and contexts that can be used when constructing an instance of this class.

As we mentioned above, the `XmlTextReader` object can read from a URL, a string in memory, or a file stream. We can construct instances of the `XmlTextReader` object by passing in either a string containing a URL or a `Stream` object. The `Stream` object, of course, can take many forms – a stream derived from an HTTP connection, a stream created from an array of bytes in memory, or a stream that pulls its information from a local file. We'll see examples of each a little later in the chapter. If we are reading from a string that has different MIME types encoded into it (such as an HTTP packet), we can also construct an `XmlTextReader` object from a `TextReader` – an object designed to handle processing of multi-part MIME streams.

We can also pass an `XmlNameTable` instance to the `XmlReader` constructor. This object type is simply a table of atomized string objects. The `XmlTextReader` will use this table to store the names of elements and attributes, saving memory consumption by reusing objects in the name table when they appear more than once in the document. Passing an `XmlNameTable` in the constructor of an `XmlTextReader` allows us to share a name table between various readers – which can save memory if we are trying to process many similar documents simultaneously. We'll see an example of this later in the chapter as well.

Finally, if we want to parse a fragment of an XML document, we can pass information about the fragment – such as its type and the context information about it – to the parser. This allows the parser to properly resolve namespaces in the fragment.

Now, let's take a look at some examples of common construction operations with `XmlTextReader`.

Loading a Document from a URL

Loading a document from a URL couldn't be simpler; we just pass a string into the `XmlTextReader` that contains the URL of the document we want to retrieve. For example, the following C# code retrieves an XML document from `localhost`:

```
// C#

string sURL = "http://localhost/sample.xml";
XmlTextReader myReader = new XmlTextReader(sURL);
// process the XML document here
myReader.Close();
```

In VB .NET, we would use the following code:

```
' VB .NET

Dim sURL As New String("http://localhost/sample.xml")
```

73

```
Dim myReader As New Xml.XmlTextReader(sURL)
' process the XML document here
myReader.Close()
```

Note that the URL has to be fully qualified, as the prefix is used to determine how to go about accessing the document. Make sure that the URL passed begins with `http://`, otherwise the `XmlReader` will throw an error. We can also use other URL prefixes (like `ftp://`) to access other types of resources.

Loading a Document from a Local File

To access an XML document that is stored in a local file, we can create a stream that reads that file. This stream needs to have read access. The stream is then passed to the constructor for the `XmlTextReader` object. Of course, if we prefer, we can also construct an `XmlTextReader` by passing it a string containing the local file name. Here's an example that assumes we have a sample document stored on our local machine:

```csharp
// C#

string sFile = "c:\\samples\\sample.xml";
FileStream myFile = new FileStream(sFile, FileMode.Open);
XmlTextReader myReader = new XmlTextReader(myFile);
// process the XML document here
myReader.Close();
myFile.Close();
```

```vbnet
' VB .NET

Dim sFile As New String("c:\samples\sample.xml")
Dim myFile As New IO.FileStream(sFile, IO.FileMode.Open)
Dim myReader As New Xml.XmlTextReader(myFile)
' process the XML document here
myReader.Close()
myFile.Close()
```

Remember to escape the backslashes if programming in a language that requires it like C#.

Loading a Document from a String in Memory

Loading a document from a string in memory is similar to loading a document from a local file – we'll use the `Stream` form of the constructor. However, in this case we'll be using a `MemoryStream`. Since `MemoryStream` only has a byte array constructor, not a string constructor, we first need to move the string into a byte array – we can then construct the `MemoryStream` object.

```csharp
// C#

string sXML = "<?xml version='1.0'?><x><y>z</y></x>";
ASCIIEncoding ae = new ASCIIEncoding();
byte[] byteXML = ae.GetBytes(sXML);
MemoryStream myStream = new MemoryStream(byteXML);
XmlTextReader myReader = new XmlTextReader(myStream);
// process the XML document here
myReader.Close();
myStream.Close();
```

```
' VB .NET

Dim sXML As New String("<?xml version='1.0'?><x><y>z</y></x>")
Dim ae As New Text.ASCIIEncoding()
Dim byteXML As Byte()
byteXML = ae.GetBytes(sXML)
Dim myStream As New IO.MemoryStream(byteXML)
Dim myReader As New Xml.XmlTextReader(myStream)
' process the XML document here
myReader.Close()
myStream.Close()
```

We might use this form of the constructor if we were passed an XML fragment from some other source, such as a database or as part of a SOAP message.

Using Name Tables

If we are writing code that needs extremely high performance, and the documents we are parsing have similar structures, we may want to reuse one `XmlNameTable` object for multiple documents. Because the `XmlTextReader` parser has to allocate string tokens for each element discovered in the process of parsing, providing a name table that already has the string tokens declared can allow the parser to simply reference the tokens already declared. This decreases the required memory footprint and makes parsing more efficient, provided that our documents all contain the same types of element names, attribute names, and so on. To reuse an `XmlNameTable`, simply create an empty one, then pass it to the constructors of all the documents we want to open using that table. Note that we need to create a `NameTable` object – this is the default implementation provided by Microsoft of the abstract class `XmlNameTable`.

```
// C#

string sURL1 = "http://localhost/sample1.xml";
string sURL2 = "http://localhost/sample2.xml";
string sURL3 = "http://localhost/sample3.xml";
NameTable myNameTable = new NameTable();
XmlTextReader myReader1 = new XmlTextReader(sURL1, myNameTable);
XmlTextReader myReader2 = new XmlTextReader(sURL2, myNameTable);
XmlTextReader myReader3 = new XmlTextReader(sURL3, myNameTable);
// the documents now share the same name table
myReader1.Close();
myReader2.Close();
myReader3.Close();
```

```
' VB .NET

Dim sURL1 As New String("http://localhost/sample1.xml")
Dim sURL2 As New String("http://localhost/sample2.xml")
Dim sURL3 As New String("http://localhost/sample3.xml")
Dim myNameTable As New Xml.NameTable()
Dim myReader1 As New Xml.XmlTextReader(sURL1, myNameTable)
Dim myReader2 As New Xml.XmlTextReader(sURL2, myNameTable)
Dim myReader3 As New Xml.XmlTextReader(sURL3, myNameTable)
' the documents now share the same name table
myReader1.Close()
myReader2.Close()
myReader3.Close()
```

Stepping Through an XML Document

Now that we know how to open XML documents, we need to learn how to parse through those documents and retrieve the information found there. Before we start looking at methods and properties, though, we need to first understand the way positions in the XML document are implemented by `XmlReader` objects.

Understanding Node Order

When an `XmlReader` parses an XML document, it effectively turns it into a list of nodes. These nodes sometimes have names, sometimes have values, and sometimes have both. The following are all the node types that can be generated by parsing an XML document with an `XmlTextReader`:

Node Type	Name	Value
Attribute	The name of the attribute	The value of the attribute
CDATA		The content of the CDATA section
Comment		The content of the comment
DocumentType	The document type name; for a DTD, this will be the same as the root element name	The internal subset of document declarations
Element	The element name	
EndElement	The element name	
EntityReference	The name of the referenced entity	
ProcessingInstruction	The target of the processing instruction	The remainder of the processing instruction (excluding the target)
SignificantWhitespace		The whitespace between markup in a mixed content model
Text		The text value
Whitespace		The whitespace that appears between markups
XmlDeclaration	The string XML	Content of the declaration (the version and encoding)

Note that there are both an `Element` and an `EndElement` node type. This is how the `XmlReader` shows nesting of elements: by sending back the `Element` node when the start tag for the element is encountered and the `EndElement` node when the end tag is reached.

Before we start looking at the different types of content we can encounter in an XML document and how to access them via `XmlReader`, let's first take a look at a quick sample program that we can use to get a feel for how the `XmlTextReader` works.

A Quick Example

Insert the following code into a Visual Studio .NET C# Console Application project, or compile it manually at the command line with this command:

>csc Example01.cs

```
// C#

// Example01.cs
using System;
using System.Xml;
using System.Text;
using System.IO;

namespace myApp
{
  class mainClass
  {
    static void Main(string[] args)
    {
      FileStream myFile = new FileStream("test.xml", FileMode.Open);
      XmlTextReader myReader = new XmlTextReader(myFile);
      Console.Write("{0,-20}{1,-20}{2,-20}\n", "Type", "Name", "Value");
      Console.Write("{0,-20}{1,-20}{2,-20}\n", "--------------------",
                    "--------------------", "--------------------");
      while(myReader.Read())
        Console.Write("{0,-20}{1,-20}{2,-20}\n",
                      myReader.NodeType.ToString(),
                      myReader.Name, myReader.Value);
      myReader.Close();
      myFile.Close();
    }
  }
}
```

This code reads the document found in the test.xml file (by repeatedly calling Read() on the XmlTextReader) and writes the node type, name, and value of each node to the console. By running this program for a couple of sample documents, we can get a feel for the kinds of information that XmlTextReader returns.

Whitespace Handling

Save the following file as test.xml in the same folder as C#Example01.cs on your system and run the preceding sample C# application with this command:

>Example01

```
<?xml version="1.0"?>
<customer>
    <name>Alfred Q. Anybody</name>
    <address>123 Anywhere Road</address>
    <city>Somewheretown</city>
    <state>PA</state>
    <postalCode>29374</postalCode>
</customer>
```

The output is a little surprising, as we can see in the following screenshot:

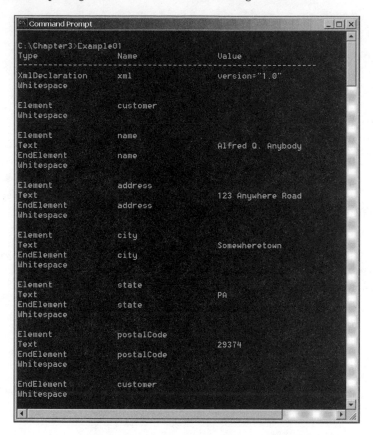

The `XmlReader` classes, by default, preserve all whitespace in an XML document – even whitespace that is not significant (as that term is defined by the W3C). This means that, when using an `XmlTextReader` "out of the box", many additional nodes will be returned that are of no use when parsing the document. To eliminate this extraneous whitespace in our returned node list, we can set the whitespace handling characteristics of our `XmlTextReader` by setting its `WhitespaceHandling` property. This property can be set to return all whitespace in the document (`All`), only significant whitespace: whitespace appearing between elements in a mixed-content element (`Significant`), or no whitespace (`None`). In most cases, the best setting for this property is `Significant`. Let's modify our test code to set the property on our `XmlTextReader` before we parse our document and try again with the amended sample:

```
// Example01a.cs
    ...
    static void Main(string[] args)
    {
        FileStream myFile = new FileStream("test.xml", FileMode.Open);
        XmlTextReader myReader = new XmlTextReader(myFile);
        myReader.WhitespaceHandling = WhitespaceHandling.Significant;
        Console.Write("{0,-20}{1,-20}{2,-20}\n", "Type", "Name", "Value");
```

Our result shows that the non-significant whitespace has been dropped:

Reading Elements

We've seen that elements that have content are returned as a node pair: an Element node indicating where the element begins, and an EndElement node indicating where the node ends. If an element is empty, however, it is only returned as one node: an Element node. To make it clear that a particular node is empty, the XmlReader class provides an isEmptyElement property – if this property (which returns a Boolean) is true, then the element is empty. If we are tracking which elements have been opened but not closed, this would be the signal that no EndElement node is to be expected for this node. Take this XML document, for example:

```
<?xml version="1.0"?>
<customer>
    <item1 />
    <item2></item2>
    <item3>Something here</item3>
    <item4>
        <structure>Some structured content here</structure>
    </item4>
</customer>
```

When parsing this document with an XmlTextReader, the Element node for the <item1> and <item2> elements would return an IsEmptyElement property of true, while the <item3> and <item4> Element nodes would return IsEmptyElement as false.

Often, elements are used to represent single atoms of information, represented as strings of text. Getting at this information using only the Read() method and the name and Value properties can be a little cumbersome. We have to use Read() until the element of interest comes up, then use Read() again to position to the text node, then pull the value from the Value property. XmlTextReader provides a handy shortcut to extract the text value of a node: ReadElementString(). This allows the text value of an element to be read while the cursor is positioned on the element, rather than requiring a second navigation to the text value. So for our previous customer example, we could extract the value of the address element with this VB .NET code:

```
' VB .NET

' Example02.vb

Imports System
Imports System.Xml
Imports System.IO

Module Module1

    Sub Main()

        Dim myFile As New IO.FileStream("test.xml", IO.FileMode.Open)
        Dim myReader As New Xml.XmlTextReader(myFile)
        myReader.WhitespaceHandling = Xml.WhitespaceHandling.Significant
        While myReader.Read()
            If myReader.NodeType = Xml.XmlNodeType.Element _
                And myReader.Name = "address" Then
                Console.WriteLine(myReader.ReadElementString())
            End If
        End While
        myReader.Close()
        myFile.Close()
    End Sub

End Module
```

Note that to compile this VB .NET Console Application at the command prompt, we must supply the compiler with extra information. We must reference the System.Xml namespace using either the /reference: or the /r: switch, supplying a parameter of System.Xml.dll:

>vbc Example02.vb /r:System.Xml.dll

If we are trying to read information from a specific location in our document, we may need to keep track of which elements have been opened in the document. For example, say we had the following sample document, test2.xml:

```
<?xml version="1.0"?>
<customer>
    <shippingAddress>
        <address>101 First Street></address>
        <city>Bluesville</city>
        <state>LA</state>
        <postalCode>12345</postalCode>
    </shippingAddress>
    <billingAddress>
        <address>202 Second Street></address>
        <city>Redsville</city>
        <state>NM</state>
        <postalCode>23456</postalCode>
    </billingAddress>
</customer>
```

Context is very important here, if we want the city part of the billing address for the customer, we can't just take the first address element we come across. One way of handling this is to create a Stack object and use it to maintain a picture of the current element stack. By looking at the stack contents, we can determine where we are in the overall document context at any time. We can use the following code sample to find our shipping address:

```
// C#

// Example03.cs
using System;
using System.Xml;
using System.Text;
using System.IO;
using System.Collections;

namespace myApp
{
  class mainClass
  {
    static void Main(string[] args)
    {
      FileStream myFile = new FileStream("test2.xml", FileMode.Open);
      XmlTextReader myReader = new XmlTextReader(myFile);
      myReader.WhitespaceHandling = WhitespaceHandling.Significant;
      Stack myStack = new Stack();
      while(myReader.Read())
        switch(myReader.NodeType)
        {
          case XmlNodeType.Element:
            if(myReader.Name=="address")
              // peek at the top of the stack - is it billingAddress?
              if(myStack.Peek().ToString() == "billingAddress")
                // it is - write the value
                Console.Write(myReader.ReadElementString() + "\n");
              if(!myReader.IsEmptyElement)
                // we're inside this one - push it onto the stack
                myStack.Push(myReader.Name);
                break;
          case XmlNodeType.EndElement:
            // we need to pop this one off the stack
            myStack.Pop();
            break;
          default:
            break;
        }
      myReader.Close();
      myFile.Close();
    }
  }
}
```

Reading Text

As we've seen, the handling of individual text nodes with an `XmlTextReader` is fairly straightforward – simply position the reader on the appropriate text node, then read the value of the text from the `Value` property of the `XmlTextReader`. If the data is enclosed in a CDATA block, the technique is similar – each CDATA block encountered by the parser will be returned as a node with the CDATA type. The contents of the CDATA block can then be read from the `Value` property of the `XmlTextReader`. On the other hand, a better way to read the information is to use the methods that read the values of attributes or elements as strings, such as the `ReadString()` or `ReadElementString()` methods. These methods automatically concatenate CDATA and text node values together into a single value, simplifying our code. For example, if the following element appears in the XML document that is being parsed:

```
<sampleMarkup>Sample start tag: <![CDATA[<customer>]]>.</sampleMarkup>
```

to read the content of the `<sampleMarkup>` element would require three calls using the `Value` property of the `XmlTextReader`. However, we can read the content of the element with one call using the `ReadElementString()` method. This method will return the following string:

```
Sample start tag: <customer>.
```

Reading Comments

Comments are returned as individual nodes by the `XmlTextReader`. When the `XmlTextReader` is pointing to a node with a `NodeType` of `Comment`, the `Value` property contains the text of the comment itself. If we want to ignore comments in the source document, we simply take no action when the parser is positioned on a comment node.

Reading Processing Instructions

Processing instructions are also returned as individual nodes by the `XmlTextReader`. When the `XmlTextReader` is pointing to a node with a `NodeType` of `ProcessingInstruction`, the target of the processing instruction can be found in the `Name` property and the remainder of the processing instruction text can be found in the `Value` property. For example, when the `XmlTextReader` is positioned on the following processing instruction:

```
<?checkID 17, "Alfred Q. Nobody">
```

the `Name` property will contain the string `checkID`, and the `Value` property will contain the string `"17, Alfred Q. Nobody"`. This makes it simple to route processing instruction requests to the appropriate processing engine.

Reading Attributes

Attributes are handled in a very different manner from other node types by the `XmlTextReader`. They do not appear as nodes when the `Read()` method is used to move through an XML document; instead, special methods are required to access the attribute nodes associated with a particular element.

The `HasAttributes` property indicates whether the element has attributes associated with it. This property only has meaning when the `XmlTextReader` is positioned on an element. If this property contains a value of `true`, then there are attributes present on the current element, which may be accessed using the attribute methods of `XmlTextReader`.

If we are looking for a specific attribute value on an element, we can obtain it by using the `GetAttribute()` method on `XmlTextReader`. This method takes the name of the attribute being sought and returns that attribute's value. For example, consider the following sample XML document, `test3.xml`:

```xml
<?xml version="1.0"?>
<Customers>
  <customer customerID="17" name="Alfred P. Somebody" />
  <customer customerID="18" name="Albert P. Somebody" />
</Customers>
```

The following code obtains the values of the `customerID` attributes on the `Customer` elements:

```csharp
// C#

// Example04.cs
using System;
using System.Xml;
```

```
using System.IO;

namespace myApp
{
  class myClass
  {
    static void Main(string[] args)
    {
      FileStream myFile = new FileStream("test3.xml", FileMode.Open);
      XmlTextReader myReader = new XmlTextReader(myFile);
      myReader.WhitespaceHandling = WhitespaceHandling.Significant;
      while(myReader.Read())
        if(myReader.NodeType==XmlNodeType.Element)
          Console.Write(myReader.GetAttribute("customerID") + "\n");
      myReader.Close();
      myFile.Close();
    }
  }
}
```

On the other hand, if we want to return all the attributes for an element but don't necessarily want to build the knowledge of the specific attribute names into our code (or don't know what attributes to expect for an element), we can use the `MoveToFirstAttribute()` and `MoveToNextAttribute()` methods to cycle through all the attributes on a particular element. Using the same example as before, the following code extracts all the attribute name-value pairs for the `Customer` element:

```
// C#

// Example05.cs
using System;
using System.Xml;
using System.IO;

namespace myApp
{
  class myClass
  {
    static void Main(string[] args)
    {
      FileStream myFile = new FileStream("test3.xml", FileMode.Open);
      XmlTextReader myReader = new XmlTextReader(myFile);
      myReader.WhitespaceHandling = WhitespaceHandling.Significant;
      while(myReader.Read())
        if(myReader.NodeType==XmlNodeType.Element && myReader.HasAttributes)
        {
          myReader.MoveToFirstAttribute();
          Console.Write(myReader.Name + ":" + myReader.Value + "\n");
          while(myReader.MoveToNextAttribute())
            Console.Write(myReader.Name + ":" + myReader.Value + "\n");
          myReader.MoveToElement();
        }
      myReader.Close();
      myFile.Close();
    }
  }
}
```

Note that we need to call the `MoveToElement()` method to position the reader back to the element with which the attributes are associated. When this program is compiled and run at the command prompt, you should see results similar to those in the following screenshot.

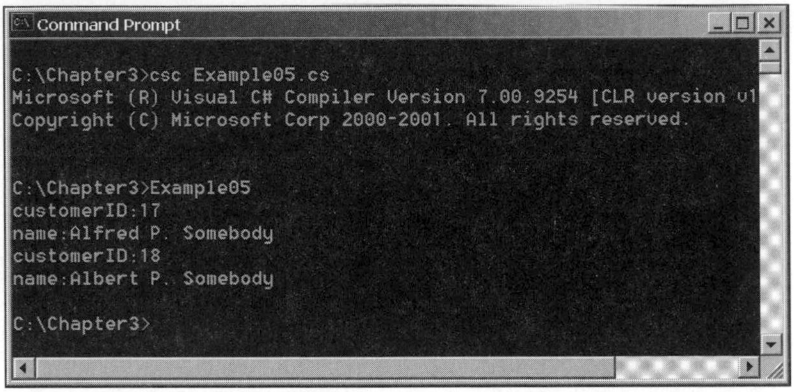

Entity Handling

The `XmlTextReader` class is not able to resolve entities – even those entities that are declared in the internal subset of the document type (that is, entities that are declared in the `DOCTYPE` declaration of the document). It is, however, able to resolve the five built-in XML entities (`&amp;`, `&apos;`, `&quot;`, `&lt;`, and `&gt;`). When parsing an XML document with the `XmlTextReader` class, these five entities will be converted to their text equivalents. Other entity references are returned as `EntityReference` node types. When the parser is positioned on an entity reference, the `Name` property contains the name of the referenced entity. If we need to use a parser that is able to resolve entity references, we should use the `XmlValidatingReader` – which we'll take a look at later in Chapter 6, *Validating XML*.

Namespace Handling

So far, we've only been using the `Name` property to return the names of elements and attributes from our `XmlTextReader`. If the `XmlTextReader` is being used to parse a document that contains namespace declarations, the `Name` property returns the qualified name of the element or attribute. For example, in the following document with namespace declarations, `test4.xml`:

```xml
<?xml version="1.0" ?>
<cust:customer xmlns:cust="http://www.wrox.com/customer">
   <cust:name>Fred Q. Someone</cust:name>
</cust:customer>
```

The following code returns the name of each element:

```csharp
// C#

// Example06.cs
using System;
using System.Xml;
using System.IO;

namespace myApp
{
  class myClass
```

```
    {
      static void Main(string[] args)
      {
        FileStream myFile = new FileStream("test4.xml", FileMode.Open);
        XmlTextReader myReader = new XmlTextReader(myFile);
        myReader.WhitespaceHandling = WhitespaceHandling.Significant;
        while(myReader.Read())
          if(myReader.NodeType==XmlNodeType.Element)
            Console.Write(myReader.Name + "\n");
        myReader.Close();
        myFile.Close();
      }
    }
}
```

This code returns the following output:

```
cust:customer
cust:name
```

Note that the actual qualifier (the selected namespace prefix) is returned, rather than the URI of the declared namespace. If we want to retrieve the namespace URI for a given node, we can also do so using the NamespaceURI property. We can also return just the local name of an element (without the namespace prefix) by using the LocalName property. Using the same sample XML document, the following code returns the namespace URI and local name of each element:

```
// C#

// Example07.cs
using System;
using System.Xml;
using System.IO;

namespace myApp
{
  class myClass
  {
    static void Main(string[] args)
    {
      FileStream myFile = new FileStream("test4.xml", FileMode.Open);
      XmlTextReader myReader = new XmlTextReader(myFile);
      myReader.WhitespaceHandling = WhitespaceHandling.Significant;
      while(myReader.Read())
        if(myReader.NodeType==XmlNodeType.Element)
          Console.Write(myReader.NamespaceURI + ":" +
                        myReader.LocalName + "\n");
      myReader.Close();
      myFile.Close();
    }
  }
}
```

This code returns the following output:

```
http://www.wrox.com/customer:customer
http://www.wrox.com/customer:name
```

The XmlNodeReader Class

The `XmlNodeReader` class is also derived from the `XmlReader` class. This class shares all of its methods with the `XmlTextReader` class, so the techniques described in the previous sections for accessing XML data will work for objects of this type as well. The main difference between `XmlNodeReader` and `XmlTextReader` is in the constructor – `XmlNodeReader` allows access to the contents of XML nodes obtained in some other way, such as part of an XPath resolution or an `XmlDocument` parse. While we haven't yet seen any examples of `XmlNode` objects, they play an important part when manipulating documents using the `XmlDocument` class (which we'll take a look at in the next chapter, *DOM Navigation of XML*) or the XPath classes (which we'll look at in Chapter 5, *XSL Transformations of XML*). For example, we can select XML document fragments using XPath document manipulation methods, then iterate through the fragments to extract their content using `XmlNodeReader` objects. By using a combination of these technologies, we can simplify our code while keeping memory consumption to a minimum. We'll take a look at an example of this once we've covered the other relevant technologies later in the book.

The XmlValidatingReader Class

The other important class derived from `XmlReader` is the `XmlValidatingReader` class. This class can be created from an existing `XmlReader`, or from a string or stream containing an XML fragment. Again, this class has all the same properties and methods as an `XmlTextReader`, so the techniques we've already examined will work for objects of this type as well. The `XmlValidatingReader` class validates the document against a specified XML schema or DTD, and throws errors if the document (or document fragment) is invalid. The `XmlValidatingReader` class is described in much more detail in Chapter 6, *Validating XML*.

Writing XML Documents

We've seen how the .NET framework provides the `XmlReader` abstract class for the serialized reading of XML documents, along with several derived classes that can be instantiated. It's probably not surprising then, that the .NET framework also provides an abstract class called `XmlWriter` for the serialized writing of XML documents, as well as derived classes that can be instantiated. Let's take a look at these classes – the `XmlWriter` abstract class and the `XmlTextWriter` derivation of that class.

The XmlWriter Abstract Class

The `XmlWriter` class is used to serialize XML documents. Since the class is abstract, it may not be instantiated – instead, we must use a class derived from `XmlWriter`. We can create our own `XmlWriter` class if we want, but it would require overriding virtually every property and method (For more information see Chapter 9, *Extending XmlReader and XmlWriter*). The .NET framework provides one class derived from `XmlWriter`, called `XmlTextWriter`, that is designed to work with text representations of XML documents. Let's take a look at how the `XmlTextWriter` class may be used to create XML documents.

The XmlTextWriter Class

This implementation of `XmlWriter` is used to serialize XML documents to strings or streams. To use an instance of `XmlTextWriter`, we specify the target of the serialization, then call methods to add content to the document in the order it needs to appear. Let's see how this is done.

Constructing an Instance of XmlTextWriter

The XmlTextWriter provides three different constructors. If we already have a TextWriter object – an object designed to facilitate the writing of character data to a stream – we can create an XmlTextWriter that sends its information to the underlying stream of that object. More commonly, though, we'll use one of the other forms of the constructor.

To create an XmlTextWriter that sends data to a stream, use the stream form of the constructor. For example, to write XML data to a memory stream, we can do something like this:

```csharp
// C#

Stream myStream = new MemoryStream();
XmlTextWriter myWriter = new XmlTextWriter(myStream, null);
// serialize data to the stream
myWriter.Close();
```

```vbnet
' VB .NET

Dim myStream As New IO.MemoryStream()
Dim myWriter As New Xml.XmlTextWriter(myStream, Nothing)
' serialize data to the stream
myWriter.Close()
```

The second parameter of the constructor, passed as a null or Nothing reference here, is the encoding to be used for the resulting XML document – if a null is passed, the encoding defaults to UTF-8. If we need to use a different encoding, for example Unicode, then we can pass an appropriate encoding object in the constructor:

```csharp
// C#

Stream myStream = new MemoryStream();
System.Text.Encoding myEncoding = new System.Text.UnicodeEncoding();
XmlTextWriter myWriter = new XmlTextWriter(myStream, myEncoding);
// serialize data to the stream
myWriter.Close();
```

```vbnet
' VB .NET

Dim myStream As New IO.MemoryStream()
Dim myEncoding As New Text.UnicodeEncoding()
Dim myWriter As New Xml.XmlTextWriter(myStream, myEncoding)
' serialize data to the stream
myWriter.Close()
```

The final form of the constructor takes a string instead of a stream parameter – this string is interpreted as a filename. This constructor also takes an encoding, with a null value indicating that the document should be encoded as UTF-8 (if we want to use a different encoding, we can do so by passing an encoding value in this parameter). For example:

```csharp
// C#

XmlTextWriter myWriter = new XmlTextWriter("doc.xml", null);
// serialize data to the stream
myWriter.Close();
```

```
' VB .NET

Dim myWriter As New Xml.XmlTextWriter("doc.xml", Nothing)
' serialize data to the stream
myWriter.Close()
```

Writing Data to an XmlTextWriter

Once the document is open, information is written to it by calling the methods on the XmlTextWriter object. Each type of XML node – elements, attributes, text, processing instructions, and so on – has a method that is used to write that type of content. Let's take a look at some of these methods.

Writing Elements

There are a couple of ways that elements can be written using an XmlTextWriter object. The most basic is to write the start element and end element tags as two separate calls – in practice, this would mean writing the start element, writing the contents of the element, and then writing the end element. Here is an example in both C# and VB .NET:

```csharp
// C#

// Example08.cs

using System;
using System.Xml;
using System.IO;

namespace Wrox
{
  class consoleApp
  {
    static void Main(string[] args)
    {
      XmlTextWriter myWriter = new XmlTextWriter("doc.xml", null);
      myWriter.WriteStartElement("rootElement");
      myWriter.WriteStartElement("myContent");
      myWriter.WriteEndElement();
      myWriter.WriteEndElement();
      myWriter.Close();
    }
  }
}
```

```vbnet
' VB .NET

' Example08.vb

Imports System
Imports System.Xml
Imports System.IO

Module Module1

    Sub Main()

        Dim myWriter As New Xml.XmlTextWriter("doc.xml", Nothing)
```

```
            myWriter.WriteStartElement("rootElement")
            myWriter.WriteStartElement("myContent")
            myWriter.WriteEndElement()
            myWriter.WriteEndElement()
            myWriter.Close()

        End Sub

    End Module
```

Note that the `WriteEndElement()` method takes no parameters – the `XmlTextWriter` object keeps a stack of open element names, and knows which end tag to write when the `WriteEndElement()` method is called. If we fail to close all the elements in our code, the `Close()` method on the `XmlTextWriter` will throw an error.

The output of the above code looks like this:

`<rootElement><myContent /></rootElement>`

Note that, in the above output, the `XmlTextWriter` used the abbreviated representation of the `<myContent>` empty element. If the consumer of the document we are creating requires the full close tag to be present for some reason (such as some HTML browsers), we can use the `WriteFullEndElement()` method instead – this forces an empty element to be written instead as a start tag followed by an end tag. If we change the above code to use `WriteFullEndElement()` instead of `WriteEndElement()`:

```
    // C#

    // Example08a.cs

        static void Main(string[] args)
        {
            XmlTextWriter myWriter = new XmlTextWriter("doc.xml", null);
            myWriter.WriteStartElement("rootElement");
            myWriter.WriteStartElement("myContent");
            myWriter.WriteFullEndElement();
            myWriter.WriteFullEndElement();
            myWriter.Close();
        }

    ' VB .NET

    ' Example08.vb

    Sub Main()

        Dim myWriter As New Xml.XmlTextWriter("doc.xml", Nothing)
        myWriter.WriteStartElement("rootElement")
        myWriter.WriteStartElement("myContent")
        myWriter.WriteFullEndElement()
        myWriter.WriteFullEndElement()
        myWriter.Close()

    End Sub
```

The output of this version of the code looks like this:

<rootElement><myContent></myContent></rootElement>

You'll notice that the output is on one line, with no formatting or indentation – this is the default behavior of the XmlTextWriter object. However, there are several formatting options we can take advantage of to improve the formatting of the resulting document – we'll take a look at those in the *Formatting Options* section later in this chapter.

The XmlTextWriter object also provides a convenient helper method. This method allows an element that has only text content to be written in one call, rather than the three calls that would be needed otherwise. The method, WriteElementString(), takes the name of the element and the text content of the element as parameters. For example, the following code uses this method to write elements with text-only content:

```csharp
// C#

// Example09.cs

XmlTextWriter myWriter = new XmlTextWriter("doc.xml", null);
myWriter.WriteStartElement("customer");
myWriter.WriteElementString("name", "John Q. Customer");
myWriter.WriteElementString("phone", "999-555-1212");
myWriter.WriteEndElement();
myWriter.Close();
```

```vbnet
' VB .NET

' Example09.vb

Dim myWriter As New Xml.XmlTextWriter("doc.xml", Nothing)
myWriter.WriteStartElement("customer")
myWriter.WriteElementString("name", "John Q. Customer")
myWriter.WriteElementString("phone", "999-555-1212")
myWriter.WriteEndElement()
myWriter.Close()
```

This code produces the following output (formatting added for clarity):

```
<customer>
  <name>John Q. Customer</name>
  <phone>999-555-1212</phone>
</customer>
```

Writing Text

There are also several methods that are provided by the XmlTextWriter class to allow the writing of text content to an XML document. The one we'll use the most often is WriteString() – this takes a string as a parameter, and sends the content of that string to the resulting XML document. Here's an example:

```csharp
// C#

// Example10.cs

XmlTextWriter myWriter = new XmlTextWriter("doc.xml", null);
```

```
myWriter.WriteStartElement("testElement");
myWriter.WriteString("This is a test.");
myWriter.WriteEndElement();
myWriter.Close();
```

```
' VB .NET

' Example10.vb

Dim myWriter As New Xml.XmlTextWriter("doc.xml", Nothing)
myWriter.WriteStartElement("testElement")
myWriter.WriteString("This is a test.")
myWriter.WriteEndElement()
myWriter.Close()
```

The output of this sample code is the following:

<testElement>This is a test.</testElement>

If we happen to have the text we want to write in a character array, we can use the WriteChars() method to send this data to the XML document. When using this method, we need to pass in a zero-based offset into the character array and the number of characters to write. For example:

```
// C#

// Example11.cs

XmlTextWriter myWriter = new XmlTextWriter("doc.xml", null);
myWriter.WriteStartElement("testElement");
char [] myChars = new char[5] {'A', 'B', 'C', 'D', 'E'};
myWriter.WriteChars(myChars, 1, 3);
myWriter.WriteEndElement();
myWriter.Close();
```

```
' VB .NET

' Example11.vb

Dim myWriter As New Xml.XmlTextWriter("doc.xml", Nothing)
myWriter.WriteStartElement("testElement")
Dim myChars(5) As Char
myChars(0) = "A"
myChars(1) = "B"
myChars(2) = "C"
myChars(3) = "D"
myChars(4) = "E"
myWriter.WriteChars(myChars, 1, 3)
myWriter.WriteEndElement()
myWriter.Close()
```

The output of this code is the following:

<testElement>BC</testElement>

Note that in Beta 2 of the .NET Framework, the documentation for this method is incorrect – the third parameter actually corresponds to the last position in the character array to copy into the target document, rather than the number of characters to be copied. Presumably, Microsoft will resolve this by the time the .NET Framework is released.

If we happen to have a string that contains XML markup, we can write the string to the XML document enclosed in a CDATA marker string. This is done by passing the string to the `WriteCData()` method, like this:

```csharp
// C#

// Example12.cs

XmlTextWriter myWriter = new XmlTextWriter("doc.xml", null);
myWriter.WriteStartElement("testElement");
myWriter.WriteCData("<sampleMarkup>");
myWriter.WriteEndElement();
myWriter.Close();
```

```vbnet
' VB .NET

' Example12.vb

Dim myWriter As New Xml.XmlTextWriter("doc.xml", Nothing)
myWriter.WriteStartElement("testElement")
myWriter.WriteCData("<sampleMarkup>")
myWriter.WriteEndElement()
myWriter.Close()
```

The output of this code is the following:

`<testElement><![CDATA[<sampleMarkup>]]></testElement>`

The `XmlTextWriter` class also provides a couple of methods to encode binary content as printable characters before writing it to an XML document. This is necessary because binary content in an XML document can contain markup or other illegal XML characters.

To encode a piece of binary data using the BinHex algorithm, use the `WriteBinHex()` method. This method takes a byte array, an index into the array to start from, and a number of bytes as its parameters:

```csharp
// C#

// Example13.cs

XmlTextWriter myWriter = new XmlTextWriter("doc.xml", null);
myWriter.WriteStartElement("testElement");
byte[] myBytes = new byte[6] {17, 203, 119, 107, 102, 23};
myWriter.WriteBinHex(myBytes, 3, 2);
myWriter.WriteEndElement();
myWriter.Close();
```

```vbnet
' VB .NET

' Example13.vb
```

```
Dim myWriter As New Xml.XmlTextWriter("doc.xml", Nothing)
myWriter.WriteStartElement("testElement")
Dim myBytes(6) As Byte
myBytes(0) = 17
myBytes(1) = 203
myBytes(2) = 119
myBytes(3) = 107
myBytes(4) = 102
myBytes(5) = 23
myWriter.WriteBinHex(myBytes, 3, 2)
myWriter.WriteEndElement()
myWriter.Close()
```

The output of this code is the following:

<testElement>6B66</testElement>

To use the slightly more efficient Base64 encoding algorithm, use the `WriteBase64()` method instead:

```csharp
// C#

// Example14.cs

XmlTextWriter myWriter = new XmlTextWriter("doc.xml", null);
myWriter.WriteStartElement("testElement");
byte[] myBytes = new byte[6] {17, 203, 119, 107, 102, 23};
myWriter.WriteBase64(myBytes, 3, 2);
myWriter.WriteEndElement();
myWriter.Close();
```

```vbnet
' VB .NET

' Example14.vb

Dim myWriter As New Xml.XmlTextWriter("doc.xml", Nothing)
myWriter.WriteStartElement("testElement")
Dim myBytes(6) As Byte
myBytes(0) = 17
myBytes(1) = 203
myBytes(2) = 119
myBytes(3) = 107
myBytes(4) = 102
myBytes(5) = 23
myWriter.WriteBase64(myBytes, 3, 2)
myWriter.WriteEndElement()
myWriter.Close()
```

The output of this code is the following:

<testElement>a2Y=</testElement>

Writing Comments

Not surprisingly, comments are written to an XML document with the `WriteComment()` method. We pass the string content of the comment (not the comment markers, just the comment text) to the method, and it adds the comment to the XML document being generated. For example:

```
// C#

// Example15.cs

XmlTextWriter myWriter = new XmlTextWriter("doc.xml", null);
myWriter.WriteStartElement("testElement");
myWriter.WriteComment("This is my comment!");
myWriter.WriteEndElement();
myWriter.Close();
```

```
' VB .NET

' Example15.vb

Dim myWriter As New Xml.XmlTextWriter("doc.xml", Nothing)
myWriter.WriteStartElement("testElement")
myWriter.WriteComment("This is my comment!")
myWriter.WriteEndElement()
myWriter.Close()
```

This generates the following result:

<testElement><!-- This is my comment! --></testElement>

Writing Processing Instructions

The method used to write a processing instruction to an XML document, `WriteProcessingInstruction()`, takes two parameters: the string that is the name of the processing instruction, and the string that contains the remainder of the processing instruction text. For example:

```
// C#

// Example16.cs

XmlTextWriter myWriter = new XmlTextWriter("doc.xml", null);
myWriter.WriteStartElement("testElement");
myWriter.WriteProcessingInstruction("checkID", "17, 1, 32");
myWriter.WriteEndElement();
myWriter.Close();
```

```
' VB .NET

' Example16.vb

Dim myWriter As New Xml.XmlTextWriter("doc.xml", Nothing)
myWriter.WriteStartElement("testElement")
myWriter.WriteProcessingInstruction("checkID", "17, 1, 32")
myWriter.WriteEndElement()
myWriter.Close()
```

The output of this code is the following:

<testElement><?checkID 17, 1, 32?></testElement>

Writing Entity References

Entity references are written to an XML document using the `WriteEntityRef()` method. It takes the name of the entity as a string parameter and puts the entity reference declaration markers around the name before it serializes it to the target document. Here's an example:

```csharp
// C#

// Example17.cs

XmlTextWriter myWriter = new XmlTextWriter("doc.xml", null);
myWriter.WriteStartElement("testElement");
myWriter.WriteEntityRef("cust");
myWriter.WriteEndElement();
myWriter.Close();
```

```vbnet
' VB .NET

' Example17.vb

Dim myWriter As New Xml.XmlTextWriter("doc.xml", Nothing)
myWriter.WriteStartElement("testElement")
myWriter.WriteEntityref("cust")
myWriter.WriteEndElement()
myWriter.Close()
```

And the output looks like this:

```
<testElement>&cust;</testElement>
```

Writing Attributes

As with elements, there are several ways we can write attributes to our destination document. The most common way is by using the `WriteStartAttribute()` and `WriteEndAttribute()` methods. Since attribute values can contain text, entity references, or CDATA sections, this allows us to write the content of the attribute using separate methods. Here's an example:

```csharp
// C#

// Example18.cs

XmlTextWriter myWriter = new XmlTextWriter("doc.xml", null);
myWriter.WriteStartElement("testElement");
myWriter.WriteStartAttribute("myAttr", null);
myWriter.WriteString("sample");
myWriter.WriteEntityRef("val");
myWriter.WriteEndAttribute();
myWriter.WriteEndElement();
myWriter.Close();
```

```vbnet
' VB .NET

' Example18.vb

Dim myWriter As New Xml.XmlTextWriter("doc.xml", Nothing)
myWriter.WriteStartElement("testElement")
```

```
myWriter.WriteStartAttribute("myAttr", Nothing)
myWriter.WriteString("sample")
myWriter.WriteEntityRef("val")
myWriter.WriteEndAttribute()
myWriter.WriteEndElement()
myWriter.Close()
```

Note that there is no method that allows an unqualified attribute name (an attribute name with no namespace prefix) to be created; instead, both of the possible forms of the method require namespace information to be provided. To create attributes in the default namespace, simply pass a null value as the namespace parameter. Here's the resulting output:

```
<testElement myAttr="sample&val;" />
```

For attributes that have simple string content, there's a quicker way to create them. The `WriteAttributeString()` method allows us to create an attribute with a simple string value in one step. Different forms of this method are used to create attributes in namespaces or unqualified attributes. Here's an example:

```
// C#

// Example19.cs

XmlTextWriter myWriter = new XmlTextWriter("doc.xml", null);
myWriter.WriteStartElement("testElement");
myWriter.WriteAttributeString("myAttr", "sampleVal");
myWriter.WriteEndElement();
myWriter.Close();
```

```
' VB .NET

' Example19.vb

Dim myWriter As New Xml.XmlTextWriter("doc.xml", Nothing)
myWriter.WriteStartElement("testElement")
myWriter.WriteAttributeString("myAttr", "sampleVal")
myWriter.WriteEndElement()
myWriter.Close()
```

And the resulting XML output looks like this:

```
<testElement myAttr="sampleVal" />
```

Finally, if we're driving the generation of our XML document with an XmlReader, there is a helper method that will transfer all the attributes from an element in an XmlReader to the resulting element in the XmlWriter with one call. The method is called WriteAttributes(), and it takes an XmlReader as a parameter (along with a flag indicating whether default attribute values should be written to the resulting document). Rather than looking at an example of this here, we'll see how this works later in the chapter when we look at chaining an XmlReader and XmlWriter together.

Namespace Support

The XmlWriter class provides full support for namespaces. The methods that write elements and attributes have overloaded versions that allow namespace URIs and prefixes to be associated with the elements or attributes being created. XmlWriter will automatically declare the namespaces in the resulting XML document where they are needed. For example, the following code creates the Customer element in the http://localhost/cust namespace:

```
// C#

// Example20.cs

XmlTextWriter myWriter = new XmlTextWriter("doc.xml", null);
myWriter.WriteStartElement("testElement");
myWriter.WriteStartElement("customer", "http://localhost/cust");
myWriter.WriteEndElement();
myWriter.WriteEndElement();
myWriter.Close();
```

```
' VB .NET

' Example20.vb

Dim myWriter As New Xml.XmlTextWriter("doc.xml", Nothing)
myWriter.WriteStartElement("testElement")
myWriter.WriteStartElement("customer", "http://localhost/cust")
myWriter.WriteEndElement()
myWriter.WriteEndElement()
myWriter.Close()
```

The output of the above code is this:

```
<testElement><customer xmlns="http://localhost/cust" /></testElement>
```

Note that, since we didn't specify a prefix, the namespace is declared as the default namespace for the element. If there is already a namespace in scope with a prefix, that prefix is automatically added to the element or attribute name. For example, here we declare the customer namespace with a prefix, then create a customerName element with the same namespace:

```
// C#

// Example21.cs

XmlTextWriter myWriter = new XmlTextWriter("doc.xml", null);
myWriter.WriteStartElement("testElement");
myWriter.WriteStartElement("cust", "customer", "http://localhost/cust");
myWriter.WriteElementString("customerName", "http://localhost/cust",
                            "Fred Q. Person");
myWriter.WriteEndElement();
myWriter.WriteEndElement();
myWriter.Close();
```

```
' VB .NET

' Example21.vb
```

97

```
Dim myWriter As New Xml.XmlTextWriter("doc.xml", Nothing)
myWriter.WriteStartElement("testElement")
myWriter.WriteStartElement("cust", "customer", "http://localhost/cust")
myWriter.WriteElementString("customerName", "http://localhost/cust", _
                             "Fred Q. Person")
myWriter.WriteEndElement()
myWriter.WriteEndElement()
myWriter.Close()
```

The output of this code is this (formatting added for clarity):

```
<testElement>
  <cust:customer xmlns:cust="http://localhost/cust">
    <cust:customerName>Fred Q. Person</cust:customerName>
  </cust:customer>
</testElement>
```

Formatting Options

As we mentioned earlier in the chapter, `XmlTextWriter` provides a number of ways we can control the formatting of our output document. Note that this isn't necessary if our document is only going to be machine read – all formatting introduced by these options is ignored by parsers – but it will make the documents easier for a human to interpret.

To enable formatting by `XmlTextWriter`, the first thing we need to do is to set the `Formatting` property. This property takes one of two values: `Indented` or `None`, and is `None` by default. Setting this property to `Indented` instructs the `XmlTextWriter` to indent element content in the resulting XML document. Note that only elements are indented – mixed content is left as-is. We can also control the whitespace character used for formatting by setting the `IndentChar` property (the default value is a space), and the number of characters to use per level with the `Indentation` property (the default number is two). Some examples will make this clear.

In this example, the generated XML document indents elements by two spaces:

```
// C#

// Example22.cs

XmlTextWriter myWriter = new XmlTextWriter("doc.xml", null);
myWriter.Formatting = Formatting.Indented;
myWriter.WriteStartElement("testElement");
myWriter.WriteStartElement("customer");
myWriter.WriteElementString("customerName", "Fred Q. Person");
myWriter.WriteEndElement();
myWriter.WriteEndElement();
myWriter.Close();
```

```
' VB .NET

' Example22.vb

Dim myWriter As New Xml.XmlTextWriter("doc.xml", Nothing)
myWriter.Formatting = Xml.Formatting.Indented
myWriter.WriteStartElement("testElement")
myWriter.WriteStartElement("customer")
```

```
myWriter.WriteElementString("customerName", "Fred Q. Person")
myWriter.WriteEndElement()
myWriter.WriteEndElement()
myWriter.Close()
```

The output of this code is this:

```
<testElement>
  <customer>
    <customerName>Fred Q. Person</customerName>
  </customer>
</testElement>
```

However, in this example a single tab character is used for the indentation:

```
// C#
```

```
// Example23.cs
```

```
XmlTextWriter myWriter = new XmlTextWriter("doc.xml", null);
myWriter.Formatting = Formatting.Indented;
myWriter.IndentChar = '\t';
myWriter.Indentation = 1;
myWriter.WriteStartElement("testElement");
myWriter.WriteStartElement("customer");
myWriter.WriteElementString("customerName", "Fred Q. Person");
myWriter.WriteEndElement();
myWriter.WriteEndElement();
myWriter.Close();
```

```
' VB .NET
```

```
' Example23.vb
```

```
Dim myWriter As New Xml.XmlTextWriter("doc.xml", Nothing)
myWriter.Formatting = Xml.Formatting.Indented
myWriter.IndentChar = Chr(9)
myWriter.Indentation = 1
myWriter.WriteStartElement("testElement")
myWriter.WriteStartElement("customer")
myWriter.WriteElementString("customerName", "Fred Q. Person")
myWriter.WriteEndElement()
myWriter.WriteEndElement()
myWriter.Close()
```

The output of this code is this:

```
<testElement>
    <customer>
        <customerName>Fred Q. Person</customerName>
    </customer>
</testElement>
```

We can also set whether single quotes or double quotes should be used to delimit attribute values. The default is double quotes, which should be fine for most applications; however, if we prefer, we can change this. In this example, single quotes are used to delimit the attributes:

```csharp
// C#

// Example24.cs

XmlTextWriter myWriter = new XmlTextWriter("doc.xml", null);
myWriter.QuoteChar='\'';
myWriter.WriteStartElement("customer");
myWriter.WriteAttributeString("customerName", "Fred Q. Person");
myWriter.WriteAttributeString("customerID", "12345");
myWriter.WriteEndElement();
myWriter.Close();
```

```vbnet
' VB .NET

' Example24.vb

Dim myWriter As New Xml.XmlTextWriter("doc.xml", Nothing)
myWriter.QuoteChar = "'"
myWriter.WriteStartElement("customer")
myWriter.WriteAttributeString("customerName", "Fred Q. Person")
myWriter.WriteAttributeString("customerID", "12345")
myWriter.WriteEndElement()
myWriter.Close()
```

And the resulting output is this:

```
<customer customerName='Fred Q. Person' customerID='12345' />
```

A More Complex Example

Finally, let's take a look at a more typical business problem and see how the technologies we've learned in this chapter can be applied to it to help solve it.

The Problem

Our company is The Widget Factory, Inc., a manufacturer of small mechanical parts for engines. We have a large number of invoice documents stored in a document repository. These invoice documents describe the parts sold to our customers, which parts and how many, on each invoice. However, the invoice documents identify the parts using a part ID as opposed to a human-readable part name. We're setting up an online system using .NET that our customers can use to check the contents of their invoices, but we'd like to show our customers the human-readable name of the part instead of the part ID. Therefore, we'd like to create a static method that reads an invoice document from a file, changes the partID attributes on the part elements to <partName> elements, and returns the resulting document in a different file, which can then be styled for presentation on our online system. We will potentially be processing hundreds of these documents, so we'd like to keep the memory footprint down to a minimum.

Our Solution: Encapsulate a Reader and a Writer

Since we only need to make relatively minor changes to our document, the best approach is to read the document using the `XmlTextReader` streamed reader and write the document back out using the `XmlTextWriter` streamed writer. This will minimize our memory consumption. The general idea is this: we'll take a quick peek at the nodes as they are returned by the `XmlTextReader`. If the node is a `<Part>` element, then we'll go through the attributes one-by-one until we find the `PartID`; instead of writing it to the `XmlTextWriter`, we'll call a private method that returns the appropriate part name and write that to the `XmlTextWriter` as an element.

The sample input document we'll be using is `Invoice.xml`:

```
<invoice>
    <customer customerID="17">
        <mailingAddress>
            <address1>742 Evergreen Terrace</address1>
            <city>Springfield</city>
            <state>XX</state>
            <postalCode>12345</postalCode>
        </mailingAddress>
    </customer>
    <part partID="17">
        <quantity>2</quantity>
        <price>13.50</price>
    </part>
    <part partID="18">
        <quantity>3</quantity>
        <price>14.50</price>
    </part>
    <part partID="20">
        <quantity>4</quantity>
        <price>15.50</price>
    </part>
    <part partID="22">
        <quantity>5</quantity>
        <price>16.50</price>
    </part>
    <part partID="23">
        <quantity>6</quantity>
        <price>17.50</price>
    </part>
</invoice>
```

First, let's create the private static method that returns the part name for the part ID (normally this would be accessing a relational database to obtain the part name, but for the purposes of illustration we'll hardcode the part names):

```csharp
// C#

// WidgetFactory.cs
using System;
using System.Xml;
using System.IO;

namespace Wrox
{
```

```
class consoleApp
{
  static void Main(string[] args)
  {
    TranslateParts("invoice.xml", "newinvoice.xml");
  }

  static string GetPartName (string sPartID)
  {
    switch(sPartID)
    {
      case "17":
        return("2 inch grommets");
        break;
      case "18":
        return("3 inch grommets");
        break;
      case "20":
        return("2 inch widgets");
        break;
      case "22":
        return("1 inch widgets");
        break;
      default:
        return("Unknown");
        break;
    }
  }
}
```

Next, let's take a look at the code that actually moves data through the reader and the writer. First, we create an `XmlTextReader` and an `XmlTextWriter` on the supplied input and output XML filenames:

```
static void TranslateParts(string sInDoc, string sOutDoc)
{
  XmlTextReader myReader = new XmlTextReader(sInDoc);
  XmlTextWriter myWriter = new XmlTextWriter(sOutDoc, null);
```

We'll make the output a little more readable by turning on `XmlTextWriter`'s formatting capabilities:

```
myWriter.Formatting = Formatting.Indented;
```

Next, we need to move through the source document looking for `<part>` elements with `partID` attributes:

```
while(myReader.Read())
  {
    if((myReader.NodeType==XmlNodeType.Element) &&
      (myReader.Name=="part"))
    {
```

Once we've found a `<part>` element, we need to process each of the attributes individually. For attributes that are not `partID`, we simply need to write the attribute to the output document. Otherwise, we'll need to use our function to translate it into a part name:

```
myWriter.WriteStartElement(myReader.Name);
myReader.MoveToFirstAttribute();
// move through the attributes
```

```
        bool bFinished = false;
        while(!bFinished)
        {
           if(myReader.Name == "partID")
```

When we're processing the partID attribute, instead of writing it to the destination document, we're going to write a <partName> element that contains the translated name (as provided by the GetPartName() static method we described earlier):

```
              myWriter.WriteElementString("partName",
                                            GetPartName(myReader.Value));
          else
```

Otherwise, we simply copy the attribute over to the destination document:

```
              myWriter.WriteAttributeString(myReader.Name,
                                              myReader.Value);
              bFinished = !myReader.MoveToNextAttribute();
          }
          myReader.MoveToElement();
        }
      else
```

For any other type of content, we simply copy that content to the destination document. Note that for elements, we use the shortcut method described earlier in the chapter to move all of the attributes for the current <XmlReader> element to the <XmlWriter> element. This lets us avoid walking through each attribute individually:

```
      {
        switch(myReader.NodeType)
        {
        case XmlNodeType.Element:
          myWriter.WriteStartElement(myReader.Name);
          myWriter.WriteAttributes(myReader, false);
          break;
        case XmlNodeType.CDATA:
          myWriter.WriteCData(myReader.Value);
          break;
        case XmlNodeType.EndElement:
          myWriter.WriteEndElement();
          break;
        case XmlNodeType.EntityReference:
          myWriter.WriteEntityRef(myReader.Name);
          break;
        case XmlNodeType.ProcessingInstruction:
          myWriter.WriteProcessingInstruction(myReader.Name,
                                                myReader.Value);
          break;
        case XmlNodeType.Text:
        case XmlNodeType.SignificantWhitespace:
          myWriter.WriteString(myReader.Value);
          break;
        default:
          // write nothing to the result document
          break;
```

```
                }
              }
            }
        myReader.Close();
        myWriter.Close();
      }
    }
  }
```

When we run this code against our sample invoice, this is the output, `newinvoice.xml`:

```xml
<invoice>
  <customer customerID="17">
    <mailingAddress>
      <address1>742 Evergreen Terrace</address1>
      <city>Springfield</city>
      <state>XX</state>
      <postalCode>12345</postalCode>
    </mailingAddress>
  </customer>
  <part>
    <partName>4 inch grommets</partName>
    <quantity>2</quantity>
    <price>13.50</price>
  </part>
  <part>
    <partName>3 inch grommets</partName>
    <quantity>3</quantity>
    <price>14.50</price>
  </part>
  <part>
    <partName>2 inch widgets</partName>
    <quantity>4</quantity>
    <price>15.50</price>
  </part>
  <part>
    <partName>1 inch widgets</partName>
    <quantity>5</quantity>
    <price>16.50</price>
  </part>
  <part>
    <partName>Unknown</partName>
    <quantity>6</quantity>
    <price>17.50</price>
  </part>
</invoice>
```

Summary

In this chapter, we've taken a look at the forward-only mechanisms provided by the .NET framework for reading and writing XML documents. These classes perform well and have a small memory footprint; however, they may be unsuited to some tasks (such as making complex changes to the internal structure of a document or navigating pointing relationships within a document). We've also seen how chaining an `XmlReader` and an `XmlWriter` provides a efficient way to make modifications to XML documents. In the next chapter, we'll take a look at the other classes in the .NET framework designed for the loading and manipulation of XML documents – the DOM classes.

XML for .NET Developers
Professional XML for .NET Developers Professional XML

DOM Navigation of XML

In this chapter, we'll take a look at the classes provided in the .NET framework for the manipulation of XML documents using the Document Object Model, or DOM, interface. The subjects we'll be addressing include:

- ❑ The classes that provide DOM-style support, including `XmlDocument` and all the classes derived from the `XmlNode` abstract class

- ❑ The differences between the DOM classes and the streamed XML classes, and the situations where the use of each is appropriate

- ❑ Extensions to the DOM model included in the .NET classes

- ❑ Reading documents using the DOM classes

- ❑ Writing documents using the DOM classes

- ❑ Extending the DOM classes

Technologies Used

Like the previous chapter, this chapter will present its examples using the C# and VB .NET programming languages. If you prefer, it should be a simple matter to port the examples to C++ .NET as most of the code simply calls objects found in the .NET framework. Sample code will be provided in the form of Console Applications to keep the samples simple and easy to understand. You should be able to compile the samples either using the command-line .NET Framework compilers or by inserting the code into a Visual Studio .NET Console Application project.

The System.Xml Assembly

The objects we'll be using in this chapter may all be found in the System.Xml assembly in the .NET Framework. Note that if we use Visual Studio .NET to create our code, the System.Xml assembly will automatically be part of the project – so we don't need to manually add it to the list of references for the project. This assembly contains objects that operate directly on XML documents, including both forward-only access objects, similar to the Simple API for XML (SAX), and random-access objects that load entire documents into memory, similar to DOM. This assembly also includes some helper classes, such as name table classes, that are used to improve the performance of Microsoft's XML parser. This chapter addresses the classes that implement the DOM interface to XML documents.

Understanding the DOM Classes

Before we start discussing the specifics of the DOM implementation in .NET, let's take a quick look at how the .NET implementation of the DOM works and how it builds its representation of an XML document.

Document Representation

Unlike the streamed, forward-only XmlReader and XmlWriter classes that we looked at in the previous chapter, the DOM model loads an entire XML document into memory at once. The document is decomposed into individual atoms of information – elements, attributes, comments, processing instructions, and so on – and a tree structure is built from them. The individual components of the document are called **nodes**, and each one is represented by an implementation of the XmlNode abstract class (which we'll look at a little later in the chapter). Let's take a look at a quick example of a document:

```xml
<?xml version="1.0"?>
<customer customerID="cust123">
    <customerName>Fred Q. Customer</customerName>
    <address>
        <streetAddress>314 Somewhere Street</streetAddress>
        <city>Randomsville</city>
        <state>XY</state>
        <postalCode>27182</postalCode>
    </address>
</customer>
```

This simple document is represented by the DOM classes in a tree structure that looks like this:

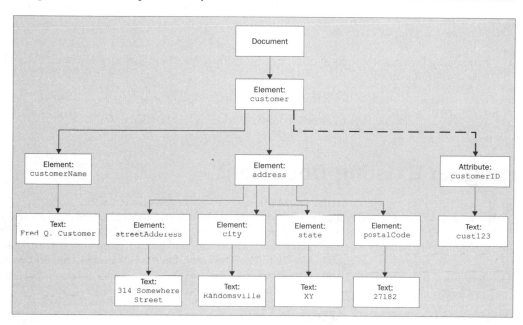

In this diagram, each box represents a node or more accurately, an instance of a class that implements the XmlNode abstract class. Note that the text content has its own node type, and since elements can have mixed text and element content (if we're marking up a text document, for example), text content needs to be represented as separate nodes. Also, note that there is a dotted line connecting the customerID attribute to the rest of the diagram. This is because attribute nodes are handled differently from other nodes in a DOM model of an XML document (as we'll see later in the chapter).

Usage Guidelines

As we've seen, the .NET classes provide two primary mechanisms for accessing and creating XML documents: the XmlReader and XmlWriter classes, and the DOM classes. Each of these methods has strengths and weaknesses. The XmlReader and XmlWriter classes stream information through memory, keeping their memory footprint very small; however, this means that documents have to be read in the order they appear in the source document (or written in the order they will appear in the destination document). This can make it difficult to work with complex documents, such as those that have IDREF pointers or other complex structures. On the other hand, the memory footprint for the DOM classes is much larger, as these classes load entire documents at once; however, this allows us to navigate around the document at will, making it easier to work with complex documents or documents that contain pointing relationships. Here are some good rules-of-thumb for when to use the XmlReader and XmlWriter classes, and when to use the DOM classes:

XmlReader and XmlWriter are better suited to:

❑ Processing many documents simultaneously – this keeps the memory footprint down

❑ Extracting relatively small amounts of information from large documents

> ❑ Working with documents that have simple structures

The DOM classes are better suited to:

> ❑ Processing fewer documents at once, or other situations where memory consumption and speed are not crucial

> ❑ Extracting most or all of the information from large documents

> ❑ Working with documents that have complex structures or IDREF pointers

Opening an Existing Document

To open an existing document using the DOM classes, we can simply use either the LoadXml() method or one of the overloads of the Load() method on an instantiated XmlDocument object. When the XML document is parsed by the XmlDocument object, that object's ChildNodes list (a collection of XmlNode objects that describe the contents of the XML document) will be populated according to the contents of the document; it can then be navigated as necessary. Let's take a look at the most common ways of opening a document using the XmlDocument class.

Opening a Document from a URL

To open a document from a URL, use the overload of the Load() method that takes a string parameter. This string represents the URL where the XML document may be found. The following demonstrates the syntax used with C#:

```
// C#

XmlDocument myDocument = new XmlDocument();
myDocument.Load("http://localhost/sample.xml");
// process the document as appropriate
myFile.Close();
```

The same can be achieved using VB .NET as follows:

```
' VB .NET
Dim myDocument As New Xml.XmlDocument()
myDocument.Load("http://localhost/sample.xml")
' process the document as appropriate
myFile.Close()
```

Opening a Document from a File

Documents may be opened from a file by first creating a FileStream object based on that file. That object should then be passed to the overload of the Load() method on the XmlDocument object that takes a stream as a parameter. The document will then be loaded and parsed from the provided stream. Let's look how this is done:

```csharp
// C#

XmlDocument myDocument = new XmlDocument();
FileStream myFile = new FileStream("mydoc.xml", FileMode.Open);
myDocument.Load(myFile);
// process the document as appropriate
myFile.Close();
```

```vbnet
' VB .NET

Dim myDocument As New Xml.XmlDocument()
Dim myFile As New IO.FileStream("mydoc.xml", IO.FileMode.Open)
myDocument.Load(myFile)
' process the document as appropriate
myFile.Close()
```

Opening a Document from a String in Memory

To parse a document that is held in a string in memory, we can use the LoadXml() method on the XmlDocument object. It interprets the string as an XML document and parses it as appropriate. We might use this method to parse an XML string passed to us as a parameter of a SOAP message, for example, or one that was selected from a relational database. For example, the following code reads the XML in the string and parses it:

```csharp
// C#

XmlDocument myDocument = new XmlDocument();
string myXML = "<customer><name>Fred Q. Somebody</name></customer>";
myDocument.LoadXml(myXML);
// process the document as appropriate
```

```vbnet
' VB .NET

Dim myDocument As New Xml.XmlDocument()
Dim myXML As String
myXML = "<customer><name>Fred Q. Somebody</name></customer>"
myDocument.LoadXml(myXML)
' process the document as appropriate
```

Navigating Through the Document

Navigating through an XML document loaded into the DOM classes is straightforward. Each node in the document has a list of child nodes associated with it, the ChildNodes collection, and also contains a pointer back to its parent node, held in the ParentNode property. Depending on the actual object type of each of the nodes, we can determine the type of content and retrieve it from the document. We'll see some specific examples of this later in the chapter.

Searching for Content in the Document

There are several methods provided by the DOM objects to assist in the quick searching of XML documents. These typically return either an XmlNode object or an XmlNodeList object that contains the node or nodes that match the provided search criteria. Let's look at a few of these methods now.

GetElementsByTagName()

This method is implemented for the XmlDocument and XmlElement classes. It returns an XmlNodeList (a collection of XmlNode objects) that corresponds to all of the elements matching the provided tag name that can be found as children of the specified XmlDocument or XmlElement. For example, using the following sample XML file:

```
<!-- consumerlist.xml -->
<customerList>
    <customer customerID="12345">
        <name>Fred Q. Somebody</name>
        <address>100 Somewhere Street</address>
        <city>Sometown</city>
       <state>XY</state>
        <postalCode>13579</postalCode>
    </customer>
    <customer customerID="23456">
        <name>Jimmy C. Anybody</name>
        <address>200 Anywhere Lane</address>
        <city>Anytown</city>
        <state>YZ</state>
        <postalCode>99999</postalCode>
    </customer>
    <customer customerID="34567">
        <name>Mark Z. Somebody</name>
        <address>300 Nowhere Avenue</address>
        <city>Nowheresville</city>
        <state>XY</state>
        <postalCode>94949</postalCode>
    </customer>
</customerList>
```

The following code gets the <city> elements that are found in the entire document, and then the <city> elements that are found in the first <customer> element:

```csharp
// C#

// consumerlist.cs
using System;
using System.Xml;
using System.IO;

namespace Wrox
{
  class consoleApp
  {
```

```csharp
    static void Main(string[] args)
    {
      XmlDocument myDocument = new XmlDocument();
      FileStream myStream =
        new FileStream("consumerlist.xml", FileMode.Open);
      myDocument.Load(myStream);
      Console.Write("City elements found in the entire document:\r\n");
      XmlNodeList myCities = myDocument.GetElementsByTagName("city");
      for(int i=0; i<myCities.Count; i++)
        Console.Write(myCities[i].ChildNodes[0].Value + "\r\n");
      Console.Write(
        "City elements found in the first customer element:\r\n");
      XmlElement firstCustomer =
        (XmlElement)myDocument.DocumentElement.ChildNodes[0];
      myCities = firstCustomer.GetElementsByTagName("city");
      for(int i=0; i<myCities.Count; i++)
        Console.Write(myCities[i].ChildNodes[0].Value + "\r\n");
      myStream.Close();
      Console.ReadLine();
    }
  }
}
```

```vbnet
' VB .NET

' consumerlist.vb
Imports System
Imports System.Xml
Imports System.IO

Module Module1

  Sub Main()

    Dim myDocument As New Xml.XmlDocument()
    Dim myStream As New IO.FileStream("consumerlist.xml", IO.FileMode.Open)
    Dim firstCustomer As Xml.XmlElement

    myDocument.Load(myStream)
    Console.WriteLine("City elements found in the entire document:")
    Dim myCities As Xml.XmlNodeList
    myCities = myDocument.GetElementsByTagName("city")
    Dim i As Integer
    For i = 0 To myCities.Count - 1
      Console.WriteLine(myCities(i).ChildNodes(0).Value )
    Next i
    Console.WriteLine( _
        "City elements found in the first customer element:")
    firstCustomer = myDocument.DocumentElement.ChildNodes(0)
    myCities = firstCustomer.GetElementsByTagName("city")
    For i = 0 To myCities.Count - 1
      Console.WriteLine(myCities(i).ChildNodes(0).Value )
    Next i
    myStream.Close()
```

```
      Console.ReadLine()

   End Sub

End Module
```

We can compile and run the C# code as follows from the Command Prompt:

>**csc consumerlist.cs**

>**consumerlist**

To compile the VB .NET code from the Command Prompt is slightly more complicated. We need to reference types in the System.Xml assembly, which the VB .NET compiler doesn't reference by default. To do this we use the /reference or /r switch as below:

>**vbc consumerlist.vb /r:System.Xml.dll**

>**consumerlist**

The output of either the VB .NET or C# code is this:

GetElementById()

This method is found on the XmlDocument object, and returns the element with an attribute of type ID that matches the specified ID. Note that this requires that the document have an associated schema or DTD – the DOM implementation does not assume that an attribute represents an ID unless it is explicitly defined as one in a DTD or schema. We will demonstrate this using the following XML file (parts.xml), which contains an internal DTD:

```xml
<?xml version="1.0"?>
<!DOCTYPE partList [
  <!ELEMENT partList (part+)>
  <!ELEMENT part (name, size, color)>
  <!ATTLIST part partID ID #REQUIRED>
  <!ELEMENT name (#PCDATA)>
  <!ELEMENT size (#PCDATA)>
  <!ELEMENT color (#PCDATA)>]>

<partList>
  <part partID="part17">
    <name>Grommets</name>
```

```
      <size>2 inch</size>
      <color>Red</color>
    </part>
    <part partID="part22">
      <name>Widgets</name>
      <size>3 inch</size>
      <color>Blue</color>
    </part>
</partList>
```

The following code returns the <part> element with partID of part17:

```
// c#

// parts.cs
using System;
using System.Xml;
using System.IO;

namespace Wrox
{
  class consoleApp
  {
    static void Main(string[] args)
    {
      XmlDocument myDocument = new XmlDocument();
      FileStream myStream = new FileStream("parts.xml", FileMode.Open);
      XmlValidatingReader myReader =
              new XmlValidatingReader(myStream, XmlNodeType.Document, null);
      myDocument.Load(myReader);
      Console.Write("Part name for part ID part17:\r\n");
      XmlElement part17 = myDocument.GetElementById("part17");
      Console.Write(part17.ChildNodes[0].ChildNodes[0].Value + "\r\n");
      myStream.Close();
      Console.ReadLine();
    }
  }
}
```

```
' VB .NET

' parts.vb
Imports System
Imports System.Xml
Imports System.IO

Module Module1

  Sub Main()

    Dim myDocument As New Xml.XmlDocument()
    Dim myStream As New IO.FileStream("parts.xml", IO.FileMode.Open)
    Dim myReader As New Xml.XmlValidatingReader(myStream, _
```

```
                                      Xml.XmlNodeType.Document, Nothing)
        myDocument.Load(myReader)
        Console.WriteLine("Part name for part ID part17: ")
        Dim part17 As Xml.XmlElement
        part17 = myDocument.GetElementById("part17")
        Console.WriteLine(part17.ChildNodes(0).ChildNodes(0).Value)
        myStream.Close()
        Console.ReadLine()

    End Sub

End Module
```

Note that we have to load the XmlDocument object using an XmlValidatingReader – otherwise, the processor does not recognize that the partID attribute is actually an ID, and the GetElementById() method will fail. We'll discuss using an XmlValidatingReader for DTD and schema validation in Chapter 6.

Compiling and running the code as in the previous example gives this output:

SelectNodes()

This method, a .NET extension to the DOM, may be found on all the objects derived from XmlNode. It allows us to select all the nodes relative to the XmlNode that match a provided XPath expression, and returns them in an XmlNodeList. (For more information about XPath, see the next chapter). This is an extremely powerful way to quickly access the content of an XML document if the location of the nodes in question is more complex than a simple element name or ID.

For example, using the customer.xml file we used earlier, the following code retrieves the value of the <city> element for all the customers whose state is XY:

```csharp
// C#

// selectNodes.cs
using System;
using System.Xml;
using System.IO;

namespace Wrox
{
  class consoleApp
  {
    static void Main(string[] args)
    {
      XmlDocument myDocument = new XmlDocument();
```

```
        FileStream myStream =
          new FileStream("consumerlist.xml", FileMode.Open);
        myDocument.Load(myStream);
        Console.Write("Cities for customers that are in the XY state:\r\n");
        XmlNodeList XYCities = myDocument.SelectNodes(
          "//customer/city/text()[../../state/text()='XY']");
        for (int i=0; i<XYCities.Count; i++)
          Console.Write(XYCities[i].Value + "\r\n");
        myStream.Close();
        Console.ReadLine();
      }
    }
  }
```

```vbnet
' VB .NET

' selectNodes.vb
Imports System
Imports System.Xml
Imports System.IO

Module Module1

  Sub Main()

    Dim myDocument As New Xml.XmlDocument()
    Dim myStream As New IO.FileStream("consumerlist.xml", IO.FileMode.Open)
    myDocument.Load(myStream)
    Console.WriteLine("Cities for customers that are in the XY state: ")
    Dim XYCities As Xml.XmlNodeList
    XYCities = myDocument.SelectNodes( _
        "//customer/city/text()[../../state/text()='XY']")
    Dim i As Integer
    For i = 0 To XYCities.Count - 1
      Console.WriteLine(XYCities(i).Value)
    Next i
    myStream.Close()
    Console.ReadLine()
  End Sub

End Module
```

The result of compiling and running this code is this:

SelectSingleNode()

This method is also found on all classes derived from `XmlNode`. Like `SelectNodes()`, it allows us to search a document using an XPath expression; however, it only returns the first node relative to the starting node (in document order) that matches the expression. Using the same sample XML file as in the previous section (`customer.xml`), the following code retrieves the city for only the first customer in the XY state:

```csharp
// C#

// selectSingleNode.cs
using System;
using System.Xml;
using System.IO;

namespace Wrox
{
  class consoleApp
  {
    static void Main(string[] args)
    {
      XmlDocument myDocument = new XmlDocument();
      FileStream myStream =
              new FileStream("consumerlist.xml", FileMode.Open);
      myDocument.Load(myStream);
      Console.Write(
              "City for the first customer that is in the XY state:\r\n");
      XmlNode XYCity = myDocument.SelectSingleNode(
                  "//customer/city/text()[../../state/text()='XY']");
      Console.Write(XYCity.Value + "\r\n");
      myStream.Close();
      Console.ReadLine();
    }
  }
}
```

```vbnet
' VB .NET

' selectSingleNode.vb
Imports System
Imports System.Xml
Imports System.IO

Module Module1

  Sub Main()

    Dim myDocument As New Xml.XmlDocument()
    Dim myStream As New IO.FileStream("consumerlist.xml", IO.FileMode.Open)
    myDocument.Load(myStream)
    Console.WriteLine( _
              "City for the first customer that is in the XY state: ")
    Dim XYCity As Xml.XmlNode
```

```
        XYCity = myDocument.SelectSingleNode( _
                        "//customer/city/text()[../../state/text()='XY']")
        Console.WriteLine(XYCity.Value)
        myStream.Close()
        Console.ReadLine()

    End Sub

End Module
```

And here is the output:

```
Command Prompt - selectSingleNode                                    _ |□| x|
C:\>selectSingleNode
City for the first customer that is in the XY state:
Sometown
```

Accessing Content

Next, let's take a look at some of the classes that are derived from the XmlNode class. We'll see how the various properties of those classes correspond to the information found in the XML document, and how to retrieve that information.

Elements

We've already seen some examples of accessing XmlElement nodes. An element's name is found in the Name property of the XmlElement object; its contents may be found in the ChildNodes collection. If we need to access the attributes of an element, we can do so via the GetAttribute() method (we'll take a look at this a little later on when we discuss attributes). For example, the next example returns the text content of the <city> element for the customer in the following document (customer.xml):

```
<?xml version="1.0"?>
<customer customerID="12345">
    <name>Fred Q. Somebody</name>
    <address>100 Somewhere Street</address>
    <city>Sometown</city>
    <state>XY</state>
    <postalCode>13579</postalCode>
</customer>
```

And here's the code that extracts the contents of the <city> element:

```
// C#

// customer.cs
using System;
using System.Xml;
using System.IO;

namespace Wrox
```

119

```
{
  class consoleApp
  {
    static void Main(string[] args)
    {
      XmlDocument myDocument = new XmlDocument();
      FileStream myStream = new FileStream("customer.xml", FileMode.Open);
      myDocument.Load(myStream);
      Console.Write("The customer's city:\r\n");
      XmlElement cityElement =
                  (XmlElement)myDocument.DocumentElement.ChildNodes[2];
      Console.Write(cityElement.ChildNodes[0].Value + "\r\n");
      myStream.Close();
      Console.ReadLine();
    }
  }
}
```

```
' VB .NET

' customer.vb
Imports System
Imports System.Xml
Imports System.IO

Module Module1

  Sub Main()

    Dim myDocument As New Xml.XmlDocument()
    Dim myStream As New IO.FileStream("customer.xml", IO.FileMode.Open)
    myDocument.Load(myStream)
    Console.WriteLine("The customer's city:")
    Dim cityElement As Xml.XmlElement
    cityElement = myDocument.DocumentElement.ChildNodes(2)
    Console.WriteLine(cityElement.ChildNodes(0).Value)
    myStream.Close()
    Console.ReadLine()

  End Sub

End Module
```

The output of this code is the following:

```
Command Prompt - customer

C:\>customer
The customer's city:
Sometown
```

We can also use the `innerText` property on the `XmlElement` object to return the text content of that element in one call. This is also a handy way to strip uninteresting markup from a mixed-content element, such as a marked-up paragraph. Here's an example, `para.xml`:

```
<?xml version="1.0"?>
<para paraID="p17">
   This is a test of the <b>Emergency Broadcast System</b>.
</para>
```

And here's the code:

```
// C#

// para.cs
using System;
using System.Xml;
using System.IO;

namespace Wrox
{
  class consoleApp
  {
    static void Main(string[] args)
    {
      XmlDocument myDocument = new XmlDocument();
      FileStream myStream = new FileStream("para.xml", FileMode.Open);
      myDocument.Load(myStream);
      Console.Write(myDocument.DocumentElement.InnerText + "\r\n");
      myStream.Close();
      Console.ReadLine();
    }
  }
}
```

```
' VB .NET

' para.vb
Imports system
Imports system.Xml
Imports system.IO

Module Module1

  Sub Main()

    Dim myDocument As New Xml.XmlDocument()
    Dim myStream As New IO.FileStream("para.xml", IO.FileMode.Open)
    myDocument.Load(myStream)
    Console.WriteLine(myDocument.DocumentElement.InnerText)
    myStream.Close()
    Console.ReadLine()

  End Sub

End Module
```

The output is this:

```
Command Prompt - para                                    _ □ ×

C:\>para
      This is a test of the Emergency Broadcast System.
```

Text

For XmlText nodes, the interesting property is the Value, which contains the actual text content of the node. The example in the preceding section shows how this property may be used to extract the value of an XmlText node. However, if the text is enclosed in a CDATA wrapper (if it contains markup characters, for example) it will be created by the parser as an XmlCDATASection node instead; and if we mix both text and CDATA-wrapped text, they will appear as separate nodes. Here's an example, sampleCode.xml:

```
<?xml version="1.0"?>
<sampleCode>
    <![CDATA[<?xml version="1.0"?>]]>
</sampleCode>
```

Here's some code that pulls out the value of the CDATA node:

```csharp
// C#

// samplecode.cs
using System;
using System.Xml;
using System.IO;

namespace Wrox
{
  class consoleApp
  {
    static void Main(string[] args)
    {
      XmlDocument myDocument = new XmlDocument();
      FileStream myStream = new FileStream("sampleCode.xml", FileMode.Open);
      myDocument.Load(myStream);
      Console.Write(
              myDocument.DocumentElement.ChildNodes[0].Value + "\r\n");
      myStream.Close();
      Console.ReadLine();
    }
  }
}
```

```vbnet
' VB .NET

' sampleCode.vb
Imports system
```

```
    Imports system.Xml
    Imports system.IO

    Module Module1

      Sub Main()

        Dim myDocument As New Xml.XmlDocument()
        Dim myStream As New IO.FileStream("sampleCode.xml", IO.FileMode.Open)
        myDocument.Load(myStream)
        Console.WriteLine(myDocument.DocumentElement.ChildNodes(0).Value)
        myStream.Close()
        Console.ReadLine()

      End Sub

    End Module
```

And here's the result:

Comments

Much like XmlText nodes, XmlComment nodes present their content using the Value property – this will contain all the text between the start comment (<!--) and end comment (-->)markers. Let's see an example, comment.xml:

```
<?xml version="1.0"?>
<sampleCode>
    <!-- This is a useful comment about the sample document. -->
</sampleCode>
```

We can actually use the same code as in the preceding section, as what we're interested in is the Value of the first child node of the document. When we run that code against this document, this is the result:

Note that there's no guarantee that other parsers won't simply ignore comments – so we should be careful not to put information that drives programmatic behavior in comments.

Processing Instructions

Processing instructions – special instructions to the XML parser that we can embed in our documents – can also be read using the DOM objects. There are two ways we can access the content of an `XmlProcessingInstruction` node. If we want to retrieve the target of the processing instruction and the remainder of the instruction separately, we can do so using the `Name` and `Data` properties of the `XmlProcessingInstruction` object. For example, we can use the following XML file, `sampleCode2.xml`:

```
<?xml version="1.0"?>
<sampleCode>
    <?refreshData targetID="t17"?>
</sampleCode>
```

We can use this code to extract the processing instruction content:

```csharp
// C#

// samplecode2.cs
using System;
using System.Xml;
using System.IO;

namespace Wrox
{
  class consoleApp
  {
    static void Main(string[] args)
    {
      XmlDocument myDocument = new XmlDocument();
      FileStream myStream =
        new FileStream("sampleCode2.xml", FileMode.Open);
      myDocument.Load(myStream);
      XmlProcessingInstruction myPI =
        (XmlProcessingInstruction)myDocument.DocumentElement.ChildNodes[0];
      Console.Write("Name: " + myPI.Name + "\r\n");
      Console.Write("Data: " + myPI.Data + "\r\n");
      myStream.Close();
      Console.ReadLine();
    }
  }
}
```

```vbnet
' VB .NET

' sampleCode2.vb
Imports System
Imports System.Xml
Imports System.IO

Module Module1
```

```
    Sub Main()

        Dim myDocument As New Xml.XmlDocument()
        Dim myStream As New IO.FileStream("sampleCode2.xml", IO.FileMode.Open)
        myDocument.Load(myStream)
        Dim myPI As Xml.XmlProcessingInstruction
        myPI = myDocument.DocumentElement.ChildNodes(0)
        Console.WriteLine("Name: " + myPI.Name )
        Console.WriteLine("Data: " + myPI.Data )
        myStream.Close()
        Console.ReadLine()

    End Sub

End Module
```

This results in the following output:

```
Command Prompt - sampleCode2                                    _ |□| x|

C:\>sampleCode2
Name: refreshData
Data: targetID="t17"
```

Attributes

As we mentioned earlier in the chapter, attributes are handled differently from other node types in the DOM model. Since attributes are order-neutral (there is no significance to the order they are specified in an element start tag), they are handled as an unordered collection of nodes associated with a particular XmlElement node, rather than as child nodes of that node. If we want to access a list of all the attribute nodes associated with a particular XmlElement, we can use the Attributes property of the XmlElement object. This returns a collection of attributes that may be iterated against or searched by name. Each XmlAttribute object in the collection may then be accessed via that object's Name and Value properties. For example, take the following sample XML document, attributes.xml:

```
<?xml version="1.0"?>
<customer customerID="12345"
          name="Fred Q. Somebody"
          address="100 Somewhere Street"
          city="Sometown"
          state="XY"
          postalCode="13579" />
```

The following code returns the names and values of all the attributes for the <customer> element:

```
// C#

// attributes.xml
using System;
using System.Xml;
using System.IO;
```

125

```
namespace Wrox
{
  class consoleApp
  {
    static void Main(string[] args)
    {
      XmlDocument myDocument = new XmlDocument();
      FileStream myStream = new FileStream("attributes.xml", FileMode.Open);
      myDocument.Load(myStream);
      XmlAttributeCollection myAttributes =
                          myDocument.DocumentElement.Attributes;
      for(int i=0; i<myAttributes.Count; i++)
        Console.Write("Attribute: " + myAttributes[i].Name + " = " +
                    myAttributes[i].Value + "\r\n");
      myStream.Close();
      Console.ReadLine();
    }
  }
}
```

```
' VB .NET

' attributes.vb
Imports System
Imports System.Xml
Imports System.IO

Module Module1

  Sub Main()

    Dim myDocument As New Xml.XmlDocument()
    Dim myStream As New IO.FileStream("attributes.xml", IO.FileMode.Open)
    myDocument.Load(myStream)
    Dim myAttributes As Xml.XmlAttributeCollection
    myAttributes = myDocument.DocumentElement.Attributes()
    Dim i As Integer
    For i = 0 To myAttributes.Count - 1
      Console.WriteLine("Attribute: " + myAttributes(i).Name + " = " + _
                    myAttributes(i).Value )
    Next i
    myStream.Close()
    Console.ReadLine()

  End Sub

End Module
```

The resulting output is as follows:

```
Command Prompt - attributes
C:\>attributes
Attribute: customerID = 12345
Attribute: name = Fred Q. Somebody
Attribute: address = 100 Somewhere Street
Attribute: city = Sometown
Attribute: state = XY
Attribute: postalCode = 13579
```

Alternatively, we can use one of the helper methods on XmlElement to determine the value of a particular attribute of interest. The GetAttribute() method returns the text value of an attribute having a given name on the provided element. Using our sample from above and the following code:

```csharp
// C#

// attributes2.cs
using System;
using System.Xml;
using System.IO;

namespace Wrox
{
  class consoleApp
  {
    static void Main(string[] args)
    {
      XmlDocument myDocument = new XmlDocument();
      FileStream myStream = new FileStream("attributes.xml", FileMode.Open);
      myDocument.Load(myStream);
      Console.Write("The city attribute is: " +
                    myDocument.DocumentElement.GetAttribute("city"));
      myStream.Close();
      Console.ReadLine();
    }
  }
}
```

```vbnet
' VB .NET

' attributes2.vb
Imports System
Imports System.Xml
Imports System.IO

Module Module1

  Sub Main()

    Dim myDocument As New Xml.XmlDocument()
    Dim myStream As New IO.FileStream("attributes.xml", IO.FileMode.Open)
    myDocument.Load(myStream)
    Console.Write("The city attribute is: " + _
              myDocument.DocumentElement.GetAttribute("city"))
```

```
        myStream.Close()
        Console.ReadLine()

    End Sub

End Module
```

returns the following output:

If we wish, we can use the `GetAttributeNode()` method – this will return the `XmlAttribute` object representing the attribute in question, rather than the attribute value. This is useful if an attribute's value contains unresolved entity references or other complex content, as in the following example:

```
<customer pref="&FedEx;-&Priority;" />
```

Entity Handling

While the `XmlDocument` object does not normally handle validation, it will extract entity values declared in internal or external DTD subsets (or schemas) and replace them where they are declared in the XML document. If it cannot resolve an entity declaration, it will throw an error (even though it doesn't perform any other validation of the document content). While there is an `XmlEntityReference` class, this is typically used for the creation of XML documents using the `XmlDocument` class, and will not appear in parsed XML documents.

Whitespace Handling

The `XmlDocument` object provides a property, `PreserveWhitespace`, that handles how whitespace (tabs, space characters, hard returns, etc.) is managed by the DOM parser. It has two different meanings, depending on its value during `Load()` (or `LoadXml()`) method calls and `Save()` method calls.

If the `PreserveWhitespace` property is set to `true` on the `XmlDocument` object when the `Load()` (or `LoadXml()`) method is called, then whitespace nodes are preserved. The .NET implementation of the DOM provides two special node types – `XmlWhitespace` and `XmlSignificantWhitespace` – that represent whitespace in a source document. Whitespace is deemed significant in an XML document if it appears between other non-whitespace text nodes. Note that only whitespace other than a single space will be treated this way. These nodes will appear in a generated DOM model if the `PreserveWhitespace` property is set to `true`, but will not be created otherwise. The default for the `PreserveWhitespace` property is `false`. For example, with the following source document, `para2.xml`:

```
<?xml version="1.0"?>
<para paraID="p17">
   This is a test of the <b>Emergency Broadcast System.</b>
   <i>This sentence is entirely in italics.</i>
</para>
```

The following code does not preserve the whitespace nodes:

```csharp
// C#

// para2.cs
using System;
using System.Xml;
using System.IO;

namespace Wrox
{
  class consoleApp
  {
    static void Main(string[] args)
    {
      XmlDocument myDocument = new XmlDocument();
      FileStream myStream = new FileStream("para2.xml", FileMode.Open);
      myDocument.Load(myStream);
      for(int i=0; i<myDocument.DocumentElement.ChildNodes.Count; i++)
      {
        XmlNode myNode = myDocument.DocumentElement.ChildNodes[i];
        Console.Write("Node type: " + myNode.NodeType.ToString() + "\r\n");
      }
      myStream.Close();
      Console.ReadLine();
    }
  }
}
```

```vbnet
' VB .NET

' para2.vb
Imports System
Imports System.Xml
Imports System.IO

Module Module1

  Sub Main()

    Dim myDocument As New Xml.XmlDocument()
    Dim myStream As New IO.FileStream("para2.xml", IO.FileMode.Open)
    myDocument.Load(myStream)
    Dim i As Integer
    For i = 0 To myDocument.DocumentElement.ChildNodes.Count - 1
      Dim myNode As Xml.XmlNode
      myNode = myDocument.DocumentElement.ChildNodes(i)
      Console.WriteLine("Node type: " + myNode.NodeType.ToString())
    Next i
    myStream.Close()
    Console.ReadLine()
```

```
      End Sub

End Module
```

resulting in the following output:

```
C:\>para2
Node type: Text
Node type: Element
Node type: Element
```

However, loading the document after turning on whitespace preservation (as in this code):

```csharp
// C#

// para3.cs
using System;
using System.Xml;
using System.IO;

namespace Wrox
{
  class consoleApp
  {
    static void Main(string[] args)
    {
      XmlDocument myDocument = new XmlDocument();
      FileStream myStream = new FileStream("para2.xml", FileMode.Open);
      myDocument.PreserveWhitespace = true;
      myDocument.Load(myStream);
      for(int i=0; i<myDocument.DocumentElement.ChildNodes.Count; i++)
      {
        XmlNode myNode = myDocument.DocumentElement.ChildNodes[i];
        Console.Write("Node type: " + myNode.NodeType.ToString() + "\r\n");
      }
      myStream.Close();
      Console.ReadLine();
    }
  }
}
```

```vbnet
' VB .NET

' para3.vb
Imports System
Imports System.Xml
Imports System.IO

Module Module1

  Sub Main()
```

```
       Dim myDocument As New Xml.XmlDocument()
       Dim myStream As New IO.FileStream("para2.xml", IO.FileMode.Open)
       MyDocument.PreserveWhitespace = True
       myDocument.Load(myStream)
       Dim i As Integer
       For i = 0 To myDocument.DocumentElement.ChildNodes.Count - 1
         Dim myNode As Xml.XmlNode
         myNode = myDocument.DocumentElement.ChildNodes(i)
         Console.WriteLine("Node type: " + myNode.NodeType.ToString() )
       Next i
       myStream.Close()
       Console.ReadLine()

    End Sub

  End Module
```

results in the following output:

Typically, we should set `PreserveWhitespace` to `true` when loading text-style documents (where whitespace can be quite important), and leave it set to `false` when loading data-style documents.

When calling the `Save()` method, if the `PreserveWhitespace` flag is set to `true`, all whitespace nodes in the tree (nodes of the `XmlWhitespace` or `XmlSignificantWhitespace` types) are expressed in the output, and no additional formatting is performed. However, if `PreserveWhitespace` is set to `false`, whitespace nodes in the tree are discarded, and the `Save()` method automatically formats the output.

Namespace Support

Namespaces provide a way to identify elements as belonging to a specified group in XML. This is done by adding a namespace declaration and prefixing relevant nodes with a namespace identifier. Often, this is used to provide additional clues to the processor as to how to use the information. For example, the XSLT namespace is used to tell the processor that elements with that prefix represent XSLT instructions. The .NET implementation of the DOM provides full namespace support. The `XmlNode` abstract class provides two properties – `NamespaceURI` and `Prefix` – that together define the namespace for a particular node. For example we can use the following C# or VB .NET code to return namespace information from the following sample XML document, `customer2.xml`:

```
<?xml version="1.0"?>
<cust:customer xmlns:cust="http://localhost/customer">
   <cust:name>Fred Q. Anybody</cust:name>
</cust:customer>
```

The following code returns namespace information about the root element:

```csharp
// C#

// customer2.cs
using System;
using System.Xml;
using System.IO;

namespace Wrox
{
  class consoleApp
  {
    static void Main(string[] args)
    {
      XmlDocument myDocument = new XmlDocument();
      FileStream myStream = new FileStream("customer2.xml", FileMode.Open);
      myDocument.Load(myStream);
      Console.Write("Namespace: " +
                  myDocument.DocumentElement.NamespaceURI + "\r\n");
      Console.Write("Prefix:    " +
                  myDocument.DocumentElement.Prefix + "\r\n");
      Console.Write("LocalName: " +
                  myDocument.DocumentElement.LocalName + "\r\n");
      myStream.Close();
      Console.ReadLine();
    }
  }
}
```

```vbnet
' VB .NET

' customer2.vb
Imports System
Imports System.Xml
Imports System.IO

Module Module1

  Sub Main()

    Dim myDocument As New Xml.XmlDocument()
    Dim myStream As New IO.FileStream("customer2.xml",IO.FileMode.Open)
    myDocument.Load(myStream)
    Console.WriteLine("Namespace: " + _
                  myDocument.DocumentElement.NamespaceURI )
    Console.WriteLine("Prefix:    " + _
                  myDocument.DocumentElement.Prefix )
    Console.WriteLine("LocalName: " + _
                  myDocument.DocumentElement.LocalName )
    myStream.Close()
    Console.ReadLine()
```

```
      End Sub

   End Module
```

produces this output:

```
Command Prompt - customer2

C:\>customer2
Namespace: http://localhost/customer
Prefix:    cust
LocalName: customer
```

Note that we're using `LocalName` to retrieve the name of the element – if we use the `Name` prop retrieve the name of an element with a namespace prefix, the entire name (including the prefix and the colon) is returned. These properties may be accessed from any of the classes derived from `XmlNode`; however, for the classes that do not provide namespace support (such as `XmlText`) these properties have no effect.

Validation

The DOM implementation itself does not perform DTD or schema validation for documents loaded using the `Load()` or `LoadXml()` methods. If we need to perform validation on our documents, first load the document using an `XmlValidatingReader` object and pass that object to the constructor of the `XmlDocument` object. To learn more about using `XmlValidatingReader` to validate a document against a DTD or Schema, see Chapter 6, *Validating XML*.

Modifying a Document

So far, so good – at this point, we've seen how to load existing documents and extract their content. However, the real power of the `XmlDocument` DOM model is its ability to easily add and remove content anywhere in the XML document tree. Let's see how this is done.

Deleting Content

Deleting content from a loaded XML document couldn't be easier. For non-attribute content, we remove individual nodes by calling the `RemoveChild()` method of that node's parent. For example, say we wanted to remove the `<postalCode>` element from the customer in the following file, `customer3.xml`:

```
<?xml version="1.0"?>
<customer>
   <name>Fred Q. Anybody</name>
   <address>1 Anywhere Road</address>
   <city>Anytown</city>
   <state>XY</state>
   <postalCode>58757</postalCode>
</customer>
```

code accomplishes that:

```csharp
// customer3.cs
using System;
using System.Xml;
using System.IO;

namespace Wrox
{
  class consoleApp
  {
    static void Main(string[] args)
    {
      XmlDocument myDocument = new XmlDocument();
      FileStream myStream = new FileStream("customer3.xml", FileMode.Open);
      myDocument.Load(myStream);
      XmlElement pcElement =
        (XmlElement)myDocument.GetElementsByTagName("postalCode")[0];
      myDocument.DocumentElement.RemoveChild(pcElement);
      myDocument.Save("customer4.xml");
      myStream.Close();
    }
  }
}
```

```vbnet
' VB .NET

' customer3.vb
Imports System
Imports System.Xml
Imports System.IO

Module Module1

  Sub Main()

    Dim myDocument As New Xml.XmlDocument()
    Dim myStream As New IO.FileStream("customer3.xml", IO.FileMode.Open)
    myDocument.Load(myStream)
    Dim pcElement As Xml.XmlElement
    pcElement = myDocument.GetElementsByTagName("postalCode")(0)
    myDocument.DocumentElement.RemoveChild(pcElement)
    myDocument.Save("customer4.xml")
    myStream.Close()

  End Sub

End Module
```

The result is a new file (called `customer4.xml` in this case) shown below:

If we need to remove an attribute from an element, the method is similar – there are several helper methods on the `XmlElement` node that allow us to easily remove an attribute from the attribute list for that element. The most useful is `RemoveAttribute()`, which removes an attribute with a particular name. For example, with the following sample XML document, `customer5.xml`:

```
<?xml version="1.0"?>
<customer name="Fred Q. Anybody"
          address="1 Anywhere Road"
          city="Anytown"
          state="XY"
          postalCode="58757" />
```

we can use this code removes the `postalCode` attribute from the `<customer>` element:

```csharp
// C#

// customer5.cs
using System;
using System.Xml;
using System.IO;

namespace Wrox
{
  class consoleApp
  {
    static void Main(string[] args)
    {
      XmlDocument myDocument = new XmlDocument();
      FileStream myStream = new FileStream("customer5.xml", FileMode.Open);
      myDocument.Load(myStream);
      myDocument.DocumentElement.RemoveAttribute("postalCode");
      myDocument.Save("customer6.xml");
      myStream.Close();
    }
  }
}
```

```
' VB .NET

' customer5.vb
Imports System
Imports System.Xml
Imports System.IO

Module Module1

  Sub Main()

    Dim myDocument As New Xml.XmlDocument()
    Dim myStream As New IO.FileStream("customer5.xml", IO.FileMode.Open)
    myDocument.Load(myStream)
    myDocument.DocumentElement.RemoveAttribute("postalCode")
    myDocument.Save("customer6.xml")
    myStream.Close()
  End Sub

End Module
```

The result is a new file (called `customer6.xml` in this case), shown below:

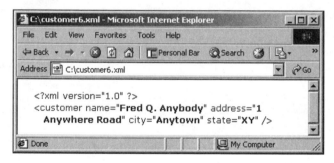

Modifying Content

Modifying existing nodes in an XML document is a little more tricky. Since the name of a node in the `XmlDocument` model is read-only, renaming an element (for example) requires creating a new node, copying over all of the relevant child nodes, and then substituting the new node in place of the old in the document tree. However, changing the values of nodes is more straightforward. Let's look at the following example XML file, `customerlist2.xml`:

```
<?xml version="1.0"?>
<customerList>
   <customer>
      <name>Fred Q. Anybody</name>
      <address>1 Anywhere Road</address>
      <city>Anytown</city>
      <state>XY</state>
      <postalCode>18743</postalCode>
   </customer>
   <customer>
```

```
        <name>John X. Somebody</name>
        <address>2 Somewhere Street</address>
        <city>Someville</city>
        <state>YZ</state>
        <postalCode>99999</postalCode>
    </customer>
</customerList>
```

The following code changes all <postalCode> elements to the full American Zip+4 format:

```csharp
// C#

// customerlist2.cs
using System;
using System.Xml;
using System.IO;

namespace Wrox
{
  class consoleApp
  {
    static void Main(string[] args)
    {
      XmlDocument myDocument = new XmlDocument();
      FileStream myStream =
                new FileStream("customerlist2.xml", FileMode.Open);
      myDocument.Load(myStream);
      XmlNodeList zipValues =
                myDocument.SelectNodes("//customer/postalCode/text()");
      for(int i=0; i<zipValues.Count; i++)
        zipValues[i].Value = zipValues[i].Value + "-0000";
      myDocument.Save("customerlist3.xml");
      myStream.Close();
    }
  }
}
```

```vbnet
' VB .NET

' customerlist2.vb
Imports System
Imports System.Xml
Imports System.IO

Module Module1

  Sub Main()

    Dim myDocument As New Xml.XmlDocument()
    Dim myStream As New IO.FileStream("customerlist2.xml", IO.FileMode.Open)
    myDocument.Load(myStream)
    Dim zipValues As Xml.XmlNodeList
    zipValues = myDocument.SelectNodes("//customer/postalCode/text()")
    Dim i As Integer
```

```
      For i = 0 To zipValues.Count - 1
        zipValues(i).Value = zipValues(i).Value + "-0000"
      Next i
      myDocument.Save("customerlist3.xml")
      myStream.Close()

    End Sub

  End Module
```

Here is the resulting XML document, `customerlist3.xml`:

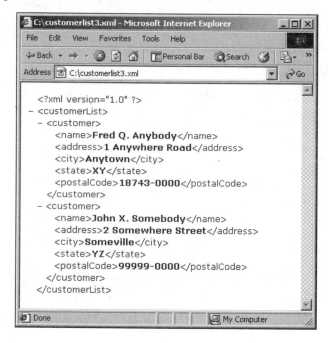

Creating New Content

As we mentioned earlier in the chapter, the constructors of the various `XmlNode` classes (with the obvious exception of `XmlDocument`) are protected – we can't create new instances of these classes directly, as they need to be associated with a particular document. Instead, we have to use the factory methods provided on the `XmlDocument` object to create these nodes – there is a factory method for each derivation of `XmlNode`. For example, take the following example document, `part2.xml`:

```
<?xml version="1.0"?>
<part>
    <name>Grommets</name>
    <size>2 in.</size>
</part>
```

The following code creates a `<color>` element and appends it to the `<part>` element's children:

```csharp
//C#

// part2.cs
using System;
using System.Xml;
using System.IO;

namespace Wrox
{
  class consoleApp
  {
    static void Main(string[] args)
    {
      XmlDocument myDocument = new XmlDocument();
      FileStream myStream = new FileStream("part2.xml", FileMode.Open);
      myDocument.Load(myStream);
      XmlElement colorElement = myDocument.CreateElement("color");
      XmlText colorText = myDocument.CreateTextNode("red");
      colorElement.AppendChild(colorText);
      myDocument.DocumentElement.AppendChild(colorElement);
      myDocument.Save("part3.xml");
      myStream.Close();
    }
  }
}
```

```vbnet
' VB .NET

' part2.vb
Imports System
Imports System.Xml
Imports System.IO

Module Module1

  Sub Main()

    Dim myDocument As New Xml.XmlDocument()
    Dim myStream As New IO.FileStream("part2.xml", IO.FileMode.Open)
    myDocument.Load(myStream)
    Dim colorElement As Xml.XmlElement
    colorElement = myDocument.CreateElement("color")
    Dim colorText As Xml.XmlText
    colorText = myDocument.CreateTextNode("red")
    colorElement.AppendChild(colorText)
    myDocument.DocumentElement.AppendChild(colorElement)
    myDocument.Save("part3.xml")
    myStream.Close()

  End Sub

End Module
```

The resulting XML document, part3.xml looks like this:

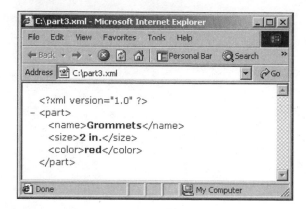

Inserting Content

Inserting content, like deleting content, is straightforward. To insert non-attribute nodes into the content of another node, we simply use one of the methods inherited from XmlNode. We saw an example of this in the previous sample code when we inserted a text node into an element node, and the element node into another element node. There are other methods that allow us to select exactly where in an element child list an element will appear. The PrependChild() method puts a child node at the beginning of the parent node's list of children, while InsertChildBefore() and InsertChildAfter() specify an existing child that the new child should be positioned relative to.

Adding Attributes

Adding attributes to an existing element is straightforward. We can either manipulate the XmlAttributeCollection for that element directly, or use one of the helper functions on the XmlElement object itself. The most useful is SetAttribute(), which sets the value of the attribute we specify for a particular element. For example, using the following example XML document, part2.xml:

```
<?xml version="1.0"?>
<part>
    <name>Grommets</name>
    <size>2 in.</size>
</part>
```

the following code adds a partID attribute to the <part> element:

```
// C#

// part4.cs
using System;
using System.Xml;
using System.IO;

namespace Wrox
{
```

```
    class consoleApp
    {
      static void Main(string[] args)
      {
        XmlDocument myDocument = new XmlDocument();
        FileStream myStream = new FileStream("part2.xml", FileMode.Open);
        myDocument.Load(myStream);
        myDocument.DocumentElement.SetAttribute("partID", "p17");
        myDocument.Save("part5.xml");
        myStream.Close();
      }
    }
}
```

```vbnet
' VB .NET

' part4.vb
Imports System
Imports System.Xml
Imports System.IO

Module Module1

  Sub Main()

    Dim myDocument As New Xml.XmlDocument()
    Dim myStream As New IO.FileStream("part2.xml", IO.FileMode.Open)
    myDocument.Load(myStream)
    myDocument.DocumentElement.SetAttribute("partID", "p17")
    myDocument.Save("part5.xml")
    myStream.Close()

  End Sub

End Module
```

Here is the resulting XML file, part5.xml:

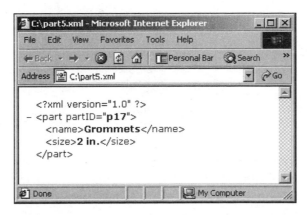

Creating a Document from Scratch

A document can easily be created from scratch using the XmlDocument class. Simply call the XmlDocument constructor with no parameters as usual – at this point, the XmlDocument is empty. Next, create the root element using the CreateElement() method on the document, and set it to be the root element of the document by calling the AppendChild() method on the XmlDocument object. After that, simply create elements, attributes, and so on as necessary by calling the appropriate methods on the XmlDocument element, and build the document tree by calling methods like AppendChild(). Let's see an example. Say we want to create the following document, part6.xml:

The following code accomplishes this:

```csharp
// C#

// part6.cs
using System;
using System.Xml;
using System.IO;

namespace Wrox
{
  class consoleApp
  {
    static void Main(string[] args)
    {
      XmlDocument myDocument = new XmlDocument();
      XmlElement partElement = myDocument.CreateElement("part");
      partElement.SetAttribute("partID", "p17");
      myDocument.AppendChild(partElement);
      XmlElement nameElement = myDocument.CreateElement("name");
      XmlText nameText = myDocument.CreateTextNode("Grommets");
      nameElement.AppendChild(nameText);
      partElement.AppendChild(nameElement);
      XmlElement sizeElement = myDocument.CreateElement("size");
      XmlText sizeText = myDocument.CreateTextNode("2 in.");
      sizeElement.AppendChild(sizeText);
      partElement.AppendChild(sizeElement);
      myDocument.Save("part6.xml");
    }
  }
}
```

```
' VB .NET

' part6.vb
Imports System
Imports System.Xml
Imports System.IO

Module Module1

  Sub Main()

    Dim myDocument As New Xml.XmlDocument()
    Dim partElement As Xml.XmlElement
    partElement = myDocument.CreateElement("part")
    partElement.SetAttribute("partID", "p17")
    myDocument.AppendChild(partElement)
    Dim nameElement As Xml.XmlElement
    nameElement = myDocument.CreateElement("name")
    Dim nameText As Xml.XmlText
    nameText = myDocument.CreateTextNode("Grommets")
    nameElement.AppendChild(nameText)
    partElement.AppendChild(nameElement)
    Dim sizeElement As Xml.XmlElement
    sizeElement = myDocument.CreateElement("size")
    Dim sizeText As Xml.XmlText
    sizeText = myDocument.CreateTextNode("2 in.")
    sizeElement.AppendChild(sizeText)
    partElement.AppendChild(sizeElement)
    myDocument.Save("part6.xml")

  End Sub

End Module
```

Bear in mind that the document only exists as a DOM model in memory until we call some method, such as Save(), that serializes the document to a file or other medium.

A More Complex Example

To close out this chapter, let's take a look at how a programmer can extend the functionality of the DOM objects provided by the .NET framework by looking at a more complex example.

The Business Problem

In our day-to-day processing of XML documents, we work with a great deal of relational-style data – data that is related in our XML documents using IDREF to ID pointers. Unfortunately, while this link is really two-way, it may only be traversed one way by the default implementation of the DOM in the .NET framework – an element may be found with a given ID field, but there's no easy way to find out which elements have attributes that point to a given ID. We'd like to have a helper method that makes this easier to do.

The Solution: Extend the XmlDocument Class

Our solution to the problem is to inherit from the `XmlDocument` class and add a `GetElementsReferencingID()` method to it. This method will take a string as a parameter and return an `XmlNodeList` containing all the elements that point to the provided string. Since the .NET implementation of the DOM doesn't allow us programmatic access to the attribute declarations in the DTD or schema, we'll assume that any attribute that ends in `IDREF` is of type `IDREF`, and any attribute whose name ends in `IDREFS` is of type `IDREFS`. Let's take a look at the code that does this.

First, since we want to use `XmlNodeList` and it's an abstract class, we'll need to derive from it. We'll call our derived class `ElementList`. The class keeps its list of elements in an `ArrayList` object – this gives us the `IEnumerator` interface we need to override the abstract methods, and is fairly easy to work with.

```csharp
// C#

// order.cs
using System;
using System.Xml;
using System.IO;
using System.Collections;

namespace CSOrder
{
  class Class1
  {
    class ElementList : XmlNodeList
    {
      private ArrayList myElements;

      public override int Count
      {
        get
        {
          return(myElements.Count);
        }
      }

      public override XmlNode Item(int iItem)
      {
        return((XmlNode)myElements[iItem]);
      }

      public override IEnumerator GetEnumerator()
      {
        return(myElements.GetEnumerator());
      }

      public void addNode(XmlNode newNode)
      {
        if(myElements==null)
          myElements = new ArrayList();
        myElements.Add(newNode);
      }
    }
```

Next, we need to write our class that is derived from XmlDocument – for lack of imagination, we'll call it XmlDocumentPlus. We'll add a method, called GetElementsReferencingID(), that looks up the elements that have pointers to a particular ID that we're interested in.

```
class XmlDocumentPlus : XmlDocument
{
  public XmlNodeList GetElementsReferencingID (string sID)
  {
    ElementList myList = new ElementList();
    AddReferencingElements(this.DocumentElement, myList, sID);
    return(myList);
  }
}
```

Since we need to check all the elements in the document, we'll use some recursion here – the first call to AddReferencingElements() checks the root element, and then AddReferencingElements() will call itself for every child element of the element passed to it. The rest of the code is straightforward – it just examines the attributes for each node and determines whether the element points to the provided ID string or not.

```
private void AddReferencingElements(XmlElement myElement,
                                    ElementList myList, string sID)
{
  for(int i=0; i<myElement.Attributes.Count; i++)
  {
    string sWork=myElement.Attributes[i].Name;
    if(sWork.EndsWith("IDREF"))
    {
      // do we have a match?
      if(myElement.Attributes[i].Value==sID)
      {
        // we do, add it to the list
        myList.addNode(myElement);
      }
    }
    else if (sWork.EndsWith("IDREFS"))
    {
      // do we have a match in this string?
      sWork = myElement.Attributes[i].Value;
      string[] sIDTokens = sWork.Split(' ');
      for(int j=0; j<sIDTokens.Length; j++)
      {
        if(sIDTokens[j]==sID)
        {
          // add it to the list
          myList.addNode(myElement);
        }
      }
    }
  }
  // and we need to check all the child elements of this node
  for (int i=0; i<myElement.ChildNodes.Count; i++)
  {
    if(myElement.ChildNodes[i].NodeType==XmlNodeType.Element)
```

```
                {
                    AddReferencingElements(
                        (XmlElement)myElement.ChildNodes[i], myList, sID);
                }
            }
        }
    }
```

Finally, we add a Main() procedure that calls the methods and returns all the customers who ordered part p2:

```
    static void Main(string[] args)
    {
        XmlDocumentPlus myDoc = new XmlDocumentPlus();
        myDoc.Load("order.xml");
        ElementList myList =
            (ElementList)myDoc.GetElementsReferencingID("p2");
        Console.WriteLine("Customers that ordered part p2:");
        for(int i=0; i<myList.Count; i++)
        {
            Console.WriteLine(myList[i].ChildNodes[0].InnerText);
        }
    }
}
```

If we use the following source document, order.xml:

```
<?xml version="1.0"?>
<orderInfo>
    <customer customerID="c1" partIDREFS="p1 p2">
        <name>Andy B. Somebody</name>
    </customer>
    <customer customerID="c2" partIDREFS="p1">
        <name>Fred G. Anybody</name>
    </customer>
    <customer customerID="c3" partIDREFS="p2">
        <name>David Q. Nobody</name>
    </customer>
    <part partID="p1">
        <name>Grommets</name>
        <size>2 in.</size>
    </part>
    <part partID="p2">
        <name>Widgets</name>
        <size>1 in.</size>
    </part>
</orderInfo>
```

The output of the program is as below:

```
Command Prompt                                              _ □ x

C:\>order
Customers that ordered part p2:
Andy B. Somebody
David Q. Nobody
```

For VB .NET programmers, here is the entire program listing in VB .NET:

```vbnet
' VB .NET

' order.vb
Imports System
Imports System.Xml
Imports System.IO
Imports System.Collections
Module Module1

  Sub Main()
    Dim myDoc As New XmlDocumentPlus()
    myDoc.Load("order.xml")
    Dim myList As ElementList
    myList = myDoc.GetElementsReferencingID("p2")
    Console.WriteLine("Customers that ordered part p2:")
    Dim i As Integer
    For i = 0 To myList.Count - 1
      Console.WriteLine(myList(i).ChildNodes(0).InnerText)
    Next i
  End Sub

  Class ElementList
    Inherits Xml.XmlNodeList

    Dim myElements As ArrayList

    Public Overrides ReadOnly Property count() As Integer
      Get
        count = myElements.Count
      End Get
    End Property

    Public Overrides Function Item(ByVal iItem As Integer) As Xml.XmlNode
      Item = myElements(iItem)
    End Function

    Public Overrides Function GetEnumerator() As IEnumerator
      GetEnumerator = myElements.GetEnumerator()
    End Function

    Public Function addNode(ByVal newNode As Xml.XmlNode)
      If myElements Is Nothing Then
        myElements = New ArrayList()
```

```
           End If
         myElements.Add(newNode)
      End Function

   End Class

   Class XmlDocumentPlus
      Inherits Xml.XmlDocument

      Public Function GetElementsReferencingID(ByVal sID As String) As _
                                         Xml.XmlNodeList
         Dim myList As New ElementList()
         AddReferencingElements(Me.DocumentElement, myList, sID)
         GetElementsReferencingID = myList
      End Function

      Private Sub AddReferencingElements(ByVal myElement As Xml.XmlElement, _
                                    ByVal myList As ElementList, _
                                    ByVal sID As String)

         Dim i As Integer
         For i = 0 To myElement.Attributes.Count - 1
           Dim sWork As String
           sWork = myElement.Attributes(i).Name
           If (sWork.EndsWith("IDREF")) Then
             ' do we have a match?
             If (myElement.Attributes(i).Value = sID) Then
               ' we do, add it to the list
               myList.addNode(myElement)
             End If
           ElseIf (sWork.EndsWith("IDREFS")) Then
             ' do we have a match in this string?
             sWork = myElement.Attributes(i).Value
             Dim sIDTokens As String()
             sIDTokens = sWork.Split(" ")
             Dim j As Integer
             For j = 0 To sIDTokens.Length - 1
               If (sIDTokens(j) = sID) Then
                 ' add it to the list
                 myList.addNode(myElement)
               End If
             Next j
           End If
         Next i

         ' and we need to check all the child elements of this node
         For i = 0 To myElement.ChildNodes.Count - 1
           If (myElement.ChildNodes(i).NodeType = Xml.XmlNodeType.Element) Then
             AddReferencingElements(myElement.ChildNodes(i), myList, sID)
           End If
         Next i
      End Sub
   End Class

End Module
```

Summary

In this chapter, we've taken a brief look at the DOM functionality in the .NET framework. We've seen how to load documents into memory, manipulate them while they are there, and serialize them back out to XML strings. We also took a look at the differences between the `XmlDocument` object and the `XmlReader`/`XmlWriter` objects, and where using each is more appropriate. Finally, we created a class derived from the `XmlDocument` class, to show how easy it is to add functionality to the classes in the .NET framework. If you learn to use the techniques described in this chapter, you'll be well on the way to reading and modifying XML documents with ease.

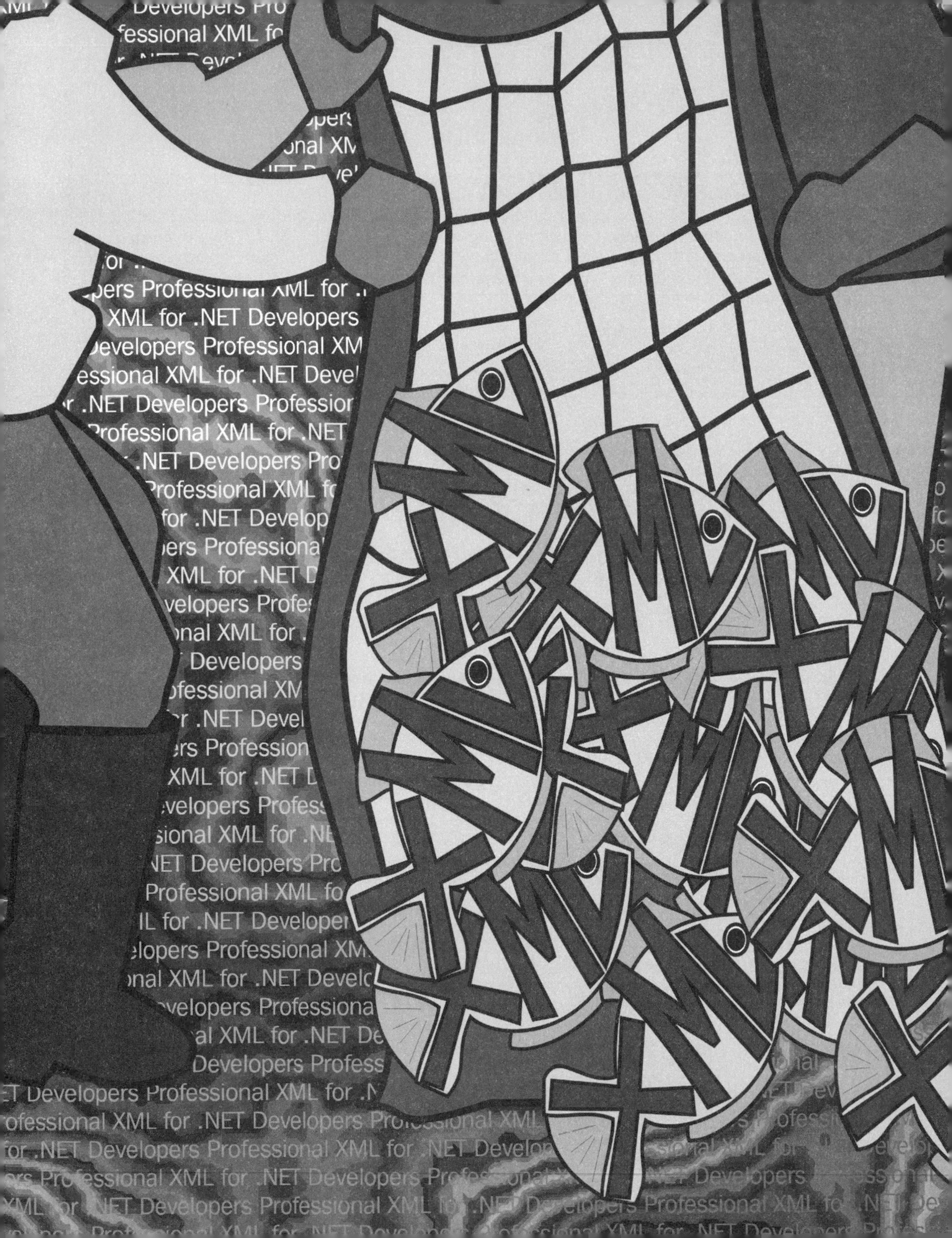
Professional XML for .NET Developers

5

XSL Transformations of XML

In this chapter, we'll talk about the support for the **Extensible Stylesheet Language for Transformation** (**XSLT**) and the **XML Path Language** (**XPath**) in the .NET framework. The subjects we'll be discussing include:

- ❑ Performing "traditional" document styling using the .NET Framework
- ❑ Embedding scripts in stylesheets
- ❑ Passing arguments to a transformation
- ❑ Extending stylesheet functionality with .NET code
- ❑ Navigating through documents using XPath expressions
- ❑ Optimizing XSLT transformations

Technologies Used

Like the previous chapter, this chapter will present its examples using both C# and VB .NET. If you like, it should be a simple matter to port the examples to C++ .NET – most of what we'll be doing is leveraging objects found in the .NET framework. Sample code will be provided in the form of Console Applications to keep the samples simple and easy to understand. You should be able to compile the samples either using the command-line .NET framework compilers or by inserting the code into a Visual Studio .NET project. As always, all examples are available for download from the Wrox web site at http://www.wrox.com/.

The System.Xml.Xsl Namespace

The `System.Xml.Xsl` namespace contains the classes that are used to perform XSLT transformations. The `XslTransform` class is used to perform transformations, and the `XsltArgumentList` class is used to pass in arguments to the transform. This namespace also includes two exception classes, `XsltCompileException` and `XsltException`, which describe errors encountered when parsing and processing XSLT stylesheets, respectively. If we want to use the XSLT engine in .NET, we must add the `System.Xml.Xsl` namespace to our project.

The System.Xml.XPath Namespace

The `System.Xml.XPath` namespace contains the XPath expression parser and evaluator. XPath is a locator language for XML documents – it enables us to select one or more nodes from an XML document that match the conditions in the locator (such as retrieving all the customer nodes whose shipping address is in California). When we parse a document using the classes in the .NET framework, these classes are used to process the XPath expressions found in the stylesheet. We can also use these classes directly to select or match against nodes using XPath expressions. The `XPathDocument` class is an XML document representation tuned for XSLT processing. The `XPathExpression` class represents a compiled XPath expression, and the `XPathNavigator` class provides mechanisms to access XML documents with XPath expressions. Later in the chapter, we'll see how these classes may be used to manipulate XML documents.

XSLT Processing

First, we'll take a look at "traditional" XSLT processing – in other words, the processing of one XML document with an XML stylesheet to produce another XML document. The most common use of XSLT is to transform an XML document into some renderable form, such as XHTML or WML. However, XSLT can also be used to transform documents from one structure to another (to make them conform to different standards), or even to create flattened (not marked-up) files.

XSLT files are just XML files – they include instructions for the creation of the structure and content of a resulting XML document, based on a source XML document. For example, the following stylesheet, run against a customer XML document, creates an XHTML document showing the customer's name in an `<H1>` element:

```
<xsl:stylesheet xmlns:xsl="http://www.w3.org/1999/XSL/Transform"
                version="1.0">
   <xsl:template match="*">
      <html>
         <body>
            <h1>
               <xsl:value-of select="//customer/name/text()" />
            </h1>
         </body>
      </html>
   </xsl:template>
</xsl:stylesheet>
```

Note that a full discussion of XSLT and XPath syntax is outside the scope of this chapter – for more information on XML and XSLT, see *Professional XSLT 2nd Edition*, ISBN 1-86100-5-06-7 by Michael Kay, also published by Wrox Press.

The XslTransform Class

XML documents are transformed in the .NET framework using the XslTransform class. This class's constructor takes no parameters. The following demonstrate this:

```csharp
// C#
XslTransform myTransform = new XslTransform();
```

```vbnet
' VB .NET
Dim myTransform As New Xml.Xsl.XslTransform()
```

Once we've created an instance of XslTransform, we need to use one of the forms of the Load() method to load the stylesheet to be used for the transforms. Let's take a look at the various forms of the Load() method and how they work.

Loading a Stylesheet

There are several different ways we can load an XSLT stylesheet into the XslTransform object. Different methods will be appropriate based on the other processing that is being performed. To load an XSLT document from a URL, we use the Load(string) version of the method, as follows:

```csharp
// C#
XslTransform myTransform = new XslTransform();
myTransform.Load("styleCustomer.xsl");
```

```vbnet
' VB .NET
Dim myTransform As New Xml.Xsl.XslTransform()
myTransform.Load("styleCustomer.xsl")
```

If we already have the XML document parsed into an XmlReader or XmlDocument, we can use the appropriate form of the Load() method to load it into the XslTransform object. This version of the method can be useful if we have generated the XSLT stylesheet programmatically (perhaps as the output of another transform), or if the stylesheet is already parsed for some other reason (such as being passed as part of the payload of a SOAP message). For example, the following code styles one stylesheet with another, then uses the result to style a third document:

```csharp
// C#

// transform.cs
using System;
using System.Xml;
using System.Xml.XPath;
using System.Xml.Xsl;

namespace Wrox
{
  class consoleApp
  {
    static void Main(string[] args)
    {
      XslTransform myTransform = new XslTransform();
      XmlDocument myDoc = new XmlDocument();
      XmlDocument myFinal = new XmlDocument ();
      XmlReader myResult;
      XmlReader myFinalResult;
```

```
                    myTransform.Load("styleCustomer.xsl");
                    myDoc.Load("customerPrefs.xsl");
                    myFinal.Load("customer1.xml");
                    myResult = myTransform.Transform(myDoc, null);
                    myTransform.Load(myResult);
                    myFinalResult = myTransform.Transform(myFinal, null);
            }
        }
}
```

```
' VB .NET

' transform.vb
Imports System
Imports System.Xml
Imports System.Xml.XPath
Imports System.Xml.Xsl

Module Module1

  Sub Main()

    Dim myTransform As New Xml.Xsl.XslTransform()
    Dim myDoc As New Xml.XmlDocument()
    Dim myFinal As New Xml.XmlDocument()
    Dim myResult As Xml.XmlReader
    Dim myFinalResult As Xml.XmlReader

    myTransform.Load("styleCustomer.xsl")
    myDoc.Load("customerPrefs.xsl")
    myFinal.Load("customer1.xml")
    myResult = myTransform.Transform(myDoc, Nothing)
    myTransform.Load(myResult)
    myFinalResult = myTransform.Transform(myFinal, Nothing)

  End Sub

End Module
```

Transforming XML Documents

Like the Load() method, the Transform() method has several overloads. In this case, however, it's important to carefully consider which form of the method will be used to perform the transformation. Ideally, we should use an instance of XPathDocument to hold the document being transformed. The XPathDocument class is optimized for XPath processing – it doesn't contain all the validation and structure overhead of the other document classes, and will provide the best performance. Here's an example:

```
' VB .NET

    Dim myDoc As New System.Xml.XPath.XPathDocument("customer1.xml")
    Dim myResult As System.Xml.XmlReader
    Dim myTransform As New System.Xml.Xsl.XslTransform()
    myTransform.Load("styleCustomer.xsl")
    myResult = myTransform.Transform(myDoc, Nothing)
```

```
// C#

    XPathDocument myDoc = new XpathDocument("customer1.xml");
```

```
        XmlReader myResult;
        XslTransform myTransform = new XslTransform();
        myTransform.Load("styleCustomer.xsl");
        myResult = myTransform.Transform(myDoc, null);
```

We can also transform a document found at a URL by using the string version of the method:

```
' VB .NET

myTransform.Transform("customer1.xml","newCust1.xml")
```

```
// C#

myTransform.Transform("customer1.xml","newCust1.xml");
```

However, note that this method will only write the output to a file – if we need to do something else with the output, we're better off loading the source document into an `XPathDocument` object first (otherwise, we'll need to load the document from the file system and reparse it).

These two methods are all that are necessary to transform XML documents using stylesheets that conform to the W3C XSLT specification (which can be found at http://www.w3.org/TR/xslt). However, Microsoft provides a couple of mechanisms that significantly enhance the functionality available to us when creating stylesheets. Let's take a look at these next.

Using Embedded Scripting with msxsl:script

The XSLT transformation objects in the .NET framework provide support for embedded scripts in XSLT documents using the script extension element. Scripting languages provide a richer set of functionality than that provided by pure XSLT, and can often be used to perform more complex manipulation of document contents (such as applying scientific functions or accessing external information sources). The script extension element must be declared in the `urn:schemas-microsoft-com:xslt` namespace. The .NET parser will accept scripts coded in C#, VB .NET, VBScript, or JScript. In the script element, we define the namespace for the function calls by providing an `implements-prefix` attribute. Let's look at an example. Here is a stylesheet that contains an embedded C# function, `weather.xsl`:

```
<xsl:stylesheet xmlns:xsl="http://www.w3.org/1999/XSL/Transform"
                xmlns:msxsl="urn:schemas-microsoft-com:xslt"
                xmlns:myScript="urn:scripts"
                version="1.0">
  <xsl:template match="weatherForecast">
    <weatherForecast>
      <xsl:apply-templates />
    </weatherForecast>
  </xsl:template>

  <xsl:template match="day">
    <day>
      <xsl:copy-of select="date" />
      <highCelsius>
        <xsl:value-of select="myScript:fahrenheitToCelsius
                              (highFahrenheit)" />
      </highCelsius>
      <lowCelsius>
```

```
        <xsl:value-of select="myScript:fahrenheitToCelsius
                              (lowFahrenheit)" />
      </lowCelsius>
    </day>
  </xsl:template>
  <msxsl:script language="C#" implements-prefix="myScript">
    public double fahrenheitToCelsius(double fahrenheit)
      {
        double celsius = (fahrenheit - 32) * 5 / 9;
        return celsius;
      }
  </msxsl:script>
</xsl:stylesheet>
```

The following code, when compiled, uses the `weather.xsl` stylesheet to style a sample document named `weather.xml`:

```csharp
// C#

// weather.cs
using System;
using System.Xml;
using System.Xml.XPath;
using System.Xml.Xsl;

namespace Wrox
{
  class consoleApp
  {
    static void Main(string[] args)
    {
      XslTransform myTransform = new XslTransform();
      myTransform.Load("weather.xsl", null);
      myTransform.Transform("weather.xml","weatherCelsius.xml");
    }
  }
}
```

```vbnet
' VB .NET

' weather.vb
Imports System
Imports System.Xml
Imports System.Xml.Xsl
Imports System.Xml.XPath

Module Module1

  Sub Main()

    Dim myTransform As New Xml.Xsl.XslTransform()
    myTransform.Load("weather.xsl", Nothing)
    myTransform.Transform("weather.xml","weatherCelsius.xml")

  End Sub

End Module
```

We can use the C# or VB .NET code to run `weather.xsl` against `weather.xml` (below):

```xml
<?xml version="1.0"?>
<weatherForecast>
  <day>
    <date>8/1/2001</date>
    <highFahrenheit>85</highFahrenheit>
    <lowFahrenheit>60</lowFahrenheit>
  </day>
  <day>
    <date>8/2/2001</date>
    <highFahrenheit>92</highFahrenheit>
    <lowFahrenheit>82</lowFahrenheit>
  </day>
</weatherForecast>
```

either in Visual Studio .NET or from the command line. To compile and run the C# code from the command line:

>**csc weather.cs**

>**weather**

To compile the VB .NET code from the **Command Prompt** is slightly more complicated. We need to reference types in the `System.Xml` assembly, which the VB .NET compiler doesn't reference by default. To do this we use the `/reference` or `/r` switch as below:

>**vbc weather.vb /r:System.Xml.dll**

>**weather**

The result is exactly the same with either the C# or the VB .NET code, `weatherCelsius.xml`:

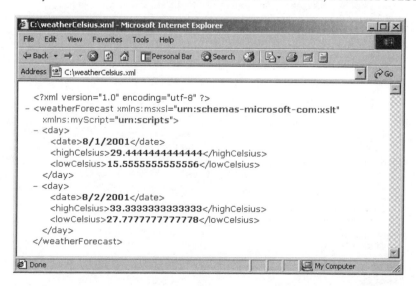

Note that it takes a second or two to load the stylesheet – that's because the C# compiler needs to be loaded and run against the embedded C# script before the script can be processed. We'll take a look at a better-performing way to extend XSLT stylesheet functionality – using extension objects – later in the chapter.

Passing Arguments to a Transformation

XSLT provides a mechanism for working with arguments within a stylesheet. To use an argument, it must be "declared" within the stylesheet by including an `<xsl:param>` element in the `<xsl:stylesheet>` element; it may then be referenced like a variable (by prefixing the param name with the dollar sign).

When using the .NET framework to transform an XML document using a stylesheet with parameters, the values of the parameters are passed to the transformation engine in an `XsltArgumentList` object. We simply create a new `XsltArgumentList` object and call the `AddParam()` method on it to create the parameter. Let's see how this is done. We'll extend our previous example to accept a parameter that indicates whether the temperature in the output document should be computed in Celsius or Kelvin. We implement this in our stylesheet (`weather2.xsl`) by adding a parameter to our C# embedded script:

```
<xsl:stylesheet xmlns:xsl="http://www.w3.org/1999/XSL/Transform"
                xmlns:msxsl="urn:schemas-microsoft-com:xslt"
                xmlns:myScript="urn:scripts"
                version="1.0">
  <xsl:param name="Format" />
  <xsl:template match="weatherForecast">
    <weatherForecast>
      <xsl:apply-templates />
    </weatherForecast>
  </xsl:template>

  <xsl:template match="day">
    <day>
      <xsl:copy-of select="date" />
      <highTemp>
        <xsl:value-of
          select="myScript:convertTemp(highFahrenheit, $Format)" />
      </highTemp>
      <lowTemp>
        <xsl:value-of
          select="myScript:convertTemp(lowFahrenheit, $Format)" />
      </lowTemp>
    </day>
  </xsl:template>
  <msxsl:script language="C#" implements-prefix="myScript">
    public double convertTemp(double fahrenheit, string targetFormat)
    {
      switch(targetFormat)
        {
        case "Kelvin":
          double kelvin = (fahrenheit - 32) * 5 / 9 + 273;
          return kelvin;
        case "Celsius":
          double celsius = (fahrenheit - 32) * 5 / 9;
          return celsius;
        default:
          return 0.0;
        }
    }
  </msxsl:script>
</xsl:stylesheet>
```

Using the same source XML document as in the previous example (`weather.xml`), we use the following code to transform the temperatures into Celsius by setting an argument for the stylesheet:

```
' VB .NET

' weather2.vb
Imports System
Imports System.Xml
Imports System.Xml.Xsl
Imports System.Xml.XPath
Imports System.IO
Imports System.Text

Module Module1

  Sub Main()

    Dim myTransform As New System.Xml.Xsl.XslTransform()
    Dim myArgList As New System.Xml.Xsl.XsltArgumentList()
    Dim myOut As New System.IO.FileStream("weatherNew.xml", _
                                    System.IO.FileMode.Create)
    Dim myDoc As New System.Xml.XPath.XPathDocument("weather.xml")

    myTransform.Load("weather2.xsl")
    myArgList.AddParam("Format", "", "Celsius")
    myTransform.Transform(myDoc, myArgList, myOut)

  End Sub

End Module
```

```
// C#

// weather2.cs
using System;
using System.Xml;
using System.Text;
using System.IO;
using System.Xml.XPath;
using System.Xml.Xsl;

namespace myApp
{
  class mainClass
  {
    static void Main(string[] args)
    {
      XslTransform myTransform = new XslTransform();
      XsltArgumentList myArgList = new XsltArgumentList();
      FileStream myOut = new FileStream("weatherNew.xml",
                                    System.IO.FileMode.Create);
      XPathDocument myDoc = new XPathDocument("weather.xml");

      myTransform.Load("weather2.xsl");
      myArgList.AddParam("Format", "", "Celsius");
      myTransform.Transform(myDoc, myArgList, myOut);
    }
  }
}
```

We can compile and run the code as in the previous example. The output of the either the C# or VB .NET code is the same XML document, weatherNew.xml:

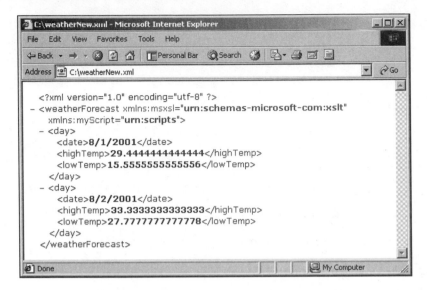

If we change the parameter in the code, instructing the stylesheet to transform the document to degrees Kelvin rather than Celsius:

```
' VB .NET
    myArgList.AddParam("Format", "", "Kelvin")
```

```
// C#
    myArgList.AddParam("Format", "", "Kelvin");
```

then the output of the programs (weather3.cs and weather3.vb in the code download) will now be this document, weatherNew2.xml:

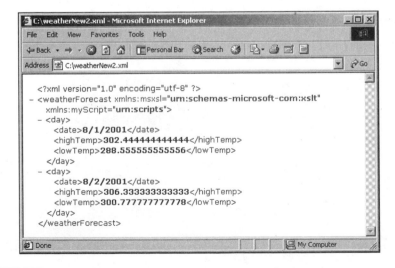

Extending Stylesheets with Extension Objects

One of the most powerful techniques available to the programmer when working with stylesheets using the .NET framework is the ability to associate methods with XSLT `select` expressions, in particular namespaces in a stylesheet. By adding an association of the extension object with the `select` expression to an `XsltArgumentList` object, we can actually instruct the transformation engine to run a method in our code. The method to be called may take any number of arguments, and should return the value we want to have substituted in our code for the select expression in the stylesheet. Here's an example, where we move the code from our first embedded script example into an extension object, `weather3.xsl`:

```
<xsl:stylesheet xmlns:xsl="http://www.w3.org/1999/XSL/Transform"
                xmlns:msxsl="urn:schemas-microsoft-com:xslt"
                xmlns:myFunc="urn:objs"
                version="1.0">
  <xsl:template match="weatherForecast">
    <weatherForecast>
      <xsl:apply-templates />
    </weatherForecast>
  </xsl:template>

  <xsl:template match="day">
    <day>
      <xsl:copy-of select="date" />
      <highTemp>
        <xsl:value-of select="myFunc:convertTemp(highFahrenheit)" />
      </highTemp>
      <lowTemp>
        <xsl:value-of select="myFunc:convertTemp(lowFahrenheit)" />
      </lowTemp>
    </day>
  </xsl:template>
</xsl:stylesheet>
```

Below is the code with the extension object we will be using:

```csharp
// C#

// weather4.cs
using System;
using System.Xml;
using System.Xml.XPath;
using System.Xml.Xsl;

namespace Wrox
{
  class consoleApp
  {
    static void Main(string[] args)
    {
      XslTransform myTransform = new XslTransform();
      XsltArgumentList myArgs = new XsltArgumentList();
      XPathDocument myDoc = new XPathDocument("weather.xml");

      // create an instance of the util class to be used to process
      // XSLT extension object calls
      util utilObj = new util();
      myArgs.AddExtensionObject("urn:objs", utilObj);
```

```
        System.IO.FileStream myOut = new System.IO.FileStream(
          "weatherNew3.xml", System.IO.FileMode.Create);
        myTransform.Load("weather3.xsl", null);
        myTransform.Transform(myDoc, myArgs, myOut);
      }
  }
  class util
  {
    public double convertTemp (double fahrenheit)
    {
      double celsius = (fahrenheit - 32) * 5 / 9;
      return celsius;
    }
  }
}
```

```vbnet
' VB .NET

' weather4.vb
Imports System
Imports System.Xml
Imports System.Xml.Xsl
Imports System.Xml.XPath

Module Module1

  Sub Main()

    Dim myTransform As New Xml.Xsl.XslTransform()
    Dim myArgs As New Xml.Xsl.XsltArgumentList()
    Dim myDoc As New Xml.Xpath.XPathDocument("weather.xml")

    ' create an instance of the util class to be used to process
    ' XSLT extension object calls
    Dim utilObj As New util()
    myArgs.AddExtensionObject("urn:objs", utilObj)
    Dim myOut As New IO.FileStream("weatherNew3.xml", IO.FileMode.Create)
    myTransform.Load("weather3.xsl", Nothing)
    myTransform.Transform(myDoc, myArgs, myOut)

  End Sub

  Class util

    Public Function convertTemp(ByVal fahrenheit As Double) As Double
      Dim celsius As Double
      celsius = (fahrenheit - 32) * 5 / 9
      convertTemp = celsius
    End Function

  End Class

End Module
```

The output XML document, `weatherNew3.xml`, looks like this:

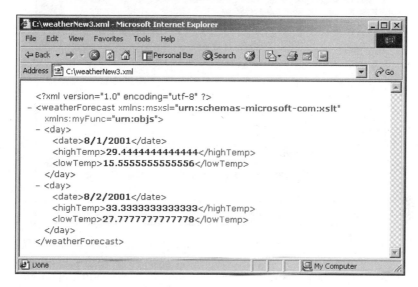

We can also change the behavior of stylesheet objects that contain extension objects by changing the functions to which the extension objects are bound. If we change our `convertTemp()` method to convert the temperature to Kelvin, rather than Celsius:

```csharp
// C#

  class util
  {
    public double convertTemp (double fahrenheit)
    {
      double kelvin = (fahrenheit - 32) * 5 / 9 + 273;
      return kelvin;
    }
  }
```

```vbnet
// VB .NET

  Class util

    Public Function convertTemp(ByVal fahrenheit As Double) As Double
      Dim kelvin As Double
      kelvin = (fahrenheit - 32) * 5 / 9 + 273
      convertTemp = kelvin
    End Function

  End Class
```

without changing the source document or the stylesheet, the output (of `weather5.cs` and `weather5.vb`) now becomes `weatherNew4.xml`:

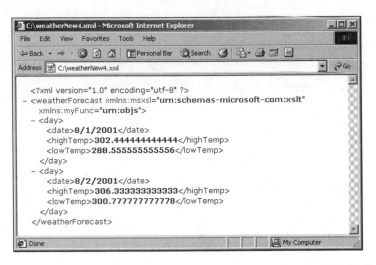

There are some advantages and disadvantages to using extension objects instead of embedded scripts:

❑ Portability – Embedded scripts are more portable than extension objects, since any .NET platform can correctly transform a stylesheet with an embedded script. A stylesheet using extension objects, on the other hand, can only be transformed by a piece of code (either .NET or some other platform that supports extension objects) that correctly implements an extension object associated with the appropriate namespace and name.

❑ Size – A stylesheet that relies on extension objects will be smaller and more maintainable than a stylesheet containing embedded scripts.

❑ Flexibility – As we have seen, stylesheets that rely on extension objects can change their behavior based on the extension object to which they are bound. Stylesheets using embedded scripts will always behave as the embedded script dictates.

❑ Performance – Because extension objects are precompiled, rather than being compiled just-in-time, scripts using extension objects will perform somewhat better than those that contain embedded scripts (depending on various factors, including how often stylesheets are loaded and how much scripting is embedded).

❑ Maintainability – Stylesheets using extension objects can be somewhat more difficult to troubleshoot and modify, as the actual code being executed is split between the stylesheet and the code providing the extension object implementation. Embedded scripts, while a bit slower, have the advantage of keeping all the code in one place.

We can decide whether extension objects or embedded scripts are appropriate for our stylesheets by taking the above factors into consideration.

Tuning XSLT Transformations for Performance

The performance of the XSLT styling engine in the .NET framework has been improved dramatically over the MSXML libraries. However, for situations where performance is critical, there are some ways we can tune our code to ensure the best styling performance.

Avoid Multiple Loads of Stylesheets

The first performance tip seems obvious, but it's very important. If we need to use a stylesheet over and over again, we can load it into an `XslTransform` object once and reuse that object rather than loading it each time it is needed. For example, say we have the following code that processes all the document filenames in a collection:

```
' VB .NET

  Sub TransformDocs(ByVal colDocuments As System.Collections.ArrayList)

    Dim i As Integer
    Dim sSrcDoc As String
    Dim sDestDoc As String
    Dim myTransform As New System.Xml.Xsl.XslTransform()

    For i = 0 To colDocuments.Count - 1
      myTransform.Load("customerXHTML.xsl")
      sSrcDoc = colDocuments(i)
      sDestDoc = sSrcDoc.Substring(0, sSrcDoc.IndexOf(".")) + "XHTML.xml"
      myTransform.Transform(sSrcDoc, sDestDoc)
      myTransform.Load("customerWML.xsl")
      sDestDoc = sSrcDoc.Substring(0, sSrcDoc.IndexOf(".")) + "WML.xml"
      myTransform.Transform(sSrcDoc, sDestDoc)
    Next

  End Sub
```

```
// C#

static void TransformDocs(ArrayList colDocuments)
{

  int i;
  string sSrcDoc;
  string sDestDoc;
  XslTransform myTransform = new XslTransform();

  for(i=0; i<colDocuments.Count; i++)
  {
    myTransform.Load("customerXHTML.xsl");
    sSrcDoc = (string)colDocuments[i];
    sDestDoc = sSrcDoc.Substring(0, sSrcDoc.IndexOf(".")) + "XHTML.xml";
    myTransform.Transform(sSrcDoc, sDestDoc);
    myTransform.Load("customerWML.xsl");
    sDestDoc = sSrcDoc.Substring(0, sSrcDoc.IndexOf(".")) + "WML.xml";
    myTransform.Transform(sSrcDoc, sDestDoc);
  }
}
```

There is significant overhead involved in loading the stylesheet into the `XslTransform` object each time. A better form of this code would be to create two `XslTransform` objects, load the stylesheets into those objects, and then reuse them in the loop:

```vb.net
' VB .NET

Sub TransformDocs(ByVal colDocuments As System.Collections.ArrayList)

    Dim i As Integer
    Dim sSrcDoc As String
    Dim sDestDoc As String
    Dim myTransformXHTML As New System.Xml.Xsl.XslTransform()
    Dim myTransformWML As New System.Xml.Xsl.XslTransform()

    myTransformXHTML.Load("customerXHTML.xsl")
    myTransformWML.Load("customerWML.xsl")

    For i = 0 To colDocuments.Count - 1
      sSrcDoc = colDocuments(i)
      sDestDoc = sSrcDoc.Substring(0, sSrcDoc.IndexOf(".")) + "XHTML.xml"
      myTransformXHTML.Transform(sSrcDoc, sDestDoc)
      sDestDoc = sSrcDoc.Substring(0, sSrcDoc.IndexOf(".")) + "WML.xml"
      myTransformWML.Transform(sSrcDoc, sDestDoc)
    Next

  End Sub
```

```csharp
// C#

static void TransformDocs(System.Collections.ArrayList colDocuments)
{
  int i;
  string sSrcDoc;
  string sDestDoc;

  XslTransform myTransformXHTML = new XslTransform();
  XslTransform myTransformWML = new XslTransform();

  myTransformXHTML.Load("customerXHTML.xsl");
  myTransformWML.Load("customerWML.xsl");

  for(i=0; i<colDocuments.Count; i++)
  {
    sSrcDoc = (string)colDocuments[i];
    sDestDoc = sSrcDoc.Substring(0, sSrcDoc.IndexOf(".")) + "XHTML.xml";
    myTransformXHTML.Transform(sSrcDoc, sDestDoc);
    sDestDoc = sSrcDoc.Substring(0, sSrcDoc.IndexOf(".")) + "WML.xml";
    myTransformWML.Transform(sSrcDoc, sDestDoc);
  }
}
```

Use XPathDocument Objects

As we have stated earlier in the chapter, the System.Xml.XPath namespace contains a class called XPathDocument. This class is a document representation that is tuned for XPath expression resolution – it drops strong document validation and node identification to improve XPath performance. In most situations when we are receiving documents from a trusted source (such as a document repository we have created), this is the best way to drive stylesheets.

Use Smart Pipelining

If our code involves repeated styling of documents, it's important to code these in such a way that we avoid repeated loading and parsing of the documents. For example, the following code runs two stylesheets on a source document, one after the other:

```csharp
// C#

using System;
using System.Xml;
using System.IO;
using System.Xml.XPath;
using System.Xml.Xsl;

namespace Wrox
{
  class consoleApp
  {
    static void Main(string[] args)
    {
      XslTransform myTransform1 = new XslTransform();
      XslTransform myTransform2 = new XslTransform();
      MemoryStream interimStream = new MemoryStream();
      MemoryStream finalStream = new MemoryStream();

      XPathDocument myDoc = new XPathDocument("startDoc.xml");

      myTransform1.Load("style1.xsl");
      myTransform2.Load("style2.xsl");

      myTransform1.Transform(myDoc, null, interimStream);
      XPathDocument myInterimResult = new XPathDocument(interimStream);
      myTransform2.Transform(myInterimResult, null, finalStream);
    }
  }
}
```

```vbnet
' VB .NET

Imports System
Imports System.Xml
Imports System.IO
Imports System.Xml.XPath
Imports System.Xml.Xsl

Module Module1

  Sub Main()

    Dim myTransform1 As New Xml.Xsl.XslTransform()
    Dim myTransform2 As New Xml.Xsl.XslTransform()
    Dim interimStream As New System.IO.MemoryStream()
    Dim finalStream As New System.IO.MemoryStream()

    Dim myDoc As New Xml.XPath.XPathDocument("startDoc.xml")

    myTransform1.Load("style1.xsl")
    myTransform2.Load("style2.xsl")
```

```
      myTransform1.Transform(myDoc, Nothing, interimStream)
      Dim myInterimResult As New Xml.XPath.XPathDocument(interimStream)
      myTransform2.Transform(myInterimResult, Nothing, finalStream)

  End Sub

End Module
```

As the intermediate result is being written to a stream, the code has to re-parse the intermediate document before it can be styled the second time. A better approach would be to write the intermediate result to an XmlReader, which allows the second stylesheet to run against the already parsed result of the first transformation:

```csharp
// C#

using System;
using System.Xml;
using System.IO;
using System.Xml.XPath;
using System.Xml.Xsl;

namespace Wrox
{
  class consoleApp
  {
    static void Main(string[] args)
    {
      XslTransform myTransform1 = new XslTransform();
      XslTransform myTransform2 = new XslTransform();
      XmlReader interimReader;
      MemoryStream finalStream = new MemoryStream();

      XPathDocument myDoc = new XPathDocument("startDoc.xml");

      myTransform1.Load("style1.xsl");
      myTransform2.Load("style2.xsl");

      interimReader = myTransform1.Transform(myDoc, null);
      XPathDocument myInterimResult = new XPathDocument(interimReader);
      myTransform2.Transform(myInterimResult, null, finalStream);
    }
```

```vbnet
' VB .NET

Imports System
Imports System.Xml
Imports System.IO
Imports System.Xml.XPath
Imports System.Xml.Xsl

Module Module1

  Sub Main()

    Dim myTransform1 As New Xml.Xsl.XslTransform()
    Dim myTransform2 As New Xml.Xsl.XslTransform()
    Dim interimReader As Xml.XmlReader
    Dim finalStream As New System.IO.MemoryStream()
```

```
        Dim myDoc As New Xml.XPath.XPathDocument("startDoc.xml")

        myTransform1.Load("style1.xsl")
        myTransform2.Load("style2.xsl")

        interimReader = myTransform1.Transform(myDoc, Nothing)
        Dim myInterimResult As New Xml.XPath.XPathDocument(interimReader)
        myTransform2.Transform(myInterimResult, Nothing, finalStream)

    End Sub

End Module
```

Other XPath Functions

The System.Xml.XPath doesn't only provide support for XSLT transforms – it contains some classes that allow XPath expressions to be run directly against documents (without being in the context of an XSLT stylesheet). Let's see how these classes work.

The XPathNavigator Abstract Class

The System.Xml.XPath namespace contains a class called XPathNavigator that is designed to facilitate XPath expression evaluation for a document. The XSLT processing engine uses the XPathNavigator class to evaluate the XPath expressions found in a stylesheet. However, since these methods are public, we can use them to evaluate XPath expressions against a document ourselves. Instances of XPathNavigator cannot be created directly – instead, we create an XPathNavigator by calling the CreateNavigator() method of any object that implements the IXPathNavigable interface. In the .NET framework, these objects are XmlNode and XPathDocument. Once we have an XPathNavigator for a document, we can navigate through the document using a number of different methods, similar to those available to an XmlReader (but more flexible). Let's take a look at a couple of the most useful methods.

Testing Nodes Against XPath Expressions

If we are navigating through an XML document using an XPathNavigator object, we can check to see if the current node matches an XPath expression using the Matches() method. This can be useful, for example, if we want to walk through all the element nodes in a document and check them one by one to see if they have a particular attribute value. Let's see an example. In the following code, we check all the <Customer> elements in the CustomerList document. When we encounter one that has a CustomerID attribute, we write its name to the console:

```
' VB .NET

' customerList.vb
Imports System
Imports System.Xml
Imports System.Xml.XPath
Imports System.Collections

Module Module1
```

```vb
   Sub Main()

     Dim myDoc As New System.Xml.XmlDocument()
     Dim myNav As System.Xml.XPath.XPathNavigator
     Dim bContinue As Boolean

     myDoc.Load("customerList.xml")
     myNav = myDoc.CreateNavigator()

     ' move to the customerList element
     myNav.MoveToFirstChild()
     ' move to the first customer element
     myNav.MoveToFirstChild()
     bContinue = True
     While bContinue
       ' check to see if this node has a customerID attribute
       If myNav.Matches("/customerList/customer[@customerID]") Then
         Console.WriteLine(myNav.GetAttribute("customerName", ""))
       End If
       ' if the MoveToNext method returns False, then there are no more
       ' nodes in the doc
       bContinue = myNav.MoveToNext()
     End While
     Console.ReadLine()
   End Sub

End Module
```

```csharp
// C#

// customerList.cs
using System;
using System.Xml;
using System.Xml.XPath;
using System.Collections;

namespace myApp
{
  class mainClass
  {
    static void Main(string[] args)
    {
      XmlDocument myDoc = new XmlDocument();
      XPathNavigator myNav;
      bool bContinue;

      myDoc.Load("customerList.xml");
      myNav = myDoc.CreateNavigator();

      // move to the customerList element
      myNav.MoveToFirstChild();
      // move to the first customer element
      myNav.MoveToFirstChild();
      bContinue = true;
      while(bContinue)
      {
        // check to see if this node has a customerID attribute
        if(myNav.Matches("/customerList/customer[@customerID]"))
        {
```

```
              Console.WriteLine(myNav.GetAttribute("customerName", ""));
          }
          // if the MoveToNext method returns False, then there are no more
          // nodes in the doc
          bContinue = myNav.MoveToNext();
       }
       Console.ReadLine();
    }
  }
}
```

If we run this code against the following sample document, `customerList.xml`:

```
<?xml version="1.0"?>
<customerList>
  <customer customerName="Frank Jones" customerID="1" />
  <customer customerName="James Smith" />
  <customer customerName="David Williams" customerID="2" />
  <customer customerName="William Brown" customerID="3" />
  <customer customerName="Roger Black" />
</customerList>
```

this output is produced:

Selecting Nodes Using XPath Expressions

The most useful method of `XPathNavigator` is the `Select()` method. This allows us to retrieve a list of nodes in the document that match a particular XPath expression. The list is returned as an `XPathNodeIterator` – a simple, forward-only iterator that allows us to programmatically inspect each node and process it as necessary. For example, the following code selects all the `<Customer>` elements from the document whose `customerType` attribute is `Corporate`, and writes the customer names for those customers:

```
// C#

// customerList2.cs
using System;
using System.Xml;
using System.IO;
using System.Xml.XPath;
using System.Xml.Xsl;

namespace Wrox
{
  class consoleApp
  {
    static void Main(string[] args)
```

```
    {
      XPathDocument myDoc = new XPathDocument("customerList2.xml");
      XPathNavigator myNav;
      XPathNodeIterator myNodes;

      myNav = myDoc.CreateNavigator();
      myNodes = myNav.Select(
        "/customerList/customer[@customerType='Corporate']");

      while(myNodes.MoveNext())
      {
        Console.WriteLine(myNodes.Current.GetAttribute("customerName", ""));
      }
      Console.ReadLine();
    }
  }
}
```

```
' VB .NET

' customerList2.vb
Imports System
Imports System.Xml
Imports System.IO
Imports System.Xml.XPath
Imports System.Xml.Xsl

Module Module1

  Sub Main()

    Dim myDoc = New Xml.XPath.XPathDocument("customerList2.xml")
    Dim myNav As Xml.XPath.XPathNavigator
    Dim myNodes As Xml.XPath.XPathNodeIterator

    myNav = myDoc.CreateNavigator()
    myNodes = _
      myNav.Select("/customerList/customer[@customerType='Corporate']")

    While myNodes.MoveNext()
      Console.WriteLine(myNodes.Current.GetAttribute("customerName", ""))
    End While

    Console.ReadLine()

  End Sub

End Module
```

If we run this code using the following sample source document, `customerList2.xml`:

```
<?xml version="1.0"?>
<customerList>
  <customer customerName="Big Widgets, Inc." customerType="Corporate" />
  <customer customerName="James Smith" customerType="Consumer" />
  <customer customerName="Ed's Pagination" customerType="Corporate" />
  <customer customerName="Magpie Technologies" customerType="Corporate" />
  <customer customerName="Roger Black" customerType="Consumer"/>
</customerList>
```

the output is this:

```
Command Prompt - customerList2                                    _ □ X
C:\>customerList2
Big Widgets, Inc.
Ed's Pagination
Magpie Technologies
```

Precompiling XPath Expressions

To improve the performance of XPath evaluations when using an instance of XPathNavigator, we can precompile the XPath expressions. Since the parser doesn't have to optimize the expression each time it is used, evaluation of the expression will be quicker. This is done by creating an XPathExpression object that represents a compiled form of the expression. All of the methods of XPathNavigator that take a string XPath expression as a parameter can also take an XPathExpression object. For example, we can improve the performance of the Matches() example, above, by precompiling the XPath expression we use for the test:

```vb
' VB.NET

' customerListPrecompiled.vb
Imports System
Imports System.Xml
Imports System.Xml.XPath
Imports System.Collections

Module Module1

  Sub Main()

    Dim myDoc As New System.Xml.XmlDocument()
    Dim myNav As System.Xml.XPath.XPathNavigator
    Dim bContinue As Boolean
    Dim myExpr As System.Xml.XPath.XPathExpression

    myDoc.Load("customerList.xml")
    myNav = myDoc.CreateNavigator()

    myExpr = myNav.Compile("//customer[@customerID]")

    myNav.MoveToFirstChild()
    myNav.MoveToFirstChild()
    bContinue = True
    While bContinue
      If myNav.Matches(myExpr) Then
        Console.WriteLine(myNav.GetAttribute("customerName", ""))
      End If
      bContinue = myNav.MoveToNext()
    End While
    Console.ReadLine()
  End Sub

End Module
```

```csharp
// C#

// customerListPrecompiled.cs
using System;
using System.Xml;
using System.Xml.XPath;
using System.Collections;

namespace myApp
{
  class mainClass
  {
    static void Main(string[] args)
    {
      XmlDocument myDoc = new XmlDocument();
      XPathNavigator myNav;
      bool bContinue;
      XPathExpression myExpr;

      myDoc.Load("customerList.xml");
      myNav = myDoc.CreateNavigator();

      myExpr = myNav.Compile("//customer[@customerID]");

      myNav.MoveToFirstChild();
      myNav.MoveToFirstChild();
      bContinue = true;
      while(bContinue)
      {
        if(myNav.Matches(myExpr))
        {
          Console.WriteLine(myNav.GetAttribute("customerName", ""));
        }
        bContinue = myNav.MoveToNext();
      }
      Console.ReadLine();
    }
  }
}
```

Summary

The .NET framework provides robust support for XSLT and XPath processing. While it fully supports the XSLT and XPath specifications as defined by the W3C, it also provides many helpful extensions to these specifications that enhance the usability of stylesheets within .NET applications. These include:

❏ Embedding scripts in stylesheets in a variety of languages

❏ Using extension objects to extend the XSLT functionality

❏ Applying XPath expressions to a document without requiring the context of a stylesheet

As always, when deciding which parts of this functionality to use in our programs, we need to think about the long-term requirements for our code. Does it need to be portable to other .NET-enabled systems? Does it need to be portable to non-.NET systems? If we keep the advantages and disadvantages of each technique in mind, we can create code that performs well and suits our requirements.

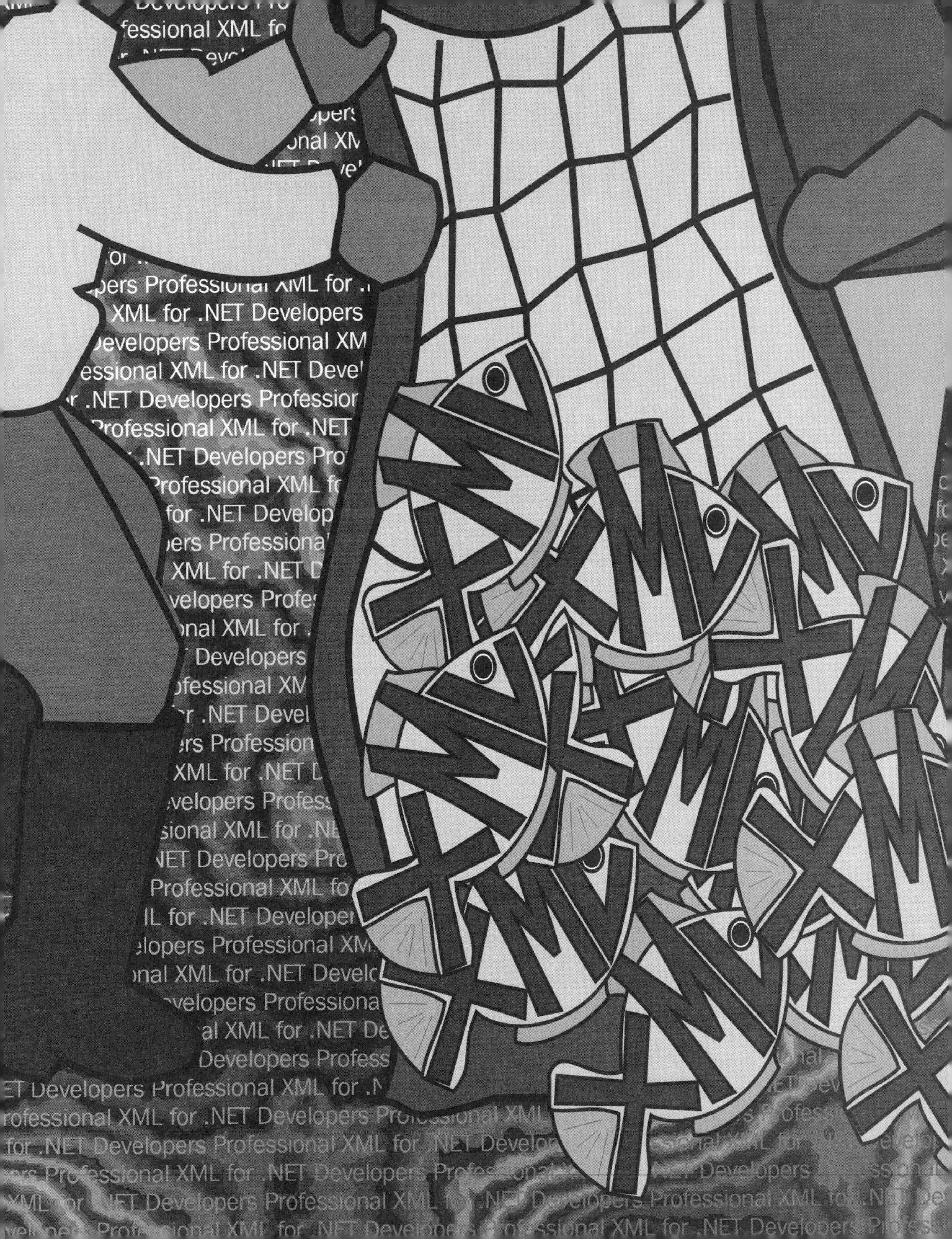
Professional XML for .NET Developers

6

Validating XML

A schema defines the grammar for a family of XML documents. In the early days of XML, each software vendor used its own proprietary notation for schemas. One of the notable early runners was Microsoft's XML-Data Reduced (XDR) schema syntax, which was supported by the XML parser shipped with Microsoft Internet Explorer 5.0.

In May 2001, the World Wide Web Consortium published the XML Schema Definition Language (XSD) recommended standard. The arrival of this standard brings much needed consistency to the scene, and software vendors have been eager to fall in line and follow this standard. For example, the Microsoft XML parser MSXML (version 4.0) supports the XSD standard.

The Microsoft .NET Framework provides extensive support for the XSD standard. XSD is so tightly interwoven into the fabric of the .NET Framework, it's hard to imagine how everything would hang together without it. For example, the .NET Framework uses XSD schemas to define the structure of data in an ADO.NET dataset (see Chapter 10 for details). XSD also has an important role to play in Web Services, as you'll see in Chapter 13, *Web Services and SOAP*.

In this chapter, we will look at creating an XSD schema using a variety of useful tools in Visual Studio .NET. We will also show how to represent an XSD schema as a collection of objects in memory, using Microsoft's Schema Object Model (SOM). This allows us to create, modify, and delete schema definitions programmatically, and write the schema out to disk (or elsewhere) when we've finished.

Another important use of schemas is for document validation. In the .NET Framework, we use an `XmlValidatingReader` object to test whether an XML document complies with the required grammar. We'll show you how to perform validation at the end of this chapter.

To get things going, we'll begin with a brief recap of XSD syntax. We'll also review Document Type Definitions, and Microsoft's XDR schema syntax.

Defining a Grammar for XML Documents

The XML Information Set (Infoset) defines an abstract model for XML documents. Every well formed XML document that conforms to the rules for XML namespace will have an XML infoset. The infoset describes the information items in the document, such as the document node, elements, attributes, and so on.

The XML Infoset does not make any predictions about the grammar of an XML document. A grammar defines the set of allowable elements and attributes in the document, and can also define allowed data types for elements and attributes.

There are three different ways to define an XML grammar in the .NET Framework:

❑   Document Type Definitions (DTDs)

❑   Microsoft XML-Data Reduced (XDR) schemas

❑   W3C XML Schema Definition Language (XSD) schemas

If you are developing a new XML solution, you should use XSD schemas. The .NET Framework provides extensive support for XSD schemas, and the wider XML community is also heading down this route.

Having said that, there are still roles for DTDs and XDR schemas to play. DTDs are an approved W3C standard – there are many XML grammars currently defined using DTDs, and it's unlikely these will migrate to XSD overnight. Likewise, XDR schemas are used extensively in Microsoft BizTalk Server, to define grammars for business documents exchanged between applications and organizations.

If possible, you might like to consider converting DTDs and XDR schemas to XSD schemas, so that you can take advantage of the rich support in the .NET Framework. As you'll see later in this chapter, Visual Studio .NET includes tools to help us convert XDR schemas into XSD format.

For the sake of completeness, we'll take a brief look at each of these technologies in the next few sections. We won't attempt to describe each technology in detail – there are plenty of books that do a fine job of that already (for example: *Professional XML 2nd Edition* ISBN 1-861005-05-9 and *Professional XML Schemas* ISBN 1-861005-47-4 also published by Wrox Press).

Instead, we'll show a complete example of a DTD, an XDR schema, and an XSD schema for the following XML document, DefiningGrammars\Company.xml, which you can download, along with all other examples in this book, from the Wrox web site at http://www.wrox.com:

```xml
<?xml version="1.0"?>
<Company>

  <CompanyName>My Cool Startup Company</CompanyName>
  <RegDate>1997-07-02</RegDate>

  <Employee EmpNum="123" JobTitle="Director">
    <Name>Chris Peterson</Name>
    <Tel>222-7777-123</Tel>
    <Salary>79500.00</Salary>
  </Employee>

  <Employee EmpNum="456" JobTitle="Manager">
    <Name>Emily Williams</Name>
```

```
      <Tel>222-7777-456</Tel>
      <Salary>52750.00</Salary>
   </Employee>

   <Employee EmpNum="789" JobTitle="Programmer">
     <Name>Thomas Smith</Name>
     <Tel>222-7777-789</Tel>
     <DailyRate>425.00</DailyRate>
   </Employee>

</Company>
```

This document highlights several important XML issues, which we'll pick up on when we look at the DTD, XDR schema, and XSD schema in a moment. Note the following points:

❑ The <Company> element has a <CompanyName> child element, a <RegDate> child element, and any number (zero or more) of <Employee> child elements.

❑ <CompanyName> has a string value, and <RegDate> has a date value.

❑ <Employee> has an EmpNum attribute, which can be any string value. <Employee> also has a JobTitle attribute, which must have a value of either "Director", "Manager", or "Programmer".

❑ <Employee> has three child elements: <Name> (a string), <Tel> (also a string), and either <Salary> or <DailyRate> (both are fractional numbers).

Defining a Grammar Using a DTD

DTDs have a special relationship with XML, because they are defined in the XML Specification. Despite the advent of the XSD standard, DTDs will be around for a while yet. Here is the DTD for the above sample XML document, DefiningGrammars\Company.dtd:

```
<!ELEMENT Company (CompanyName, RegDate, Employee*)>

<!ELEMENT CompanyName (#PCDATA)>
<!ELEMENT RegDate (#PCDATA)>
<!ELEMENT Employee (Name, Tel, (Salary | DailyRate))>

<!ATTLIST Employee
   EmpNum CDATA #REQUIRED
   JobTitle (Director | Manager | Programmer) #REQUIRED>

<!ELEMENT Name (#PCDATA)>
<!ELEMENT Tel (#PCDATA)>
<!ELEMENT Salary (#PCDATA)>
<!ELEMENT DailyRate (#PCDATA)>
```

<!ELEMENT> declarations specify element content, and <!ATTLIST> declarations specify the list of attributes for an element. The #PCDATA and CDATA keywords are euphemisms for "text", but we cannot specify particular data types in a DTD.

There are several other limitations with DTDs. The most important restriction is that DTDs don't support namespaces – this is likely to become more important as XML developers use namespaces more widely in the future. Another weakness with DTDs is that they offer limited extensibility – for example, you cannot define an element or attribute type in terms of other types in the DTD.

For more information about DTDs, see *Professional XML 2nd Edition* 1-861005-05-9 from Wrox Press. For some examples of DTDs, see http://www.oasis-open.org/cover/xml.html, and http://www.dublincore.org/.

Defining a Grammar Using a Microsoft XDR Schema

Microsoft introduced XDR as a preliminary schema syntax, before the emergence of the XSD standard. XML developers from the last millennium might be familiar with XDR schemas, but if you've never encountered them before you can probably ignore them now (although XDR schemas are still used in BizTalk Server). The future is XSD schemas, not XDR.

Having said all that, let's take a look at the XDR schema for the sample XML document we saw earlier, `DefiningGrammars\Company.xdr`:

```xml
<?xml version="1.0"?>
<Schema name="CompanySchema" xmlns="urn:schemas-microsoft-com:xml-data"
        xmlns:dt="urn:schemas-microsoft-com:datatypes">

  <ElementType name="Company" content="eltOnly">
    <element type="CompanyName"/>
    <element type="RegDate"/>
    <element type="Employee" minOccurs="0" maxOccurs="*"/>
  </ElementType>

  <ElementType name="CompanyName" content="textOnly" dt:type="string"/>
  <ElementType name="RegDate"     content="textOnly" dt:type="date"/>

  <ElementType name="Employee" content="eltOnly">
    <attribute type="EmpNum"   required="yes"/>
    <attribute type="JobTitle" required="yes"/>
    <element type="Name"/>
    <element type="Tel"/>
    <group order="one">
      <element type="Salary"/>
      <element type="DailyRate"/>
    </group>
  </ElementType>

  <AttributeType name="EmpNum"   dt:type="string"/>
  <AttributeType name="JobTitle" dt:type="enumeration"
              dt:values="Director Manager Programmer"/>

  <ElementType name="Name"      content="textOnly" dt:type="string"/>
  <ElementType name="Tel"       content="textOnly" dt:type="string"/>
  <ElementType name="Salary"    content="textOnly" dt:type="fixed.14.4"/>
  <ElementType name="DailyRate" content="textOnly" dt:type="fixed.14.4"/>

</Schema>
```

XDR schemas are XML documents, with a `Schema` document element and various namespace declarations. Inside the XDR schema we use `<ElementType>` to define element types, and use `<AttributeType>` to define attribute types. We then use `element type="..."` to indicate that a particular element is required at this location in the document. Likewise, we use `attribute type="..."` to indicate that a particular attribute is required.

Defining a Grammar Using an XSD Schema

The XML Schema Definition Language was recommended by the W3C on May 2, 2001. XML parser writers have readily supported this standard, and the .NET Framework provides extensive API and tool support.

Here is the complete listing of the XSD schema for the XML sample document, DefiningGrammars\Company.xsd:

```
<?xml version="1.0"?>
<xsd:schema xmlns:xsd="http://www.w3.org/2001/XMLSchema">

  <xsd:element name="Company" type="CompanyType"/>

  <xsd:complexType name="CompanyType">
    <xsd:sequence>
      <xsd:element name="CompanyName" type="xsd:string"/>
      <xsd:element name="RegDate"      type="xsd:date"/>
      <xsd:element name="Employee"     type="EmployeeType"
                   minOccurs="0" maxOccurs="unbounded"/>
    </xsd:sequence>
  </xsd:complexType>

  <xsd:complexType name="EmployeeType">
    <xsd:sequence>
      <xsd:element name="Name" type="xsd:string"/>
      <xsd:element name="Tel"  type="xsd:string"/>
      <xsd:choice>
        <xsd:element name="Salary"    type="xsd:double"/>
        <xsd:element name="DailyRate" type="xsd:double"/>
      </xsd:choice>
    </xsd:sequence>
    <xsd:attribute name="EmpNum"   use="required" type="xsd:string"/>
    <xsd:attribute name="JobTitle" use="required" type="JobTitleType"/>
  </xsd:complexType>

  <xsd:simpleType name="JobTitleType">
    <xsd:restriction base="xsd:string">
      <xsd:enumeration value="Director"/>
      <xsd:enumeration value="Manager"/>
      <xsd:enumeration value="Programmer"/>
    </xsd:restriction>
  </xsd:simpleType>

</xsd:schema>
```

The document element in an XSD schema is <schema>. The namespace URI http://www.w3.org/2001/XMLSchema is required, to indicate that this is an XSD schema document. The namespace prefix xsd is used by convention in XSD schema documents.

Inside the XSD schema we use <xsd:element> and <xsd:attribute> to define an occurrence of an element and attribute, respectively. For example, <xsd:element name="Company" type="CompanyType"> specifies an element named <Company> in the XML instance document (this will be the document element in the XML instance document).

We use <xsd:complexType> to define the complex content for an element. For example, <xsd:complexType name="CompanyType"> defines the complex content of the <Company> element. The <Company> element will have a <CompanyName> child element, followed by a <RegDate> child element, followed by any number of <Employee> elements.

181

We use `<xsd:simpleType>` to define new simple types. For example, `<xsd:simpleType name="JobTitleType">` creates a new type of `string` that can only have one of the values `"Director"`, `"Manager"`, or `"Programmer"`.

For an introduction to XSD schemas, see http://www.w3.org/TR/xmlschema-0/. For a detailed description of XSD structures, see http://www.w3.org/TR/xmlschema-1/. For a detailed description of XSD data types, see http://www.w3.org/TR/xmlschema-2/.

Creating an XSD Schema in Visual Studio .NET

For early adopters of the XSD standard, the only way to create an XSD schema was to type it in manually using a text editor. We can still do this if we like, but the XSD standard is long and complex, so writing an XSD Schema from scratch is not a trivial undertaking.

Fortunately, Visual Studio .NET includes several tools to help us create an XSD schema more easily. We can create an XSD schema as follows:

❑   From scratch, using the XML Designer

❑   From a database, using the Server Explorer

❑   From an XML document or XDR schema, using the XSD Generator

> Note: The **xsd** prefix may not work with RC1 of the .NET Framework; the **xs** prefix should be used instead, however the namespace,
> `http://www.w3.org/2001/XMLSchema`, remains the same. For updated information watch http:www.msdn.microsoft.com/.

Creating an XSD Schema Using the XML Designer

The **XML Designer** allows us to create an XSD schema graphically, rather than writing the schema definitions manually. The XML Designer supports the W3C XSD Recommendation dated 2 May, 2001; it does not support earlier versions of the XSD standard, Microsoft XDR schemas, or DTDs.

To create a new XSD schema in Visual Studio .NET, invoke the File | New | File menu command. Alternatively, if we want to add an XSD schema to an existing project, we can invoke the Project | Add New Item menu command.

Select the XML Schema template as follows:

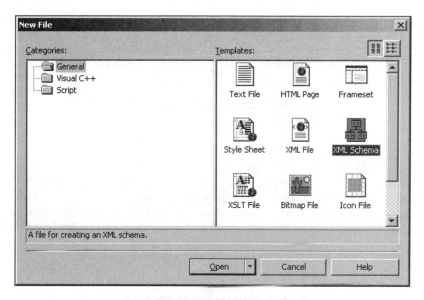

A blank schema appears in the XML Designer window. The Toolbox has an XML Schema tab, containing items we can drag-and-drop onto the new schema. This is how the Toolbox appears:

When we drag items onto the schema, the XML Designer generates the corresponding schema definitions in the schema document. To view and edit these definitions, click the XML tab at the bottom of the XML Designer window.

Example of Creating an XSD Schema Using the XML Designer

Let's see how to create the XSD schema document we saw earlier in this chapter, for a company and its employees.

The first step is to drag an element onto the schema. This global element definition will represent the document element in XML instance documents. In the caption bar for the new element, type Company in the first field – this sets the name of the element. Then type CompanyType in the second field in the caption bar – this sets the type of the element. The element should now appear as follows:

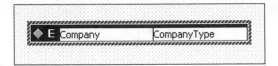

Now drag a complexType onto the schema, and set its name to CompanyType. On the first row, click the small box at the start of the row. A drop-down list appears. Choose the element option. This adds an element to the complexType. Set the name of the element to CompanyName, and set its type to string. On the second row, repeat these steps to add an element. Set the name of the element to RegDate, and set its type to date. On the third row, repeat these steps to add an element named Employee with a type of EmployeeType.

This is how CompanyType will appear after you have made these changes:

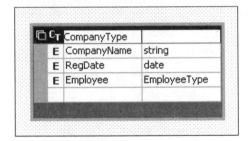

View the Properties window for the Employee element. Set its minOccurs property to 0, and set its maxOccurs property to unbounded. This will allow the <Company> element to have any number of <Employee> child elements in an XML source document.

To define the content for the <Employee> element, drag a complexType and set its name to EmployeeType. Define the following content for this complexType:

- ❑ Define an element called Name with a string data type.

- ❑ Define an element called Tel with a string data type.

- ❑ Define a choice, to represent a choice of elements. The XML Designer automatically creates a new group box named (group1), where you can define the choice of elements. In the new group box, define an element called Salary with a double data type. Also define an element called DailyRate with a double data type.

- ❑ Back in the EmployeeType box, add an attribute called EmpNum with a string data type. In the Properties window, set the use property to required. This indicates that the EmpNum attribute is mandatory.

- ❑ Add another attribute called JobTitle with a JobTitleType data type (we will define this data type shortly). Set the use property to required for this attribute.

This is how EmployeeType will appear after you have made these changes:

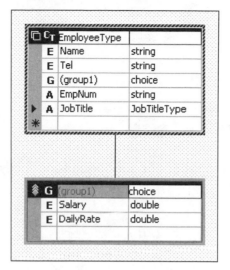

The last step is to create the JobTitleType simple type, which specifies the allowable job titles for employees. Drag a simpleType, and configure it as follows:

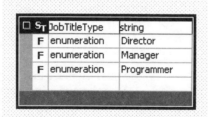

If you've followed these steps as described, the schema should now appear as shown overleaf. You can download this XSD schema as CreatingSchema\CompanyWithDesigner.xsd (the XML Schema Designer also generates a file named CompanyWithDesigner.xsx, which holds layout information for components on the designer surface):

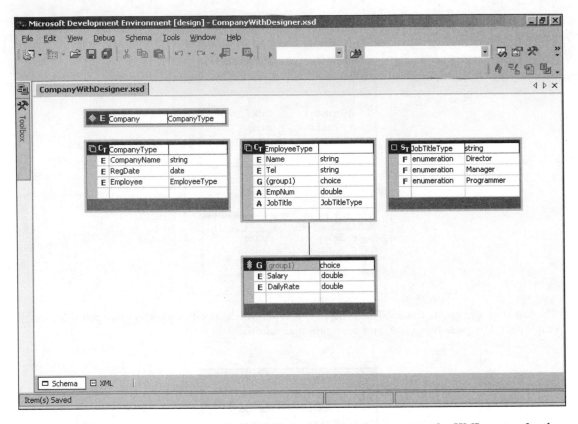

Click on the XML tab at the bottom of the XML Designer window, to view the XML syntax for the schema. The schema is semantically equivalent to the one at the beginning of the chapter.

Let's now take a look at how to generate an XSD schema from a database.

Creating an XSD Schema from a Database

One of the useful tools provided in Visual Studio .NET is the **Server Explorer**. To use the Server Explorer, invoke the View | Server Explorer menu command. The Server Explorer allows us to view and manage any servers to which we have network access, all within the Visual Studio .NET environment:

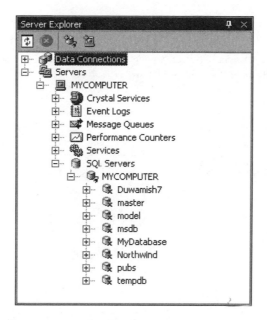

We can use the Server Explorer to open database connections to a SQL Server database (or another database such as Oracle) and work with the tables, views, indexes, and stored procedures in the database. We can also modify database structures, add new tables, and so on. The **Data Connections** node lists all the database connections we have made to a server. The **SQL Servers** node lists all the SQL Server databases available on a particular server.

Visual Studio .NET enables us to create an XSD schema from a table, view, or from the resultset returned by a stored procedure. This is extremely useful, because the task of mapping relational data to XML format is a common requirement for many developers. To create a schema from a database table, select the database table in the Server Explorer and drag it onto your schema.

Example of Creating an XSD Schema from a Database Table

In this example, we'll create a new database in SQL Server, and add a simple table containing employee data. We'll then use the Server Explorer to generate an XSD schema for the database table. (The reason we're creating a new database and a new table is to avoid damaging any existing data in the database – you can use an existing database and table if you prefer.)

To create a new database in SQL Server, follow these steps (if you use a different database product, use the appropriate database management tool to create the new database):

❑   From the **Start** menu, select **Programs | Microsoft SQL Server | Query Analyzer**.

❑   A **Connect to SQL Server** dialog box appears. Enter appropriate connection information, and press **OK**.

❑   In the Query Pane in Query Analyzer, type the following SQL statement. This statement creates a new database named `MyDatabase`:

```
CREATE DATABASE MyDatabase
```

❑ Click the green triangle on the toolbar, to execute this SQL statement. A message should appear in the Results Pane, indicating that the database was created successfully.

❑ Take a look in the Object Browser, to see the new database (if the Object Browser isn't visible, select the menu item **Tools | Object Browser | Show/Hide**). In the Object Browser, right-click the computer name and select **Refresh** from the shortcut menu. There should be an entry for **MyDatabase**, as follows:

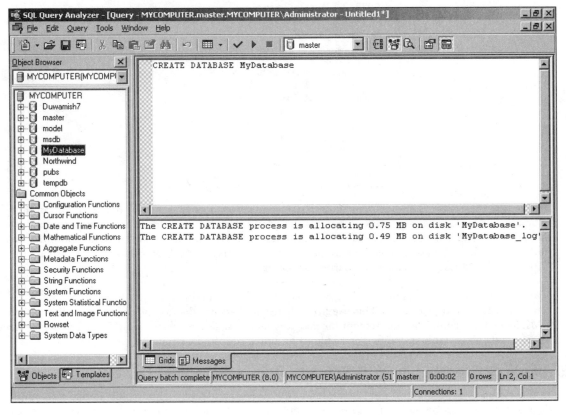

Now that we have created the database, we can create a new table in the database. To create a new table, follow these steps:

❑ In the Query Pane in Query Analyzer, type the following SQL statement. This statement creates a new table named `Employee` in the `MyDatabase` database:

```
USE MyDatabase
CREATE TABLE Employee
(
    EmployeeId int NOT NULL PRIMARY KEY,      /* Primary key column */
    Salary money NOT NULL,                    /* Required column */
    HireDate datetime NULL,                   /* Optional column */
    EmployeeName varchar(30) NOT NULL         /* Required column */
)
```

❑ Click the green triangle on the toolbar, to execute this SQL statement. A message should appear in the Results Pane, indicating that the command completed successfully.

❑ In the Object Browser, click the + sign next to **MyDatabase**, to expand this entry. Also expand **User Tables**, then **dbo.Employee**, then **Columns**. The new **Employee** table should appear as follows in the Object Browser:

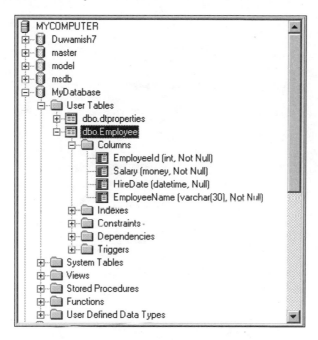

The final step is to generate an XSD schema for this database table, using Visual Studio .NET. Follow these steps:

❑ Launch Visual Studio .NET.

❑ Create a new XSD schema, or open an existing XSD schema.

❑ If the Server Explorer isn't visible, select the menu item **View | Solution Explorer** to make it so.

❑ In the Server Explorer, locate the **MyDatabase** table and select the **Employee** table. The following screenshot will help you find what you're looking for:

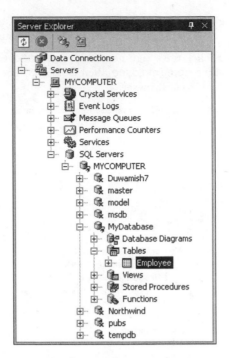

❑   Drag the **Employee** table onto the XSD Schema. The XML Designer creates the following schema:

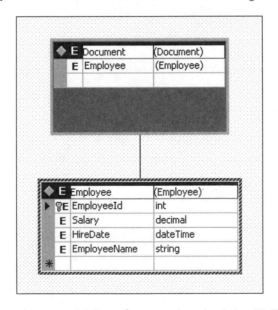

The full definition for the schema is as follows (you can download this XML document as `CreatingSchema\EmployeeFromDatabase.xml`):

```xml
<?xml version="1.0" encoding="utf-8" ?>
<xsd:schema targetNamespace="http://tempuri.org/XMLSchema.xsd"
            elementFormDefault="qualified"
            xmlns="http://tempuri.org/XMLSchema.xsd"
            xmlns:xsd="http://www.w3.org/2001/XMLSchema"
            xmlns:msdata="urn:schemas-microsoft-com:xml-msdata">

  <xsd:element name="Document">
    <xsd:complexType>
      <xsd:choice maxOccurs="unbounded">
        <xsd:element name="Employee">
          <xsd:complexType>
            <xsd:sequence>
                <xsd:element name="EmployeeId" type="xsd:int" />
                <xsd:element name="Salary" type="xsd:decimal" />
                <xsd:element name="HireDate" type="xsd:dateTime"
                             minOccurs="0"/>
                <xsd:element name="EmployeeName" type="xsd:string"/>
            </xsd:sequence>
          </xsd:complexType>
        </xsd:element>
      </xsd:choice>
    </xsd:complexType>

    <xsd:unique name="DocumentKey1" msdata:PrimaryKey="true">
      <xsd:selector xpath=".//Employee" />
      <xsd:field xpath="EmployeeId" />
    </xsd:unique>
  </xsd:element>

</xsd:schema>
```

Notice the following points about this schema:

❑   The name of the database table, Employee, is mapped to an element named <Employee> in the schema. Each row of data in the Employee table will map to a separate <Employee> element in an XML source document.

❑   Each column in the Employee table is mapped to an XML child element with the same name. You can change these element names if you like, or use attributes instead of elements. If you do modify the XSD schema, you should provide supporting documentation to describe how the XSD schema maps to the database structure. Application developers need this information, so that they can retrieve data from the database into the correct place in the XML document (and also write XML data to the correct columns in the database table).

❑   The data types for table columns are mapped to equivalent XSD data types. For example, the Salary column in the database has a money type. This is mapped to the decimal XSD data type.

❑   The EmployeeID primary key in the database table is mapped to a primary key element in the schema.

❑   The HireDate column is declared as optional in the database table. The schema uses minOccurs="0" to achieve this effect.

Creating an XSD Schema Using the XSD Generator

As well as creating XSD schemas within the Visual Studio .NET IDE, you can use a command-line tool called the **XSD Generator**. This tool ships as part of Visual Studio .NET, and offers us several additional ways to create an XSD schema using:

❑ An existing XML source document

❑ An existing Microsoft XDR schema

❑ Data types in a `.DLL` or `.EXE` assembly file

You can also use the XSD Generator tool for two additional tasks:

❑ To create a **serializable class** from an XSD schema document. The XSD Generator uses the XSD schema to define how public data in an object can be serialized into XML format. A common scenario is for one application to serialize an object to XML, and send the XML to another application. The receiving application can deserialize the XML data, to reconstitute the object in memory. Serialization is used extensively in the .NET Framework, such as to pass objects to and from a Web Service. See Chapter 7 for more information about serialization and XML.

❑ To create a **typed dataset class** from an XSD schema document. The typed dataset class makes it much easier to access tables, rows, and columns in the dataset. See Chapter 10, *ADO.NET* for more information about datasets and XML.

Creating an XSD Schema from an XML Document

To create an XSD schema from an XML document, open a Command Prompt window and run the XSD Generator tool as follows:

>xsd file.xml [/outputdir:directory]

If you get an error trying to run the XSD Generator tool, make sure the tool is on your path. The default installation directory for the tool is \Program Files\Microsoft.NET\FrameworkSDK\Bin.

The tool generates an XSD schema with the same name as the XML document, but with an **.xsd** file extension. The schema is placed in the specified output directory, or in the current directory if the **/outputdir:** parameter is omitted.

Consider this simple XML document, `CreatingSchema\CompanySummary.xml`:

```
<?xml version="1.0"?>
<CompanySummary CompanyName="My Cool Startup Company">
    <RegDate>1997-07-02</RegDate>
    <NumEmps>3</NumEmps>
</CompanySummary>
```

The XSD Generator tool creates the following XSD schema for this document. The XSD Generator tool analyzes the structure of the XML document, and reverse-engineers an XSD schema to describe the structure it sees. Using the XSD Generator tool on the above file should produce the following output `CreatingSchema\CompanySummaryFromXML.xsd`:

```
<?xml version="1.0" encoding="utf-8"?>
<xsd:schema id="NewDataSet" targetNamespace="" xmlns=""
            xmlns:xsd="http://www.w3.org/2001/XMLSchema"
            xmlns:msdata="urn:schemas-microsoft-com:xml-msdata">

  <xsd:element name="CompanySummary">
    <xsd:complexType>
      <xsd:sequence>
        <xsd:element name="RegDate" type="xsd:string"
                     minOccurs="0" msdata:Ordinal="0" />
        <xsd:element name="NumEmps" type="xsd:string"
                     minOccurs="0" msdata:Ordinal="1" />
      </xsd:sequence>
      <xsd:attribute name="CompanyName" type="xsd:string" />
    </xsd:complexType>
  </xsd:element>

  <xsd:element name="NewDataSet" msdata:IsDataSet="true"
               msdata:Locale="en-GB">
    <xsd:complexType>
      <xsd:choice maxOccurs="unbounded">
        <xsd:element ref="CompanySummary" />
      </xsd:choice>
    </xsd:complexType>
  </xsd:element>

</xsd:schema>
```

You might have noticed that the XSD Generator assigns the `"xsd:string"` data type to all the elements in the schema. This is because the XML document doesn't convey enough information for the XSD Generator to specify any other data type with confidence. You will probably want to modify the schema manually, to use the correct data types.

Also, notice the `msdata:Locale="en-GB"` attribute in the element rule `<xsd:element name="NewDataSet">`. The `msData:Locale` attribute value depends on your locale settings. For example, the English Speaking Canadian locale is `msdata:Locale="en-CA"`.

Creating an XSD Schema from an XDR Schema

To create an XSD schema from a Microsoft XDR schema, open a Command Prompt window and run the XSD Generator tool as follows:

>**xsd file.xdr [/outputdir:directory]**

The tool generates an XSD schema with the same name as the XDR schema, but with an `xsd` file extension. Consider this simple XDR schema, which describes a room reservation at a hotel, `CreatingSchema\Reservation.xdr`:

```
<?xml version="1.0"?>
<Schema xmlns="urn:schemas-microsoft-com:xml-data"
        xmlns:dt="urn:schemas-microsoft-com:datatypes">

  <ElementType name="Reservation" content="eltOnly">
    <attribute type="PersonName" required="yes"/>
    <element type="ArrivalDate"/>
```

```
            <element type="NumNights"/>
        </ElementType>

        <AttributeType name="PersonName" dt:type="string"/>
        <ElementType name="ArrivalDate" dt:type="date"/>
        <ElementType name="NumNights" dt:type="int"/>

    </Schema>
```

The XSD Generator tool creates the following XSD schema from this XDR schema (you can download this XSD schema as `CreatingSchema\ReservationFromXDR.xsd`):

```xml
<?xml version="1.0" encoding="utf-8"?>
<xsd:schema id="NewDataSet" targetNamespace="" xmlns=""
            xmlns:xsd="http://www.w3.org/2001/XMLSchema"
            xmlns:msdata="urn:schemas-microsoft-com:xml-msdata">

  <xsd:element name="NewDataSet"
               msdata:IsDataSet="true" msdata:Locale="en-GB">
    <xsd:complexType>
      <xsd:choice maxOccurs="unbounded">
        <xsd:element name="Reservation">
          <xsd:complexType>
            <xsd:sequence>
              <xsd:element name="ArrivalDate" type="xsd:date"
                           minOccurs="0" msdata:Ordinal="1" />
              <xsd:element name="NumNights" type="xsd:int"
                           minOccurs="0" msdata:Ordinal="2" />
            </xsd:sequence>
            <xsd:attribute name="PersonName" type="xsd:string" />
          </xsd:complexType>
        </xsd:element>
      </xsd:choice>
    </xsd:complexType>
  </xsd:element>

</xsd:schema>
```

Creating an XSD Schema from an Assembly

An assembly is a `.DLL` or `.EXE` file that contains Common Language Runtime (CLR) classes and other resources, such as icons and bitmaps.

We can use the XSD Generator tool to create an XSD schema to match the classes in an assembly. This is useful with serialization, where an object's public fields are written out as XML format and passed to other parts of the system. The XSD Generator tool enables us to generate an XSD schema, to describe the XML structure that will be generated when instances of a class are serialized. See Chapter 7, *Serializing XML*, for details about serialization.

Open a Command Prompt window, and run the XSD Generator tool as follows:

xsd {file.dll | file.exe} [/outputdir:directory] [/type:typename [...]]

Use the `/type:` parameter to specify particular classes in the assembly. If we omit the `/type:` parameter, the XSD Generator tool will create a schema for all the classes in the assembly.

Using the Schema Object Model

The Microsoft **Schema Object Model** (SOM) is an extensive collection of classes in the `System.Xml.Schema` namespace, to give a "classes and objects" view of an XSD schema. SOM comprises classes such as `XmlSchema`, `XmlSchemaElement`, `XmlSchemaComplexType`, and so on. These classes correspond directly to constructs in the XSD language, such as `xsd:schema`, `xsd:element`, and `xsd:complexType`.

We can use SOM to read an existing XSD schema into memory. The `XmlSchema` class has a static (shared) `Read()` method, which reads an XSD schema and builds a SOM object tree in memory. At the top of the tree is a single `XmlSchema` object, which represents the `xsd:schema` element in the XSD schema. Beneath the `XmlSchema` object, the object tree contains other SOM objects to match the structure of the XSD schema document.

We can use SOM to modify the structure of the schema programmatically in memory. We can add new objects to the tree, modify existing objects, and delete unwanted objects. We can also create an entirely new schema if necessary, and populate it programmatically with the SOM objects of our choice.

Once we've made our changes to the SOM object tree in memory, we can write the schema to disk. However, we must first verify that the object tree represents a valid XSD schema. For example, we might have forgotten to add an `XmlSchemaComplexType` object where it is expected, or specified an unrecognized data type for an element or attribute. To check for such errors, the `XmlSchema` class provides a `Compile()` method. This method verifies the syntax and structure of the schema, and raises a validation event if there are any problems.

As you might have noticed, there is a clear analogy between SOM and DOM (the Document Object Model). SOM allows you to manipulate schema documents, whereas DOM allows you to manipulate instance documents. If you're familiar with the DOM APIs, you'll feel quite at home with the SOM APIs too.

In the following section, we'll take a closer look at the SOM classes in the `System.Xml.Schema` namespace. After that, we'll work through a complete example to illustrate common tasks, such as creating complex types, defining elements and attributes, and so on.

The Schema Object Model Class Hierarchy

The Schema Object Model encapsulates the entire XSD language. Every element defined in the XSD standard has a corresponding SOM class in the `System.Xml.Schema` namespace. For example, `xsd:element` is represented by the class `XmlSchemaElement`, and `xsd:attribute` is represented by the class `XmlSchemaAttribute`.

The SOM classes are arranged in an inheritance hierarchy, as shown in the following diagram. This diagram shows the principal SOM classes – for full information about all SOM classes, see the `System.Xml.Schema` namespace hierarchy in .NET Framework Help:

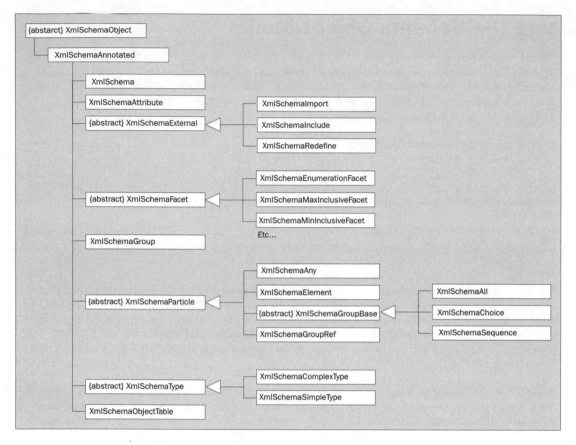

Take note of the following points:

❑ All SOM classes inherit from XmlSchemaObject. This class contains generic information that applies for any kind of XSD element. For example, the LineNumber and LinePosition properties tell us the location of an XSD element (if we read the XSD schema document from a file).

❑ The XmlSchemaImport, XmlSchemaInclude, and XmlSchemaRedefine classes allow us to reference external XSD schema documents. This is very useful. It means we can define common data types in a generic XSD schema document, then reuse or customize these data types as needed in other schemas.

❑ The XmlSchemaFacet class has a wide range of subclasses, representing the various facets defined in the XSD standard. Facets allow us to fine-tune data types. For example, XmlSchemaEnumerationFacet specifies an enumerated value for a data type.

❑ The XmlSchemaParticle class has several important subclasses. Most notably, the XmlSchemaElement class represents the xsd:element element. Also notice the classes XmlSchemaAll, XmlSchemaChoice, and XmlSchemaSequence. These represent the XSD compositors <xsd:all>, <xsd:choice>, and <xsd:sequence>, which define how content is organized in a complex type (<xsd:all> means all the child elements must appear, but in any order; <xsd:choice> means only one of the child elements is allowed; and <xsd:sequence> means all the child elements must appear in the specified order).

□ The XmlSchemaType class has two subclasses, XmlSchemaComplexType and XmlSchemaSimpleType, which allow you to define new types in the schema.

Creating a Schema Using the Schema Object Model

One of the issues you'll face when you start using SOM is the sheer number of classes involved. At the beginning, this can seem rather overwhelming. However, most developers only use a small subset of these classes on a regular basis.

Another issue that will soon become apparent is that SOM is fairly verbose. Even the simplest task can take several lines of code to achieve. The code isn't particularly difficult, there's just a lot of it. In all likelihood, SOM will be used primarily by developers who need to create Schema generators (such as the XSD Generator we saw earlier in this chapter).

The best way to understand SOM is to look at a worked example. In the coming pages, we'll write a program that uses SOM to generate an XSD schema for a simple XML document.

Requirements for the Sample Application

Our sample application will generate an XSD schema for the following XML document. We don't need this XML document to generate the XSD schema – the XML document is only listed here to help describe the required structure of the XSD schema (you can download this XML document as Employee.xml from the folders SchemaObjectModelCS and SchemaObjectModelVB):

```xml
<?xml version="1.0"?>
<Employee EmpNum="789" JobTitle="Programmer">
    <Name>Thomas Smith</Name>
    <Tel>222-7777-789</Tel>
    <Tel>333-8888-564</Tel>
    <DailyRate>425.00</DailyRate>
</Employee>
```

For illustrative purposes, we will restrict the JobTitle attribute so that it must be "Director", "Manager", or "Programmer". Also, we'll allow an employee to have any number (zero or more) of <Tel> elements. Finally, we'll allow an employee to have either a <DailyRate> or a <Salary>.

Our sample application will generate the following XSD schema document, to describe the structure of the XML document (you can download this XSD schema as Employee.xsd from the folders SchemaObjectModelCS and SchemaObjectModelVB):

```xml
<?xml version="1.0"?>
<schema targetNamespace="" xmlns="http://www.w3.org/2001/XMLSchema">

  <element name="Employee">
    <complexType>
      <sequence>
        <element name="Name" type="string" />
        <element name="Tel"  type="string"
                 minOccurs="0" maxOccurs="unbounded"/>
        <choice>
          <element name="Salary"    type="double" />
          <element name="DailyRate" type="double" />
```

```
        </choice>
      </sequence>

      <attribute name="EmpNum" type="string" use="required" />

      <attribute name="JobTitle" use="required">
        <simpleType>
          <restriction base="string">
            <enumeration value="Director" />
            <enumeration value="Manager" />
            <enumeration value="Programmer" />
          </restriction>
        </simpleType>
      </attribute>

    </complexType>
  </element>
</schema>
```

To generate this XSD schema document, our sample application will create the following object tree in memory. Each box in this diagram represents a SOM object. The diagram shows how each SOM object will map to an element in the generated XSD schema document, when the object tree is written to disk:

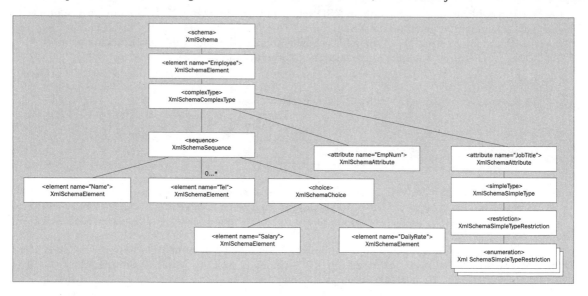

Creating a New Schema

Now that we've described the aims and scope of the sample application, it's time to write some code! We'll start by creating an empty Console Application, and add code one step at a time to programmatically generate the required XSD schema.

Launch Visual Studio .NET, and select the menu item File | New | Project. In the New Project dialog box, choose either C# or Visual Basic as the project type (depending on your language preference). Choose the Console Application template, and enter an appropriate Name and Location for the new project. Click OK, to create the new project.

Visual Studio .NET creates a new file, containing the main class for the Console Application. Add the following using statements (C#) or Imports statements (Visual Basic), to expose various .NET namespaces in the application:

```
// C#
using System.IO;              // File handling
using System.Xml;             // General XML classes and types
using System.Xml.Schema;      // XSD schema classes and types
```

```
' VB .NET
Imports System.IO            ' File handling
Imports System.Xml           ' General XML classes and types
Imports System.Xml.Schema    ' XSD schema classes and types
```

We are now ready to start creating the XSD schema. To create a schema we need to create an instance of the XmlSchema class. This corresponds to the xsd:schema element in an XSD schema document. Set the TargetNamespace property if the schema is targeted at a particular namespace.

Add the following code in the Main() method. In this example, we create a schema with no target namespace:

```
// C#
XmlSchema schema = new XmlSchema();
```

```
' VB .NET
Dim schema As XmlSchema = New XmlSchema()
```

Creating Element Definitions

To create an element definition, create an XmlSchemaElement object. Set its Name property, and add the element to the appropriate location in the SOM object tree.

Add the following code to the Main() method, in which we create an element object for the XSD schema element <xsd:element name="Employee"/>. We then add the element to the list of items beneath the <xsd:schema> element in the SOM object tree:

```
// C#
XmlSchemaElement elementEmployee = new XmlSchemaElement();
elementEmployee.Name = "Employee";
schema.Items.Add(elementEmployee);
```

```
' VB .NET
Dim elementEmployee As XmlSchemaElement = New XmlSchemaElement()
elementEmployee.Name = "Employee"
schema.Items.Add(elementEmployee)
```

Creating a Complex Type

To create a complex type, create an XmlSchemaComplexType object. Set its Name property, if you need to refer to this complex type by its name elsewhere in the schema. Also set its Particle property to one of the compositor types:

- ❑ XmlSchemaSequence – this complexType defines sequential child elements.

- ❑ XmlSchemaChoice – this complexType defines mutually exclusive child elements.

- ❑ XmlSchemaAll – this complexType defines child elements that can appear in any order.

- ❑ XmlSchemaGroupRef – this complexType refers to an <xsd:group> element. <xsd:group> elements are useful if you want to define a group of elements that appear in several different places in an XML document.

Add the following code to the Main() method. In this code, we create an anonymous complex type and add it beneath the <element name="Employee"> element. We specify an XmlSchemaSequence as the compositor for the complex type:

```csharp
// C#
XmlSchemaComplexType ct = new XmlSchemaComplexType();
elementEmployee.SchemaType = ct;
XmlSchemaSequence seq = new XmlSchemaSequence();
ct.Particle = seq;
```

```vbnet
' VB .NET
Dim ct As XmlSchemaComplexType = New XmlSchemaComplexType()
elementEmployee.SchemaType = ct
Dim seq As XmlSchemaSequence = New XmlSchemaSequence()
ct.Particle = seq
```

Specifying Detailed Information for an Element

When you create an XmlSchemaElement object, you can set various properties to configure the element. For example, you can set SchemaTypeName to define a simple type (such as xsd:string). Also, you can set MinOccurs, MaxOccurs, Default, and Final if necessary.

Add the following code to the Main() method. In this code, we create an XmlSchemaElement for the <Name> element (string data type). We also create an XmlSchemaElement for the <Tel> element (string data type, minOcurs="0", maxOccurs="unbounded"). We use the XmlQualifiedName class to reference the XSD-standard string data type:

```csharp
// C#
XmlSchemaElement elementName = new XmlSchemaElement();
elementName.Name = "Name";
elementName.SchemaTypeName = new XmlQualifiedName("string",
                                "http://www.w3.org/2001/XMLSchema");
seq.Items.Add(elementName);

XmlSchemaElement elementTel = new XmlSchemaElement();
elementTel.Name = "Tel";
elementTel.SchemaTypeName = new XmlQualifiedName("string",
                                "http://www.w3.org/2001/XMLSchema");
elementTel.MinOccurs = 0;
elementTel.MaxOccursString = "unbounded";
seq.Items.Add(elementTel);
```

```vbnet
' VB .NET
Dim elementName As XmlSchemaElement = New XmlSchemaElement()
elementName.Name = "Name"
```

```
elementName.SchemaTypeName = New XmlQualifiedName("string", _
                              "http://www.w3.org/2001/XMLSchema")
seq.Items.Add(elementName)

Dim elementTel As XmlSchemaElement = New XmlSchemaElement()
elementTel.Name = "Tel"
elementTel.SchemaTypeName = New XmlQualifiedName("string", _
                             "http://www.w3.org/2001/XMLSchema")
elementTel.MinOccurs = 0
elementTel.MaxOccursString = "unbounded"
seq.Items.Add(elementTel)
```

Let's take stock of the situation so far. At this stage in proceedings, we have created the following parts of the SOM tree:

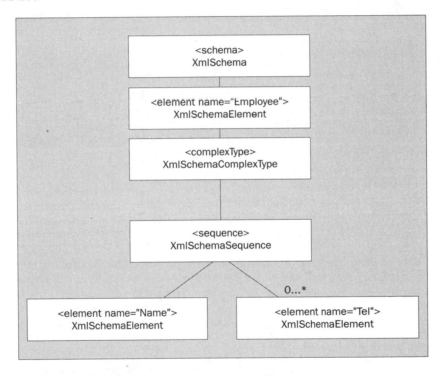

Creating a Choice of Elements

In an XSD schema, the <choice> element allows you to specify a set of mutually exclusive elements. To represent a <choice> element in SOM, create an XmlSchemaChoice object and add the appropriate XmlSchemaElement objects.

Add the following code to the Main() method. In this code, we create an XmlSchemaChoice object and add two XmlSchemaElement objects representing the <Salary> and <DailyRate> elements:

```
// C#
XmlSchemaChoice choice = new XmlSchemaChoice();
seq.Items.Add(choice);
```

```
XmlSchemaElement elementSalary = new XmlSchemaElement();
elementSalary.Name = "Salary";
elementSalary.SchemaTypeName = new XmlQualifiedName("double",
                              "http://www.w3.org/2001/XMLSchema");
choice.Items.Add(elementSalary);

XmlSchemaElement elementDailyRate = new XmlSchemaElement();
elementDailyRate.Name = "DailyRate";
elementDailyRate.SchemaTypeName = new XmlQualifiedName("double",
                              "http://www.w3.org/2001/XMLSchema");
choice.Items.Add(elementDailyRate);
```

```
' VB .NET
Dim choice As XmlSchemaChoice = New XmlSchemaChoice()
seq.Items.Add(choice)

Dim elementSalary As XmlSchemaElement = New XmlSchemaElement()
elementSalary.Name = "Salary"
elementSalary.SchemaTypeName = New XmlQualifiedName("double", _
                              "http://www.w3.org/2001/XMLSchema")
choice.Items.Add(elementSalary)

Dim elementDailyRate As XmlSchemaElement = New XmlSchemaElement()
elementDailyRate.Name = "DailyRate"
elementDailyRate.SchemaTypeName = New XmlQualifiedName("double", _
                              "http://www.w3.org/2001/XMLSchema")

choice.Items.Add(elementDailyRate)
```

Creating Attributes

To create an attribute definition, create an `XmlSchemaAttribute` object. Set its `Name` property, plus any other relevant properties, such as `SchemaTypeName`, `Use`, and so on. Then add the attribute to the appropriate location in the SOM object tree.

Add the following code to the `Main()` method. In this code, we define the `EmpNum` attribute (`string` data type, `use="required"`) and the `JobTitle` attribute (`use="required"`). We don't set the data type for `JobTitle`, because it needs to be an enumerated type. We'll deal with that issue in a moment:

```
// C#
XmlSchemaAttribute attrEmpNum = new XmlSchemaAttribute();
attrEmpNum.Name = "EmpNum";
attrEmpNum.SchemaTypeName = new XmlQualifiedName("string",
                              "http://www.w3.org/2001/XMLSchema");
attrEmpNum.Use = XmlSchemaUse.Required;
ct.Attributes.Add(attrEmpNum);

XmlSchemaAttribute attrJobTitle = new XmlSchemaAttribute();
attrJobTitle.Name = "JobTitle";
attrJobTitle.Use = XmlSchemaUse.Required;
ct.Attributes.Add(attrJobTitle);
```

```
' VB .NET
Dim attrEmpNum As XmlSchemaAttribute = New XmlSchemaAttribute()
attrEmpNum.Name = "EmpNum"
attrEmpNum.SchemaTypeName = New XmlQualifiedName("string", _
                              "http://www.w3.org/2001/XMLSchema")
```

```
attrEmpNum.Use = XmlSchemaUse.Required
ct.Attributes.Add(attrEmpNum)

Dim attrJobTitle As XmlSchemaAttribute = New XmlSchemaAttribute()
attrJobTitle.Name = "JobTitle"
attrJobTitle.Use = XmlSchemaUse.Required
ct.Attributes.Add(attrJobTitle)
```

Creating a Simple Type

In an XSD schema, the <simpleType> element allows you to create new simple types in your schema. You base the new type on an existing base type, and then specify how the new type differs from this type.

Add the following code to the Main() method. In this code, we create a new simple type that restricts the standard string type (the restricted string type will only allow the values "Director", "Manager", and "Programmer"). We create three XmlSchemaEnumerationFacet objects to define an enumerated list of allowed values for this new type:

```csharp
// C#
XmlSchemaSimpleType st = new XmlSchemaSimpleType();
attrJobTitle.SchemaType = st;

XmlSchemaSimpleTypeRestriction restriction =
                          new XmlSchemaSimpleTypeRestriction();
restriction.BaseTypeName = new XmlQualifiedName("string",
                          "http://www.w3.org/2001/XMLSchema");
st.Content = restriction;

XmlSchemaEnumerationFacet e1 = new XmlSchemaEnumerationFacet();
XmlSchemaEnumerationFacet e2 = new XmlSchemaEnumerationFacet();
XmlSchemaEnumerationFacet e3 = new XmlSchemaEnumerationFacet();
e1.Value = "Director";
e2.Value = "Manager";
e3.Value = "Programmer";
restriction.Facets.Add(e1);
restriction.Facets.Add(e2);
restriction.Facets.Add(e3);
```

```vbnet
' VB .NET
Dim st As XmlSchemaSimpleType = New XmlSchemaSimpleType()
attrJobTitle.SchemaType = st

Dim restriction As XmlSchemaSimpleTypeRestriction = _
                          New XmlSchemaSimpleTypeRestriction()
restriction.BaseTypeName = New XmlQualifiedName("string", _
                          "http://www.w3.org/2001/XMLSchema")
st.Content = restriction

Dim e1 As XmlSchemaEnumerationFacet = New XmlSchemaEnumerationFacet()
Dim e2 As XmlSchemaEnumerationFacet = New XmlSchemaEnumerationFacet()
Dim e3 As XmlSchemaEnumerationFacet = New XmlSchemaEnumerationFacet()
e1.Value = "Director"
e2.Value = "Manager"
e3.Value = "Programmer"
restriction.Facets.Add(e1)
```

```
restriction.Facets.Add(e2)
restriction.Facets.Add(e3)
```

Compiling the Schema

We have now added all the objects we need to the SOM object tree. The next step is to compile the schema, using the `Compile()` method in the `XmlSchema` object. This verifies the syntactic and semantic correctness of the schema. For example, the `Compile()` method checks that the XSD schema is a well formed XML document, obeys XSD syntax rules, and uses valid XSD data types.

The `Compile()` method takes a single parameter, which specifies a call-back method to receive any validation events when the schema is compiled. Add the following code to the `Main()` method. This code calls the `Compile()` method, specifying a validation event handler method:

```
// C#
schema.Compile(new ValidationEventHandler(MyHandler));
```

```
' VB .NET
schema.Compile(New ValidationEventHandler(AddressOf MyHandler))
```

After the end of the `Main()` method, implement the validation event handler method, `MyHandler()`, as follows:

```
// C# -- The event handler method is declared 'static' in this example,
//          because the sample program is a Console Application with a
//          'static' Main method. If you're building a different type of
//          solution (such as a Windows Application or an ASP.NET Web
//          Application), you may not need the 'static' qualifier.

public static void MyHandler(object sender, ValidationEventArgs e)
{
    Console.WriteLine(e.Message);
}
```

```
' VB .NET
Public Sub MyHandler(ByVal sender As Object, _
                      ByVal e As ValidationEventArgs)
    Console.WriteLine(e.Message)
End Sub
```

Writing the Schema Out

The final step in our sample application is to write the schema to a file. The `XmlSchema` object has a `Write()` method, which allows us to write the schema to a `Stream`, `TextWriter`, or `XmlWriter` object.

At the end of the `Main()` method, add the following code. This code writes the schema to the console, and then writes the schema to a file named `Employees.xsd` in the root directory (for simplicity):

```
// C#
schema.Write(Console.Out);
Console.WriteLine("\nSchema written to console");
```

```
FileStream fs = new FileStream("C:\\Employee.xsd",
                                FileMode.OpenOrCreate,
                                FileAccess.Write);
schema.Write(fs);
Console.WriteLine("Schema written to file C:\\Employee.xsd");
```

```
' VB .NET
schema.Write(Console.Out)
Console.WriteLine(vbCrLf & "Schema written to console")

Dim fs As FileStream = New FileStream("C:\Employee.xsd", _
                                FileMode.OpenOrCreate, _
                                FileAccess.Write)
schema.Write(fs)
Console.WriteLine("Schema written to file C:\Employee.xsd")
```

Building and Running the Sample Application

We are now ready to build and run the sample application. In Visual Studio .NET, select the menu item Build | Build. Fix any compiler errors that might arise. Then select the menu item Debug | Start Without Debugging, to execute the application,

The application generates an XSD schema in memory, and displays it on the console as follows:

```
<?xml version="1.0" encoding="ibm850"?>
<schema targetNamespace="" xmlns="http://www.w3.org/2001/XMLSchema">
  <element name="Employee">
    <complexType>
      <sequence>
        <element name="Name" type="string" />
        <element minOccurs="0" maxOccurs="unbounded" name="Tel" type="string" />

        <choice>
          <element name="Salary" type="double" />
          <element name="DailyRate" type="double" />
        </choice>
      </sequence>
      <attribute name="EmpNum" type="string" use="required" />
      <attribute name="JobTitle" use="required">
        <simpleType>
          <restriction base="string">
            <enumeration value="Director" />
            <enumeration value="Manager" />
            <enumeration value="Programmer" />
          </restriction>
        </simpleType>
      </attribute>
    </complexType>
  </element>
</schema>
Schema written to console
Schema written to file C:\Employee.xsd
Press any key to continue
```

The application also writes the XSD schema to C:\Employee.xsd. Open Internet Explorer, and type C:\Employee.xsd in the address field. The XSD schema appears as follows:

```
C:\Employee.xsd                                                              _ □ ×
File   Edit   View   Favorites   Tools   Help
← Back  ▾  →  ▾  ⊗  ⌂  △  | ⊘Search  ⌂Favorites  ⊛Media  ⊗  ⌂▾  ⌂  ⌂  ⌂
Address  ⌂ C:\Fmployee.xsd                                             ▾   ⌂Go

  <?xml version="1.0" ?>
- <schema targetNamespace="" xmlns="http://www.w3.org/2001/XMLSchema">
  - <element name="Employee">
    - <complexType>
      - <sequence>
          <element name="Name" type="string" />
          <element minOccurs="0" maxOccurs="unbounded" name="Tel" type="string" />
        - <choice>
            <element name="Salary" type="double" />
            <element name="DailyRate" type="double" />
          </choice>
        </sequence>
        <attribute name="EmpNum" type="string" use="required" />
      - <attribute name="JobTitle" use="required">
        - <simpleType>
          - <restriction base="string">
              <enumeration value="Director" />
              <enumeration value="Manager" />
              <enumeration value="Programmer" />
            </restriction>
          </simpleType>
        </attribute>
      </complexType>
    </element>
  </schema>

⊛ Done                                                    ⌨ My Computer
```

Sample Applications Online

You can download complete sample applications for this topic from the Wrox Press web site for this book:

❏   C# sample folder: Chapter6\Examples\SchemaObjectModelCS

❏   Visual Basic sample folder: Chapter6\Examples\SchemaObjectModelVB

Validating XML in the .NET Framework

So far in this chapter, we've seen how to use a schema to define the grammar for an XML document. We've also seen how to represent an XSD schema as a set of objects in memory, using the Schema Object Model.

Another use of schemas (and DTDs) is to validate an XML document against a grammar. This is important if you receive an XML document from another application or organization – it's essential to know that the document complies with the expected grammar.

The .NET Framework also lets you validate an XML document programmatically, using any of the following:

- ❏ DTD
- ❏ XDR schema
- ❏ XSD schema

Before you can perform validation, you must tell the parser which DTD or schema to use. Let's briefly recap how to do this for a DTD, XDR schema, and XSD schema. Then we'll look at how to perform validation using the .NET Framework APIs.

Linking an XML Document to a DTD or Schema

When you create an XML document, you can include a static reference to a DTD, XDR schema, or XSD schema. This informs the parser which file to use to validate the XML document.

Defining a static reference to a DTD or schema is appropriate if you know which DTD or schema to use, such as when you are developing an in-house application and you have the DTD or schema available. You can also apply a schema dynamically, using an XmlSchemaCollection object. You'll see how to do this in the section, *Caching Schemas*, later in this chapter.

Linking an XML Document to a DTD

To link an XML document to a DTD, specify a <!DOCTYPE> declaration in the prolog of the XML document. Here's a simple example of an XML document that links to a DTD file named CompanySummary.dtd (you can download this document as CompanySummaryWithDTD.xml from the folders ValidateCS and ValidateVB):

```
<?xml version="1.0"?>
<!DOCTYPE CompanySummary SYSTEM "CompanySummary.dtd">
<CompanySummary CompanyName="My Cool Startup Company">
    <RegDate>1997-07-02</RegDate>
    <NumEmps>3</NumEmps>
</CompanySummary>
```

The DTD for this XML document, CompanySummary.dtd, is as follows:

```
<!ELEMENT CompanySummary (RegDate, NumEmps)>
<!ATTLIST CompanySummary CompanyName CDATA #REQUIRED>
<!ELEMENT RegDate (#PCDATA)>
<!ELEMENT NumEmps (#PCDATA)>
```

Linking an XML Document to an XDR Schema

To link an XML document to an XDR schema, specify a namespace declaration with the following syntax in the document element of the XML document:

```
xmlns="x-schema:url-of-XDR-schema"
```

For example, the following XML document links to an XDR schema named CompanySummary.xdr (you can download this document as CompanySummaryWithXDR.xml from the folders ValidateCS and ValidateVB):

```
<?xml version="1.0"?>
<CompanySummary CompanyName="My Cool Startup Company"
                xmlns="x-schema:file://CompanySummary.xdr">
   <RegDate>1997-07-02</RegDate>
   <NumEmps>3</NumEmps>
</CompanySummary>
```

We've already seen the XDR schema for this document (see the section, *Creating an XSD Schema from an XDR Schema*, earlier in this chapter).

Linking an XML Document to an XSD Schema

To link an XML document to an XSD schema, the situation is more complicated because an XML document can be linked to multiple XSD schemas. This happens if different parts of the XML document are qualified by different namespaces; you can link a separate XSD schema for each namespace.

The syntax for linking an XML document to an XSD schema depends on whether or not the document content is qualified with a namespace. We'll look at both possibilities.

Unqualified Content in the XML Document

If the content of the XML document isn't qualified by a namespace, add the following declarations to link the document to an XSD schema:

```
xmlns:xsi="http://www.w3.org/2001/XMLSchema-instance"
xsi:noNamespaceSchemaLocation="url-of-XSD-schema"
```

For example, the following document links to an XSD schema named CompanySummary.xsd (you can download the XML document as CompanySummaryWithXSD.xml from the folders ValidateCS and ValidateVB):

```
<?xml version="1.0"?>
<CompanySummary CompanyName="My Cool Startup Company"
                xmlns:xsi="http://www.w3.org/2001/XMLSchema-instance"
                xsi:noNamespaceSchemaLocation="file://CompanySummary.xsd">
   <RegDate>1997-07-02</RegDate>
   <NumEmps>3</NumEmps>
</CompanySummary>
```

Namespace-Qualified Content in the XML Document

If the content of the XML document is qualified by a namespace, add the following declarations to the XML document:

```
xmlns:xsi="http://www.w3.org/2001/XMLSchema-instance"
xsi:schemaLocation="namespace-uri   url-of-XSD-schema"
```

You can have any number of xsi:schemaLocation declarations, one for each namespace in the XML document. Also, you can still use xsi:noNamespaceSchemaLocation if the XML document has unqualified content.

The following XML document uses the namespace URI urn:MyUri, and links to an XSD schema named CompanySummaryNS.xsd to describe the content in this namespace (you can download this document as CompanySummaryWithXSDAndNS.xml from the folders ValidateCS and ValidateVB):

```
<?xml version="1.0"?>
<CompanySummary CompanyName="My Cool Startup Company"
                xmlns="urn:MyUri"
                xmlns:xsi="http://www.w3.org/2001/XMLSchema-instance"
                xsi:schemaLocation="urn:MyUri file://CompanySummaryNS.xsd">
    <RegDate>1997-07-02</RegDate>
    <NumEmps>3</NumEmps>
</CompanySummary>
```

You must also modify the XSD Schema, to specify the namespace used in the instance document:

```
<xsd:schema xmlns:xsd="http://www.w3.org/2001/XMLSchema"
            targetNamespace="namespace-uri" elementFormDefault="qualified">
```

Performing Validation

The .NET Framework provides the XmlValidatingReader class for validating XML documents. XmlValidatingReader inherits from XmlReader, which acts as a fast, forward-only cursor through an XML document. XmlValidatingReader inherits these capabilities, and adds support for XML validation. In addition, XmlValidatingReader resolves any general entities in the XML document, and fills in any default attributes specified in the DTD or schema.

The following diagram shows the inheritance hierarchy for XML reader classes:

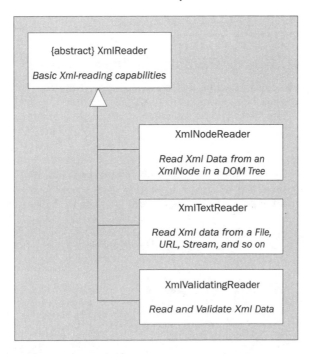

In the coming pages, we'll write a program that validates an XML document using a DTD, XDR schema, and XSD schema. We'll start by creating an empty Console Application, and add code one step at a time to perform the following tasks:

❑ Create a validating reader object

❑ Specify the type of validation required

❑ Register an event handler method, to deal with validation errors

❑ Read and validate the document

❑ Provide an implementation for the validation event handler method

Full C# and Visual Basic code listings are given in the download.

Creating a New Console Application

Launch Visual Studio .NET, and create a new C# or Visual Basic project for a Console Application. Visual Studio .NET creates a new file, containing the main class for the Console Application. Add the following using statements (C#) or Imports statements (Visual Basic), to expose various .NET namespaces in the application:

```
// C#
using System;
using System.Xml;            // General XML classes and types
using System.Xml.Schema;     // XSD schema classes and types
```

```
' VB .NET
Imports System
Imports System.Xml           ' General XML classes and types
Imports System.Xml.Schema    ' XSD schema classes and types
```

Creating a Validating Reader Object

To perform validation, you need to create an XmlValidatingReader object. You can create an XmlValidatingReader object from an existing XmlReader object, or from a portion of XML in a String or a Stream. For full details, see the XmlValidatingReader constructor in Visual Studio .NET Online Help.

The following example shows how to create an XmlValidatingReader object to validate an XML document on disk. First, we create an XmlTextReader object to read the XML document from disk. XmlTextReader doesn't have any validation capabilities, so we create an XmlValidatingReader object and associate it with the XmlTextReader. Add this code to the start of your Main() method:

```
// C# - using CompanySummaryWithXSD.xml (see downloads)
XmlTextReader tr = new XmlTextReader("CompanySummaryWithXSD.xml");
XmlValidatingReader vr = new XmlValidatingReader(tr);
```

```
' Visual Basic - using CompanySummaryWithXSD.xml (see downloads)
Dim tr As XmlTextReader = New XmlTextReader("CompanySummaryWithXSD.xml")
Dim vr As XmlValidatingReader = New XmlValidatingReader(tr)
```

Specifying the Type of Validation Required

The XmlValidatingReader object supports validation using DTDs, XDR schemas, or XSD schemas. To indicate which particular type of validation you want, set the ValidationType property to one of the following values:

- ❑ ValidationType.DTD – uses the DTD specified in the XML document.

- ❑ ValidationType.XDR – uses the XDR specified in the XML document. You can also create a schema cache to specify which schema(s) to use – see the section, *Caching Schemas*, later in this chapter.

- ❑ ValidationType.Schema – uses the XSD schema(s) specified in the XML document, or in the schema cache.

- ❑ ValidationType.Auto – uses the most appropriate type of validation, depending on the validation information specified in the XML document.

- ❑ ValidationType.None – does not perform validation.

Add the following code to the Main() method. This code requests XSD validation:

```
// C#
vr.ValidationType = ValidationType.Schema;
```

```
' VB .NET
vr.ValidationType = ValidationType.Schema
```

Registering a Validation Event Handler Method

The validation event handler method receives notifications about validation errors. Add the following code to the Main() method. This code registers an event handler method named MyHandler (we'll implement this method shortly):

```
// C#
vr.ValidationEventHandler += new ValidationEventHandler(MyHandler);
```

```
' VB .NET
AddHandler vr.ValidationEventHandler, AddressOf MyHandler
```

Reading and Validating the Document

XmlValidatingReader has a Read() method, inherited from XmlReader, which allows you to read the content of the XML document. Each time you call the Read() method, you get the next node in the document. The Read() method returns false when you reach the end of the document. You should close the XmlValidatingReader at this time.

The XmlValidatingReader reports any validation errors it detects while reading the XML document. The validation event handler method will be called, with information about the validation error. Also, an XmlException can occur under certain circumstances, such as a missing XML document or schema. Therefore, you should enclose your code in a try...catch block, to catch an XmlException if it happens.

Add the following code to the `Main()` method. This code uses the `Read()` method to read the entire content of the XML document. The `XmlValidatingReader` validates the XML document as it goes. The example also illustrates the data processing capabilities of the `XmlValidatingReader`, by outputting the value of the `<NumEmps>` element. The entire code is enclosed in a `try...catch` block. Notice that we close the `XmlValidatingReader` in the `finally` block; this automatically closes the underlying `XmlTextReader` as well:

```
// C#
try
{
  while (vr.Read())
  {
    if (vr.NodeType == XmlNodeType.Element && vr.LocalName == "NumEmps")
    {
      int num;
      num = XmlConvert.ToInt32(vr.ReadElementString());
      Console.WriteLine("Number of employees: " + num);
    }
  }
}
catch (XmlException ex)
{
  Console.WriteLine("XMLException occurred: " + ex.Message);
}
finally
{
  vr.Close();
}
```

```
' VB .NET
Try
  While vr.Read()
    If vr.NodeType = XmlNodeType.Element And vr.LocalName = "NumEmps"
      Dim num As Int32
      num = XmlConvert.ToInt32(vr.ReadElementString())
      Console.WriteLine("Number of employees: " & num)
    End If
  End While

Catch ex As XmlException
  Console.WriteLine("XMLException occurred: " & ex.Message)

Finally
  vr.Close()

End Try
```

Implementing the Validation Event Handler Method

Here is a simple validation event handler method, to deal with any validation errors that the `XmlValidatingReader` detects as it traverses the XML document. Add this code after the end of the `Main()` method:

```
// C#
public static void MyHandler(object sender, ValidationEventArgs e)
{
  Console.WriteLine("Validation Error: " + e.Message);
}
```

```
// Visual Basic
Public Sub MyHandler(ByVal sender As Object, _
                     ByVal e As ValidationEventArgs)
  Console.WriteLine("Validation Error: " & e.Message)
End Sub
```

> The **ValidationEventArgs** parameter type is located in the **System.Xml.Schema** namespace, not **System.Xml**.

Building and Running the Sample Application

We are now ready to build and run the sample application. In Visual Studio .NET, select the menu item Build | Build. Then select the menu item Debug | Start Without Debugging, to execute the application. The application parses and validates the XML document `CompanySummaryWithXSD.xml`. The application should not detect any problems with this document. (Note that `CompanySummary.xsd` and `CompanySummaryWithXSD.xml` must be in the `bin` folder to be detected as the code stands at the moment.)

Modify `CompanySummaryWithXSD.xml`, to make it invalid. For example, delete the <NumEmps> element. Run the application again – the application should detect the validation error and display an error message. (Remember to undo your edits to `CompanySummaryWithXSD.xml` to make it valid again.)

Caching Schemas

The .NET Framework includes an `XmlSchemaCollection` class, which allows you to cache schemas in memory rather than reloading them each time you want to validate a document. This can improve run-time performance, especially if you have many XML documents to validate.

The `XmlSchemaCollection` class associates schemas with XML namespaces. This enables you to preload all the schemas you might need to validate a range of different XML documents. It's also useful if you have an XML document with multiple namespaces, where you need several schemas to achieve validation.

Add the following code at the start of your `Main()` method. This code creates an `XmlSchemaCollection` object, and loads two schemas. The first schema is `"CompanySummaryNS.xsd"`, and deals with XML content qualified with the `"urn:MyUri"` namespace. The second schema is `"CompanySummary.xsd"`, and deals with XML content that has no namespace qualification (both of these XSD schemas are included in the download for this chapter):

```
// C#
XmlSchemaCollection sc = new XmlSchemaCollection();
sc.Add("urn:MyUri", "CompanySummaryNS.xsd");
sc.Add("", "CompanySummary.xsd");
```

```
' VB .NET
Dim sc As XmlSchemaCollection = New XmlSchemaCollection()
sc.Add("urn:MyUri", "CompanySummaryNS.xsd")
sc.Add("", "CompanySummary.xsd")
```

Next, amend the code in the line declaring the XMLTextReader object so that the file CompanySummaryWithXSDAndNS.xml will be read:

```
// C# - using CompanySummaryWithXSDAndNS.xml (see downloads)
XmlTextReader tr = new XmlTextReader("CompanySummaryWithXSDAndNS.xml");
```

```
' VB .NET - using CompanySummaryWithXSDAndNS.xml (see downloads)
Dim tr As XmlTextReader = _
        New XmlTextReader("CompanySummaryWithXSDAndNS.xml")
```

Once you have loaded schemas into an XmlSchemaCollection, you can advise the XmlValidatingReader object to use the schemas in this cache. The XmlValidatingReader has a Schemas property, which is the XmlSchemaCollection of schemas used by the XmlValidatingReader during validation.

Add the following code to your Main() method, just after the statement that sets the ValidationType for the XmlValidatingReader object. This code adds your schema cache to the XmlValidatingReader schema cache:

```
// C#
vr.Schemas.Add(sc);
```

```
' VB .NET
vr.Schemas.Add(sc)
```

An added benefit of using XmlSchemaCollection is that the XML document doesn't need to specify which schemas to use for validation. The XmlSchemaCollection now contains this linkage information.

Building and Running the Sample Application

Build and run the application. The application validates CompanySummaryWithXSD.xml, using the XSD schema CompanySummary.xsd. Experiment with the XML document, to ensure the application detects validation errors.

Modify your code, so the XmlValidatingReader reads CompanySummaryWithXSDAndNS.xsd (this XML document uses the namespace URI urn:MyUri). Build and run the application again. The application validates CompanySummaryWithXSDAndNS.xml, using the XSD schema CompanySummaryNS.xsd. Experiment with the XML document, to ensure the application detects validation errors.

Sample Applications Online

You can download complete sample applications for this topic (including all XML documents, DTDs, and schemas) from the Wrox Press web site for this book:

- ❑ C# sample folder: Chapter6\Examples\ValidateCS
- ❑ Visual Basic sample folder: Chapter6\Examples\ValidateVB

Summary

In this chapter, you have seen how to create an XSD schema using various tools in Visual Studio .NET. If you have a sample XML document or a Microsoft XDR schema, you can use the XSD Generator tool to create the equivalent XSD schema. Alternatively, if you need to map relational data to XML format, you can use the Server Explorer to automatically generate an XSD schema from the database. If none of these options are feasible, you can create a new XSD schema easily using the XML Designer. This saves you from the anguish of learning XSD syntax – but learn it anyway, you'll feel better for it.

You can manipulate an XSD schema programmatically, using the Schema Object Model (SOM). SOM is a large collection of classes in the System.Xml.Schema namespace, and allows you to create, modify, and delete structural information in an XSD schema.

You can also use an XSD schema to validate an XML document, to check that the document complies with the required grammar. Use the XmlValidatingReader object to read and validate the XML document. The XmlValidatingReader supports validation using XSD schemas, XDR schemas, and DTDs. For optimum performance, use XmlSchemaCollection to keep a cache of schemas in memory.

In the next chapter, you'll find out how to serialize objects into XML data. This makes it easier to pass objects between applications and web services, over any protocol.

7

Serializing XML

As you have already seen in previous chapters, the .NET Framework provides extensive and extensible support for building distributed applications and services.

One of the issues you must address when you build a distributed system is how to get objects from one part of the system to another. For example, imagine a traveling sales person who uses a Windows Forms application to create new `Customer` and `Order` objects during the working day. At the end of the day, after our weary traveler has checked into a motel room, he or she needs to send the `Customer` and `Order` objects to corporate headquarters. How can this be achieved in the .NET Framework?

To satisfy this requirement, the .NET Framework implements a serialization mechanism based upon XML. You can serialize an object into XML format so that all its `public` fields and properties are written out in XML format. You can then send the XML data anywhere you like, because XML is an open and widely supported standard. The recipient application deserializes the XML data, to reconstitute the objects in memory.

In this chapter, we describe the serialization process and show how to take control over how objects are serialized and deserialized. The `System.Xml.Serialization` namespace has a set of classes to support XML serialization. The most important class is `XmlSerializer`, which has methods to serialize and deserialize objects as XML. We'll begin by showing how simple fields and properties are serialized and deserialized. Then we'll investigate some more complex issues, such as dealing with arrays, composite objects, and inheritance.

The serialization mechanism is extremely customizable, so you can control how your objects are serialized into XML format. For example, you can choose whether a value should be serialized as an element, as an attribute, or as text content. You can also specify the desired element name, attribute name, namespace URI, and so on – the .NET Framework provides a suite of attribute classes to achieve this flexibility.

XSD schemas also have an important role to play in the XML serialization process. As you learned in the previous chapter, XSD schemas allow you to define the structure and content of an XML document. In this chapter, we'll show how to use XSD schemas to define the structure of XML documents that are generated during serialization.

At the end of the chapter, we'll introduce an alternative serialization mechanism that uses formatter classes called `BinaryFormatter` and `SoapFormatter`.

`BinaryFormatter` serializes objects into binary format rather than XML. This is typically used in **Remoting**, where an application invokes a method in a separate application running in a different address space. `BinaryFormatter` enables you to serialize objects in binary format, for efficient transmission to the remote application.

`SoapFormatter` serializes objects into Simple Object Access Protocol (SOAP) format. SOAP is an XML-based notation for defining method calls, parameters, and return values. SOAP is a vital ingredient in Web Services, because it enables client applications to invoke Web Service methods using open standards such as HTTP and XML. When you pass object parameters into a Web Service method, or return objects from a Web Service method, `SoapFormatter` serializes the objects into SOAP format for transmission.

Serializing an Object as XML Data

XML serialization provides us with an easy way to save the current state of an object. This can be useful in many different situations. For example, you might have a simple Windows application that needs to store object data on the local disk when the application shuts down. The next time the application is launched, it loads the data from the local disk to recreate the object in memory.

Serialization is also useful in n-tier applications, where you need to pass object data between different parts of the system. You can serialize objects as XML format, and write the XML data to a stream or file. The recipient service or application can deserialize the objects easily, and without reams of programming.

To use serialization, you define a `public` class with `public` fields and properties. You can then serialize instances of this class to XML documents. By default, each `public` field and property in the object is serialized to an element with the same name in the XML document. The class name is used for the document element name.

In the following pages, we'll describe how to serialize simple objects to a file. You can download a complete sample application from the Wrox Press web site for this book:

❑ C# sample folder: `Chapter7\SerializeSimpleCS`

❑ VB .NET sample folder: `Chapter7\SerializeSimpleVB`

To open a sample application in Visual Studio .NET, select the menu item File | Open Solution and choose the solution file (`.sln`) for the sample application.

Defining a Class for Use in Serialization

Consider the following class, which we will use to illustrate simple serialization:

```
// C#
public class Employee
{
    public string Name;
    public decimal Salary;
}
```

```
' VB.NET
Public Class Employee
    Public Name As String
    Public Salary As Decimal
End Class
```

Notice that the Employee class is public, which is essential if you want to serialize Employee instances. If you try to serialize a class that isn't public, XMLSerializer throws an exception at run time.

Inside the class, you can declare members with any access specifier (such as public, private, or protected). However, XMLSerializer only serializes public members; non-public members will not be serialized. If you really do want to serialize non-public members, use BinaryFormatter or SoapFormatter instead (these classes are discussed later in this chapter).

Creating Objects to be Serialized

Once you've defined a public class, you can create instances of this class in the usual way. For example:

```
// C#
Employee employee1 = new Employee();
employee1.Name = "Thomas Smith";
employee1.Salary = 25000;

Employee employee2 = new Employee();
employee2.Name = "Emily Jones";
employee2.Salary = 32500;
```

```
' VB.NET
Dim employee1 As New Employee()
employee1.Name = "Thomas Smith"
employee1.Salary = 25000

Dim employee2 As New Employee()
employee2.Name = "Emily Jones"
employee2.Salary = 32500
```

Creating an XML Serializer

To serialize objects, you must create an XmlSerializer object for that type. Each XmlSerializer object serializes and deserializes objects of a specific type.

The following example shows how to create an XmlSerializer object to serialize (and deserialize) Employee objects:

```
// C#
using System.Xml.Serialization;

XmlSerializer serializer = new XmlSerializer(typeof(Employee));
```

```
' VB.NET
Imports System.Xml.Serialization

Dim serializer As New XmlSerializer(GetType(Employee))
```

If your application needs to serialize and deserialize many different types of object, you can create an array of XmlSerializer objects – a separate XmlSerializer for each data type you need to serialize or deserialize. The XmlSerializer class has a static (Shared) method named FromTypes() to achieve this task. The FromTypes() method takes an array of Types, and returns an array of XmlSerializer objects as follows:

```
// C# - assume we have classes Employee, Address, and Manager
Type[] types = new Type[3];
types[0] = typeof(Employee);
types[1] = typeof(Address);
types[2] = typeof(Manager);

XmlSerializer[] serializers = new XmlSerializer[3];
serializers = XmlSerializer.FromTypes(types);
```

```
' VB.NET - assume we have classes Employee, Address, and Manager
Dim types(3) As Type
types(0) = GetType(Employee)
types(1) = GetType(Company)
types(2) = GetType(Manager)

Dim serializers(3) As XmlSerializer
serializers = XmlSerializer.FromTypes(types)
```

Serializing Objects

To serialize an object, call the `Serialize()` method on the `XmlSerializer` object. The `Serialize()` method is overloaded, to enable you to serialize your object to one of the following destinations. Use the appropriate version of the `Serialize()` method, depending on where you want to serialize your object:

❑ A `Stream` - Store bytes of data to a disk file (using a `FileStream` object), to memory (using a `MemoryStream` object), to a network socket (using a `NetworkStream` object), or to any other type of `Stream`.

❑ A `TextWriter` - Store character data to a stream (using `StreamWriter`) with a specified character encoding (such as `System.Text.Unicode` or `System.Text.ASCII`). Alternatively, you can write data to a `string` (using `StringWriter`), to an HTTP output stream (using `HttpWriter`), or generate HTML content in an ASP.NET Web Application (using `HtmlTextWriter`).

❑ An `XmlWriter` - Use an `XmlWriter` to write XML data to a `Stream`, `TextWriter`, or file. The `XmlWriter` provides a fast, non-cached, forward-only way to generate XML content.

The following example shows how to serialize two `Employee` objects to files named `Employee1.xml` and `Employee2.xml` in the `C:\` folder:

```
// C#
TextWriter writer1 = new StreamWriter("C:\\Employee1.xml");
serializer.Serialize(writer1, employee1);
writer1.Close();

TextWriter writer2 = new StreamWriter("C:\\Employee2.xml");
serializer.Serialize(writer2, employee2);
writer2.Close();
```

```
' VB.NET
Dim writer1 As New StreamWriter("C:\Employee1.xml")
serializer.Serialize(writer1, employee1)
writer1.Close()

Dim writer2 As New StreamWriter("C:\Employee2.xml")
serializer.Serialize(writer2, employee2)
writer2.Close()
```

Examining Serialized Data in an XML Document

Now that we've seen how to serialize an object, let's see how the XML data appears after serialization.

If you've been using the sample application from our web site, you can run the application in Visual Studio .NET. Select the menu item **Debug | Start Without Debugging**. The application generates two XML documents named `C:\Employees1.xml` and `C:\Employees2.xml`.

`C:\Employees1.xml` appears as follows:

```
<?xml version="1.0" encoding="utf-8"?>
<Employee xmlns:xsi="http://www.w3.org/2001/XMLSchema-instance"
          xmlns:xsd="http://www.w3.org/2001/XMLSchema">
   <Name>Thomas Smith</Name>
   <Salary>25000</Salary>
</Employee>
```

`C:\Employees2.xml` appears as follows:

```
<?xml version="1.0" encoding="utf-8"?>
<Employee xmlns:xsi="http://www.w3.org/2001/XMLSchema-instance"
          xmlns:xsd="http://www.w3.org/2001/XMLSchema">
   <Name>Emily Jones</Name>
   <Salary>32500</Salary>
</Employee>
```

Notice that the document element maps to the class name (`Employee`), and the child elements map to the `public` fields (`Name` and `Salary`) in the `Employee` class. Also notice the XSD namespaces in the XML documents. This is a hint to the important role of XSD schemas in serialization. We'll return to this issue later in this chapter.

Deserializing XML Data into an Object

Deserializing XML data back into objects is essentially the reverse of serialization. Create an `XmlSerializer` object for your desired class type, and call the `Deserialize()` method to deserialize an XML document into a new instance of your class type.

In the following pages, we'll describe how to deserialize XML documents, to reconstitute serialized data into objects in memory. You can download a complete sample application from the Wrox Press web site for this book:

❑ C# sample folder: `Chapter7\DeserializeSimpleCS`

❑ VB .NET sample folder: `Chapter7\DeserializeSimpleVB`

To open a sample application in Visual Studio .NET, select the menu item File | Open Solution and choose the solution file (`.sln`) for the sample application.

Defining a Class for Use in Deserialization

To deserialize an XML document into an object, your application must have a class with the same name as the document element in the XML document. Otherwise, you'll get a run-time exception when you try to deserialize the XML document.

The fields and properties in the class should match the child elements in the XML document. If any elements are missing in the XML document, the corresponding fields or properties in the deserialized object are not assigned. If the XML document contains additional (unexpected) content, this is ignored during deserialization. You can fine-tune this behavior if you like – for details, see the section *Dealing with Unexpected XML Content*, later in this chapter.

Creating an XML Serializer for a Particular Type

To deserialize objects of a particular type, you must create an XmlSerializer object for that type. The following example creates an XmlSerializer, ready to deserialize data into Employee objects:

```csharp
// C#
using System.Xml.Serialization;

XmlSerializer serializer = new XmlSerializer(typeof(Employee));
```

```vbnet
' VB.NET
Imports System.Xml.Serialization

Dim serializer As New XmlSerializer(GetType(Employee))
```

Deserializing Objects

To deserialize an object, call the Deserialize() method on the XmlSerializer object. The Deserialize() method is overloaded, just like the Serialize() method, to enable you to deserialize from a variety of different sources.

The Deserialize() method creates an instance of the appropriate class, and populates the instance with data from the XML document. The method returns an object data type, so you'll probably want to cast this into your specific class type (Employee in this example).

The following example deserializes two XML documents named C:\Employee1.xml and C:\Employee2.xml, to create two new Employee objects:

```csharp
// C#
TextReader reader1 = new StreamReader("C:\\Employee1.xml");
Employee employee1 = (Employee)serializer.Deserialize(reader1);
reader1.Close();

TextReader reader2 = new StreamReader("C:\\Employee2.xml");
Employee employee2 = (Employee)serializer.Deserialize(reader2);
reader2.Close();
```

```vbnet
' VB.NET
Dim reader1 As New StreamReader("C:\Employee1.xml")
Dim employee1 As Employee = CType(serializer.Deserialize(reader1), _
                                  Employee)
reader1.Close()

Dim reader2 As New StreamReader("C:\Employee2.xml")
Dim employee2 As Employee = CType(serializer.Deserialize(reader2), _
                                  Employee)
reader2.Close()
```

Using a Deserialized Object

Once you've deserialized XML data to an object, you can use the object as normal. The following example displays the Name and Salary for the two deserialized Employee objects, employee1 and employee2:

```
// C#
Console.WriteLine("employee1 name: " + employee1.Name +
                  ", salary: " + employee1.Salary);

Console.WriteLine("employee2 name: " + employee2.Name +
                  ", salary: " + employee2.Salary);
```

```
' VB.NET
Console.WriteLine("employee1 name: " & employee1.Name & _
                  ", salary: " & employee1.Salary)

Console.WriteLine("employee2 name: " & employee2.Name & _
                  ", salary: " & employee2.Salary)
```

If you run the sample application in Visual Studio .NET, the application displays the following output:

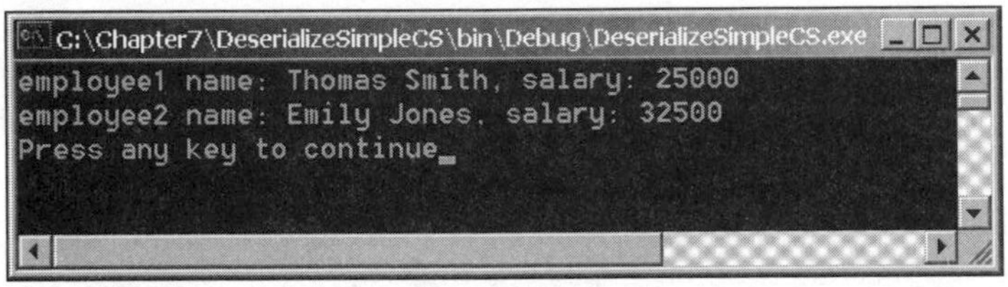

Dealing with Unexpected XML Content

When you deserialize an XML document to create a new object, you need to consider what might happen if the document contains unexpected content. What does the XmlSerializer do if it encounters unexpected elements, attributes, or other types of node in the document?

In the following pages, we'll describe how to deal with unexpected content in the XML document. You can download a complete sample application from the Wrox Press web site for this book:

❑   C# sample folder: Chapter7\DeserializeUnknownCS

❑   VB .NET sample folder: Chapter7\DeserializeUnknownVB

To open a sample application in Visual Studio .NET, select the menu item File | Open Solution and choose the solution file (.sln) for the sample application.

The example uses the familiar Employee class, identical to the one used in the previous examples.

Earlier in this chapter, you saw code to create an Employee object with a Name of Thomas Smith and a Salary of 25000. When this object is serialized, the XML document has the following structure (this XML document is provided as GoodEmployee.xml in the Online Samples):

```
<?xml version="1.0" encoding="utf-8"?>
<Employee xmlns:xsi="http://www.w3.org/2001/XMLSchema-instance"
          xmlns:xsd="http://www.w3.org/2001/XMLSchema">
   <Name>Thomas Smith</Name>
   <Salary>25000</Salary>
</Employee>
```

However, the document might pass through several applications before the time comes to deserialize the document. These applications might add new content to the document, perhaps to support business rules in another part of the company.

The following example shows an additional attribute, element, and CDATA section in the document (this XML document is provided as ExtraEverything.xml in the Online Samples):

```
<?xml version="1.0" encoding="utf-8"?>
<Employee EmpNum="789"
          xmlns:xsi="http://www.w3.org/2001/XMLSchema-instance"
          xmlns:xsd="http://www.w3.org/2001/XMLSchema">
   <Name>Thomas Smith</Name>
   <Salary>25000</Salary>
   <Tel>222-7777-789</Tel>
   <![CDATA[Age range: < 40]]>
</Employee>
```

When the XmlSerializer reads the XML document, it generates events if it encounters unexpected content. There are three different types of event:

❑ UnknownAttribute event – XmlSerializer found an unexpected attribute

❑ UnknownElement event – XmlSerializer found an unexpected element

❑ UnknownNode event – XmlSerializer found any type of unexpected node

If you don't handle these events in your code, the XmlSerializer skips the offending content. If you want to be notified about unexpected content, provide event handlers for these events in your application. This will alert you to any possible discrepancies in the serialized data format your application expects to receive. It can also be useful for diagnostic purposes. For example, you could use these events to create a log file that describes any unexpected content found in the XML document.

Handling Unexpected Attributes

To handle unexpected attributes in the XML document, you can register an event handler for the UnknownAttribute event as follows in your application:

```
// C#
XmlSerializer serializer = new XmlSerializer(typeof(Employee));
...
serializer.UnknownAttribute +=
            new XmlAttributeEventHandler(MyUnknownAttributeHandler);
```

```
' VB.NET
Dim serializer As New XmlSerializer(GetType(Employee))
...
AddHandler serializer.UnknownAttribute, _
           AddressOf MyUnknownAttributeHandler
```

In the following example, `MyUnknownAttributeHandler` is an event handler method for the `UnknownAttribute` event. Implement this event handler method as follows:

```csharp
// C#
public void MyUnknownAttributeHandler(object sender,
                                      XmlAttributeEventArgs e)
{
    string type = e.ObjectBeingDeserialized.GetType().ToString();
    Console.WriteLine("Unknown attribute when deserializing " + type);
    Console.WriteLine("Line number: "   + e.LineNumber);
    Console.WriteLine("Line position: " + e.LinePosition);
    Console.WriteLine("Attribute name: " + e.Attr.Name);
    Console.WriteLine("Attribute XML: " + e.Attr.OuterXml);
}
```

```vbnet
' VB.NET
Public Sub MyUnknownAttributeHandler(ByVal sender As Object, _
                                     ByVal e As XmlAttributeEventArgs)

    Dim type As String = e.ObjectBeingDeserialized.GetType().ToString()
    Console.WriteLine("Unknown attribute when deserializing " & type)
    Console.WriteLine("Line number: "   & e.LineNumber)
    Console.WriteLine("Line position: " & e.LinePosition)
    Console.WriteLine("Attribute name: " & e.Attr.Name)
    Console.WriteLine("Attribute XML: " & e.Attr.OuterXml)

End Sub
```

The `XmlAttributeEventArgs` parameter contains information about the unexpected attribute, such as its location in the XML document. The parameter also has an `Attr` property, which describes the attribute as an `XmlAttribute` DOM object.

Run the sample application in Visual Studio .NET. The application asks you for an XML filename; type `C:\ExtraAttribute.xml`. This XML document contains an unexpected `EmpNum` attribute in the `<Employee>` element. When the sample application deserializes the document, it displays the following message on the console (note: the C# example displays the `Employee` class name as `DeserializeUnknownCS.Employee`, because it is defined in the `DeserializeUnknownCS` namespace):

```
C:\Chapter7\DeserializeUnknownCS\bin\Debug\DeserializeUnknownCS.exe
Please enter the XML filename: C:\ExtraAttribute.xml

Unknown attribute when deserializing DeserializeUnknownCS.Employee
Line number: 3
Line position: 19
Attribute name: EmpNum
Attribute XML: EmpNum="789"
----------------------------------------------------------
Employee name: Thomas Smith
Employee salary: 25000
Press any key to continue_
```

Handling Unexpected Elements

To handle unexpected elements in the XML document, register an event handler for the
UnknownElement event as follows in your application. This code registers a method named
MyUnknownElementHandler() to handle unknown elements:

```csharp
// C#
serializer.UnknownElement +=
            new XmlElementEventHandler(MyUnknownElementHandler);
```

```vbnet
' VB.NET
AddHandler serializer.UnknownElement, AddressOf MyUnknownElementHandler
```

You can now add the following method to your class. This method will be called if an unexpected XML
element is found during deserialization:

```csharp
// C#
public void MyUnknownElementHandler(object sender,
                            XmlElementEventArgs e)
{
    string type = e.ObjectBeingDeserialized.GetType().ToString();
    Console.WriteLine("Unknown element when deserializing " + type);
    Console.WriteLine("Line number: "   + e.LineNumber);
    Console.WriteLine("Line position: " + e.LinePosition);
    Console.WriteLine("Element name: "  + e.Element.Name);
    Console.WriteLine("Element XML: "   + e.Element.OuterXml);
}
```

```vbnet
' VB.NET
Public Sub MyUnknownElementHandler(ByVal sender As Object, _
                            ByVal e As XmlElementEventArgs)

    Dim type As String = e.ObjectBeingDeserialized.GetType().ToString()
    Console.WriteLine("Unknown element when deserializing " & type)
    Console.WriteLine("Line number: "   & e.LineNumber)
    Console.WriteLine("Line position: " & e.LinePosition)
    Console.WriteLine("Element name: "  & e.Element.Name)
    Console.WriteLine("Element XML: "   & e.Element.OuterXml)

End Sub
```

As you might expect, the `XmlElementEventArgs` parameter contains information about the unexpected element.

Run the sample application again in Visual Studio .NET. The application asks you for an XML filename; type `C:\ExtraElement.xml`. This XML document contains an unexpected `<Tel>` child element within `<Employee>`. When the sample application deserializes the document, it displays the following message on the console:

```
C:\Chapter7\DeserializeUnknownVB\bin\DeserializeUnknownVB.exe
Please enter the XML filename: C:\ExtraElement.xml
Unknown element when deserializing DeserializeUnknownVB.Employee
Line number: 12
Line position: 3
Element name: Tel
Element XML: <Tel>222-7777-789</Tel>
--------------------------------------------------------------
Employee name: Thomas Smith
Employee salary: 25000
Press any key to continue_
```

Handling General Unexpected Nodes

To handle general unexpected nodes in the XML document, register an event handler for the `UnknownNode` event as follows (note: this statement is currently commented-out in the sample applications; un-comment this statement now):

```
// C#
serializer.UnknownNode += new XmlNodeEventHandler(MyUnknownNodeHandler);
```

```
' VB.NET
AddHandler serializer.UnknownNode, AddressOf MyUnknownNodeHandler
```

Implement the `UnknownNode` event handler method as follows:

```
// C#
public void MyUnknownNodeHandler(object sender, XmlNodeEventArgs e)
{
    string type = e.ObjectBeingDeserialized.GetType().ToString();
    Console.WriteLine("Unknown node when deserializing " + type);
    Console.WriteLine("Line number: "   + e.LineNumber);
    Console.WriteLine("Line position: " + e.LinePosition);
    Console.WriteLine("Node name: "     + e.Name);
    Console.WriteLine("Node text: "     + e.Text);
    Console.WriteLine("Node type: "     + e.NodeType.ToString());
}
```

```
' VB.NET
Public Sub MyUnknownNodeHandler(ByVal sender As Object, _
                        ByVal e As XmlNodeEventArgs)

    Dim type As String = e.ObjectBeingDeserialized.GetType().ToString()
```

```
        Console.WriteLine("Unknown node when deserializing " & type)
        Console.WriteLine("Line number: "    & e.LineNumber)
        Console.WriteLine("Line position: " & e.LinePosition)
        Console.WriteLine("Node name: "      & e.Name)
        Console.WriteLine("Node text: "      & e.Text)
        Console.WriteLine("Node type: "      & e.NodeType.ToString())

    End Sub
```

The `XmlNodeEventArgs` parameter contains information about the unexpected node, such as its location in the XML document.

Notice the expression `e.NodeType.ToString()` on the last line, which displays the `NodeType` property as a string. The `NodeType` property is an enumeration value such as `XmlNodeType.Element`, `XmlNodeType.Attribute`, or `XmlNodeType.CDATA`. These enumeration values will be displayed as the strings `"Element"`, `"Attribute"`, and `"CDATA"` respectively.

Run the sample application again in Visual Studio .NET. The application asks you for an XML filename; type `C:\ExtraEverything.xml`. This XML document contains an unexpected attribute, an unexpected element, and an unexpected CDATA section. When the sample application deserializes the document, it displays the following message on the console:

Notice that the application now displays several warning messages:

- ❑ The first message is due to a general unexpected node (the EmpNum attribute)

- ❑ The second message is due to an unexpected attribute (the EmpNum attribute again)

- ❑ The third message is due to a general unexpected node (the <Tel> element)

- ❑ The fourth message is due to an unexpected element (the <Tel> element again)

- ❑ The final message is due to a general unexpected node (the CDATA section)

Serializing and Deserializing Complex Objects

The examples we have seen so far deal with simple classes, which contain a few public fields using primitive data types. Classes can get a lot more complicated than that, and XmlSerializer is capable of dealing with these complexities.

In this section, you will learn how to serialize and deserialize objects that contain the following features:

- ❑ Properties
- ❑ Enumeration values
- ❑ Arrays
- ❑ Composite objects
- ❑ Objects that use inheritance

In the following pages, we'll describe how to serialize and deserialize complex objects. You can download complete sample applications from the Wrox Press web site for this book:

- ❑ C# folder for serialization: Chapter7\SerializeComplexCS
- ❑ C# folder for deserialization: Chapter7\DeserializeComplexCS
- ❑ VB .NET folder for serialization: Chapter7\SerializeComplexVB
- ❑ VB .NET folder for deserialization: Chapter7\DeserializeComplexVB

If you want to work along with these sample applications as we go through the following pages, we suggest you open up two copies of Visual Studio .NET. In the first instance of Visual Studio .NET, open the "serialization" solution. In the other instance of Visual Studio .NET, open the "deserialization" solution.

Serializing and Deserializing Properties

Classes can contain public properties, to represent read/write values in an object. You can use properties to encapsulate private or internal (Friend) fields in your class.

XmlSerializer serializes and deserializes public properties as follows:

- ❑ During serialization, XmlSerializer creates an XML element for each public property. The element name is the same as the property name. The element value is obtained using the get accessor for the property.

❑ During deserialization, XmlSerializer reads the XML element that represents the property. XmlSerializer then uses the set accessor to set the value for this property in the deserialized object.

The following example defines a get/set property named TelephoneExtension in the Employee class. There is also a private field named FullTelNum, to hold the employee's full telephone number internally:

```csharp
// C# - inside the Employee class
public string TelephoneExtension
{
   get
   {
      return FullTelNum.Substring(9, 3);  // Return last 3 digits
   }
   set
   {
      FullTelNum = "222-7777-" + value;   // Prefix with company number
   }
}
private string FullTelNum;                 // Hold full number internally
```

```vbnet
' VB.NET - inside the Employee class
Public Property TelephoneExtension() As String

   Get
      Return FullTelNum.Substring(9, 3)    ' Return last 3 digits
   End Get

   Set(ByVal Value As String)
      FullTelNum = "222-7777-" + Value     ' Prefix with company number
   End Set

End Property

Private FullTelNum As String               ' Hold full number internally
```

In your "serialization" application, you can set the value of this property as follows (see the Main() method in the "serialization" example):

```csharp
// C#
employee1.TelephoneExtension = "283";
```

```vbnet
' VB.NET
employee1.TelephoneExtension = "283"
```

When you serialize the employee1 object, the TelephoneExtension property is serialized as a <TelephoneExtension> element in the XML document, as follows (don't run the sample application just now – it generates a lot of additional XML content we haven't described yet!):

```xml
<?xml version="1.0" encoding="utf-8"?>
<Employee xmlns:xsi="http://www.w3.org/2001/XMLSchema-instance"
          xmlns:xsd="http://www.w3.org/2001/XMLSchema">
```

```
      <Name>Thomas Smith</Name>
      <Salary>25000</Salary>
      <TelephoneExtension>283</TelephoneExtension>
   </Employee>
```

When you deserialize the object, the `<TelephoneExtension>` element value is used to set the `TelephoneExtension` property in the new `Employee` object. In your "deserialization" application, you can display the deserialized value as follows – the value 283 will be displayed (see the `Main()` method in the "deserialization" example):

```
// C#
Console.WriteLine("Extension number: " + employee1.TelephoneExtension);
```

```
' VB.NET
Console.WriteLine("Extension number: " & employee1.TelephoneExtension)
```

Serializing and Deserializing Enumeration Values

Classes can use enumerated data types to represent fields (or properties) that have a restricted set of allowed values.

Let's see how `XmlSerializer` deals with enumeration values. The following example creates an enumerated type called `JobStatusType`, and declares a field named `JobStatus` with this type (see the `Employee` class in the "serialization" and "deserialization" examples):

```
// C# - inside the Employee class
public enum JobStatusType
{
    FullTime,
    Contractor
}
public JobStatusType JobStatus;
```

```
' VB.NET - inside the Employee class
Public Enum JobStatusType
    FullTime
    Contractor
End Enum
Public JobStatus As JobStatusType
```

In your "serialization" application, you can set this enumerated field as follows (see the `Main()` method in the "serialization" example):

```
// C#
employee1.JobStatus = Employee.JobStatusType.FullTime;
```

```
' VB.NET
employee1.JobStatus = Employee.JobStatusType.FullTime
```

When you serialize the employee1 object (as earlier), the JobStatus field is serialized as a
<JobStatus> element in the XML document, as follows:

```
<?xml version="1.0" encoding="utf-8"?>
<Employee xmlns:xsi="http://www.w3.org/2001/XMLSchema-instance"
          xmlns:xsd="http://www.w3.org/2001/XMLSchema">
  <Name>Thomas Smith</Name>
  <Salary>25000</Salary>
  <JobStatus>FullTime</JobStatus>
  <TelephoneExtension>283</TelephoneExtension>
</Employee>
```

To deserialize this data, the "deserialization" class must have the same enumeration definitions as the
"serialization" class. You can then deserialize and display the enumeration value as follows – the value
FullTime will be displayed (see the Main() method in the "deserialization" example):

```
// C#
Console.WriteLine("Job status: " + employee1.JobStatus);
```

```
' VB.NET
Console.WriteLine("Job status: " & employee1.JobStatus.ToString())
```

Later in this chapter, we'll discuss how to use XSD schemas during serialization and deserialization. At
that stage, you'll see that enumerated values in an object get mapped to <xsd:enumeration> values in
the XSD schema. See the section, *Using XSD Schemas with Serialization*, for details.

Serializing and Deserializing Arrays

Classes can contain arrays of primitive types or class types. XmlSerializer serializes and deserializes
arrays as follows:

❑   During serialization, XmlSerializer creates an XML element representing the array as a
    whole. By default, the XML element name is the same as the array name. XmlSerializer
    then creates an XML child element for each item in the array. The child elements are named
    after the data type of the array. For example, if you have an array of string objects,
    XmlSerializer will create a <string> element for each item in the array.

❑   During deserialization, XmlSerializer counts the number of XML elements representing
    array data. It then creates an array of the appropriate length in the deserialized object, and
    populates the array using the XML data.

In this section, we'll continue to use the sample applications we introduced earlier. The following
example adds an array field to the Employee class, representing a list of contact names for the
employee (see the Employee class in the "serialization" and "deserialization" examples):

```
// C# - inside the Employee class
public string [] Contacts;
```

```
' VB.NET
Public Contacts As String()
```

In your "serialization" application, you can create and initialize an array for this field as follows (see the `Main()` method in the "serialization" example):

```csharp
// C#
employee1.Contacts = new string[]{"Mary Smith", "Mungo Evans", "Midge Yo" };
```

```vbnet
' VB.NET
employee1.Contacts = New String(){"Mary Smith", "Mungo Evans", "Midge Yo"}
```

When you serialize the `employee1` object (as earlier), the `Contacts` array is serialized as a `<Contacts>` element in the XML document. Each item in the array is serialized as a child `<string>` element as follows:

```xml
<?xml version="1.0" encoding="utf-8"?>
<Employee xmlns:xsi="http://www.w3.org/2001/XMLSchema-instance"
          xmlns:xsd="http://www.w3.org/2001/XMLSchema">
   <Name>Thomas Smith</Name>
   <Salary>25000</Salary>
   <TelephoneExtension>283</TelephoneExtension>
   <JobStatus>FullTime</JobStatus>
   <Contacts>
       <string>Mary Smith</string>
       <string>Mungo Evans</string>
       <string>Midge Yo</string>
   </Contacts>
 </Employee>
```

When you deserialize this data in your "deserialization" application, you can display the `Contacts` array as follows – the three values Mary Smith, Mungo Evans, and Midge Yo will be displayed (see the `Main()` method in the "deserialization" example):

```csharp
// C#
Console.WriteLine("There are " + employee1.Contacts.Length + " contacts:");

foreach(string contact in employee1.Contacts)
{
    Console.WriteLine(contact);
}
```

```vbnet
' VB.NET
Console.WriteLine("There are " & employee1.Contacts.Length & " contacts:")

Dim contact As String
For Each contact In employee1.Contacts
    Console.WriteLine(contact)
Next
```

Serializing and Deserializing Composite Objects

Object-oriented programming is all about defining objects for the abstractions in your system. It is quite natural for an object to contain other objects, to build a composite type.

For example, an `Employee` object might have an `Address` object named `HomeAddress`, and another `Address` object named `WorkAddress` as follows:

```csharp
// C#
public class Employee
{
    public Address HomeAddress;
    public Address WorkAddress;
    ... etc. ...
}


public class Address
{
    public string Street;
    public string Area;
    public string City;
}
```

```vbnet
' VB.NET
Public Class Employee
    Public HomeAddress As Address
    Public WorkAddress As Address
    ... etc. ...
End Class


Public Class Address
    Public Street As String
    Public Area As String
    Public City As String
End Class
```

This is how `XmlSerializer` serializes and deserializes composite objects:

❑ During serialization, the `public` inner object is serialized to an XML element with the same name as that object. The `public` members of the inner object are serialized as XML child elements. This process works recursively if the inner object is itself a composite object.

❑ During deserialization, `XmlSerializer` creates the inner object and initializes it with the XML child elements representing that object.

In your "serialization" application, you can create and initialize a composite object as follows (see the `Main()` method in the "serialization" example):

```csharp
// C#
employee1.HomeAddress = new Address();
employee1.HomeAddress.Street = "4 Sunshine Villas";
employee1.HomeAddress.Area = "Bay";
employee1.HomeAddress.City = "Nirvana";
```

```
employee1.WorkAddress = new Address();
employee1.WorkAddress.Street = "1 Main St";
employee1.WorkAddress.Area = "Downtown";
employee1.WorkAddress.City = "SlogCity";
```

```
' VB.NET
employee1.HomeAddress = New Address()
employee1.HomeAddress.Street = "4 Sunshine Villas"
employee1.HomeAddress.Area = "Bay"
employee1.HomeAddress.City = "Nirvana"

employee1.WorkAddress = New Address()
employee1.WorkAddress.Street = "1 Main St"
employee1.WorkAddress.Area = "Downtown"
employee1.WorkAddress.City = "SlogCity"
```

When you serialize the employee1 object (as earlier), the HomeAddress and WorkAddress objects are serialized as <HomeAddress> and <WorkAddress> elements as follows:

```
<?xml version="1.0" encoding="utf-8"?>
<Employee xmlns:xsi="http://www.w3.org/2001/XMLSchema-instance"
          xmlns:xsd="http://www.w3.org/2001/XMLSchema">
   <Name>Thomas Smith</Name>
   <Salary>25000</Salary>
   <TelephoneExtension>283</TelephoneExtension>
   <JobStatus>FullTime</JobStatus>
   <Contacts>
      <string>Mary Smith</string>
      <string>Mungo Evans</string>
      <string>Midge Yo</string>
   </Contacts>
   <HomeAddress>
      <Street>4 Sunshine Villas</Street>
      <Area>Bay</Area>
      <City>Nirvana</City>
   </HomeAddress>
   <WorkAddress>
      <Street>1 Main St</Street>
      <Area>Downtown</Area>
      <City>SlogCity</City>
   </WorkAddress>
</Employee>
```

When you deserialize this data in your "deserialization" application, the XmlSerializer recreates all the inner objects as necessary (see the Main() method in the "deserialization" example):

```
// C#
Console.WriteLine("Home city: " + employee1.HomeAddress.City);
... etc. ...
```

```
' VB.NET
Console.WriteLine("Home city: " & employee1.HomeAddress.City)
... etc. ...
```

Using Methods to Simplify Class Usage

The previous example could be simplified greatly by adding suitable methods to the Address class. This doesn't affect serialization in any way – XmlSerializer simply ignores the methods when it serializes and deserializes the object.

We will add three methods to the Address class:

- ❑ A constructor. You can use this constructor to initialize Address objects when you create them for the first time in your application.

- ❑ A no-argument constructor. XmlSerializer requires this as part of the deserialization process. When XmlSerializer tries to deserialize XML data into an object, it has to create a new object to house this data. The only constructor the XmlSerializer is capable of calling is the no-argument constructor (XmlSerializer can't call any constructors that take arguments, because it wouldn't know what values to pass into these arguments).

- ❑ A ToString() method, to display all the Address fields in a single method call.

Here is the revised Address class definition, containing the three new methods:

```
// C#
public class Address
{
    public string Street;
    public string Area;
    public string City;

    // Constructor
    public Address(string streetParam, string areaParam, string cityParam)
    {
        Street = streetParam;
        Area = areaParam;
        City = cityParam;
    }

    // No-argument constructor
    public Address()
    {
        // No-arg constructor, to enable object to be deserialized
    }

    // Return object data as a string
    public override string ToString()
    {
        return Street + ", " + Area + ", " + City;
    }
}
```

```vbnet
' VB.NET
Public Class Address

    Public Street As String
    Public Area As String
    Public City As String

    ' Constructor
    Public Sub New(ByVal streetParam As String, _
                   ByVal areaParam As String, _
                   ByVal cityParam As String)
        Street = streetParam
        Area = areaParam
        City = cityParam
    End Sub

    ' No-argument constructor
    Public Sub New()
        ' No-arg constructor, to enable object to be deserialized
    End Sub

    ' Return object data as a string
    Public Overrides Function ToString() As String
        Return Street & ", " & Area & ", " & City
    End Function

End Class
```

With these changes in place, your "serialization" application can create and display Address objects much more easily than before (see the Main() method in the "serialization" example). Notice how concise the code is now, compared to the earlier example before the constructors and ToString() method were added:

```csharp
// C#
employee1.HomeAddress = new Address("4 Sunshine Villas", "Bay", "Nirvana");
employee1.WorkAddress = new Address("1 Main St", "Downtown", "SlogCity");
...
Console.WriteLine(employee1.HomeAddress.ToString());
Console.WriteLine(employee1.WorkAddress.ToString ());
```

```vbnet
' VB.NET
employee1.HomeAddress = New Address("4 Sunshine Villas", "Bay", "Nirvana")
employee1.WorkAddress = New Address("1 Main St", "Downtown", "SlogCity")
...
Console.WriteLine(employee1.HomeAddress.ToString())
Console.WriteLine(employee1.WorkAddress.ToString())
```

Serializing and Deserializing with Inheritance

XmlSerializer supports serialization and deserialization on inherited types. When you serialize an object, XmlSerializer automatically serializes the public fields and properties in its superclass. This process continues recursively up the inheritance tree.

Consider the following example of inheritance. The simplified Employee class represents a generic type of employee, and is declared as an abstract (MustInherit) class. The Manager class inherits from Employee, and represents a specific type of employee:

```csharp
// C#
public abstract class Employee
{
    public string Name;
}

public class Manager : Employee
{
    public int GolfHandicap;
}
```

```vbnet
' VB.NET
Public MustInherit Class Employee
    Public Name As String
End Class

Public Class Manager
        Inherits Employee
   Public GolfHandicap As Integer
End Class
```

You can create and serialize a Manager object as follows in your "serialization" application (see the Main() method in the "serialization" example):

```csharp
// C#
Manager mgr = new Manager();
mgr.Name = "Thomas Smith";
mgr.GolfHandicap = 5;

XmlSerializer serializer = new XmlSerializer(typeof(Manager));
TextWriter writer1 = new StreamWriter("C:\\Manager1.xml");
serializer.Serialize(writer1, mgr);
writer1.Close();
```

```vbnet
' VB.NET
Dim mgr As New Manager()
mgr.Name = "Thomas Smith"
mgr.GolfHandicap = 5

Dim serializer As New XmlSerializer(GetType(Manager))
Dim writer1 As New StreamWriter("C:\Manager1.xml")
serializer.Serialize(writer1, mgr)
writer1.Close()
```

239

This is how the XML document appears after the `Manager` object has been serialized:

```
<?xml version="1.0" encoding="utf-8" ?>
<Manager xmlns:xsi="http://www.w3.org/2001/XMLSchema-instance"
         xmlns:xsd="http://www.w3.org/2001/XMLSchema">
  <Name>Thomas Smith</Name>
  <GolfHandicap>5</GolfHandicap>
</Manager>
```

To deserialize this data, use the following code in your "deserialization" application (see the `Main()` method in the "deserialization" example):

```
// C#
XmlSerializer serializer = new XmlSerializer(typeof(Manager));
TextReader reader1 = new StreamReader("C:\\Manager1.xml");
Manager mgr = (Manager)serializer.Deserialize(reader1);
reader1.Close();
```

```
' VB.NET
Dim serializer As New XmlSerializer(GetType(Manager))
Dim reader1 As New StreamReader("C:\Manager1.xml")
Dim mgr As Manager = CType(serializer.Deserialize(reader1), Manager)
reader1.Close()
```

Fine-Tuning the Serialization Process

For the remainder of the chapter, we look at various ways to fine-tune the serialization process. In this section, we show how to control the format of the XML data generated by `XmlSerializer` during serialization. In the next section, we'll see how to use XSD schemas with serialization.

The first question to ask is: why would you want to control the format of the XML data during serialization? Well, if you're using serialization for internal consumption within a closed system, it doesn't really matter how the XML data is formatted. However, if you need to exchange serialized objects with external applications and services, the chances are that these applications and services will require the XML data to be in a particular format.

You can add **.NET Framework attributes** to your class, to control how instances are serialized into XML data. For example, you can specify the element names to use when fields or properties are serialized to the XML document. You can also specify that a field or property should be serialized as an attribute rather than as an element, or as simple text content within a containing element. It's also possible to specify namespace information for elements and attributes in the XML document.

> **The .NET Framework SDK refers to these as "attributes". To avoid confusion with XML attributes, we will use the phrase .NET Framework attribute in this chapter.**

The general syntax of a .NET Framework attribute is as follows:

```
// C#
[ name-of-.NET-Framework-attribute(property = property-value,...) ]
```

```
' VB.NET
< name-of-.NET-Framework-attribute(property := property-value,...) >
```

In the following pages, we'll describe how to use .NET Framework attributes to fine-tune the serialization process. You can download complete sample applications from the Wrox Press web site for this book:

❑ C# folder: Chapter7\FineTuningSimpleCS

❑ VB .NET folder: Chapter7\FineTuningSimpleVB

Download these sample applications, and open one in Visual Studio .NET. Take a look at the Employee class. Notice that it contains various .NET Framework attributes, such as XmlRoot and XmlElement. We'll describe what these all mean in the coming pages.

Let's consider a simplified version of the Employee class first. The following class definition has a Name field, which is qualified with an XmlElement attribute. The XmlElement attribute causes the Name field to be serialized as an XML element called <FullName> (without the XmlElement attribute, the Name field would just be serialized as <Name>):

```
// C#
using System.Xml.Serialization;      // Need this for [XmlElement]

public class Employee
{
    [XmlElement(ElementName="FullName")]
    public string Name;
}
```

```
' VB.NET
Imports System.Xml.Serialization      ' Need this for <XmlElement>

Public Class Employee
    <XmlElement(ElementName:="FullName")> _
    Public Name As String
End Class
```

This is how an Employee instance appears after serialization:

```
<?xml version="1.0" encoding="utf-8" ?>
<Employee xmlns:xsi="http://www.w3.org/2001/XMLSchema-instance"
          xmlns:xsd="http://www.w3.org/2001/XMLSchema">
    <FullName>Thomas Smith</FullName>
</Employee>
```

.NET Framework attributes correspond to classes in the System.Xml.Serialization namespace. For example, the XmlElement attribute corresponds to the XmlElementAttribute class. The attribute classes inherit from the Attribute class in the System namespace – see Online Help for full details of these classes.

Defining Simple Formatting for Serialization

In this section, we'll describe how to achieve simple formatting during serialization. These features enable you to generate specific XML content, which can be useful if you need to comply with a prescribed XML grammar.

We'll show how to use the following .NET Framework attributes:

❑ XmlRoot – Format the XML document element

❑ XmlElement – Format elements in the XML document

❑ XmlAttribute – Format attributes in the XML document

❑ XmlText – Format text content in the XML document

For a full list of .NET Framework attributes, see the XmlSerializer class in the .NET Framework Online Help.

Formatting the XML Document Element

The XmlRoot attribute controls how the document element is formatted during serialization. The XmlRoot attribute has a property called ElementName, to set the name of the document element. There is also a property called Namespace, to set a namespace URI for all the elements in the document. See the XmlRootAttribute class in Online Help for a full list of available properties.

Consider the following class definition (we've omitted the System.Xml.Serialization namespace for brevity in these examples):

```
// C#
[XmlRoot(ElementName="StaffMember", Namespace="urn:MyNamespaceURI")]
public class Employee
{
    public string Name;
    public decimal Salary;
}

' VB.NET
<XmlRoot(ElementName:="StaffMember", Namespace:="urn:MyNamespaceURI")> _
Public Class Employee
    Public Name As String
    Public Salary As Decimal
End Class
```

When an instance of this class is serialized, the document element is called <StaffMember> rather than <Employee>. Also, a default namespace "urn:MyNamespaceURI" is defined for the document:

```
<?xml version="1.0" encoding="utf-8" ?>
<StaffMember xmlns="urn:MyNamespaceURI"
             xmlns:xsi="http://www.w3.org/2001/XMLSchema-instance"
             xmlns:xsd="http://www.w3.org/2001/XMLSchema">
    <Name>Thomas Smith</Name>
    <Salary>25000</Salary>
</StaffMember>
```

Defining Qualified Namespaces

XML enables you to qualify the namespace URI with a prefix. This can be useful if you have an XML document that contains contents from several different namespaces.

If you want to use qualified namespaces, you have to change the way you serialize the object in your code. The `Serialize()` method in the `XmlSerializer` class can take an `XmlSerializerNamespaces` parameter, to associate namespace URIs with namespace prefixes.

The following example shows how to create an `XmlSerializerNamespaces` object, and associate the namespace URI `"urn:MyNamespaceURI"` with the namespace prefix `myNS`. The `XmlSerializerNamespaces` object is then passed into the `Serialize()` method, to tell the `XmlSerializer` to use the prefix `myNS` with the namespace URI `"urn:MyNamespaceURI"` (this code is in the `Main()` method in the sample applications):

```csharp
// C#
// Associate namespace prefix "myNS" with URI "urn:MyNamespaceURI"
XmlSerializerNamespaces ns = new XmlSerializerNamespaces();
ns.Add("myNS", "urn:MyNamespaceURI");

// Serialize employee1 object, using the XmlSerializerNamespaces
XmlSerializer serializer = new XmlSerializer( typeof(Employee) );
TextWriter writer1 = new StreamWriter("C:\\Employee1.xml");
serializer.Serialize(writer1, employee1, ns);
writer1.Close();
```

```vbnet
' VB.NET
' Associate namespace prefix "myNS" with URI "urn:MyNamespaceURI"
Dim ns As New XmlSerializerNamespaces()
ns.Add("myNS", "urn:MyNamespaceURI")

' Serialize employee1 object, using the XmlSerializerNamespaces
Dim serializer = New XmlSerializer(GetType(Employee))
Dim writer1 = New StreamWriter("C:\Employee1.xml")
serializer.Serialize(writer1, employee1, ns)
writer1.Close()
```

When an `Employee` instance is serialized, the namespace prefix `myNs` appears explicitly on each element:

```xml
<?xml version="1.0" encoding="utf-8"?>
<myNS:StaffMember xmlns:myNS="urn:MyNamespaceURI">
    <myNS:Name>Thomas Smith</myNS:Name>
    <myNS:Salary>25000</myNS:Salary>
</myNS:StaffMember>
```

Formatting XML Elements

The `XmlElement` attribute controls how individual elements are formatted during serialization. The `XmlElement` attribute has a property called `ElementName`, to set the name of the element. There is also a property called `Namespace`, to set a local namespace URI for just this element. See the `XmlElementAttribute` class in Online Help for a full list of available properties.

Consider the following class definition:

```csharp
// C#
[XmlRoot(ElementName="StaffMember", Namespace="urn:MyNamespaceURI")]
public class Employee
{
    [XmlElement(ElementName="FullName", Namespace="urn:MyLocalURI")]
    public string Name;

    public decimal Salary;
}
```

```vbnet
' VB.NET
<XmlRoot(ElementName:="StaffMember", Namespace:="urn:MyNamespaceURI")> _
Public Class Employee

    <XmlElement(ElementName:="FullName", Namespace:="urn:MyLocalURI")> _
    Public Name As String

    Public Salary As Decimal

End Class
```

When an instance of this class is serialized, the Name field is serialized as a <FullName> element, with a local namespace URI of "urn:MyLocalURI":

```xml
<?xml version="1.0" encoding="utf-8"?>
<myNS:StaffMember xmlns:myNS="urn:MyNamespaceURI">
  <FullName xmlns="urn:MyLocalURI">Thomas Smith</FullName>
  <myNS:Salary>25000</myNS:Salary>
</myNS:StaffMember>
```

Formatting XML Attributes

The XmlAttribute attribute controls how individual XML attributes are formatted during serialization. You can use XmlAttribute on its own, to indicate that a field or property should be serialized as an attribute rather than as an element. If you want to specify an explicit attribute name or namespace, you can set the AttributeName and Namespace properties. See the XmlAttributeAttribute class in Online Help for a full list of available properties.

Consider the following class definition:

```csharp
// C#
[XmlRoot(ElementName="StaffMember", Namespace="urn:MyNamespaceURI")]
public class Employee
{
    [XmlElement(ElementName="FullName", Namespace="urn:MyLocalURI")]
    public string Name;

    [XmlAttribute(AttributeName="EmpNum")]
    public string ID;
```

```
    public decimal Salary;
}


' VB.NET
<XmlRoot(ElementName:="StaffMember", Namespace:="urn:MyNamespaceURI")> _
Public Class Employee

    <XmlElement(ElementName:="FullName", Namespace:="urn:MyLocalURI")> _
    Public Name As String

    <XmlAttributeAttribute(AttributeName:="EmpNum")> _
    Public ID As String

    Public Salary As Decimal

End Class
```

When an instance of this class is serialized, the ID field is serialized as an EmpNum attribute in the enclosing element, <StaffMember>:

```
<?xml version="1.0" encoding="utf-8" ?>
<myNS:StaffMember
    EmpNum="789"
    xmlns:myNS="urn:MyNamespaceURI">

    <FullName xmlns="urn:MyLocalURI">Thomas Smith</FullName>
    <myNS:Salary>25000</myNS:Salary>

</myNS:StaffMember>
```

Formatting Text Content

The XmlText attribute indicates that a field or property in a class should be serialized as text content in the XML document, rather than as an element or attribute.

Consider the following class definition:

```
// C#
[XmlRoot(ElementName="StaffMember", Namespace="urn:MyNamespaceURI")]
public class Employee
{
    [XmlElement(ElementName="FullName", Namespace="urn:MyLocalURI")]
    public string Name;

    [XmlAttribute(AttributeName="EmpNum")]
    public string ID;

    public decimal Salary;

    [XmlText]
    public string Bio;
}
```

```
' VB.NET
<XmlRoot(ElementName:="StaffMember", Namespace:="urn:MyNamespaceURI")> _
Public Class Employee

    <XmlElement(ElementName:="FullName", Namespace:="urn:MyLocalURI")> _
    Public Name As String

    <XmlAttributeAttribute(AttributeName:="EmpNum")> _
    Public ID As String

    Public Salary As Decimal

    <XmlText()> _
    Public Bio As String

End Class
```

When an instance of this class is serialized, the Bio field is serialized as text content in the enclosing element, <StaffMember>:

```
<?xml version="1.0" encoding="utf-8"?>
<myNS:StaffMember
    EmpNum="789"
    xmlns:myNS="urn:MyNamespaceURI">

    <FullName xmlns="urn:MyLocalURI">Thomas Smith</FullName>

    <myNS:Salary>25000</myNS:Salary>

    Thomas is a cool guy (a great bloke)

</myNS:StaffMember>
```

Advanced Fine-Tuning Issues

In this section, we'll describe how to use some of the more sophisticated .NET Framework attributes to control the serialization process. We'll describe the following topics:

- ❑ Ignorable fields and properties
- ❑ Enumeration identifiers
- ❑ Polymorphic arrays
- ❑ Nullable object references

In the following pages, we'll describe how to use these .NET Framework attributes to control advanced aspects of serialization. You can download complete sample applications from the Wrox Press web site for this book:

- ❑ C# folder: Chapter7\FineTuningComplexCS
- ❑ VB .NET folder: Chapter7\FineTuningComplexVB

Download these sample applications, and open one in Visual Studio .NET. The application contains three classes – Employee, Manager, and Perk – to illustrate the advanced serialization techniques. There are several important concepts here, and plenty of new syntax. Hold on tight, here we go!

Defining Ignorable Fields and Properties

The XmlIgnore attribute indicates that a field or property should be ignored during serialization and deserialization. When an instance of the class is serialized, the field or property is not written out to the XML document. When the document is deserialized, the field or property is not assigned a value from the XML document.

The XmlIgnore attribute can be useful for fields or properties that hold a transient or computed value, which would have no meaning when the object is deserialized later. Another use of XmlIgnore is to reduce the number of fields and properties that need to be serialized; this can decrease the amount of information that needs to be exchanged between applications, and potentially offer better performance as a result.

In the following example, the Employee class has a Timestamp field indicated the date and time when the object was created. The constructor sets this field when an Employee object is created. The field is marked with XmlIgnore, because there's no point in serializing its value:

```csharp
// C#
public class Employee
{
    public string Name;


    [XmlIgnore()]
    public DateTime Timestamp;

    public Employee()
    {
        Timestamp = DateTime.Now;
    }

}
```

```vbnet
' VB.NET
Public Class Employee

    Public Name As String

    <XmlIgnore()> _
    Public Timestamp As DateTime

    Public Sub New()
        Timestamp = DateTime.Now
    End Sub

End Class
```

When an instance of this class is serialized, the Timestamp field is omitted:

```
<?xml version="1.0" encoding="utf-8"?>
<Employee xmlns:xsi="http://www.w3.org/2001/XMLSchema-instance"
          xmlns:xsd="http://www.w3.org/2001/XMLSchema">
  <Name>Thomas Smith</Name>
</Employee>
```

When this document is deserialized, XmlSerializer first calls the no-arg constructor in Employee to perform preliminary initialization (such as setting the Timestamp field to the current date and time). XmlSerializer then sets the other fields and properties using data from the XML document.

Defining Enumeration Identifiers

Earlier in this chapter, we showed how to use enumeration values with serialization (see the section, *Serializing and Deserializing Enumeration Values*). As we described at the time, the default serialization process for enumeration types is to write one of the enumeration identifiers to the XML document.

If you want XmlSerializer to write out different values for enumeration types, you can use the XmlEnum attribute on each enumeration identifier. This enables the XML document to contain more meaningful text strings for enumerated values, rather than the enumeration identifiers used in your program, which may not easy to understand.

In the following example, the Employee class has a JobStatusType enumeration type. Each of the enumeration identifiers is qualified with an XmlEnum attribute, to specify the value to use when serializing that identifier (this doesn't affect how you use the enumeration type in your application – you still use the identifiers Employee.JobStatusType.FullTime and Employee.JobStatusType.Contractor).

```
// C#
public class Employee
{
    public String Name;

    public enum JobStatusType
    {
        [XmlEnum(Name="Full time staff member")]
        FullTime,

        [XmlEnum(Name="Contracted worker")]
        Contractor
    }
    public JobStatusType JobStatus;
    ...
}

' VB.NET
Public class Employee

    Public Name As String

    Public Enum JobStatusType
        <XmlEnum(Name:="Full time staff member")> _
        FullTime
```

```
        <XmlEnum(Name:="Contracted worker")> _
        Contractor
    End Enum
    Public JobStatus As JobStatusType
        ...
    End Class
```

When an instance of this class is serialized, the `JobStatus` field is serialized using the appropriate `XmlEnum` name. For example:

```
<?xml version="1.0" encoding="utf-8"?>
<Employee xmlns:xsi="http://www.w3.org/2001/XMLSchema-instance"
          xmlns:xsd="http://www.w3.org/2001/XMLSchema">
    <Name>Thomas Smith</Name>
    <JobStatus>Full time staff member</JobStatus>
</Employee>
```

Defining Polymorphic Arrays

A polymorphic array is one that contains objects of different types, all inherited from a common superclass.

Polymorphic arrays are extremely powerful, and are used a great deal in object-oriented applications. For example, imagine you have an array containing different types of `Employee` objects, such as a `Programmer`, `Manager`, and `CEO` objects. You can loop through the array, and call the `PayRise()` method on each object. Let's assume each type of employee implements the `PayRise()` method in a different way (sadly, unless you're the CEO of course). Polymorphism means that the correct version of `PayRise()` will always be called, depending on what type of employee is getting the pay rise.

Unfortunately, `XmlSerializer` throws an exception if you try to serialize or deserialize a polymorphic array. The problem arises because `XmlSerializer` doesn't know what types of object might appear in the array, and throws its hands up in horror when it finds an unexpected type of object.

Fortunately, the solution is quite straightforward. Declare `XmlArrayItem` attributes on the array, to indicate all the subclass types that *might* appear in the array. This keeps `XmlSerializer` happy. The general syntax for declaring `XmlArrayItem` attributes is as follows:

```
// C# syntax for XmlArrayItem attributes
[XmlArrayItem( Type = typeof(subclass-type) ),
 XmlArrayItem( Type = typeof(another-subclass-type) ),
 ... ]
public superclass-type [] array-name;
```

```
' VB.NET syntax for XmlArrayItem attributes
<XmlArrayItem( Type := GetType(subclass-type) ), _
 XmlArrayItem( Type := GetType(another-subclass-type) ), _
 ... >
Public array-name As superclass-type()
```

To illustrate this concept, we'll use a simple inheritance hierarchy representing the different types of perk for an employee in a company. The superclass is called `Perk`, and there are two subclasses named `CompanyCar` and `BonusPayment`:

```csharp
// C# inheritance hierarchy for perks

// Perk is the superclass for all types of perks
public abstract class Perk
{
}

// CompanyCar is a type of perk
public class CompanyCar : Perk
{
   public string Model;

   public CompanyCar()
   {
   }

   public CompanyCar(string m)
   {
      Model = m;
   }
}

// BonusPayment is another type of perk
public class BonusPayment : Perk
{
   public decimal Amount;

   public BonusPayment()
   {
   }

   public BonusPayment(decimal amt)
   {
      Amount = amt;
   }
}
```

```vbnet
' VB.NET inheritance hierarchy for perks

' Perk is the superclass for all types of perk
Public MustInherit Class Perk
End Class

' CompanyCar is a type of perk
Public Class CompanyCar
    Inherits Perk

    Public Model As String

    Public Sub New()
    End Sub

    Public Sub New(ByVal m As String)
        Model = m
```

```
        End Sub

End Class

' BonusPayment is another type of perk
Public Class BonusPayment
    Inherits Perk

    Public Amount As Decimal

    Public Sub New()
    End Sub

    Public Sub New(ByVal amt As Decimal)
        Amount = amt
    End Sub

End Class
```

You can now declare a Perk array in the Employee class, to indicate that an employee can have many perks. To avoid serialization exceptions, you must use XmlArrayItem attributes to inform XmlSerializer what types of object might appear in this array at run-time (CompanyCar and BonusPayment). You can also define an element name to represent each subclass type during serialization. In the following code, we specify that CompanyCar objects should be serialized as <Car> elements, and BonusPayment objects should be serialized as <Bonus> elements:

```csharp
// C# definition of the Employee class
public class Employee
{
    public string Name;

    [XmlArrayItem( ElementName="Car", Type=typeof(CompanyCar) ),
     XmlArrayItem( ElementName="Bonus", Type=typeof(BonusPayment) )]
    public Perk [] JobPerks;
    ...
}
```

```vbnet
' VB.NET definition of the Employee class
Public Class Employee

    Public Name As String

    <XmlArrayItem( ElementName:="Car", Type:=GetType(CompanyCar) ), _
     XmlArrayItem( ElementName:="Bonus", Type:=GetType(BonusPayment) )> _
    Public JobPerks As Perk()
    ...
End Class
```

In your application, you can create an array of different types of perk as follows:

```csharp
// C# code to create an array of perks for employee1
employee1.JobPerks = new Perk[] {
                        new CompanyCar("BMW 525i"),
```

```
                                     new BonusPayment(2000),
                                     new BonusPayment(1500)
                         };
```

```
' VB.NET code to create an array of perks for employee1
employee1.JobPerks = New Perk() { _
                         New CompanyCar("BMW 525i"), _
                         New BonusPayment(2000), _
                         New BonusPayment(1500) _
                     }
```

This is how the array appears when the employee1 object is serialized:

```xml
<?xml version="1.0" encoding="utf-8"?>
<Employee xmlns:xsi="http://www.w3.org/2001/XMLSchema-instance"
          xmlns:xsd="http://www.w3.org/2001/XMLSchema">
    <Name>Thomas Smith</Name>
    <JobPerks>
        <Car>
            <Model>BMW 525i</Model>
        </Car>
        <Bonus>
            <Amount>2000</Amount>
        </Bonus>
        <Bonus>
            <Amount>1500</Amount>
        </Bonus>
    </JobPerks>
</Employee>
```

Defining Nullable Object References

Earlier in this chapter, we showed how to serialize and deserialize composite objects that contain nested objects (see the section, *Serializing and Deserializing Composite Objects*). We used an example of an Employee containing two Address objects.

One issue we haven't considered yet is what happens if you serialize an object that contains a null object reference. For example, imagine you assign an Address object to the HomeAddress field, but leave the WorkAddress field as null in C#, or Nothing in VB .NET:

```csharp
// C#
employee1.HomeAddress = new Address("4 Sunshine Villas", "Bay", "Nirvana");
employee1.WorkAddress = null;
```

```vbnet
' VB.NET
employee1.HomeAddress = New Address("4 Sunshine Villas", "Bay", "Nirvana")
employee1.WorkAddress = Nothing
```

When you serialize the employee1 object, XmlSerializer writes the HomeAddress field as expected. However, since the WorkAddress field is a null object reference, XmlSerializer writes a <WorkAddress xsi:nil=true> placeholder element for the WorkAddress field. xsi:nil=true is an XSD schema mechanism for indicating missing content in the XML document:

```
<?xml version="1.0" encoding="utf-8"?>
<Employee xmlns:xsi="http://www.w3.org/2001/XMLSchema-instance"
          xmlns:xsd="http://www.w3.org/2001/XMLSchema">
   <Name>Thomas Smith</Name>
   <HomeAddress>
      <Street>4 Sunshine Villas</Street>
      <Area>Bay</Area>
      <City>Nirvana</City>
   </HomeAddress>
   <WorkAddress xsi:nil="true" />
</Employee>
```

If you are happy with this situation, skip forward to the next section.

If you don't want the placeholder <WorkAddress xsi:nil=true/> element appearing in the XML document, modify the Employee class definition as shown below. This suppresses the XSD warning (xsi:nil="true"), so there is no indication that the <WorkAddress> element is missing in the serialized data:

```
// C#
public class Employee
{
    [XmlElement(IsNullable=false)]
    public Address HomeAddress;

    [XmlElement(IsNullable=false)]
    public Address WorkAddress;
    ...
}


' VB.NET
Public Class Employee

    <XmlElement(IsNullable:=False)> _
    Public HomeAddress As Address

    <XmlElement(IsNullable:=False)> _
    Public WorkAddress As Address
    ...
End Class
```

The IsNullable property on the XmlElement attribute suppresses placeholder elements from appearing for null objects. This is how the XML document will appear now – notice there is no mention of the null WorkAddress object reference:

```
<?xml version="1.0" encoding="utf-8" ?>
<Employee xmlns:xsi="http://www.w3.org/2001/XMLSchema-instance"
          xmlns:xsd="http://www.w3.org/2001/XMLSchema">
   <Name>Thomas Smith</Name>
   <HomeAddress>
      <Street>4 Sunshine Villas</Street>
      <Area>Bay</Area>
      <City>Nirvana</City>
```

```
        </HomeAddress>
    </Employee>
```

That concludes our investigation into the use of .NET Framework attributes to control how objects are serialized into XML documents.

In the next section, we'll look at how to use XSD schemas to influence the serialization process. This is a fairly simple discussion, but an important one nonetheless. XSD schemas define XML document structures, and you can use XSD schemas to specify the format of XML documents generated during serialization.

Using XSD Schemas with Serialization

We discussed XSD schemas in great detail in the previous chapter. As you know, an XSD schema describes the structure and allowable content in a family of related XML documents.

XSD schemas have an important role to play in the serialization process. You can use an XSD schema to ensure that objects are serialized into a particular XML grammar. This is important if your application needs to generate serialized data that complies with an industry-wide or in-house XML document structure.

There are two different ways to use XSD schemas to influence serialization. Here is a brief summary – details follow shortly:

❑   If you already have a class definition for serializable objects, the class describes how XML documents will appear when instances are serialized. If you need to let other developers know the structure of this XML document, you can generate an XSD schema from the class definition. You use the XSD Generator tool to generate this XSD schema. The XSD Generator tool takes into account all the `public` fields and properties in the class definition, plus any .NET Framework attributes in the class. Using this information, the XSD Generator can "reverse engineer" an XSD schema definition to describe the XML document structure obtained during serialization.

❑   Now consider the reverse scenario, where you have to serialize an object into a preordained XML document structure. For example, imagine there is some sort of industry standard for the XML document structure, and your objects must be serialized into this format. In this situation, you must carefully design your class so that it generates the correct XML during serialization. As you saw in the previous sections, this can be quite a tricky task. Fortunately, the XSD Generator tool comes to the rescue again. You can use this tool to generate a class definition in C#, VB .NET, or Jscript .NET, to comply with a prescribed XSD schema during serialization.

Generating an XSD Schema from a Class

To generate an XSD schema from a serializable class, use the XSD Generator tool as follows at the Windows Command Prompt:

>xsd {file.dll | file.exe} [/outputdir:directory] [/type:typename [...]]

The default installation folder is `C:\Program Files\Microsoft.NET\FrameworkSDK\Bin`.

As this syntax shows, you provide the name of a .DLL or .EXE assembly that contains serializable class definitions. The /type parameter is optional, and enables you to select specific class types that you wish to be expressed in the XSD schema. If you don't specify the /type parameter, the XSD Generator tool will parse all classes in the assembly and generate an XSD schema that encompasses all these classes. The generated XSD schema is named schema0.xsd.

Example of Generating an XSD Schema from a Class

As an example, we'll use the Employee, Address, and Manager classes from earlier in this chapter – see the section, *Serializing and Deserializing Complex Objects*, for details. You can download the sample applications from the following folders:

- ❑ C# folder: Chapter7\SerializeComplexCS
- ❑ VB .NET folder: Chapter7\SerializeComplexVB

We'll begin with the Employee class. To generate XSD schema rules for the Employee class, follow these steps:

- ❑ Open a Windows Command Prompt.
- ❑ Navigate to the folder that contains the executable file for the sample application. In C#, the executable file is located in the bin\Debug subfolder. In VB .NET, the executable file is located in the bin subfolder.
- ❑ Type the following command, to run the XSD Generator tool (specify the name of the executable file as SerializeComplexCS.exe or SerializeComplexVB.exe, depending on whether you are using the C# or VB .NET sample application):

>xsd SerializeComplexCS.exe /type:Employee

or

>xsd SerializeComplexVB.exe /type:Employee

The XSD Generator creates the following XSD schema. The fields in the class map to <element> definitions in the XSD schema. Notice that the JobStatusType enumeration maps to a <simpleType> named "JobStatusType", and the Contacts array maps to a <complexType> named "ArrayOfString". Also notice the nillable="true" on all elements, except those that represent primitive types (such as decimal) in the Employee class:

```
<!-- Part of the XSD schema, showing rules for Employee element -->
<element name="Employee" nillable="true" type="Employee" />
<complexType name="Employee" abstract="true">
   <sequence>
      <element name="Name" nillable="true" type="string" />
      <element name="Salary" type="decimal" />
      <element name="JobStatus" type="JobStatusType" />
      <element name="Contacts" nillable="true" type="ArrayOfString" />
      <element name="HomeAddress" nillable="true" type="Address" />
      <element name="WorkAddress" nillable="true" type="Address" />
      <element name="TelephoneExtension" nillable="true" type="string" />
   </sequence>
```

```
    </complexType>

<simpleType name="JobStatusType">
   <restriction base="string">
      <enumeration value="FullTime" />
      <enumeration value="Contractor" />
   </restriction>
</simpleType>

<complexType name="ArrayOfString">
   <sequence>
      <element minOccurs="0" maxOccurs="unbounded"
               name="string" nillable="true" type="string" />
   </sequence>
</complexType>
```

Now let's look at the `Address` class. Run the XSD Generator as before, but specify `/type:Address` rather than `/type:Employee`. The XSD Generator tool generates the following XSD schema rules for the `Address` class. There are no surprises here:

```
<!-- Part of the XSD schema, showing rules for Address element -->
<element name="Address" nillable="true" type="Address" />
<complexType name="Address">
   <sequence>
      <element name="Street" nillable="true" type="string" />
      <element name="Area" nillable="true" type="string" />
      <element name="City" nillable="true" type="string" />
   </sequence>
</complexType>
```

Finally, let's look at the `Manager` class. Run the XSD Generator as before, but this time specify `/type:Manager`. The XSD Generator tool generates the following XSD schema rules for the `Manager` class. Notice the `<extension base="Employee">` element, which indicates that the `Manager` type is inherited from the `Employee` type. Type extensibility is a powerful feature of XSD schemas:

```
<!-- Part of the XSD schema, showing rules for Manager element -->
<element name="Manager" nillable="true" type="Manager" />
<complexType name="Manager">
   <complexContent mixed="false">
      <extension base="Employee">
         <sequence>
            <element name="GolfHandicap" type="int" />
         </sequence>
      </extension>
   </complexContent>
</complexType>
```

Generating a Class from an XSD Schema

To generate a class definition from an XSD schema, you can use the XSD Generator tool. Open a Windows Command Prompt, and type the following command:

```
>xsd  file.xsd  /classes
    [/element:an-element-name]  [/element:another-element-name] ...
    [/uri:namespace-uri-to-generate-content-for]
    [/language:CS | VB | JS]
    [/namespace:runtime-namespace-for-generated-class]
```

As this syntax shows, you provide the name of an XSD schema file and specify the /classes flag. If you are only interested in specific elements in the XSD schema, use the /element flag to specify which elements are relevant. Likewise, you can use the /uri flag to selectively process elements in a particular namespace.

The XSD Generator tool generates a class that encompasses the rules defined in the XSD schema. The default language is C#, but you can specify the /language flag to generate VB .NET or JScript .NET if you prefer. By default, the new class is placed in a run-time namespace called Schemas. Use the /namespace flag to specify a different run-time namespace.

Example of Generating a Class from an XSD Schema

Consider the following simple XSD schema, which defines the required format for serialized Address objects. This file provided in the code download Chapter7\GenerateClass\Address.xsd:

```xml
<?xml version="1.0" encoding="utf-8"?>
<xsd:schema targetNamespace=""
          xmlns:xsd="http://www.w3.org/2001/XMLSchema">

  <xsd:element name="Address" nillable="true" type="Address" />

  <xsd:complexType name="Address">
    <xsd:sequence>
      <xsd:element name="Street" nillable="true" type="xsd:string" />
      <xsd:element name="Area"   nillable="true" type="xsd:string" />
      <xsd:element name="City"   nillable="true" type="xsd:string" />
    </xsd:sequence>
  </xsd:complexType>

</xsd:schema>
```

To generate a class from this XSD schema, run the XSD Generator tool as follows:

>xsd Address.xsd /classes /language:CS

or:

>xsd Address.xsd /classes /language:VB

If you choose the C# language, the XSD Generator tool creates the following C# class definition from this XSD schema. Notice how .NET Framework attributes are used to ensure instances of this class are serialized into the required XML format:

```
//------------------------------------------------------------------- --------
// <autogenerated>
//     This code was generated by a tool.
//     Runtime Version: 1.0.2914.16
//
//     Changes to this file may cause incorrect behavior and will be lost
//     if the code is regenerated.
// </autogenerated>
//-------------------------------------------------------------------

//
// This source code was auto-generated by xsd, Version=1.0.2914.16.
//
using System.Xml.Serialization;

[System.Xml.Serialization.XmlRootAttribute(Namespace="", IsNullable=true)]
public class Address {

    [System.Xml.Serialization.XmlElementAttribute(IsNullable=true)]
    public string Street;

    [System.Xml.Serialization.XmlElementAttribute(IsNullable=true)]
    public string Area;

    [System.Xml.Serialization.XmlElementAttribute(IsNullable=true)]
    public string City;
}
```

Here is the equivalent class definition in VB .NET:

```
'-------------------------------------------------------------------
' <autogenerated>
'     This code was generated by a tool.
'     Runtime Version: 1.0.2914.16
'
'     Changes to this file may cause incorrect behavior and will be lost
'     if the code is regenerated.
' </autogenerated>
'-------------------------------------------------------------------

Option Strict Off
Option Explicit On

Imports System.Xml.Serialization

'
'This source code was auto-generated by xsd, Version=1.0.2914.16.
'

<System.Xml.Serialization.XmlRootAttribute([Namespace]:="", IsNullable:=true)> _
Public Class Address

    <System.Xml.Serialization.XmlElementAttribute(IsNullable:=true)> _
    Public Street As String
```

```
<System.Xml.Serialization.XmlElementAttribute(IsNullable:=true)> _
Public Area As String

<System.Xml.Serialization.XmlElementAttribute(IsNullable:=true)> _
Public City As String

End Class
```

Mapping XSD Types to Common Language Runtime Types

The previous examples raise an interesting question: how are XSD data types mapped to Common Language Runtime (CLR) data types in a .NET Framework application? For example, if you specify the type "xsd:string" in an XSD schema, what is the equivalent CLR type?

OK, that was an easy one. Other XSD schema types aren't quite so straightforward. The following table shows how each XSD schema type is mapped to a CLR type:

XSD data type	CLR data type
anyURI	System.Uri
Base64Binary	Byte[]
boolean	bool
byte	SByte
date	DateTime
dateTime	DateTime
decimal	decimal
double	double
duration	TimeSpan
ENTITIES	string
ENTITY	string
float	single
gDay	DateTime
gMonth	DateTime
gMonthDay	DateTime
gYear	DateTime
gYearMonth	DateTime
hexBinary	Byte[]
ID	string
IDREF	string

Table continued on following page

XSD data type	CLR data type
IDREFS	string
int	Int32
integer	Int64
language	string
long	Int64
Name	string
NCName	string
negativeInteger	Int64
NMTOKEN	string
NMTOKENS	string
nonNegativeInteger	UInt64
nonPositiveInteger	Int64
normalizedString	string
NOTATION	string
positiveInteger	UInt64
QName	string
short	Int16
string	string
time	DateTime
unsignedByte	Byte
unsignedLong	UInt64
unsignedShort	UInt16
unsignedInt	UInt32

Serializing Object Graphs

An object graph is a network of objects that can potentially include circular references. XmlSerializer cannot serialize object graphs that contain circular references – this limitation stems from the fact that XmlSerializer does not store object identities during serialization. To deal with circular references, you must use the BinaryFormatter or SoapFormatter class, rather than XmlSerializer:

❑   The BinaryFormatter class is defined in the namespace System.Runtime.Serialization.Formatters.Binary, and serializes object graphs to a binary stream. This is a compact and efficient way to represent serialized data, which is an important issue when you need to exchange objects between distributed applications.

❑ The `SoapFormatter` class is defined in the namespace
`System.Runtime.Serialization.Formatters.Soap`, and serializes object graphs into
Simple Object Access Protocol (SOAP) format. SOAP is an XML-based industry standard for
invoking methods and exchanging data over the Internet.

`BinaryFormatter` and `SoapFormatter` are used extensively in **Remoting** and **Web Services**.

❑ Remoting is the .NET Framework term for invoking methods on remote objects. When you
invoke a method that takes object parameters or returns an object result, the objects are
serialized using `BinaryFormatter` or `SoapFormatter` (you can programmatically control
which formatter is used – see Chapter 15 for details).

❑ Web Services are an open way of exposing component functionality using HTTP and SOAP
protocols. The .NET Framework uses `SoapFormatter` to pass serialized objects in
SOAP format.

To use `BinaryFormatter` or `SoapFormatter` for serialization or deserialization, you must ensure all
the classes involved are qualified with the `Serializable` attribute as follows:

```csharp
// C#
using System;        // Required for the Serializable attribute

[Serializable()]
public class MyClass
{
    ...
}
```

```vbnet
' VB.NET
Imports System        ' Required for the Serializable attribute

<Serializable()> _
Public Class MyClass
    ...
End Class
```

To serialize the object, create a `BinaryFormatter` or `SoapFormatter` object in your application and
call its `Serialize()` method to serialize an object graph to a stream:

```csharp
// C# serialization using BinaryFormatter or SoapFormatter
using System;
using System.IO;

// Use one of the following two statements:
using System.Runtime.Serialization.Formatters.Binary; // Binary formatting
using System.Runtime.Serialization.Formatters.Soap;   // SOAP formatting
...
MyClass myObject = new MyType(...);
FileStream fileStream = File.Create("MyFile.dat");

// Use one of the following two statements:
BinaryFormatter formatter = new BinaryFormatter();    // Binary formatting
SoapFormatter formatter = new SoapFormatter();         // SOAP formatting
```

```
formatter.Serialize(fileStream, myObject);
fileStream.Close();
```

```
' VB.NET serialization using BinaryFormatter or SoapFormatter
Imports System
Imports System.IO

' Use one of the following two statements:
Imports System.Runtime.Serialization.Formatters.Binary ' Binary formatting
Imports System.Runtime.Serialization.Formatters.Soap   ' SOAP formatting
...
Dim myObject As New MyType(...)
Dim fileStream As FileStream = File.Create("MyFile.dat")

' Use one of the following two statements:
Dim formatter As New BinaryFormatter()                 ' Binary formatting
Dim formatter As New SoapFormatter()                   ' SOAP formatting

formatter.Serialize(fileStream, myObject)
fileStream.Close()
```

This serializes the object, plus any other objects in the object graph, to a binary or SOAP stream. To deserialize the stream, create a `BinaryFormatter` or `SoapFormatter` object and call its `Deserialize()` method as follows:

```
// C# deserialization using BinaryFormatter or SoapFormatter
...
FileStream fileStream = File.OpenRead("MyFile.dat");

// Use one of the following two statements:
BinaryFormatter formatter = new BinaryFormatter();     // Binary formatting
SoapFormatter formatter = new SoapFormatter();         // SOAP formatting

MyClass obj = (MyClass) formatter.Deserialize(fileStream);
fileStream.Close();
```

```
' VB.NET deserialization using BinaryFormatter or SoapFormatter
...
Dim fileStream As FileStream = File.OpenRead("MyFile.dat")

' Use one of the following two statements:
Dim formatter As New BinaryFormatter()                 ' Binary formatting
Dim formatter As New SoapFormatter()                   ' SOAP formatting

Dim obj As MyClass = CType(formatter.Deserialize(fileStream), MyClass)
fileStream.Close()
```

Example of Serializing Object Graphs

In the following pages, we'll describe how to use BinaryFormatter and SoapFormatter to serialize an object graph in binary and SOAP format, respectively. You can download complete sample applications from the Wrox Press web site for this book:

❑ C# folder for binary formatting: Chapter7\BinaryFormattingCS

❑ C# folder for SOAP formatting: Chapter7\SOAPFormattingCS

❑ VB .NET folder for binary formatting: Chapter7\BinaryFormattingVB

❑ VB .NET folder for SOAP formatting: Chapter7\SOAPFormattingVB

This example uses a reflexive class named Person. The Person class has a field called Spouse, which refers to another Person object (or null if the person isn't married). The Person class has a Marry() method, so two people can marry each other. This is how the Person objects will look when they get married:

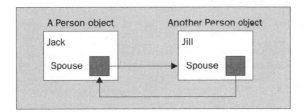

Here is the class definition for the Person class. Notice the Serializable attribute in the class definition, to allow Person instances to be serialized using BinaryFormatter or SoapFormatter. Also notice that the Name and Spouse fields are private (BinaryFormatter and SoapFormatter serialize all fields and properties, whereas XmlSerializer only serializes the public fields and properties):

```
// C#
using System;
...
[Serializable()]
public class Person
{
   private string Name;
   private Person Spouse;

   public Person(string n)
   {
      Name = n;
   }

   public void Marry(Person Other)
   {
      Spouse = Other;       // I'm married to the other person ...
      Other.Spouse = this;  // ... and the other person is married to me
   }

   public override string ToString()
```

```
        {
            if (Spouse == null)
                return Name + " (single)";
            else
                return Name + " (married to " + Spouse.Name + ")" ;
        }
    }
```

```
' VB.NET
Imports System

<Serializable()> _
Public Class Person

    Private Name As String
    Private Spouse As Person

    Public Sub New(ByVal n As String)
        Name = n
    End Sub

    Public Sub Marry(ByRef Other As Person)
        Spouse = Other        ' I'm married to the other person ...
        Other.Spouse = Me    ' ... and the other person is married to me
    End Sub

    Public Overrides Function ToString() As String
        If IsNothing(Spouse) Then
            Return Name & " (single)"
        Else
            Return Name & " (married to " & Spouse.Name & ")"
        End If
    End Function

End Class
```

The following code creates two `Person` objects, marries them, and serializes the `gentleman` object. This automatically causes the `lady` object to be serialized as well, and maintains the relationship between these two objects during serialization:

```
// C#
using System;
using System.IO;

// Use one of the following two statements:
using System.Runtime.Serialization.Formatters.Binary; // Binary formatting
using System.Runtime.Serialization.Formatters.Soap;   // SOAP formatting
...
Person gentleman = new Person("Jack");
Person lady = new Person("Jill");
gentleman.Marry(lady);
```

```csharp
FileStream fileStream = File.Create("SerializedData.dat");

// Use one of the following two statements:
BinaryFormatter formatter = new BinaryFormatter();      // Binary formatting
SoapFormatter formatter = new SoapFormatter();          // SOAP formatting

formatter.Serialize(fileStream , gentleman);
fileStream.Close();
```

```vbnet
' VB.NET
Imports System
Imports System.IO

' Use one of the following two statements:
Imports System.Runtime.Serialization.Formatters.Binary ' Binary formatting
Imports System.Runtime.Serialization.Formatters.Soap    ' SOAP formatting
...
Dim gentleman As New Person("Jack")
Dim lady As New Person("Jill")
gentleman.Marry(lady)

Dim fileStream As FileStream = File.Create("SerializedData.dat")

' Use one of the following two statements:
Dim formatter As New BinaryFormatter()      ' Binary formatting
Dim formatter As New SoapFormatter()        ' SOAP formatting

formatter.Serialize(fileStream, gentleman)
fileStream.Close()
```

The following code deserializes the object graph from the binary stream or SOAP stream. After deserialization, Jack and Jill are still married to each other:

```csharp
// C#
FileStream fileStream = File.OpenRead("SerializedData.dat");

// Use one of the following two statements:
BinaryFormatter formatter = new BinaryFormatter();      // Binary formatting
SoapFormatter formatter = new SoapFormatter();          // SOAP formatting

Person person = (Person)formatter.Deserialize(fileStream);
fileStream.Close();
```

```vbnet
' VB.NET
Dim fileStream As FileStream = File.OpenRead("SerializedData.dat")

' Use one of the following two statements:
Dim formatter As New BinaryFormatter()      ' Binary formatting
Dim formatter As New SoapFormatter()        ' SOAP formatting

Dim person As person = CType(formatter.Deserialize(fileStream), Person)
fileStream.Close()
```

Summary

In this chapter, you have seen how to serialize objects as XML data using the XmlSerializer class. You have also seen how to deserialize the XML document, to reconstitute the object in memory. Serialization is an important part of the .NET Framework, because it provides an open and configurable way of exchanging object data between distributed applications and services.

If you need to serialize your objects to a particular XML document format, you can use .NET Framework attributes to fine-tune the serialization process. You can use the XmlRoot attribute to define the document element name and namespace URI. You can also use XmlElement, XmlAttribute, and XmlText to control other aspects of the generated XML document. You can use attributes such as XmlEnum and XmlArrayItem to control some of the finer aspects of serialization.

XmlSerializer works well for the majority of classes, but it cannot serialize object graphs or private fields. To do this, you must use BinaryFormatter or SoapFormatter instead. These formatters preserve object identity information during serialization, which allows you to serialize and deserialize complex object graphs.

BinaryFormatter and SoapFormatter are used with Web Services and Remoting. For details about Web Services and SOAP, see Chapter 13. For details about Remoting, see Chapter 15.

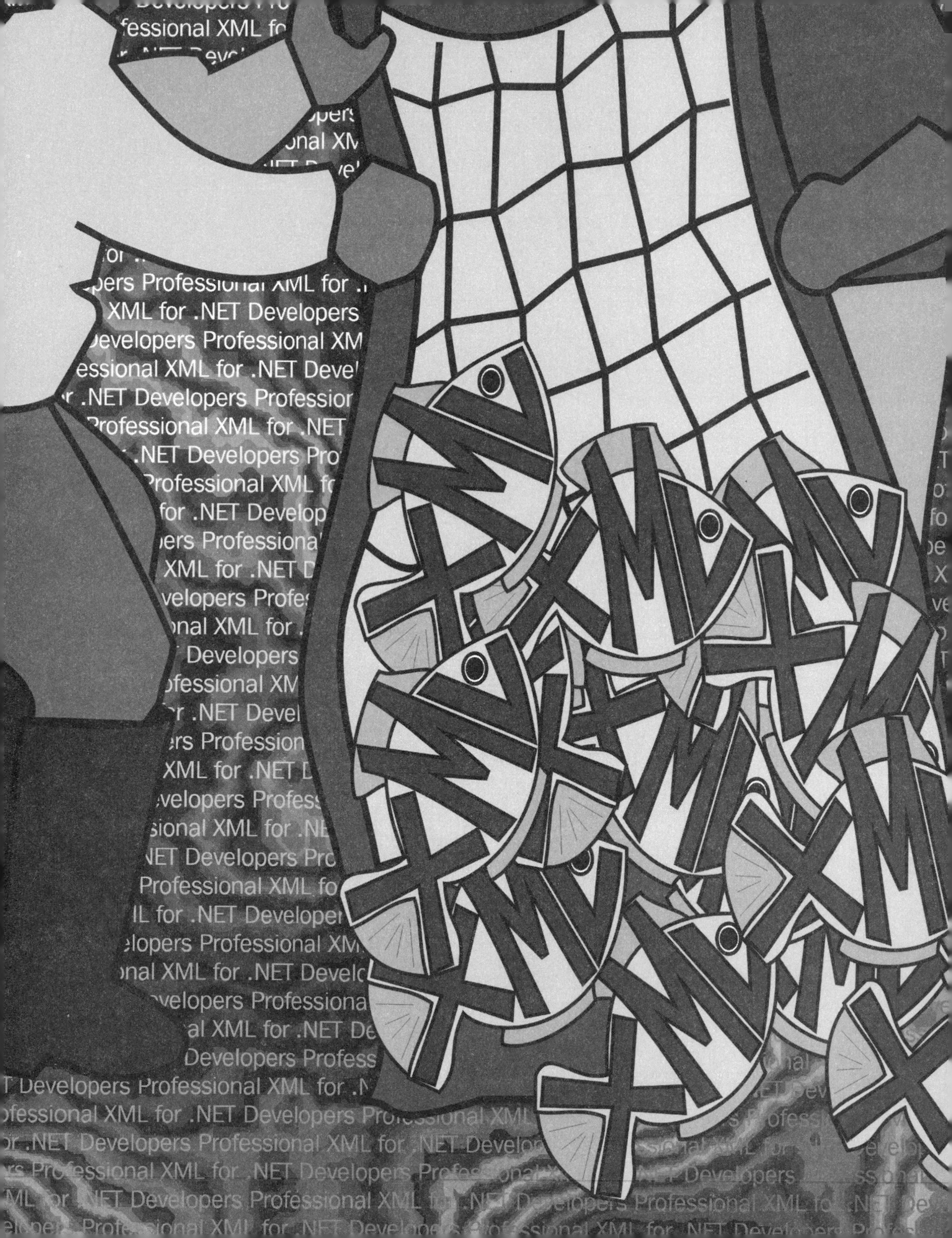

8

MSXML

Many of us were introduced to programming using XML with the release of one of the Microsoft XML software development kits. These enabled programmers to explore the different features and capabilities of XML while we were programming in the old 'unmanaged' world. Obviously, the focus of this book is to provide us with all of the XML support that exists in the new managed .NET world. However, it may be useful for those of us transitioning between the two worlds, to take a look at the similarities and differences between them.

Even if you have had limited exposure to MSXML, this chapter will give you enough background to understand the relationship between managed and unmanaged XML. For those of us who are more familiar with MSXML, we will also look at when it might be appropriate to call upon features of MSXML from the managed world.

The main points we want to address in this chapter are:

- ❑ The background of MSXML
- ❑ MSXML's DOMDocument vs. .NET's XmlDocument
- ❑ MSXML's XMLHTTP
- ❑ MSXML's XSLTemplate vs. .NET's XslTransform
- ❑ SAX
- ❑ Using MSXML in .NET
- ❑ What is next for MSXML?

What is MSXML?

When we talk about MSXML, we are referring to Microsoft's XML Parser and SDK. Unless specified differently, we will be referring to MSXML version 3.0 in this chapter.

Brief History of MSXML

With the advent of XML, Microsoft provided an XML parser for its Internet Explorer browser, version 4.0. Since XML and related technologies were a work in progress, so were the parsers and SDKs provided by Microsoft. During the early evolutionary phases when specifications were uncertain, features were added to each release of MSXML to either map to working draft specifications, or introduce enhancements for the development community to take advantage of. However, many of us kept looking to the World Wide Web Consortium (W3C) for Recommendation status regarding XML standards, and felt cautious about embracing XML techniques in our development.

However, with the release of MSXML 3.0, important behaviors were implemented. For instance, the parser was now totally compliant with the W3C-standardized XSLT and XPath expressions. Improvements were also made in the event-driven parsing approach using the Simple API for XML (SAX). Additional support was provided for namespaces in the Document Object Model (DOM). And server-safe enhancements were provided for the notable HTTP support objects in the SDK.

Thereafter, MSXML was accepted by a growing audience of developers in the Microsoft community. Use of MSXML was seen in client-side scripts, ASP, and middle-tier components.

However, MSXML 3.0 is still admittedly a work in progress. For example, its support for schemas was Microsoft's XML-Data Reduced (XDR) language, which was meant to overcome the limitations of DTDs, even though it would eventually be replaced by the W3C-standardized XML Schema Definition (XSD). At the time of writing, MSXML 4.0 was released – we'll take a brief look at this at the end of the chapter.

Since it's not entirely obvious which version of the XML component may or may not be installed on a given machine, it is important to identify the file names and version numbers for the more recent releases. A good review of MSXML can be found at http://www.perfectxml.com/msxml.asp. Different products might have installed a particular version of MSXML as part of their installation process. As noted earlier, throughout this chapter we'll assume that you are using and have installed version 3.0 release. Note that certain versions are hosted in different DLLs, and it is therefore possible to have multiple releases installed at the same time.

To find out what versions are currently installed on your machine, the MSXML DLL(s) can be found in the System32 directory (usually located under C:\WINDOWS\ or C:\WINNT\). If you right-click on a DLL and choose the Property option, the file version can be found under the Version tab:

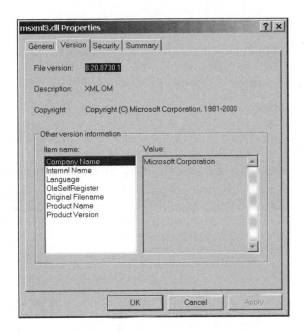

MSXML Object Model

The objective of this section is not simply to provide an explanation of the MSXML objects. As we explore what may be familiar territory for the 'unmanaged' developer, we will also map these objects to their .NET counterparts (if one exists or comes close). This is not a comprehensive listing of all the various interfaces, events, or enumerations associated with MSXML. Rather, the information below targets the principal objects and behaviors as they relate to .NET. In this section, we will consider the objects like DOMDocument and FreeThreadedDOMDocument, XMLHTTP, and XSLTemplate.

Let's start by looking at what is arguably the core of MSXML, the XML Document Object Model (DOM).

DOMDocument and FreeThreadedDOMDocument

The DOMDocument is the foundation of the XML Document Object Model (DOM). This object provides the following capabilities:

- ❑ Load or create a document
- ❑ Gather parsing or validation errors, if any
- ❑ Access and manipulate the information and structures contained within the document
- ❑ Include members for retrieving and creating other XML objects
- ❑ Save the document back to an XML file, if necessary

The XML document can actually be created using either a rental-threaded model (DOMDocument) or a free-threaded model (FreeThreadedDOMDocument). The free-threaded model manages concurrent access among threads, and thus performs a notch below the rental-threaded approach. We cannot combine nodes or documents that are created using different threading models. Regardless of which threading model is used, the behavior of the objects is identical, thus containing the same properties, methods, and events.

Since DOMDocument plays such a significant role in MSXML, we are going to take a detailed look at how it compares to its closest equivalent in .NET, the XmlDocument class. Recall that we've already looked at the functionality encapsulated in XmlDocument in Chapter 4.

Comparing Properties of DOMDocument and XmlDocument

In the first table, we will consider all of the property names of the DOMDocument in the first column. In the second column, the corresponding XmlDocument property (or method, in one case) is listed, if one exists. The final column contains a brief comment regarding the purpose of the property and any mapping details.

DOMDocument	XmlDocument	Comments
Async	n/a	Indicates whether asynchronous download is permitted. XmlDocument does not support this behavior.
Attributes	Attributes	Returns the list of attributes for this node.
BaseName	LocalName	Returns the right-hand side of a namespace-qualified name. For example, it returns "name" for the element <nmspc:name>.
ChildNodes	ChildNodes	Contains a node list containing the child nodes.
DataType	n/a	Specifies the data type for this node. Data type information is not preserved with XmlDocument.
Definition	n/a	Returns the definition of the node in the DTD or Schema. Definition information is not preserved with XmlDocument.
Doctype	DocumentType	Gets the node containing the DOCTYPE declaration.
DocumentElement	Document Element	Returns the root element of the document.
FirstChild	FirstChild	Returns the first child of this node.
Implementation	Implementation	An XML DOM application can use objects from multiple implementations. This property provides access to an "implementation" object that handles this document.

DOMDocument	XmlDocument	Comments
lastChild	LastChild	Returns the last child of this node.
namespaceURI	NamespaceURI	Returns the Uniform Resource Identifier (URI) for the namespace.
nextSibling	NextSibling	Returns the next sibling of this node in the parent's child list.
NodeName	Name	Contains the qualified name of the element, attribute, or entity reference, or a fixed string for other node types.
NodeType	NodeType	Specifies the XML DOM node type.
nodeTypedValue	n/a	Contains this node's value, expressed in its defined data type. Data type information is not preserved with XmlDocument.
nodeTypeString	NodeType.ToString()	Returns the node type in string form. Note that a property of DOMDocument corresponds to a method within XmlDocument in this case.
NodeValue	Value	Gets or sets the value of the node. The value returned depends on the node type.
ondataavailable	n/a	Specifies the event handler for the ondataavailable event. XmlDocument does not support this behavior.
onreadystatechange	n/a	Specifies the event handler to be called when the readyState property changes. XmlDocument does not support this behavior.
ontransformnode	n/a	Specifies the event handler for the ontransformnode event. XmlDocument does not support this behavior. Transformations are accomplished through use of the XslTransfrom class.
ownerDocument	OwnerDocument	Returns the root of the document that contains this node.
parentNode	ParentNode	Returns the parent node (for nodes that can have parents).

Table continued on following page

DOMDocument	XmlDocument	Comments
Parsed	n/a	Returns `True` if this node and all descendants have been parsed and instantiated; `False` if any nodes remain to be parsed. `XmlDocument` does not support this behavior.
parseError	n/a	Returns a "parse error" object that contains information about the parsing error. If the `XmlDocument` encounters parsing or loading errors, an `XmlException` is thrown.
Prefix	Prefix	In MSXML, this returns the namespace prefix and is read-only. In .NET, this property is read/write.
preserveWhite Space	Preserve Whitespace	Gets or sets a value indicating whether to preserve whitespace.
previousSibling	Previous Sibling	Returns the previous sibling of this node in the parent's child list.
readyState	n/a	Indicates the current state of the XML document when loading asynchronously. `XmlDocument` does not support this behavior.
resolveExternals	XmlResolver	Indicates whether external definitions (resolvable namespaces, DTD external subsets, and external entity references) are to be resolved at parse time, independent of validation.
specified	n/a	Indicates whether the node (usually an attribute) is explicitly specified or derived from a default value in the DTD or schema. `XmlDocument` does not *directly* support this behavior. To determine whether an attribute is explicitly specified or derived, use the `XmlAttribute.Specified` property.
Text	InnerText	Gets or sets the concatenated values of the node and all its child nodes.
url	BaseURI	Returns the location or canonicalized URL for the last loaded XML document.

DOMDocument	XmlDocument	Comments
validateOnParse	n/a	Indicates whether the parser should validate this document. XmlDocument does not support this behavior. Validation is accomplished through use of the XmlValidatingReader class.
Xml	OuterXml	Contains the XML representation of the node and all its descendants.

Note the three MSXML DOMDocument events, ondataavailable, onreadystatechange, and ontransformnode, listed in the properties table above. The .NET XmlDocument has no corresponding events to these, although it does have events to respond to Node modifications.

Comparing Methods of DOMDocument and XmlDocument

Now let's take a look at the DOMDocument's listing of methods using the same approach we used for examining properties:

DOMDocument	XmlDocument	Comments
Abort()	n/a	Aborts an asynchronous download in progress. XmlDocument does not support this behavior.
AppendChild()	AppendChild()	Appends the specified node to the end of the list of child nodes of this node.
cloneNode()	Clone()	Creates a duplicate node that is an exact clone of this node.
createAttribute()	Create Attribute()	Creates a new attribute with the specified name.
createCDATASection()	CreateCData Section()	Creates a CDATA section node that contains the supplied data.
createComment()	CreateComment()	Creates a comment node that contains the supplied data.
createDocument Fragment()	CreateDocument Fragment()	Creates an empty DocumentFragment object.
createElement()	CreateElement()	Creates an element node.
createEntity Reference()	CreateEntity Reference()	Creates a new "Entity Reference" object.
createNode()	CreateNode()	Creates a node using the supplied type, name, and namespace.

Table continued on following page

DOMDocument	XmlDocument	Comments
createProcessing Instruction()	Create Processing Instruction()	Creates a processing instruction node that contains the supplied target and data.
CreateTextNode()	CreateText Node()	Creates a text node that contains the supplied data.
getElementsBy TagName()	GetElementsBy TagName()	Returns a list of elements that match the specified name.
hasChildNodes()	HasChildNodes	Returns True if this node has child nodes. Note that in this case a method of DOMDocument maps to a property of XMLDocument.
insertBefore()	InsertBefore()	Inserts the specified node immediately before the specified reference node.
Load()	Load()	Loads an XML document from the specified location.
loadXML()	LoadXml()	Loads an XML document using the supplied string.
nodeFromID()	GetElement ByID()	Returns the element node whose ID attribute matches the supplied value.
removeChild()	RemoveChild()	Removes the specified child node from the list of child nodes and returns it.
replaceChild()	ReplaceChild()	Replaces the specified old child node with the supplied new child node in the set of child nodes of this node, and returns the new child node.
Save()	Save()	Saves an XML document to the specified location.
selectNodes()	SelectNodes()	Selects a list of nodes matching the XPath expression.
selectSingleNode()	SelectSingle Node()	Selects the first node that matches the XPath expression.
transformNode()	n/a	Processes this node and its child nodes using the supplied XSLT style sheet and returns the resulting transformation. XmlDocument does not support this behavior. Transformations are accomplished through use of the XslTransfrom class.

DOMDocument	XmlDocument	Comments
transformNodeTo Object()	n/a	Processes this node and its child nodes using the supplied XSLT style sheet and returns the resulting transformation in the supplied object. XmlDocument does not support this behavior. Transformations are accomplished through use of the XslTransfrom class.

For the most part, the behavior that existed in DOMDocument carried over to XmlDocument. Where there was a match in behavior, the name of the property or method was also usually the same (or very similar) between both classes.

Exclusive Features of DOMDocument

Some clear distinctions can be discerned from the tables above. The following list identifies the capabilities not *directly* available with XmlDocument:

❑ Support for asynchronous loading of an XML document

❑ Event handler for node transformations

❑ Validation of XML document when parsed

❑ Node transformations

As implied by the italicized use of 'directly' above, these behaviors can be replicated through use of other .NET classes. These processes will not be covered here, as they are demonstrated elsewhere in this book.

Exclusive Features of XmlDocument

All of the properties, methods, and events for the DOMDocument were listed in the tables above, with corresponding methods and properties from XmlDocument where they existed. What shouldn't escape our notice is that many of the features of the XmlDocument did *not* exist in its COM predecessor. Here is a list of some of the capabilities available in XmlDocument that are not supported with DOMDocument:

❑ Better searching, manipulation, and status retrieval for nodes.

See the following XmlDocument methods: CreateSignificantWhitespace(), CreateWhitespace(), GetEnumerator(), ImportNode(), InsertAfter(), Normalize(), PrependChild(), and RemoveAll().

Also see the following XmlDocument properties: InnerXml, IsReadOnly, and Item.

❑ New events to control node changes.

See the following XmlDocument events: NodeChanged, NodeChanging, NodeInserted, NodeInserting, NodeRemoved, and NodeRemoving.

❑ More support for namespaces, XML declarations, and future support.

See the following XmlDocument methods: GetNamespaceOfPrefix(), GetPrefixOfNamespace(), CreateXmlDeclaration(), and Supports().

❑   Support for interfacing with other .NET objects.

See the following `XmlDocument` methods: `ReadNode()`, `WriteContentTo()`, and `WriteTo()`.

With the above information, it should be easier for developers comfortable with the `DOMDocument` object to identify the similarities and differences with `XmlDocument`.

> **For more information on `XmlDocument` and related classes, please refer to Chapter 4, *DOM Navigation of XML*.**

XMLHTTP

One of the most celebrated objects made available in the MSXML component is `XMLHTTP`. This object allows us to create a small HTTP client, which can make requests to a web server, and receive responses from that web server. It is integrated with MSXML to support sending requests from and parsing responses into the `DOMDocument`.

A typical approach to using the `XMLHTTP` object involves the following steps:

1. Instantiate the `XMLHTTP` object.

2. Call the `open()` method, supplying parameters (some optional) to indicate the HTTP method, URL, whether the call is asynchronous, and user/password information.

3. Optionally set any custom header information with the `setRequestHeader()` method.

4. Make the HTTP request by invoking the `send()` method.

5. Check the response from the server by checking one of the following read-only properties:

`responseBody` – returns response in an array of unsigned bytes

`responseStream` – returns response in a stream

`responseText` – returns response as a string

`responseXML` – returns response as `DOMDocument` of the XML

The next section will provide code to demonstrate the required steps above.

Using XMLHTTP in VBScript

Let's take a look at some code, `client.vbs`, written in VBScript, that will display a message to the user revealing the contents of an XML file accessed through an HTTP request. To execute the code, just double-click the file. (This will fail if the Microsoft Windows Script Host is not installed on your machine.)

```
Dim xmlhttp

' Instantiate the XMLHTTP object
Set xmlhttp = CreateObject("Msxml2.XMLHTTP")
```

```
' Call the open method, setting the request to be synchronous
xmlhttp.open "GET", "http://localhost/virdir/sample.xml", false

' Invoke the request
xmlhttp.send

' Display the response
MsgBox xmlhttp.responseXML.xml
```

For the script to work, it is assumed that a `sample.xml` file exists in a http://localhost/virdir virtual directory on the local machine, with the following contents:

```
<?xml version="1.0"?>
<root>
  <Message>Hello World!</Message>
</root>
```

The results of this VBScript execution would be:

This object has provided us with a means of interacting with the server from the client. These requests can be made transparently, allowing us to provide a level of streaming data from the server. However, use of this object has many possibilities, and many developers have even used it in non-XML-related situations!

Given its popularity, the next question to be answered is: Does .NET provide a counterpart to the features mentioned above?

Comparing XMLHTTP to Classes in the System.Net Namespace

Although there is no direct class in the .NET library to compare `XMLHTTP` to, there are several classes that can still give us similar behavior. In particular, here we are going to take a quick look at the following classes:

❑   `WebRequest`

❑   `HttpWebRequest`

❑   `HttpWebResponse`

We'll investigate how we could use these classes from the `System.Net` namespace in our .NET programs to mimic what `XMLHTTP` is capable of doing.

A similar step-by-step approach is typically used to make an HTTP request. The steps are:

1.   Instantiate an `HttpWebRequest` object by calling the static (shared in VB. NET) `Create()` method of the `WebRequest` class.

2.   Optionally set HTTP request attributes such as method type, custom headers, or other credentials.

3. Invoke the request by calling either the GetResponse() (synchronous) or the BeginGetResponse() (asynchronous) method of the HttpWebRequest object. This returns an HttpWebResponse object.

4. Extract information from the HttpWebResponse object created in Step 3. This is likely to involve calling the GetResponseStream() method of the HttpWebResponse object to capture the body of the response.

5. Finally, call the Close() method of either the HttpWebResponse or Stream object to release the connection for reuse.

Given the same example situation presented for using XMLHTTP in VBScript, let's see how to accomplish the same behavior using .NET. The below example, XMLHTTPExample, is provided in both C# (.cs) and VB .NET (.vb):

```csharp
// C#
using System;
using System.Net;
using System.Xml;
using System.Windows.Forms;

namespace Wrox.Samples.MSXML
{
  public class XMLHTTPExample
  {
    public static void Main()
    {
      string site="http://localhost/virdir/sample.xml";

      // Instantiate HttpWebRequest object by calling the static
      // Create() method of the WebRequest object.
      HttpWebRequest req = (HttpWebRequest)WebRequest.Create(site);

      // Capture the HttpWebResponse object by calling the
      // GetResponse() method of the HttpWebRequest object.
      HttpWebResponse rsp = (HttpWebResponse)req.GetResponse();

      // Create and populate XmlDocument with response stream.
      XmlDocument xd = new XmlDocument();
      xd.Load(rsp.GetResponseStream());

      // Close the response stream to release the connection.
      rsp.Close();

      // Display contents of XML in message box.
      MessageBox.Show(xd.OuterXml);
    }
  }
}
```

```vbnet
' VB .NET
Option Explicit On
Option Strict On

Imports System
Imports System.Net
Imports System.Xml
```

```
Imports System.Windows.Forms

Namespace Wrox.Samples.MSXML
  Public Class XMLHTTPExample
    Shared Sub Main
      Dim site As String = "http://localhost/virdir/sample.xml"

      ' Instantiate HttpWebRequest object by calling the shared
      ' Create() function of the WebRequest object.
      Dim req As HttpWebRequest = _
        CType(WebRequest.Create(site), HttpWebRequest)

      ' Capture the HttpWebResponse object by calling the
      ' GetResponse() function of the HttpWebRequest object.
      Dim rsp As HttpWebResponse = _
        CType(req.GetResponse(), HttpWebResponse)

      ' Create and populate XmlDocument with response stream.
      Dim xd As XmlDocument = New XmlDocument()
      xd.Load(rsp.GetResponseStream())

      ' Close the response stream to release the connection.
      rsp.Close()

      ' Display contents of XML in message box.
      MessageBox.Show(xd.OuterXml)

    End Sub
  End Class
End Namespace
```

When compiling the examples above, references need to be set to the System.dll, System.Xml.dll, and System.Windows.Forms.dll (for the MessageBox). When either of the examples is compiled and executed, the following message box appears:

Because the XMLHTTP object is packaged in with the XML parser, it shouldn't surprise us to see that additional support for XML was provided directly in the class. An example of this is seen in the responseXML property, which returns a parsed DOMDocument contained in the body of the HTTP response.

In .NET, the HttpWebResponse object does not have a corresponding method to return an XmlDocument. However, as our above code examples demonstrate, by passing the response stream into the Load() method of XmlDocument, the same behavior can be realized.

XSLTemplate

The MSXML XSLTemplate object provides a compiled, cached XSLT stylesheet. This is provided as an alternative to using the transformNodeToObject() and transformNode() methods of the DOMDocument, especially when executed within an iterative process. The reason for this is that the template rules and parse tree are not retained in memory between method calls. Therefore, to improve performance, the XSLTemplate object provides caching of a compiled XSLT stylesheet to be reused throughout the application.

281

The actual transformation is accomplished by creating an IXSLProcessor object, which is returned by calling the createProcessor() method of XSLTemplate. The IXSLProcessor contains methods to gather source and output information to complete the transformation.

The usual process for using this object is the following:

1. Synchronously load the XSLT stylesheet into a FreeThreadedDOMDocument object

2. Instantiate an XSLTemplate object

3. Set the stylesheet property of the XSLTemplate object to the documentElement property of the FreeThreadedDOMDocument object containing the XSLT stylesheet

4. Create an XSLProcessor object to manage the transformation by calling the createProcessor() method of the XSLTemplate object

5. Assign the source XML node to the input property of the XSLProcessor object

6. Invoke the transformation by calling the transform() method of the XSLProcessor object

7. Obtain the results of transformation from the output property of the XSLProcessor object

The next section demonstrates the above steps using JavaScript.

Using XSLTemplate in JavaScript

The following HTML page, transform.html, contains a <script> element to implement the steps stated above:

```
<html>
<head>
<script type="text/javascript">
<!--
  function doTransform()
  {
    // Create FreeThreadedDOMDocument
    var oStyleSheet = new ActiveXObject("MSXML2.FreeThreadedDOMDocument");

    // Load the XSLT stylesheet
    oStyleSheet.async = false;
    oStyleSheet.load("xslt.xsl");

    // Create the XSLTemplate object
    var oXSLT = new ActiveXObject("MSXML2.XSLTemplate");

    // Link XSLT stylesheet to XSLTemplate object
    oXSLT.stylesheet = oStyleSheet.documentElement;

    // Create the XSLProcessor object
    var oXSLTProc = oXSLT.createProcessor();

    // Load XML source in DOMDocument
    var oXMLSource = new ActiveXObject("MSXML2.DOMDocument");
```

```
        oXMLSource.async = false;
        oXMLSource.load("regions.xml");

        // Add a global parameter
        oXSLTProc.addParameter("TableOnly", "Yes", "");

        // Assign XML source to XSLProcessor object
        oXSLTProc.input = oXMLSource;

        // Invoke the transformation
        oXSLTProc.transform();

        // Use output of transformation
        results.innerHTML = oXSLTProc.output;
    }
-->
</script>
</head>

<body onload="doTransform()">
<div id="results" />
</body>

</html>
```

The script references the stylesheet xslt.xsl, the contents of which are:

```
<?xml version="1.0" encoding="UTF-8" ?>
<xsl:stylesheet xmlns:xsl="http://www.w3.org/1999/XSL/Transform" version="1.0">
  <xsl:output method="html"/>
  <xsl:param name="TableOnly" select="'Yes'" />

  <xsl:template match="/">
    <xsl:choose>
      <xsl:when test="$TableOnly='No'">
        <xsl:call-template name="HTML" />
      </xsl:when>
      <xsl:otherwise>
        <xsl:call-template name="Table" />
      </xsl:otherwise>
    </xsl:choose>
  </xsl:template>

  <xsl:template name="HTML">
    <html>
    <head>
      <title>XSLT Example</title>
    </head>
    <body>
      <xsl:call-template name="Table" />
    </body>
    </html>
  </xsl:template>

  <xsl:template name="Table">
    <h1>Regions</h1>
    <table border="1">
      <tr>
        <th>Number</th>
```

```
        <th>Description</th>
      </tr>
      <xsl:apply-templates select="//region" />
    </table>
  </xsl:template>

  <xsl:template match="region">
    <tr>
      <td><xsl:value-of select="number" /></td>
      <td><xsl:value-of select="description" /></td>
    </tr>
  </xsl:template>

</xsl:stylesheet>
```

The above stylesheet is designed to transform `<region>` elements in the source document, `regions.xml`:

```
<?xml version="1.0"?>
<regions>
  <region>
    <number>1</number>
    <description>North</description>
  </region>
  <region>
    <number>2</number>
    <description>South</description>
  </region>
  <region>
    <number>3</number>
    <description>East</description>
  </region>
  <region>
    <number>4</number>
    <description>West</description>
  </region>
</regions>
```

Assuming that all the files exist in the same folder, the results on the screen when `transform.html` is loaded into Internet Explorer are:

Comparing XSLTemplate to XslTransform

In .NET, the closest match to XSLTemplate is XslTransform (recall that we discussed this class in detail in Chapter 5). XslTransform, like XSLTemplate, allows for caching of XSLT stylesheets, and is in itself a processor implementation of the XSLT version 1.0 recommendation.

The minimal steps needed to use XslTransform in managed code are as follows:

1. Instantiate an XslTransform object

2. Load an XSLT stylesheet into XslTransform object using the Load() method

3. Invoke the transformation using the Transform() method, supplying the XML source and the target output (the Transform() method is overloaded and supports other means of handling input and output for the transformation)

Just three easy steps! Although more steps could be introduced (such as providing parameters), the above list is much simpler than the steps required for XSLTemplate.

Using the same files as in the previous example, let's take a look at how to code the same behavior using the XslTransform class in .NET. This example is called XSLTransformExample, and is shown here in both C# and VB .NET:

```
// C#
using System;
using System.IO;
using System.Xml;
using System.Xml.XPath;
using System.Xml.Xsl;

namespace Wrox.Samples.MSXML
{
  public class XslTransformExample
  {
public static void Main()
```

```
      {
          StreamWriter output = new StreamWriter("output.html", false);

          // Instantiate the XslTransform object (Step 1)
          XslTransform xslt = new XslTransform();

          // Load the XSLT style sheet (Step 2)
          xslt.Load("xslt.xsl");

          // Create and define the XsltArgumentList.
          XsltArgumentList xslArg = new XsltArgumentList();
          xslArg.AddParam("TableOnly", "", "No");

          // Load XML source
          XPathDocument sourceXML = new XPathDocument("regions.xml");

          // Invoke the transform (Step3)
          xslt.Transform(sourceXML, xslArg, output);

          // Close the StreamWriter
          output.Close();
      }
   }
}
```

```
' VB.NET
Option Explicit On
Option Strict On

Imports System
Imports System.IO
Imports System.Xml
Imports System.Xml.XPath
Imports System.Xml.Xsl

Namespace Wrox.Samples.MSXML
   Public Class XslTransformExample
     Shared Sub Main
        Dim output As StreamWriter = New StreamWriter("output.html", false)

        ' Instantiate the XslTransform object (Step 1)
        Dim xslt As XslTransform = New XslTransform()

        ' Load the XSLT style sheet (Step 2)
        xslt.Load("xslt.xsl")

        ' Create and define the XsltArgumentList.
        Dim xslArg As XsltArgumentList = New XsltArgumentList()
        xslArg.AddParam("TableOnly", "", "No")

        ' Load XML source
        Dim sourceXML As XPathDocument = New XPathDocument("regions.xml")

        ' Invoke the transform (Step 3)
        xslt.Transform(sourceXML, xslArg, output)

        ' Close the StreamWriter
        output.Close()
     End Sub
   End Class
End Namespace
```

When compiling the examples above, references need to be set to `System.dll` and `System.Xml.dll`. The three main steps required to perform the transformation are highlighted in both the language examples. Note how the global parameter "`TableOnly`" which is passed into the XSLT stylesheet is assigned a value of "`No`". This indicates that the transformation is expected to return a full HTML document.

On running the above code, an output file, `output.html`, is produced. Opening this file in Internet Explorer, you should see exactly the same result as the `transform.html` document produced earlier using MSXML's `XSLTemplate` object.

SAX

SAX, or the Simple API for XML, is a publicly developed interface that enables us to read data in an XML document using events-based methods. A SAX reader is fast, forward-only, and read-only.

SAX2 is the latest version of the API, and is available in MSXML 3.0.

SAX vs. DOM

SAX does not demand resources for an in-memory representation of the document, and is therefore an alternative to the Document Object Model (DOM). However, the gains in performance or resources come at a price. For instance, SAX does not support random access to the XML document.

Here is a typical list of situations when a developer would consider using SAX over DOM:

❑   When XML documents are large

❑   When small amounts of information are needed from the XML document

❑   When we need to abort parsing

Comparing SAX to XmlReader

Note that there are no SAX classes explicit in the .NET Framework class library. However, recall that in Chapter 3 we compared SAX to the non-cached, forward-only, read-only access to XML documents provided by the .NET `XmlReader` class. At first glance the object model seems to be identical to that of the SAX reader. The difference is that `XmlReader` is a "pull" model, allowing us to read nodes at will. For example, we can skip forward in the XML document to particular nodes that the programmer specifies. In comparison, SAX is a "push" model, where events are pushed from the parser to the application to notify us when nodes are read.

It would be simple to build a SAX reader on top of the .NET `XmlReader` class, but we won't be going into that here.

Using MSXML in .NET Code

So far, this chapter has been focused on how the objects available in MSXML compare to similar objects in .NET. This section is focused on providing us with information on how we can use MSXML in our .NET applications.

Why would we want to do that? There are numerous reasons why a developer would directly use MSXML in a .NET application. Some may prefer MSXML's `DOMDocument` to .NET's `XmlDocument`. Others may have code they would like to slowly transition to .NET, which is currently making heavy use of MSXML objects. The point is that we can do it if we need to.

However, in order for us to use MSXML in .NET, we need to understand how to reference it from the managed .NET world.

Runtime Callable Wrappers

At the start of this chapter, we referred to an old world where unmanaged code lived. In many cases, these legacy pieces of code were known as COM components. How can applications living in the new managed world communicate with such code from days of old?

This is where Runtime Callable Wrappers (RCWs) bridge the gap. In simple terms, an RCW is a .NET proxy for the COM component. It wraps around a COM component and provides an interface to that component that .NET applications can understand.

How do we create RCWs? If we are using Visual Studio .NET (discussed in the next chapter), we could select **Project** from the menu bar, select the **Add Reference** option, and under the **COM** tab, choose the component to use in our .NET project. Examples of doing this are given in Chapter 9, *Extending XmlReader and XmlWriter*.

However, there is also a command-line tool that we can use to create our RCW proxy, which we'll look at next.

tlbimp.exe

The .NET SDK provides a command-line tool called `tlbimp.exe` that generates the .NET RCW proxies. The name of the tool is a shortened form of 'Type Library Importer'. As the name implies, it translates the COM component's type library into a format that is recognizable by .NET code.

In the case of MSXML, we create a RCW as follows. At a command-line prompt, type:

>tlbimp msxml3.dll /out:msxmlRCW.dll

(You may need to check that `tlbimp` is on the PATH of your machine. It is usually located in `Program Files\Microsoft.net\frameworksdk\bin\.`) This will create a DLL in the current directory named `msxmlRCW.dll`. Now, to use MSXML in our .NET applications, all we need to do is copy this DLL into the application directory and reference it when compiling.

> Note: A series of warnings may appear when executing the `tlbimp.exe` tool. These warnings should be read, as certain access points in the COM component may require pointers and thus code in .NET will be marked as unsafe to operate.

We could have named the DLL anything, such as `xmlnerd.dll`. It was just a matter of convention to name it `msxmlRCW.dll`.

The following example, `RCWExample`, demonstrates how to use MSXML in a .NET application. (Create this as a Console Application if you are using Visual Studio .NET.)

```
// C#
using System;
using msxmlRCW;

namespace Wrox.Samples.MSXML
{
  public class RCWExample
  {
    public static void Main()
    {
```

```
            // Instantiate the DOMDocument30 object
            DOMDocument30 dom = new DOMDocument30();

            // Synchronously load an XML document
            dom.async=false;
            dom.load("regions.xml");

            // Write the contents to the console
            Console.WriteLine(dom.xml);
        }
    }
}
```

```
' VB.NET
Option Explicit On
Option Strict On

Imports System
Imports msxmlRCW

Namespace Wrox.Samples.MSXML
  Public Class RCWExample
    Shared Sub Main
      ' Instantiate the DOMDocument30 object
      Dim dom As DOMDocument30 = New DOMDocument30()

      ' Synchronously load an XML document
      dom.async=false
      dom.load("regions.xml")

      ' Write the contents to the console
      Console.WriteLine(dom.xml)
    End Sub
  End Class
End Namespace
```

Both examples assume that the regions.xml file and the msxmlRCW.dll that we just created exist in the same directory. After either code example is compiled (referencing the msxmlRCW.dll), the output to the screen is as follows:

As you can see, using MSXML in .NET applications is not difficult to do, if that is our endeavor.

What is Next for MSXML?

Managed use of XML has not deprecated MSXML itself. As of the writing of this book, the Microsoft XML Core Services (MSXML) 4.0 was available at Microsoft's web site for download: http://www.microsoft.com/downloads/release.asp?ReleaseID=33037.

Note the new name. What was formerly called the MSXML Parser is now Microsoft XML Core Services. What features have been added? Here is a list of some of the major enhancements:

- ❑ Support for XML Schema Definition (XSD)
- ❑ XPath Extension Functions for XSD support
- ❑ Improved namespace management
- ❑ DOM to SAX and SAX to DOM support
- ❑ Schema Object Model (SOM)

In addition, the Microsoft XML Core Services 4.0 SDK ships with better documentation and more code examples.

Note that there is no direct support for .NET code in this newest release. Therefore, we still need to encapsulate it in an RCW to use it (if desired) in our managed code.

Summary

In this chapter we explored MSXML from various standpoints. After reviewing a brief history of MSXML, we looked closely at some of its principal objects, and how they compare to related objects in .NET.

We took an especially close look at DOMDocument, and how it compared to XmlDocument. We also demonstrated how to use classes in the System.Net namespace that perform similarly to the XMLHTTP object. We examined how to do transformations using cached style sheets in either environment. We finally compared SAX to XmlReader.
For situations in which we need to use MSXML objects in our .NET applications, we covered using Runtime Callable Wrappers.

With the release Microsoft XML Core Services 4.0, we realize that despite the overwhelming support for XML in .NET, the legacy of MSXML still lives on.

9

Extending XmlReader and XmlWriter

In this chapter we shall take the `XmlReader` and `XmlWriter` abstract classes, whose purpose and context were discussed in Chapter 3, build abstract `XmlSimpleReader` and `XmlSimpleWriter` classes which extend and simplify them, and then implement these to read from and write to COM applications.

To do this we shall use .NET Runtime Callable Wrappers (RCWs) to implement a client-server link to MS Visio 2000 and MS Word 2000. In other words, what we will be reading and writing is, at the other end, MS Visio diagrams and MS Word tables. In fact, since `XmlReaders` and `XmlWriters` can be chained, so that you just have a stream of parse-events going from one to the other, the XML messages need never exist as recognizable marked-up text, though the XML text can of course be generated on demand for calling programs.

This will have some attractive consequences. Firstly, .NET applications that use these XML interfaces will be blissfully unaware of the complexities of the MS Visio and MS Word COM object models. Secondly, once we have the data as XML, we can exploit .NET's powerful XML-processing infrastructure to raise our productivity. And finally, by defining the data model of our message in XML Schema, we have a specification that is independent of the target application or implementation programming language.

In other words, loose-coupling the link between two components is normally justifiable on grounds of good practice alone. But loose-coupling two applications, by using `XmlReader` and `XmlWriter`, brings extra productivity and power.

Why Extend XmlReader and XmlWriter?

Why should anyone want to use `XmlReader` and `XmlWriter` as interfaces to other programs instead of doing simple component calls? I would break this question into two parts: firstly, when is it worth using an XML based API and, secondly, when is it worth using a stream-based XML interface instead of an object-based interface?

Why Use an XML Interface at All?

As someone with a programming background, it took me quite a long time to work out that, while getting code right was a good challenge and great fun, the really expensive process was getting the data right, and that revisions to a project's data structures typically cost far more in time and money than did revisions to its function. This was, and is, particularly true for the cross-platform integration projects that I've had some experience in. I now view any API that works at the level of individual string or numeric parameters as sadly inadequate for high-level business programming because any change to the data structures being passed requires re-coding, re-compiling, and re-testing of the interfaces, as well as those parts of the system that actually generate or consume the data.

A good alternative is to pass XML documents as parameters. This way any changes to the structure of the data being passed are invisible to the interface code and only affect those parts of the system that really need to know about them.

I've also experienced many different ways of defining data buffers, ranging from COBOL copy books and data dictionary reports to SQL system tables and various forms of structured English. None have been as expressive, standard, and cross-platform as XML Schema, and that, to me, is a major benefit – if we can give analysts the right tools and training to write XML Schemas for message APIs, then we can automate a substantial chunk of otherwise tedious and expensive development.

Why Use XmlReader/XMLWriter for the Interface?

Assuming we have an application where XML is a persuasive option for the interface, when should we use an object-based interface as opposed to a stream-based interface?

The options here are passing one or more entire XML message as strings or DOM (Document Object Model) objects in a single call, as opposed to doing multiple calls for each event in the parsing or composition of a message.

The DOM option is probably simpler to code and use, but may have performance implications. The recipient of an XML message may not be able to start processing it before it has the whole document, and if the recipient is another process – or even on another machine – then it will have to start by re-parsing the message.

By contrast, a stream-based approach requires less parsing and gives greater opportunity for overlapping processing. For example, an application that graphed slowly arriving or slowly calculated data would be able to provide a better user experience than one which couldn't display anything until the incoming data set was complete. Another example would be a messaging application where the task of creating or re-cycling DOMs for tens or hundreds of messages per second has been known to lead to performance and memory problems. A final example would be processing a single continuous audit log of indeterminate length, which can only be done through a stream approach.

So, although a stream-based interface requires greater initial development, it does offer higher scalability.

Project Scope

To complete this project you will need the following:

❑   .Net beta 2 SP2 or later

❑   MS Word 2000 SR1 and/or MS Visio 2000 SR1.

To make the project interesting, we're going to invent a "little language" to represent States and Transitions, which is simply a way of talking about diagrams with circles linked by arrows. Since we're going to implement this in XML, we won't need a parser or any of the other traditional clutter – the "language" will simply be an expandable XML data structure. Also, in the interests of simplicity, we're not going to label the Transitions with event labels or list the actions associated with the States – basically, the aim is to come up with the simplest model that can be interestingly represented in both MS Visio and MS Word. This language will naturally have an XML grammar too. We'll call it **Flow**.

Here's a Flow diagram for paragliding (I'm not an expert in this, but I can testify that it's a once done, never forgotten experience), shown in MS Visio 2000, `paraglide.vsd`:

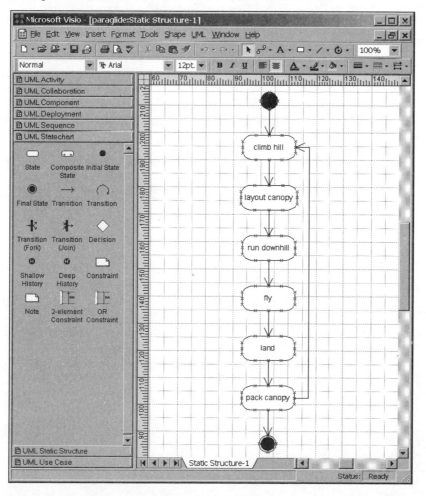

Each arrow in the MS Visio diagram above represents a Transition from one State to another.

Here's how the same Flow model can be represented in MS Word 2000, paraglide.doc:

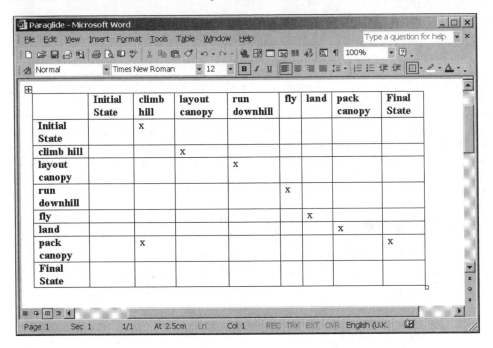

Each 'x' in the MS Word diagram above represents a Transition from the row State to the column State. Note that the table doesn't tell us anything about how the diagram is laid out. We're going to assume that it gets laid out effectively, but with this table we can understand each State and Transition that we care about when reading or writing this model.

And here is the same Flow represented in XML, paraglide.xml:

```
<root>
    <State><ID>Initial State</ID></State>
    <State><ID>Climb Hill</ID></State>
    <State><ID>Layout Canopy</ID></State>
    <State><ID>Run Downhill</ID></State>
    <State><ID>Fly</ID></State>
    <State><ID>Land</ID></State>
    <State><ID>Pack Canopy</ID></State>
    <State><ID>Final State</ID></State>
    <Transition>
        <FromStateID>Initial State</FromStateID>
        <ToStateID>Climb Hill</ToStateID>
    </Transition>
    <Transition>
        <FromStateID>Climb Hill</FromStateID>
        <ToStateID>Layout Canopy</ToStateID>
    </Transition>
    <Transition>
        <FromStateID>Layout Canopy</FromStateID>
```

```
            <ToStateID>Run Downhill</ToStateID>
        </Transition>
        <Transition>
            <FromStateID>Run Downhill</FromStateID>
            <ToStateID>Fly</ToStateID>
        </Transition>
        <Transition>
            <FromStateID>Fly</FromStateID>
            <ToStateID>Land</ToStateID>
        </Transition>
        <Transition>
            <FromStateID>Land</FromStateID>
            <ToStateID>Pack Canopy</ToStateID>
        </Transition>
        <Transition>
            <FromStateID>Pack Canopy</FromStateID>
            <ToStateID>Climb Hill</ToStateID>
        </Transition>
        <Transition>
            <FromStateID>pack canopy</FromStateID>
            <ToStateID>Final State</ToStateID>
        </Transition>
    </root>
```

The `<State>` elements have separate `<ID>` sub-elements in order to allow for expansion; a desirable next step would be to introduce `<Action>` sub-elements. Each `<Transition>` element contains one `<FromStateID>` element and one `<ToStateID>` element. This document makes it pretty clear which information we're interested in.

For completeness, here is a schema for the Flow XML grammar, `Flow.xsd`. We're not going to use it for interactive run-time validation, but it makes a good, unambiguous build-time specification:

```
<xs:schema xmlns:xs="http://www.w3.org/2001/XMLSchema">
    <xs:element name="root">
        <xs:complexType>
            <xs:choice maxOccurs="unbounded">
                <xs:element name="State" type="StateType"/>
                <xs:element name="Transition" type="TransitionType">
                    <!-- ensure that we have a valid FromStateID -->
                    <xs:keyref name="FromState" refer="StateID">
                        <xs:selector xpath="FromStateID"/>
                        <xs:field xpath="."/>
                    </xs:keyref>
                    <!-- ensure that we have a valid ToStateID -->
                    <xs:keyref name="ToState" refer="StateID">
                        <xs:selector xpath="ToStateID"/>
                        <xs:field xpath="."/>
                    </xs:keyref>
                </xs:element>
            </xs:choice>
        </xs:complexType>
        <!-- enforce uniqueness and permit referential integrity -->
        <xs:key name="StateID">
            <xs:selector xpath="State"/>
            <xs:field xpath="ID"/>
        </xs:key>
        <!-- enforce uniqueness for transitions -->
```

```
      <xs:unique name="TransitionID">
        <xs:selector xpath="Transition"/>
        <xs:field xpath="FromStateID"/>
        <xs:field xpath="ToStateID"/>
      </xs:unique>
    </xs:element>
    <xs:complexType name="StateType">
      <xs:sequence>
        <xs:element ref="ID"/>
      </xs:sequence>
    </xs:complexType>
    <xs:complexType name="TransitionType">
      <xs:all>
        <xs:element ref="FromStateID"/>
        <xs:element ref="ToStateID"/>
      </xs:all>
    </xs:complexType>
    <xs:element name="ID" type="xs:string"/>
    <xs:element name="FromStateID" type="xs:string"/>
    <xs:element name="ToStateID" type="xs:string"/>
  </xs:schema>
```

The root element has an anonymous complexType definition, which specifies various logical constraints as well as which sub-elements are permitted. These logical constraints are equivalent to referential integrity in databases – they permit us to say that there should never be an arrow that doesn't start and finish at existing cells. There's more logic here than you might expect, because referential integrity constraints are inserted directly into element declarations, not indirectly through type definitions.

The StateID and TransitionID constraints are outside the anonymous xs:complexType because they apply to the root element directly, not through its type. The final constraints are some relatively straightforward type definitions.

We've made this schema fairly strict in order to simplify our implementation. We've specified uniqueness constraints on States and Transitions, and referential integrity for the <FromStateID> and <ToStateID> elements, and this guarantees that the data will map sensibly to tables and graphs. In Visio terms, that means that there will never be more than one cell with a particular name, that any two cells will only have one arrow going between them in any a particular direction, and that every arrow will start and end at a cell. Try translating that into Word table terms as an interesting exercise. For more on uniqueness constraints, see Chapter 9 of the Wrox Press book **Professional XML Schemas**, ISBN 1-861005-47-4, by Stephen Mohr et al.

We will now implement readers and writers for implementing this language in MS Word and MS Visio. These won't be general XML readers and writers, their semantics will be specialized to understand Flow documents. As seen above, Flow itself will be implemented using a minimal subset of XML syntax. Attributes, namespaces, entities, processing instructions, mixed content (text and sub-elements within the same element) or XML declarations will neither be required for Flow documents nor implemented in our Flow device drivers.

Although talking to MS Office components can be very detailed and complex (which is why there's a lot of code commentary below), you will see a common pattern emerge. Basically, you start by getting a handle to the application, to which you can issue COM commands. You then use this handle to drill down to the window or document that you want to manipulate, then use a handle to that to drill down to where you might use a cursor or selection if you were doing it manually, and finally you apply menu options to the current selection or cursor location. All this is rather easier in Word than in Visio, because Word allows you to record macros, and these macros demonstrate which function calls you need to make to the COM object.

Setting Up the Project

We need to start by doing some configuration. It's best to use Microsoft Visual Studio .NET because of the complexity of the application-specific COM calls. In order to give ourselves a simple test form, we'll choose a C# Windows Application project type for our new project and call it Flow Test. Here's the Flow Test form, with four appropriately named and labeled buttons, to which we will attach code as we work through the chapter and test our readers and writers, and a text label, which we will use both to display the results of read operations, and to buffer data to reuse for write tests. This code is also downloadable from the Wrox web site:

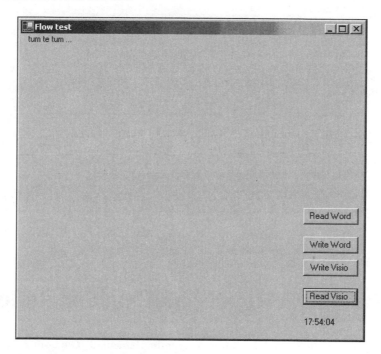

Creating a Runtime Callable Wrapper

To create an RCW for MS Word and MS Visio, go to the project menu and choose Add Reference. Choose the COM tab in the dialog that appears, then scroll down to Visio 2000 Type Library and hit Select, then repeat for Microsoft Word 9.0 Object Library:

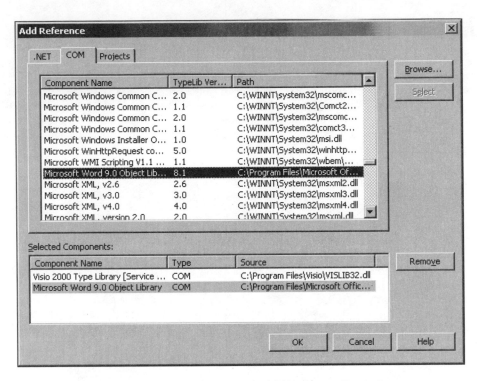

When we hit **OK**, for each application we will be asked "Would you like to have a wrapper generated for you?". Choose **Yes** for each application.

Building XmlSimpleReader and XmlSimpleNode

The XmlReader provided in .NET is an abstract class. Although there are 38 abstract members to be coded for any implementation, much has already been implemented. The bonus is that not only do we end up with an XmlReader compatible component, but it's clear how the internal bits fit together, so it's a bit like painting by numbers.

Since we are implementing Flow with a small subset of XML syntax features (see http://www.docuverse.com/smldev/minxml.html for a suitably succinct specification of Minimal XML) we can implement most of these member functions or accessors with stubs. Even so, we don't want to do this once each for the MS Visio reader and the MS Word reader, so we'll build an intermediate abstract class called XmlSimpleReader, which we'll add to the project as a C# file with that name.

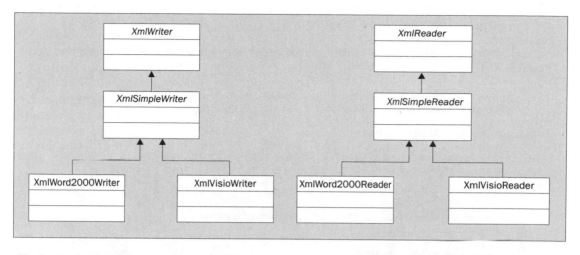

The basic idea behind an `XmlReader` is that it should buffer and report a series of nodes. These nodes reflect the process of parsing an XML document, so there are node types for Element, Text, and EndElement, as well as for Attribute, CDATA, Processing Instruction, and Notation (which we are not interested in, and will be absent from our documents). The `XmlReader` also records how deep it is in the XML element stack. Apart from functionality to do with the current node, it also provides helper functions to skip nodes or move to the next node of a particular type, and to report the XML content of the current element.

Let's take a look at the code, with the repetitive bits stripped out (the complete class can be downloaded as `XmlSimpleReader.cs`) and with some commentary inserted:

```
using System;
using System.Xml;
using System.Text;

namespace Flow
{
    ///<summary>
    ///   provide code stubs for any XmlReader features
    ///   not needed in Minimal XML.
    ///</summary>
    public abstract class XmlSimpleReader: XmlReader
    {
```

The following flags and states are scoped as `protected` because they have to be accessible to classes that implement this class:

```
    protected ReadState state = ReadState.Initial;
    protected int depth = 0;
```

`int depth` is the obvious basis for the required `Depth` accessor, which will be updated by the application-specific `Read()` method, and read by `ReadInnerXml()` and `ReadOuterXml()` in this class. If accessors are new to you, just think of them of object features that can be implemented as if they were methods but used as if they were variables. The `Depth` accessor is going to tell us when we've got back to an XML-nesting level that we started from, or when we've got back to the root:

```
        protected XmlSimpleNode currentNode;
```

XmlSimpleNode is a separate class used to return nodes from application-specific implementations, and is described below:

```
    protected XmlNameTable xnt = new NameTable();
    protected XmlNodeType nodeType = XmlNodeType.None;

    public XmlSimpleReader():
      base(){}
    ///<summary>AttributeCount is always zero</summary>
    override public int AttributeCount
    {
      get{return 0;}
    }
    ///<summary>BaseURI is always empty</summary>
    override public string BaseURI
    {
      get{return String.Empty;}
    }
    ///<summary>set state to closed</summary>
    override public void Close()
    {
      state = ReadState.Closed;
    }
```

We have dropped twenty three similar stub functions dropped for clarity.

The Read() function below is left abstract to document the fact that it needs to be coded in application-specific implementations. This function is where the rubber meets the road:

```
    ///<summary>make the signature visible</summary>
    abstract override public bool Read();

    ///<summary>no attributes</summary>
    override public bool ReadAttributeValue()
    {
      return false;
    }
```

ReadInnerXml() and ReadOuterXml() have to be implemented, but need not know anything about specific external applications provided that Read() updates currentNode with an XmlSimpleNode. Both require the XmlReader to be positioned on an element or attribute, but since we've already excluded the use of attributes we only need to test that we're on an element:

```
    ///<summary>loop through current element content</summary>
    override public string ReadInnerXml()
    {
      // return empty string unless node type is an element or attribute
      if (this.currentNode.nodeType != XmlNodeType.Element)
      {
        return String.Empty;
      }
      else
      {
```

We're on the right kind of node, so we need to generate a single XML string for the current element's content. First, we'll get a `StringBuilder` and note the current depth of element nesting:

```
StringBuilder xml = new StringBuilder();
int d = this.Depth;
```

Next we're going to keep reading nodes until we've come back to our current depth, adding open element tags, text, and close element tags. Of course, we've guaranteed that we won't meet any other types of nodes, which means we only need a three-way `switch` structure inside the loop to cope with the three node types:

```
// read each node in the tree
do
{
  switch (this.currentNode.nodeType)
  {
    case XmlNodeType.Element:
      if (this.depth > d)
        xml.Append("<" + currentNode.text + ">");
      break;
    case XmlNodeType.Text:
      xml.Append(currentNode.text);
      break;
    case XmlNodeType.EndElement:
      if (this.depth > d)
        xml.Append("</" + currentNode.text + ">");
      break;
  }
} while (this.depth >= d & this.Read());
```

Finally, we'll return the contents of our `StringBuilder` as a string:

```
    return xml.ToString();
  }
}
```

`ReadOuterXml()` is substantially similar to `ReadInnerXml()`, except that we no longer have to exclude the start and end tags for the current element.

```
///<summary>loop through current element tags and content</summary>
override public string ReadOuterXml()
{
  // return empty string unless node type is an element or attribute
  if (this.currentNode.nodeType != XmlNodeType.Element)
  {
    return String.Empty;
  }
  else
  {
    StringBuilder xml = new StringBuilder();
    int d = this.Depth;

    // read each node in the tree
    do
    {
```

```
        switch (this.currentNode.nodeType)
        {
          case XmlNodeType.Element:
            xml.Append("<" + currentNode.text + ">");
            break;
          case XmlNodeType.Text:
            xml.Append(currentNode.text);
            break;
          case XmlNodeType.EndElement:
            xml.Append("</" + currentNode.text + ">");
            break;
        }
      } while (this.depth >= d & this.Read());
      return xml.ToString();
    }
  }
```

We've omitted another eight stub functions for clarity

```
    }
  }
```

That's it for XmlSimpleReader. There are two genuine functions coded; the rest is simply a matter of providing accessors to state variables, or of saying "we don't do this".

Finally, in this section let's look at XmlSimpleReader's little helper class, XmlSimpleNode. The purpose of this class is to hold the data returned in response to each Read(). One counter-intuitive aspect of the XmlReader and XmlWriter models is that they use the term "Node" to refer to parse-events like EndElement, which are not considered "Nodes" in other XML contexts, such as XPath or DOM. Add this to your project as a C# class, XmlSimpleNode.cs:

```
using System;
using System.Xml;

namespace Flow
{
  ///<summary>contains only a nodeType and a value</summary>
  public class XmlSimpleNode
  {
    public XmlNodeType nodeType = XmlNodeType.None;
    public string text = String.Empty;

    public XmlSimpleNode(XmlNodeType n, string t)
    {
      nodeType = n;
      text = t;
    }
  }
}
```

All this class contains is a constructor and a couple of public properties. The nodeType is an instance of XmlNodeType, which is a supplied enumeration.

So what is left to be done in order to implement specific XmlReaders? Implementations of XmlSimpleReader will have to:

❑ Provide a constructor class that connects to the target application

❑ Provide a `Read()` function that updates `currentNode` in `XmlSimpleReader` with an `XmlSimpleNode`

❑ Update the `XmlSimpleReader`'s `depth`, `nodeType`, and `State` flags following each new `Read()`

We'll have a look at writing `XmlWord2000Reader` in the next section.

Building XmlWord2000Reader

This will be the simplest of the four application-specific components to write. We make some simplifying assumptions, such as the Flow data being contained in the first table in the document. In many ways working with MS Word is easier than working with MS Visio. The key advantage is that MS Word has a **Record Macro** option, which allows you to see how any user interaction can be emulated with COM calls.

On the other hand, the MS Word COM interface does have one peculiarity; a very heavy use of `ref` parameters. We know that when we pass an object, or what C# refers to as a reference object, as a parameter, we really pass a handle to the object. That is, if the called procedure updates the object, the calling procedure can see the changes, although the called procedure can't change *which* object the calling procedure's handle points to, only the *value* of the object. In other words, they're both looking at the same object. If we pass a primitive "value object" then the calling procedure can't see any changes the called procedure makes to its parameters. The technical shorthand for this distinction is "pass by value" as opposed to "pass by reference".

But of course there are exceptions, and C# provides the `ref` modifier for parameters to allow functions to pass back otherwise un-passable changes to their parameters. Since an object handle could start pointing to an object of one type and end up pointing to a different object of a different type, these parameters should be declared as being of type `object`.

A second peculiarity is that several MS Word COM calls have many optional parameters, which you can set to the special value `Missing` that .Net provides for this purpose.

So what we have to do here is:

❑ Open a copy of MS Word 2000 and a source Word file

❑ Provide a `Read()` function that steps through the array, updating the parent `XmlSimpleReader` appropriately for each new node

To start with, add a new C# class to your project and call it `XmlWord2000Reader.cs`:

```
using System;
using System.Xml;
using System.Collections;
using System.Reflection;
using Word;

namespace Flow
{
    ///<summary>minimal XML reader from Word 2000 State Transition Tables</summary>
    public class XmlWord2000Reader : XmlSimpleReader
    {
```

We will define variables for the MS Word application and document, and for common `ref` parameters:

```
        private Word.Application app;
        private Word._Document doc;
        static object missing = Missing.Value;
        static object _true = true;
        static object _false = false;
        static object _wdCell = Word.WdUnits.wdCell;
        static object _wdLine = Word.WdUnits.wdLine;
        static object _wdOpenFormatAuto = Word.WdOpenFormat.wdOpenFormatAuto;
        static object _1 = 1;
```

Next, the `ArrayList` called `nodeStream` will be used to hold a sequence of `XmlSimpleNode` elements, which will in fact be loaded in by the constructor but fed back by the `Read()` function to simulate the sequence of parse events on which the `XmlReader` is modeled. The integer `i` will mark the current `Read()` position in this sequence:

```
        private ArrayList nodeStream = new ArrayList();
        private int i;
```

Next, we programmatically open MS Word and the specified document, then go to the table and start reading from it:

```
        public XmlWord2000Reader(string docName) :
          base()
        {
          // open Word doc
```

If you have correctly added a RCW for Word as described in the *Setting Up the Project* section, MS-Visual Studio. NET should kick in with auto-completion once you get past the dot in `Word.Application` in the line below – this is our handle to a `Word` object, and will be used for all our Word manipulation.

```
          app = new Word.Application();
          app.Visible = true;
          object _docName = docName;
          doc = app.Documents.Open(ref _docName, ref _false, ref _false,
                          ref _false, ref missing, ref missing, ref _false,
                          ref missing, ref missing, ref _wdOpenFormatAuto,
                          ref missing, ref _true);
```

We'll measure the size of the table by selecting it, then query how many columns the selected object has. Note that this only works for columns since MS Word gets easily confused between table rows and lines, so a row label that breaks over two lines is hard to distinguish from two different cells:

```
          // go to States / Transitions table
          Word.Window win = app.ActiveWindow;
          Word.Selection sel = win.Selection;
          win.Selection.Tables.Item(1).Select();
```

```
    // get number of states
    int statesCount = sel.Columns.Count - 1;
    object _statesCount = statesCount;
    sel.MoveUp(ref _wdLine, ref _1, ref missing);

    // start filling up the nodeStream
    nodeStream.Add(new XmlSimpleNode(XmlNodeType.Element,
                                     xnt.Add("root")));
```

Let's get a list of each state from the column headers, add them to the nodeStream buffer, and then return to the top left cell:

```
    // get states
    ArrayList states = new ArrayList(statesCount);
    for (int i = 0; i < statesCount; i++)
    {
      sel.MoveRight(ref _wdCell, ref _1, ref missing);
      nodeStream.Add(new XmlSimpleNode(XmlNodeType.Element,
                                       xnt.Add("State")));
      addTextElement("ID", sel.Text);
      states.Add(sel.Text);
      nodeStream.Add(new XmlSimpleNode(XmlNodeType.EndElement,
                                       xnt.Add("State")));
    }
    sel.MoveLeft(ref _wdCell, ref _statesCount, ref missing);
```

Now, we'll get each Transition and add them to the nodeStream buffer. Let's do this in the totally obvious way, as a nested loop. We'll return to the left-hand column at the end of every row, and to the top left after the last row:

```
    // get transitions
    object _row, _col;
    for (int row = 0; row < statesCount; row++)
    {
      // move down one row
      sel.MoveDown(ref _wdLine, ref _1, ref missing);
      for (int col = 0; col < statesCount; col++)
      {
        // move right one col
        sel.MoveRight(ref _wdCell, ref _1, ref missing);
```

Let's add the Transition if the cell is marked with an x:

```
        if (sel.Text == "x")
        {
          // add transition
          nodeStream.Add(new XmlSimpleNode(XmlNodeType.Element,
                                           xnt.Add("Transition")));
          // add fromStateID
          addTextElement("FromStateID", (string)states[row]);
```

```
            // add toStateID
            addTextElement("ToStateID", (string)states[col]);
            // close transition
            nodeStream.Add(new XmlSimpleNode(XmlNodeType.EndElement,
                                       xnt.Add("Transition")));
      }
    }
    // move back all cols
    sel.MoveLeft(ref _wdCell, ref _statesCount, ref missing);
  }
  // move up all rows
  sel.MoveUp(ref _wdLine, ref _statesCount, ref missing);
  // add final close tag
  nodeStream.Add(new XmlSimpleNode(XmlNodeType.EndElement,
                               xnt.Add("root")));

  // and initialise the currentNode to our first element tag
  this.nodeType = XmlNodeType.None;
}
```

The Read() function is called by the parent XmlSimpleReader whenever it wants the next node. It uses the nodeStream ArrayList to decouple itself from the complexities of MS Word. The results of the read operation are communicated by updating the parent's state, currentNode, and (via the update() function) depth flags:

```
/// <summary>override Read() for our subset of ReadStates</summary>
override public bool Read()
{
  switch (this.state)
  {
    case ReadState.Initial:
      this.state = ReadState.Interactive;
      i = 0;
      update(i++);
      break;
    case ReadState.Interactive:
      if (i == this.nodeStream.Count)
        this.state = ReadState.EndOfFile;
      else
        update(i++);
      break;
    case ReadState.EndOfFile:
      break;
    case ReadState.Closed:
      break;
  }
  // need true, or false if EOF
  return !EOF;
}
```

This helper method is simply a way of encapsulating the logic for updating the depth property of the XmlSimpleWriter:

```
///<summary>update state of reader for new currentNode</summary>
private void update(int newNode)
{
  this.currentNode = (XmlSimpleNode) nodeStream[newNode];
```

```
        this.nodeType = currentNode.nodeType;
        switch (currentNode.nodeType)
        {
          case XmlNodeType.Element:
            this.depth++;
            break;
          case XmlNodeType.Text:
            break;
          case XmlNodeType.EndElement:
            this.depth--;
            break;
        }
      }
    }
```

Finally, we have a little helper function to add a simple text element to the `nodeStream ArrayList` in a single shot:

```
    ///<summary>add a whole text element</summary>
    private void addTextElement(string name, string text)
    {
      nodeStream.Add(new XmlSimpleNode(XmlNodeType.Element, xnt.Add(name)));
      nodeStream.Add(new XmlSimpleNode(XmlNodeType.Text, xnt.Add(text)));
      nodeStream.Add(new XmlSimpleNode(XmlNodeType.EndElement,
                                       xnt.Add(name)));
    }
  }
}
```

We're now ready to test this out. This is how we'll attach a test procedure to the **Read Word** button in `Form1.cs` (note that the method name reflects the button's name, not its text):

```
private void readWord_Click(object sender, System.EventArgs e)
{
  if(this.openFileDialogWord2000.ShowDialog() == DialogResult.OK)
  {
    // load our reader
    XmlWord2000Reader xwr = new XmlWord2000Reader(
                          this.openFileDialogWord2000.FileName);
    xwr.MoveToContent();
    XmlDocument xDoc = new XmlDocument();
    string xml = xwr.ReadOuterXml();
    xDoc.LoadXml(xml);
    content.Text = xDoc.OuterXml;
  }
}
```

Building XmlSimpleWriter

Again, we're going to write a single abstract class to simplify the task of writing our two application-specific writers. The XmlSimpleWriter requires thirty one member functions to be implemented, largely concerned with writing various kinds of nodes. Given the restrictions that we've imposed on our XML most of these can be stubbed out with error messages or passed through to simpler functions. For example, concepts like CDATA are pretty meaningless for any non-text serialization of XML. Having implemented these basic methods we get a bonus. XmlWriter has already implemented WriteNode() for us using these lower-level functions. WriteNode() takes an XmlReader as a parameter and copies everything from the current XmlReader node and below through to the XmlWriter in one call.

Reusability decisions often have to be based on hypothetical scenarios. In order to simplify the process of writing Flow models to our target applications, we will in fact cache write calls to a DOM object. This will allow us to write States to the application first, and then link our Transitions to them. I could have put the code that caches XML parse events into the parent XmlSimpleWriter since it is in fact the same for both of these implementations, but I chose to hide it in the specific writers, so that XmlSimpleWriter could be used for genuinely streaming writers too.

Here's the next C# class for the project, XmlSimpleWriter.cs:

```csharp
using System;
using System.Xml;
using System.Text;

namespace Flow
{
    ///<summary>Minimal XML writer</summary>
    public abstract class XmlSimpleWriter : XmlWriter
    {
        protected WriteState wState = WriteState.Start;

        public XmlSimpleWriter()
        {}
        ///<summary>dummy - only Close() takes effect</summary>
        public override void Flush(){}
        ///<summary>dummy - we don't support namespaces</summary>
        public override string LookupPrefix(string p)
        {
            return null;
        }
```

Here another twenty two stub or pass-through methods are omitted for brevity:

```csharp
    }
}
```

This leaves the responsibility for implementing methods to write text and element tags to the specific implementations. Again, we get a bonus by working with XmlWriter. Some fairly substantial methods, like WriteNode(), are in fact implemented in the root XmlWriter class and do not have to be re-implemented by us.

We'll implement an XmlSimpleWriter in the next section.

Building XmlWord2000Writer

We'll start with writing to Word 2000 since we can compare the results of our write operation with the diagram we originally read.

The basic approach will be to open Word in our constructor, but cache all the written nodes into an XmlDocument, and finally update Word when we get a Close() call. This will allow us to reorder the data as necessary; specifically, to write the column and row labels in the State table before we start marking the Transitions by putting "x" in the link cells. Add XmlWord2000Writer.cs to the project:

```
using System;
using System.Xml;
using System.Collections;
using System.Reflection;
using System.Threading;

using Word;

namespace Flow
{
    /// <summary>
    ///    minimal XML writer for Word 2000 State Transition Tables
    /// </summary>
    public class XmlWord2000Writer : XmlSimpleWriter
    {
```

Assign various objects with common values, so that the values can be passed in as ref parameters – they must be objects because the compiler checks that ref parameters are writable objects even if they don't in fact get updated:

```
        static object missing = Missing.Value;
        static object _true = true;
        static object _false = false;
        static object _wdCell = Word.WdUnits.wdCell;
        static object _wdLine = Word.WdUnits.wdLine;
        static object _wdWord9TableBehavior =
                     Word.WdDefaultTableBehavior.wdWord9TableBehavior;
        static object _wdAutoFitFixed = Word.WdAutoFitBehavior.wdAutoFitFixed;
        static object _wdAutoFitContent =
                     Word.WdAutoFitBehavior.wdAutoFitContent;
```

Several Word variables allow us to open the application in the constructor but update it in Close(), and dom is the XmlDocument that will be used to cache everything until we perform the update:

```
        private Word.Application app;
        private Word.Document doc;
        private XmlDocument dom = new XmlDocument();
        private XmlNode currentNode;
        private string fileName;
```

The following code opens MS Word (this doesn't have any error detection to cope with the case that MS Word is already open), note the target filename, and initialize the parent WriteState:

```
/// <summary>
/// constructor to write State Transition Tables to MS Word from
/// minimal XML
/// </summary>
/// <param name="fileName">name to be saved as</param>
public XmlWord2000Writer(string fileName) :
  base()
{
  // get Word handle
  app = new Word.Application();
  app.Visible = true;
  // get document
  doc = new Word.Document();
  //  save fileName
  this.fileName = fileName;

  // initialize object state data
  wState = WriteState.Start;
  currentNode = dom.DocumentElement;
}
```

`Close()` does the real work of creating the table in Word. First it will create a single-cell table, then add each `State` to the table as a new column and row, then store the offset in `UmlStates` keyed by `StateID`, and finally fill in the Transitions by adding "x" symbols to the appropriate cells:

```
///<summary>
///  write the data structure to the Word doc and save it
///</summary>
public override void Close()
{
  Hashtable UmlStates = new Hashtable();
  XmlNodeList matches;
  string shapeName;
  // create the table
  Word.Range rng = doc.Range(ref missing, ref missing);
  Thread.Sleep(2000);
  Word.Window win = app.ActiveWindow;
  Word.Selection sel = win.Selection;
  // create the table
  doc.Tables.Add(rng, 1, 1, ref _wdWord9TableBehavior,
                 ref _wdAutoFitContent);
  // select it - so now our 'selected' pointer (sel) will reference it
  win.Selection.Tables.Item(1).Select();
```

Note that `SelectNodes()` allows us to use an XPath expression to extract data from an `XmlDocument`. XPath is covered in Chapter 4, and is well worth learning because this query language is at a far higher level and far more productive than navigating the `XmlDocument` by hand. This is one reason why the nodes were cached in an `XmlDocument`, rather than just as an `ArrayList` of `XmlSimpleNodes`.

The other reason for using an `XmlDocument` here is `WriteEndDocument()`, which involves adding all the element close events required to complete a document, but which becomes totally redundant if you are caching to a real tree structure rather than an event list:

```
    // extract initial state and write it
    matches = dom.SelectNodes("/root/State[ID = 'Initial State']");
    if (matches.Count == 1)
    {
      shapeName = "Initial State";
      addState(sel, shapeName, UmlStates.Count);
      UmlStates.Add(shapeName, UmlStates.Count);
    }
    // extract other states and write them
    matches = dom.SelectNodes(
            "/root/State[ID != 'Initial State'][ID != 'Final State']");
    foreach (XmlNode currentNode in matches)
    {
      // set shape name
      shapeName = currentNode.SelectSingleNode("ID").InnerText;
      addState(sel, shapeName, UmlStates.Count);
      UmlStates.Add(shapeName, UmlStates.Count);
    }
    // extract final state and write it
    matches = dom.SelectNodes("/root/State[ID = 'Final State']");
    if (matches.Count != 0)
    {
      shapeName = "Final State";
      addState(sel, shapeName, UmlStates.Count);
      UmlStates.Add(shapeName, UmlStates.Count);
    }
```

Now that we have a table with a column and row for each State, we need to get a list containing each Transition. For each Transition we'll move to the right until we're in the same column as the ToStateID, then down until we're in the same row as the FromStateID, then we'll mark the spot with an "x"and return to the top left cell:

```
    // extract connections and write them
    matches = dom.SelectNodes("/root/Transition");
    foreach (XmlNode currentNode in matches)
    {
      string fromName =
            currentNode.SelectSingleNode("FromStateID").InnerText;
      int from = (int)UmlStates[fromName] + 1;
      string toName = currentNode.SelectSingleNode("ToStateID").InnerText;
      int to = (int)UmlStates[toName] + 1;

      object _from = from;
      object _to = to;
      sel.MoveRight(ref _wdCell, ref _to, ref missing);
      sel.MoveDown(ref _wdLine, ref _from, ref missing);
      sel.TypeText("x");
      sel.MoveUp(ref _wdLine, ref _from, ref missing);
      sel.MoveLeft(ref _wdCell, ref _to, ref missing);
    }
    // autoformat table
    object _tableFormat = Word.WdTableFormat.wdTableFormatSimple2;
    sel.Tables.Item(1).AutoFormat(ref _tableFormat, ref _true, ref _true,
                    ref _true, ref _true, ref _true, ref _false,
                    ref _true, ref _false, ref _true);
```

```
        // save file
        object _fileName = (object) fileName;
        doc.SaveAs(ref _fileName, ref missing, ref missing, ref missing,
                   ref missing, ref missing, ref missing, ref missing,
                   ref missing, ref missing, ref missing);
    }
```

A couple of stubbed-out or pass-through methods follow:

```
    ///<summary>dummy - not needed: we use an internal XmlDocument</summary>
    public override void WriteEndDocument(){}
    ///<summary>pass through to WriteString</summary>
    public override void WriteRaw(string s)
    {
      WriteString(s);
    }
```

Here are the methods to write element tags and strings update the XmlDocument. The method WriteString() adds text content to the current element node, and updates the WriteState:

```
    ///<summary>create a new element provided we're in the right state</summary>
    public override void WriteString(string s)
    {
      if (currentNode.ParentNode == null)
        return;
      if(wState != WriteState.Element && wState != WriteState.Content)
        throw new XmlException("Can only write a string into an element.",
                               null);
      // create new text node
      XmlText text = dom.CreateTextNode(s);
      currentNode.AppendChild(text);
      wState = WriteState.Content;
    }
```

Since we're using an XmlDocument, where the idea of an EndElement node is meaningless, all that WriteEndElement() does is change context to the current XmlDocument node's parent:

```
    ///<summary>pop back up to the parent of the current element</summary>
    public override void WriteEndElement()
    {
      currentNode = currentNode.ParentNode;
    }
```

Provided we're in the start or content states, we create an element node with the correct name, and update the WriteState:

```
    ///<summary>provided we're in element or content mode</summary>
    public override void WriteStartElement(string prefix, string name,
                                           string ns)
    {
      if (wState != WriteState.Element && wState != WriteState.Content
             && wState != WriteState.Start)
        throw new XmlException("can't write a new element in this state.",
                               null);
```

```
      // we don't support namespaces so ignore other arguments
      XmlElement el = dom.CreateElement(name);
      if (dom.DocumentElement == null)
        currentNode = dom.AppendChild(el);
      else
        currentNode = currentNode.AppendChild(el);
      wState = WriteState.Element;
    }
```

That just leaves a helper function, addState(), which assumes that the cursor is currently in the top left corner of a table, and adds a row and column at the specified offset, typing the StateID in as the left and top labels. Finally, it returns the cursor to the top left cell:

```
    private void addState(Word.Selection sel,
                          string stateName, int stateCount)
    {
      // add the column
      object _cols = stateCount;
      object _1 = 1;
      sel.MoveRight(ref _wdCell, ref _cols, ref missing);
      sel.InsertColumnsRight();
      sel.TypeText(stateName);
      // add the row
      sel.MoveDown(ref _wdLine, ref _cols, ref missing);
      sel.InsertRowsBelow(ref _1);
      sel.TypeText(stateName);
      // need to move up one further this time
      _cols = ((int)_cols) + 1;
      sel.MoveRight(ref _wdCell, ref _1, ref missing);
      sel.MoveUp(ref _wdLine, ref _cols, ref missing);
      sel.MoveLeft(ref _wdCell, ref _1, ref missing);
    }
  }
}
```

We can test our new component from the Flow test form with a writeWord_Click procedure like the following. I've hard-coded test parameters for the target directory and file name, and for a temporary XML file that shows how our XmlWriter can be chained with the built-in XmlTestReader:

```
private void writeWord_Click(object sender, System.EventArgs e)
{
  TextWriter writer = new StreamWriter("c:\\projects\\dotNetXml\\temp.xml");
  writer.WriteLine(content.Text);
  writer.Close();
  XmlTextReader reader =
            new XmlTextReader("c:\\projects\\dotNetXml\\temp.xml");
  XmlWord2000Writer xwr =
            new XmlWord2000Writer("c:\\projects\\dotNetXml\\temp.doc");
  xwr.WriteNode(reader, false);
  xwr.Close();
}
```

As you can see above, this test depends on having done a read of some kind first, so that content.Text is populated with some valid XML.

Now that we can read from and write to MS Word, let's do the same exercise with MS Visio. This code has been tested with Visio 5 and may not work with earlier versions, in which case you could try writing a driver for another graphics application, such as the open source **graphviz dot.exe**.

Building XmlVisioReader

Essentially, all this class has to do is three tasks:

❑ It should open a copy of MS Visio and the target file, for instance `paraglide.vsd`, which is shown in the earlier diagram

❑ It should then load the shapes in the current page into an array

❑ Finally, it should provide a `Read()` function that steps through the array, updating the parent `XmlSimpleReader` appropriately for each new node

Let's look at the at our new class, `XmlVisioReader.cs`:

```
using System;
using System.Xml;
using System.Collections;

namespace Flow
{
    ///<summary>minimal XML reader from Visio UML State diagrams</summary>
    public class XmlVisioReader : XmlSimpleReader
    {
        private Visio.Application app;
        private ArrayList nodeStream = new ArrayList();
        private int i;

        public XmlVisioReader(string docName):
            base()
        {
```

First we'll open MS Visio and the document. We'll make sure that the document isn't already open on the desktop to avoid MS Visio errors:

```
            // open Visio doc
            app = new Visio.Application();
            app.Documents.Open(docName);

            // start filling up the nodeStream
            nodeStream.Add(new XmlSimpleNode(XmlNodeType.Element,
                                    xnt.Add("root")));
```

We'll grab the active page in the document, and start looping through its shapes. We need a four-way `if-else-else if` structure to cope with the four different kinds of MS Visio shapes we're interested in; ordinary States, Transitions, the special Initial State shape, and the special Final State shape.

MS Visio will not necessarily give us the State and Connection shapes in any particular order. This is fine, since no order is specified in the Schema.

The `xnt` object is an XML name table in `XmlSimpleWriter`. This is used to ensure that otherwise identical strings are not multiplied unnecessarily. In other words, if there are fifty elements in a document with the text content **layout canopy**, then this should be result in the application containing fifty references to just one character string:

```
Visio.IVPage p = app.ActivePage;
foreach (Visio.IVShape s in p.Shapes)
{
  // state shape
  if (s.Name == "State" | s.Name.StartsWith("State."))
  {
    nodeStream.Add(new XmlSimpleNode(XmlNodeType.Element,
                                     xnt.Add("State")));
    addTextElement("ID", s.Text);
    nodeStream.Add(new XmlSimpleNode(XmlNodeType.EndElement,
                                     xnt.Add("State")));
  }
```

MS Visio has a powerful and complex interface, which is documented interactively from the help menu **Developer Reference** option, and in an installable help file, `DVS.PDF`, which by default would be deployed to `C:\program files\Visio\Docs\DVS.PDF`. It uses `Connect` objects to glue shapes like Transitions to shapes such as States. Each `Connect` object has a `FromPart` property, which can be used to tell what part of a shape it connects to. Since Transitions are one-dimensional, these `Connects` will have a link to either the beginning or end of the Transition shape:

```
  // transition shape
  else if (s.Name == "Transition" | s.Name.StartsWith("Transition."))
  {
    nodeStream.Add(new XmlSimpleNode(XmlNodeType.Element,
                   xnt.Add("Transition")));
    // search connects
    foreach (Visio.IVConnect connect in s.Connects)
    {
      if(connect.FromPart == (short)Visio.VisFromParts.visBegin)
      {
        if (connect.ToSheet.Name == "Initial State")
          addTextElement("FromStateID", connect.ToSheet.Name);
        else
          addTextElement("FromStateID", connect.ToSheet.Text);
      }
      else if(connect.FromPart == (short)Visio.VisFromParts.visEnd)
      {
        if (connect.ToSheet.Name == "Final State")
          addTextElement("ToStateID", connect.ToSheet.Name);
        else
          addTextElement("ToStateID", connect.ToSheet.Text);
      }
    }
    nodeStream.Add(new XmlSimpleNode(XmlNodeType.EndElement,
                                     xnt.Add("Transition")));
  }
  // start shape
  else if (s.Name == "Initial State")
  {
    nodeStream.Add(new XmlSimpleNode(XmlNodeType.Element,
                                     xnt.Add("State")));
    addTextElement("ID", s.Name);
```

317

```
                    nodeStream.Add(new XmlSimpleNode(XmlNodeType.EndElement,
                                              xnt.Add("State")));
            }
            // end shape
            else if (s.Name == "Final State")
            {
                nodeStream.Add(new XmlSimpleNode(XmlNodeType.Element,
                                          xnt.Add("State")));
                addTextElement("ID", s.Name);
                nodeStream.Add(new XmlSimpleNode(XmlNodeType.EndElement,
                                          xnt.Add("State")));
            }
        }
        // add final close tag
        nodeStream.Add(new XmlSimpleNode(XmlNodeType.EndElement,
                                    xnt.Add("root")));

        // and initialise the currentNode to our first element tag
        this.nodeType = XmlNodeType.None;
    }
```

`Read()`, `addTextElement()`, and `update()` are identical to their equivalents in
`XmlWord2000Reader`, so have been omitted here for brevity:

```
    }
 }
```

We can test this out by creating a Flow diagram using the MS Visio **UML Statechart** template (or
downloading `paraglide.vsd` from **www.wrox.com**), and calling it from our test form. We'll add this
code as a single-click procedure on the **Read Visio** button, which references a `fileDialog` object and
the main text area as `content`:

```
    if(this.openFileDialogVSD.ShowDialog() == DialogResult.OK)
    {
        // load our reader
        xvr = new XmlVisioReader(this.openFileDialogVSD.FileName);
        xvr.MoveToContent();
        content.Text = xvr.ReadOuterXml();
    }
```

Building XmlVisioWriter

The basic approach will be to open MS Visio in our constructor, but to cache all the written nodes into
an `XmlDocument`, and only update MS Visio when we get a `Close()` call. This will allow us to reorder
the data if necessary; specifically, to add all the State shapes before we start adding the Transitions. This
file can be downloaded as `XmlVisioWriter.cs`:

```
using System;
using System.Xml;
using System.Collections;
```

```
namespace Flow
{
    ///<summary>minimal XML writer for Visio UML State diagrams</summary>
    public class XmlVisioWriter : XmlSimpleWriter
    {
```

Like the Word 2000 component, we'll open the application in our constructor but store the values until we update the document and save it in our `Close()` method. These private class variables will pass the document between the two methods:

```
private Visio.Application app;
private Visio.IVDocument template;
private Visio.IVDocument stencil;
private Visio.IVPage page;
private XmlDocument dom = new XmlDocument();
private XmlNode currentNode;
private string fileName;
```

The constructor opens a copy of MS Visio with the UML Statechart stencil, notes the target filename, and initializes the `WriteState` flag of the parent `XmlSimpleWriter`:

```
///<summary>write UML state charts to Visio from minimal XML</summary>
///<param name="fileName">name to be saved as</param>
public XmlVisioWriter(string fileName) :
    base()
{
    // get visio handle
    app = new Visio.Application();
    // get stencil, loading it if necessary
    template = app.Documents.OpenEx("UML Model Diagram.vst",
            (short)Visio.VisOpenSaveArgs.visOpenCopy);
    // get the template
    stencil = app.Documents["UML Statechart.vss"];
    // get page
    page = app.ActivePage;
    // note fileName
    this.fileName = fileName;

    // initialize object state data
    wState = WriteState.Start;
    currentNode = dom.DocumentElement;
}
```

Taking a similar approach to `XmlVisioWriter`, the `Close()` method does the hard work. First, it writes the States to the diagram, turning `Initial State` and `Final State` into the appropriate special shapes, and storing a handle to each state in a `Hashtable`, keyed by the State's `ID`:

```
///<summary>
///   write the data structure to the Visio page and save it
///</summary>
public override void Close()
{
    Hashtable UmlStates = new Hashtable();
    XmlNodeList matches;
    Visio.IVMaster master;
```

```
Visio.IVShape state, transition;
Visio.IVCell bCell, eCell;
string shapeName;
// extract initial state and write it
matches = dom.SelectNodes("/root/State[ID = 'Initial State']");
if (matches.Count == 1)
{
  // get master
  master = stencil.Masters["Initial State"];
  // drop master on page
  state = page.Drop(master, 1, 1);
  UmlStates.Add("Initial State", state);
}
// extract other states and write them
matches = dom.SelectNodes(
          "/root/State[ID != 'Initial State'][ID != 'Final State']");
foreach (XmlNode currentNode in matches)
{
  // set shape name
  shapeName = "State";
  // get master
  master = stencil.Masters[shapeName];
  // drop master on page
  state = page.Drop(master, 1, 1);
  // set the State name
  state.Name += "." + currentNode.SelectSingleNode("ID").InnerText;
  state.Text = currentNode.SelectSingleNode("ID").InnerText;
  UmlStates.Add(state.Text, state);
}
// extract final state and write it
matches = dom.SelectNodes("/root/State[ID = 'Final State']");
if (matches.Count != 0)
{
  // get master
  master = stencil.Masters["Final State"];
  // drop master on page
  state = page.Drop(master, 1, 1);
  UmlStates.Add("Final State", state);
}
```

We can now add the Transitions, knowing that all the States referred to have been added and can be located using the UmlStates Hashtable. For each Transition that we add, we want to glue its beginning to the State shape referred to in the FromStateID, and its end to the ToStateID. This involves logic and entities that are best explained by the online Developer's Reference from the Visio help menu, and by a lot of trial and error:

```
// extract connections and write them
matches = dom.SelectNodes("/root/Transition");
int i = 0;
foreach (XmlNode currentNode in matches)
{
  // set shape name
  shapeName = "Transition";
  // get master
  master = stencil.Masters[shapeName];
  // drop master on page
  transition = page.Drop(master, 1, 1);
```

```
            // set the Transition name
            transition.Name += "." + i;
            // connect transition to fromState
            string fromName =
                    currentNode.SelectSingleNode("FromStateID").InnerText;
            object fromState = UmlStates[fromName];
            state = (Visio.IVShape)fromState;
            bCell = transition.get_Cells("BeginX");
            bCell.GlueTo(state.get_Cells("AlignBottom"));
            // connect transition to toState
            state =(Visio.IVShape)UmlStates[
                    currentNode.SelectSingleNode("ToStateID").InnerText];
            eCell = transition.get_Cells("EndX");
            eCell.GlueTo(state.get_Cells("AlignTop"));
        }
```

Now MS Visio does its party trick. We've created all the shapes in one corner of the diagram, but MS Visio will lay them out neatly using just two function calls. Once that is done we can save the file:

```
        // select all shapes and layout
        app.ActiveWindow.SelectAll();
        page.Layout();
        // save file
        app.ActiveDocument.SaveAsEx(fileName,
                        (short)Visio.VisOpenSaveArgs.visSaveAsWS);
    }
```

WriteEndDocument(), WriteString(), WriteEndElement(), and WriteStartElement() are identical to the equivalents in XmlWord2000Writer, so I've truncated them here, though the downloadable files are of course complete.

```
    }
  }
```

Again, we can test this from the Flow test form. I attached this code to the writeVisio_Click procedure – it shows, among other things, how you can chain XmlReaders and XmlWriters, and it also gives us the XML as a text file:

```
  private void writeVisio_Click(object sender, System.EventArgs e)
  {
    TextWriter writer = new StreamWriter("c:\\projects\\dotNetXml\\temp.xml");
    writer.WriteLine(content.Text);
    writer.Close();
    XmlTextReader reader =
                new XmlTextReader("c:\\projects\\dotNetXml\\temp.xml");
    XmlVisioWriter xvr =
                new XmlVisioWriter("c:\\projects\\dotNetXml\\temp.vsd");
    xvr.WriteNode(reader, false);
    xvr.Close();
  }
```

Obviously, the above test procedure depends on having clicked the Read Visio button in order to put some XML into content.Text in the first place.

Now we can read from and write to both Word and Visio, this is a good moment to give yourself the satisfaction of validating the project by round-tripping a document – from Visio to Word, and from Word to Visio; you should find that nothing has changed except the automatic layout.

Summary

We have extended XmlReader and XmlWriter to communicate the grammar specified in the schema Flow.xsd with two target applications.

Using XmlReader and XmlWriter gave us various build-time advantages. Our components are automatically compatible with XmlTextReader and XmlTextWriter, and with XmlDocument, which in turn gives us access to XPath (and XSLT) support. We also inherited some of our functionality for free, for example, the Move() methods in our XmlReaders and the WriteNode() method in our XmlWriters.

The fact that the objects we are reading and writing are specified using XML Schema gives us a clear specification that will allow them to be transported to other applications and platforms, independent of the implementation language or target system.

By separating XmlSimpleReader and XmlSimpleWriter from the specific application components, we have simplified the development task, and also concealed the fact that we are doing single-shot reads and writes. In principle, we could also use XmlSimpleReader and XmlSimpleWriter to implement components that do truly interactive or streaming reading and writing, such as data loggers.

Now think of the alternatives. We could have written ad hoc APIs into each target application, but then we wouldn't have had an easy way of storing the models outside the apps, and we might have had to do serious analysis and testing to ensure that all models from each app would be acceptable to the other.

We could have written a traditional mini-language, but we'd have had to write our own parser for it. Our language specification might have been in some form of Extended Backus-Naur Form, but wouldn't have had the infrastructure support of XML Schema – for instance the ability to generate a Web Service for serializing, sending, receiving, and de-serializing compliant documents.

This exercise demonstrates that identifying good opportunities for extending XmlReader and XmlWriter will lead us to new levels of productivity, maintainability, and infrastructure integration.

In the next chapter we take a look ADO.NET.

10

ADO.NET

Data access is critical to almost every program. In today's world, *how* the data is requested, packaged, and transmitted affects the interoperability, performance, and scalability of enterprise applications. It is no wonder then that we give attention to the .NET Framework's answer to data access: ADO.NET.

The `System.Data` namespace, which contains classes, interfaces, delegates, and enumerations, is at the heart of ADO.NET. It should also come as no surprise that at the core of ADO.NET is XML. While this chapter is not an in-depth coverage of ADO.NET, it will take a deep look at how to utilize XML in our data access.

This chapter covers the following areas:

- ❑ XML in ADO.NET
- ❑ ADO.NET compared to ADO
- ❑ Data providers
- ❑ The `DataSet` class
- ❑ Reading and writing XML with `DataSets`
- ❑ Strongly typed `DataSets`
- ❑ The `XmlDataDocument` class
- ❑ Retrieving XML from SQL Server 2000

Through it all, we will explore lots of code examples and offer insight as to which classes or methods are best suited for a given scenario.

Role of XML in ADO.NET

As was mentioned earlier in this book, there is much hype over the use of XML in the .NET Framework. ADO.NET is no exception with regard to how it employs the benefits of XML within its class libraries. These libraries provide a variety of classes and methods to manipulate relational data as XML, or load XML data and view it in a relational format. This enables the developer to choose the appropriate design technique depending on the needs of the application.

Consider some of the possibilities:

- ❑ Load *any* XML document from file or through HTTP, and...
    - ❑ Access and modify it through a table/row format
    - ❑ Filter and sort using relational expressions
    - ❑ Use it as the source for data-bound controls such as `DataGrid` control of ASP.NET
- ❑ Load data from a database, such as SQL Server, and...
    - ❑ Access, modify, and persist the data as a hierarchical XML document
    - ❑ Apply XSLT stylesheet transformations to the data
    - ❑ Search the data with XPath expressions

This is just a glimpse of the XML features we use programmatically with ADO.NET. Internally, the data itself is represented and transmitted as XML. Therefore data can be transported across HTTP – not hindered by firewalls. This is especially valuable in today's ever-growing number of web-based applications.

ADO.NET vs. ADO

In order to fully appreciate the new XML features with ADO.NET, we should briefly take a look at how it compares with ADO. Immediately we see a major difference in that ADO is built on COM, whereas ADO.NET is a collection of classes within the .NET Framework responsible for data access.

Any Similarities?

Clearly, the two models are entirely separate entities in terms of programming technique and object hierarchies. However, there is evidence that ADO.NET has been influenced by its ADO predecessor.

Where ADO.NET appears familiar to ADO programmers is with the ADO `Connection` and `Command` objects. Depending on the managed target provider (discussed later this chapter), the ADO `Connection` object corresponds to an ADO.NET class that must implement the `System.Data.IDbConnection` interface. Likewise, the ADO `Command` object maps to a class that must implement the `Sytem.Data.IDbCommand` interface. These mappings are far from exact, but are intuitive for ADO programmers to grasp, at a higher level. In other words, a "connection" object is responsible for providing a unique session with the data source (as in ADO), and a "command" object executes updates or query statements against the data source (again, as in ADO). The methods and properties are different, but the behavior embodied within the classes is mostly the same.

How Different?

As noted above, these are two very different object models. The differences are at almost every level. This section aims to reflect the differences between the objects and their respective behaviors.

The typical objects used by ADO are seen below.

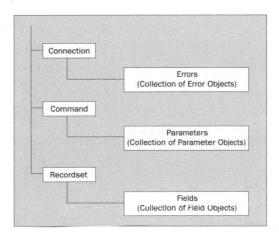

Although some of these objects could act independently from one another, a general approach to accessing data involved creating a `Connection` object, executing a `Command` object associated with the `Connection` object, and (possibly) working with the resulting `RecordSet` object. We also had the ability to set the cursor location and cursor type. An example might be setting the `CursorLocation` property to server-side, or defining a read-only or dynamic cursor. `Property` objects could also be employed to suit the need of a given data provider.

Although the object model was relatively easy to learn, ADO did have its drawbacks. It lacked in interoperability and, to a degree, scalability. With the advent of ADO.NET, these areas of concern are addressed by its use of XML. Let's consider some of the major differences between the two technologies.

Limitations with COM

Because ADO is COM-based, therein lays some limitations. Although within a homogenous environment data is transferred efficiently in compact binary format, what if a client of the data is a non-Windows platform? Even within a Windows environment, marshaling a `RecordSet` involved a significant amount of processing time toward type conversions. It was also the responsibility of the developer to ensure that the data values were recognized by COM. ADO.NET solves these issues by making XML a universal transmission format. Provided a data consumer can use XML, the developer can ensure data access across heterogeneous environments. In addition, as long as all parties agree on data types defined within a schema, conversions to COM data types are unnecessary. This greatly increases interoperability, and potentially performance.

Cursors

There is also no *explicit* implementation of cursors in ADO.NET. Whereas ADO defined cursor types such as `ReadOnly`, `Static`, `Keyset`, and `Dynamic`, these behaviors are realized *implicitly* by our choice of .NET classes when working with data. These behaviors will become evident with the discussion of the `System.Data.DataSet` class and `System.Data.IDataReader` interface later this chapter.

What about cursor locations? The .NET Framework does not support server-side cursors. To obtain this ability, it is necessary to import the ADO type library. As implied, this makes native ADO objects available in our .NET project. Importing this COM type library for server-side cursor support is an alternative for accessing extremely large data sets.

Recordset vs. ?

ADO.NET has no direct counterpart for the ADO `Recordset`. Perhaps the closest .NET class to the ADO `Recordset` is `System.Data.DataTable`. Why? Both `Recordset` and `DataTable` represent a single table of data. However, the `DataTable` doesn't need to be aware of the origin of the data it contains. And for other reasons that will become apparent shortly, the role of `DataTable` is significantly different within the .NET Framework from that of the ADO `Recordset`.

XML in ADO

ADO provided limited support for XML. An example of how ADO made use of XML is in the `Save()` method of the `Recordset` object. By specifying `adPersistXML` as the `PersistFormat`, we could either generate an XML file of the `Recordset` or send its contents as XML via a stream. However, we did not have the ability to define the structure of the XML or handle complex hierarchies. We also didn't have a means within the API to view or traverse the data as XML.

Disconnected Data

ADO supported disconnected recordsets. We had the ability to bring data to the client and drop the connection to the underlying data source. The disconnected data could be modified by the client, and updates were propagated back to the data source when the connection was re-established. This required careful coding on the part of the developer.

What benefits are realized by using disconnected data? Once the data is acquired on the client, local processing is much faster. The precious resource of a connection to a relational database is not kept open unnecessarily. Connection-based locking issues are minimized. All of these features enriched our distributed applications with scalability and performance.

ADO.NET was designed with the value of disconnected data in mind. Within the .NET Framework, data cached on the client is always disconnected from the data source. That is, we do not have to introduce complexity to our code to achieve the benefits of disconnected data. So, where does XML come into the picture? Since ADO.NET incorporates XML as the universal transmission language, we have the option to handle the data accordingly. Whereas ADO provided a relational view to the data, ADO.NET also makes it possible to expose the data as XML.

So what can be done with local XML data? Searches can be executed with XPath, node values can be modified, and transformations can be applied. And if that isn't enough, ADO.NET provides the ability to reflect the changes back to the underlying data source once a connection is made again.

Consider this perspective – could we use ADO.NET to open an XML document (even with an arbitrary structure) and view it as if it were relational data? Absolutely! Since the data is disconnected, we could read or make changes to it by accessing information in a column/row format. Once again, we can simply apply the changes by persisting it back to its source document.

> The key point here is that whenever we work with the data, where it comes from or what it was will not dictate how we use it.

Managed Data Providers

So how do we get to the data? We will discuss how to access XML document files with ADO.NET later this chapter. But what about popular data sources such as Oracle or SQL Server? If you are familiar with ADO, then consider **managed data providers** as the counterpart to OLE DB providers. Managed data providers are the liaisons between our data-aware applications and the underlying data source.

Let's briefly consider the managed data providers available at the time of this writing.

SQL Server .NET Data Provider

The classes for this managed data provider are located in the `System.Data.SqlClient` namespace. The provider accesses SQL Server directly, an improvement over the OLE DB or ODBC layer imposed by ADO. In order to use this provider, keep the following requirements in mind:

- Installation of Microsoft Data Access Components (MDAC) version 2.6 or later. (MDAC 2.7 is installed by the .NET framework.)
- SQL Server 7.0 (or later).

For previous versions of SQL Server, consider our next provider, OLE DB for .NET.

OLE DB .NET Data Provider

The classes for this managed data provider are located in the `System.Data.OleDb` namespace. This allows our applications to communicate via native OLE DB. Currently, the supported providers are:

- Microsoft.JET.OLEDB.4.0   for Access databases
- SQLOLEDB   for SQL Server 6.5 (or lower)
- MSDAORA   for Oracle

The use of connection strings is virtually identical to how they are used in ADO.

Note that the OLE DB provider MSDASQL for ODBC is disabled. Therefore, all access through ODBC must be handled through another managed provider. So, what if we need to access a data source via ODBC? Microsoft has answered the call, which brings us to the discussion of the next provider.

ODBC .NET Data Provider Beta 1

As of Beta 2 of the .NET SDK, the ODBC .NET data provider is not provided during installation. It is available for download at Microsoft's web site at http://msdn.microsoft.com/downloads. Once installed, the classes for this managed data provider are located in the `System.Data.Odbc` namespace. It is also dependant on MDAC 2.6 (or higher) being installed.

Common Model

All of the managed data providers inherit from a common set of classes and interfaces. These common classes and interfaces can be found in the `System.Data` and `System.Data.Common` namespaces. This makes it possible to write "generic" code that is not tied to a specific provider.

For example, observe the following code block (`wrox.samples.adonet.common.cs` – the corresponding `wrox.samples.adonet.common.vb` is provided in the code download), which determines the count of columns in the returning data. It runs against the `Northwind` database provided with SQL Server.

> *There are several pieces of code in this chapter (clearly commented) that need SQL Server's* `Northwind` *database to run. However, only the code in the final section needs the latest version, SQL Server 2000.*

Note that two managed data providers are used – SQL Server and OLE DB. The output is the same, regardless of which provider is used.

```
// C#
using System;
using System.Data;
using System.Data.SqlClient;
using System.Data.OleDb;

namespace Wrox.Samples.ADONET
{
  public class Common
  {
    public IDbConnection GetSqlConnection(string connectionString)
    {
      IDbConnection cn = new SqlConnection(connectionString);
      return cn;
    }
    public IDbConnection GetOleDbConnection(string connectionString )
    {
      IDbConnection cn = new OleDbConnection(connectionString);
      return cn;
    }
    public void Demo(IDbConnection connect, string commandText)
    {
      try
      {
        // connectObject could be either a SqlConnection or
        // an OleDbConnection
        connect.Open();

        // CreateCommand returns an IDbCommand object
        IDbCommand cmd = connect.CreateCommand();
```

```
            cmd.CommandText = commandText;

            // ExecuteReader returns an IDataReader object
            DisplayFieldCount(cmd.ExecuteReader());
        }
        catch(Exception e)
        {
            Console.WriteLine(e.ToString());
        }
        finally
        {
            if (!(connect == null))
            {
                connect.Close();
            }
        }
    }

    private void DisplayFieldCount(IDataReader reader)
    {
        // As long as the reader is open with records to read...
        if (!( reader.IsClosed ) && ( reader.Read()))
        {
            Console.WriteLine("Total fields = {0} \n", reader.FieldCount);
            reader.Close();
        }
    }

    public static void Main()
    {
        string myCommandText;
        string mySqlConnectionString =
            "data source=(local);user id=sa;password=;initial catalog=Northwind";
        string myOleDbConnectionString =
            "Provider=SQLOLEDB;" + mySqlConnectionString;

        // Create an instance of this class
        Common c = new Common();

        myCommandText = "Select * From Employees";
        Console.WriteLine("Accessing data with SQL Server .NET Provider..." );

        // Display the number of columns using SqlConnection object
        c.Demo(c.GetSqlConnection( mySqlConnectionString), myCommandText );

        myCommandText = "Select FirstName, LastName From Employees";
        Console.WriteLine("Accessing data with OLE DB .NET Provider..." );

        // Display the number of columns using OleDbConnection object
        c.Demo(c.GetOleDbConnection( myOleDbConnectionString), myCommandText);
    }
    }
}
```

First, we need to compile the code. Here is how to achieve this at the command prompt:

>csc.exe /t:exe /out:common.CS.exe /reference:System.dll,System.Data.dll,System.Xml.dll wrox.samples.adonet.common.cs

The /out:common.CS.exe option informs the compiler to generate an executable file named common.cs.exe. Note also the /reference option, indicating all of the .dll files our code needs to reference.

> *The VB. NET code can be run with a similar command, using the vbc.exe compiler. The command line compilation of all other files within this chapter is also done in a similar manner.*

Once compiled and executed, this is the resulting text in the console:

Observe the use of interfaces in the code above. Since the SqlConnection and OleDbConnection classes implement the IDbConnection interface, two methods were created to return an IDbConnection object from each provider. When the object reference is passed into the Demo() method, it is no longer important which provider was being used, as long as we just use the common behaviors available through the interfaces.

Of course if we need to use provider-specific behavior, then we need to code accordingly. An example of this will be seen later when we exploit the XML features of SQL Server 2000 using the SQL Server managed data provider.

DataSets

The System.Data.DataSet class was designed to work with disconnected data. Think of a DataSet object as an in-memory representation of data records. The object itself is really a container for other objects, which map to entities such as columns, rows, tables, relationships, and constraints.

With the growing number of articles and books that cover this class in detail, our objective is to explore this powerful addition to ADO.NET with an *XML perspective*. However, for those who have had little or no background on using DataSets, we will highlight the essentials along the way.

DataSet vs. ADO Recordset

There really is no comparison to be made here. As we mentioned earlier this chapter, the ADO Recordset maps closer to the DataTable (of which DataSets make heavy use) or IDataReader (discussed below). Conversely, DataSets have no counterpart whatsoever in ADO. This paradigm shift is the result of the issues ADO could not easily resolve in today's demanding programming environments.

DataSet vs. IDataReader

The real question is: what determines whether it is more appropriate to use a DataSet or an IDataReader object? The answer lies in the behavior of each object, and the requirements of the application.

What is `IDataReader`? It is an interface usually implemented by a managed .NET Data Provider (that is, `OleDbDataReader` or `SqlDataReader`) and is designed for forward-only, read-only, connection-based scrolling of the data. Each row in the result is examined one at a time until the `Read()` method returns `false`. Note that this approach requires an open connection to the database. Until the `Close()` method is called, the connection to the database is kept open.

In comparison, `DataSets` contain objects representing data. The data is truly disconnected, can be viewed in any direction, and can be modified with updates, inserts, and deletes.

DataSet Collections

The three primary collections of the `DataSet` are accessible through public instance properties of the class. They are as follows:

Collection	**DataSet** Property
PropertyCollection	ExtendedProperties
DataRelationCollection	Relations
DataTableCollection	Tables

The collections may contain objects, that contain other collections, as in the case of `DataTableCollection`. A `DataTable` contains a collection of `DataColumns` and `DataRows`. We will visit these collections later in this section.

PropertyCollection

The `PropertyCollection` exposed by the `ExtendedProperties` property allows for custom information to be stored with the `DataSet` object. This could be anything – company name, auditing information, `SELECT` statements, whatever metadata we want. This information persists with the `DataSet` if we should view it as XML.

Here is an example (`extendedpropertiesexample`) of using the `ExtendedProperties` property. As with most examples in this chapter, we give the code in both C# and VB. NET. We'll start with C#:

```
// C#
using System;
using System.Data;

namespace Wrox.Samples.ADONET
{
  public class ExtendedPropertiesExample
  {
    public static void Main()
    {
      DataSet ds = new DataSet("MyDataSet");

      // Add properties
      ds.ExtendedProperties.Add("Publisher", "Wrox");
      ds.ExtendedProperties.Add("Book", "Professional .NET XML");
```

```
        // Access properties in code
        Console.WriteLine(ds.ExtendedProperties["Publisher"]);
        Console.WriteLine(ds.ExtendedProperties["Book"]);

        // Persist schema of DataSet to file
        ds.WriteXml("MyDataSet.XML", XmlWriteMode.WriteSchema);
    }
  }
}
```

This is the VB. NET version of `extendedpropertiesexample`:

```
' VB .NET
Option Explicit On
Option Strict On

Imports System
Imports System.Data

Namespace Wrox.Samples.ADONET
  Public Class ExtendedPropertiesExample

    Shared Sub Main
      Dim ds As DataSet = New DataSet("MyDataSet")

      ' Add properties
      ds.ExtendedProperties.Add("Publisher", "Wrox")
      ds.ExtendedProperties.Add("Book", "Professional .NET XML")

      ' Access properties
      Console.WriteLine(ds.ExtendedProperties("Publisher"))
      Console.WriteLine(ds.ExtendedProperties("Book"))

      ' Persist schema of DataSet to file
      ds.WriteXml("MyDataSet.xml", XmlWriteMode.WriteSchema)
    End Sub
  End Class
End Namespace
```

The console output when either the C# or VB. NET code is compiled and executed is:

In addition, an XML file named `MyDataSet.xml` is written to the application directory. This is accomplished by calling the `WriteXml()` method of the `DataSet`. We will cover this and related methods in more detail later this chapter. The point here is to establish how the custom properties persist with the `DataSet` in the inline schema. Here is the content of the resulting XML file:

```
<?xml version="1.0" standalone="yes" ?>
<MyDataSet>
  <xsd:schema id="MyDataSet" targetNamespace="" xmlns=""
              xmlns:xsd="http://www.w3.org/2001/XMLSchema"
```

```
                xmlns:msdata="urn:schemas-microsoft-com:xml-msdata"
                xmlns:msprop="urn:schemas-microsoft-com:xml-msprop">
     <xsd:element name="MyDataSet" msdata:IsDataSet="true"
              msprop:Publisher="Wrox"
              msprop:Book="Professional .NET XML">
       <xsd:complexType>
         <xsd:choice maxOccurs="unbounded" />
       </xsd:complexType>
     </xsd:element>
   </xsd:schema>
</MyDataSet>
```

The extended properties map to attributes in the schema and are associated with the urn:schemas-microsoft-com:xml-msprop namespace.

DataTableCollection

This collection is accessed through the Tables property of the DataSet. The DataTableCollection is at the heart of the DataSet, because all the data is located in its DataTables. To appreciate how the data is stored, let's take a closer look at the DataTable itself.

DataTable

This object stores data in a column/row format, and provides public instance properties to gain access to corresponding collections. Familiarity with relational database concepts helps identify the role of each collection. Here is a mapping of the collections to their respective DataTable properties:

Collection	DataTable Property
DataColumnCollection	Columns
DataRowCollection	Rows
ConstraintCollection	Constraints
DataRelationCollection	ChildRelations
DataRelationCollection	ParentRelations
PropertyCollection	ExtendedProperties

Note that, like the DataSet, a DataTable has its own ExtendedProperties property, which behaves in the same manner.

Adding a DataTable to the DataSet

To add a DataTable object to the DataSet, we use the Add() method of the DataTableCollection. Here is an example of doing so in C#:

```
// C#
DataSet ds = new DataSet("MyDataSet");
DataTable dt = new DataTable("Employee");

// Define table Employee with columns and rows here ...

// Add DataTable to DataSet's DataTableCollection through Tables property
ds.Tables.Add(dt);
```

Here is the same code snippet in VB. NET:

```
' VB .NET
Dim ds As DataSet = New DataSet("MyDataSet")
Dim dt As DataTable = New DataTable("Employee")

' Define table Employee with columns and rows here ...

' Add DataTable to DataSet's DataTableCollection through Tables property
ds.Tables.Add(dt)
```

In either example, we passed a string ("Employee") into the constructor of the DataTable to provide it a name we can reference later.

DataColumnCollection

In the above code snippets, we left out the code defining the structure or **schema** of the DataTable. One way to define the schema of the DataTable is programmatically by creating or modifying DataColumns. We access this collection through the Columns property of the DataTable. Observe the code, columnsexample, below in C#:

```csharp
//C#
using System;
using System.Data;

namespace Wrox.Samples.ADONET
{
  public class ColumnsExample
  {
    public static void Main()
    {
      DataSet ds = new DataSet("MyDataSet");
      DataTable dt = new DataTable("Employee");

      // Add columns
      dt.Columns.Add("EmployeeID", System.Type.GetType("System.Int32"));
      dt.Columns.Add("LastName", System.Type.GetType("System.String"));
      dt.Columns.Add("FirstName", System.Type.GetType("System.String"));
      dt.Columns.Add("DisplayName", System.Type.GetType("System.String"));
      dt.Columns.Add("Notes", System.Type.GetType("System.String"));

      // Display columns
      foreach (DataColumn dc in dt.Columns)
      {
        Console.WriteLine("Column={0}, DataType={1}", dc.ColumnName,
                          dc.DataType);
      }

      // Add DataTable to DataSet
      ds.Tables.Add(dt);

      // Persist schema of DataSet to file
      ds.WriteXml("MyDataSet.xml", XmlWriteMode.WriteSchema);
    }
  }
}
```

Here is the same example in VB .NET:

```
'VB .NET
Option Explicit On
Option Strict On

Imports System
Imports System.Data

Namespace Wrox.Samples.ADONET
  Public Class ColumnsExample
    Shared Sub Main
      Dim ds As DataSet = New DataSet("MyDataSet")
      Dim dt As DataTable = New DataTable("Employee")

      ' Add properties
      dt.Columns.Add("EmployeeID", System.Type.GetType("System.Int32"))
      dt.Columns.Add("LastName", System.Type.GetType("System.String"))
      dt.Columns.Add("FirstName", System.Type.GetType("System.String"))
      dt.Columns.Add("DisplayName", System.Type.GetType("System.String"))
      dt.Columns.Add("Notes", System.Type.GetType("System.String"))

      ' Display columns
      Dim dc as DataColumn
      For Each dc in dt.Columns
        Console.WriteLine("Column={0}, DataType={1}", _
        dc.ColumnName, dc.DataType)
      Next

      ' Add DataTable to DataSet
      ds.Tables.Add(dt)

      ' Persist schema of DataSet to file
      ds.WriteXml("MyDataSet.xml", XmlWriteMode.WriteSchema)
    End Sub
  End Class
End Namespace
```

The result of compiling and running either example on the console screen is:

In addition, the XML Schema `MyDataSet.xml` is written to the application directory. We'll be talking in detail about the `WriteXml()` method that acheives this later. For now, notice that `MyDataSet.xml` has the following content:

```
<?xml version="1.0" standalone="yes"?>
<MyDataSet>
  <xsd:schema id="MyDataSet" targetNamespace="" xmlns=""
            xmlns:xsd="http://www.w3.org/2001/XMLSchema"
```

```
                  xmlns:msdata="urn:schemas-microsoft-com:xml-msdata">
       <xsd:element name="MyDataSet" msdata:IsDataSet="true">
         <xsd:complexType>
           <xsd:choice maxOccurs="unbounded">
             <xsd:element name="Employee">
               <xsd:complexType>
                 <xsd:sequence>
                   <xsd:element name="EmployeeID" type="xsd:int"
                                minOccurs="0" />
                   <xsd:element name="LastName" type="xsd:string"
                                minOccurs="0" />
                   <xsd:element name="FirstName" type="xsd:string"
                                minOccurs="0" />
                   <xsd:element name="DisplayName" type="xsd:string"
                                minOccurs="0" />
                   <xsd:element name="Notes" type="xsd:string"
                                minOccurs="0" />
                 </xsd:sequence>
               </xsd:complexType>
             </xsd:element>
           </xsd:choice>
         </xsd:complexType>
       </xsd:element>
     </xsd:schema>
   </MyDataSet>
```

Note that the Employee table is mapped to the XML Schema as an element, and all the columns are defined as child elements of <Employee>. The data type we set for each column is mapped to a corresponding data type in the schema.

DataColumn

We can control the XML representation of a DataTable by setting a special property on the DataColumn object – ColumnMapping. This property can be set to determine behaviors such as whether the value in the column should map to an element or attribute in an XML document. The possible values are seen in the following table. The ColumnMapping property is set to a MappingType enumeration:

Enumeration Name	Description
MappingType.Attribute	Attribute in XML document
MappingType.Element	Element in XML document
MappingType.SimpleContent	Text node in XML document
MappingType.Hidden	No mapping to XML document, used internally

The default value is MappingType.Element. This will render an element-centric document as the preceding example demonstrates. Let's look at a revision to the example above (columnsexample) by adding the following snippets (after the addition of the columns), which set the ColumnMapping property for a couple of the DataColumns. This example is called mappingtypeexample.

```
// C#

// Set ColumnMapping values
dt.Columns["EmployeeID"].ColumnMapping = MappingType.Attribute;
dt.Columns["DisplayName"].ColumnMapping = MappingType.Hidden;
```

```
' VB .NET

' Set ColumnMapping values
dt.Columns("EmployeeID").ColumnMapping = MappingType.Attribute
dt.Columns("DisplayName").ColumnMapping = MappingType.Hidden
```

The schema changes with these revisions. Look at how the <Employee> element is now defined:

```
<xsd:element name="Employee">
  <xsd:complexType>
    <xsd:sequence>
      <xsd:element name="LastName" type="xsd:string" minOccurs="0"
                   msdata:Ordinal="1" />
      <xsd:element name="FirstName" type="xsd:string"
                   minOccurs="0" msdata.Ordinal="2" />
      <xsd:element name="Notes" type="xsd:string" minOccurs="0"
                   msdata:Ordinal="4" />
    </xsd:sequence>
    <xsd:attribute name="EmployeeID" type="xsd:int" />
    <xsd:attribute name="DisplayName" type="xsd:string"
                   use="prohibited" />
  </xsd:complexType>
</xsd:element>
```

The "EmployeeID" column is now expressed as an attribute. The "DisplayName" column is also mapped to an attribute; however, it is marked in the schema as "prohibited", meaning it cannot be included in any instance documents. A reason for doing this is when we need to work with data values in our code that should not be available outside in any resulting XML document.

You may also notice the addition of msdata.Ordinal attributes to the <xsd:element> elements. This relates to the original column number corresponding to these elements in the original DataSet.

Note that MappingType.SimpleContent should only be set when no other DataColumn in the current DataTable is mapped to MappingType.Element; otherwise an exception will be thrown.

Before we move on, be aware that DataColumn also contains an ExtendedProperties property, which behaves exactly like the DataSet and DataTable properties. This allows for additional metadata at many levels.

DataRowCollection

This collection, which is accessed through the Rows property of the DataTable, represents the data at the record level. As the name implies, this is a collection of DataRow objects, which correspond to rows in a table. Adding a new row is rather easy, and the basic steps to follow are:

- ❑ Create a new `DataRow` object
- ❑ Set the new `DataRow` object to the reference returned by the `DataTable`'s `NewRow()` method
- ❑ Assign column values
- ❑ Add the new `DataRow` to the `DataTable`'s `DataRowCollection` through the `Rows` property

We'll continue by revising the previous example (`mappingtypeexample`) to our new example `wrox.samples.adonet.rowsexample`. As well as altering the class name, the end of the file should be modified as follows. The code then populates the `DataTable` with a new row of data. Here's the C# version:

```csharp
// C#
    // Set ColumnMapping values
    dt.Columns["EmployeeID"].ColumnMapping = MappingType.Attribute;
    dt.Columns["DisplayName"].ColumnMapping = MappingType.Hidden;

    // Create a new DataRow
    DataRow dr = dt.NewRow();
    dr["EmployeeID"] = 10;
    dr["LastName"] = "Doe";
    dr["FirstName"] = "John";
    dr["DisplayName"] = "Mr. John Doe";
    dr["Notes"] = "Employee history...";

    // Add new DataRow to DataRowCollection of DataTable
    dt.Rows.Add(dr);

    // Add DataTable to DataSet
    ds.Tables.Add(dt);

    // Save contents of DataSet to file
    ds.WriteXml("MyDataSet.xml");
    }
  }
}
```

Here it is in VB .NET:

```vbnet
    ' Set ColumnMapping values
    dt.Columns("EmployeeID").ColumnMapping = MappingType.Attribute

    dt.Columns("DisplayName").ColumnMapping = MappingType.Hidden

    ' Create a new DataRow
    Dim dr As DataRow = dt.NewRow()
    dr("EmployeeID") = 10
    dr("LastName") = "Doe"
    dr("FirstName") = "John"
    dr("DisplayName") = "Mr. John Doe"
    dr("Notes") = "Employee history..."

    ' Add new DataRow to DataRowCollection of DataTable
    dt.Rows.Add(dr)

    ' Add DataTable to DataSet
    ds.Tables.Add(dt)
```

```
            ' Save contents of DataSet to file
            ds.WriteXml("MyDataSet.xml")
        End Sub
    End Class
End Namespace
```

The above example adds one row of data to the DataTable. When the code is compiled and executed, it writes an XML document called MyDataSet.xml to the application directory with the following contents:

```
<?xml version="1.0" standalone="yes"?>
<MyDataSet>
    <Employee EmployeeID="10">
        <LastName>Doe</LastName>
        <FirstName>John</FirstName>
        <Notes>Employee history...</Notes>
    </Employee>
</MyDataSet>
```

As we should expect, the "EmployeeID" column is mapped to an attribute, and the "DisplayName" column is nowhere to be seen.

At this point, we can define other DataTables and add them to the DataSet as well. In many cases, it is not only necessary to store data in different tables, but also to establish relationships between fields in one table and fields in another. That is the focus of the next topic.

DataRelationCollection

The Relations property of the DataSet gives us access to this collection, which enables us to define relationships between DataTables. Each relationship is defined in a DataRelation object. A relationship can be column-to-column or columns-to-columns as in typical relational database environments. Under the covers, this is represented as an XML Schema document with constraints defined to enforce the relationships.

Consider the following example, relateexample, which creates three tables: Employee, Customer, and Order. Each table is joined to the others by creating DataRelation objects matching the respective columns. Here is the C# code:

```csharp
//C#
using System;
using System.Data;

namespace Wrox.Samples.ADONET
{
  public class RelateExample
  {
    // Create first DataTable
    public DataTable CreateOrderTable()
    {
      DataTable dt = new DataTable("Order");
      dt.Columns.Add("OrderID", System.Type.GetType("System.Int32"));

      // This will be used to join Customer table
      dt.Columns.Add("CustomerID", System.Type.GetType("System.Int32"));

      // This will be used to join Employee table
      dt.Columns.Add("EmployeeID", System.Type.GetType("System.Int32"));
```

```
      dt.Columns.Add("OrderDate", System.Type.GetType("System.DateTime"));
      dt.Columns.Add("PurchaseOrder", System.Type.GetType("System.String"));
      return dt;
}


// Create second DataTable
public DataTable CreateCustomerTable()
{
   DataTable dt = new DataTable("Customer");
   dt.Columns.Add("CustomerID", System.Type.GetType("System.Int32"));

   // This will be used to join Employee table
   dt.Columns.Add("EmployeeID", System.Type.GetType("System.Int32"));
   dt.Columns.Add("CustomerName", System.Type.GetType("System.String"));
   return dt;
}


// Create third DataTable
public DataTable CreateEmployeeTable()
{
   DataTable dt = new DataTable("Employee");

   // This will be used to join Customer & Order tables
   dt.Columns.Add("EmployeeID", System.Type.GetType("System.Int32"));
   dt.Columns.Add("LastName", System.Type.GetType("System.String"));
   dt.Columns.Add("FirstName", System.Type.GetType("System.String"));
   return dt;
}

public DataSet CreateMyDataSet()
{
   // Create DataSet object and add tables
   DataSet ds = new DataSet("MyDataSet");
   ds.Tables.Add(CreateOrderTable());
   ds.Tables.Add(CreateCustomerTable());
   ds.Tables.Add(CreateEmployeeTable());

   // Create relationships between tables
   DataRelation dr;

   dr = new DataRelation("Employee2Order",
     ds.Tables["Employee"].Columns["EmployeeID"],
     ds.Tables["Order"].Columns["EmployeeID"]);
   ds.Relations.Add(dr);

   dr = new DataRelation("Employee2Customer",
     ds.Tables["Employee"].Columns["EmployeeID"],
     ds.Tables["Customer"].Columns["EmployeeID"]);
   ds.Relations.Add(dr);

   dr = new DataRelation("Customer2Order",
     ds.Tables["Customer"].Columns["CustomerID"],
     ds.Tables["Order"].Columns["CustomerID"]);
   ds.Relations.Add(dr);

   return ds;
}
```

```csharp
      public static void Main()
      {
        RelateExample re = new RelateExample();
        DataSet ds = re.CreateMyDataSet();

        // Persist schema of DataSet to file
        ds.WriteXml("MyDataSet.xml", XmlWriteMode.WriteSchema);
      }
    }
  }
```

The VB .NET code is similar, and can be found in the code download.

When either of the examples is compiled and executed, a file named MyDataSet.xml is created in the application directory. Here are the contents of that document:

```xml
<?xml version="1.0" standalone="yes"?>
<MyDataSet>
  <xsd:schema id="MyDataSet" targetNamespace=""
              xmlns="" xmlns:xsd="http://www.w3.org/2001/XMLSchema"
              xmlns:msdata="urn:schemas-microsoft-com:xml msdata">
    <xsd:element name="MyDataSet" msdata:IsDataSet="true">
      <xsd:complexType>
        <xsd:choice maxOccurs="unbounded">
          <xsd:element name="Order">
            <xsd:complexType>
              <xsd:sequence>
                <xsd:element name="OrderID" type="xsd:int" minOccurs="0" />
                <xsd:element name="CustomerID" type="xsd:int"
                             minOccurs="0" />
                <xsd:element name="EmployeeID" type="xsd:int"
                             minOccurs="0" />
                <xsd:element name="OrderDate" type="xsd:dateTime"
                             minOccurs="0" />
                <xsd:element name="PurchaseOrder" type="xsd:string"
                             minOccurs="0" />
              </xsd:sequence>
            </xsd:complexType>
          </xsd:element>
          <xsd:element name="Customer">
            <xsd:complexType>
              <xsd:sequence>
                <xsd:element name="CustomerID" type="xsd:int"
                             minOccurs="0" />
                <xsd:element name="EmployeeID" type="xsd:int"
                             minOccurs="0" />
                <xsd:element name="CustomerName" type="xsd:string"
                             minOccurs="0" />
              </xsd:sequence>
            </xsd:complexType>
          </xsd:element>
          <xsd:element name="Employee">
            <xsd:complexType>
              <xsd:sequence>
                <xsd:element name="EmployeeID" type="xsd:int"
                             minOccurs="0" />
                <xsd:element name="LastName" type="xsd:string"
                             minOccurs="0" />
```

```
                    <xsd:element name="FirstName" type="xsd:string"
                                 minOccurs="0" />
                </xsd:sequence>
              </xsd:complexType>
            </xsd:element>
          </xsd:choice>
        </xsd:complexType>
        <xsd:unique name="Constraint1">
          <xsd:selector xpath=".//Customer" />
          <xsd:field xpath="CustomerID" />
        </xsd:unique>
        <xsd:unique name="Employee_Constraint1"
                    msdata:ConstraintName="Constraint1">
          <xsd:selector xpath=".//Employee" />
          <xsd:field xpath="EmployeeID" />
        </xsd:unique>
        <xsd:keyref name="Employee2Customer" refer="Employee_Constraint1">
          <xsd:selector xpath=".//Customer" />
          <xsd:field xpath="EmployeeID" />
        </xsd:keyref>
        <xsd:keyref name="Customer2Order" refer="Constraint1">
          <xsd:selector xpath=".//Order" />
          <xsd:field xpath="CustomerID" />
        </xsd:keyref>
        <xsd:keyref name="Employee2Order" refer="Employee_Constraint1">
          <xsd:selector xpath=".//Order" />
          <xsd:field xpath="EmployeeID" />
        </xsd:keyref>
      </xsd:element>
    </xsd:schema>
</MyDataSet>
```

The relationships we built in code are preserved in the resulting XSD schema through use of `<xsd:unique>` and `<xsd:keyref>` elements, as seen at the end of the schema above. First, we specify that each `<Customer>` element must contain an `<CustomerID>` element with a unique value, and each `<Employee>` element must contain a `<EmployeeID>` element with a unique value. Then we specify that the value of every `<EmployeeID>` beneath a `<Customer>` must correspond to the value of an `<EmployeeID>` beneath an `<Employee>`, the value of every `<CustomerID>` beneath an `<Order>` must correspond to the value of a `<CustomerID>` beneath a `<Customer>`, and the value of every `<EmployeeID>` beneath an `<Order>` corresponds to the value of an `<EmployeeID>` beneath an `<Employee>`.

Reading and Writing XML with DataSets

We mentioned previously that an ADO `Recordset` is capable of persisting its contents as XML. However, the usage or control of the XML was quite limited. ADO.NET has provided easy-to-use methods to provide rich control over how XML should be used in our code.

WriteXml Method

Looks familiar? We have used this method in many of our examples up to this point to generate an XML document to review the underlying schema. One of our examples (see `wrox.samples.adonet.rowsexample`) even generated an XML document of the data without including the schema. We can control how and where to persist the `DataSet` by using one of the following overloaded methods:

```
// C#
public void WriteXml(parameter1, XmlWriteMode);
```

```
' VB
Overloads Public Sub WriteXml(paramter1, XmlWriteMode)
```

Parameter1 can take a `Stream`, string, `TextWriter`, or `XmlWriter`, depending on whether you want to populate a `Stream`, file, `TextWriter`, or `XmlWriter`. *XmlWriteMode* is optional. Depending on the `XmlWriteMode` given, the resulting XML document may include schema information, data, changes to the data, or a combination thereof. Understanding the `XmlWriteMode` enumeration is the key to enabling specific behavior.

XmlWriteMode

This table provides a brief explanation of the different members of this enumeration:

Enumeration Member	Description
XmlWriteMode.IgnoreSchema (Default)	Writes the contents of the `DataSet` without including inline schemas. *(As of Beta 2, the Framework documentation suggests that* `WriteSchema` *is the default, but in practice* `IgnoreSchema` *seems to be the default.)*
XmlWriteMode.DiffGram	Writes the contents of the `DataSet` as a DiffGram. (**DiffGrams** are an XML serialization of the original and current state of the data.)
XmlWriteMode.WriteSchema	Writes the contents of the `DataSet` as XML data, including inline schemas to define relational structure.

If we choose `XmlWriteMode.IgnoreSchema` and the `DataSet` is not populated with data, nothing is written. Likewise if `XmlWriteMode.WriteSchema` is chosen and there is no schema in the `DataSet`, nothing is written. When would we want to choose `XmlWriteMode.DiffGram`? SQL Server 2000 installed with the latest Web Release (version 2) allows for modifications to the database using **UpdateGrams**. DiffGrams, which are a subset of UpdateGrams, can be sent to an instance of SQL Server 2000 to make data changes. We'll see a bit more about the capabilites of the latest Web Release of SQL Server later in the chapter.

WriteXmlSchema Method

This method is similar to `WriteXml()`. It is also overloaded to support writing to a `Stream`, file, `TextWriter`, or `XmlWriter`, but since the method employs a specific behavior (writing a schema), there is no need to specify `XmlWriteModes`. The major difference between using `WriteXml()` with `XmlWriteMode.WriteSchema` mode selected and `WriteXmlSchema()` is that the latter writes only the XSD schema of the `DataSet`, rather than the schema and any data that the `DataSet` is populated with. Therefore, whether data is populated or not, this is a great way to extract just the schema information.

GetXml and GetXmlSchema Methods

What if our code simply needed to extract an XML representation of the `DataSet` as a string? That is what the `GetXml()` and `GetXmlSchema()` methods do. As the names imply, `GetXml()` returns a string of XML representing the data content, whereas the `GetXmlSchema()` method returns a string representing the schema. The next example, `xmlstringexample`, demonstrates using each method. Here is the C# code:

```csharp
//C#
using System;
using System.Data;

namespace Wrox.Samples.ADONET
{
  public class XmlStringExample
  {
    // Create Employee table with 3 columns
    public DataTable CreateEmployeeTable()
    {
      DataTable dt = new DataTable("Employee");
      dt.Columns.Add("EmployeeID", System.Type.GetType("System.Int32"));
      dt.Columns.Add("LastName", System.Type.GetType("System.String"));
      dt.Columns.Add("FirstName", System.Type.GetType("System.String"));
      return dt;
    }

    // This adds a row to the Employee table
    public void AddEmployee(DataTable employeeTable, int employeeID,
                            string lastName, string firstName)
    {
      DataRow dr = employeeTable.NewRow();
      dr["EmployeeID"]=employeeID;
      dr["LastName"]=lastName;
      dr["FirstName"]=firstName;
      employeeTable.Rows.Add(dr);
    }

    // Returns a DataSet object with an Employee table
    public DataSet CreateMyDataSet()
    {
      DataSet ds = new DataSet("MyDataSet");
      ds.Tables.Add(CreateEmployeeTable());
      return ds;
    }

    public static void Main()
    {
      XmlStringExample xse = new XmlStringExample();
      // Creates a DataSet object with an Employee table
      DataSet MyDataSet = xse.CreateMyDataSet();
      // Add two employees
      xse.AddEmployee(MyDataSet.Tables["Employee"], 1, "Doe", "John");
      xse.AddEmployee(MyDataSet.Tables["Employee"], 2, "Ominous", "Ann");

      Console.WriteLine("Contents of DataSet as XML");
      Console.WriteLine(MyDataSet.GetXml());

      Console.WriteLine("\nXSD Schema of DataSet");
      Console.WriteLine(MyDataSet.GetXmlSchema());
```

```
      }
    }
  }
```

And here is the VB .NET code:

```vbnet
' VB .NET
Option Explicit On
Option Strict On

Imports System
Imports System.Data

Namespace Wrox.Samples.ADONET
  Public Class XmlStringExample

    ' Create Employee table with 3 columns
    Public Function CreateEmployeeTable() As DataTable
      Dim dt As DataTable = New DataTable("Employee")
      dt.Columns.Add("EmployeeID", System.Type.GetType("System.Int32"))
      dt.Columns.Add("LastName", System.Type.GetType("System.String"))
      dt.Columns.Add("FirstName", System.Type.GetType("System.String"))
      Return dt
    End Function

    ' This adds a row to the Employee table
    Public Sub AddEmployee(employeeTable As DataTable, _
      employeeID As Integer, lastName As String, firstName As String)
      Dim dr As DataRow = employeeTable.NewRow()
      dr("EmployeeID")=employeeID
      dr("LastName")=lastName
      dr("FirstName")=firstName
      employeeTable.Rows.Add(dr)
    End Sub

    ' Returns a DataSet object with an Employee table
    Public Function CreateMyDataSet() As DataSet
      Dim ds As DataSet = New DataSet("MyDataSet")
      ds.Tables.Add(CreateEmployeeTable())
      Return ds
    End Function

    Shared Sub Main
      Dim xse As XmlStringExample = New XmlStringExample()
      ' Creates a DataSet object with an Employee table
      Dim MyDataSet As DataSet = xse.CreateMyDataSet()
      ' Add two employees
      xse.AddEmployee(MyDataSet.Tables("Employee"), 1, "Doe", "John")
      xse.AddEmployee(MyDataSet.Tables("Employee"), 2, "Ominous", "Ann")

      Console.WriteLine("Contents of DataSet as XML")
      Console.WriteLine(MyDataSet.GetXml())

      Console.WriteLine()
      Console.WriteLine("XSD Schema of DataSet")
      Console.WriteLine(MyDataSet.GetXmlSchema())
    End Sub
  End Class
End Namespace
```

Once this code is compiled and executed, this is what is written to the screen:

```
Contents of DataSet as XML
<MyDataSet>
  <Employee>
    <EmployeeID>1</EmployeeID>
    <LastName>Doe</LastName>
    <FirstName>John</FirstName>
  </Employee>
  <Employee>
    <EmployeeID>2</EmployeeID>
    <LastName>Ominous</LastName>
    <FirstName>Ann</FirstName>
  </Employee>
</MyDataSet>

XSD Schema of DataSet
<xsd:schema id="MyDataSet" targetNamespace="" xmlns=""
      xmlns:xsd="http://www.w3.org/2001/XMLSchema"
      xmlns:msdata="urn:schemas-microsoft-com:xml-msdata">
  <xsd:element name="MyDataSet" msdata:IsDataSet="true">
    <xsd:complexType>
      <xsd:choice maxOccurs="unbounded">
        <xsd:element name="Employee">
          <xsd:complexType>
            <xsd:sequence>
              <xsd:element name="EmployeeID" type="xsd:int"
                    minOccurs="0" />
              <xsd:element name="LastName" type="xsd:string"
                    minOccurs="0" />
              <xsd:element name="FirstName" type="xsd:string"
                    minOccurs="0" />
            </xsd:sequence>
          </xsd:complexType>
        </xsd:element>
      </xsd:choice>
    </xsd:complexType>
  </xsd:element>
</xsd:schema>
```

What makes this example intriguing? We created an in-memory `DataSet` and `DataTable`, populated it with some data, and easily retrieved the XML representation with a single method call! Note that the XSD schema properly mapped the data types of each column, as is seen with `EmployeeID`.

ReadXml Method

This method gives us the ability to perform actions such as loading schemas into a `DataSet`, loading data into tables, or applying data changes. Here is the list of the overloaded signatures:

```
// C#
public XmlReadMode ReadXml(parameter1, XmlReadMode);
```

```
' VB
Overloads Public Function ReadXml(parameter1, XmlReadMode) As XmlReadMode
```

The method returns the XmlReadMode used to access the XML data.

Again, *parameter1* can take a Stream, string, TextReader, or XmlReader, depending on whether we want to read XML from a Stream, file, TextReader, or XmlReader. *XmlReadMode* is optional; it can be used to determine how the data should be accessed. What options are available? Let's take a closer look.

XmlReadMode

Setting the XmlReadMode in the ReadXml() method can have a significant impact on the actions produced. The members of this enumeration are explained in the following table:

Enumeration Member	Description
XmlReadMode.Auto *(Default)*	The Runtime determines the most appropriate method of reading based on the document's data, presence of an inline schema, and/or the existence of a schema in the DataSet.
XmlReadMode.DiffGram	Reads and applies modifications from a DiffGram. (The DiffGram is typically provided by the WriteXml() method of another DataSet)
XmlReadMode.Fragment	Reads inline *XDR* schemas, as are generated with SQL Server 2000 FOR XML statements.
XmlReadMode.IgnoreSchema	Ignores inline schemas and maps data in the XML document to schema in the DataSet. If no match is found, the data is discarded.
XmlReadMode.InferSchema	Ignores inline schemas and infers a schema into the DataSet based on the structure of the data.
XmlReadMode.ReadSchema	Reads inline schemas and loads the data. Conflicts between the schema and DataSet result in an exception being thrown.

In most cases, we will likely know how and why we are reading XML into the DataSet. Therefore, it is better to choose a specific mode than leave it up to the Runtime to determine the best course of action. This is what happens when the default mode (XmlReadMode.Auto) is in effect.

When reading XML into the DataSet, we are likely to want one or more of the following actions to take place:

❑ Load data

❑ Modify existing data

❑ Load schema

Choosing the appropriate XmlReadMode for loading data is dependent on a variety of factors. For starters, does a schema already exist in the DataSet? If a schema does not exist in the DataSet, is there an inline schema with the XML data? What if there isn't a schema on either side?

If we need to load data into a DataSet that has a schema already defined, we use the XmlReadMode.IgnoreSchema with ReadXml(). For instance, suppose we have the following XML file named MyData.xml available in our application folder:

```xml
<?xml version="1.0" standalone="yes"?>
<MyDataSet>
  <xsd:schema id="MyDataSet" targetNamespace="" xmlns=""
              xmlns:xsd="http://www.w3.org/2001/XMLSchema"
              xmlns:msdata="urn:schemas-microsoft-com:xml-msdata">
    <xsd:element name="MyDataSet" msdata:IsDataSet="true">
      <xsd:complexType>
        <xsd:choice maxOccurs="unbounded">
          <xsd:element name="Employee">
            <xsd:complexType>
              <xsd:sequence>
                <xsd:element name="LastName" type="xsd:string"
                             minOccurs="0" msdata:Ordinal="1" />
                <xsd:element name="FirstName" type="xsd:string"
                             minOccurs="0" msdata:Ordinal="2" />
                <xsd:element name="Notes" type="xsd:string"
                             minOccurs="0" msdata:Ordinal="4" />
              </xsd:sequence>
              <xsd:attribute name="EmployeeID" type="xsd:int" />
              <xsd:attribute name="DisplayName" type="xsd:string"
                             use="prohibited" />
            </xsd:complexType>
          </xsd:element>
        </xsd:choice>
      </xsd:complexType>
    </xsd:element>
  </xsd:schema>
  <Employee EmployeeID="10">
    <LastName>Doe</LastName>
    <FirstName>John</FirstName>
    <Notes>Employee history...</Notes>
  </Employee>
</MyDataSet>
```

Notice the above XML document contains an inline schema. The document element is <MyDataSet>. Now, let's take a look at code, ignoreschemaexample, which will read this into a DataSet. Here's the C# code:

```csharp
// C#
using System;
using System.Data;

namespace Wrox.Samples.ADONET
{
  public class IgnoreSchemaExample
  {
    public DataSet CreateMyDataSet()
    {
      DataSet ds = new DataSet("Employees");
      DataTable dt = new DataTable("Employee");
```

```
            dt.Columns.Add("LastName", System.Type.GetType("System.String"));
            dt.Columns.Add("FirstName", System.Type.GetType("System.String"));
            ds.Tables.Add(dt);
            return ds;
        }

        public static void Main()
        {
            IgnoreSchemaExample ise = new IgnoreSchemaExample();
            DataSet MyDataSet = ise.CreateMyDataSet();
            MyDataSet.ReadXml("MyData.xml", XmlReadMode.IgnoreSchema);

            Console.WriteLine("Contents of DataSet as XML");
            Console.WriteLine(MyDataSet.GetXml());

            // Use \n to skip a line
            Console.WriteLine("\nXSD Schema of DataSet");
            Console.WriteLine(MyDataSet.GetXmlSchema());
        }
    }
}
```

And here's the VB .NET version of the code:

```
' VB
Option Explicit On
Option Strict On

Imports System
Imports System.Data

Namespace Wrox.Samples.ADONET
  Public Class IgnoreSchemaExample
    Public Function CreateMyDataSet() As DataSet
      Dim ds As DataSet = New DataSet("Employees")
      Dim dt As DataTable = New DataTable("Employee")
      dt.Columns.Add("LastName", _
        System.Type.GetType("System.String"))
      dt.Columns.Add("FirstName", _
        System.Type.GetType("System.String"))
      ds.Tables.Add(dt)
      Return ds
    End Function

    Shared Sub Main
      Dim ise As IgnoreSchemaExample = New IgnoreSchemaExample()
      Dim MyDataSet As DataSet  = ise.CreateMyDataSet()
      MyDataSet.ReadXml("MyData.xml", XmlReadMode.IgnoreSchema)

      Console.WriteLine("Contents of DataSet as XML")
      Console.WriteLine(MyDataSet.GetXml())

      ' Skip a line
      Console.WriteLine()
      Console.WriteLine("XSD Schema of DataSet")
      Console.WriteLine(MyDataSet.GetXmlSchema())
    End Sub
  End Class
End Namespace
```

When the above code is compiled and executed, the output to the screen is as follows:

```
Contents of DataSet as XML
<Employees>
  <Employee>
    <LastName>Doe</LastName>
    <FirstName>John</FirstName>
  </Employee>
</Employees>
```

```
XSD Schema of DataSet
<xsd:schema id="Employees" targetNamespace="" xmlns=""
xmlns:xsd="http://www.w3.org/2001/XMLSchema"
xmlns:msdata="urn:schemas-microsoft-com:xml-msdata">
  <xsd:element name="Employees" msdata:IsDataSet="true">
   <xsd:complexType>
    <xsd:choice maxOccurs="unbounded">
     <xsd:element name="Employee">
      <xsd:complexType>
       <xsd:sequence>
        <xsd:element name="LastName" type="xsd:string"
                minOccurs="0" />
        <xsd:element name="FirstName" type="xsd:string"
                minOccurs="0" />
       </xsd:sequence>
      </xsd:complexType>
     </xsd:element>
    </xsd:choice>
   </xsd:complexType>
  </xsd:element>
</xsd:schema>
```

In the preceeding code we used the `XmlReadMode.IgnoreSchema` value in the `ReadXml()` method of the `DataSet`. By doing so, the data in the XML document was matched up to the schema already defined in the `DataSet`, through the definition of tables and columns. Any data that did not match, such as the `EmployeeID`, was discarded. Notice that the schema of the `DataSet` remained unchanged from how we defined it in our code.

Changing the `XmlReadMode` will alter the results. For instance, in the above example, only the matching data was introduced to the `DataSet`. What if we wanted to fill the `DataSet` with all of the data in an XML document even though there isn't a matching schema? Wouldn't it be great if somehow the Runtime could generate a schema based on the structure of the data? That is when we should choose `XmlReadMode.InferSchema`.

Let's observe how making just one change to our previous example has an impact on the structure and data of the `MyDataSet` object. Here is the only change to `ignoreschemaexample`, giving us the example `inferschemaexample`.

```
// C#
MyDataSet.ReadXml("MyData.xml", XmlReadMode.InferSchema);
```

```
' VB
MyDataSet.ReadXml("MyData.xml", XmlReadMode.InferSchema)
```

How will this affect the results? Here is the new output to the screen:

```
Contents of DataSet as XML
<MyDataSet>
  <Employee EmployeeID="10">
    <LastName>Doe</LastName>
    <FirstName>John</FirstName>
    <Notes>Employee history...</Notes>
  </Employee>
</MyDataSet>
```

```
XSD Schema of DataSet
<xsd:schema id="MyDataSet" targetNamespace=""
xmlns="" xmlns:xsd="http://www.w3.org/2001/XMLSchema"
xmlns:msdata="urn:schemas-microsoft-com:xml-msdata">
  <xsd:element name="MyDataSet" msdata:IsDataSet="true">
    <xsd:complexType>
      <xsd:choice maxOccurs="unbounded">
        <xsd:element name="Employee">
          <xsd:complexType>
            <xsd:sequence>
              <xsd:element name="LastName" type="xsd:string" minOccurs="0"
                        msdata:Ordinal="0" />
              <xsd:element name="FirstName" type="xsd:string" minOccurs="0"
                        msdata:Ordinal="1" />
              <xsd:element name="Notes" type="xsd:string" minOccurs="0"
                        msdata:Ordinal="2" />
            </xsd:sequence>
            <xsd:attribute name="EmployeeID" type="xsd:string" />
          </xsd:complexType>
        </xsd:element>
      </xsd:choice>
    </xsd:complexType>
  </xsd:element>
</xsd:schema>
```

In this case, all of the data from the document populated the DataSet, and new schema definitions were generated. First of all, notice how the <MyDataSet> element took precedence over the <Employees> element from the previous ouput. In order to accommodate any data that did not have a column defined to hold it, new columns were added. The columns added reflected the proper mapping, as in the case of the attribute EmployeeID. However, note that the Runtime did not automatically assume that EmployeeID should be an integer just because a number was found. This is also proof that XmlReadMode.InferSchema ignores any inline schemas, as the XML document that was used in this example did.

Understanding the Inference Process

What process is used to determine how the structure of an XML document is defined in a DataSet? In other words, how does the Runtime decide whether an XML node is a DataColumn, DataTable, DataRelation, or even a DataSet object? The following table provides a summary of the rules used to map XML nodes to DataSet objects.

XML Node	DataSet
Attribute	DataColumn
Element containing attributes or child elements	DataTable
Repeated elements (siblings)	DataTable
Non-repeating elements *void* of attributes or child elements	DataColumn
Document or root element *void* of attributes or elements inferred as DataColumns	DataSet
Document or root element containing either attributes or elements inferred as DataColumns	DataTable
Elements inferred as DataTables nested in elements inferred as DataTables	DataRelation
Text of element *void* of child elements	DataColumn
Text of element containing child elements	(Ignored)

Loading Schema Information into the DataSet

One way or another, the ReadXml() method populates data into the DataSet. Although schema information could also be derived from the XML, that is not the primary usage of ReadXml. The two methods we employ when all we want to do is extract schema information are ReadXmlSchema() and InferXmlSchema(). Let's take a look at each method and when to choose one over the other.

ReadXmlSchema Method

This method is an attractive option when the requirements are to load only schema information into the DataSet. It contains overloaded signatures similar to that of ReadXml(), without specifying an XmlReadMode. If we pass in an XML document containing schema information (XSD or XDR), it will use the schema found to generate the appropriate structure in the DataSet. If the XML document contains only data, it will infer the schema much like using ReadXml() with XmlReadMode.InferSchema. The difference with ReadXmlSchema() is that no data is loaded, just – you guessed it – schema information.

For example, the following code, readxmlschmaexample, will read the MyData.xml document used in previous examples to load the inline schema into the DataSet. Here's the C# code:

```
// C#
using System;
using System.Data;

namespace Wrox.Samples.ADONET
{
  public class ReadXmlSchemaExample
  {
    public static void Main()
    {
      DataSet MyDataSet = new DataSet();
      MyDataSet.ReadXmlSchema("MyData.xml");
```

```
          Console.WriteLine("Contents of DataSet as XML");
          Console.WriteLine(MyDataSet.GetXml());

          Console.WriteLine("\nXSD Schema of DataSet");
          Console.WriteLine(MyDataSet.GetXmlSchema());
      }
    }
  }
```

And here's the VB .NET code:

```
' VB
Option Explicit On
Option Strict On

Imports System
Imports System.Data

Namespace Wrox.Samples.ADONET
  Public Class ReadXmlSchemaExample
    Shared Sub Main
      Dim MyDataSet As DataSet = New DataSet()
      MyDataSet.ReadXmlSchema("MyData.xml")

      Console.WriteLine("Contents of DataSet as XML")
      Console.WriteLine(MyDataSet.GetXml())

      Console.WriteLine()
      Console.WriteLine("XSD Schema of DataSet")
      Console.WriteLine(MyDataSet.GetXmlSchema())
    End Sub
  End Class
End Namespace
```

When the code is compiled and executed, the results we expected are output to the screen:

```
Contents of DataSet as XML
 <MyDataSet />

XSD Schema of DataSet
 <xsd:schema id="MyDataSet" targetNamespace="" xmlns=""
xmlns:xsd="http://www.w3.org/2001/XMLSchema"
xmlns:msdata="urn:schemas-microsoft-com:xml-msdata">
  <xsd:element name="MyDataSet" msdata:IsDataSet="true">
   <xsd:complexType>
<xsd:choice maxOccurs="unbounded">
  <xsd:element name="Employee">
   <xsd:complexType>
      <xsd:sequence>
        <xsd:element name="LastName" type="xsd:string" minOccurs="0"
                    msdata:Ordinal="1" />
        <xsd:element name="FirstName" type="xsd:string" minOccurs="0"
                    msdata:Ordinal="2" />
        <xsd:element name="Notes" type="xsd:string" minOccurs="0"
                    msdata:Ordinal="4" />
```

```
            </xsd:sequence>
            <xsd:attribute name="EmployeeID" type="xsd:int" />
            <xsd:attribute name="DisplayName" type="xsd:string" use="prohibited" />
          </xsd:complexType>
        </xsd:element>
      </xsd:choice>
    </xsd:complexType>
  </xsd:element>
</xsd:schema>
```

The first output to the screen confirmed that no data was loaded, as is seen in the empty element `MyDataSet`. However, the complete schema was loaded and the `DataSet` can now be populated with data using whatever means are required by the application.

InferXmlSchema Method

This method should be used when an inline schema is not available and a schema needs to be generated based on the structure of the instance document. The additional advantage to using this method over `ReadXmlSchema()` is that we can choose to ignore certain namespaces from the source. The overloaded signatures of this method are similar to that of `ReadXmlSchema()`, with a second argument accepting a string array of the namespaces to be ignored. This can greatly affect the way the schema is inferred.

Suppose we wanted to infer a schema into a `DataSet` from the following XML document named `Employees.xml`:

```
<?xml version="1.0" standalone="yes"?>
<Employees xmlns="http://tempuri.org/"
           xmlns:wrx="urn:Wrox-DotNET-ADONET-DataSet:InferXmlSchema">
  <Employee wrx:internal-code="EID" EmployeeID="1" >
    <LastName wrx:internal-code="LN">Doe</LastName>
    <FirstName wrx:internal-code="FN">John</FirstName>
  </Employee>
  <Employee wrx:internal-code="EID" EmployeeID="2" >
    <LastName wrx:internal-code="LN">Ominous</LastName>
    <FirstName wrx:internal-code="FN">Ann</FirstName>
  </Employee>
</Employees>
```

Based on the rules of inference covered earlier this chapter, how many tables would be added to the `DataSet`? Because the `<Employee>` element and all of its children contain attributes, each element maps to a `DataTable`. However, it may appear more logical to just have an `Employee` table, with columns for `EmployeeID`, `LastName`, and `FirstName`. What if we want to ignore the attributes associated with the `urn:Wrox-DotNET-ADONET-DataSet:InferXmlSchema` namespace? Would that change how the schema is inferred?

Let's take a look at some code to demonstrate what happens. This time, note how the code, `inferxmlschemaexample.cs`, written in C# specifies a namespace to ignore, while the code, `inferxmlschemaexample.vb`, written in VB.NET is passed an empty string. Here's the C# code:

```
// C#
using System;
using System.Data;
```

```
namespace Wrox.Samples.ADONET
{
  public class InferXmlSchemaExample
  {
    public static void Main()
    {
      DataSet MyDataSet = new DataSet();

      // Infer schema, ignoring nodes with the supplied namespace
      MyDataSet.InferXmlSchema("Employees.xml",
        new string[] {"urn:Wrox-DotNET-ADONET-DataSet:InferXmlSchema"});

      // Display the number of tables, and each name
      Console.WriteLine("Tables in the {0} DataSet:",
        MyDataSet.DataSetName);
      foreach (DataTable dt in MyDataSet.Tables)
      {
        Console.WriteLine(dt.TableName);
      }
    }
  }
}
```

And here's the VB .NET code:

```
' VB .NET
Option Explicit On
Option Strict On

Imports System
Imports System.Data

Namespace Wrox.Samples.ADONET
  Public Class InferXmlSchemaExample
    Shared Sub Main
      Dim MyDataSet As DataSet  = New DataSet()

      ' Infer schema, and ignore nothing
      MyDataSet.InferXmlSchema("Employees.xml", New String(){""})

      ' Display the number of tables, and each name
      Console.WriteLine("Tables in the {0} DataSet:", MyDataSet.DataSetName)
      Dim dt As DataTable
      For Each dt in MyDataSet.Tables
        Console.WriteLine(dt.TableName)
      Next
    End Sub
  End Class
End Namespace
```

When both examples are compiled and executed, the screen output for the code written in C# is:

```
Wrox.Samples.ADONET                                    _ □ X
Tables in the Employees DataSet:
Employee
```

Note that only one table is defined. Here is the output from the code written in VB. NET:

```
Wrox.Samples.ADONET                                    _ □ X
Tables in the Employees DataSet:
Employee
LastName
FirstName
```

This output identifies three tables, as we predicted.

In either example, the *data* in the Employees.xml document was never loaded into the DataSet.

XML Namespaces

The previous section provided an example of how namespaces could be factored out when inferring a schema into a DataSet. Many of the classes we have been introduced to so far this chapter provide properties to set or retrieve namespace information. This gives us the ability to programmatically manage namespaces in our code.

Prefix and Namespace Properties

To control namespaces and the prefixes that alias them, we simply use the Prefix and Namespace properties. These properties are members of the DataSet, DataTable, and DataColumn classes.

The following example, prefixnamespaceexample, loads the Employees.xml file from the last example and infers a schema into the DataSet including all namespaces. We check for the namespace of the DataSet, and then define our own prefix for that namespace. We then output the contents as XML. Here is the C# code:

```csharp
// C#
using System;
using System.Data;

namespace Wrox.Samples.ADONET
{
  public class PrefixNamespaceExample
  {
    public static void Main()
    {
      DataSet MyDataSet = new DataSet();
      MyDataSet.ReadXml("Employees.xml", XmlReadMode.InferSchema);

      // Get the value of the namespace for the DataSet
      Console.WriteLine("Namespace of DataSet: {0}", MyDataSet.Namespace);
```

```
        // Set the prefix of the namespace
        MyDataSet.Prefix = "tmp";

        Console.WriteLine(MyDataSet.GetXml());
      }
    }
}
```

And here's the VB .NET code:

```
' VB
Option Explicit On
Option Strict On

Imports System
Imports System.Data

Namespace Wrox.Samples.ADONET
  Public Class PrefixNamespaceExample
    Shared Sub Main
      Dim MyDataSet As DataSet  = New DataSet()
      MyDataSet.ReadXml("Employees.xml", XmlReadMode.InferSchema)

      ' Get the value of the namespace for the DataSet
      Console.WriteLine("Namespace of DataSet: {0}", MyDataSet.Namespace)
      ' Set the prefix of the namespace
      MyDataSet.Prefix = "tmp"

      Console.WriteLine(MyDataSet.GetXml())
    End Sub
  End Class
End Namespace
```

This is what is written to the screen once the code is compiled and executed:

```
Namespace of DataSet: http://tempuri.org/
<tmp:Employees xmlns:tmp="http://tempuri.org/">
  <Employee wrx:internal-code="EID" EmployeeID="1"
 xmlns:wrx="urn:Wrox-DotNET-ADONET-DataSet:InferXmlSchema" xmlns="http://tempuri.org/">
    <LastName wrx:internal-code="LN">Doe</LastName>
    <FirstName wrx:internal-code="FN">John</FirstName>
  </Employee>
  <Employee wrx:internal-code="EID" EmployeeID="2"
 xmlns:wrx="urn:Wrox-DotNET-ADONET-DataSet:InferXmlSchema" xmlns="http://tempuri.org/">
    <LastName wrx:internal-code="LN">Ominous</LastName>
    <FirstName wrx:internal-code="FN">Ann</FirstName>
  </Employee>
</tmp:Employees>
```

Notice the use of the `tmp` prefix for the `<Employees>` root element. Also, be aware of the impact that namespaces have when defined in the `DataSet`, `DataTable`, or `DataColumn` objects. When loading data into a `DataSet` from an XML document, conflicting namespaces from the source document will be ignored. Keep this in mind when troubleshooting data loading from an XML document.

Strongly Typed DataSets

Another feature that deserves attention here is the use of **strongly typed** DataSets. A strongly typed DataSet is a subclass of DataSet with all the features we have learned so far. In addition, DataTables and DataColumns can be referenced through strongly typed names, as opposed to the collections we have been using so far. The advantages of using a strongly typed DataSet include the IntelliSense of typed DataSet members, easy to read code, and compiler-caught type-mismatch errors.

Although we could take on the task of writing our own strongly typed DataSet, the .NET Framework includes a very nice tool to handle the bulk of the work. The xsd.exe tool can create a source code file (in the language of our choice) for the strongly typed DataSet from an XSD schema. Once the code is generated, we can compile it and use it in our programs.

Let's walk through an example. The following schema is stored in a file named MySchema.xsd:

```xml
<?xml version="1.0" standalone="yes"?>
<xsd:schema id="Employees" targetNamespace="http://tempuri.org/"
            xmlns:xsd="http://www.w3.org/2001/XMLSchema">
  <xsd:element name="Employee">
    <xsd:complexType>
      <xsd:sequence>
        <xsd:element name="LastName" type="xsd:string" minOccurs="0" />
        <xsd:element name="FirstName" type="xsd:string" minOccurs="0" />
      </xsd:sequence>
      <xsd:attribute name="EmployeeID" type="xsd:int" />
    </xsd:complexType>
  </xsd:element>
</xsd:schema>
```

To generate the strongly typed DataSet code in C#, type the following at a DOS prompt:

>xsd.exe /d /l:C# MySchema.xsd /n:Wrox.Samples.ADONET

The /d directive indicates that we want a DataSet. The /l option indicates what language we want the resulting code to be. (We could just as easily have created the strongly typed DataSet in VB .NET, rather than C#.) The /n option allows us to specify the .NET namespace (not to be confused with the DataSet.Namespace property) of the new DataSet class. The resulting file is named MySchema.cs, and contains over 300 lines of code. Instead of listing all of that code here (it is provided in the code download), let's see how we can put it to use. First we need to compile the source code. At the DOS prompt, type the following:

>csc.exe /target:library /r:system.dll,system.data.dll myschema.cs

This will create the myschema.dll. Notice that we needed to reference the system.data.dll for this to compile. Now, let's take a look at how we can put this strongly typed DataSet to work. Observe the following code, stronglytypeddatasetexample, which adds two rows to our new DataSet named Employees. Here's the C# code:

```csharp
// C#
using System;
using System.Data;
using Wrox.Samples.ADONET;
```

```
namespace Wrox.Samples.ADONET
{
  public class StronglyTypedDataSetExample
  {
    public static void Main()
    {
      // Employees is our strongly typed DataSet
      Employees e = new Employees();
      e.Employee.AddEmployeeRow(1,"Doe","John");
      e.Employee.AddEmployeeRow(2,"Ominous","Ann");
      Console.WriteLine(e.GetXml());
    }
  }
}
```

And here's the same code in VB .NET:

```
' VB
Option Explicit On
Option Strict On

Imports System
Imports System.Data
Imports Wrox.Samples.ADONET

Namespace Wrox.Samples.ADONET
  Public Class StronglyTypedDataSetExample
    Shared Sub Main
      ' Employees is our strongly typed DataSet
      Dim e As Employees = New Employees()
      e.Employee.AddEmployeeRow(1,"Doe","John")
      e.Employee.AddEmployeeRow(2,"Ominous","Ann")
      Console.WriteLine(e.GetXml())
    End Sub
  End Class
End Namespace
```

As you can see, strongly typed DataSets are very easy to use and read! When we compile the above code (referencing the myschema.dll) and execute it, this is the result on the screen:

Notice how the schema information remained intact, such as the default namespace and XML structure.

XmlDataDocument

Up to this point we have been exploring the XML features of the DataSet class, which allows us to get a relational view of the data. Although the DataSet class is impressive on its own merits, it does lack a few important features. What if we wanted to view the data hierarchically? What if our code made extensive use of XPath queries or XSL Transformations? What if the data source is an XML document that needs its fidelity (exact XML structure) preserved? How could we do this without making unnecessary copies of the data?

Fortunately, Microsoft has integrated XML support so tightly with ADO.NET that these questions are easy to address. Perhaps the greatest link between hierarchical and relational data is seen in the relationship between DataSet and XmlDataDocument. We can achieve synchronized access to data from either class! That is, once synchronized, both objects are working with the same set of data.

We could load an XML document into an XmlDataDocument, synchronize it with a DataSet, and bind it to an ASP.NET DataGrid. (We'll be looking at these in more detail in Chapter 11, *ASP.NET*.) Or, we could access SQL Server and load a DataSet, synchronize it with an XmlDataDocument, and perform XML Transformations on the data. We don't have to choose between these technologies, because each is readily available in ADO.NET.

As you may have guessed or assumed, XmlDataDocument extends XmlDocument, so the power of the DOM is at our fingertips. The features we have learned so far about XmlDocument in this book (mainly in Chapter 4) are also inherited in XmlDataDocument.

Synchronizing with a DataSet

There are a couple of ways to synchronize an XmlDataDocument with a DataSet, as well as a few tips to keep in mind to avoid exceptions being thrown. In order to choose the appropriate means to synchronize the objects, the first question we should ask is which object is the source of the data? Let's examine what to do in either case.

When XmlDataDocument is the Data Source

If we load an XmlDataDocument with data, and wish to view it as relational data, here is what we could do. First, we need to define the schema in the DataSet to map against the nodes we want to expose in the source document. In other words, we need to provide the DataSet with information on which elements and attributes in the XmlDataDocument we want a relational view of.

With this in mind, let us look at some code that will load an XML file into an XmlDataDocument. Our example in C#, XDD2DSexample.cs, will demonstrate how to synchronize with a DataSet using the DataSet property of the XmlDataDocument.

```
// C#
using System;
using System.Data;
using System.Xml;

namespace Wrox.Samples.ADONET
{
  public class XDD2DSExample
  {
    public static DataSet CreateEmployeesDataSet(DataSet employeeDataSet)
```

```
    {
      // DataSet schema generated, but no data loaded
      employeeDataSet.DataSetName = "Employees";
      employeeDataSet.Namespace = "http://tempuri.org/";
      DataTable dt = new DataTable("Employee");
      dt.Columns.Add("EmployeeID", System.Type.GetType("System.Int32"));
      dt.Columns["EmployeeID"].ColumnMapping = MappingType.Attribute;
      dt.Columns.Add("LastName", System.Type.GetType("System.String"));
      dt.Columns.Add("FirstName", System.Type.GetType("System.String"));
      employeeDataSet.Tables.Add(dt);
      return employeeDataSet;
    }

    public static void Main()
    {
      XmlDataDocument xdd = new XmlDataDocument();
      // DataSet synchronized with XmlDataDocument
      DataSet myDataSet = CreateEmployeesDataSet(xdd.DataSet);
      // After DataSet schema is defined, load the data
      xdd.Load("TwoEmployees.xml");

      // Create DataRow array of employees in descending order
      DataRow[] sortedRows =
        myDataSet.Tables["Employee"].Select("", "EmployeeID DESC");
      for (int i=0; i<sortedRows.Length; i++)
        Console.WriteLine("{0}: {1}, {2}",
          sortedRows[i]["EmployeeID"],
          sortedRows[i]["LastName"],
          sortedRows[i]["FirstName"]);
    }
  }
}
```

However, the example in VB. NET, XDD2DSexample.vb, will use a different approach – passing a DataSet object into the constructor of the XmlDataDocument:

```
' VB
Option Explicit On
Option Strict On

Imports System
Imports System.Data
Imports System.Xml

Namespace Wrox.Samples.ADONET
  Public Class XDD2DSExample
    Public Shared Function CreateEmployeesDataSet() As DataSet
      ' DataSet schema generated, but no data loaded
      Dim ds As DataSet = New DataSet("Employees")
      ds.Namespace = "http://tempuri.org/"
      Dim dt As DataTable = New DataTable("Employee")
      dt.Columns.Add("EmployeeID", System.Type.GetType("System.Int32"))
      dt.Columns("EmployeeID").ColumnMapping = MappingType.Attribute
      dt.Columns.Add("LastName", System.Type.GetType("System.String"))
      dt.Columns.Add("FirstName", System.Type.GetType("System.String"))
      ds.Tables.Add(dt)
      Return ds
    End Function
  End Class
```

```
    Shared Sub Main
      ' Generate DataSet schema
      Dim myDataSet As DataSet = CreateEmployeesDataSet()

      ' Synchronize DataSet with XmlDataDocument
      Dim xdd As XmlDataDocument = New XmlDataDocument(myDataSet)

      ' Load the data from XML document
      xdd.Load("TwoEmployees.xml")

      ' Create DataRow array of employees in descending order
      Dim sortedRows() as DataRow = _
      myDataSet.Tables("Employee").Select("", "EmployeeID DESC")

      Dim i As Integer
      For i = 0 to sortedRows.GetUpperBound(0)
        Console.WriteLine("{0}: {1}, {2}", _
          sortedRows(i)("EmployeeID"), _
          sortedRows(i)("LastName"), _
          sortedRows(i)("FirstName"))
      Next
    End Sub
  End Class
End Namespace
```

Note that when synchronizing a DataSet with an XmlDataDocument (which is the source of the data), the schema must be defined in the DataSet before the data is loaded. (In our example, the schema is generated just by creating the tables and columns of the DataSet.)

This is the TwoEmployees.xml document loaded in both examples:

```
<?xml version="1.0" standalone="yes"?>
<Employees xmlns="http://tempuri.org/">
  <Employee EmployeeID="1" >
    <LastName>Doe</LastName>
    <FirstName>John</FirstName>
    <Notes>
      This is ignored by DataSet
    </Notes>
  </Employee>
  <Employee EmployeeID="2">
    <LastName>Ominous</LastName>
    <FirstName>Ann</FirstName>
    <Notes>
      However, this is seen by XmlDataDocument
    </Notes>
  </Employee>
</Employees>
```

The output to the screen is the same in each case:

This example demonstrates one of the exciting features of ADO.NET. Although the source of our data was in an XML document, we were able to view it with relational tools. In this case, we took advantage of the `DataTable.Select` property to display the data in descending order. With larger `DataSets`, we could have easily applied filters as well.

At this point, a question could be raised as to what was gained by introducing `XmlDataDocument` into our code in the first place. As we already learned in this chapter, we could also have loaded the XML document directly into the `DataSet`, bypassing the `XmlDataDocument`. To answer the concern raised, consider that the schema generated for the `DataSet` did not include a column for `Notes`. The data in the `<Notes>` element is still available to us in `XmlDataDocument`. In addition, `XmlDataDocument` preserves the fidelity of the XML, remembering element order, hierarchical information, and whitespace. The `WriteXml()` method of the `DataSet` could format the XML dramatically differently from the original document. Finally, each object is sharing the same set of data – so that changes in one object will be seen in the other.

When DataSet is the Data Source

As we just explained, the `DataSet` could be populated from an XML document. But what if the source of the data is a table in a SQL Server database? Whatever it may be that populated the `DataSet`, we can access it hierarchically with the `XmlDataDocument`.

Let's consider the following example, `DS2XDDexample`, which returns employee information from the Northwind sample database that comes with SQL Server. Once we have the data populated in the `DataSet`, we will synchronize it with an `XmlDataDocument` and perform an `XPath` search for specific nodes. Here's the C# code:

```
// C#
using System;
using System.Data;
using System.Xml;
using System.Data.SqlClient;

namespace Wrox.Samples.ADONET
{
  public class DS2XDDExample
  {
    public static DataSet CreateNWEmployeesDataSet()
    {
      string connect =
        "data source=(local);user id=sa;password=;initial catalog=Northwind";
      string query =
        "SELECT EmployeeID, LastName, FirstName, Title FROM Employees";

      DataSet ds = new DataSet("NWEmployees");
      ds.Tables.Add(new DataTable("Employee"));

      // Connect to the database and fill the DataSet
      SqlConnection sqlCN = new SqlConnection(connect);
      try
      {
        sqlCN.Open();
        SqlDataAdapter sqlDA = new SqlDataAdapter();
        sqlDA.SelectCommand = new SqlCommand(query, sqlCN);
        sqlDA.Fill(ds.Tables["Employee"]);
      }
      catch (Exception e)
```

```
      {
        Console.WriteLine(e.ToString());
      }
      finally
      {
        if (!(sqlCN == null))
        {
          sqlCN.Close();
        }
      }
      return ds;
    }

  public static void Main()
  {
    DataSet myDataSet = CreateNWEmployeesDataSet();
    // XmlDataDocument synchronized with DataSet
    XmlDataDocument xdd = new XmlDataDocument(myDataSet);
    string xpathQuery = "/NWEmployees/Employee[EmployeeID='4']";
    XmlNode xn = xdd.SelectSingleNode(xpathQuery);
    if (!(xn==null))
      Console.WriteLine(xn.OuterXml);
    else
      Console.WriteLine("Nothing found...");
  }
 }
}
```

And here's the VB .NET code:

```
' VB
Option Explicit On
Option Strict On

Imports System
Imports System.Data
Imports System.Xml
Imports System.Data.SqlClient

Namespace Wrox.Samples.ADONET
  Public Class DS2XDDExample
    Public Shared Function CreateNWEmployeesDataSet() As DataSet
      Dim connect As String = _
        "data source=(local);user id=sa;password=;initial catalog=Northwind"

      Dim query As String = _
        "SELECT EmployeeID, LastName, FirstName, Title FROM Employees"

      Dim ds As DataSet = New DataSet("NWEmployees")
      ds.Tables.Add(New DataTable("Employee"))

      ' Connect to the database and fill the DataSet
      Dim sqlCN As SqlConnection = _
      New SqlConnection(connect)

      Try
        sqlCN.Open()
        Dim sqlDA As SqlDataAdapter = New SqlDataAdapter()
        sqlDA.SelectCommand = New SqlCommand(query, sqlCN)
        sqlDA.Fill(ds.Tables("Employee"))
```

```
        Catch e As Exception
           Console.WriteLine(e.ToString())
        Finally
           If Not (sqlCN Is Nothing) Then
              sqlCN.Close()
           End If
        End Try
        Return ds
     End Function

     Shared Sub Main
        Dim myDataSet As DataSet  = CreateNWEmployeesDataSet()

        ' XmlDataDocument synchronized with DataSet
        Dim xdd As XmlDataDocument = New XmlDataDocument(myDataSet)

        Dim xpathQuery As String = _
        "/NWEmployees/Employee[EmployeeID='4']"

        Dim xn As XmlNode = xdd.SelectSingleNode(xpathQuery)
        If Not (xn Is Nothing) Then
           Console.WriteLine(xn.OuterXml)
        Else
           Console.WriteLine("Nothing found...")
        End If
     End Sub
  End Class
End Namespace
```

When the examples are compiled and executed, the following data is output to the console (formatted here for easy reading):

```
<Employee>
  <EmployeeID>4</EmployeeID>
  <LastName>Peacock</LastName>
  <FirstName>Margaret</FirstName>
  <Title>Sales Representative</Title>
</Employee>
```

Note that data should not be loaded into the XmlDataDocument prior to synchronization of a populated DataSet or else an exception is thrown.

The above code demonstrates the flexibility we have when working with data. Although the DataSet was populated from a relational database, we were still able to synchronize it with an XmlDataDocument and perform a node search using XPath expressions.

Element and Row Conversions

The XmlDataDocument class contains two methods to easily convert smaller segments of data from one format to another. It might be that our application requires only one row in a table or one element from an XML document for processing. Again, whether our data came from an XML document or a relational database, we can code our solution with whatever technology makes sense for our needs.

GetElementFromRow Method

This method takes a `DataRow` parameter and returns the `XmlElement` object representation of that row. Here is a brief example, `GetElementFromRowexample`, of how to use this method. Again, it uses `Northwind` that comes with SQL Server. We'll just look at the C# code – the VB .NET code is very similar and can be found in the code download:

```csharp
// C#
using System;
using System.Data;
using System.Xml;
using System.Data.SqlClient;

namespace Wrox.Samples.ADONET
{
  public class GetElementFromRowExample
  {
    public static DataSet CreateNWEmployeesDataSet()
    {
      string connect =
        "data source=(local);user id=sa;password=;initial catalog=Northwind";
      string query =
        "SELECT EmployeeID, LastName, FirstName, Title FROM Employees";

      DataSet ds = new DataSet("NWEmployees");
      ds.Tables.Add(new DataTable("Employee"));

      // Connect to the database and fill the DataSet
      SqlConnection sqlCN = new SqlConnection(connect);
      try
      {
        sqlCN.Open();
        SqlDataAdapter sqlDA = new SqlDataAdapter();
        sqlDA.SelectCommand = new SqlCommand(query, sqlCN);
        sqlDA.Fill(ds.Tables["Employee"]);
      }
      catch (Exception e)
      {
        Console.WriteLine(e.ToString());
      }
      finally
      {
        if (!(sqlCN == null))
        {
          sqlCN.Close();
        }
      }
      return ds;
    }

    public static void Main()
    {
      // Populate DataSet with data from NorthWind database
      DataSet myDataSet = CreateNWEmployeesDataSet();
      // XmlDataDocument synchronized with DataSet
      XmlDataDocument xdd = new XmlDataDocument(myDataSet);
```

```
            // Get the first row
            DataRow firstRow = myDataSet.Tables[0].Rows[0];
            // Get the element representation of the first row
            XmlElement xe = xdd.GetElementFromRow(firstRow);
            Console.WriteLine(xe.OuterXml);
        }
    }
}
```

The resulting output to the screen is the XML representation of the first row in the Northwind Employees table:

```
<Employee>
 <EmployeeID>1</EmployeeID>
 <LastName>Davolio</LastName>
 <FirstName>Nancy</FirstName>
 <Title>Sales Representative</Title>
</Employee>
```

GetRowFromElement Method

As the name of this method implies, the DataRow representation of the supplied XmlElement is returned. Here is an example, GetRowFromElementexample, of how it is done. This time we'll look at the VB .NET code – the C# code can be found in the download:

```
' VB
Option Explicit On
Option Strict On

Imports System
Imports System.Data
Imports System.Xml

Namespace Wrox.Samples.ADONET
  Public Class GetRowFromElementExample
    Shared Sub Main
      ' Create the XmlDataDocument object
      Dim xdd As XmlDataDocument = New XmlDataDocument()

      ' Infer schema from XML document
      xdd.DataSet.InferXmlSchema("TwoEmployees.xml", Nothing)

      ' Load the data
      xdd.Load("TwoEmployees.xml")

      ' Create XmlNamespaceManager object for resolving namespaces
      Dim xnm As XmlNamespaceManager =
        New XmlNamespaceManager(xdd.NameTable)
      xnm.AddNamespace("e", "http://tempuri.org/")

      ' Get first employee element
      Dim xe As XmlElement =
        CType(xdd.DocumentElement.FirstChild, XmlElement)

      ' Display current text of FirstName child node
      Console.WriteLine("Name before update = {0}",
        xe.SelectSingleNode("e:FirstName", xnm).InnerText)
```

```
        ' Get DataRow from XmlElement
        Dim dr As DataRow = xdd.GetRowFromElement(xe)

        ' Change value of first name through DataRow
        dr("FirstName") = "Jane"

        ' Display updated text of FirstName child node
        Console.WriteLine("Name after update = {0}",
            xe.SelectSingleNode("e:FirstName", xnm).InnerText)
     End Sub
  End Class
End Namespace
```

Each example uses the `TwoEmployees.xml` file from a prior example in this chapter. When compiled and executed, the result on the screen is:

Retrieving XML from SQL Server 2000

The SQL Server .NET managed data provider enables us to take advantage of the XML features within SQL Server 2000. Although our previous example showed us how to view relational data from a SQL Server database as XML, this section will cover how to retrieve XML content directly from the server.

Using FOR XML

SQL Server 2000 allows us to add a FOR XML clause to our queries to generate the results in XML format. We can request the results using one of three options:

FOR XML Mode	Description
RAW	Returns query results using generic <row> elements, with non-null column values mapped to attributes in the element.
AUTO	Returns query results as nested XML elements. Tables map to elements, and columns map to attributes (although element-centric results are possible by adding the ELEMENTS option).
EXPLICIT	By writing the query in a special way, the writer can shape the result of the XML.

The above table provides a fundamental understanding of each option available with FOR XML clauses. There is more information regarding specific syntax and other options in *SQL Server Books Online* (documentation that ships with SQL Server) and *Professional SQL Server 2000 XML* from Wrox Press ISBN 1-861005-46-6.

The following code example, `forxmlexample`, uses the FOR XML AUTO, ELEMENTS clause in the query. We'll look at the C# code – the VB .NET code can be found in the book's code download:

```csharp
// C#
using System;
using System.Xml;
using System.Data;
using System.Data.SqlClient;

namespace Wrox.Samples.ADONET
{
  public class FORXMLExample
  {
    public static void Main()
    {
      string cmdText = "SELECT EmployeeID, LastName, FirstName" +
                       " FROM Employees FOR XML AUTO, Elements";

      string connect =
        "data source=(local);initial catalog=Northwind;" +
        "user id=sa;password=;";

      // Create SqlConnection
      SqlConnection sqlCN = new SqlConnection(connect);
      try
      {
        sqlCN.Open();

        // Create SqlCommand
        SqlCommand sqlCMD = new SqlCommand(cmdText, sqlCN);

        // Execute SqlCommand and load XmlReader
        XmlReader xr = sqlCMD.ExecuteXmlReader();
        Console.WriteLine("Employee Last Names")
        Console.WriteLine("===================");
        while (xr.Read())
        {
          if (xr.Name=="LastName")
            Console.WriteLine(xr.ReadElementString());
        }
        xr.Close();
      }
      catch (Exception e)
      {
        Console.WriteLine(e.ToString());
      }
      finally
      {
        if (!(sqlCN == null))
        {
          sqlCN.Close();
        }
      }
    }
  }
}
```

Once again, we have demonstrated that when the data is in XML format, we can do just about anything we want. In our code, we called upon the ExecuteXmlReader() method of the SqlCommand object to return an XmlReader. With the XmlReader, we searched for nodes with the "LastName" name and printed out the contents if found. Here is a screenshot of the results:

Retrieving XML from SQL Server 2000 is rather straightforward and easy to do. The steps involved required a connection to the database, passing in a FOR XML query, and populating the results of the ExecuteXmlReader() method into an XmlReader object. If we wanted to, we could have easily passed the resulting XmlReader into the ReadXml() method of DataSet. Our options seem unending!

SQLXML Managed Classes

At the time of the writing of this book, XML for SQL Server 2000 Web Release 2, Beta 2 became available. (See http://www.microsoft.com/sql/.) With this release came .NET support through SQLXML managed classes, which fall under the Microsoft.Data.SqlXml namespace. They make it easy for us to access SQL Server using SQL, XPath, or Template queries. The new classes are:

❑   SqlXmlCommand

❑   SqlXmlParameter

❑   SqlXmlAdapter

In addition to retrieving data, support is provided through the SqlXmlAdapter class for updating the server through DiffGrams.

We won't be looking at these classes in detail here, but let's explore a quick example that demonstrates how to use an XPath query to generate an XML response from SQL Server 2000 using the SqlXmlCommand class. The following code example, sqlxmlexample, references the Microsoft.Data.SqlXml.dll (installed with Web Release 2) when compiling. Here's the VB .NET code – the C# code can be found in the code download:

```
' VB
Option Explicit On
Option Strict On

Imports System
Imports System.Data
```

```vb
Imports System.Xml
' Namespace of SQLXML managed classes
Imports Microsoft.Data.SqlXml

Namespace Wrox.Samples.ADONET
  Public Class SqlXmlExample
    Shared Sub Main
      ' Create an OLEDB connection string
      Dim cn As String = _
"Provider=SQLOLEDB;Server=(local);database=Northwind;user id=sa;password="

      ' Instantiate SqlXmlCommand object
      Dim cmd As SqlXmlCommand = New SqlXmlCommand(cn)

      With cmd
        ' Assign command type for XPath queries
        .CommandType = SqlXmlCommandType.XPath

        ' Provide location of mapping schema
        .SchemaPath="Employees.xsd"

        ' Set command text to XPath expression
        .CommandText="Employee[@EmployeeID=4]"

        ' Set the root node of resulting XML
        .RootTag="Northwind-Employees"
      End With

      ' Create XmlReader object capture resulting XML
      Dim reader As XmlReader = cmd.ExecuteXmlReader()

      ' Create XmlDataDocument
      Dim xmlDoc As XmlDataDocument = New XmlDataDocument()

      ' Load XmlReader object
      xmlDoc.Load(reader)

      ' Close XmlReader
      reader.Close()

      ' Write contents of XmlDataDocument to screen
      Console.WriteLine(xmlDoc.OuterXml)
    End Sub
  End Class
End Namespace
```

The result of compiling and running this code (plus some formatting here for ease of reading) is:

```xml
<?xml version="1.0" encoding="utf-8"?>
  <Northwind-Employees>
   <Employee EmployeeID="4">
    <FirstName>
     Margaret
    </FirstName>
    <LastName>
     Peacock
    </LastName>
   </Employee>
  </Northwind-Employees>
```

However, if an error occurs, the resulting XML document will contain a processing instruction node with a structure similar to this:

```
<?MSSQLError HResult="" Source="" Description=""?>
```

Summary

There is no doubt that ADO.NET is rich with XML features. We have learned that wherever the data comes from, we can either view it hierarchically or relationally. We covered the capabilities of the `DataSet` class, including reading and writing XML, and programmatically accessing or changing its XML representation. We highlighted how to synchronize `DataSets` with `XmlDataDocuments`, and why we would do so. We also covered the advantages of strongly typed `DataSets`. Finally, we took a glimpse at how to access some of the XML features available with SQL Server 2000.

With ADO.NET, we are empowered to make application design decisions based on the business needs at hand, not restricted to a given service or technology. Because we can use XML features so easily in our data access, ADO.NET is sure to be one of the greatest crowd-pleasers in the .NET Framework.

11

ASP.NET

Introduction

In previous chapters you have been introduced to the various XML classes from the `System.Xml` namespaces and MSXML, as well as ADO.NET. As you must have figured out, .NET has harnessed the power and flexibility of XML in every possible way. ASP.NET – the next generation of Active Server Pages (ASP) – is no exception. With ASP.NET, ASP technology has evolved into a more scalable, easy-to-program, and reliable model.

This chapter is intended to introduce you to some of the basics of ASP.NET – it will in no way provide you with everything you need to know about ASP.NET, since doing so would require a book of its own. However, we will talk about the main features of ASP.NET, such as Web Forms and Web Controls, but again we do not intend to provide a complete reference of these topics. In the next chapter, *Case Study: Using Web Services*, we will demonstrate both these areas further. For more information about ASP.NET see Professional ASP.NET, by Alex Homer et al., ISBN 1-861004-88-5, also from Wrox Press.

We will focus more on the relationship between ASP.NET and XML. In particular, we will try to show you:

❑ How ASP.NET Web Controls follow XML syntax

❑ Which Web Controls ASP.NET provides that can deal with XML data

❑ How ASP.NET uses XML for Web Application configuration

This chapter assumes basic familiarity with ASP, the XML Document Object Model (DOM) and ADO.NET. If you are not familiar with the DOM, please refer to Chapter 4, which covers DOM Navigation. To learn more about ADO.NET refer to Chapter 10.

What is ASP.NET?

ASP.NET is the next generation of ASP technology and differs significantly from its predecessors. In fact, Microsoft has completely re-engineered the product. ASP.NET is more scalable and robust than previous releases of ASP and it provides a whole new way of programming web applications in an efficient and easy way. We can still use the existing ASP pages along with ASP.NET; however, there are limitations to this backward compatibility. All the built-in objects like Request and Response are still available to ASP.NET, so that you can still code in the old ASP way if you wish. However, considering the limitations of this (covered later) and the rich features that ASP.NET offers, it is highly recommended to avoid using ASP.NET along with traditional ASP pages. In the following sections we will examine some areas that mark ASP.NET as distinct from ASP.

Language-Neutral Execution

In traditional ASP, the choice of programming languages is limited, with VBScript and Jscript the primary options available to the programmers. In addition, VBScript has its own set of limitations, like the lack of strong data types, and the lack of objected-oriented features (which even VB 6 lacks), etc.

> In VB 6 inheritance was limited to 'interface inheritance'. VB .NET now provides true inheritance. There is now a difference in 'implementing' and 'inheriting'. VB .NET also has introduced many new keywords like `MustInherit`, `NonInheritable` and `Overridable` that you can use while developing your classes.

ASP.NET provides a true language-neutral execution framework for Web applications to use. This provides language independence as long as the language outputs the Microsoft Intermediate Language that is understood by the .NET Framework. This means that whether we use C#, VB .NET, JScript .NET, managed C++ .NET, or Perl, our code will be compiled to Intermediate Language (IL) and then executed by the .NET Framework. There are many third-party efforts to develop .NET-compatible versions of existing languages. This also means that ASP.NET now can take full advantage of rich .NET Framework base classes via any compliant language.

Compiled Execution

One of the drawbacks of traditional ASP pages is that they are parsed each time they are requested, even though the same logic is to be performed every time. This naturally makes ASP execution slower. ASP.NET changes this behavior. When we execute an ASP.NET page for the first time, it gets compiled into a binary `.dll` (dynamic link library) and then gets executed. If you are following code-behind coding technique (discussed later) then you can compile the page class into a `.dll` even before deploying the pages. All future requests are served by this compiled code, making execution faster. Don't worry about file modifications either – ASP.NET automatically detects the changes and recompiles the page whenever necessary.

Also, previous versions of ASP required that you restart the web application when you changed files like `global.asa`. ASP.NET now detects changes to files automatically and recompiles them. This means that there is no server down time experienced by the user.

Event-Driven Processing and Web Forms

Every ASP.NET page is called as a Web Form rather than as a simple page. This is because, just like tools such as Visual Basic, ASP.NET now provides an event-driven programming model to developers. ASP developers typically use form postbacks to handle any server-side processing, but there are no server-side events generated by the HTML `<form>` elements that they can handle. ASP.NET changes this and introduces server-side events. This means that we can write code that will be executed on the server when a user clicks on a button in their browser. This makes ASP.NET programming much easier and is similar to event-driven tools like VB.

Server-Side Controls

Server-side controls are an exciting addition in ASP.NET. Server-side controls are controls such as textboxes and checkboxes, which are processed by the server and reduce coding to a great extent. In fact, we can now build Web Forms without using `<%` and `%>` tags or HTML `input` tags at all, and this is one of the most important advances in web development enabled by ASP.NET: separation of code from presentation.

The beauty of server-side controls lies in the fact that, even though we are not directly using HTML `<form>` elements, ASP.NET will finally render everything as HTML. So no worries about browser compatibility! Server-side controls wrap the functionality of HTML form controls in an object oriented way. Each server-side control is actually a class that has properties, methods, and events.

Here are some advantages of server-side controls:

- ❏ We can design forms without using native HTML controls. Although server-side controls provide similar structure, the attribute names and usage are more consistent than with HTML.

- ❏ ASP.NET server controls are capable of maintaining their state without complex code. The programmer need not keep track of values entered by the user in form controls while redisplaying the same form. Behind the scenes, ASP.NET uses hidden form fields to accomplish this.

- ❏ ASP.NET also provides many advanced controls like `DataGrid`, `DataList`, `Repeater`, and `Calendar`, which provide rich functionality and save the programmer from lots of code.

- ❏ All the ASP.NET server controls are finally rendered in HTML 3.2 equivalents, so any browser that supports HTML 3.2 and above can display them without any compatibility issues.

- ❏ Server-side controls allow us to handle events on the server side. For example, we can write `click` event handlers for buttons, which will be processed at the server end.

- ❏ With normal HTML controls we can only access their values via forms. Server-side controls allow access to all the properties on the server-side. This implies that we can do tasks like changing the appearance of controls (color, font, etc.) on the fly by using their properties, while processing the page at server-side.

- ❏ We can data-bind many server-side controls like `DataGrid`, `DataList`, etc. The data-bound controls eliminate much of the code required for tasks like paging and navigation. The data binding does not simply mean binding with database tables but also with arrays, object collections, and XML files.

ASP.NET server-side controls come in two flavors:

❏ **HTML controls**: These represent standard HTML controls but run at the server end. The markup inside the ASP.NET Web Form matches closely with normal HTML form controls, but it has an additional `runat` attribute, which is set to `server`, so that it can be processed server-side. This is provided for programmers who may want to stick to old-style HTML syntax.

❏ **Web Controls**: ASP.NET offers a set of controls that provide consistent properties, methods and events. Some Web Controls like `DataGrid`, validation controls, and calendar control provide advanced features that are not available with standard HTML controls.

Note that even though there are two flavors of server-side controls, essentially they are rendered the same way to the web browser. In the sections to come, we will be concentrating on Web Controls rather than HTML controls.

Custom Web Controls

In traditional ASP, the most common method of reusing code is with COM components and `include` files. Typically, COM components are used to encapsulate our business logic, whereas `include` files are used to encapsulate repeatedly used HTML markup and general functions that do not fit in a component. While ASP.NET allows us to wrap our business logic in components, it provides yet another method of code reuse in the form of custom Web Controls. Custom Web Controls are similar to ActiveX controls in that we can create reusable Web Controls by assembling various built-in controls. However, custom Web Controls emit pure HTML code. For example, we may assemble a complete login form in a custom Web Control and use it across multiple web applications. Just like built-in Web Controls, custom Web Controls can have methods, properties, and events of their own.

Error Handling and Tracing

ASP.NET provides highly customized ways to handle application errors. Each Web Form can have its own "error page" that is shown for any unhandled errors originating from that Web Form. We can also configure our application to have a generic error page that is displayed for all the unhandled errors throughout the application. We can also customize the error pages that are displayed for HTTP server responses like 404 – File Not Found, and 401 – Access Denied, via the configuration file itself. In addition to custom error handling, ASP.NET allows a powerful tracing feature for Web Forms. This comes in handy when debugging code. Instead of outputting various values on screen via `Response.Write`, trace gives a list of HTTP headers, session cookie IDs, etc., at the end of the page in a very systematic manner. We can also insert additional values in the trace output.

Server-Side Caching

ASP.NET provides powerful caching features, which help to improve the overall performance of our application. We can cache page outputs as well as our data and objects. ASP.NET provides a separate set of caching APIs that offer control on what we cache and the lifetime of the cached object. Cached objects can be refreshed or removed, based on some fixed time interval, certain idle time, or even external dependencies. Caching does not simply mean your Web Forms but also custom controls. There are various parameters based on which ASP.NET maintains cached versions of your pages, for instance Form parameters, query string parameters, HTTP header information, etc.

Configuration and Deployment

Prior to ASP.NET, configuring a web application required programmers to sit in front of an IIS snap-in and change individual configuration settings. The settings include things like the default page language or session time-out values. ASP.NET allows very flexible and easy configuration via special XML files. Another area where the traditional ASP programmer had to spend considerable efforts was COM component registration. Unlike COM components, .NET components (often referred to as assemblies) do not require any kind of registration in the Registry. This is possible due to the fact that .NET components store all the information about themselves in some thing known as an Assembly Manifest. Now we can deploy our applications by using the XCOPY utility to copy the web application folder to the web server without needing to go to the server to perform configuration changes and component registrations. However, note that configuring the physical directory as a web application still needs to be done prior to running any of your ASP.NET pages. (By the way, for those of you who are unfamiliar with DOS commands, XCOPY is a DOS command that copies the entire directory tree, that is, a directory and all its sub-directories, from one location to another.)

Compatibility with ASP

Even though ASP.NET provides exciting new features, one thing we should note is that there are already many applications up and running developed in traditional ASP. In cases like transition from ASP to ASP.NET and extending current ASP applications, we may want to use ASP alongside ASP.NET. Microsoft recognized this need and hence provided ways so that you may use ASP.NET along with ASP. In traditional ASP, every page is stored with an extension of .asp. In ASP.NET, each page is stored with an extension of .aspx. The processors for each of these extensions are entirely different. Also, the global.asa file of ASP has the equivalent file global.asax in ASP.NET. Your web application may contain both .aspx and .asp files. However, there are some limitations to be aware of. A major limitation is that we cannot share application or session state between our ASP and ASP.NET pages. Also, global.asa events are fired only for ASP pages, whereas global.asax events are fired only for .aspx pages. This means that application and session events are fired separately for ASP and ASPX pages. Because of these limitations, it is recommended that you do not mix up ASP and ASP.NET unless it is absolutely necessary.

ASP.NET and XML

Having seen some basics about ASP.NET, let us see how ASP.NET and XML are related to one another. The relation between ASP.NET and XML is in two major ways:

❑ ASP.NET uses XML extensively to represent Web Controls and configuration settings.

❑ ASP.NET provides Web Controls that can deal with XML data and display it as per our requirement. The representation can be tabular or stylesheet-based.

Here are some areas in which ASP.NET and XML go hand in hand:

❑ **Representation of Web Forms and Web Controls:** Each ASP.NET application typically consists of one or more Web Forms that, in turn, consist of various Web Controls. The Web Form consists of HTML and markup for Web Controls. The markup used for the Web Controls is actually XML. We will see some examples of this in later sections.

❑   **Functionality of MSXML and the System.XML namespace:** ASP.NET can use the full functionality provided by the `System.Xml` namespace and MSXML. The `System.Xml` namespace and MSXML are discussed in detail in previous chapters.

❑   **Data-bound controls like DataGrid and DropDownList to display XML data:** ASP.NET provides many controls like the `DataGrid` and `DropDownList` that are used typically to display data from database tables. However, we can also use them to display data from XML documents.

❑   **XML Control to quickly display XML documents formatted with XSL stylesheets:** There are many times when we want to show our XML data after applying an XSL stylesheet to it. We can do this by using MSXML or `System.Xml` objects. However, ASP.NET allows us to perform the same task without much of the coding via the XML Web Control.

❑   **Web Application configuration via an XML document:** ASP.NET relies on a special XML document for configuration purpose. This document exists as a disk file called `web.config`. We will explore `web.config` in later sections.

❑   **Web Services:** Web Services offer services over the web. They provide a "black-box" programming model where the functionality is requested over the Web. For example, you may get stock quotes, daily news, or weather information by calling a Web Service from your web application or even desktop application. The communication between your application and a Web Service occurs via the HTTP protocol using standards like SOAP (Simple Object Access Protocol). Web Services and SOAP are discussed in detail in Chapters 13 and 14.

We'll now take a closer look at Web Forms, and show the XML syntax of Web Controls in action. Following this, we'll move on to the more exciting Web Controls that allow us to display XML documents.

Web Forms and Web Controls

ASP.NET calls each `.aspx` page as a Web Form. By now, you may be wondering what the differences between traditional ASP pages and Web Forms are. Here is a list covering major points:

❑   ASP pages typically contain HTML `<form>` elements and forms are posted back to the server by some action, such as clicking a Submit button. Web Form `<form>` tags contain an additional attribute called `runat`, whose value must be set to `server`. This form tells the web server that this form is to be processed at the server end. The following code illustrates how it looks:

```
<FORM id="Form1" runat="server" >
   ...
</FORM>
```

❑   Traditional ASP pages are just a mixture of HTML and code blocks. They do not have any "object model" behind them. ASP.NET Web Forms provide an object-oriented programming model. Each Web Form is derived from the `System.Web.UI.Page` class and offers various properties, methods, and events. You can also write properties and methods of your own.

❑   Separating HTML markup and code is often difficult in ASP. However, ASP.NET provides a way to separate our code from rest of the markup by using "code-behind" files. A code-behind file is nothing more than a sourcecode file that contains various event handlers and functions. We simply refer to this file from our `.aspx` page. The following example will make this clear:

```
<%@ page language="vb" codebehind="webform1.vb"
        Inherits="Mynamespace.WebForm1" %>
```

This code-behind approach provides several advantages. These include:

- ❑   The code is truly separated from display markup
- ❑   The code can be deployed as a compiled DLL, which means you can hide your business logic from casual eyes
- ❑   The page becomes easier to maintain and any changes are easy to perform
- ❑   The display markup can be "imported" from the web designer team

On the other side, disadvantages of code-behind can be:

- ❑   You have to add certain page-level attributes that provide information about class and namespace names
- ❑   If you want to compile the code-behind files, you have to take extra steps
- ❑   You have to deploy code-behind files along with .aspx files

However, the code-behind approach is more sophisticated and is used extensively by VS .NET

If we want to avoid writing our code in separate code-behind files then we can also write our code in <script> blocks that are marked with runat="server" in the .aspx page itself:

```
<script language="VB" runat="server">
    ...
</script>
```

ASP uses traditional HTML controls. These control values can be accessed at server side only through a Form or QueryString collection. In contrast, ASP.NET Web Controls are actually classes that have properties, methods, and events and can be programmed just like any other objects. Web Controls are represented by special XML markup at design time. Just like Web Forms they are also marked to run at "server". This means that various events of the controls are handled at the server and these events can refer to other controls in an objected-oriented way. At run time they are rendered as HTML. ASP.NET provides several in-built Web Controls out of the box, and we can also develop our own controls.

The figure overleaf shows how ASP.NET Web Forms are processed by the web server (IIS):

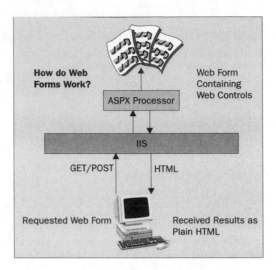

The following are the stages involved in Web Form processing:

1. We request a Web Form by entering its URL in the web browser (or navigate to it via some link).

2. IIS detects that we have requested a Web Form from the extension `.aspx`.

3. IIS routes the request for further processing to the ASP.NET processor, which is a DLL named `aspnet_isapi.dll`.

4. The ASP.NET processor starts processing the Web Form and associated code behind (if any). If your Web Form is being called for the first time it will be compiled into a DLL and the same DLL is used for any future requests to the page.

5. `Page_Init` and `Page_Load` events of the Web Form are fired. Note that these events are always fired before firing any of the Web Control events.

6. Web control events are then fired. For example, if you submit a Web Form by clicking on a button then `Page_Init` is fired first followed by `Page_Load` and then the `Button1_Click` event is fired.

7. After processing all control events the `Page_Unload` event is fired.

8. The output is sent by IIS to the user and displayed in the browser.

Web Form and Web Controls Namespaces

All of the functionality of .NET base classes is logically encapsulated in namespaces. Web Controls are no exception. All the classes intrinsic to ASP.NET are available in the `System.Web` namespace. ASP.NET Web Forms are derived from the `Page` class that resides in the `System.Web.UI` namespace. The `System.Web` namespace further contains the `System.Web.UI.HtmlControls` and the `System.Web.UI.WebControls` namespaces, which contain classes related to HTML controls and Web Controls respectively.

Web Forms in Action – User Feedback Web Form

Let's develop a simple Web Form and examine its various parts. We will develop a user feedback screen of the type that is commonly used to accept details like name, e-mail address, gender, country, and comments. We will then store these details in an XML file. We will use VS .NET to develop our application. The complete source code is available in this chapter's folder under the `UserFeedback` sub-folder.

Creating a New Web Project in Visual Studio .NET

In order to create a new ASP.NET web project, you need to follow these steps:

❑ Open VS .NET and select **File | New | Project**. You will be prompted with a dialog box as shown below asking you the type of the project:

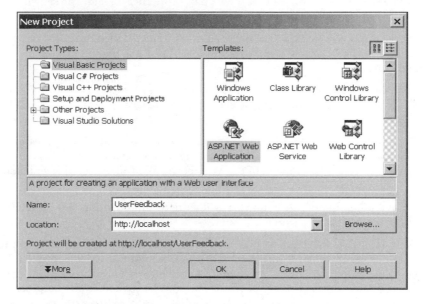

❑ Select **Visual Basic Projects** in the **Project Types** pane, and **ASP.NET Web Application** in the **Templates** pane.

❑ Type in the name for your web application as `UserFeedback` and click on **OK**.

VS .NET will create a new project and open the Web Form Designer. It will also create a virtual root under IIS with the same name as the project. We used VB .NET as our language of choice but you can also choose other languages like C#.

Once you create the project, VS .NET will open a blank Web Form in a Visual Designer ready for design and coding.

Adding Controls to the Web Form and Setting their Properties

Adding controls to the Web Form is just a matter of dragging them from the toolbox and placing them on the Web Form designer. If the toolbox is not visible on your machine you can select View | Toolbox from the menu.

Once you add the controls to the Web Form, you can set their properties. To change any of the property values, simply select the control and use the Properties window to set various property values. If properties window is not visible on your machine select View | Properties Window.

To start with, rename the default Web Form (`WebForm1.aspx`) to `UserFeedback.aspx`. Then complete the form by doing the following:

❑ Add five labels to the form and set their `Text` properties to values as shown opposite (Name :, E-mail Address :, Gender :, Country :, and Comments :).

❑ Add three textboxes to enter values for **Name, E-mail Address,** and **Comments.** Note that the `textmode` property of `Textbox3` is set to `MultiLine` so that it represents a `<textarea>` element.

❑ Add two radio buttons as shown and set their `Text` property. In order to group them together so only one of them at a time can be selected, set the `GroupName` property of both the radio buttons to `gender`.

❑ Add a `DropDownList` Web Control. We need to fill this control with a list of countries stored in a database table. We achieve this by binding it to a `DataSet`. The code to do just that is written in the `Page_Load` event of the Web Form. We will discuss this code later.

❑ Add a Button Web Control that posts the form back. Set its `Text` property to `Submit`. In the `Click` event handler of this button we will write this information to an XML file so that the web site administrator can review it later.

❑ We want to ensure that the user fills in all the required information before submitting the form. In our case; **Name, E-mail Address,** and **Comments** are mandatory fields, so we have added `RequiredFieldValidator` controls to each of the textbox controls. Set the `ControlToValidate` property of the `RequiredFieldValidator` controls to `TextBox1`, `TextBox2`, and `TextBox3` respectively. Also set the `ErrorMessage` property of the `RequiredFieldValidator` controls to some explanatory message. This message will be displayed if the user submits the form without filling the respective control.

When you have completed the above instructions, your project should look something like the following screenshot:

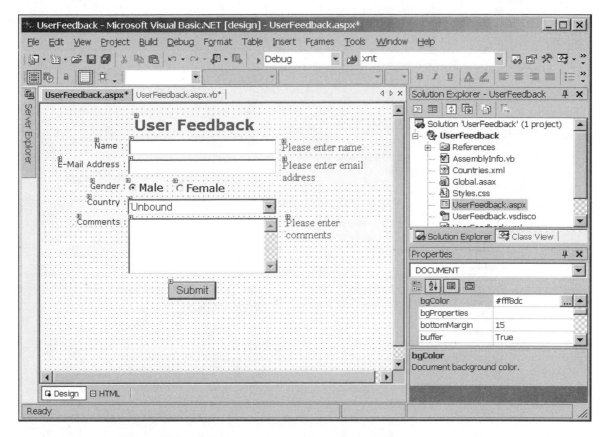

Examining the Markup Generated by Our Web Form

At this stage it might be interesting to see what markup VS .NET generated for all of the above controls. We can do this by selecting the HTML tab on the VS .NET designer window.

```
<%@ Page Language="vb" AutoEventWireup="false"
        Codebehind="UserFeedback.aspx.vb"
        Inherits="UserFeedback.UserFeedback" %>

<!DOCTYPE HTML PUBLIC "-//W3C//DTD HTML 4.0 Transitional//EN">
<HTML>
<HEAD>
    <title></title>
    <meta name="GENERATOR" content="Microsoft Visual Studio.NET 7.0">
    <meta name="CODE_LANGUAGE" content="Visual Basic 7.0">
    <meta name="vs_defaultClientScript" content="JavaScript">
    <meta name="vs_targetSchema"
          content="http://schemas.microsoft.com/intellisense/ie5">
</HEAD>
```

```
<body MS_POSITIONING="GridLayout" bgColor="cornsilk">
<form id="Form1" method="post" runat="server">
   <asp:TextBox id="TextBox1"
      style="Z-INDEX: 101; LEFT: 140px; POSITION: absolute; TOP: 55px"
      runat="server" Width="231px" Height="24px">
   </asp:TextBox>
   <asp:Label id="Label6"
      style="Z-INDEX: 111; LEFT: 79px; POSITION: absolute; TOP: 120px"
      runat="server" Font-Names="Verdana" Font-Size="Smaller">
      Gender :
   </asp:Label>
   <asp:Label id="Label5"
      style="Z-INDEX: 110; LEFT: 148px; POSITION: absolute; TOP: 19px"
      runat="server" ForeColor="#C04000" Font-Bold="True"
      Font-Names="Verdana" Font-Size="Larger">
      User Feedback
   </asp:Label>
   <asp:Label id="Label4"
      style="Z-INDEX: 109; LEFT: 58px; POSITION: absolute; TOP: 176px"
      runat="server" Font-Names="Verdana" Font-Size="Smaller">
      Comments :
   </asp:Label>
   <asp:Label id="Label3"
      style="Z-INDEX: 108; LEFT: 74px; POSITION: absolute; TOP: 145px"
      runat="server" Font-Names="Verdana" Font-Size="Smaller">
      Country :
   </asp:Label>
   <asp:Label id="Label2"
      style="Z-INDEX: 107; LEFT: 28px; POSITION: absolute; TOP: 86px"
      runat="server" Font-Names="Verdana" Font-Size="Smaller">
      E-Mail Address :
   </asp:Label>
   <asp:Label id="Label1"
      style="Z-INDEX: 106; LEFT: 86px; POSITION: absolute; TOP: 57px"
      runat="server" Font-Names="Verdana" Font-Size="Smaller">
      Name :
   </asp:Label>
   <asp:Button id="Button1"
      style="Z-INDEX: 105; LEFT: 202px; POSITION: absolute; TOP: 279px"
      runat="server" Text="Submit">
   </asp:Button>
   <asp:TextBox id="TextBox3"
      style="Z-INDEX: 104; LEFT: 139px; POSITION: absolute; TOP: 178px"
      runat="server" Width="235px" Height="88px"
      TextMode="MultiLine">
   </asp:TextBox>
   <asp:DropDownList id="DropDownList1"
      style="Z-INDEX: 103; LEFT: 138px; POSITION: absolute; TOP: 149px"
      runat="server" Width="234px" Height="22px">
   </asp:DropDownList>
   <asp:TextBox id="TextBox2"
      style="Z-INDEX: 102; LEFT: 139px; POSITION: absolute; TOP: 86px"
      runat="server" Width="232px" Height="24px">
   </asp:TextBox>
   <asp:RadioButton id="RadioButton1"
```

```
          style="Z-INDEX: 112; LEFT: 135px; POSITION: absolute; TOP: 120px"
          runat="server" Text="Male" Font-Names="Verdana" Font-Size="Smaller"
          GroupName="gender" Checked="True">
    </asp:RadioButton>
    <asp:RadioButton id="RadioButton2"
          style="Z-INDEX: 113; LEFT: 209px; POSITION: absolute; TOP: 121px"
          runat="server" Text="Female" Font-Names="Verdana" Font-Size="Smaller"
          GroupName="gender">
    </asp:RadioButton>
    <asp:RequiredFieldValidator id="RequiredFieldValidator1"
          style="Z-INDEX: 114; LEFT: 379px; POSITION: absolute; TOP: 59px"
          runat="server" ErrorMessage="Please enter name"
          ControlToValidate="TextBox1" Font-Size="Smaller">
    </asp:RequiredFieldValidator>
    <asp:RequiredFieldValidator id="RequiredFieldValidator2"
          style="Z-INDEX: 115; LEFT: 380px; POSITION: absolute; TOP: 87px"
          runat="server" Width="174px" Height="17px"
          ErrorMessage="Please enter email address"
          ControlToValidate="TextBox2" Font-Size="Smaller">
    </asp:RequiredFieldValidator>
    <asp:RequiredFieldValidator id="RequiredFieldValidator3"
          style="Z-INDEX: 116; LEFT: 385px; POSITION: absolute; TOP: 177px"
          runat="server" Width="147px" Height="38px"
          ErrorMessage="Please enter comments" ControlToValidate="TextBox3"
          Font-Size="Smaller">
    </asp:RequiredFieldValidator>
  </form>
  </body>
  </HTML>
```

As seen above, most of the markup is XML and follows the rules of XML grammar closely. Note that at the top of the page the code-behind file for the Web Form is specified using the following directive:

```
<%@ Page Language="vb" AutoEventWireup="false"
        Codebehind="UserFeedback.aspx.vb"
        Inherits="UserFeedback.UserFeedback" %>
```

This directive tells ASP.NET that all the code for this Web Form (event handlers, functions, etc.) lies in a file named UserFeedback.aspx.vb and this Web Form is inherited from the UserFeedback class found in that file. Note that we may opt for not using the code-behind style of writing code. In such cases, all the code can be put in the <script runat="server"></script> block in the page. Here are some points that are to be noted from the above markup:

❑ The <form> tag has an attribute runat that is set to server. This is the only valid value for the runat attribute.

❑ As can be seen, all of the Web Controls are marked using a specific XML vocabulary. They take generalized form of:

```
<asp:control_type runat="server" id="control_id"
                  event="event_handler"   ...  />
```

Here the `control_type` represents the type of Web Control such as: `TextBox`, `Label`, or `Button`. `id` is an identifier that uniquely identifies the control. The `event` attribute indicates a particular event and its handler `runat` attribute tells ASP.NET processor that this control is to be processed at the `server`. In addition to the above information, controls may have further attributes or nested elements:

❑ Each Web Control is identified by a unique ID, represented by an `id` attribute. This ID is used to programmatically access the control.

❑ Web Control events can be represented by attributes of type `Onxxxx` where `xxxx` is the event name. For example: `OnClick`. Note that the event attribute values are just event handler method names and do not contain any parameters, unlike JavaScript. This is because in ASP.NET (actually in .NET) all the event handlers take a unique signature, as we will see in the next sections.

As can be seen from the above code sample, the Web Controls follow many of the rules of XML grammar (even though not very strictly), such as:

❑ All start tags have matching end tags. For empty elements we use the `< ... />` style of markup.

❑ Nesting of elements is done properly. There are some controls, such as `DataGrid` and `Repeater`, which contain nested elements, as we will see in later sections.

❑ Attributes are enclosed in double quotes. This rule is not strictly followed by ASP.NET. This might be to make the HTML coder's life easier. If you are using VS .NET you will observe that it automatically puts attribute values in double quotes for you.

Note that Web Form markup is not case-sensitive. This is in line with HTML markup itself.

The following is a screenshot of our Web Form when run in Internet Explorer. Note how the red error message was displayed when we attempted to post the form without filling the **Name** field.

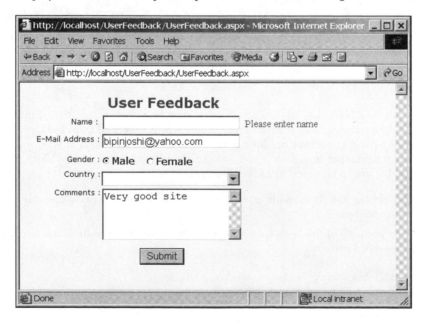

Writing Code for our Application

Now it's time to write some code to achieve the functionality we want. Go to the code view by double-clicking on the Web Form or by right-clicking on the form and selecting View Code. This will open a window as shown below:

As can be seen, UserFeedback is a class that inherits from the Page class. All the Web Controls that we placed on the Web Form are actually treated as class variables in this class. We can now write event handlers for the various controls involved. Note that every event handler has a typical syntax as shown below:

```
Sub EventHandlerFunctionName (sender as object, e as EventArgs)
```

Here, sender represents the object or control that caused the event to trigger, and e provides more information about the event.

Our first task is to fill the `DropDownList` control with country values stored in the `Countries.xml` file. The file can be found along with this chapter's source code available from the download. The `Countries.xml` file has a structure as follows:

```xml
<?xml version="1.0" encoding="utf-8" ?>
<countries>
   <country>
      <name>USA</name>
      <code>US</code>
   </country>
   <country>
      <name>UK</name>
      <code>UK</code>
   </country>
   <country>
      <name>India</name>
      <code>IN</code>
   </country>
</countries>
```

Since we will be using classes from the `System.Xml` namespace, we will add `Imports` statement at the beginning of the class as shown below:

```
Imports System.Xml
```

We will now add the following code in the `Page_Load` event handler:

```vb
If Page.IsPostBack = False Then
    Dim ds As New DataSet()
    'read country list from xml file
    ds.ReadXml(Request.PhysicalApplicationPath & "Countries.xml")
    'bind DropDownList1 with dataset
    DropDownList1.DataSource = ds
    DropDownList1.DataTextField = "Name"
    DropDownList1.DataValueField = "code"
    DropDownList1.DataBind()
End If
```

Here, we have read the contents of the `Countries.xml` file in a `DataSet` object using its `ReadXml()` method. We then set the `DataSource` property of the `DropDownList` to the `DataSet` object. We also set the `DataTextField` and `DataValueField` properties so that we will display the country name to the user via the `DisplayTextField` property, but still access `code` programmatically via the `DataValueField` property. Finally, we called the `DataBind()` method to actually bind the `DropDownList` with the data from the `DataSet` object.

Note the use of the `IsPostBack` property of the `Page` class. This property tells us whether the page is being called for the first time or if it is being loaded because of a post-back. Since Web Controls can maintain their state between post-backs, we will fill the DropDownList only if the Web Form is being loaded for the first time.

Now, let us turn our attention to storing the data in an XML file. For storing the data entered by the user, we will use an XML file named `UserFeedback.xml` having following structure:

```xml
<?xml version="1.0" encoding="utf-8" ?>
<feedback>
    <name></name>
    <email></email>
    <gender></gender>
    <country></country>
    <comments></comments>
</feedback>
```

We will do the save operation in the Click event of Button1. Double-click on Button1 in the designer to open the code window with the Click event handler skeleton added, and place the following code in it:

```vb
Private Sub Button1_Click(ByVal sender As System.Object, _
                ByVal e As System.EventArgs) Handles Button1.Click

    Dim MyDoc As New XmlDocument()
    Dim MyFeedbackElement As XmlElement
    Dim MyNameElement As XmlElement
    Dim MyEmailElement As XmlElement
    Dim MyGenderElement As XmlElement
    Dim MyCountryElement As XmlElement
    Dim MyCommentsElement As XmlElement
    Dim MyTextNode As XmlText

    MyDoc.Load(Request.PhysicalApplicationPath & "userfeedback.xml")

    MyFeedbackElement = MyDoc.CreateElement("feedback")
    MyNameElement = MyDoc.CreateElement("name")
    MyEmailElement = MyDoc.CreateElement("email")
    MyGenderElement = MyDoc.CreateElement("gender")
    MyCountryElement = MyDoc.CreateElement("country")
    MyCommentsElement = MyDoc.CreateElement("comments")

    MyTextNode = MyDoc.CreateTextNode(TextBox1.Text)
    MyNameElement.AppendChild(MyTextNode)

    MyTextNode = MyDoc.CreateTextNode(TextBox2.Text)
    MyEmailElement.AppendChild(MyTextNode)

    If RadioButton1.Checked = True Then
        MyTextNode = MyDoc.CreateTextNode("Male")
    Else
        MyTextNode = MyDoc.CreateTextNode("Female")
    End If
    MyGenderElement.AppendChild(MyTextNode)

    MyTextNode = MyDoc.CreateTextNode(DropDownList1.SelectedItem.Value)
    MyCountryElement.AppendChild(MyTextNode)

    MyTextNode = MyDoc.CreateTextNode(TextBox3.Text)
    MyCommentsElement.AppendChild(MyTextNode)

    MyFeedbackElement.AppendChild(MyNameElement)
```

```
      MyFeedbackElement.AppendChild(MyEmailElement)
      MyFeedbackElement.AppendChild(MyGenderElement)
      MyFeedbackElement.AppendChild(MyCountryElement)
      MyFeedbackElement.AppendChild(MyCommentsElement)

      MyDoc.DocumentElement.AppendChild(MyFeedbackElement)
      MyDoc.Save(Request.PhysicalApplicationPath & "userfeedback.xml")

   End Sub
```

Here, we have used objects from System.Xml namespaces. These objects, as you must have learned from the previous chapters, are DOM-compliant. We are simply creating a new <feedback> node by appending various child nodes to it. We finally save the modified document to the disk.

Now, our application is complete. We can test it by entering values in various controls and saving them in the XML file. We can also view the source of the Web Form in the browser to confirm that it is indeed a pure HTML.

From our previous discussion we know that ASP.NET is language-neutral. You can also examine the C# version of the above application from this chapter's sourcecode download. Here, we will just scan through the equivalent code written in C#.

Here is the Page_Load event handler:

```
   private void Page_Load(object sender, System.EventArgs e)
   {
      if(Page.IsPostBack == false)
      {
         DataSet ds=new DataSet();
         //read country list from xml file
         ds.ReadXml(Request.PhysicalApplicationPath + "Countries.xml");
         //bind DropDownList1 with dataset
         DropDownList1.DataSource = ds;
         DropDownList1.DataTextField = "Name";
         DropDownList1.DataValueField = "code";
         DropDownList1.DataBind();
      }
   }
```

And here is Click event handler of the button:

```
   private void Button1_Click(object sender, System.EventArgs e)
   {
      XmlDocument MyDoc =new XmlDocument();
      XmlElement MyFeedbackElement;
      XmlElement MyNameElement;
      XmlElement MyEmailElement;
      XmlElement MyGenderElement;
      XmlElement MyCountryElement;
      XmlElement MyCommentsElement;
      XmlText MyTextNode;
      MyDoc.Load(Request.PhysicalApplicationPath + "userfeedback.xml");
```

```
      MyFeedbackElement = MyDoc.CreateElement("feedback");
      MyNameElement = MyDoc.CreateElement("name");
      MyEmailElement = MyDoc.CreateElement("email");
      MyGenderElement = MyDoc.CreateElement("gender");
      MyCountryElement = MyDoc.CreateElement("country");
      MyCommentsElement = MyDoc.CreateElement("comments");
      MyTextNode = MyDoc.CreateTextNode(TextBox1.Text);
      MyNameElement.AppendChild(MyTextNode);
      MyTextNode = MyDoc.CreateTextNode(TextBox2.Text);
      MyEmailElement.AppendChild(MyTextNode);
      if(RadioButton1.Checked == true)
         MyTextNode = MyDoc.CreateTextNode("Male");
      else
         MyTextNode = MyDoc.CreateTextNode("Female");
      MyGenderElement.AppendChild(MyTextNode);
      MyTextNode = MyDoc.CreateTextNode(DropDownList1.SelectedItem.Value);
      MyCountryElement.AppendChild(MyTextNode);
      MyTextNode = MyDoc.CreateTextNode(TextBox3.Text);
      MyCommentsElement.AppendChild(MyTextNode);
      MyFeedbackElement.AppendChild(MyNameElement);
      MyFeedbackElement.AppendChild(MyEmailElement);
      MyFeedbackElement.AppendChild(MyGenderElement);
      MyFeedbackElement.AppendChild(MyCountryElement);
      MyFeedbackElement.AppendChild(MyCommentsElement);
      MyDoc.DocumentElement.AppendChild(MyFeedbackElement);
      MyDoc.Save(Request.PhysicalApplicationPath + "userfeedback.xml");

   }
```

Note that, unlike VB .NET, which uses `Handles` keyword to indicate event handlers, the C# code to attach event handlers is a bit different as shown below:

```
   private void InitializeComponent()
   {
      this.Button1.Click += new System.EventHandler(this.Button1_Click);
      this.Load += new System.EventHandler(this.Page_Load);
   }
```

In the following section we will learn more about some of the commonly used Web Controls.

Common Web Controls

ASP.NET comes with variety of Web Controls each performing a specific task. Discussing each and every control is out of scope of this book. In this section, we will look at some commonly used Web Controls. We will not go much into the syntactical details of each one of them, but rather try to understand their functions.

TextBox

The `TextBox` Web Control is used to accept some textual input from the user. It is represented by `<asp:TextBox>` and maps to HTML `input` tags of type `text` or `password`. `TextBox` Web Controls can act as single line text-box or as multiline text-boxes, in which case they are equivalent to the `textarea` control of HTML. The following is an example of using a `TextBox` Web Control:

```
<asp:TextBox id="TextBox1" Text="Hello" runat="Server" />
```

CheckBox and RadioButton

These controls are used when a certain selection is to be made from a number of possible choices. With the CheckBox Web Controls we can select multiple choices at a time, while radio button Web Controls only allow selection of a single option from a group of choices. They are represented by <asp:CheckBox> and <asp:RadioButton> respectively. They correspond to the HTML <input> element of the types checkbox and radio. The following examples show how to use these controls:

```
<asp:CheckBox id="CheckBox1" Checked="true" runat="server" />
<asp:RadioButton id="RadioButton1" Checked="true" GroupName="MyGroup"
                 runat="server" />
<asp:RadioButton id="RadioButton2" Checked="true" GroupName="MyGroup"
                 runat="server" />
```

DropDownList and ListBox

These controls provide a list of options for the user to choose from. The main difference between a DropDownList and a ListBox is in their appearance in the browser window. Also, ListBox allows multiple items to be selected at a time, which is not possible with DropDownList. They are represented by <asp:DropDownList> and <asp:ListBox> respectively. Each option is represented by <asp:ListItem>. These controls correspond to the select HTML control. These controls can be easily bound to data from a database table. The following is an example of using these controls:

```
<asp:DropDownList id="DropDownList1" runat="server">
   <asp:ListItem value="1" selected="True">List Item 1</asp:ListItem>
   <asp:ListItem value="2" selected="True">List Item 2</asp:ListItem>
</asp:DropDownList>

<asp:ListBox id="List1" selectionmode="multiple" runat="server">
   <asp:ListItem value="1" selected="True">List Item 1</asp:ListItem>
   <asp:ListItem value="2">List Item 2</asp:ListItem>
</asp:ListBox>
```

Button and LinkButton

Buttons and LinkButtons are used to indicate some kind of action like "Submit" or "OK". They are represented by <asp:Button> and <asp:LinkButton> respectively. The Button Web Control corresponds to the HTML input element of type button and the LinkButton Web Controls correspond to a hyperlink that posts back the form. The following examples illustrate their use:

```
<asp:Button id="MyButton" Text="Click Me" OnClick="OnClickHandler"
            runat="server"/>

<asp:LinkButton id="LinkButton1" Text="Click Me" OnClick="OnClickHandler"
                runat="server"/>
```

Calendar

The Calendar control is a functionality-rich Web Control that allows us to select a date. This control is similar to VB 6's Calendar control. It provides variety of ways to customize the appearance of the control and is represented by <asp:Calendar>. Here is how it is used:

```
<asp:Calendar id="Calendar1" runat="server" />
```

Validation Controls

ASP.NET contains a set of controls called validation controls. There main aim is to validate values provided by the user in the Web Form controls. There are different validation controls to perform tasks like checking mandatory fields, comparing values, checking the format of entered data, etc. These controls use client-side JavaScript by default so that form is not posted back unless all the validations succeed.

DataGrid, DataList, and Repeater

These controls offer a highly customized way to display data from a database table or XML document in a tabular format. The DataGrid control also offers capabilities like in-place editing and paging. They provide flexibility of layout in increasing order. They are represented by `<asp:DataGrid>`, `<asp:DataList>`, and `<asp:Repeater>` respectively, and are rendered as HTML tables in the browser. The following example shows the use of DataGrid in its most basic form:

```
<asp:DataGrid id="datagrid1" runat="server"  autogeneratecolumns="true"
              AllowPaging="True" />
```

XML Control

In order to display an XML document in the browser we normally apply a stylesheet to it, to format the data as per our requirement. We can do this using System.Xml or MSXML objects. The XML control provides a very easy way to perform the same task without much coding, and is represented by `<asp:XML>`. We will be covering the XML control in detail in sections to come.

Now that we know about Web Controls, let us use some controls that have XML display capabilities.

Using a DataGrid to Display an XML Document

The ASP.NET DataGrid control is a very flexible way to represent your data in a tabular format. Typically, it is used with database tables but can also be used to display XML data as well. We will focus our attention to displaying XML data in the DataGrid. We will consider two examples here:

❑ One will show how to display data from an XML file into the DataGrid

❑ The other will show how XML from an XmlDocument object is displayed in the DataGrid

In both the examples you will notice that we are actually binding our DataGrid to a DataSet. The DataSet in turn is filled by different sources. The DataSet object has a method, ReadXml(), that we will be using in our examples. The following are the two commonly used signatures of this method:

```
ReadXml (string filename)
```

and:

```
ReadXml (Stream stream)
```

The first syntax accepts the physical path of an XML document, while the second syntax accepts a Stream object containing XML data.

397

Once you have the `DataSet` ready filled with the data you want to display, you can "bind" it with the `DataGrid` Web Control. The `DataGrid` control has a property called `DataSource` that we will set to our `DataSet` instance. This tells the `DataGrid` where the data to be displayed comes from. We can then bind the `DataGrid` to the data by calling the `DataBind()` method of the `DataGrid`.

> For a more detailed discussion about the **DataSet** object and its properties and methods, please refer to Chapter 10, ADO.NET.

Displaying XML from File

In this example, we will show a sample XML document (`employees.xml`) in an ASP.NET `DataGrid` Web Control. The complete source-code for this example is available in this chapter's `DataGridXMLFile` sub-folder.

Create a new Visual Basic ASP.NET Web Application using VS .NET, and name the application `DataGridXMLFile`. Add a new XML file named `Employees.xml` to the project by selecting the **Project | Add New Item...** dialog box. This file represents an employee database where we are storing some information like Name, Age, and Department about various employees. Add the following XML markup in the file and save the file:

```xml
<?xml version="1.0" encoding="utf-8" ?>
<employees>
    <employee>
        <name>John</name>
        <age>26</age>
        <department>Sales</department>
    </employee>
    <employee>
        <name>Mular</name>
        <age>45</age>
        <department>Welfare</department>
    </employee>
    <employee>
        <name>Nicky</name>
        <age>24</age>
        <department>Design</department>
    </employee>
</employees>
```

Add a new Web Form and call it `EmployeeDataGrid.aspx`, and then set it as the default start page. Drag and drop a `DataGrid` Web Control on to the Web Form. VS .NET allows you to quickly format the `DataGrid` controls by providing some pre-built styles. Right-click on the `DataGrid` and select **Auto Format**. Select a style of your choice and click on **OK**. Switch on to HTML view and observe the markup generated by the designer:

```
<%@ Page Language="vb" AutoEventWireup="false"
        Codebehind="EmployeeDataGrid.aspx.vb"
        Inherits="DataGridXMLFile.EmployeeDataGrid"%>
<!DOCTYPE HTML PUBLIC "-//W3C//DTD HTML 4.0 Transitional//EN">

<HTML>
```

```
<HEAD>
    <title></title>
    <meta name="GENERATOR" content="Microsoft Visual Studio.NET 7.0">
    <meta name="CODE_LANGUAGE" content="Visual Basic 7.0">
    <meta name="vs_defaultClientScript" content="JavaScript">
    <meta name="vs_targetSchema"
        content="http://schemas.microsoft.com/intellisense/ie5">
</HEAD>

<body MS_POSITIONING="GridLayout">
<form id="Form1" method="post" runat="server">
    <asp:DataGrid id="DataGrid1"
        style="Z-INDEX: 101; LEFT: 23px; POSITION: absolute; TOP: 21px"
        runat="server" Width="374px" Height="133px" BorderStyle="None"
        BorderWidth="1px" BorderColor="#CC9966" BackColor="White"
        CellPadding="4">
        <FooterStyle ForeColor="#330099" BackColor="#FFFFCC"></FooterStyle>
        <HeaderStyle Font-Bold="True" ForeColor="#FFFFCC"
            BackColor="#990000"></HeaderStyle>
        <PagerStyle HorizontalAlign="Center" ForeColor="#330099"
            BackColor="#FFFFCC"></PagerStyle>
        <SelectedItemStyle Font-Bold="True" ForeColor="#663399"
            BackColor="#FFCC66"></SelectedItemStyle>
        <ItemStyle ForeColor="#330099" BackColor="White"></ItemStyle>
    </asp:DataGrid>
</form>
</body>
</HTML>
```

Now double-click on the Web Form and switch to the code window. Add following code to the
Page_Load event handler of the Web Form:

```
'create instance of dataset
Dim ds As DataSet
ds = New DataSet()
'read XML disk file into the dataset
ds.ReadXml(Request.PhysicalApplicationPath & "employees.xml")
'bind datagrid with the datagrid
DataGrid1.DataSource = ds
DataGrid1.DataBind()
```

As discussed earlier, we cannot directly bind a DataGrid to an XML file. We first read the XML file
into a DataSet via its ReadXml() method, and then bind our grid to that DataSet. The
Request.PhysicalApplicationPath gives us the web application physical disk path. Note that a
DataSet can have more than one DataTable. Our DataSet contains just a single DataTable, hence
we have not specified any particular table name to bind with. If your DataSet has multiple tables, you
can specify data table name via the DataMember property. Also, note that after reading
employees.xml file, the DataTable generated has a name employee that corresponds to
<employee> element from our file.

Build and then run the application by selecting **Debug | Start** or pressing *F5*. You should see something like the following screenshot:

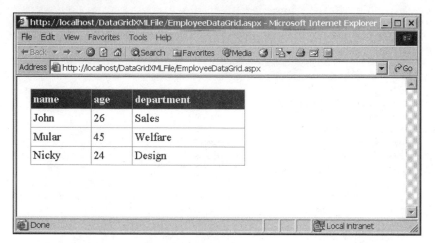

Displaying the Contents of the XMLDocument Object

The previous example showed us how we can display the contents of a static file into a `DataGrid`. What if we are loading the file in an `XmlDocument` object, manipulating it, and then want to display this changed data to the user. Our next example shows just that. The complete source-code for the example is available in this chapter's `DataGridXMLDOM` sub-folder. The following steps will guide you through the process:

- ❑ Create a new Visual Basic ASP.NET Web Application using VS .NET, and name the application `DataGridXMLDOM`.

- ❑ Copy the XML file we created the in previous example to the web application folder.

- ❑ Add a new Web Form named `EmployeeDataGridDOM` to the project.

- ❑ Add a `DataGrid` Web Control to the Web Form by dragging from the toolbox. As described in the previous example format the `DataGrid` with format of your choice.

- ❑ Add following code in the `Page_Load` event handler of the Web Form:

```
'create dataset and XmlDocument objects
Dim ds As DataSet
Dim MyDoc As XmlDocument
Dim Reader As XmlTextReader
Dim XmlText As StringReader

ds = New DataSet()
MyDoc = New XmlDocument()
'load XML disk file
MyDoc.Load(Request.PhysicalApplicationPath & "employees.xml")

  'create a new employee node and append it to the original
```

```
    'content of the file
Dim MyNewEmployee As XmlElement = mydoc.CreateElement("employee")
Dim MyNameElement As XmlElement = mydoc.CreateElement("name")
Dim MyTextNode1 As XmlText = mydoc.CreateTextNode("Nancy")
Dim MyAgeElement As XmlElement = mydoc.CreateElement("age")
Dim MyTextNode2 As XmlText = mydoc.CreateTextNode("32")
Dim MyDeptElement As XmlElement = mydoc.CreateElement("department")
Dim MyTextNode3 As XmlText = MyDoc.CreateTextNode("EDP")

MyNameElement.AppendChild(MyTextNode1)
MyAgeElement.AppendChild(MyTextNode2)
MyDeptElement.AppendChild(MyTextNode3)
MyNewEmployee.AppendChild(MyNameElement)
MyNewEmployee.AppendChild(MyAgeElement)
MyNewEmployee.AppendChild(MyDeptElement)
MyDoc.DocumentElement.AppendChild(MyNewEmployee)

XmlText = New StringReader(MyDoc.DocumentElement.OuterXml)
Reader = New XmlTextReader(XmlText)
'read the new content into the dataset
ds.ReadXml(Reader)
'bind datagrid with the dataset
DataGrid1.DataSource = ds
DataGrid1.DataBind()
```

The code works as follows:

❑ First, the XML document is loaded into the XmlDocument instance so that we can then manipulate it as required. We add a new employee node to the document.

❑ An instance of a StringReader class is created and the XML representation of the XmlDocument is passed to it via the OuterXml property.

❑ We then create an instance of the XmlTextReader by passing this StringReader as a constructor parameter.

❑ Finally, this XmlTextReader is passed to the ReadXml() method of our DataSet. Any time you change XmlDocument instance – say by adding new nodes – we can simply "ReadXml" again by passing the new instance of XmlTextReader.

As in the previous case-run the application and you should get some thing like this:

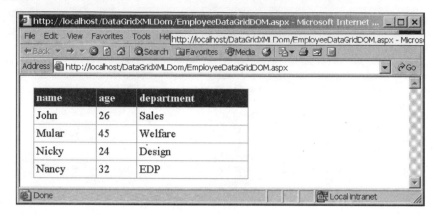

Note the last row of the `DataGrid` that displays the new employee added to the `XmlDocument`.

Using the DataGrid to Display Complex XML Documents

Up to now we have seen how to display data from simple XML documents in an ASP.NET `DataGrid`. In reality we may have XML documents with a more nested structure. When we call the `ReadXml()` method of a `DataSet`, depending on the nesting of various elements, `DataSet` creates different `DataTables` related to one another via `DataRelations`. Let us understand this through an example. We will take the following XML document that represents some companies and their branches, `companybranches.xml`:

```xml
<?xml version="1.0" encoding="utf-8" ?>
<companies>
    <company>
        <name>MyCompany Inc.</name>
        <country>USA</country>
        <branches>
            <branch>Washington</branch>
            <branch>New York</branch>
            <branch>M.A.</branch>
        </branches>
    </company>
    ...
</companies>
```

We will develop a Web Application that will display all the company names and their respective countries in one `DataGrid`. The `DataGrid` allows the user to select a record and, depending on the selection, a second `DataGrid` is shown that lists all the branches of that company.

We will begin as usual by creating a new VS .NET Web Application named `DataGridXMLFileComplex`. The complete source-code for this example can be found in the `DataGridXMLFileComplex` sub-folder of this chapter's folder. Add a Web Form named `CompanyBranches`. Also, add an XML file named `companybranches.xml` and put some data as per the above structure.

Add following code in the `Page_Load` event handler:

```
Private Sub Page_Load(ByVal sender As System.Object, _
                        ByVal e As System.EventArgs) Handles MyBase.Load
    'create instance of dataset
    ds = New DataSet()
    'read XML disk file into the dataset
    ds.ReadXml(Request.PhysicalApplicationPath & "companybranches.xml")
    'bind datagrid with the datagrid
    DataGrid1.DataSource = ds
    DataGrid1.DataMember = "company"
    DataGrid1.DataBind()

    Dim i As Integer
    For i = 0 To ds.Tables.Count - 1
        Label4.Text() = Label4.Text & ds.Tables(i).TableName & "<br>"
    Next
    For i = 0 To ds.Relations.Count - 1
        Label6.Text() = Label6.Text & ds.Relations(i).RelationName & "<br>"
    Next

End Sub
```

The code is similar to previous example except that we are displaying list of `DataTables` and `DataRelations` automatically created by `DataSet`. Note that the `DataSet` created three tables; company, branches and branch. It also created two data relations - company_branches and branches_branch. The table names and relation names are based on XML element names we used in our XML file.

Our next task is to display all the branches for a selected company. Add the `SelectedIndexChanged()` event handler for `DataGrid1` as shown below:

```
Private Sub DataGrid1_SelectedIndexChanged(ByVal sender As System.Object, _
        ByVal e As System.EventArgs) Handles DataGrid1.SelectedIndexChanged

    Dim rows() As DataRow = _
        ds.Tables("branches").Rows(DataGrid1.SelectedIndex).GetChildRows(_
    "branches_branch")
    Dim tb As New DataTable()
    Dim col As New DataColumn("BranchName")
    tb.Columns.Add(col)

    Dim row As DataRow
    Dim newrow As DataRow
    For Each row In rows
        newrow = tb.NewRow()
        newrow(0) = row(0)
        tb.Rows.Add(newrow)
    Next
    DataGrid2.DataSource = tb.DefaultView
    DataGrid2.DataBind()
End Sub
```

This code gets all the related rows and then creates a new data table. This data table contains a list of all the branches for the selected company. The DataGrid2 is bound with the DefaultView of the DataTable.

Here is how the application looks when run in Internet Explorer:

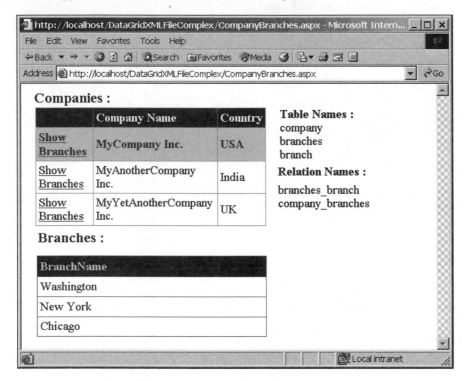

Using the XML Control to Display an XML Document

Recent versions of Internet Explorer provide support for XML and XSLT. We can display our XML data directly in the browser after applying an XSLT Stylesheet to it. We can do this using traditional MSXML objects or System.Xml classes, but ASP.NET further simplifies our task by providing a special XML Web Control. It is represented by <asp:Xml>. XML Web Control has five properties that are important for us:

- ❑ DocumentSource: This property indicates the file name of the source XML document

- ❑ TransformSource: This property indicates the file name of the XSLT stylesheet

- ❑ Document: This property points to an XmlDocument object, which in turn loads the XML document

- ❑ Transform: This property holds a reference to XmlDocument, which loads the XSL stylesheet

- ❑ DocumentContent: This property can be used if our XML data is in the form of a string rather than a disk file or XmlDocument object

Having understood the basics of XML Web Control, we will now see XML control in action. For our examples we will need one XML document and one XSLT stylesheet. We will use the same XML document (employees.xml) that we used in the previous examples. To display this document in our browser (in a tabular form) we will create an XSLT stylesheet – employees.xslt. The following markup shows what this stylesheet contains:

```
<?xml version="1.0" encoding="UTF-8" ?>
<xsl:stylesheet version="1.0"
     xmlns:xsl="http://www.w3.org/1999/XSL/Transform">

<xsl:template match="/">
    <H3>List of Employees :</H3>
    <xsl:for-each select='employees/employee'>
       <ul>
           <li>
               <div style="BORDER-RIGHT: buttonshadow 1px solid;
                    PADDING-RIGHT: 3px; BORDER-TOP: buttonshadow 1px solid;
                    PADDING-LEFT: 3px; FONT-WEIGHT: bold; PADDING-BOTTOM: 3px;
                    BORDER-LEFT: buttonshadow 1px solid; COLOR: black;
                    PADDING-TOP: 3px; BORDER-BOTTOM: buttonshadow 1px solid;
                    FONT-FAMILY: Verdana; BACKGROUND-COLOR: silver">
                   <strong><i>Name : </i></strong>
                   <xsl:value-of select='name' />
               </div>
               <div>
                   <strong><i>Age : </i></strong>
                   <xsl:value-of select='age' />
               </div>
               <div>
                   <strong><i>Department : </i></strong>
                   <xsl:value-of select='department' />
               </div>
           </li>
       </ul>
    </xsl:for-each>
</xsl:template>
</xsl:stylesheet>
```

This stylesheet simply displays various elements, <name>, <age>, and <department> in an HTML table. The complete source-code for the examples to follow is available in the XMLControl sub-folder of this chapter's folder.

Using the XML Control to Display Content from XML files

In this example, we will place an XML Web Control on the Web Form. In the Page_Load event of the form we will set the DocumentSource property to the path of our XML document and the TransformSource property to the path of XSLT stylesheet. The following series of steps will guide you in creating the application:

❑   Create a new Visual Basic ASP.NET Web Application using VS .NET. Name the application as XMLControl.

❑   Add a new Web Form by selecting Project | Add Web Form.... Name the Web Form as XMLControlFiles.

- ❏ Add the employee.xml file to the project as described in previous examples. Similarly, add employees.xslt file to the project.

- ❏ Drag and drop XML Web Control from the toolbox onto the Web Form.

- ❏ Using the **Properties** window set the DocumentSource property of the XML Web Control to employees.xml. Similarly, set the TransformSource property to employees.xslt.

Before running our application, have a look at the markup generated by VS .NET designer:

```
<%@ Page Language="vb" AutoEventWireup="false"
Codebehind="XMLControlFiles.aspx.vb" Inherits="XMLControl.XMLControlFiles"%>
<!DOCTYPE HTML PUBLIC "-//W3C//DTD HTML 4.0 Transitional//EN">
<HTML>
<HEAD>
    <title></title>
    <meta name="GENERATOR" content="Microsoft Visual Studio.NET 7.0">
    <meta name="CODE_LANGUAGE" content="Visual Basic 7.0">
    <meta name="vs_defaultClientScript" content="JavaScript">
    <meta name="vs_targetSchema"
          content="http://schemas.microsoft.com/intellisense/ie5">
</HEAD>
<BODY MS_POSITIONING="GridLayout">
    <FORM id="Form1" method="post" runat="server">
        <asp:Xml id="Xml1" runat="server" DocumentSource="Employees.xml"
          TransformSource="Employees.xslt"></asp:Xml>
    </FORM>
</BODY>
</HTML>
```

Note that we have set the properties of the XML Web Control at design time. You can also set them at run time, in the Page_Load event handler.

Run the application. Here is the output after running the Web Form:

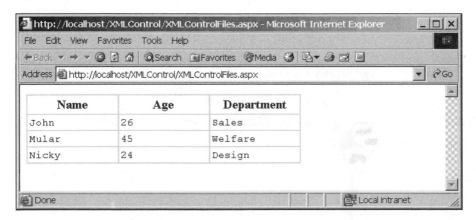

Using the XML Control with XmlDocument

In last example, we used the `DocumentSource` and `TransformSource` properties of the XML Web Control. In this example, we will use the `Document` and `Transform` properties, which take objects of `XmlDocument` class. Here we will first load the XML data file and XSL stylesheet file into `XmlDocument` objects and then set the appropriate properties of the XML Control.

- ❑ Add another Web Form named `XMLControlDOM` to the previous project.
- ❑ Add an XML Web Control to the Web Form.
- ❑ Double-click on the Web Form to open the code window. Write the following code in the `Page_Load` event handler of the Web Form:

```
Dim myxml As New XmlDocument()
Dim myxsl As New XslTransform()

myxml.Load(Request.PhysicalApplicationPath & "employees.xml")
myxsl.Load(Request.PhysicalApplicationPath & "employees.xslt")

Xml1.Document = myxml
Xml1.Transform - myxsl
```

Here, we have created objects of `XmlDocument` and `XmlTransform` and loaded our XML and XSLT files into them. We have then set `Document` and `Transform` properties to the respective objects. When you run this form you will notice that the output of the previous example and this example is exactly the same.

Using the XML Control with a String of XML Data

In this final example, we will see how to use the `DocumentContent` property of the XML Web Control. This property takes a literal XML string to which we will apply our XSL stylesheet. Add another Web Form named `XMLControlString` to the project we created in previous examples, add an XML Web Control to it, and write the following code in the `Page_Load` event handler of the Web Form.

```
Dim myxml As New XmlDocument()
Dim myxsl As New XslTransform()

myxml.Load(Request.PhysicalApplicationPath & "employees.xml")
myxsl.Load(Request.PhysicalApplicationPath & "employees.xslt")

Xml1.DocumentContent = myxml.OuterXml
Xml1.Transform = myxsl
```

Note that instead of setting the `Document` property with the `XmlDocument` object, we have set the `DocumentContent` property with the XML string returned by the `OuterXml` property of the `XmlDocument` object. Instead of this, we could have set it to any other XML string as shown in following example:

```
Dim myDatSet As New DataSet()
myDatSet.ReadXml(Request.PhysicalApplicationPath & "employees.xml")
Xml1.DocumentContent = myDatSet.GetXml()
```

The `DataSet` represents all the data it holds in XML format. In the above statement, we have obtained the XML string from a `DataSet` using the `GetXml()` method and setting it to the `DocumentContent` property of the XML Control. Note that just for the sake of simplicity we have loaded an XML document into a `DataSet` and get the XML content back. However, you can also do a similar thing with a `DataSet` being populated from a database table.

As seen from the above examples there are variety of ways in which you can combine the use of XML and Web Controls like `DataGrid` and XML. The actual usage will depend on the type of application you are developing. For example, if you are just displaying data from XML files you can use techniques that directly deal with XML files. On the other hand, if you are dynamically changing or creating the XML structure and then want to display that XML to the user, then you will need to use techniques that deal with `XmlDocument` objects.

Now that we have seen various ways of displaying XML data, let us see how ASP.NET uses XML for web application configuration.

ASP.NET Application Configuration

In previous versions of ASP, configuring a web application was a task that had to be performed manually at the server. One had to open an IIS snap-in and set various properties of a web application. The configuration properties involve things such as:

- ❑   HTTP Handlers for various types of documents involved in the application
- ❑   Script time-out values for all the pages
- ❑   Custom error pages that are used instead of default IIS error pages
- ❑   Security settings and authentication levels
- ❑   Session and session state information
- ❑   Page buffering behavior

The following figure shows a typical IIS application settings dialog.

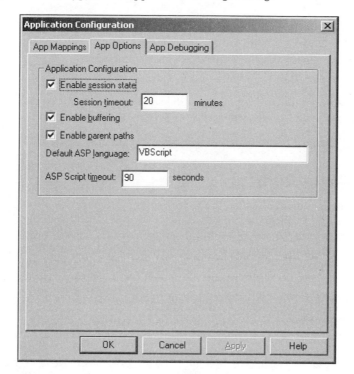

ASP.NET puts an end to the manual configuration of settings being required. ASP.NET does this through two special XML files called machine.config and web.config. During the installation process, ASP.NET generates a file named machine.config. This file represents the default configuration settings used by all the ASP.NET web applications. You can configure your individual web application using a web.config file. This file represents configuration settings for a particular application. This file is an XML document with various sections. Each section handles a specialized task. This type of configuration has various advantages such as:

❑ True XCOPY deployment to compatible host machines is possible. We simply copy all the web application files in another IIS virtual root. Since configuration is already in place, we don't need to use an IIS snap-in.

❑ Since configuration information resides in a plain text file, it can be changed very easily.

❑ The settings are automatically applied to the current folder and all its sub-folders. One web application can have more than one configuration file in different folders.

❑ Configuration of some tasks like form-based authentication is only possible through the web.config file.

❑ Unlike traditional ASP, any changes made to configuration settings are applied immediately and without manual restarting of the web server.

Note that even though ASP.NET frees us from most of the manual configuration tasks, two tasks remain manual. They are:

❑ Creation of a Web Application

❑ Mapping custom file extensions with respective applications

> It is not mandatory that our Web Application should have a `web.config` file. In the absence of a `web.config` file, configuration settings from `machine.config` will be applied.

Location of web.config

The `web.config` file is typically located in the root folder of the web application. However, this is not mandatory. In fact, it can reside in any folder of our web application. The rule that ASP.NET follows while applying settings from this file is: settings from `web.config` are applied to the folder in which it resides and all of its sub-folders. Moreover, an application can have more than one `web.config` file.

In order to understand how the settings from `web.config` are applied, consider an example of a web application that resides in the example folder, `MyShop`. This folder has two sub-folders; `Folder1` and `Folder2`. Please refer following figure for more details. There are two `web.config` files: one in the root folder `MyShop` and another in `Folder2`. As discussed earlier, all the sub-folders inherit settings from `web.config` that belong to their parent folder. So, in our case settings from the `web.config` that lies in the root folder are applied to the `MyShop` folder itself, and to both `Folder1` and `Folder2`. However, `Folder2` already has its own `web.config`. Sub-folders of `Folder2` will inherit settings from the `web.config` that lies in `Folder2` and not in `MyShop`. Any settings from this `web.config` file will override the settings from the parent file. Any settings not covered in this `web.config` file will assume values from the parent file.

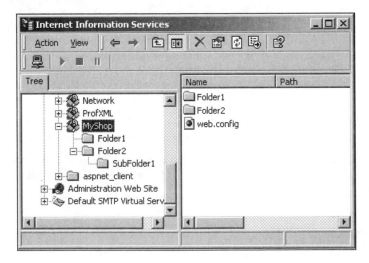

Structure of web.config

Now that we know the significance of web.config, let us see how it looks. The following is the markup from the default web.config file that gets created when we create a new Web Application in VS .NET (for the sake of clarity, descriptive comments are omitted):

```
<?xml version="1.0" encoding="utf-8" ?>
<configuration>
  <system.web>
    <compilation defaultLanguage="vb" debug="true" />
    <customErrors mode="RemoteOnly" />
    <authentication mode="Windows" />
    <authorization>
      <allow users="*" />
    </authorization>
    <trace enabled="false" requestLimit="10" pageOutput="false"
      traceMode="SortByTime" localOnly="true" />
    <sessionState mode="InProc"
      stateConnectionString="tcpip=127.0.0.1:42424"
      sqlConnectionString="data source=127.0.0.1;user id=sa;password="
      cookieless="false" timeout="20" />
    <httpHandlers>
      <add verb="*" path="*.vb"
          type="System.Web.HttpNotFoundHandler,System.Web" />
      <add verb="*" path="*.cs"
          type="System.Web.HttpNotFoundHandler,System.Web" />
      <add verb="*" path="*.vbproj"
          type="System.Web.HttpNotFoundHandler,System.Web" />
      <add verb="*" path="*.csproj"
          type="System.Web.HttpNotFoundHandler,System.Web" />
      <add verb="*" path="*.webinfo"
          type="System.Web.HttpNotFoundHandler,System.Web" />
    </httpHandlers>
    <globalization requestEncoding="utf-8" responseEncoding="utf-8" />
  </system.web>
</configuration>
```

As can be seen, the root element of the file is <configuration>. This then contains an element <system.web>, which in-turn contains various configuration sections. Unlike Web Form markup, which follows XML grammar loosely, web.config follows it strictly. All the rules of XML grammar, such as case sensitivity, element nesting, attribute quotes, matching start and end tags, etc. are followed by web.config. If we violate any of the rules, we will get a run-time error.

In the next few sections we will examine some of the important sections of the web.config file.

Sections of web.config

web.config files consist of many tags. Each such tag corresponds to what is called as a "Section". For example <authentication> or <httpHandlers> are referred to as the Authentication section and HttpHandlers section respectively. In the following text we will focus our attention on the most commonly used sections of web.config.

Authentication

Many web applications require checking that the request is coming from a valid source. This is known as authentication and ASP.NET provides various ways to authenticate the user. They are referred to as authentication "modes" within the `web.config` file. Various authentication modes are summarized below:

❑ **Windows**: In which Windows login ID's are used to authenticate the user. In this case, IIS authenticates the user via Basic, Digest, or Integrated Windows authentication. This type of authentication is best suited for intranet scenarios where participating machines are on the same network.

❑ **Forms**: In which case a custom form is presented to the user to enter their user ID and password. Once the user is validated, a cookie is issued, which is passed to and fro with each request. The presence of this cookie is used to decide whether the requesting user is authenticated or not. Sometimes form-based authentication is also called cookie authentication.

❑ **Passport**: In which the credentials of the user are stored on some passport server. It also provides single sign-on for the user if they visit more than one site using passport. For example if there are two sites that support passport authentication, then once a user logs in to either of the sites they are authenticated for the other site as well. Sites like Hotmail, MSN, and Passport use passport authentication.

The following markup indicates the usage of the authentication section for forms based authentication.

```
<authentication mode="Forms">
   <forms name="cookie_name" loginUrl="login.aspx" timeout="30" path="/" >
   </forms>
</authentication>
```

Here, we have set the `mode` attribute to `Forms` indicating that we are using form-based authentication. Next, we have set the cookie name and URL that represents the login form, via the `cookie_name` and `loginUrl` attributes of the `forms` tag respectively.

Authorization

Authentication is the process of deciding the validity of a user, where as authorization is the process of deciding whether a user is allowed to access a resource or not. We can configure our ASP.NET Web Application to accept only certain users or deny certain users. We can also authorize users based on their Windows user groups (referred to as roles in ASP.NET vocabulary) to access the resources. `Web.config` has an `authorization` section that does just that.

The following markup shows an example of using this section:

```
<authorization>
   <allow roles="administrator,dba" />
</authorization>
```

Here, only users with `administrator` or `dba` role are allowed to access the web application resources. Following are a few more examples of using the `authorization` section:

```
<authorization>
   <allow users="*" />
</authorization>
```

The above example allows all users (*) to access the resources.

```
<authorization>
    <allow users="usr1,usr2,usr3" roles="Admin,dba" />
    <deny users="?" />
</authorization>
```

The above example allows the users usr1, usr2, and usr3, as well as users from the groups Admin and dba to access the resources. It also denies access to all anonymous users (?).

CustomErrors

IIS allows us to set our own error pages for server errors. For example, many sites present some custom page for a file not found (404) error. However, we have to do these settings through an IIS snap-in. ASP.NET allows us to define custom error pages that are displayed when certain errors occur. This allows us to show user-friendly messages for any unhandled errors. The customErrors section from Web.config specifies these settings. The following is a sample using the customErrors section:

```
<customErrors defaultRedirect="myerror.aspx"  mode="On">
    <error statusCode="500" redirect="myerror500.aspx"/>
</customErrors>
```

Here, we have turned the custom errors feature on by setting the mode attribute to On . The other two possible values of this attribute are:

- ❑   Off, which turns off the custom error feature

- ❑   RemoteOnly, which causes remote users to recieve custom error pages but displays ASP.NET real error message to local users

These two settings are particularly useful when you are debugging your application. Then we have specified a default page that will be displayed if any unhandled errors take place. This page can be a static HTML page or an .aspx page. We can also set specific pages for specific error numbers using error tags as shown.

HttpHandlers

HttpHandlers are used to process incoming requests from the users of your application. For example, when a user requests an .aspx page, IIS uses the aspnet_wp.exe .aspx processor to process the request. We can write our own HttpHandlers (in a Common Language Specification-compliant language) if we wish. HttpHandlers are nothing more than special components that implement the IHttpHandler interface. They are similar to ISAPI extensions. For example we may write an HttpHandler to process files with the extension .myfile. So, whenever the user of our application requests a file of extension .myfile, IIS uses our custom HttpHandler to process the request. We can tell IIS which extensions map to which .dll via the configuration dialog box. However, ASP.NET allows us to put these settings in the HttpHandlers section of web.config. The following markup shows an httpHandlers section:

```
<httpHandlers>
    <add verb="*" path="*.vb"
         type="System.Web.HttpNotFoundHandler,System.Web" />
    <add verb="*" path="*.cs"
```

```
                type="System.Web.HttpNotFoundHandler,System.Web" />
      <add verb="*" path="*.myfile" type="MyNamespace.MyClass,MyDllName" />
   </httpHandlers>
```

The add tag is used to add an individual HttpHandler to the section. The verb attribute specifies the type of request, that is, GET/POST; * represents all types of requests. The path attribute gives the path of the files to be handled. Here, we can indicate a specific file or all files having a particular extension. The type attribute specifies the assembly and class that will handle these requests.

HttpModules

HttpModules are similar to HttpHandlers in that they affect the processing of requested resources. But, unlike HttpHandlers, which interfere only with certain types of files, HttpModules take part in the processing of every request. They implement the IHttpModule interface, and are similar to ISAPI filters. Web.config has an HttpModules section that is used to configure them.

```
<httpModules>
    <add type="myclass,mydll" name="mymodulename" />
</httpModules>
```

Pages

Often we will observe that all of our pages require similar settings of session state, buffer, etc. Instead of setting these settings for each and every page, the web.config pages section allows us to configure these settings in one place. The following example shows how:

```
<pages buffer="true" enableSessionState="false" enableViewState="true"
       autoEventWireup="false" />
```

Here, we have set a buffer attribute to true indicating that all the pages will buffer their output before sending it to the browser. We have also disabled the session state, which means that the pages cannot store values in sessions. The enableViewState attribute is set to true, which means that pages will maintain their state between post-backs.

SessionState

Configuring session state is another task commonly done by ASP programmers. Session configuration involves setting things like cookie-less sessions or sessions with cookies, session time-out values, session state information, etc. ASP.NET offers more session configuration options than ASP and they can be set via the sessionState section of the web.config file. The following markup shows a typical sessionState section:

```
<sessionState mode="Inproc" cookieless="true" timeout="3" />
```

ASP.NET session state can also be stored in a separate SQL server or state server if required. This behavior is governed by the mode attribute. In the above example, session state will be stored on the same machine as IIS. We have also set the session to be cookie-less. Once we do that, ASP.NET merges the session ID in the request URL rather than storing it in a cookie. We have also configured our session to be timed out after inactivity of 3 minutes.

As stated earlier, ASP.NET allows for storing state information in an out-of process storage location, like a separate state server or SQL server database. The following fragment shows how to configure your web application to store state in a SQL server database:

```
<sessionState mode="SQLServer"
    sqlConnectionString="data source=myserver;user id=sa;password="
    timeout="20" />
```

Here, we have set the mode attribute to SQLServer. We have also set the sqlConnectionString attribute to the connection string of the SQL server database that stores the state information

Trace

While developing an application, there will be many times when we need to track the various steps or stages of the application as it is being executed. Typically many programmers use Response.Write statements to achieve this. ASP.NET provides a facility to trace a page as it executes. All the trace information is displayed at the bottom of the page. Instead of writing Response.Write we can write to the trace directly using a trace object. We can control the trace settings via the trace section of web.config. The following is an example of using the trace section:

```
<trace enabled="true" requestLimit="20" pageOutput="true" />
```

Here, we have enabled application tracing by setting the enabled attribute to true. We have also set the pageOutput attribute to true, which causes the trace information to appear below each page. The requestLimit attribute tells the server that it should store a log of 20 requests.

appSettings

Even though web.config provides us with a lot of room for customization, we may still need to add some custom settings. The appSettings section is used just for that purpose. Note that this section is not located inside the <system.web></system.web> tags but separately inside the <configuration></configuration> tags. Database connection strings, e-mail server addresses, and log file paths are typical candidates for this section. The following example shows how this section is used:

```
<appSettings>
    <add key="logfilepath" value="c:\mylogs" />
    <add key="databasename" value="c:\databases\employee.mdb" />
<appSettings>
```

Here, we have added two custom settings, logfilepath and databasename, in the appSettings section. In order to retrieve these settings, ASP.NET provides special method to the Context object. The following code fragment shows how to do this:

```
Dim nv as NameValueCollection
Dim mydatabase as string
Nv=Context.GetConfig("appSettings")

Mydatabase=Ctype(nv("databasename"),string)
```

Using web.config Settings

Now that we know about many of the web.config settings and their usage, let us develop an application that makes use of these settings.

This application allows the user to perform mathematical operations, like addition, subtraction, multiplication, and division. Before allowing the user to perform any operation, the user is authenticated by means of form-based authentication. In the case of an error, say an invalid number for the user is supplied, the application shows a custom error page. The message displayed on the custom error page can be customized by changing its value from the <appSettings> section. The application uses the authentication, sessionState, globalization, customErrors, and appSettings sections of a web.config file.

Creating the Web Project and Modifying web.config

As usual, create a new Visual Basic ASP.NET Web Application using VS .NET. Name the application ConfigSettings. Add three Web Forms, default.aspx, login.aspx, and myerror.aspx, to the project. Set login.aspx as the start page and change the web.config file as shown below:

```xml
<?xml version="1.0" encoding="utf-8" ?>
<configuration>
  <system.web>
      <compilation defaultLanguage="vb" debug="true" />
      <customErrors mode="On"
                    defaultRedirect="myerror.aspx"></customErrors>
      <authentication mode="Forms">
         <forms name="myform" loginUrl="login.aspx">
            <credentials passwordFormat="Clear">
               <user name="John" password="john123" />
               <user name="Mular" password="mular123" />
               <user name="Nicky" password="nicky123" />
            </credentials>
         </forms>
      </authentication>
      <authorization>
         <allow users="*" /> <!-- Allow all users -->
      </authorization>
      <trace enabled="false" requestLimit="10" pageOutput="false"
            traceMode="SortByTime" localOnly="true" />
      <sessionState mode="InProc" cookieless="false" timeout="3" />
      <httpHandlers>
         <add verb="*" path="*.vb"
            type="System.Web.HttpNotFoundHandler,System.Web" />
         <add verb="*" path="*.cs"
            type="System.Web.HttpNotFoundHandler,System.Web" />
         <add verb="*" path="*.vbproj"
            type="System.Web.HttpNotFoundHandler,System.Web" />
         <add verb="*" path="*.csproj"
            type="System.Web.HttpNotFoundHandler,System.Web" />
         <add verb="*" path="*.webinfo"
            type="System.Web.HttpNotFoundHandler,System.Web" />
      </httpHandlers>
```

```
        <globalization requestEncoding="utf-8" responseEncoding="utf-8"
                        culture="en-GB" />
    </system.web>
    <appSettings>
       <add key="errmsg" value="An Application error has occurred. Please ensure
that you entered all the operands correctly." />
    </appSettings>
</configuration>
```

The code marked with bold face is of primary interest. The following are the main points to be noted:

❑ Custom errors are turned on and the default error page is set to myerror.aspx.

❑ The authentication mode is set to Forms and the login page is set to login.aspx. For the sake of simplicity, we have embedded user IDs and their passwords in the web.config file itself using the <credentials> section. In practice you would probably use a database table to store these details.

❑ We have changed the session time-out value from the default value of 20 minutes to 3 minutes.

❑ We want to display our dates in the UK format of dd/MM/yyyy. To achieve this, we have set the culture attribute of globalization section to en-GB.

❑ Finally, we have added an <appSettings> section to the web.config file. We have stored the value of the custom error message in this section.

Developing the login.aspx Page

login.aspx allows users to log in to our application so that they can use it further. Our login page should look like following screenshot:

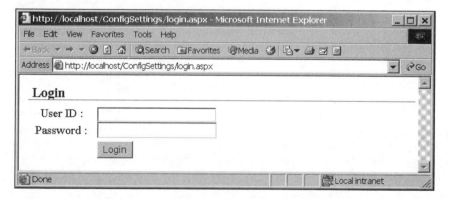

As usual, you can design the page using VS .NET designer. Double-click on the Login button and switch to the code window. Write the following code in the Click event handler of the login button:

```
If FormsAuthentication.Authenticate(TextBox1.Text, TextBox2.Text) = True Then
    FormsAuthentication.RedirectFromLoginPage(TextBox1.Text, False)
End If
```

The `FormsAuthentication` class allows us to authenticate the users based on their user ID and password. In our case, we are validating the users against user IDs and passwords stored in the `web.config` file. This is accomplished with the `Authenticate()` method as shown above. Once the user is authenticated, a cookie is issued and the user is taken to the page they requested.

Developing the default.aspx Page

`Default.aspx` is the page that allows users to perform the mathematical operations and should look something like this:

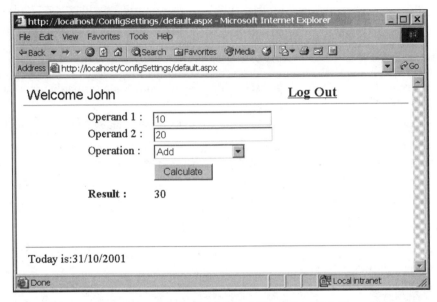

Design the page in the VS .NET designer and double-click on the Web Form to switch to the code window. Write the following code to the `Page_Load` event handler of the Web Form:

```
Label1.Text = "Welcome " & User.Identity.Name
Label7.Text = "Today is:" & DateTime.Today.ToShortDateString
```

The first line of the above code displays a welcome message to the logged in user in the top left corner of the page. Note that `User.Identity.Name` gives you the user ID that you used to log in to the system. The second line displays the current date at the bottom of the screen. Note that since we have changed `culture` to en-GB, we get all date values in the format dd/MM/yyyy. Double-click on the **Calculate** button and write the following code in the `Click` event handler of the **Calculate** button:

```
Select Case DropDownList1.SelectedItem.Value
  Case "A"
    Label5.Text = _
        (Integer.Parse(TextBox1.Text) + Integer.Parse(TextBox2.Text)).ToString
  Case "S"
    Label5.Text = _
        (Integer.Parse(TextBox1.Text) - Integer.Parse(TextBox2.Text)).ToString
  Case "M"
    Label5.Text = _
```

```
            (Integer.Parse(TextBox1.Text) * Integer.Parse(TextBox2.Text)).ToString
    Case "D"
        Label5.Text = _
            (Integer.Parse(TextBox1.Text) / Integer.Parse(TextBox2.Text)).ToString
    End Select
    Label5.Visible = True
    Label6.Visible = True
```

This code simply performs the mathematical operations requested and displays the result.

Double-click on the Log Out link button at the top of the page and write the following code in the Click event handler of the link button:

```
FormsAuthentication.SignOut()
Response.Redirect("login.aspx")
```

This code logs the user out and takes the user back to the login page.

If you enter some invalid values in the text-boxes, say some text instead of numbers, an exception will be thrown. Since we have set custom error mode to "On", instead of showing the default ASP.NET error message, the system will show our custom error page - myerror.aspx.

Developing the myerror.aspx Page

This page displays the custom error message to the user. The page picks up the message to be displayed from the web.config file's <appSettings> section. The page looks as shown below:

Add the following code to the Page_Load event handler of the page:

```
Dim nv As NameValueCollection
nv = context.GetConfig("appSettings")
Label2.Text = nv.Item("errmsg")
```

This code shows how to access settings stored in the <appSettings> section of the web.config file. The context.GetConfig() method returns a NameValueCollection of all the key-value pairs from the <appSettings> section. Individual values can then be accessed by the corresponding key.

419

Summary

In this chapter, we saw how ASP.NET and XML are related to one another. ASP.NET Web Forms and Web Controls rely extensively on XML markup to represent themselves. Even though this markup is not "pure" XML, it closely follows XML standards, like start tag and end tags, proper nesting, etc. Another area where ASP.NET uses XML extensively is web application configuration.

Web Forms allow us to develop web applications as if we were using some RAD tool like Visual Basic. They provide an object model for the page. Web Forms typically contain one or more Web Controls. Web controls provide an easy way to program interfaces and rich functionality. Even though Web Controls are represented by a special markup at design time they are rendered as plain HTML to the browser. Many Web Controls allow data binding with data sources like database tables and XML documents. The `DataGrid` and XML controls provide easy-to-use ways to display XML data. The `DataGrid` is typically used when we need to display data in tabular format, whereas the XML control is used when we have to apply some XSL stylesheet to the XML data.

ASP.NET allows us to configure our web application via a special XML document that called `web.config`. This file is a pure XML document and contains various sections to represent various configurable settings. We can configure things like custom errors, HTTP handlers, security information, and session time-outs. The file-based configuration allows easy deployment and maintenance of our web application.

12

Case Study: Using ASP.NET and ADO.NET

In the beginning, the World Wide Web was primarily a means of distributing free information to anyone who had the right software and knowledge to receive it. As time has progressed, the variety of applications that can read and utilize web information has grown, and with it the range of possible users. Among those who were exploiting these new web technologies, was the business community, which identified the Web as a way of promoting its products to the expanding Internet-enabled public. The Internet, therefore, began to revolutionize the very nature of marketing and the relationship between business and consumer across industries. The Internet enables the promotion of brands, products, and services to a far wider cross-section of consumers (potentially millions) at relatively little cost. With the Internet currently now the main means of rapid communication, the marketing possibilities seem endless.

When HTML forms were added to the HTML specification and CGI began to be used for server-side applications, it enabled the user at home to communicate with the server and obtain information. The Internet became a two-way communicating medium. Soon the business community figured out that the Internet medium could be used to reach great numbers of people. It exploited this capability and over time applications were developed to enable financial transactions over the wire and with them the ability to order and purchase products over the Internet. The concept of the online store was born.

E-commerce, as we know it today, remains in an ever-evolving state of technological advancement. There have been many different types of e-commerce applications developed with a variety of technologies ranging from ASP to C++.

Ideas took off in a grand fashion and soon there were e-commerce stores for everything, ranging from pins to planes. Not long after though, businesses realized that this was not going to work for every product as they had expected. This medium has many pros but there are still cons; you cannot get everything at once! There are pros, such as you need not leave your house for shopping and that you can get your order on your doorstep. However, the con is that this does not work for all types of products; there are some that need to be seen or felt before buying. Companies that were only doing business online were shattered by poor consumer findings, and so the Internet bubble burst. Nevertheless, there were a few ideas that worked and still work. A DVD Rental Store is one of these. A DVD application has tremendous potential. The subscribers to this store don't need to drive to the rental place, find the DVD from the showcase, and wait in the line to check the DVD out. A DVD rental store allows the subscriber to get the DVD they have chosen in their mail.

In this case study, I will present to you some of the Administration and the Client aspects of an online DVD rental store. The idea behind this is to facilitate the data entry for our DVD catalogue, and let the user browse through our system and search for the DVD that they want.

In isolation, the Rental Store is a relatively simple catalogue, but when combined with a shopping cart, an inventory, an order processing system, and a database, it becomes a very powerful system. ASP.NET and ADO.NET, combined with the power of VB .NET and XML tie these elements of the application together.

Our case study is written using Microsoft .NET, in particular ASP.NET, XSL, and ADO.NET. The programming language is VB .NET and the database engine is SQL Server 2000. As usual with .NET, XML and XSL play a major part.

Let's get started.

DVD Rental System Design

So, what are the typical requirements of a DVD Rental system? A DVD Rental application for any half-decent online store would need to fulfill the following criteria:

- ❑ Present the data to the user in friendly manner
- ❑ Have a search capability
- ❑ Allow the user to store selected items in an easily retrievable form
- ❑ Allow the user to easily modify those selected items
- ❑ Support all leading browsers

Application Scope

Let's quickly define the scope for the application. There are many books and articles covering the shopping cart and the order processing system. Over the course of this case study, we will be building the Administration side and the Client front end for an online DVD rental store. We will leave the shopping cart backend and UI, which includes user identification and Secured Payment for the reader to add. Refer to the Book "Professional ASP XML", ISBN 1-861004-02-8, also published by Wrox Press where I demonstrated an XML-based online shopping cart.

The application is defined in two parts:

❑ **Admin**: This application will be used by product managers to maintain product data
❑ **Client**: This application will be used by a subscriber to search and view the data

The Admin application will harness the functionality of ASP.NET and ADO.NET to transfer data from our online store's primary database to the data entry form, and allow the product manager to maintain data in the database.

The Client application will allow the subscriber to request information with a browser. The product data is translated from XML format into HTML using ASP.NET's XML features.

We can trigger an XSL Transformation (the transformation is explained later in the chapter) of our results, which are returned as XML by the database. We trigger the transformation in our ASP.NET environment, and then send the HTML-formatted data to the subscriber's browser for display in a user-friendly or consumer-friendly format.

In order to make our application as user-friendly as possible for the product managers and our customers, we will construct it with the following capabilities:

❑ The ability to add items to the database at the touch of a button
❑ The ability for shoppers to search, and view the data they found

These are the issues that we will need to address during the construction of our application, which we'll move on to shortly.

The Technology Setup

Earlier on, we briefly touched upon how we'll be using .NET technologies to build this application. We also discussed that we will be building Admin and Client parts of the application. Before we actually get started on the building of our Online DVD Rental application, let's just see how we're going to use ASP.NET, ADO.NET, and XML alongside other technologies to pull together the functionality we need for the application.

Take a look at the diagram below:

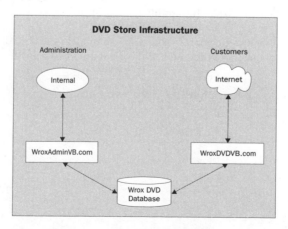

So how does each technology feature in the DVD Rental Application construction?

❑ **ASP.NET** – We'll use ASP.NET to control the processing flow of the entire application. ASP scripts will be responsible for executing the XSL transformations, implementing transaction logic (when the user proceeds with an order), and the controls for connection to the primary product database. For more details on how ASP.NET works, please refer to the Chapter 11, *ASP.NET*.

❑ **ADO.NET** – We will use ADO.NET from the web page to access the data from a SQL Server 2000 database and also use ADO.NET to save the data back to the database. We will leverage the built-in support for XML. For more details on how ADO.NET works, please refer to the Chapter 10, ADO.NET.

❑ **VB .NET** – We will use VB .NET as our primary programming language to code our application.

❑ **XML System Classes** – The data fetched from the database will be in XML format. We will apply an XSL transformation, which creates the final formatted data for display in the client browser.

❑ **SQL Server 2000** – This will act as our primary database storing all data, which is accessed from ASP.NET using ADO.NET.

Other Technical Requirements

In addition, there are some requirements for our system that we need to consider before building the online DVD application. The application can operate on Windows NT 4.0 Server (and above) with the .NET Framework installed. The application also requires Internet Information Server 5.0 and SQL Server 2000 to create the primary product database.

We also mentioned in our general criteria that a good web-based application should be browser-independent. As our Admin application *only*, runs in a controlled environment we can afford to dictate the browser type. Our Admin application will support Internet Explorer. However, our Client application runs in an uncontrolled space so we need to try to make it as browser-independent as reasonably possible. The application will support IE and Netscape.

By now you will already be equipped with a fairly comprehensive understanding of the .NET framework, ASP.NET, VB .NET, and ADO.NET; we hope that you will have also grasped the fundamentals of XML Classes that we've covered earlier in this book. For the purposes of the application, we will also be touching upon a little bit of SQL for our database; don't worry about this – it will be explained. However, if you would like more information, see the following book: "*Professional SQL Server 2000 XML*", ISBN 1-861005-46-6 published by Wrox Press.

So, now that we have established some goals for our application, let's start building the application. We will begin with setting the environment and then look at the database followed with the actual ASP.NET code.

> The source code is available from http://www.wrox.com/.

Setting up the Environment

Let's look at the two parts of the application:

- **Admin**: We are not going to try to implement all the aspects of the application within ASP script. We're going to use SQL queries to access the primary database. We already know that we're using ADO.NET to get the data from the database, and we'll use the DataGrid control to display and edit the data. The DataGrid control deserves some attention and we have a small section devoted to an explanation of the DataGrid.

- **Client**: Again, we are not going to try to implement all the aspects of the application within ASP script. We're going to use SQL queries to access the primary database. We will be using ADO.NET to get the data from the database in the XML format and apply XSL style sheets to display and edit the data. For more on XSL stylesheets and transformation please refer to the book *XSLT Programmer's reference, 2nd Edition*, ISBN 1-861005-06-7, by Michael Kay.

Note: We will be doing a server-side XSL transformation to maintain the browser independence. Client-side transformation, which needs IE, would make the application browser dependent. And one more thing to keep in mind is that using client side-transformation is not good as we can never tell which version of the parser is installed.

Before we delve into the details of the Admin and Client applications, let's take a look at the database setup.

The Product Database

> You will get the complete database script in the source code, so you need not worry how to create the procedures and the database.

The primary database for our online store holds all information in two relational tables: Item and Section:

- **Item** – We store product information in this table.

- **Section** – We store information related to the section the movie falls under in this table. This table has a one-to-many relation with the Item table.

- **Item_status** – We store the information about individual transactions in the table.

- **Customers** – We store the information about our customers in this table.

We can see how the tables link together in the diagram overleaf:

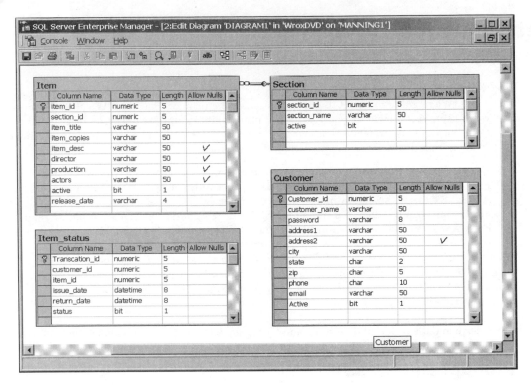

We manage the data within these tables via SQL queries that we will be called from our ASP script, but we'll look at that later on as we examine the code. You should convert the SQL queries into Stored Procedures, a few of the benefits being:

❑ We let the Database do the heavy load and leave the web server to display the data

❑ If we have to make a change to the business logic on the database side we need not change the ASP pages but just make a change to the stored procedure

Adding a New Section to the Section Table

The first requirement for the product manager is to create new sections in the `Section` table. The section represents the category the DVD movie falls under. We can add a new section with the following SQL query, which adds a new record to the `Section` table:

```
INSERT INTO Section (section_name , active)
VALUES (@section_name,1)
```

The `INSERT` query generates the unique ID for the `section_id`.

Editing a Row from the Section

We've implemented the functionality to add a new section, but of course this isn't very useful unless we can modify the sections we added. We use the following query to make this possible:

```
UPDATE Section
SET section_name='@section_name', active='@active'
WHERE section_id='@section_id'
```

This query is called from the ASP page called `Section.aspx`.

So, at this point we've created ways to add and update rows in the section table. What about a delete facility? What happens if we no longer support a section? In the above UPDATE query we can set `active` to `false`. This will prevent the section from appearing on the client page as we select the records for the active sections only. We could permanently delete the record from the database but then we will have to maintain the data base integrity and do a cascading delete. If we delete the record permanently then to keep the rental histories would be very difficult.

Adding a New Item to the Item Table

Another requirement for the product manager is to create new items as and when a new DVD is released. We can add a new item with the following SQL query, which adds a new record to the `Item` table:

```
INSERT INTO Item (section_id,item_title, item_copies,item_desc, director,
                  production, actors, active, release_date)
  VALUES (@section_id, @item_title, @item_copies, @item_desc, @director,
          @production, @actors, 1, @release_date)
```

This INSERT query generates the unique ID for the item. The `uniqueidentifier` data type stores 16-byte binary values that operate as globally unique identifiers (GUIDs). A GUID is a unique binary number; no other computer in the world will generate a duplicate of that GUID value. The main use for a GUID is for assigning an identifier that must be unique in a network that has many computers at many sites.

This SQL command is used in the `AddItem.aspx` page.

Editing a Row from the Item Table

We've implemented the functionality to add a new item, but of course this isn't very useful unless we can modify the items we have already added. We can use the following SQL command to make this possible:

```
UPDATE Item
SET item_title=@item_title,
    section_id=@section_id,
    item_copies=@item_copies,
    item_desc=@item_desc,
    Director=@director,
    production=@production,
    release_Date=@releasae_date,
    active=@active
WHERE item_id=@item_id
```

This SQL command is called from the `Item.aspx` page, using the `DoItemUpdate()` function.

At this point, we've created ways to add and update rows in the `Item` table, but what happens if we no longer support an item? Well, in the update query we can set the `active` to `false` in a similar fashion to the way we did for the `Section` table.

Displaying the Contents on the Browser

The display is the most visual aspect of an application, and it is also one of the easiest to implement. On the admin side, we will be using a `DataGrid` to implement this, but on the client side we will be using XSL to achieve this. We will do a server-side transformation for XSL transformation. We will look at this in detail later. First of all let's look at the code that gets the content information for us, which we later display.

Admin

There is nothing difficult about getting the data from the databases. The following SQL query selects data from the `Item` table:

```
SELECT Item.* FROM Item
```

Again, `Item.aspx` calls this SQL query.

The similar SQL query that selects data from the `Section` table is:

```
SELECT Section.* FROM Section
```

Again, `Section.aspx` calls this SQL query.

Before we proceed let's look at the queries we will be doing on the client side.

Client

On the client side we can search for the movie title using two criteria:

❑ Section

❑ Item Title

Here is the SQL to search on the section:

```
SELECT Item.* FROM Section, item
WHERE Item.section_id = Section.section_id
     AND Section.section_name LIKE '% + strToSearch + %'
     AND Item.active = 1
FOR XML AUTO
```

Here is the SQL query needed to search for a particular movie based its name:

```
SELECT Item.*, section.section_name FROM Item , Section
WHETE Item.item_title like '%" + strToSearch + "%'
     AND item.active = 1
     AND section.section_id = item.section_id
FOR XML AUTO
```

We'll use `strToSearch` hold the value of the search we want to do. If the search returns negative we will display that the search did not return any result.

The `FOR XML AUTO` command is a SQL Server-specific command that causes the output of the query to be presented as XML-formatted data.

The ASP.NET Code

The ASP code in this case study provides a large amount of functionality. It has to communicate with our SQL Server database, find the data that's required, and control the formatting of the data that appears in the user's browser. The ASP files in this chapter rely on this connection string. The connection string is in the file `Global.asax` as an application variable:

```
Sub Application_OnStart()
    Application("strConnect") = _
        "server=localhost;database=wroxDvd;uid=WroxDvd;pwd="
End Sub
```

We use this connection string to connect to the database. You can create a user control to encapsulate the connection string in the project. All you need to do to connect to your database is alter this file accordingly.

As the groundwork is done, let's start looking at the applications one at a time, starting with the Admin interface.

When the user follows the URL to the DVD Rental site (and hence the Admin screen), the user loads the `WebForm1.aspx`. We'll look at this page next.

The Admin Application

To start with, create a new Visual Basic ASP.NET Web Application in Visual Studio .NET and name it `WroxAdminVB`. See Chapter 11, *ASP.NET*, for full details of setting up Web Applications in Visual Studio .NET. The main screen for our Admin application looks like this:

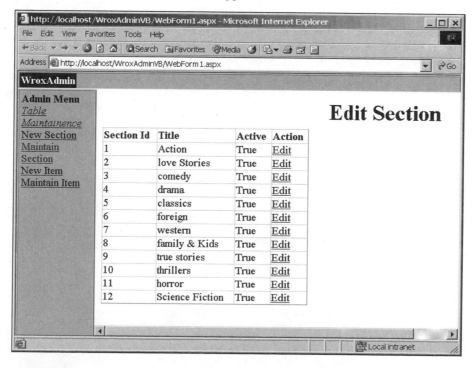

If you look closely, we have two framesets in `WebForm1.aspx`. The page loaded into the first frameset is called `Top.aspx` (and displays the **WroxAdmin** page). The two pages that are loaded into the second frameset are `Side.aspx` page (which displays the **Admin Menu**) and `Section.aspx` (which defaults to the **Edit Section**). We will not discuss the `Top.aspx` or `Side.aspx` pages further as they are mainly presentational. The code for these is, of course, available in the code download.

Let's look at the code for `WebForm1.aspx`:

```
<%@OutputCache Duration="10" VaryByParam="*" VaryByCustom="browser" %>
<%@ Page Language="vb" AutoEventWireup="false"
        Codebehind="WebForm1.aspx.vb" Inherits="WroxAdminVB.WebForm1"%>
<html>
    <head>
        <title></title>
    </head>
    <frameset frameborder="1" framespacing="0" rows="32px,*">
        <frame src="top.aspx" noresize="true" marginheight="0"
                marginwidth="0" scrolling="no">
        <frameset cols="145px,*" frameborder="0" framespacing="0">
            <frame src="side.aspx" noresize="true" marginheight="0"
                    marginwidth="0" scrolling="no">
            <frame src="section.aspx" noresize="true" marginheight="0"
                    marginwidth="0" id="main" name="main">
        </frameset>
    </frameset>
    <body MS_POSITIONING="GridLayout">
        <form id="Form1" method="post" runat="server">
        </form>
    </body>
</html>
```

Notice the first line of code:

```
<%@OutputCache Duration="10" VaryByParam="*" VaryByCustom="browser" %>
```

We are caching the content per the browser type. This will make sure that different versions of the browsers will get different copies of the page. This way we need not worry about Netscape getting an incompatible copy of the page. To read more on caching, please refer to the Chapter 11, *ASP.NET*.

The auto-generated VB .NET code from the `WebForm1.aspx.vb` looks like this:

```
Public Class WebForm1
    Inherits System.Web.UI.Page

#Region " Web Form Designer Generated Code "

    'This call is required by the Web Form Designer.
    <System.Diagnostics.DebuggerStepThrough()> _
    Private Sub InitializeComponent()

    End Sub

    Private Sub Page_Init(ByVal sender As System.Object, _
        ByVal e As System.EventArgs) Handles MyBase.Init
        'CODEGEN: This method call is required by the Web Form Designer
```

```
            'Do not modify it using the code editor.
            InitializeComponent()
        End Sub

    #End Region

        Private Sub Page_Load(ByVal sender As System.Object, _
            ByVal e As System.EventArgs) Handles MyBase.Load
            'Put user code to initialize the page here
        End Sub

    End Class
```

As we have seen the main screen, now let's proceed to the other pages: `AddSection.aspx`, `Section.aspx`, `AddItem.aspx`, and `Item.aspx`.

AddSection.aspx

We will look quickly at adding records to our `Section` table. Add a file called `AddSection.aspx` to the project.

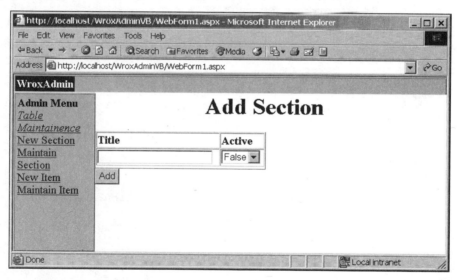

The following is the code that adds records. Firstly, we need to add some code to the **Add** button's event handler:

```
Private Sub btAdd_Click(ByVal sender As Object, _
                        ByVal e As System.EventArgs) Handles btAdd.Click
    DoSectionAdd(txtTitle.Text, ctlActive.SelectedIndex)
End Sub
```

We trap the button click and call the `DoSectionAdd()` function. This function uses the values from the textbox and dropdown to create a SQL statement:

```
Sub DoSectionAdd(ByVal strTitle As String, ByVal txtActive As String)

    Dim objTitle, objActive As String
```

```
    objTitle = strTitle
    objActive = txtActive

    'create a suitable SQL statement and execute it
    Dim strSQL As String
    strSQL = _
      "Insert into Section values ('" & objTitle & "','" & objActive & "')"
    ExecuteSQLStatement(strSQL)

End Sub
```

In the last line we call another function, `ExecuteSQLStatement()`. We will be using this function to execute the all the queries in our application. This function accepts a string as its only parameter, which is used to amend the database as necessary:

```
Sub ExecuteSQLStatement(ByVal strSQL)
    Try
        Dim objConnect As New SqlConnection(Application("strConnect"))
        objConnect.Open()
        Dim objCommand As New SqlCommand(strSQL, objConnect)
        objCommand.CommandType = CommandType.Text
        objCommand.CommandText = strSQL
        objCommand.ExecuteNonQuery()
        Response.Write("Record Added")
        txtTitle.Text = ""
    Catch objError As Exception
        'display error details
        Response.Write("<b>* Error while adding data</b>.<br />" _
            & objError.Message & "<br />" & objError.Source & "<p />")
        Exit Sub  ' and stop execution
    End Try
End Sub
```

Section.aspx

We have already discussed that we can add and edit sections from `Section.aspx`. Now let's see the code:

```
<%@ Page Language="vb" AutoEventWireup="false" Codebehind="Section.aspx.vb"
        Inherits="WroxAdminVB.Section"%>
<!DOCTYPE HTML PUBLIC "-//W3C//DTD HTML 4.0 Transitional//EN">
<html>
  <head>
    <title>Edit Section</title>
  </head>
  <body MS_POSITIONING="GridLayout">
    <center>
      <h1>
        Edit Section
      </h1>
    </center>
    <form id="Form1" method="post" runat="server">
      <ASP:DataGrid id="MyDataGrid" runat="server"
                  HeaderStyle-Font-Bold
                  EditItemStyle-BackColor="yellow"
                  DataKeyField="section_id" OnEditCommand="DoItemEdit"
                  OnUpdateCommand="DoItemUpdate"
                  OnCancelCommand="DoItemCancel"
```

```
                      AutoGenerateColumns="False">
        <EditItemStyle BackColor="silver"></EditItemStyle>
        <Columns>
          <ASP:BoundColumn DataField="section_id" HeaderText="Section ID"
                           HeaderStyle-Font-Bold ReadOnly="True" />
          <asp:TemplateColumn HeaderText="Title">
            <ItemTemplate>
              <ASP:Label Text='<%# Container.DataItem("section_name") %>'
                         runat="server" ID="Label2" />
            </ItemTemplate>
            <EditItemTemplate>
              <ASP:TextBox id="txtSection"
                           Text='<%# Container.DataItem("section_name") %>'
                           runat="server" />
            </EditItemTemplate>
          </asp:TemplateColumn>
          <asp:TemplateColumn HeaderText="Active">
            <ItemTemplate>
              <ASP:Label Text='<%# Container.DataItem("active") %>'
                         runat="server" ID="Label1" />
            </ItemTemplate>
            <EditItemTemplate>
              <ASP:TextBox id="txtActive"
                           Text='<%# Container.DataItem("active") %>'
                           runat="server" />
            </EditItemTemplate>
          </asp:TemplateColumn>
          <asp:EditCommandColumn headerStyle-Font-Bold HeaderText="Action"
                                 ButtonType="LinkButton"
                                 UpdateText="Update" CancelText="Cancel"
                                 EditText="Edit">
          </asp:EditCommandColumn>
        </Columns>
      </ASP:DataGrid>
    </form>
  </body>
</html>
```

If we look at the code, we can see that we are using a few ASP server-side controls, namely one DataGrid, one TextBox, two TemplateColumn, one BoundColumn, one EditCommandColumn, and two labels.

DataGrid

The DataGrid control displays the data in tabular format with the capability of editing, sorting, and paging the data. The DataGrid binds a column to each field in the data source.

Note: In our code we have used AutoGenerateColumns="False"*, which enables us to generate our own column names.*

Each data field is displayed in a separate column in the order it is stored in the database.

TextBox

We will use this control to display the data when we click the Edit link.

Section.aspx.vb

Let's start by listing the entire contents of the file Section.aspx.vb:

```
Imports System.Data
Imports System.Data.SqlClient

Public Class Section
    Inherits System.Web.UI.Page
    Protected WithEvents lblSQL As System.Web.UI.WebControls.Label
    Protected WithEvents MyDataGrid As System.Web.UI.WebControls.DataGrid
    Protected WithEvents form1 As System.Web.UI.HtmlControls.HtmlForm

#Region " Web Form Designer Generated Code "

    'This call is required by the Web Form Designer.
    <System.Diagnostics.DebuggerStepThrough()> _
        Private Sub InitializeComponent()

    End Sub

    Private Sub Page_Init(ByVal sender As System.Object, _
                            ByVal e As System.EventArgs) Handles MyBase.Init
        'CODEGEN: This method call is required by the Web Form Designer
        'Do not modify it using the code editor.
            InitializeComponent()
    End Sub

#End Region

    Private Sub Page_Load(ByVal sender As System.Object, _
                            ByVal e As System.EventArgs) Handles MyBase.Load
        If Not Page.IsPostBack Then
            BindDataGrid() 'create data set and bind to grid control
        End If
    End Sub

    Sub DoItemEdit(ByVal objSource As Object, _
                ByVal objArgs As DataGridCommandEventArgs)

        'set the EditItemIndex property of the grid to this item's index
        MyDataGrid.EditItemIndex = objArgs.Item.ItemIndex
        BindDataGrid()   'bind the data and display it

    End Sub

    Sub DoItemUpdate(ByVal objSource As Object, _
                ByVal objArgs As DataGridCommandEventArgs)

        Dim objSection, objActive As TextBox
        objSection = CType(objArgs.Item.FindControl("txtSection"), TextBox)
        objActive = CType(objArgs.Item.FindControl("txtActive"), TextBox)
        'objArgs.Item.Cells(2).Controls(0)

        If (UCase(objActive.Text) = UCase("True")) Then
            objActive.Text = 1
        ElseIf (UCase(objActive.Text) = UCase("False")) Then
            objActive.Text = 0
        End If

        'create a suitable SQL statement and execute it
        Dim strSQL As String
```

```
            strSQL = "UPDATE section SET section_name='" & _
                    objSection.Text & "', " & _
                    "active='" & objActive.Text & "' " & _
                    "WHERE section_id='" & _
                    MyDataGrid.DataKeys(objArgs.Item.ItemIndex) & "'"
        ExecuteSQLStatement(strSQL)

        MyDataGrid.EditItemIndex = -1
        BindDataGrid()   'bind the data and display it

    End Sub

    Sub DoItemCancel(ByVal objSource As Object, _
                    ByVal objArgs As DataGridCommandEventArgs)

        'set EditItemIndex property of grid to -1 to switch out of Edit mode
        MyDataGrid.EditItemIndex = -1
        BindDataGrid()   'bind the data and display it

    End Sub

    Sub ExecuteSQLStatement(ByVal strSQL)
        Try
            Dim objConnect As New SqlConnection(Application("strConnect"))
            objConnect.Open()
            Dim objCommand As New SqlCommand(strSQL, objConnect)
            objCommand.CommandType = CommandType.Text
            objCommand.CommandText = strSQL
            objCommand.ExecuteNonQuery()

        Catch objError As Exception
            'display error details
            Response.Write("<b>* Error while updating data</b>.<br />" _
                & objError.Message & "<br />" & objError.Source & "<p />")
            Exit Sub  ' and stop execution
        End Try
    End Sub

    Sub BindDataGrid()
        'create a SQL statement to select some rows from the database
        Dim strSQL As String
        strSQL = "Select section.* from section"
        Dim myDataReader As SqlDataReader
        Try
            Dim objConnect As New SqlConnection(Application("strConnect"))
            objConnect.Open()
            Dim objCommand As New SqlCommand(strSQL, objConnect)
            myDataReader = objCommand.ExecuteReader()

        Catch objError As Exception

            'display error details
            Response.Write("<b>* Error while accessing data</b>.<br />" _
                & objError.Message & "<br />" & objError.Source & "<p />")
            Exit Sub  ' and stop execution

        End Try
```

```
            'set the DataSource property and bind the grid
         MyDataGrid.DataSource = myDataReader
         MyDataGrid.DataBind()
      End Sub
   End Class
```

Let's look at the code that generates the page with data bound to the `DataGrid`.

```
Private Sub Page_Load(ByVal sender As System.Object, _
                      ByVal e As System.EventArgs) Handles MyBase.Load
   If Not Page.IsPostBack Then
      BindDataGrid() 'create data set and bind to grid control
   End If
End Sub
```

The `Page_Load()` function is called by default when the page is executed. Now what is `Page.IsPostBack`? It is a value indicating that the page is being loaded in response to a client postback, or that it is being loaded and accessed for the first time. The `True` property means that the page is loaded in response to the client postback.

If `Page.IsPostBack` is `False`, then we call a function named `BindDataGrid()`, which does the data binding to the grid. We are using `SqlConnection` to create the connection, and then creating a `SqlCommand` object to execute the query and apply the result to a `SqlDataReader` object. Then we bind the `DataGrid` data source to the `SqlDataReader` object. To use the SQL objects we need to declare the following namespaces:

```
Imports System.Data
Imports System.Data.SqlClient
```

Using this code we get the data from our SQL Server and bind our `DataGrid` with the data. Now let's look again at the editing feature in `Section.aspx`:

```
<ASP:DataGrid id="MyDataGrid" runat="server"
              HeaderStyle-Font-Bold
              EditItemStyle-BackColor="yellow"
              DataKeyField="section_id" OnEditCommand="DoItemEdit"
              OnUpdateCommand="DoItemUpdate"
              OnCancelCommand="DoItemCancel"
              AutoGenerateColumns="False">
```

We have a few functions that are bound to the `DataGrid`, such as `DoItemEdit()`, `DoItemUpdate()`, and `DoItemCancel()`. Each of these functions has a fairly self-explanatory name and will be explained shortly.

Whenever we click on the Edit link the color or row being edited is set to silver. Please refer to the Edit Screen shown opposite:

```
<EditItemStyle BackColor="silver"></EditItemStyle>
```

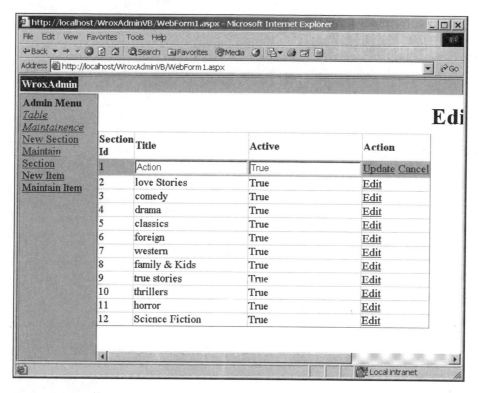

Handling the Edit Events

We have to write event handlers to react on the `OnEditCommand`, `OnUpdateCommand`, and `OnCancelCommand` events.

The `OnEditCommand` event is raised when the user clicks on the Edit link. For this event we have our `DoItemEdit` event handler specified. Within this event handler, we set the `EditItemIndex` property of the `DataGrid` to the index of the row that was clicked. We get this index from the `DataGridCommandEventArgs` parameter that was passed to the event handler. Lastly, we rebind our `DataGrid` by calling the `BindDataGrid()` function that we covered earlier:

```
Sub DoItemEdit(ByVal objSource As Object, _
               ByVal objArgs As DataGridCommandEventArgs)

    'set the EditItemIndex property of the grid to this item's index
    MyDataGrid.EditItemIndex = objArgs.Item.ItemIndex
    BindDataGrid()   'bind the data and display it

End Sub
```

The `DataGrid` control has the default value of −1 for the `EditItemIndex` property, which indicates that no rows are under the "Edit Mode". When we assign a different value to the `EditItemIndex` the `DataGrid` control will automatically render the specified row with the contents of `<EditItemTemplate>`. In our case, we specified a `<EditItemTemplate>` but we can use bound text box controls too.

```
<ASP:BoundColumn DataField="section_id" HeaderText="Section ID"
                 HeaderStyle-Font-Bold ReadOnly="True" />
<asp:TemplateColumn HeaderText="Title">
  <ItemTemplate>
    <ASP:Label Text='<%# Container.DataItem("section_name") %>'
               runat="server" ID="Label2" />
  </ItemTemplate>
  <EditItemTemplate>
    <ASP:TextBox id="txtSection"
                 Text='<%# Container.DataItem("section_name") %>'
                 runat="server" />
  </EditItemTemplate>
</asp:TemplateColumn>
```

This first line of code makes our Section_id column read-only so that we can stop the user from editing it as it is the primary key for our table and therefore cannot be amended.

Handling Update and Cancel

Handling the Cancel action is the easiest task of all. In the DoItemCancel() event handler we set the EditItemIndex property to –1 and then rebind the DataGrid.:

```
Sub DoItemCancel(ByVal objSource As Object, _
              ByVal objArgs As DataGridCommandEventArgs)

    'set EditItemIndex property of grid to -1 to switch out of Edit mode
    MyDataGrid.EditItemIndex = -1
    BindDataGrid()  'bind the data and display it

End Sub
```

If the user clicks the Update link then the DoItemUpdate() event handler is called. In this handler, we get the values from the editable boxes and create a SQL query to execute the update using the same ExecuteSQLStatement() function we used earlier. Then we rebind the DataGrid to get the updated data from the database and display that data. Here is the code to do this:

```
Sub DoItemUpdate(ByVal objSource As Object, _
              ByVal objArgs As DataGridCommandEventArgs)

    Dim objSection, objActive As TextBox
    objSection = CType(objArgs.Item.FindControl("txtSection"), TextBox)
    objActive = CType(objArgs.Item.FindControl("txtActive"), TextBox)
    'objArgs.Item.Cells(2).Controls(0)

    If (UCase(objActive.Text) = UCase("True")) Then
        objActive.Text = 1
    ElseIf (UCase(objActive.Text) = UCase("False")) Then
        objActive.Text = 0
    End If

    'create a suitable SQL statement and execute it
    Dim strSQL As String
    strSQL = "UPDATE section SET section_name='" & _
            objSection.Text & "', " & _
            "active='" & objActive.Text & "' " & _
            "WHERE section_id='" & _
```

```
                MyDataGrid.DataKeys(objArgs.Item.ItemIndex) & "'"
        ExecuteSQLStatement(strSQL)

        MyDataGrid.EditItemIndex = -1
        BindDataGrid()   'bind the data and display it

    End Sub
```

Let's see what we are actually doing here. Remember that we discussed earlier that we declared an `<EditItemTemplate>` to facilitate the edit. We declared an `<ASP:TemplateColumn>` for the fields we want to edit. Inside the `<ASP:TemplateColumn>` we have declared `<EditItemTemplate>`, which lets us see the data inside the `TextBox`.

```
<EditItemTemplate>
    <ASP:TextBox id="txtSection"
                Text='<%# Container.DataItem("section_name") %>'
                runat="server" />
</EditItemTemplate>
```

Well, as we are clear on how to define the `DataGrid` let's proceed with the event handler code. We declare two variables and assign them the data from the grid:

```
Dim objSection, objActive As TextBox
objSection = CType(objArgs.Item.FindControl("txtSection"), TextBox)
objActive = CType(objArgs.Item.FindControl("txtActive"), TextBox)
```

We are using the `FindControl()` method of the item that is contained in the `DataGridCommandEventArgs`, which is passed to our handler as a parameter. We have to "Type Cast" the return type to the correct type; in our case it is a `TextBox` object.

There is one more technique to extract the data. We need to declare the control as a bound control in our ASP page:

```
<asp:BoundColumn DataField="active" HeaderText="Active"></asp:BoundColumn>
```

If you are using this technique then to access the data you would use:

```
var = objArgs.Item.Cells(2).Controls(0)
```

OK, what we are doing here is accessing the `Cells` collection for the `item` contained in the `DataGridCommandEventArgs` object. From the third cell in the row (indexed 2 our `Active` column) we can use the controls collection of that cell to find the reference to the bound column it is attached to. This is best used when the column is a normal `BoundColumn` or autogenerated column.

I recommend using the `FindControl()` technique, though it is your choice to use whichever technique you want.

Once we have the values in the variables then our task is to build the SQL statement and execute the statement. We get the section ID from `MyDataGrid.DataKeys(objArgs.Item.ItemIndex)`, which we will be using to update the correct row in the table. We accept the data from the ASP page and pass the data to the SQL statement. Then we call the function `ExecuteSQLStatement()` that actually performs the update functionality:

```
Sub ExecuteSQLStatement(ByVal strSQL)
    Try
        Dim objConnect As New SqlConnection(Application("strConnect"))
        objConnect.Open()
        Dim objCommand As New SqlCommand(strSQL, objConnect)
        objCommand.CommandType = CommandType.Text
        objCommand.CommandText = strSQL
        objCommand.ExecuteNonQuery()

    Catch objError As Exception
        'display error details
        Response.Write("<b>* Error while updating data</b>.<br />" _
            & objError.Message & "<br />" & objError.Source & "<p />")
        Exit Sub   ' and stop execution
    End Try
End Sub
```

Notice how we use a `Try ... Catch` structure to incorporate error handling. We perform the update if there is no error, or display an error message if there is.

AddItem.aspx

We just saw how to add and edit a section, let's now see how to add and update the `Item` information. The Add Item page should look something like the following screenshot:

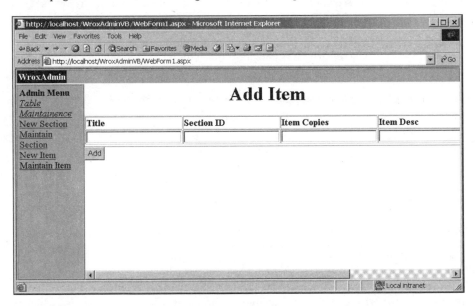

Well, the code in `AddItem.aspx.vb` is essentially the same as in `AddSection.aspx.vb`, with the exception of the SQL statement that contained in the `DoAddItems()` function:

```
Sub DoItemAdd(ByVal strTitle As String, ByVal strSectionID As String, _
            ByVal strItemCopies As String, ByVal strItemDesc As String, _
            ByVal strReleaseDate As String, ByVal strActive As String)
    'create a suitable SQL statement and execute it
    Dim strSQL As String
```

```
       strSQL = "INSERT INTO item (item_title,section_id, item_Copies, " & _
                          "item_desc, release_date,active) " & _
             "VALUES ('" & strTitle & "','" & strSectionID & "','" _
                   strItemCopies & "','" & strItemDesc & "','" & & _
                   strReleaseDate & "','" & strActive & "')"

       ExecuteSQLStatement(strSQL)
End Sub
```

Item.aspx

We just saw how the Section.aspx works, now let's look at Item.aspx, which is shown in the following screenshot.

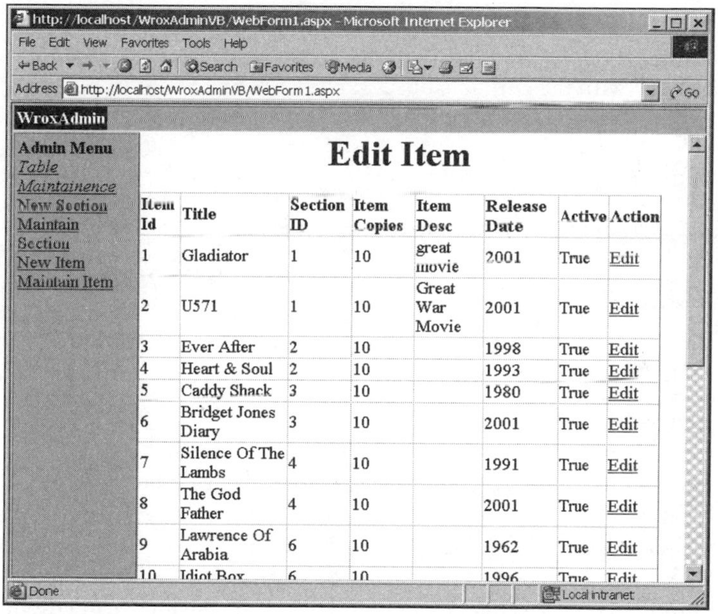

We will not list the code in Item.aspx in full here, but as always it is available in the download. However, let's look at the code for the DataGrid:

```
<ASP:DataGrid id="MyDataGrid" runat="server"
              HeaderStyle-Font-Bold DataKeyField="item_id"
              OnEditCommand="DoItemEdit" OnUpdateCommand="DoItemUpdate"
              OnCancelCommand="DoItemCancel" AutoGenerateColumns="False">
```

As with Section.aspx, we specify handlers for various events.

Handling the Edit Events

We have to write event handlers to react on the OnEditCommand, OnUpdateCommand, and OnCancelCommand events.

The `OnEditCommand` event is raised when the user clicks on the **Edit** link. For this event, we have our `DoItemEdit` event handler specified. Within this handler we set the `EditItemIndex` property of the `DataGrid` to the index of the row that was clicked. We get this index from the parameters of the event handler. Our code passed a `DataGridCommandEventArgs`, which exposed the `ItemIndex` property of the item that was selected. Lastly we rebind our `DataGrid` by calling the `BindDataGrid` function. Refer to the code for `Section.aspx`. The data binding code is same as in the `Section.aspx` with the exception of binding the `DataGrid` to `Item` table:

```
Sub DoItemEdit(ByVal objSource As Object, _
              ByVal objArgs As DataGridCommandEventArgs)
    'set the EditItemIndex property of the grid to this item's index
    MyDataGrid.EditItemIndex = objArgs.Item.ItemIndex
    BindDataGrid()  'bind the data and display it
End Sub
```

When we assign a different value to the `EditItemIndex`, the `DataGrid` control will automatically render the specified row with the contents of `<EditItemTemplate>`. In our case, we specified a `<EditItemTemplate>` but you can use bound `TextBox` controls too.

```
<asp:TemplateColumn HeaderText="Title">
   <ItemTemplate>
      <ASP:Label Text='<%# Container.DataItem("item_Title") %>'
                 runat="server" ID="Label1" />
   </ItemTemplate>
   <EditItemTemplate>
      <ASP:TextBox id="txtTitle"
                   Text='<%# Container.DataItem("item_Title") %>'
                   runat="server" />
   </EditItemTemplate>
</asp:TemplateColumn>
```

This line of code makes our `Item_id` column read-only so we cannot edit it:

```
<ASP:BoundColumn DataField="Item_ID" HeaderText="Item Id" ReadOnly="True" />
```

We will then be presented with a screen like the following in which we can edit the individual fields (Note due to space limitations we have scrolled over to the right-hand side of the page):

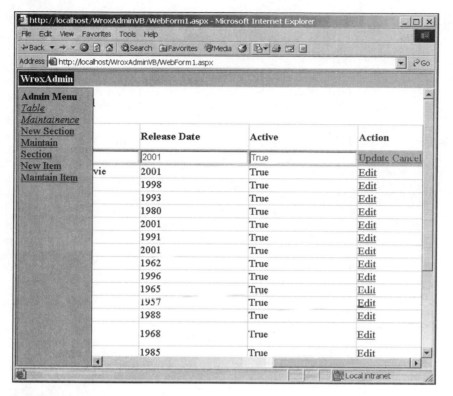

Handling Update and Cancel

Handling the **Cancel** link is as easy as it was with the `Section.aspx.vb` page. We set the `EditItemIndex` to `-1` and rebind the `DataGrid`:

```
Sub DoItemCancel(ByVal objSource As Object, _
            ByVal objArgs As DataGridCommandEventArgs)
   'set EditItemIndex property of grid to -1 to switch out of Edit mode
   MyDataGrid.EditItemIndex = -1
   BindDataGrid()  'bind the data and display it
End Sub
```

If the user clicks the **Update** link then the `DoItemUpdate` event handler is called. In this handler we get the values from the editable boxes and create a SQL statement to execute the update. Then we rebind the grid to get the updated data from the database and display the data. Here is the code to do this:

```
Sub DoItemUpdate(ByVal objSource As Object, _
            ByVal objArgs As DataGridCommandEventArgs)
   'get a reference to the title and publication date text boxes
   Dim objItemTitle, objSectionID, objCopies, objDesc, objDirector, _
       objProduction, objActors, objReleaseDate, objActive As TextBox

   objItemTitle = CType(objArgs.Item.FindControl("txtTitle"), TextBox)
   objSectionID = CType(objArgs.Item.FindControl("txtSectionId"), TextBox)
   objCopies = CType(objArgs.Item.FindControl("txtItemCopies"), TextBox)
   objDesc = CType(objArgs.Item.FindControl("txtItemDesc"), TextBox)
```

```
    objDirector = CType(objArgs.Item.FindControl("txtDirector"), TextBox)
    objProduction = _
        CType(objArgs.Item.FindControl("txtProduction"), TextBox)
    objActors = CType(objArgs.Item.FindControl("txtActors"), TextBox)
    objReleaseDate = _
        CType(objArgs.Item.FindControl("txtReleaseDate"), TextBox)
    objActive = CType(objArgs.Item.FindControl("txtActive"), TextBox)

    If (UCase(objActive.Text) = UCase("True")) Then
        objActive.Text = 1
    ElseIf (UCase(objActive.Text) = UCase("False")) Then
        objActive.Text = 0
    End If

    'create a suitable SQL statement and execute it
    Dim strSQL As String
    strSQL = "UPDATE Item SET item_title='" & objItemTitle.Text & "', " & _
             "section_id='" & objSectionID.Text & "', " & _
             "item_copies='" & objCopies.Text & "', " & _
             "item_desc='" & objDesc.Text & "', " & _
             "release_Date='" & objReleaseDate.Text & "', " & _
             "active='" & objActive.Text & "' " & _
             "WHERE item_id='" & _
             MyDataGrid.DataKeys(objArgs.Item.ItemIndex) & "'"

    ExecuteSQLStatement(strSQL)

    MyDataGrid.EditItemIndex = -1
    BindDataGrid()  'bind the data and display it

End Sub
```

As before, we are using the FindControl() method of the item that is contained in the DataGridCommandEventArgs, which is passed to our handler as a parameter. We have to "cast" the return type to the correct type; in our case it is a TextBox object.

Once we have the values in the variables our task is to build the SQL statement and execute it. We get the section ID from MyDataGrid.DataKeys(objArgs.Item.ItemIndex), which we will be using to update the correct row in the table.

Then we call the function ExecuteSQLStatement(), which actually performs the update functionality. Refer to the code for ExecuteSQLStatement() in the Section.aspx Section.

The complete code for the Item.aspx.vb is available in the download. Now as we are set with the Admin application and we have some data in the database, let's delve into the Client application.

The Client Application

When we login to the Client application we are presented with the following page. The screen is very simple but you can always add images of your own and jazz up the screen:

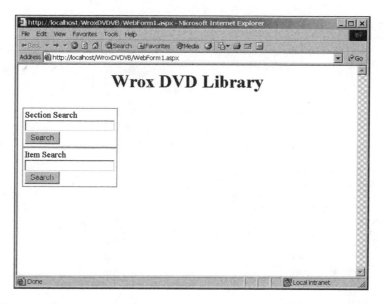

By using the Client application we can search for a movie with two criteria: Section and Item. What we are we doing is searching for the movie in the database, getting the data as XML, and applying the XSL stylesheet to the XML to display the data on the client browser.

Let's delve into the code.

WebForm1.aspx

The code to build the above screen is fairly straightforward, so we'll not list it here. Let's look at how the search is accomplished.

> Note that we must declare the `System.Web.UI.WebControls.Xml` class in our code.

Search by Section

When the user enters data in the Section textbox and clicks on its associated Search button, we call the event handler for the btnSearch.

```
Private Sub btnSearch_Click(ByVal sender As Object, _
             ByVal e As System.EventArgs) Handles btnSearch.Click
    GetSection(txtSection.Text)
End Sub
```

We call the function GetSection() that gets the data from the database in XML format. Then we apply the XSL stylesheet to the XML and display the result in the client browser. Why are we using the XSL and XML? Our XSL contains the code to convert the XML to HTML. This is a cleaner way to generate HTML:

```
Private Sub GetSection(ByVal strToSearch As String)

    Dim SQL, sXML, outXML As String
    SQL = "SELECT item.*  FROM item , section  " & _
```

```
                "WHERE  item.active = 1 AND section.active=1 AND " & _
                "section.section_id = item.section_id AND " & _
                "section.section_name LIKE '%" + strToSearch + "%' FOR XML AUTO"

        Try
            Dim objConnect As New SqlConnection(Application("strConnect"))
            objConnect.Open()
            Dim objCommand As New SqlCommand(SQL, objConnect)
            Dim xmlReader As XmlTextReader

            xmlReader = objCommand.ExecuteXmlReader()

            Dim objStrBuilder As New StringBuilder()
            objStrBuilder.Append(xmlReader.GetRemainder().ReadToEnd())

            xmlReader.Close()
            objConnect.Close()
            outXML = "<xml>" & objStrBuilder.ToString & "</xml>"

            Xml1.DocumentContent = outXML
            Xml1.TransformSource = "item.xsl"
            Response.Write(Xml1.Transform)

        Catch objError As Exception
            'display error details
            Response.Write("<b>* Error while accessing data</b>.<br />" _
                & objError.Message & "<br />" & objError.Source & "<p />")
            Exit Sub  ' and stop execution

        End Try

    End Sub
```

First we build our query to get the data from the database in XML format. Note that this SQL command
will only work with SQL Server 2000 as FOR XML AUTO is the special new feature in SQL Server 2000
that returns the data in the XML format along with other XML-related features.

We declare an XmlTextReader object and assign the result of the
objcommand.ExecuteXmlReader() call to that variable. We must append the <xml> tags to the data
to have a well formed XML.

We assign the XML and XSL to the ASP:xml control named Xml1 on the page and write the results to
the client browser, as shown in the following screenshot:

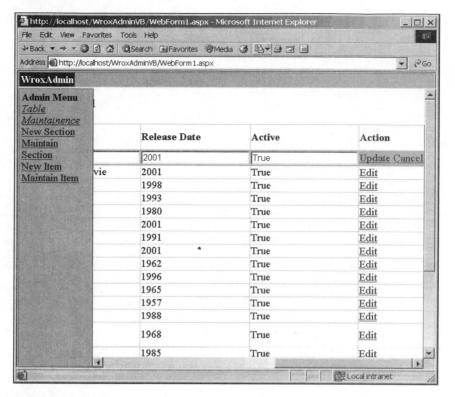

Handling Update and Cancel

Handling the **Cancel** link is as easy as it was with the `Section.aspx.vb` page. We set the `EditItemIndex` to -1 and rebind the `DataGrid`:

```
Sub DoItemCancel(ByVal objSource As Object, _
                 ByVal objArgs As DataGridCommandEventArgs)
    'set EditItemIndex property of grid to -1 to switch out of Edit mode
    MyDataGrid.EditItemIndex = -1
    BindDataGrid()  'bind the data and display it
End Sub
```

If the user clicks the **Update** link then the `DoItemUpdate` event handler is called. In this handler we get the values from the editable boxes and create a SQL statement to execute the update. Then we rebind the grid to get the updated data from the database and display the data. Here is the code to do this:

```
Sub DoItemUpdate(ByVal objSource As Object, _
                 ByVal objArgs As DataGridCommandEventArgs)
    'get a reference to the title and publication date text boxes
    Dim objItemTitle, objSectionID, objCopies, objDesc, objDirector, _
        objProduction, objActors, objReleaseDate, objActive As TextBox

    objItemTitle = CType(objArgs.Item.FindControl("txtTitle"), TextBox)
    objSectionID = CType(objArgs.Item.FindControl("txtSectionId"), TextBox)
    objCopies = CType(objArgs.Item.FindControl("txtItemCopies"), TextBox)
    objDesc = CType(objArgs.Item.FindControl("txtItemDesc"), TextBox)
```

```
        objDirector = CType(objArgs.Item.FindControl("txtDirector"), TextBox)
        objProduction = _
            CType(objArgs.Item.FindControl("txtProduction"), TextBox)
        objActors = CType(objArgs.Item.FindControl("txtActors"), TextBox)
        objReleaseDate = _
            CType(objArgs.Item.FindControl("txtReleaseDate"), TextBox)
        objActive = CType(objArgs.Item.FindControl("txtActive"), TextBox)

        If (UCase(objActive.Text) = UCase("True")) Then
            objActive.Text = 1
        ElseIf (UCase(objActive.Text) = UCase("False")) Then
            objActive.Text = 0
        End If

        'create a suitable SQL statement and execute it
        Dim strSQL As String
        strSQL = "UPDATE Item SET item_title='" & objItemTitle.Text & "', " & _
                "section_id='" & objSectionID.Text & "', " & _
                "item_copies='" & objCopies.Text & "', " & _
                "item_desc='" & objDesc.Text & "', " & _
                "release_Date='" & objReleaseDate.Text & "', " & _
                "active='" & objActive.Text & "' " & _
                "WHERE item_id='" & _
                MyDataGrid.DataKeys(objArgs.Item.ItemIndex) & "'"

        ExecuteSQLStatement(strSQL)

        MyDataGrid.EditItemIndex = -1
        BindDataGrid()  'bind the data and display it

    End Sub
```

As before, we are using the FindControl() method of the item that is contained in the DataGridCommandEventArgs, which is passed to our handler as a parameter. We have to "cast" the return type to the correct type; in our case it is a TextBox object.

Once we have the values in the variables our task is to build the SQL statement and execute it. We get the section ID from MyDataGrid.DataKeys(objArgs.Item.ItemIndex), which we will be using to update the correct row in the table.

Then we call the function ExecuteSQLStatement(), which actually performs the update functionality. Refer to the code for ExecuteSQLStatement() in the Section.aspx Section.

The complete code for the Item.aspx.vb is available in the download. Now as we are set with the Admin application and we have some data in the database, let's delve into the Client application.

The Client Application

When we login to the Client application we are presented with the following page. The screen is very simple but you can always add images of your own and jazz up the screen:

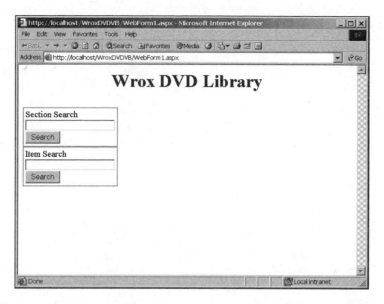

By using the Client application we can search for a movie with two criteria: Section and Item. What we are we doing is searching for the movie in the database, getting the data as XML, and applying the XSL stylesheet to the XML to display the data on the client browser.

Let's delve into the code.

WebForm1.aspx

The code to build the above screen is fairly straightforward, so we'll not list it here. Let's look at how the search is accomplished.

> Note that we must declare the `System.Web.UI.WebControls.Xml` class in our code.

Search by Section

When the user enters data in the Section textbox and clicks on its associated Search button, we call the event handler for the btnSearch.

```
Private Sub btnSearch_Click(ByVal sender As Object, _
              ByVal e As System.EventArgs) Handles btnSearch.Click
    GetSection(txtSection.Text)
End Sub
```

We call the function GetSection() that gets the data from the database in XML format. Then we apply the XSL stylesheet to the XML and display the result in the client browser. Why are we using the XSL and XML? Our XSL contains the code to convert the XML to HTML. This is a cleaner way to generate HTML:

```
Private Sub GetSection(ByVal strToSearch As String)

    Dim SQL, sXML, outXML As String
    SQL = "SELECT item.*  FROM item , section  " & _
```

447

```
            "WHERE   item.active = 1 AND section.active=1 AND " & _
            "section.section_id = item.section_id AND " & _
            "section.section_name LIKE '%" + strToSearch + "%' FOR XML AUTO"

        Try
            Dim objConnect As New SqlConnection(Application("strConnect"))
            objConnect.Open()
            Dim objCommand As New SqlCommand(SQL, objConnect)
            Dim xmlReader As XmlTextReader

            xmlReader = objCommand.ExecuteXmlReader()

            Dim objStrBuilder As New StringBuilder()
            objStrBuilder.Append(xmlReader.GetRemainder().ReadToEnd())

            xmlReader.Close()
            objConnect.Close()
            outXML = "<xml>" & objStrBuilder.ToString & "</xml>"

            Xml1.DocumentContent = outXML
            Xml1.TransformSource = "item.xsl"
            Response.Write(Xml1.Transform)

        Catch objError As Exception
            'display error details
            Response.Write("<b>* Error while accessing data</b>.<br />" _
                & objError.Message & "<br />" & objError.Source & "<p />")
            Exit Sub  ' and stop execution

        End Try

    End Sub
```

First we build our query to get the data from the database in XML format. Note that this SQL command will only work with SQL Server 2000 as FOR XML AUTO is the special new feature in SQL Server 2000 that returns the data in the XML format along with other XML-related features.

We declare an XmlTextReader object and assign the result of the objcommand.ExecuteXmlReader() call to that variable. We must append the <xml> tags to the data to have a well formed XML.

We assign the XML and XSL to the ASP:xml control named Xml1 on the page and write the results to the client browser, as shown in the following screenshot:

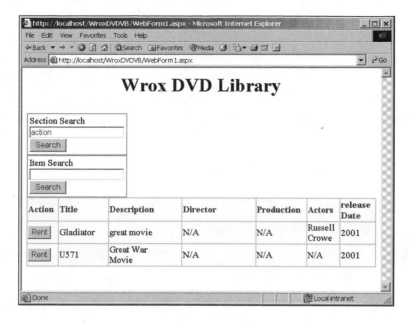

Search by Title:

When the user enters data in the Items textbox and clicks on its associated Search button, we call the event handler for the btnSearch.

```
Private Sub btnItemSearch_Click(ByVal sender As Object, _
            ByVal e As System.EventArgs) Handles btnItemSearch.Click
    ExecuteSQLStatement(txtItem.Text)
End Sub
```

We call the function ExecuteSQLStatement() that gets the data from the database in XML format. Then we apply the items.xsl XSL stylesheet to the XML and display the result in the client browser. Much of the code is similar to the code in the search by section, but the SQL statement will be different:

```
Private Sub ExecuteSQLStatement(ByVal strToSearch As String)

    Dim SQL, sXML, outXML As String
    SQL = "SELECT item.* FROM item " & _
        "WHERE item.item_title " & _
        "LIKE '%" + strToSearch + "%' AND item.active = 1 FOR XML AUTO"

    Try
        Dim objConnect As New SqlConnection(Application("strConnect"))
        objConnect.Open()
        Dim objCommand As New SqlCommand(SQL, objConnect)
        Dim xmlReader As XmlTextReader

        xmlReader = objCommand.ExecuteXmlReader()

        Dim objStrBuilder As New Stringbuilder()
        objStrBuilder.Append(xmlReader.GetRemainder().ReadToEnd())

        xmlReader.Close()
```

```
        objConnect.Close()
        outXML = "<xml>" & objStrBuilder.ToString & "</xml>"

        'Create a resolver and set the credentials to use.
        Dim resolver As XmlUrlResolver = New XmlUrlResolver()
        Dim myCred As NetworkCredential = _
                New NetworkCredential("wroxdvd", "wrox", "dinarhome")
        resolver.Credentials = myCred
        Xml1.DocumentContent = outXML
        Xml1.TransformSource = "item.xsl"
        Response.Write(Xml1.Transform)

    Catch objError As Exception

        'display error details
        Response.Write("<b>* Error while accessing data</b>.<br />" _
            & objError.Message & "<br />" & objError.Source & "<p />")
        Exit Sub  ' and stop execution

    End Try

End Sub
```

We start by building our SQL query to get the data from the database in XML format. We declare an XmlReader object and assign the result of the objcommand to the variable.

The xmlReader object will generate runtime error if the input is a non-XML document. We append the data to the objStrBuilder object till the end of data.

We append the <xml> tags to the data to have well-formed XML. We assign the XML and XSL to the ASP:xml named Xml1 control on the page and write the results to the client browser, as shown in the following screenshot:

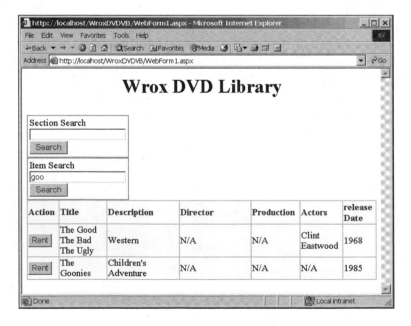

Items.xsl

Here is the XSL stylesheet `items.xsl` that we used for transformation of the XML:

```
<?xml version="1.0"?>
<xsl:stylesheet version="1.0"
                xmlns:xsl="http://www.w3.org/1999/XSL/Transform"
                xmlns:fo="http://www.w3.org/1999/XSL/Format">
  <xsl:template match="/">
    <xsl:apply-templates/>
  </xsl:template>

  <xsl:template match="/">

  <xsl:comment>
    .clsA     { color: blue; }
    a:active    { color: Red; }
    a:visited  { color: blue; }
    a:hover    { color: Red; }
  </xsl:comment>

  <table border="1" bgcolor="#FFFCEE" bordercolor="#CCCCCC"
       cellspacing="0" width="100%">
    <tr>
       <td width="30">
          <font color="#990000"><b>Action</b></font>
       </td>
       <td width="70">
          <font color="#990000"><b>Title</b></font>
       </td>
       <td width="50">
          <font color="#990000"><b>Description</b></font>
       </td>
       <td width="135">
          <font color="#990000"><b>Director</b></font>
       </td>
       <td width="30">
          <font color="#990000"><b>Production</b></font>
       </td>
       <td width="30">
          <font color="#990000"><b>Actors</b></font>
       </td>
       <td width="30">
          <font color="#990000"><b>release Date</b></font>
       </td>
    </tr>
    <xsl:for-each select="xml/item">
    <tr>
       <td width="30">
          <xsl:element name="button">
             <xsl:attribute name="item_id">
                <xsl:value-of select="@item_id"/>
             </xsl:attribute>
             <xsl:attribute name="onClick">
                AddToCart()
             </xsl:attribute>
             Rent
          </xsl:element>
       </td>
       <td width="90">
          <xsl:choose>
```

```
            <xsl:when test="string-length(@item_title)>0">
                <xsl:value-of select="@item_title"/>
            </xsl:when>
            <xsl:otherwise>N/A</xsl:otherwise>
        </xsl:choose>
    </td>
    <td width="135">
        <xsl:choose>
            <xsl:when test="string-length(@item_desc)>0">
                <xsl:value-of select="@item_desc"/>
            </xsl:when>
            <xsl:otherwise>N/A</xsl:otherwise>
        </xsl:choose>
    </td>
    <td width="30">
        <xsl:choose>
            <xsl:when test="string-length(@director)>0">
                <xsl:value-of select="@director"/>
            </xsl:when>
            <xsl:otherwise>N/A</xsl:otherwise>
        </xsl:choose>
    </td>
    <td width="30">
        <xsl:choose>
            <xsl:when test="string-length(@production)>0">
                <xsl:value-of select="@production"/>
            </xsl:when>
            <xsl:otherwise>N/A</xsl:otherwise>
        </xsl:choose>
    </td>
    <td width="30">
        <xsl:choose>
            <xsl:when test="string-length(@actors)>0">
                <xsl:value-of select="@actors"/>
            </xsl:when>
            <xsl:otherwise>N/A</xsl:otherwise>
        </xsl:choose>
    </td>
    <td width="30">
        <xsl:choose>
            <xsl:when test="string-length(@release_date)>0">
                <xsl:value-of select="@release_date"/>
            </xsl:when>
            <xsl:otherwise>N/A</xsl:otherwise>
        </xsl:choose>
    </td>
    <xsl:element name="input">
        <xsl:attribute name="type">hidden</xsl:attribute>
        <xsl:attribute name="name">
            x_desc_<xsl:value-of select="@item_id"/>
        </xsl:attribute>
        <xsl:attribute name="id">
            x_<xsl:value-of select="@item_id"/>
        </xsl:attribute>
        <xsl:attribute name="value">
            <xsl:value-of select="@item_id"/>
        </xsl:attribute>
    </xsl:element>
</tr>
```

```
      </xsl:for-each>
    </table>
  </xsl:template>
</xsl:stylesheet>
```

See Chapter 5, *XSL Transformations of XML*, for a more information about XSL.

Cart.aspx

Let's see how to add the item to the cart. I won't be implementing the complete cart here but demonstrate how to add the item to the cart. When the user clicks on the Rent button, we pass the item ID to the page that will perform the actual add to the cart.

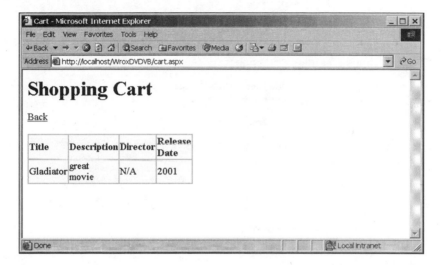

Let's look at the code that performs this. We use the JavaScript code below to pass the item_id to Cart.aspx. This code is in the file WebForm1.aspx.

```
<script language="JavaScript">
<!--
   function AddToCart()
   {
      // assign the values from the form for display while doing update
      var nitem_id = window.event.srcElement.item_id;
      var sdesc = frmMain["x_desc_" + nitem_id].value;

      document.frmMain.item_id.value= sdesc;
      document.frmMain.action ="cart.aspx"
      document.frmMain.submit ();
   }
//-->
```

We then use the item_id in the page Cart.aspx to get the data from the database. On the loading of the page, we call the GetCart() function and pass the item_id as parameter.

```
Private Sub Page_Load(ByVal sender As System.Object, _
                        ByVal e As System.EventArgs) Handles MyBase.Load
    'Put user code to initialize the page here
    GetCart(Request("item_id"))
End Sub
```

The GetCart() function is similar to the GetSection() function we saw earlier with the changes done to the SQL statement, and we apply a new XSL stylesheet, cart.xsl:

```
Private Sub GetCart(ByVal itemId As String)

    Dim SQL, sXML, outXML As String
    SQL = "SELECT item_title , item_desc, director, release_date " & _
          "FROM item WHERE Item_id = " & itemId & " FOR XML AUTO"

    Try
        Dim objConnect As New SqlConnection(Application("strConnect"))
        objConnect.Open()
        Dim objCommand As New SqlCommand(SQL, objConnect)
        Dim xmlReader As XmlTextReader

        xmlReader = objCommand.ExecuteXmlReader()

        Dim objStrBuilder As New StringBuilder()
        objStrBuilder.Append(xmlReader.GetRemainder().ReadToEnd())

        xmlReader.Close()
        objConnect.Close()
        outXML = "<xml>" & objStrBuilder.ToString & "</xml>"

        Xml1.DocumentContent = outXML
        Xml1.TransformSource = "cart.xsl"
        Response.Write(Xml1.Transform)

    Catch objError As Exception
        'display error details
        Response.Write("<b>* Error while accessing data</b>.<br />" _
            & objError.Message & "<br />" & objError.Source & "<p />")
        Exit Sub  ' and stop execution

    End Try
End Sub
```

We'll not list cart.xsl here, but it's in the download as you would expect.

Summary

In this case study, we took a look at one specific application of an online DVD store, and demonstrated how the application can be implemented without large chunks of complicated code. we also saw how to make our online store available to all potential customers regardless of the browser their client machine was running, making our real-world example as consumer-friendly as possible.

There are a few things you can add to this application:

- ❑ A shopping cart
- ❑ An easy checkout facility
- ❑ Integration with an Order Processing System
- ❑ E-mail facilities to let the user know that the movie is in the mail

In particular we have looked at:

- ❑ Features of ASP.NET and server-side controls
- ❑ How to open a database connection using ADO.NET and reading the data in XML format
- ❑ How ADO.NET has built-in support for XML
- ❑ Making an application browser-independent using server-side XSL

XML for .NET Developers
essional XML for .NET Devel
Professional XML for .NET
ofessional XML for .NET Developers Professional XML
or .NET Developers Professional XML for .NET Develo

13

Web Services and SOAP

Web Services are one of the most talked about Internet development concepts around today. In their simplest form, Web Services are pieces of application functionality exposed or delivered via XML and protocols such as HTTP. Web Services give developers a new approach to distributed application development that is platform- and implementation-independent.

Distributed application models are not new. There exist, among others, a number of commonly recognized distributed application models including DCOM, RMI, and CORBA. In many ways, Web Services attempt to deliver the same functionality as these models, but via a fundamentally different method enabling disparate systems, written in different development languages running on different platforms, to interact with that functionality. As we will see, the advent of XML, HTTP, and other Internet standards has created a climate capable of supporting this new approach to distributed application development. This has resulted into a new level of program interoperability using universally accepted Internet technologies.

Consumers (consumers can be users, applications, or a combination) of a Web Service are fortunate since they don't need to know anything about the particular implementation of that service. The only requirement for a client is an understanding of a Web Service's particular interface – the messages it expects to receive as an input and the messages it generates as an output. As we'll see, there is even a standardization effort underway to help Web Service clients match their particular needs with published Web Service functionality, and XML plays a vital role in this effort. In fact, XML is very important in many aspects of Web Service design and operation. We can describe Web Service interfaces using a standardized XML Schema, and Web Service messages are most often encoded in XML.

Seeing the opportunity presented by Web Services, Microsoft has geared up a large part of its .NET initiative towards Web Services development and use. We'll find several .NET tools making the development and use of Web Services easier. First, ASP.NET provides an easy way to develop and configure Web Services. Everything from wrapping functional code and keeping it from interface layers, to creating and managing underlying .NET configuration files, is included in ASP.NET's simplified development model. Secondly, the .NET namespaces provide functionality specifically for Web Services. Finally, Visual Studio .NET allows us to build, debug, and describe Web Services. As we will soon see, Visual Studio .NET makes working with the XML-oriented aspects of building, deploying, and running Web Services rather simple.

In this chapter, we will cover the following topics:

- ❏ We'll cover some background information on Web Services, and review some of the concepts that make Web Services so powerful. We'll look at a possible Web Service application, discuss some of the market and technological trends that are making Web Service adoption and usage more likely, and we'll start talking about the role of .NET in Web Services, or rather the role of Web Services in .NET.

- ❏ After the overview, we'll jump into building a simple ASP.NET Web Service. This will give us an opportunity to learn some common .NET Web Service concepts, and look at what Visual Studio .NET does for us in terms of making Web Service development easier. Along the way, we'll highlight some important Visual Studio. NET constructs and discuss their roles in running Web Services.

- ❏ A key requirement for the goal of implementation and platform-independence of Web Services is the capability to transport messages via different wire formats. To fulfill this requirement, .NET Web Services support three commonly accepted protocols known as HTTP GET, HTTP POST, and SOAP. HTTP must be familiar to most web users and developers. We will see that SOAP is a tremendously useful combination of XML and HTTP. In fact, the future promise of Web Services and the widespread acceptance of SOAP are directly proportional.

- ❏ All Web Services have the ability to provide a large amount of descriptive information about the interfaces they expose, and the types of messages they expect to receive as input and return as output. Using that information, we can create localized representations of Web Services, which make creating applications using Web Services much easier. We'll see that Visual Studio. NET does quite a bit of work for us by generating Web Service proxy classes.

- ❏ Web Services employ a particularly useful set of standard technologies that support 'Directory, Discovery, and Descriptions' services. These three services are delivered using standards named **UDDI** (**Uniform Description, Discovery, and Integration**) and **WSDL** (**Web Services Description Language**). We will explore each of these services, and examine how Visual Studio .NET helps us in this regard.

- ❏ We'll expand our simple Web Service application example and explore the issues of Web Service Security, State Management, and Deployment. We will also spend some time looking at how Visual Studio .NET supports building Web Service client applications, either web applications or desktop applications.

Let's get started by understanding some important Web Service concepts.

Web Services Overview

Web Services take the concept of 'software as a service' and actually put it into practice. As we've already seen, Web Services are merely pieces of functionality exposed in a universal way. Consider those pieces of functionality as small services with which consumers interact by sending and receiving messages. By interacting, or as it is sometimes called, subscribing, to a particular service, a consumer agrees to follow an interface contract published by the Web Service. The Web Service agrees to provide some advertised function. We'll get to the contract definition and how exactly services are advertised or published shortly; but for now the concept of writing software as services and implementing or subscribing to those software services is an important one to bring out.

Microsoft isn't the only organization that is realizing the potential of Web Services. Some developers could argue that Web Services functionality has existed for a long time. If they follow the rules of a universal interface and a universal data format, they'd have a strong argument. In fact, developers don't have to use any Microsoft products to develop or consume Web Services; but Microsoft is trying to take the lead with Web Service development tools, especially in .NET technology.

Market and Technological Forces

In case of Web Services, Microsoft is likely to be interested in positioning itself ahead of its competitors for a couple of reasons. First, Web Services are a good idea that is likely to be widely adopted. Since Web Services are inherently multi-platform and implementation-independent, it is in Microsoft's interest to beat the rest of the market with a good Web Service development platform. This will ensure for Microsoft that its development tools get used, and Microsoft operating systems are used as platforms for deploying Web Services. Secondly, Microsoft is trying hard to sell its entire .NET initiative, and by fielding a good, solid approach to Web Services, create credibility about its .NET tools.

Regardless of what exactly Microsoft is doing with .NET and its approach to Web Services, some current market and technical trends make the widespread adoption of Web Services highly possible. Let's consider following issues:

❑ Widespread acceptance of HTTP/HTTPS and XML – As we've mentioned earlier, Web Services are based on a common protocol called SOAP. SOAP consists of a transport protocol such as HTTP/HTTPS, and XML. Over the past few years, we've seen HTTP being well received on the Web. Most platforms support HTTP in some form, and many developers are now writing HTTP applications. Additionally, HTTP/HTTPS is consistently allowed through firewalls on port 80, whereas other protocols or serialization methods supported by DCOM or RMI require changes for requests to make it through most firewalls.

XML itself is transcending its buzzword status – XML-enabled applications are becoming more and more common, and XML parsers have been ported to most operating platforms.

❑ Evolution of Internet applications – Looking at the spectrum of Internet applications, we find that many high-end web applications would significantly gain from the real benefits provided by Web Services. In particular, there are ample examples of application-to-application integration scenarios that lend themselves nicely to Web Services. The integration of financial systems at the transaction level or data sharing applications between sales automation systems are just two examples of functionality users are expecting as Internet and Web applications evolve. Web Services may just be coming along at a time when designers and users expect the next step in application functionality, interconnectivity, and overall value.

❑ Real-time application integration – More so than ever before, we are seeing new applications come into the market that require real-time integration with partner applications, particularly legacy applications. As enterprises move their operations to the Web, quick easy access to legacy or partner application data is becoming a need. The abstract, loosely coupled interface that Web Services provide to transactional, service-based software functionality, on demand, may be an attractive solution.

❑ Developers looking for better distributed application models – Many application developers have been building distributed systems for years. These developers have most likely been working with models like DCOM, RMI, or CORBA/IIOP. Knowing the strengths and weaknesses of these models, a new, simplified approach to distributed application development may be well received if it lives up to its billing as a widely available method of deploying functionality.

New Distributed Computing Model

Web Services, irrespective of .NET technology, are partly based on the idea of distributing functionality by making the data portable, not the code itself. By creating a universal mechanism via SOAP, Web Services function by moving messages containing payloads of application-relevant data from consumer to service and back.

As we'll see in more depth later in the chapter, Web Services depend upon the construction of abstract, loosely coupled interfaces. Loosely coupled interfaces allow developers to create black-box-like components that are inherently flexible because their interfaces are not directly tied to a particular implementation. As a good object-oriented development practice, applications that hide their implementation behind an abstract, unchanging interface are generally easier to work with, and therefore, more likely to gain widespread acceptance.

Web Services are said to be competitive with existing distributed computing models like DCOM, RMI, and CORBA/IIOP. First, Web Services are said to be completely platform-independent. To gain maximum advantage of CORBA/IIOP or DCOM, they should be used on particular platforms; they have some limitations as compared to Web services.

Web Services are implementation-neutral. That is, the particular development environment, compiler or operating system used to construct a Web Service are irrelevant to its consumers, assuming the Web Service was written in as universal a manner as possible. Consumer applications do not necessarily dictate the implementation of a Web Service. Any application written by a well-behaved Web Service consumer merely has to know what messages to send to the Web Service, and what to expect in return (if needed). Remember, when all is said and done, most Web Services will support interfaces that devolve into two key parts, HTTP/HTTPS and XML.

.NET and Web Services

According to Microsoft, .NET is a platform for Web Services. As we'll see shortly, if we have built a simple ASP.NET application, we can easily create a Web Service using Visual Studio .NET.

The .NET initiative, including Visual Studio .NET and ASP.NET, is clearly being positioned to be the early development tool and platform of choice for building Web Services. Microsoft, with IBM and others, is a key proponent of the SOAP specification, another building block of the Web Services movement. As you'll see later in the chapter, Visual Studio .NET makes working with SOAP-enabled Web Services very easy.

Building a Simple Web Service

In this chapter, we will be building a couple of Web Service examples to illustrate key points of Web Service construction and usage. First, we'll look at a very simple example of building an ASP.NET Web Service using Visual Studio .NET. As an exercise, it will allow us to take a look at basic Web Service structure, in terms of ASP.NET code and VB .NET classes.

Let's take an example of a little string handling Web Service that takes an individual's name formatted as "Last, First" as its input and returns it as a proper full name in "First Last" format. The idea comes from applications like Microsoft Outlook where the first and last names are best displayed together for readability but sorting and searching are done on the last name. Let's call the "Last, First" format the *listname* and the normal name format the the *fullname*.

Creating a Web Service in Visual Studio .NET

In order to create our Web Service in Visual Studio .NET, let's create a new Visual Basic project, using an ASP.NET Web Service template as shown in the following dialog box:

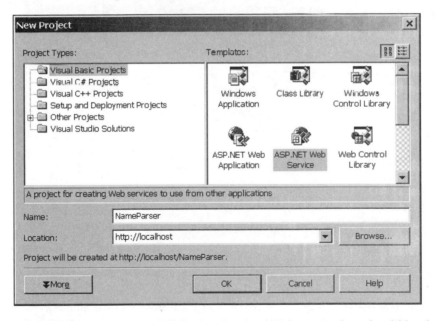

We'll name this project NameParser, and the location in the above window should be the name of the running IIS instance on our machine (normally it's localhost, so the location is http://localhost). As soon as we press the OK button, Visual Studio .NET will create a new virtual directory in IIS, and we will get a status message as shown overleaf:

Notice that if IIS is not configured correctly or it isn't running, we'll receive error messages and the project won't be created. In fact, whenever we open a Web Service or ASP.NET application, Visual Studio .NET will try to open the virtual web associated with that project, resulting in errors if IIS isn't available.

Now, we should have the **Solution Explorer** window for `NameParser` showing the following file structure:

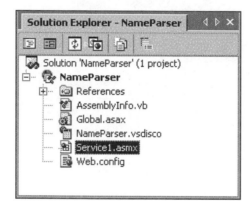

For organizatioal purposes, let's rename the `Service1.asmx` Web Service file to `NameParser.asmx`, by right-clicking on it.

Before we start writing our Web Service, let's briefly review what files have been created for us by Visual Studio .NET, and how we might use them. In many cases, we won't be required to modify these base files that are created by Visual Studio .NET. However, as we build more complex Web Services, having an understanding of some of these files will useful:

❑ **References** – This is a list of references and exists in any Visual Studio .NET application. This list is a convenient method of managing references to .NET namespaces, COM components, or other .NET projects. Previous Microsoft development environments supported the same concept to help developers create references to other COM components. One interesting feature of Visual Studio .NET is the ability to create a reference to a .NET component over the Web. Later in the chapter, we'll see how and why we would create a Web Service reference.

❑ **AssemblyInfo.vb** – This is an XML-encoded file containing Web Service assembly information including Title, Description, and GUID for COM (if applicable). We can make changes to this file by opening it in the editor window.

- ❑ **Global.asax** – This is similar to `global.asa` file in ASP. This file contains the `Global` class, which exposes `BeginRequest`, `AuthenticateRequest`, and `Error` events. You can find more about this file in Chapter 11, *ASP.NET*.

- ❑ **NameParser.vsdisco** – This file contains Web Service 'Discovery' information. We'll look at the concepts behind 'Discovery' and the contents of this file in the section titled *Directory, Discovery, and Description*. For now, understand that the contents of this file enable other applications to find your Web Service and help explain the functionality it exposes.

- ❑ **NameParser.asmx** – This file (we renamed it from `Service1.asmx`) contains the VB .NET code for the actual implementation of our Web Service. Apparently, the file extension `.asmx` doesn't stand for anything in particular; it isn't an abbreviation as well. However, whenever you see a file with an extension `.asmx`, you can be sure it is a Web Service file since only Web Services use that extension.

- ❑ **Web.config** – This is another XML-encoded file that serves as the configuration file for the ASP.NET application. Even though we are creating a Web Service, we still get the benefits of an ASP.NET application.

Writing Code for Our Simple Web Service

Let's move on to writing code in order to create our `NameParser` Web Service. Remember that our Web Service will take the *listname* ("Last, First") as an input contained in one string parameter, and output the *fullname* formatted as "First Last", also totally contained within a single string parameter.

If we open our `NameParser.asmx` file, it will contain the following lines of code (along with auto-generated code and a commented Web Service example):

```
Imports System.Web.Services

Public Class Service1
    Inherits System.Web.Services.WebService

Web Services Designer Generated Code

    ...

' Web Service Example
    '...


End Class
```

Note that when Visual Studio .NET creates the `.asmx` file for us, it names the public class generated in this file as `Service1`, by default. Since we renamed the `Service1.asmx` file to `NameParser.asmx`, we'll change the name of this public class to `NameParser`.

Also, look at the code automatically generated by VS .NET. It is generally compressed into one line that reads `Web Services Designer Generated Code`. We won't be modifying any auto-generated VS .NET code in this chapter. Visual Studio .NET also creates a sample Web Service example in the Web Service file. Since this example is inserted as comments, our code isn't affected. Hence, for brevity, the code samples in this chapter won't include the designer-generated code and the example.

Let's create a `GetFullName()` function, which takes a string as input and returns a string as output. The input string will contain the last name and the first name separated by a comma, and the output string will be the first name followed by a space and the last name. The code for this function will be as follows:

```
Public Function GetFullName(ByVal strListName As String) As String
    Dim arrName() as String

    arrName = Split(strListName, ",")
    Return arrName(1) & " " & arrName(0)
End Function
```

In this function, the *listname* parameter, `strListName` is passed into the `Split()` function using a comma as the delimiter. The output of `Split()` is a two dimensional string array, `arrName()`, where `arrName(0)` holds the last name and `arrName(1)` holds the first name. Since the purpose of `GetFullName()` function is to return the name components in the *fullname* format, the last line returns a string consisting of the first name concatenated to the last name with a space in between.

To expose `GetFullName()` via the Web Service, let's add an attribute called `WebMethod()`, immediately before the function definition. Used in Web Services, the `WebMethod()` attribute actually exposes our individual functions through the Web Service. The `WebMethod()` attribute will be added like this:

```
<WebMethod()> Public Function GetFullName(ByVal strListName As String)_
                                    As String
```

Now, we have to give our code access to the `System.Web.Services` namespace. In VB .NET, this is accomplished by the following line of code, which is added automatically above our `NameParser` class definition:

```
Imports System.Web.Services
```

Among other things, this namespace contains the `WebService` base class that provides basic Web Service functionality and access to ASP.NET objects for managing session state.

Let's make a small change in inheriting the `WebService` base class that we just gained access to, via the `Imports` statement we just added. Inside our `NameParser` class, next to the function definition, we'll add the following line:

```
Inherits System.Web.Services.WebService
```

It is possible to build a Web Service without deriving from the `WebService` base class; but getting access to session management objects and other ASP.NET application objects is more difficult.

At this point, we should have a functional Web Service that exposes one simple function, `GetFullName()`. The full code for this Web service will now be as follows:

```
Imports System.Web.Services

Public Class NameParser
    Inherits System.Web.Services.WebService

    <WebMethod()> Public Function GetFullName(ByVal strListName _
                                        As String) As String
        Dim arrName() As String

        arrName = Split(strListName, ",")
```

```
            Return arrName(1) & " " & arrName(0)
        End Function
    End Class
```

Testing Our Simple Web Service

With the help of ASP.NET, we can now test our Web Service very easily. At this point, our Web Service is not different from any other ASP.NET page, except for the different file extension.

Let's save our Visual Studio .NET project and start it after building it. Visual Studio .NET will now open a browser window and open the `NameParser.asmx` page, which should look something like the following:

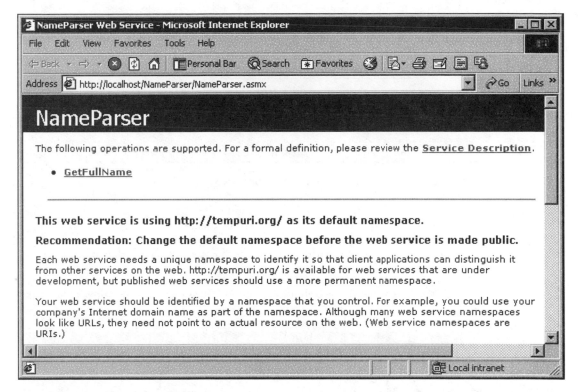

In the browser, we see a nice looking page that shows the name of the Web Service as a heading and an hyperlink named as our method `GetFullName()`. As you might guess, clicking on this **GetFullName** link will tell us more about that particular method. As you could also probably deduce, any method in our code tagged with the `WebMethod()` attribute will also be displayed when you browse this page. Now, let's click on this **GetFullName** link and we'll see something like the following:

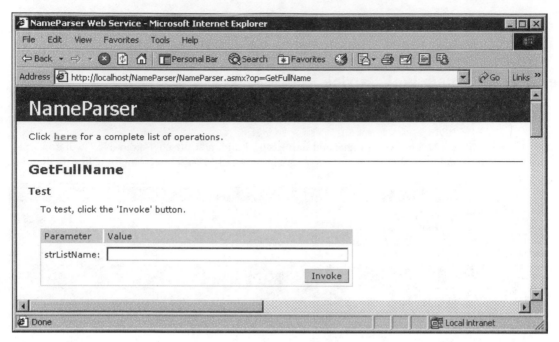

If we look at the Address bar, we will find that even though we are still browsing the NameParser.asmx file, we now have an ASP.NET querystring, op=GetFullName. This is a command indicating that we want to see the details of the Web Method called GetFullName(). What we get is a simple HTML form containing a table of every parameter our method specifies, in this case just strListName. The Web Service test page also contains its sample request and a response for SOAP, HTTP GET, and HTTP POST protocols, with placeholders that are replaced with actual values.

We can use this form to pass values to GetFullName() and test the results. If we type "Last, First" into the text box and press the Invoke button, we should see another browser window appear that looks something like this:

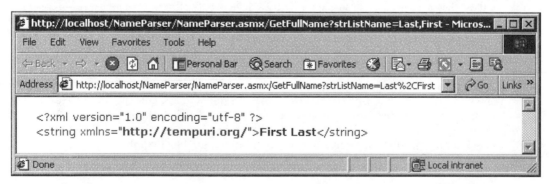

What we get back is XML generated by the web method. Looking closely at the URL of this, we get some insight into how the Web Service testing facility provided by ASP.NET works. The URL contains a query string that has our input parameter. It happens to be reformatted to conform to proper query string requirements, as in Last5%C+First. This is an HTTP GET protocol, one of three protocols .NET Web Services supports.

The XML we get is worth looking at too. Our GetFullName() function defines the return type as a string; therefore the element that represents the return value of our WebMethod() is named <string>. Notice that if you got all the way through to seeing the return XML, we now have a working Visual Studio .NET Web Service.

Let's see what happens if we have other return types. For instance, can we return something more useful than a simple string? Let's try returning an object representing our name parts.

To do this, we'll add a new function GetFullNameObject() to our Web Service that returns an instance of a class called Name. We will insert this function before our existing GetFullName() function. Our GetFullNameObject() function will look like this:

```
<WebMethod()> Public Function GetFullNameObject( _
                    ByVal strListName As String) As Name

    Dim arrName() as String
    Dim oNamePart As New Name()

    arrName = Split(strListName, ",")
    oNamePart.First = arrName(1)
    oNamePart.Last = arrName(0)
    Return oNamePart
End Function
```

Now we'll add the Name class to the project by selecting **Project | Add Class**. To keep it simple, the Name class doesn't do much. It looks like this:

```
Public Class Name

    Private strFirst As String
    Private strLast As String

    Public Property First() As String
        Get
            Return strFirst
        End Get
        Set(ByVal Value As String)
            strFirst = Value
        End Set
    End Property

    Public Property Last() As String
        Get
            Return strLast
        End Get
        Set(ByVal Value As String)
            strLast = Value
        End Set
    End Property
End Class
```

If we now rebuild the project and run it again, our new Web Service test page will show both the method names:

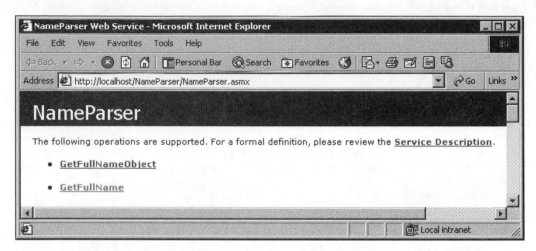

Now, let's explore the GetFullNameObject link and enter the same "Last, First" combination in the textbox. The XML we get back this time is similar to the first test we did, but formatted as shown below:

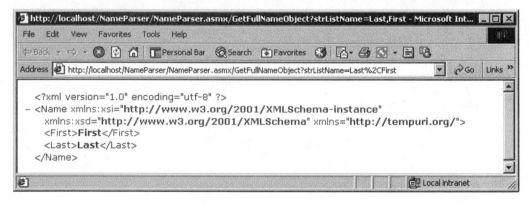

Instead of a <string> element containing our function's return value, it has been replaced with another element called <Name>, representing our Name class, that contains our two Name properties, <First> and <Last>, as child elements.

This simple example has implications that we'll explore in more detail later in the chapter. For now, however, imagine the flexibility of an interface that supports multiple input and output data types described in XML. Any application that supports an XML parser could understand the results of this particular Web Service.

Now that we have a simple Web Service running, we shall delve a little more deeply into the details behind making Web Services work. In the following sections, we'll take a look at the protocols Web Services support, focusing primarily on SOAP, building proxy classes to represent Web Services in our client applications, and some of the features included in Visual Studio .NET to make building Web Services easier.

Web Service Protocols

As we've already seen, Web Services are built on universally accepted standards. Web Service technology includes the adoption of standards for describing a particular Web Service, advertising its existence to the rest of the world, and so on. One other standard Web Services have adopted is HTTP as a protocol for exchanging data.

HTTP GET and HTTP POST

Specifically, Web Services support both HTTP GET and HTTP POST protocols. HTTP GET passes parameters in the form of UUencoded (using Unix to Unix encoding) text, what ASP developers call a query string.

HTTP GET only allows simple data types, a limitation that we've already run up against with our `GetFullNameObject` example returning an instance of a class we created called `Name`. In the test page of this example, we can see the sample request and response using HTTP GET protocol. However, to send and receive complex data types using HTTP, we have HTTP POST protocol. If we scroll down the `GetFullNameObject` test page, we'll see the HTTP GET request and response as seen below:

```
GET /NameParser/NameParser.asmx/GetFullNameObject?strListName=string HTTP/1.1
Host: localhost
```

```
HTTP/1.1 200 OK
Content-Type: text/xml; charset=utf-8
Content-Length: length

<?xml version="1.0" encoding="utf-8"?>
<Name xmlns="http://tempuri.org/">
  <First>string</First>
  <Last>string</Last>
</Name>
```

HTTP POST as a protocol works a little differently by passing name-value pairs in the body of the actual HTTP request message instead of as a part of the query string. For our `GetFullNameObject` web method, the request and response for HTTP POST will look like:

```
POST /NameParser/NameParser.asmx/GetFullNameObject HTTP/1.1
Host: localhost
Content-Type: application/x-www-form-urlencoded
Content-Length: length

strListName=string
```

```
HTTP/1.1 200 OK
Content-Type: text/xml; charset=utf-8
Content-Length: length

<?xml version="1.0" encoding="utf-8"?>
```

```
<Name xmlns="http://tempuri.org/">
  <First>string</First>
  <Last>string</Last>
</Name>
```

If we wanted, we could build an HTML form with one textbox that executed an HTTP POST to our Web Service. Again, this is a simple example, but think of the possibilities of creating a centralized, subscription or usage-based service implemented as a Web Service that allowed conventional ASP clients around the world to post data and get simple results back. Credit card authorization comes to mind as a possible example of this scenario.

SOAP

HTTP GET and HTTP POST are very useful in their own right, but the real promise of Web Services lies with SOAP, the **Simple Object Access Protocol**. It is a lightweight, XML-based protocol for exchanging information on the Web. It has a consistent format or structure but it can be used for just about any information exchange application. SOAP lends itself perfectly to Web Services for a couple of reasons. First, it will bind to just about any transport protocol, including HTTP. Second, it is encoded in XML.

A SOAP request for the `GetFullNameObject()` web method we developed earlier, including the HTTP headers, looks like this:

```
POST /NameParser/NameParser.asmx HTTP/1.1
Host: localhost
Content-Type: text/xml; charset=utf-8
Content-Length: 50
SOAPAction: "http://tempuri.org/GetFullNameObject"

<?xml version="1.0" encoding="utf-8"?>
<soap:Envelope xmlns:xsi="http://www.w3.org/2001/XMLSchema-instance"
               xmlns:xsd="http://www.w3.org/2001/XMLSchema"
               xmlns:soap="http://schemas.xmlsoap.org/soap/envelope/">
  <soap:Body>
    <GetFullNameObject xmlns="http://tempuri.org/">
       <strListName>string</strListName>
    </GetFullNameObject>
  </soap:Body>
</soap:Envelope>
```

We'll get into the details in a moment, but by scanning quickly through this XML, a few things may jump out at you. First, notice the child element of the `<soap:Body>` element, named `<GetFullNameObject>`; that's our web method name. As we continue to scan the XML, we might expect to see our input variables. On the next line, we see element `<strListName>`. Ignore rest of the XML for the moment.

SOAP is merely another way of getting the same information that our HTTP POST and HTTP GET methods delivered. However, we have a lot more control over some of the ways our SOAP messages are sent and received.

Now, we've seen a simple SOAP request. Including HTTP headers, the SOAP response looks like this:

```
HTTP/1.1 200 OK
Content-Type: text/xml; charset=utf-8
Content-Length: 50

<?xml version="1.0" encoding="utf-8"?>
<soap:Envelope xmlns:xsi="http://www.w3.org/2001/XMLSchema-instance"
               xmlns:xsd="http://www.w3.org/2001/XMLSchema"
               xmlns:soap="http://schemas.xmlsoap.org/soap/envelope/">
   <soap:Body>
      <GetFullNameObjectResponse xmlns="http://tempuri.org/">
         <GetFullNameObjectResult>
            <First>First</First>
            <Last>Last</Last>
         </GetFullNameObjectResult>
      </GetFullNameObjectResponse>
   </soap:Body>
</soap:Envelope>
```

Let's scan through this XML looking for familiar data. The first thing you may notice is the child element of the `<soap:Body>` element, which is similar to our web method name; but is changed to `<GetFullNameObjectResponse>` since we are looking at a SOAP response to the `GetFullNameObject()` method call. Immediately below this element we find the `<GetFullNameObjectResult>` and its children `<First>` and `<Last>`, the same elements we got from our HTTP GET test.

SOAP messages, regardless of their application, have some things in common. We will most likely find the four following components in a SOAP message. Note that these components could be mandatory or optional:

Component	Description
Envelope	The envelope is the root element of the SOAP XML document, and represents the message by expressing what features are represented in a message. It's a mandatory component of a SOAP message.
Header	SOAP headers were engineered to allow developers to create modularity and extra flexibility in their SOAP messages. The most common payload delivered via these optional components is security or authentication information.
Body	This mandatory element actually contains data intended for the message recipient. It can take the form of an RPC marshaling-like command as in our GetFullNameObject example earlier.
Fault	This element represents an error from Web Services. A SOAP Fault follows a specific standard that contains several pieces of information including the faultcode, faultstring, faultactor, and detail that combine to form a SOAP response that might look like the following code, without the HTTP headers. Since this component deals with errors it's not mandatory.

471

Here is a SOAP response that contains the above components:

```
<?xml version="1.0" encoding="utf-8"?>
<soap:Envelope xmlns:xsi="http://www.w3.org/2001/XMLSchema-instance"
               xmlns:xsd="http://www.w3.org/2001/XMLSchema"
               xmlns:soap="http://schemas.xmlsoap.org/soap/envelope/">
  <soap:Body>
    <GetFullNameObjectResponse xmlns="http://tempuri.org/">
      <GetFullNameObjectResult>
        <soap:Fault>
           <faultcode> Server</faultcode>
           <faultstring>General Error</faultstring>
           <detail>No Last name provided.</detail>
        </soap:Fault>
      </GetFullNameObjectResult>
    </GetFullNameObjectResponse>
  </soap:Body>
</soap:Envelope>
```

Now, we know a little more about the structure of a SOAP message as an RPC-like (Remote Procedure Call) request. We've also seen what a SOAP response looks like. What happens if we want to send the Web Service more information than input or output parameter values? Maybe we want to build a Web Service that performs authentication for every request it receives, but we don't want to include a user ID and password in every function we write. The way to do this is by extending the SOAP header.

Using the SOAP Header

SOAP headers were included in the specification to allow developers to create modular, extensible messages. The most common header payload contents are things like authentication, transaction management, and payment information, that is, items that have little to do with the purpose or contents of the message. However, header contents are data that support the main content of the SOAP message in some way.

Developers can extend the basic purpose of a SOAP message (a request for some action with accompanying data) to perform several other functions. As we've already mentioned, we can include a variety of support content to help our Web Service do its job better, or to better meet the needs of our Web Service clients.

Let's take an example of using SOAP headers in a particular Web Service application for user authentication. We'll create a SOAP header and include a subscriber ID, a user ID, and a password. If the credentials are properly authenticated then we'll process the Web Service request and return some response. In case you were wondering, the subscriber ID could be used to represent some company or organization that we allow access to our Web Service. There could very easily be duplicate user IDs between two organizations. In addition, it might be nice to have that extra piece of information for tracking our Web Service's usage for performance or even billing purposes.

Let's consider a Web Service that allows subscribers to review the contents of invoices. Subscribers could be customers, our own sales people, or maybe business partners with whom we have a close relationship (like a collection agency). Among other things, we might need a simple Web Service that takes an invoice number as input and returns an XML-encoded representation of that invoice with all the information our database contains regarding invoice detail items, amounts, taxes, shipping, etc. Let's call the web method GetInvoiceDetail() in a Web Service named SOAPHeaderSimple, and write some code in Visual Studio .NET.

To accomplish this task, we'll create a new VB .NET project and call it SOAPHeaders. Like our earlier example, rename the Service1.asmx file to SOAPHeaderSimple.asmx, and the automatically generated public class Service1 to public class SOAPHeaderSimple. Our code still requires the Imports System.Web.Services line, and our SOAPHeaderSimple class inherits the System.Web.Services.WebService base class. The contents of our SOAPHeaderSimple.asmx will be as follows:

```
Imports System.Web.Services

Public Class SOAPHeaderSimple
    Inherits System.Web.Services.WebService

    <WebMethod()> _
        Public Function GetInvoiceDetail( _
                    ByVal strInvoiceNo As String) As String

        ' Input:  Any valid InvoiceNo.
        ' Output: An XML encoded invoice including line item details.
        ' Notes:  A real implementation would require some database activity
        '             to find the invoice and its related detail and return
        '             some XML representation.

        Dim strInvoiceXML As String

        ' Ordinarily this next line would execute database code.
        ' Let's just return the Invoice Number as we got it.
        strInvoiceXML = "<invoice>" & strInvoiceNo & "</invoice>"

        Return strInvoiceXML
    End Function

End Class
```

Notice that this is the entire Web Service without the auto-generated code and example Visual Studio .NET creates. We now have a straightforward Web Service that expects a SOAP document that looks like this:

```
<?xml version="1.0" encoding="utf-8"?>
<soap:Envelope xmlns:xsi="http://www.w3.org/2001/XMLSchema-instance"
               xmlns:xsd="http://www.w3.org/2001/XMLSchema"
               xmlns:soap="http://schemas.xmlsoap.org/soap/envelope/">

    <soap:Body>
        <GetInvoiceDetail xmlns="http://tempuri.org/">
            <strInvoiceNo>string</strInvoiceNo>
        </GetInvoiceDetail>
    </soap:Body>
</soap:Envelope>
```

Now using this code and this SOAP message we can illustrate how to create a SOAP header and pass infrastructure-related information into our web method. In this case, we want a subscriber ID, a user ID, and a password.

Let's create a class called AuthInfo in our SOAPHeaderSimple Web Service that represents the SOAP header:

```
Public Class AuthInfo
    Inherits SoapHeader

    Public SubscriberID As String
    Public UserID As String
    Public Password As String
End Class
```

The class is very simple, but notice the `Inherits Soapheader` line. This tells the compiler that our little `AuthInfo` class is to be derived from the `SoapHeader` class. That means `AuthInfo` now inherits all of the properties, methods, and events from `SoapHeader`. It also means that we have to add another `Imports` line into our Web Service, otherwise we'll receive a compile time error (and a design time error since Visual Studio .NET is always watching out for us). We'll look at the entire Web Service code again with our changes, but for now if you are typing code as we go along, add the following line to the Web Service right below the existing `Imports` statement:

```
Imports System.Web.Services.Protocols
```

If you haven't seen it before, the `Imports` statement makes the contents of whatever namespace we identified available to our code. In this case, the `SoapHeader` class is defined in the `System.Web.Services.Protocols` namespace.

The next step is to tell our existing function, `GetInvoiceDetail()`, what header to expect. This requires making two changes.

The first thing we have to do is create a public instance of `AuthInfo` to actually represent our SOAP header, as the following code shows:

```
Public myHeader As AuthInfo
```

The `myHeader` instance of `SoapHeader` has to be declared as `Public` within the `SOAPHeaderSimple` class. If we don't define our SOAP header class as `Public`, its definition is not exposed, and we get an unhandled exception when we try to build and run our new Web Service.

Now we have to tell our `GetInvoiceDetail()` about the header class we've created. This is done via the `SoapHeader` attribute of the `WebMethod()` property:

```
<WebMethod(), SoapHeader("myHeader")> _
    Public Function GetInvoiceDetail( _
                    ByVal strInvoiceNo As String) As String
```

The previous code instructs the `GetInvoiceDetail()` function to expect a SOAP header represented by the class `myHeader`. It also helps tell any Web Service client that this particular method supports the use of a header as defined by `AuthInfo`.

Assuming all has gone well to this point, we should be able to have a look at the entire SOAP message that contains our `GetInvoiceDetail()` method definition as well as our new header definition. From Visual Studio .NET, build and run the Web Service and take a look at the detail for `GetInvoiceDetail()`. The SOAP request should look something like the following:

```
<?xml version="1.0" encoding="utf-8"?>
<soap:Envelope xmlns:xsi="http://www.w3.org/2001/XMLSchema-instance"
               xmlns:xsd="http://www.w3.org/2001/XMLSchema"
               xmlns:soap="http://schemas.xmlsoap.org/soap/envelope/">
    <soap:Header>
       <AuthInfo xmlns="http://tempuri.org/">
          <SubscriberID>string</SubscriberID>
          <UserID>string</UserID>
          <Password>string</Password>
       </AuthInfo>
    </soap:Header>
    <soap:Body>
       <GetInvoiceDetail xmlns="http://tempuri.org/">
          <strInvoiceNo>string</strInvoiceNo>
       </GetInvoiceDetail>
    </soap:Body>
</soap:Envelope>
```

Notice that the `<soap:Header>` element has an `<AuthInfo>` child that contains our three pieces of authentication information. Since this is the SOAP request definition produced for us, the value of each of our authentication parameters is a particular data type. They are all defined as strings.

Now, let's use the SOAP header contents in code for some processing logic. Let's assume that we have a rule that states anyone with `SubscriberID` = admin and `UserID` = admin gets some kind of special treatment to use our Web Service. We would have to evaluate the values contained in our SOAP header and execute whatever that special processing happened to be.

At this point, gaining access to the contents of our SOAP header structure is trivial. Recall that we have a member variable called `myHeader` that represents `AuthInfo`, and that `myHeader` is an instance of the class `AuthInfo`. Although we won't be incorporating this kind of logic into our sample code now, if we want to compare the subscriber ID and user ID values to some string, the code would be straightforward. If we wanted to, we could add the following code somewhere inside our `GetInvoiceDetail()` function:

```
If myHeader.SubscriberID = "admin" And myHeader.UserID = "admin" Then
     ' Do some special processing
Else
     ' Carry on as usual
End If
```

Controlling Header Direction

SOAP headers are sent from the Web Service client to the Web Service, by default. It is possible to modify that behavior using the `Direction` property of the `SoapHeader` attribute. Instead of just receiving SOAP headers from clients, it may be useful to receive SOAP headers and return the same header to a client. It may also be useful, based on application requirements, to include only header data in the response sent back to the client.

The three values of the `Direction` property are defined by an enumeration containing members defined in the following table:

Member	Description
In	Indicates that SOAP header is sent to the Web Service
Out	Indicates that SOAP header is sent to the Web Service client
InOut	Indicates that SOAP header is sent to both the Web Service and the Web Service client

If we wanted to return our `AuthInfo` data to our Web Service clients for some reason, we could control that by making the following code change in our web method. Notice that the assignment syntax uses ':=' instead of just '='; you will get an error if you miss that detail:

```
<WebMethod(), SoapHeader("myHeader", _
                        Direction:=SoapHeaderDirection.InOut)>_
   Public Function GetInvoiceDetail( _
                    ByVal strInvoiceNo As String) As String
```

By making this change, and rebuilding and running the Web Service in Visual Studio .NET, we get the following SOAP Response definition with our `<soap:Header>` included:

```
<?xml version="1.0" encoding="utf-8"?>
<soap:Envelope xmlns:xsi="http://www.w3.org/2001/XMLSchema-instance"
               xmlns:xsd="http://www.w3.org/2001/XMLSchema"
               xmlns:soap="http://schemas.xmlsoap.org/soap/envelope/">
   <soap:Header>
      <AuthInfo xmlns="http://tempuri.org/">
         <SubscriberID>string</SubscriberID>
         <UserID>string</UserID>
         <Password>string</Password>
      </AuthInfo>
   </soap:Header>
   <soap:Body>
      <GetInvoiceDetailResponse xmlns="http://tempuri.org/">
         <GetInvoiceDetailResult>string</GetInvoiceDetailResult>
      </GetInvoiceDetailResponse>
   </soap:Body>
</soap:Envelope>
```

The Web Service client will now receive our authentication information in their SOAP Response. That data doesn't magically get included. We still have to assign values in our code, but that's very straightforward, as we've already seen.

Requiring SOAP Headers

We've seen how to define SOAP header contents and use them in our Web Service code. We have also seen how to control the flow of header data from client to Web Service and back, if we choose so. How do we require SOAP headers if our application design calls for such a thing? By default, if we define a SOAP header, it is required unless we add a property named `Required` to the `SoapHeader` attribute:

```
<WebMethod(), SoapHeader("myHeader", Required:=False, _
                      Direction:=SoapHeaderDirection.InOut)> _
Public Function GetInvoiceDetail(ByVal strInvoiceNo As String) As String
```

Since the header isn't required anymore, we have to add a quick check to make sure we have a SOAP header before we try to do something with it, as in the following:

```
If Not (myHeader Is Nothing) Then
    If myHeader.SubscriberID = "admin" And _
       myHeader.UserID = "admin" Then
       ' Do some special processing
    Else
        ' Carry on as usual
    End If
End If
```

Handling SOAP Header Errors

When a Web Service comes across a SOAP header error, a specific exception, SoapHeaderException, should be thrown. Pulling this off in code is rather easy. Taking our simple example a little further, we'll throw an exception if our Web Service client sends SubscriberID and UserID both equal to admin, but the Password is empty. We can extend our existing GetInvoiceDetail() code to throw a SoapHeaderException without a lot of effort:

```
If Not (myHeader Is Nothing) Then
    If myHeader.SubscriberID = "admin" And myHeader.UserID = "admin" Then
        If myHeader.Password = vbNullString Then
            Throw New SoapHeaderException("Invalid password for Admin.", _
                                    SoapException.ClientFaultCode)
        Else
            ' Do some special processing
        End If
    Else
        ' Carry on as usual
    End If
End If
```

As we've seen, Web Services support three wire formats – HTTP GET, HTTP POST, and SOAP. We've given SOAP the largest amount of coverage, as that appears to be the future of Web Service protocols.

Now that we have a functional, albeit extraordinarily simple, Web Service running on the server with some SOAP headers, let's take a look at implementing a Web Service client that uses this functionality. We'll see how to send messages to our Web Service, how to recieve messages from it, and what is required on the client to implement our Web Service.

Using Web Service Proxy Classes

Proxy classes are used to represent a Web Service that a client wants to use. A proxy is something that is said to stand in the place of something else. In a non-software context, a proxy is most often used to describe a person who is filling the place of, and has the same rights and responsibilities as, someone else.

In a software context, proxies work the same way. As the client of a Web Service, we can create a proxy class that represents a particular Web Service. Later in the chapter, we will see that by using some information exposed by the Web Service we can create a new class that represents our Web Service. The proxy allows a developer to use the remote service as if it was a local object. Our proxy not only creates representative methods; it handles all of the lower-level Web Service connectivity for us, including building any required SOAP requests and parsing SOAP responses. This is much easier than working with the SOAP request via string handling or the XML DOM.

Now, we'll create another simple Web Service, complete with SOAP header data like our previous example. This Web Service will represent a stock quote service by exposing a function that accepts a stock symbol as input and returns a structure representing the quoted price. We'll mimic the price lookup function because our focus is on the Web Service, its proxy class, and the client application that implements the proxy class. Then, to illustrate proxy classes and their implementation in .NET, we'll build a desktop client.

Creating Our StockQuote Web Service

Since we are focusing on proxy classes in this section, let's keep our StockQuote Web Service very simple. We'll create one public method called GetQuote() that accepts a single input parameter named TickerSymbol. Regardless of what TickerSymbol we receive, we'll always return the same price. Actually implementing a real price lookup function, tied into real market data or containing running database functionality, is beyond our scope here. Our SOAP header will contain the same three pieces of information we used in the previous example – SubscriberID, UserID, and Password.

We've already covered Web Service basics and, we've spent some time working with SOAP headers, so we'll move past the Web Service implementation and talk about how a client might use this Web Service. Here's the Web Service code in the StockQuote.asmx file:

```
Imports System.Web.Services
Imports System.Web.Services.Protocols

' Definition of our standard SOAP header
Public Class AuthInfo
    Inherits SoapHeader

    Public SubscriberID As String
    Public UserID As String
    Public Password As String
End Class

' Represents a price quote, returned from GetQuote method.
Public Class PriceQuote
    Public TickerSymbol As String
    Public Price As Long
```

```
      Public DateTime As Date
   End Class

   Public Class StockQuote
      Inherits System.Web.Services.WebService

      Public AuthInfoValue As AuthInfo

      <WebMethod(), SoapHeader("AuthInfoValue")> Public Function _
            GetQuote(ByVal strTickerSymbol As String) As PriceQuote

         Dim oPrice As New PriceQuote()

         ' Make sure we received date in our header.
         If Not (AuthInfoValue Is Nothing) Then
            oPrice.DateTime = Now()
            oPrice.TickerSymbol = strTickerSymbol
            oPrice.Price = 100
         Else
            Throw New SoapHeaderException("Invalid Header data. " & _
               "SubscriberID, UserID, and Password are required elements.", _
               SoapException.ClientFaultCode)
         End If

         Return oPrice

      End Function
   End Class
```

The SOAP request includes our StrTickerSymbol input parameter and our header information:

```xml
<?xml version="1.0" encoding="utf-8"?>
<soap:Envelope xmlns:xsi="http://www.w3.org/2001/XMLSchema-instance"
               xmlns:xsd="http://www.w3.org/2001/XMLSchema"
               xmlns:soap="http://schemas.xmlsoap.org/soap/envelope/">
  <soap:Header>
    <AuthInfo xmlns="http://tempuri.org/">
      <SubscriberID>string</SubscriberID>
      <UserID>string</UserID>
      <Password>string</Password>
    </AuthInfo>
  </soap:Header>
  <soap:Body>
    <GetQuote xmlns="http://tempuri.org/">
      <strTickerSymbol>string</strTickerSymbol>
    </GetQuote>
  </soap:Body>
</soap:Envelope>
```

The SOAP response contains an XML representation of the PriceQuote class:

```xml
<?xml version="1.0" encoding="utf-8"?>
<soap:Envelope xmlns:xsi="http://www.w3.org/2001/XMLSchema-instance"
               xmlns:xsd="http://www.w3.org/2001/XMLSchema"
```

```
                    xmlns:soap="http://schemas.xmlsoap.org/soap/envelope/">
    <soap:Body>
      <GetQuoteResponse xmlns="http://tempuri.org/">
        <GetQuoteResult>
          <TickerSymbol>string</TickerSymbol>
          <Price>long</Price>
          <DateTime>dateTime</DateTime>
        </GetQuoteResult>
      </GetQuoteResponse>
    </soap:Body>
  </soap:Envelope>
```

Creating a Web Service Client Application

Using the `StockQuote` Web Service we've just created, let's build a desktop client that will get price quotes for users. As with every other example in this chapter the business functionality is trivial. We are interested in the interaction between the Web Service and the client proxy.

To create a Web Service client using Visual Studio .NET, let's create a new Visual Basic project, `PriceQuoteClient`, of type **Windows Application**, at a location where we'd like the project stored. If we don't specify the location the default location is used, which means a new directory will be created with the same name as the project.

Visual Studio .NET will create a new Windows application with a single form. Rename the default form `Form1` to `PriceQuote`, and add textboxes and labels so that it looks like the following:

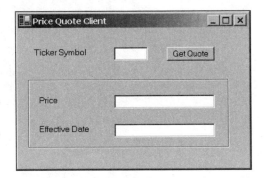

Let's rename the **Ticker Symbol** textbox is as `txtTickerSymbol`, and the **Get Quote** button as `cmdGetQuote`. Let's set the `Text` property of the form to `Price Quote Client`. We will rename the **Price** textbox as `txtPrice` and the **Effective Date** textbox as `txtDate`.

Before moving ahead let's talk about ticker symbols. Ticker symbols are short, unique abbreviations of three or four alphabetical characters that are used to identify particular stocks. These are most commonly used for reporting market information and retrieval applications like the one we are about to build. There is an assumption in financial markets that one knows the ticker symbol for any stock of interest or that one has access to a mechanism for looking up ticker symbols.

The form is relatively simple; you can probably guess how we'll add code to make it work. Pressing the **Get Quote** button will pass the contents of the **Ticker Symbol** textbox to our `StockQuote` Web Service, and we'll display the price and date we receive in the Web Service response in the appropriate textboxes.

Adding a Web Reference

We've already seen how Visual Studio .NET makes our work easier. Setting a reference to our StockQuote Web Service is yet another way .NET tools make developing Web Services easier and faster. In Visual Studio .NET, we have the ability to create what is called a **Web Reference**. Visual Studio .NET still supports adding COM references to a solution, except it now supports the ability to add references to namespaces as well.

Anyway, we are adding a reference to a Web Service, so that qualifies as a Web Reference. To add the reference, we'll right-click on the References node in the Solution Explorer window in our PriceQuoteClient project. Let's select Add Web Reference and a dialog will appear like this:

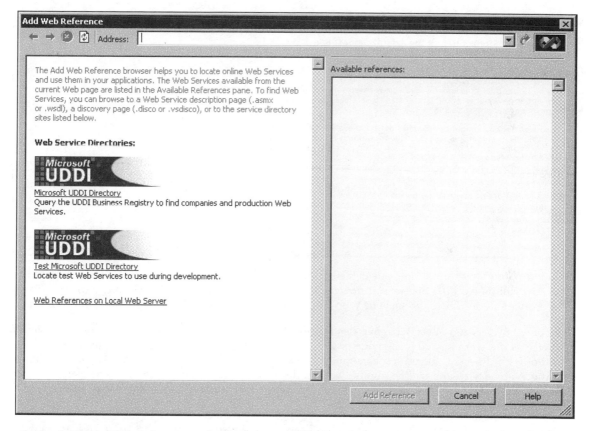

In the Address field, let's type in the location of our StockQuote Web Service. If the name of your server is localhost, and you had saved StockQuote.asmx in a folder named StockQuote, the Address would be http://localhost/StockQuote/StockQuote.asmx.

As soon as the Add Web Reference wizard finds our Web Service, the display in the left pane changes to something we see in the following screenshot. The right pane actually controls the contents of the left, which is a little counter-intuitive. If Visual Studio .NET found your Web Service, we should be looking at a dialog that looks this:

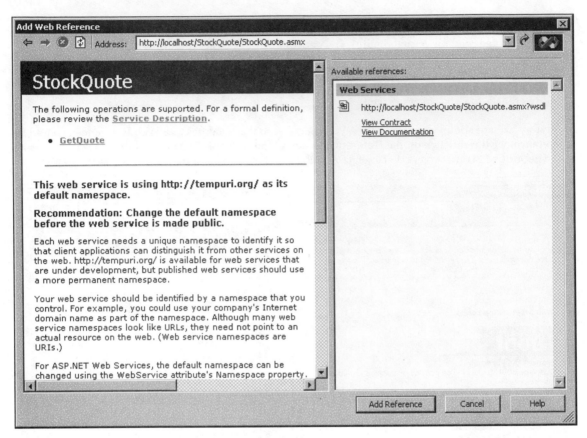

Click the **Add Reference** button near the bottom right of the dialog box and our **Solution Explorer** window will look a little different. It now contains a **Web References** node as a sibling to the existing **References** node. The child node of **Web References** should be the IIS Server name, `localhost`.

We now have a valid Web Reference that represents our Web Service. In code, we can refer to the Web Service as if it were a local namespace or COM component. Let's leave the issue of how exactly Visual Studio .NET does that for us (it is accomplished using an XML standard called WSDL that is published by the Web Service and will be covered later in the chapter), and focus on getting some code to send a value to the Web Service and get some kind of response. We'll come back to the details of our Web Reference in a moment.

We can now add code to the form, which has been renamed from `Form1` to `PriceQuote`, to send data to our Web Service, and expect some kind of response. Double-click on the `cmdGetQuote` button and add the following line of code inside its `Click` event:

```
Dim oStockQuote As New localhost.StockQuote()
```

This line of code dimensions a new object of type `StockQuote` found in the namespace `localhost` (or the IIS Server name). Obviously, `StockQuote` is our Web Service name. The server name hosting the Web Service is included to keep naming conflicts from occurring frequently. At this point, we can treat any web service methods we may invoke via `oStockQuote` as if they are local to our application.

We can complete the `cmdGetQuote_click` event code by creating an instance of the object returned from our Web Service and assigning its properties to our UI controls. The entire `PriceQuote` form class looks like this:

```
Public Class PriceQuote
    Inherits System.Windows.Forms.Form

    Private Sub cmdGetQuote_Click(ByVal sender As System.Object, _
            ByVal e As System.EventArgs) Handles cmdGetQuote.Click

        Dim oStockQuote As New localhost.StockQuote()
        Dim oPriceQuote As localhost.PriceQuote
        Dim oAuthInfo as New localhost.AuthInfo()

        oAuthInfo.SubscriberID = "Wrox"
        oAuthInfo.UserID = "author"
        oAuthInfo.Password = "easytocrack"

        oStockQuote.AuthInfoValue = oAuthInfo

        Try
            oPriceQuote = oStockQuote.GetQuote(txtTickerSymbol.Text)
        Catch ex As Exception
            MessageBox.Show(ex.Message, "Web Service Client Exception", _
                        MessageBoxButtons.OK, MessageBoxIcon.Error)
        End Try

        If Not (oPriceQuote Is Nothing) Then
            txtPrice.Text = oPriceQuote.Price
            txtDate.Text = oPriceQuote.DateTime
        End If

    End Sub
End Class
```

Remember to replace `localhost` with the name of your own server, if needed. We've simply dimensioned an `oStockQuote`, which represents the entire Web Service, and an `oPriceQuote`, which represents the structure we expect to get back from the Web Service. `oStockQuote` is the Web Service proxy class in this example. Being a proxy, it stands in the place of the real `StockQuote` Web Service, locally on our machine. As we'll see in a moment, the under-the-covers implementation of the `oStockQuote` instance is rather clever in how it actually communicates with the `StockQuote` Web Service. First let's finish our desktop example.

Notice that the SOAP header, `AuthInfoValue`, is populated with hard-coded data. We aren't being very sophisticated about how we get the data. An important thing to notice is that a local instance `oAuthInfo` of `AuthInfo` is created, and set to `oStockQuote.AuthInfoValue`. Without that line of code, you'll get an error message that reads "Value null was found where an instance of an object was required."

One other item of note in the code above is the `Try...Catch...End Try` structure wrapped around the `oStockQuote.GetQuote()` method call. Since we are dealing in network communications there are a multitude of problems we could encounter. Even though this sample code will be running on the same machine as the Web Service itself, including this block for any network or remote method invocation is a good habit to start. If the `oStockQuote.GetQuote()` fails for any reason, the code simply raises a message box and displays the `Message` property of whatever exception was raised (hardly a production-ready error-handling scheme).

Since we have code that sends a ticker symbol from `txtTickerSymbol` to the `StockQuote` Web Service, let's give this thing a try and see what happens. Set the startup object to `PriceQuote` in the project properties, build the project, and then run it. We should see our form running now. Let's type in a sample ticker symbol (remember it doesn't matter what you send in, you'll always get a price of 100 back), and press the **Get Quote** button. The `PriceQuote` form will now contain a price of 100 and whatever the date and time happened to be when the request was made.

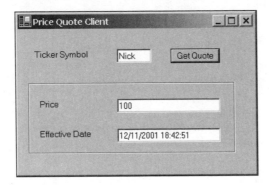

Web Service Proxy Code

Now, letting Visual Studio .NET build a proxy for us is easily accomplished. Let's take a look at what the proxy actually looks like.

In our **Solution Explorer** window, if we click on the toolbar button **Show All Files,** our file tree expands. When we told Visual Studio .NET to create a new Web Reference, we used a neat feature of the product. Using the path we specified in the **Add Web Reference** wizard, Visual Studio .NET interrogated our Web Service to learn about its methods and their parameters, and returned values and the internal structure of our Web Service. Visual Studio .NET then generated code for us to represent that Web Service, without us having to worry about building and serializing XML or HTTP connections. We can find the generated code in the file named as `StockQuote.vb`, which is found down the **Web References** branch in our **Solution Explorer** window. `StockQuote.vb` is literally the proxy class in this project for the Web Service named `StockQuote`.

Let's look at the code in the proxy class before we move on and create a web client that uses this same Web Service:

```
Option Strict Off
Option Explicit On

Imports System
Imports System.Diagnostics
```

```vb
Imports System.Web.Services
Imports System.Web.Services.Protocols
Imports System.Xml.Serialization

Namespace localhost

<System.Web.Services.WebServiceBindingAttribute(Name:="StockQuoteSoap", _
[Namespace]:="http://tempuri.org/")> _
Public Class StockQuote
    Inherits System.Web.Services.Protocols.SoapHttpClientProtocol

    Public AuthInfoValue As AuthInfo

    <System.Diagnostics.DebuggerStepThroughAttribute()> _
    Public Sub New()
       MyBase.New()
       Me.Url = "http://localhost/StockQuote/StockQuote.asmx"
    End Sub

    <System.Web.Services.Protocols.SoapHeaderAttribute("AuthInfoValue"), _
    System.Diagnostics.DebuggerStepThroughAttribute(), _
    System.Web.Services.Protocols.SoapDocumentMethodAttribute( _
    "http://tempuri.org/GetQuote", _
    Use:=System.Web.Services.Description.SoapBindingUse.Literal, _
ParameterStyle:=System.Web.Services.Protocols.SoapParameterStyle.Wrapped)> _
    Public Function GetQuote(ByVal strTickerSymbol As String) As PriceQuote

        Dim results() As Object = _
           Me.Invoke("GetQuote", New Object() {strTickerSymbol})
        Return CType(results(0), PriceQuote)

     End Function

    <System.Diagnostics.DebuggerStepThroughAttribute()> _
    Public Function BeginGetQuote(ByVal strTickerSymbol As String, _
                ByVal callback As System.AsyncCallback, _
                ByVal asyncState As Object) As System.IAsyncResult

       Return Me.BeginInvoke("GetQuote", _
          New Object() {strTickerSymbol}, callback, asyncState)

    End Function

    <System.Diagnostics.DebuggerStepThroughAttribute()> _
    Public Function EndGetQuote( _
                ByVal asyncResult As System.IAsyncResult) As PriceQuote

       Dim results() As Object = Me.EndInvoke(asyncResult)
       Return CType(results(0), PriceQuote)

    End Function
End Class

<System.Xml.Serialization.XmlRootAttribute( _
```

```
   [Namespace]:="http://tempuri.org/", IsNullable:=False)> _
Public Class AuthInfo
    Inherits SoapHeader

    Public SubscriberID As String
    Public UserID As String
    Public Password As String
End Class

<System.Xml.Serialization.XmlTypeAttribute( _
[Namespace]:="http://tempuri.org/")> _
Public Class PriceQuote

    Public TickerSymbol As String
    Public Price As Long
    Public DateTime As Date
End Class

End Namespace
```

The code obviously creates a new namespace called localhost. Visual Studio .NET picks whatever
your machine's name happens to be (for consistency, let's leave the namespace named as it is, but it
might be a good idea to start a consistent naming pattern). This explains why our proxy client required
the namespace in the following two lines of code:

```
Dim oStockQuote As New localhost.StockQuote()
Dim oPriceQuote As localhost.PriceQuote
Dim oAuthInfo as New localhost.AuthInfo()
```

Notice that the proxy code creates three familiar classes – StockQuote itself, AuthInfo to represent our
header information, and PriceQuote, which is used as the return data structure from the GetQuote() web
method. Let's look at the line immediately above the declaration for the public class StockQuote:

```
<System.Web.Services.WebServiceBindingAttribute(Name:="StockQuoteSoap", _
[Namespace]:="http://tempuri.org/")> _
```

This line declares the binding the Web Service is implementing within this class, called
StockQuoteSoap, and tells us which namespace to use.

Within the StockQuote class, we find that it inherits SoapHttpClientProtocol. This enables the
proxy to access the properties and methods necessary to communicate with the StockQuote Web
Service. For instance, the StockQuote constructor uses the SoapHttpClientProtocol.Url to set
the base URL of our Web Service:

```
<System.Diagnostics.DebuggerStepThroughAttribute()> _
Public Sub New()
  MyBase.New()
  Me.Url = "http://localhost/StockQuote/StockQuote.asmx"
End Sub
```

The code above creates a new instance of the StockQuote class by calling MyBase.New(). The keyword MyBase allows access to members of an object's base class. The next line of code sets the inherited SoapHttpClientProtocol.Url property to the location of our Web Service.

Moving down the code, we find the function GetQuote() described by three attributes:

```
<System.Web.Services.Protocols.SoapHeaderAttribute("AuthInfoValue"), _
System.Diagnostics.DebuggerStepThroughAttribute(), _
System.Web.Services.Protocols.SoapDocumentMethodAttribute( _
"http://tempuri.org/GetQuote", _
Use:=System.Web.Services.Description.SoapBindingUse.Literal, _
ParameterStyle:=System.Web.Services.Protocols.SoapParameterStyle.Wrapped)> _
Public Function GetQuote(ByVal strTickerSymbol As String) As PriceQuote
```

The first, shown above, indicates what SOAP header to use. In our case, the required SOAP header is named as AuthInfoValue. The second line contains debugging information. The final of our three attributes for GetQuote() tells us about how this web method is to be used.

The SoapDocumentMethodAttribute class is used to control the format of the XML within our SOAP requests and responses. The first property we encounter is called Use. There are two possible values for Use, either SoapBindingUse.Literal or SoapBindingUse.Encoded. Literal indicates that individual parameters for this Web Service are encoded using individual XSD schemas. Encoded indicates that parameters are encoded according to the guidelines set out in the SOAP specification. Since Visual Studio .NET defaults to Literal, we'll stick with that.

The next property, ParameterStyle, gives us some more control over the SOAP request and response. Specifically, it allows us to indicate whether our input or output parameters are direct children of the <Body> element, or are wrapped by another element used to logically group our parameters. Since most of our SOAP messages consist of mainly parameter data, choosing one ParameterStyle over the other may have an impact on our applications.

If we use the Visual Studio .NET default, that is, ParameterStyle as Wrapped, then our SOAP request will look like this:

```
<soap:Body>
    <GetQuote xmlns="http://tempuri.org/">
        <strTickerSymbol>string</strTickerSymbol>
    </GetQuote>
</soap:Body>
```

<GetQuote> is a child of the <soap:Body> element, and contains our parameter data. We would also expect our response to be wrapped as in this fragment:

```
<soap:Body>
    <GetQuoteResponse xmlns="http://tempuri.org/">
        <GetQuoteResult>
            <TickerSymbol>string</TickerSymbol>
            <Price>long</Price>
            <DateTime>dateTime</DateTime>
        </GetQuoteResult>
    </GetQuoteResponse>
</soap:Body>
```

Now, if we selected the other `ParameterStyle` setting (`ParameterStyle` as `Bare`), our SOAP request would look a little different; we no longer have the `<GetQuote>` wrapper:

```
<soap:Body>
    <strTickerSymbol>string</strTickerSymbol>
</soap:Body>
```

Similarly, our response using the `Bare` option will have a simpler structure than its `Wrapped` alternative:

```
<soap:Body>
  <GetQuoteResult>
    <TickerSymbol>string</TickerSymbol>
    <Price>long</Price>
    <DateTime>dateTime</DateTime>
  </GetQuoteResult>
</soap:Body>
```

Now that we have the SOAP attributes out of the way, let's take a look at the proxy `GetQuote()` function. Since we've already seen that a proxy is something that stands in the place of something else, we might expect to find code in the proxy function that mimics the behavior of our `GetQuote()` web method. That is, in effect, exactly what the proxy class attempts to do. The public function `GetQuote()` is the main working method in this class. It stands in the place of the `GetQuote` Web Service that we've already built. If you look at the code, we find two lines that do all the work. The first line creates an array of objects, `results()`, which serves as a container for any outbound parameters the Web Service produces:

```
Dim results() As Object = _
    Me.Invoke("GetQuote", New Object() {strTickerSymbol})
```

The `results()` array is populated using the `Invoke()` method, a member of the `SoapHttpClientProtocol` class our proxy class inherits. The `Invoke()` method is used by Web Service proxy classes to synchronously execute Web Services. It requires two parameters – the name of the Web Service method and an object array of parameters. In one line of code, the proxy function invokes the Web Service method, passes in our `strTickerSymbol`, and places any outbound parameters into an object array. The next line of code exists solely to coerce our `results()` array into another data type that, our applications will expect to be returned from the Web Service method, an instance of `PriceQuote`:

```
Return CType(results(0), PriceQuote)
```

Since we know the Web Service method returns only one parameter, `oPrice`, our `results(0)` will refer to our only outbound parameter. `Ctype()` is the inline, explicit conversion of our `results()` object array to an instance of `PriceQuote`.

Using Web Service Proxies Asynchronously

Up to this point, we've been using our Web Service synchronously. Among other things, that means our client code has to wait for the Web Service to return something to us. In our small example, waiting for return values is a not an issue. The Web Service method doesn't do anything (go back and look at the code, it always returns a price of 100 with the current date and time, regardless of the ticker symbol). In the real world, that's not always an effective design. Issues like database or network capacity will have an impact on how quickly a Web Service will return a result to our client applications. In addition, keep in mind that you may know very little about the authors of any Web Services to which you subscribe. As we discussed early in this chapter, part of the Web Service vision is for one group of developers to expose functionality to other developers, with little regard to under-the-covers implementation details being exposed.

There may be times we want our client applications to call a Web Service method, and continue working or display something useful to the user indicating that a request has been submitted. Visual Studio .NET again makes this easy for us by creating two other public functions in our proxy class – BeginGetQuote() and EndGetQuote(). Let's quickly have a look at both the functions and extend our simple Web Service client to support the StockQuote Web Service asynchronously:

```
<System.Diagnostics.DebuggerStepThroughAttribute()> _
Public Function BeginGetQuote(ByVal strTickerSymbol As String, _
            ByVal callback As System.AsyncCallback, _
            ByVal asyncState As Object) As System.IAsyncResult

    Return Me.BeginInvoke("GetQuote", _
        New Object() {strTickerSymbol}, callback, asyncState)

End Function

<System.Diagnostics.DebuggerStepThroughAttribute()> _
Public Function EndGetQuote( _
            ByVal asyncResult As System.IAsyncResult) As PriceQuote

    Dim results() As Object = Me.EndInvoke(asyncResult)
    Return CType(results(0), PriceQuote)

End Function
```

The BeginGetQuote() function is used to initiate the Web Service method. You'll find that the Visual Studio .NET proxy class builder prefixes the words Begin and End to the actual Web Service method name for the asynchronous function calls. BeginGetQuote() requires some different input parameters from our standard synchronous GetQuote() method. As you can see below, we still pass in strTickerSymbol, but the function also requires a callback object and another object for monitoring process state.

The second and third parameters become crucial in the implementation of the new asynchronous Web Service. In the client application we are about to build, the second parameter, callback object, is used to execute code when the Web Service has finished. The asynchState object, the third parameter, is used to match Web Service method results with our client code using the EndGetQuote() function.

The only line of code in BeginGetQuote() calls BeginInvoke() and starts the asynchronous conversation with the Web Service. EndGetQuote() has a simple purpose. Using the IAsyncResult returned by BeginGetQuote(), it will end the asynchronous invocation of our Web Service and coerce the results of the Web Service method into our PriceQuote class.

Writing client code to invoke the Web Service asynchronously using our proxy class gets a bit more complicated only because of the callback object used by BeginGetQuote(). Listed below is a new class, based on our previous GetQuote example, which starts the Web Service asynchronously and raises a standard message box when it is complete.

Let's create a new form similar to the existing PriceQuoteClient form, but with the command button named cmdGetQuoteAsynch. Now we'll create a new class file named PriceQuoteAsynch.vb with the code shown below:

```vb
Public Class PriceQuoteAsynch
    Inherits System.Windows.Forms.Form

    Private Sub cmdGetQuoteAsynch_Click(ByVal sender As System.Object, _
        ByVal e As System.EventArgs) Handles cmdGetQuoteAsynch.Click

        Dim oStockQuote As New localhost.StockQuote()
        Dim oAuthInfo as New localhost.AuthInfo()
        Dim cb As AsyncCallback

        cb = New AsyncCallback(AddressOf PriceQuoteAsynch.GetQuoteCallback)

        oAuthInfo.SubscriberID = "Wrox"
        oAuthInfo.UserID = "author"
        oAuthInfo.Password = "easytocrack"

        oStockQuote.AuthInfoValue = oAuthInfo

        Dim ar As IAsyncResult = oStockQuote.BeginGetQuote( _
                            txtTickerSymbol.Text, cb, oStockQuote)
    End Sub

    Public Shared Sub GetQuoteCallback(ByVal ar As IAsyncResult)

        Dim oStockQuote As localhost.StockQuote = ar.AsyncState
        Dim oPriceQuote As localhost.PriceQuote

        ' Get the completed results
        oPriceQuote = oStockQuote.EndGetQuote(ar)

        Call MsgBox("Your price quote request for " & _
                    oPriceQuote.TickerSymbol & _
                    " has been received with the following results. " & _
                    "Price: " & oPriceQuote.Price & "; DateTime: " & _
                    oPriceQuote.DateTime, MsgBoxStyle.Information, _
                    "Asynch Web Service Example")
    End Sub
End Class
```

The button click event handler now calls `oStockQuote.BeginGetQuote()` instead of `oStockQuote.GetQuote()` as in our previous example. Notice that `BeginGetQuote()` requires a couple more input parameters. We still pass in our ticker symbol, `txtTickerSymbol.Text`. The second parameter is an instance of a `callback` object that we created using the first line of highlighted code. In effect, we are telling the `BeginGetQuote()` function to execute the code found at the `AddressOf` the function `PriceQuoteAsynch.GetQuoteCallBack()`. The third parameter is the instance of the `StockQuote`. We'll see how this gets used in `GetQuoteCallBack()`.

At this point, we've invoked our Web Service method named `BeginGetQuote()`. We are waiting for the callback object to begin execution of our function named `GetQuoteCallback()`. When that function is started, the first thing it does is call `EndGetQuote()` to get a local instance of `PriceQuote` containing our ticker symbol, price and the quote date.

Let's set a debug breakpoint on `BeginGetQuote()` and `EndGetQuote()` in the proxy class, and another on `GetQuoteCallBack()`. If we run the code now, since our simple Web Service method requires little time to complete, we'll immediately get a response, just like the synchronous implementation; but the results of the code above generate the message box showing the values for our ticker symbol, price, and quote date.

Now we have seen the mechanism by which Visual Studio .NET or other applications can learn about Web Services, their definitions, the interfaces they expose, how to format messages for each Web Service method, etc. The following section will delve into that mechanism and other supporting standards for describing your Web Services and advertising their presence.

Directory, Discovery, and Description

Up to now, we've been building our sample Web Services as if we were the only users and had some knowledge as to where the Web Services existed and how to talk to them. In other words, we knew what URL to use to locate them and what SOAP requests and responses they required. In the real world, of course, our Web Services consumers will not have the same level of knowledge we do about our Web Services. We need some mechanism to publish our Web Services' presence, to describe their SOAP or other messaging interface, and to describe what functionality they provide.

Web Service Directories – UDDI

Early in this chapter, we discussed the potential benefits of Web Services, like the ability for applications to share business functionality with little regard to behind-the-scenes implementation, making reusable and easily distributable applications that are easy to build and ultimately sell. One of the largest advantage is that the demanders of Web Service functionality can find suppliers, and once the Web Service functionality search is completed, the functionality demanders have enough useful information to make decisions about which particular Web Service is best for their application, how best to use a particular Web Service, etc.

The attempt to address the obvious need arising between finding Web Services and having your Web Services found is being led by Microsoft, Ariba, IBM, and others in something called the **UDDI Project**. UDDI stands for **Universal Description, Discovery, and Integration**. In time, it is to become the standard location to find Web Services for our consumer client applications as well as to publish our Web Services.

As with any standards movement, UDDI, is evolving over time as more companies join the project. Refer to http://www.uddi.org/ for details on the UDDI Project and any published public standards.

UDDI provides two services. The first is an XML Schema for Business Descriptions. In a way, you can think of UDDI as a yellow pages or portal for Web Services. In fact, UDDI takes the yellow pages metaphor a step further to describe the contents of the XML Schema contents by describing it in three parts:

❑   White Pages – information including the Web Service publisher's contact information, address, etc.

❑   Yellow Pages – information including industrial classifications

❑   Green pages – detailed technical information including specifications on the Web Service itself

The second service provided by UDDI is a Web Registry of Web Services. In this registry, we find several pieces of information like business information, service information, and binding and technical specifications for each service.

Business Information – The businessEntity Structure

The highest level of the information hierarchy published by UDDI is the <businessEntity> element. It is a structure that represents information about the business or entity, that is, information about the publishing entity as well as the services it provides. The <businessEntity> is defined by the following XSD specification:

```
<element name = "businessEntity">
  <complexType>
    <sequence>
      <element ref = "discoveryURLs" minOccurs = "0"/>
      <element ref = "name" maxOccurs = "unbounded"/>
      <element ref = "description" minOccurs = "0"
                             maxOccurs = "unbounded"/>
      <element ref = "contacts" minOccurs = "0"/>
      <element ref = "businessServices" minOccurs = "0"/>
      <element ref = "identifierBag" minOccurs = "0"/>
      <element ref = "categoryBag" minOccurs = "0"/>
    </sequence>
    <attribute ref = "businessKey" use = "required"/>
    <attribute ref = "operator"/>
    <attribute ref = "authorizedName">
  </complexType>
</element>
```

Descriptions of the constituent parts of the <businessEntity> element are contained in the following table:

Field	Description
discoveryURLS	This optional element contains a list of URLs that point to file-based service discovery mechanisms. Each URL in this list points to a web-addressable discovery document (using HTTP GET).
name	This mandatory element contains human readable names for the <businessEntity>. This element is allowed to repeat because names can be expressed in multiple languages as specified by the unique xml:lang value to signify the language that they are expressed in.
description	This is an optional element containing human readable descriptions with a unique xml:lang value similar to the name element.
contacts	This is a list of contact information including a useType attribute, which describes the type of contact, the contact's name, phone, e-mail, and address. This is an optional element.
businessServices	This is an optional element, which provides a way of describing groups of Web Services.
identifierBag	This optional element contains a list of name-value pairs containing common identifiers or unique tax identifies useful in searches.
categoryBag	This optional element contains a list of name-value pairs useful in categorizing <businessEntity> elements, using industry-specific codes for instance.
businessKey	This required attribute contains the unique identifier for this <businessEntity>.
authorizedName	This is a required attribute that contains the name of the individual who published the <businessEntity> data.
operator	This required attribute contains the name of the UDDI site that manages the registry for this <businessEntity>.

Service Information – The businessService Structure

Each logical Service can be grouped according to business process such as invoicing services, document management services, workflow services, etc. The <businessService> element is a structure used to describe each of these logical groups. Each <businessService> structure contains one or more technical Web Service descriptions. The <businessService> UDDI specification is as follows:

```
<element name = "businessService">
  <complexType>
    <sequence>
      <element ref = "name" maxOccurs = "unbounded"/>
      <element ref = "description" minOccurs = "0"
                               maxOccurs = "unbounded"/>
```

```
            <element ref = "bindingTemplates"/>
            <element ref = "categoryBag" minOccurs = "0"/>
        </sequence>
        <attribute ref = "serviceKey" use = "required"/>
        <attribute ref = "businessKey"/>
    </complexType>
</element>
```

The constituent parts of the `<businessService>` element can be described as in the following table:

Field	Description
name	This is a required element containing repeating, language-qualified `<businessService>` names.
description	This optional element contains language-qualified descriptions of the `<businessService>`.
bindingTemplates	This is an element containing a structure of descriptive technical information about a group of Services. We will discuss the `<bindingTemplate>` element in the next section.
categoryBag	This optional element contains a list of name-value pairs for classification of this `<businessService>`.
serviceKey	This required attribute contains the unique identifier for this particular `<businessService>`.
businessKey	This is an optional attribute that contains a businessKey value.

Technical Service Descriptions – The bindingTemplate Structure

Finally, we come to some technical specification concerning our individual Web Services. This technical information is contained within the `<bindingTemplate>` structure. Each `<bindingTemplate>` structure is contained within one `<businessService>` structure, which is contained within one `<businessEntity>` structure.

The UDDI specification for the bindingTemplate structure is as follows:

```
<element name = "bindingTemplate">
  <complexType>
    <sequence>
      <element ref = "description" minOccurs = "0"
                                   maxOccurs = "unbounded"/>
      <choice>
        <element ref = "accessPoint" minOccurs = "0"/>
        <element ref = "hostingRedirector" minOccurs = "0"/>
      </choice>
      <element ref = "tModelInstanceDetails"/>
    </sequence>
    <attribute ref = "bindingKey" use = "required"/>
    <attribute ref = "serviceKey"/>
  </complexType>
</element>
```

Descriptions of the constituent parts of the `<bindingTemplate>` element are contained in the following table:

Field	Description
description	This optional element contains language-qualified descriptions of the `<businessService>`.
accessPoint	This element is used to convey the entry point for calling a particular Web Service. Either `accessPoint` or `hostingRedirector` is present, not both simultaneously.
hostingRedirector	This element is required if `accessPoint` is not provided.
tModelInstanceDetails	This is an optional element containing a list of `<tModelInstanceInfo>` elements.
bindingKey	This mandatory attribute contains the unique identifier for the `<bindingTemplate>`.
serviceKey	This optional attribute is generally not necessary when the `<bindingTemplate>` is contained within a fully qualified UDDI hierarchy.

The UDDI API

We've seen the amount of detail used to describe Web Services in the UDDI specification; but there is more defined in the specification. Included within the UDDI specification are definitions for programmatic Web Service access to the registry. This access is exposed in an API made of two parts, the **Inquiry API** and the **Publisher API**.

The Inquiry API gives applications the ability to locate other businesses that publish Web Services, and individual Web Services and their particular specifications. The Publisher API exists to allow programmers to manipulate (edit and delete) existing UDDI Registry data.

UDDI certainly makes finding Web Services much easier than it would be without the standard, particularly given the high-profile Internet software companies behind the UDDI Project. However, finding a particular Web Service by searching the UDDI Registry is only half the battle. We need a mechanism to detail what exactly a particular Web Service does, explain the structure of the SOAP request and responses, and detail the data types of the input and output parameters, among other things. This mechanism is called **WSDL**, **Web Services Description Language**.

Web Services Description Language

WSDL is an incredibly useful mechanism for describing several facets of Web Service behavior. WSDL provides the tools necessary to describe Web Service behavior by defining a standardized XML grammar for describing Web Service details.

WSDL treats Web Services as a "collection of communication endpoints capable of exchanging messages". The standard uses the following six major elements to define Web Services:

WSDL Element	Description
types	A container for data type definitions like XSD, although not exclusively limited to XSD
message	A typed definition of the data being communicated from Web Service to client, and back again if necessary
portType	A set of abstract operations
binding	A protocol and data format for a port
port	An endpoint definition
service	A collection of related endpoints

WSDL is an XML standard being backed by significant industry players including Microsoft and IBM. Among other things, it tells other applications:

❑ Where to find a particular Web Service

❑ How to communicate (using SOAP, etc.) with a Web Service

❑ How to auto-generate proxy code to represent a Web Service

Now, let's have a look at what Visual Studio .NET does for us when we create a Web Service. Let's go back to the StockQuote Web Service and run it. Once the code is running we should see the now familiar browser window used to test our Web Service. We'll see a Service Description link on the next line of our Web Service name. We ignored this previously, and went immediately to testing the GetQuote() Web Service method.

If we click on the Service Description link, the URL in the browser window should change to http://localhost/StockQuote/StockQuote.asmx?WSDL. Notice that we are calling our StockQuote.asmx page again, but this time we are sending a query string with a single value, WSDL. This tells the Web Service to return to us to the service description.

If we look at the WSDL displayed in our browser window, we will see that the root element of the WSDL for our StockQuote Web Service is <definitions>. The WSDL specification (http://www.w3.org/TR/wsdl) says that the root element is named <definitions> because WSDL itself is merely a set of definitions.

WSDL Types

After the namespace definitions for this document, we come across the <types> element. Recall that WSDL types are used to define data types that are used in Web Service messages. In our WSDL, our first type definition is a structure named GetQuote that contains one and only one child named strTickerSymbol. The actual XML for GetQuote, if you recall, could look something like the following:

```
<GetQuote xmlns="http://tempuri.org/">
    <strTickerSymbol>string</strTickerSymbol>
</GetQuote>
```

The structure of the result returned by our `StockQuote` Web Service, is also defined here. Remember the `AuthInfo` class that defined a `SubscriberID`, `UserId`, and `Password`. Its WSDL definition looks like this:

```
<s:complexType name="AuthInfo">
  <s:sequence>
    <s:element minOccurs="1" maxOccurs="1" name="SubscriberID"
               nillable="true" type="s:string" />
    <s:element minOccurs="1" maxOccurs="1" name="UserID"
               nillable="true" type="s:string" />
    <s:element minOccurs="1" maxOccurs="1" name="Password"
               nillable="true" type="s:string" />
  </s:sequence>
</s:complexType>
```

Although this section of the WSDL is merely an XSD Schema, exposing this level of detail via WSDL gives us all sorts of possibilities including the auto-generation of Web Service proxy classes by Visual Studio .NET.

WSDL Messages

The `StockQuote` Web Service example has three defined messages. Recall that messages define the format in which a Web Service expects to receive SOAP requests, and the format in which it returns SOAP responses. The first two `<message>` elements in our sample code support parameters via the `Parameters` attribute value. The final message, `GetQuoteAuthInfo`, is our SOAP header:

```
<message name="GetQuoteSoapIn">
  <part name="parameters" element="s0:GetQuote" />
</message>
<message name="GetQuoteSoapOut">
  <part name="parameters" element="s0:GetQuoteResponse" />
</message>
<message name="GetQuoteAuthInfo">
  <part name="AuthInfo" element="s0:AuthInfo" />
</message>
```

WSDL PortTypes

The following code defines the types of ports available to our Web Service. The types of ports available to a Web Service are analogous to the protocols it supports – HTTP GET, HTTP POST, and SOAP:

```
<portType name="StockQuoteSoap">
  <operation name="GetQuote">
    <input message="s0:GetQuoteSoapIn" />
    <output message="s0:GetQuoteSoapOut" />
  </operation>
</portType>
<portType name="StockQuoteHttpGet" />
<portType name="StockQuoteHttpPost" />
```

Notice that the `StockQuoteSoap` port type includes an operation definition for that particular port type as well as a definition of our input and output messages.

WSDL Bindings

The WSDL `<binding>` element defines message formats and protocol details for operations for each `<portType>`. Using the `name` attribute as a unique identifier, we can have multiple `<binding>` elements in any WSDL document:

```
<binding name="StockQuoteSoap" type="s0:StockQuoteSoap">
   <soap:binding transport="http://schemas.xmlsoap.org/soap/http"
         style="document" />
   <operation name="GetQuote">
      <soap:operation soapAction="http://tempuri.org/GetQuote"
         style="document" />
      <input>
         <soap:body use="literal" />
         <soap:header n1:required="true" message="s0:GetQuoteAuthInfo"
                    part="AuthInfo" use="literal"
                    xmlns:n1="http://schemas.xmlsoap.org/wsdl/" />
      </input>
      <output>
         <soap:body use="literal" />
      </output>
   </operation>
</binding>
```

WSDL Service Definition

Finally, we come to the actual service definition. A `<service>` element is a collection of ports, or endpoints, that the service supports. Notice that in our `StockQuote` Web Service, we support all three port types named `StockQuoteSoap`, `StockQuoteHttpGet`, and `StockQuoteHttpPost`:

```
<service name="StockQuote">
  <port name="StockQuoteSoap" binding="s0:StockQuoteSoap">
    <soap:address location="http://localhost/StockQuote/StockQuote.asmx" />
  </port>
  <port name="StockQuoteHttpGet" binding="s0:StockQuoteHttpGet">
    <http:address location="http://localhost/StockQuote/StockQuote.asmx" />
  </port>
  <port name="StockQuoteHttpPost" binding="s0:StockQuoteHttpPost">
    <http:address location="http://localhost/StockQuote/StockQuote.asmx" />
  </port>
</service>
```

Now that we have seen the basics of Web Service construction and some of the standards and specifications that make them work, let's look at some issues we are likely to encounter as we try to take our own Web Service from a test environment to a production environment. In the following sections, we'll discuss:

❑ State Management in Web Services, and the implications of using ASP.NET `Session` and `Application` objects

❑ Transactions in Web Service execution and some common design issues

❑ Deployment of Web Services

State Management in Web Services

As we've seen, in Visual Studio .NET, Web Services are really ASP.NET applications that have been rearranged a bit. As such, our Web Services have access to many of the same capabilities and features that a regular ASP.NET application would have. A perfect example of the overlap between ASP.NET applications and Web Services is state management.

ASP introduced two objects, Session and Application, which make managing state easy. ASP.NET has kept similar objects by the same name. As an ASP.NET application, Web Services have access to Application and Session objects just like any other web application.

The Session object allows the data to be stored for a particular client. The Application object is used to store data that is accessible to all code running within a Web application. Any class derived from System.Web.Services.WebService has access to the Session and Application objects.

Using the Session Object

Storing data using the Session object for an ASP.NET Web Service is relatively straightforward. To enable the Session object we need only modify the WebMethod() attribute by setting the EnableSession property to True as the following code shows:

```
Imports System.Web.Services

Public Class StateManagement
    Inherits System.Web.Services.WebService

    <WebMethod(EnableSession:=True)> _
        Public Function SessionStateExample() As String

        Session("UsageCount") = Session("UsageCount") + 1
        SessionStateExample = Session("UsageCount")

    End Function
End Class
```

By using the EnableSession:=True statement in the preceding example, we initialize the Session object, which is really the HttpSessionState object. In fact, any Web Service configured with this statement will behave just like any other ASP.NET application as far as session management is concerned. The code in the above example counts the total number of times a particular client calls the SessionStateExample() Web Service method. The value of Session("UsageCount") starts at zero and increments by one each time the Web Service is invoked. The Web Service returns a string containing the Session("UsageCount") value. Since, we are not concerned with proper typecasting, we just let VB .NET take care of it for us.

Early in this chapter, we used the built-in HTTP GET binding provided by Visual Studio .NET Web Services for testing. Let's do the same again with our StateManagement Web Service. We'll create a new ASP.NET Web Service project and a StateManagement.asmx file with the code listed above. Let's build and run the project and we should see the now familiar browser window with an Invoke button. If we press the Invoke button, we get a simple XML document in a new browser window:

Now, let's close the result window and click the Invoke button again in the Web Service test page. We'll get a new result window that displays the incremented value of 2 for our SessionStateExample return string. If we repeat the process, the result value will be 3. Obviously our Session("UsageCount") variable is being incremented. If we were to run two clients against the SessionStateExample method, and watch each client's Session("UsageCount") increment, we would notice each client was incremented independently of the other. Remember that Session values are unique to each client. In fact, Session values are literally unique to each browser instance; closing a browser and restarting it will create new Session values.

Using the Application Object

Similar to the Session object, ASP.NET exposes the Application object for storing data that is available to any web client running that particular application. However, using the Application object for persisting data from one client request to another is sometimes an unwise technique because of performance implications. The code that uses the Application object to mimic the Session example we just ran looks like this:

```
<WebMethod()> Public Function ApplicationStateExample() As String
    Application("UsageCount") = Application("UsageCount") + 1
    ApplicationStateExample = Application("UsageCount")
End Function
```

Notice that enableSession:=True isn't necessary to use the Application object; it's there already. When we include this code in our StateManagement Web Service, and invoke the ApplicationStateExample() method, we'll see exactly the same results. Now, if we open another browser and invoke the ApplicationStateExample() with two browsers, we'll see that Application("UsageCount") increments for every invocation.

Transaction Support in ASP.NET Web Services

.NET Web Services support transactions just like any other application that uses the Common Language Runtime (CLR). CLR transaction support is based on the same model used by MTS and COM+ Components Services. That is, each Web Service can indicate the type of transaction processing it supports.

Since Web Services are based on a stateless HTTP protocol, any COM objects that a transactional Web Service invokes will execute within the same transaction. If one transactional Web Service starts another transactional Web Service, each will be executed in its own separate transaction. If no exception is thrown within the Web Service itself or any components it uses, the transaction is automatically committed.

ASP.NET Web Services and any other .NET application that supports transactions have the ability to specify what level of transactional support they require. In the case of Web Services, we can indicate whether a web method is a transaction, by setting the `TransactionOption` property to one of five possible values described in the table below:

TransactionOption Value	Description
Disabled	Indicates that a Web Service method does not run within a transaction and is the default value. By either setting this value explicitly or assuming transactions are disabled by default, the application will ignore any currently active transaction.
NotSupported	Indicates that a Web Service method does not run within a transaction. When `TransactionOption` equals `NotSupported`, the Web Service code will run outside of any current transactions.
Supported	Indicates that a Web Service will share a transaction if one exists, but a transaction is not required.
Required	Indicates that a transaction is required; a new transaction will be started or an existing transaction will be shared if it already exists.
RequiresNew	Indicates that a new transaction is required regardless of the existing transaction context.

To transaction-enable any Web Service method, we simply add the `TransactionOption` property to the `WebMethod()` attribute, as the following code fragment illustrates:

```
Imports System
Imports System.Web.Services
Imports System.EnterpriseServices

Public Class TransactionSample
    Inherits WebService

    <WebMethod(TransactionOption := TransactionOption.RequiresNew)> _
            Public Sub ExecuteSQL(strSQL as String)

    ' Code to execute the SQL contained in strSQL

    End Sub
End Class
```

In this case, we've specified that the method `ExecuteSQL()` requires a new transaction regardless of whether a transaction context already exists. Also, notice that we've had to include a new namespace, `System.EnterpriseServices`, which contains `TransactionOption`.

Deploying Web Services

Deploying our Web Service is a rather simple matter. .NET supports something called **XCopy Deployment**, which means putting an ASP.NET application into production (as simple as copying files to a specified directory) and following a few simple rules.

The first step in deployment is to understand the directory structure of our development and test environments. If we let Visual Studio .NET create and manage our project structures, we will notice a simple, consistent pattern. (At least when you are getting started, this is recommended. The author speaks from the experience of closing a non-working Web Service project and recreating it in a new project only because he messed with files and their locations).

Most ASP.NET applications (remember Web Services are merely ASP.NET applications that have different file extensions) follow a directory structure like `Inetpub\wwwroot\Web Application Directory\bin`.

The `\Web Application Directory` folder contains web application files, in other words the `.asmx` and `.aspx` files. The `\bin` folder contains assemblies not included in the .NET framework that may be referenced by your application. For example, proxy classes or Web Service classes not in an `.asmx` file will be located here in built `.dll` files.

Web Service Design Considerations

Given all the ground we've covered up to this point, some issues are worth discussing that directly relate to how you design your Web Services. In this section, we'll talk about the types and content of Web Server messages your services use, running Web Services in a stateless environment, taking advantage of asynchronous Web Service capabilities, and the application of good object-oriented design philosophy.

Message Design – Bigger Messages vs. More Traffic

As we've seen earlier in this chapter, we have quite a bit of flexibility in designing our Web Service requests and responses. However, there are some things to keep in mind when we design our messages. One of the first issues you'll encounter is deciding on whether our Web Service publishes a smaller number of methods that return a lot of information for each client request, or more methods that return filtered information.

Using the first approach, building larger messages that contain more information per request-response pair, has several advantages. Let's take an online stock quote Web Service as an example. Maybe this stock quote service does more than just give one price at a particular time like our `StockQuote` example. Let's say this is a service that not only provides stock price based on time but also gives us the ability to get historical data like the last ten closing prices and the one, five and ten year highs and lows. If we assume that most of our service clients will want to see the current price but will also want to see some historical data, then it makes sense to have that data available to the client without requiring another round-trip back to our service. Using this technique to include more information in the first response back to the client, we can potentially avoid the expense of a second connection to our server and the time it takes to process another response.

When designing our Web Service methods and input and output parameters, we should think about how our clients will most likely use the data we make available to them. We may even go so far as to create several methods that perform similar functions but return different levels of detail.

Stateless Environment

Another item to keep in mind when designing our Web Services is that they live in an inherently stateless environment. Web Services usually rely on HTTP, which is stateless. The connections between web clients and our Web Services are broken after every request-response transaction is completed.

The design of our Web Services will have to consider this. We've seen how we can leverage the ASP.NET `Session` and `Application` objects to maintain data, and expose that to successive client requests to a Web Service or make the data available to any client using a particular web application. However, there is overhead associated with the technique. In some cases, the overhead (particularly with the `Application` object) can be fatal to a Web Service that is being asked to scale and serve many clients in a short amount of time.

Most Web Service functions should be granular, that is, they should be asked to do one task or a small number of tasks with a single request from a client. The Web Service should perform the task, and report results, if appropriate, back to the user. At that point, the connection is lost until the client attempts to reconnect.

Synchronous vs. Asynchronous Web Services

As we illustrated earlier in this chapter, .NET Web Services support synchronous and asynchronous implementations. In the case of potentially long running services or services that return quite a bit of data, supporting asynchronous clients may be advantageous.

Asynchronous clients can start a service and continue performing some other task. When the Web Service completes or raises an event back to the Visual Studio .NET proxy class, the client code could take appropriate action including informing the user or modifying some status display device. The result of providing asynchronous services is more effective client software. Logic would hold that Web Services that make Web Service clients easier to use are more likely to be adopted by a larger group of consumers.

Loosely Connected Pieces of Functionality

A good object-oriented development practice is building components with abstract, unchanging interfaces that hide most of their implementation details. Well-designed Web Services rely on this approach.

In theory, at least, a good Web Service interface requires no data that is implementation-specific. In other words, the Web Service should be designed so that a behind-the-scenes implementation change should not affect the SOAP request and response format or contents significantly (or at all in the best case). Think of this as maintaining binary compatibility in a COM environment. The interface for your Web Services, once in production, should rarely change. Additionally, application logic changes should continue to support existing Web Service clients.

Summary

In this chapter, we studied the basic concepts of, and some possible applications for, a Web Service. We discussed the advantages of Web Services over existing computing models, and the current market and technological trends that point to an embracing of Web Services in the near future. To experience the use of Web Services in the .NET environment, we created and tested a simple Web Service in Visual Studio .NET and studied the files created during this process.

We saw how Web Services support three wire formats – HTTP GET, HTTP POST, and SOAP. We emphasized that SOAP is XML-based, and is going to be the future of Web Services. We also covered the structure of SOAP messages including their common elements (<Envelope>, <Header>, <Body>, and <Fault>), and discussed and illustrated the use of SOAP Headers and the code necessary to implement them.

We then moved on to implementing a Web Service client that uses Web Services proxy classes. We saw how to send and receive messages from our Web Service and what is required on the client to implement our Web Service. We then saw how proxy classes are useful to application developers implementing Web Services and how proxies can be used synchronously and asynchronously.

Next, we looked at UDDI, a mechanism by which Visual Studio .NET or other applications can learn about Web Services, their definitions, the interfaces they expose, and how to format messages for each Web Service method, etc. We showed how WSDL helps consumers know exactly what particular Web Services do, how it explains the structure of SOAP requests/responses, and how it gives details of the data types of the input and output parameters. We also looked at the usage of WSDL elements.

Then we dealt with some common Web Service development issues. We saw how to manage different sessions and different applications in Web Services. We also took a brief look at transaction support and deployment of .NET Web Services

We then discussed the various things to be considered when designing a Web Service, such as the possible ways clients could use the data made available to them. We looked at why we should try to keep Web Services in a stateless environment (that is, after a Web Service performs any task and returns the results, if any, the connection to the Web Service should be lost until the client attempts to reconnect), and why supporting asynchronous clients might be advantageous if the Web Service returns a huge amount of data or is a long running service. Finally, we looked at designing a Web Service with an object-oriented approach kept in mind, so that any implementation change will not affect the SOAP request and response format or contents significantly (or at all in the best case).

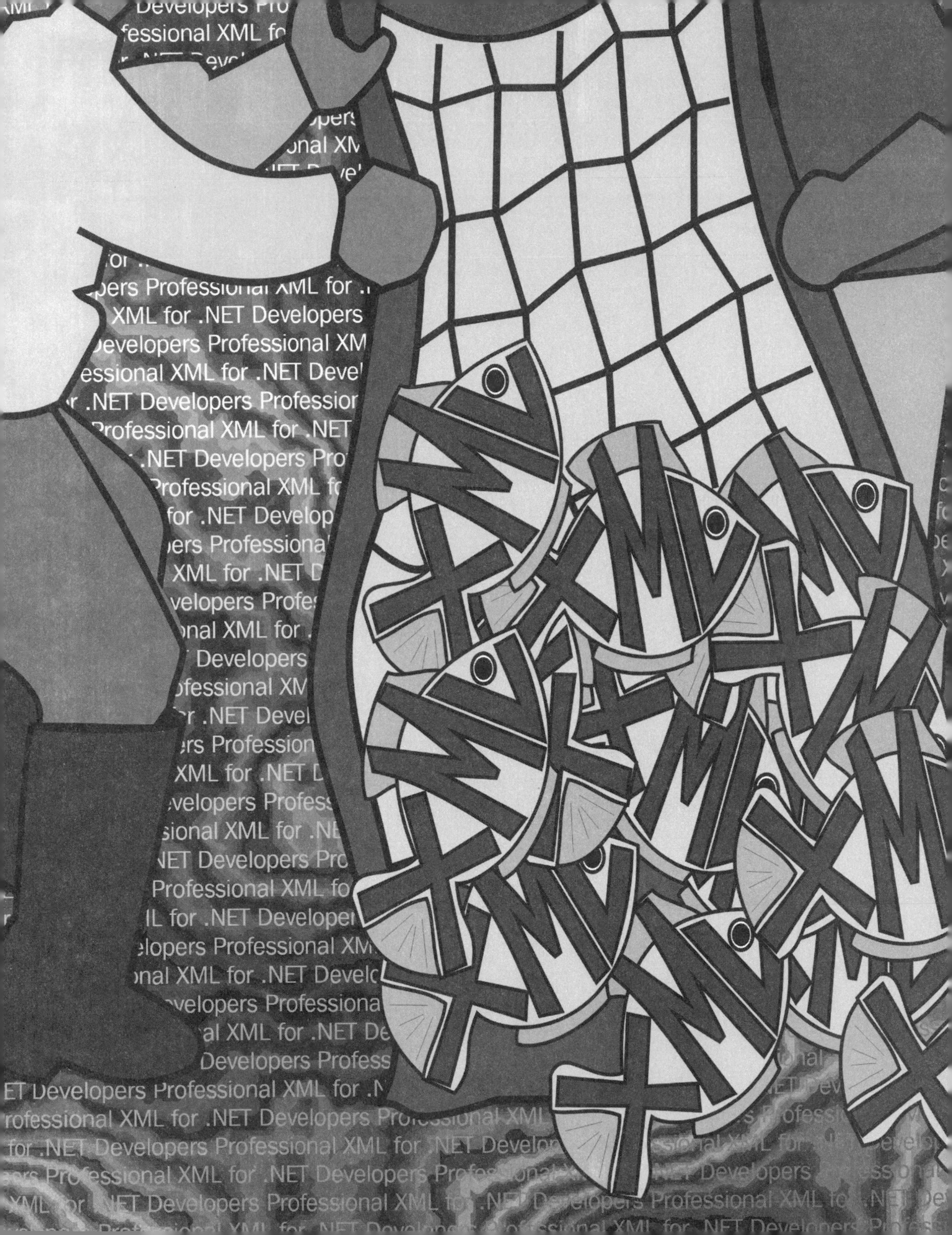
Professional XML for .NET Developers

Case Study: Using Web Services

As previous chapters have shown, .NET Web Services give us a whole new way to build distributed applications. The purpose of this chapter is to illustrate the fundamentals of building a Web Service and building client applications that use that Web Service. We'll eventually get into the details of building the application, but, since this is a case study, we'll also be covering some important details about any application development project – business and functional requirements and issues like that. So, the contents of this chapter are:

❑ Case Study Application – in this chapter we will be building a calendar application that uses a Web Service as the mechanism for storing and retrieving appointments, and tasks and a couple of client applications to illustrate how applications can consume a Web Service.

❑ Project Information – business and functional requirements, a description of our clients, a few use cases to indicate how we expect our application to be used, and any assumptions under which we will be operating for this case study.

❑ Detailed Design – to be useful throughout the case study, we'll cover in some detail our database tables and other structural information that may be of some use for any reader interested in creating this case study on their own machines.

❑ Functional Specifications – here is where we see the details of what our Web Services are going to be asked to do. We'll discuss each Web Service in turn and note important or interesting issues regarding their construction. Additionally, we'll discuss the types of Web Services clients we expect to subscribe to our application and the bounds of our client development for this case study.

❑ Web Service Implementation – definitely the bulk of this case study's material will focus on the development and coding of our Web Services and their client applications. This first implementation section will focus on how exactly we constructed our Web Services. We will cover in some detail the code that makes our Web Services run and the technical information necessary for readers to build their own Web Services.

❑   Client Implementation – since Web Services contain the promise of client- and platform-independence, it is important that this case study explores that potential. We will be reviewing two types of client application – a browser-based Web Application and a desktop-based Window Forms application.

Application Background

Now that the drama has been building on what type of application we will construct in this case study, let's unveil it. We will be building a calendaring application. Now, don't go to another chapter, stay with us for a moment. You might be thinking that a calendar application is relatively boring and has no real significance in the context of Web Services. That may be true, but we will have to fake it. Hang in there a little bit longer and we'll cover why Web Services are indeed applicable in this type of application. And, maybe, we'll discover how an existing application with a defined set of functionality can be extended via Web Services to add more value to what we currently have.

As we've already mentioned, we'll be building a Web Service that exposes calendaring functionality. At first glance, you may wonder why or how a calendar application lends itself to implementation as a Web Service, but I think you'll find it quite interesting. Consider that most calendar functionality is somewhat commodity-like. That is, showing a list of appointments for a particular week or tasks due by a particular time is functionality that you find in many places and, for the most part, it all works about the same. A user creates an appointment by giving a date, a time, and a duration. They may also provide a location and some other information. Most calendar or appointment systems operate along the same lines. Also, consider the fact that many applications in production require calendaring functions – a to-do or reminder list, a collection of tasks to be completed, or a list of scheduled events are common features. Now, envision providing base calendaring functions to any and all applications with an internet connection that need those types of features. You'll find that such a service might be very useful.

The calendar application that we will build consists of three main parts:

❑   An event list that shows any scheduled calendar event for a given day, week, or month. Events are items like appointments, meetings, or other time-based activities that have some predictable duration.

❑   A task list that shows any previously scheduled or created tasks. Tasks are generally simple to-do list type items.

❑   A reminder list that shows any reminders that have been raised. Any event or task can have reminders associated with it. Reminders are time-based notifications that get raised to a particular user.

You can find calendars online like those at MSN.com or Yahoo.com. These calendar applications have much more functionality than we'll be producing in this chapter, but they do have the same basic set of information – events, tasks, and reminders.

We'll add a few twists to our events and tasks, like having the ability to share them with other authorized users, and we'll add the ability to get our lists of information from just about any device that supports a browser. OK, let's qualify that last statement. We will add the ability to get our lists of information from any client to which we can deploy .NET applications – an ASP.NET browser application, a VB .NET Windows Forms application and a Mobile Toolkit application for the Pocket PC. In this case study, you can look forward to an ASP.NET application as well as a Window Forms application for the Windows desktop.

Web Services can add some new value to a calendar application by exposing event, task, and reminder information to any client that supports Web Services. As simple as this seems, the flexibility that exposure gives to application designers is significant. Now any application that might need calendaring or reminder functionality doesn't have to maintain a data model for calendaring data. Rather, the only requirement placed on the application itself is the ability to send and receive XML messages.

One thing that you will notice as we move along is, since this entire book is oriented toward .NET, we will take some liberties with the platform and environmental pureness of our Web Service input and output parameters. As you'll soon find when we look at our Web Service code, the output of most of our calendar Web Services are .NET `DataSet`s. That means our client applications will inherently understand the `DataSet` and be able to use it. For a detailed description of .NET `DataSet`s, refer back to Chapter 10, *ADO.NET*.

Application Purpose

The purpose of the application that we'll develop through the course of this case study is multi-faceted:

❑ We want to build an application that showcases Web Services and Web Service clients. This means reviewing code, showing screenshots, and looking at different implementation methods. It also means deliberately simplifying some issues we encounter. You'll find those issues will be noted as we move along.

❑ We want to build an application that exposes straightforward functionality for managing a simple calendar. Using MSN's online calendar or the Outlook desktop calendar as a guide, we will be building an application that supports managing events and tasks and assigning reminders to events and tasks. (See the *Functional Requirements* section below for more details as to what exactly the application is to do.)

❑ We want to build appropriately designed client consumers of our Web Services. We've already mentioned the web, desktop, and mobile applications. The purpose of including the first two in this case study is to discuss the implications of consuming or subscribing to Web Services, and the implications of using Web Services on different platforms.

❑ We want to introduce sample code to be reviewed, improved, and used by other developers, regardless of the application domain.

So, there's the 'why', the purpose of what we are doing. Let's jump into the details from a project standpoint including requirements, a description of users, and client platforms in the next section. From there, we will move into design issues and finally the code.

Project Description

As most of you can attest, developing good software is hard enough without having to wonder what exactly is it you have been asked to build. How many times have you started a project and the users or management have changed the scope, your target requirements, or something else that impacts on your feature set, underlying design, or schedule estimates? Probably more than once.

A good software project, however small, should start with some sort of a vision statement. In larger projects, it is best written down and agreed to by all hands. For small projects involving only a few developers, a shared vision is still critical. Even for the simplest application, people's perceptions of the same design conversation are influenced by their individual experiences and competencies. All of that could lead to different ideas about the task at hand. Take the time to develop a vision of what you are about to build; share that with your team members, users, and other technical staff. It will pay off down the road.

Project Vision

My vision of this project when complete is a set of Web Services that manage calendar events, tasks, and reminders. The functionality to work with events, tasks, and reminders will be made available to any client that consumes Web Services. The Web Service application will expose functions allowing client applications to request calendar data by date and user. The Web Service clients will be responsible for initiating the requests and formatting and displaying any data returned by the Web Service application.

The Web Services themselves will be responsible for managing database issues, such as connections, and for implementing security.

The following diagram illustrates the structure of this application including the interface between the Calendar Service clients and the Calendar Service server components.

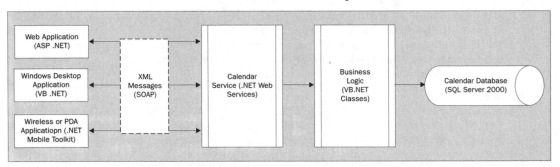

This may not be a bullet-proof vision that anticipates everything, but the preceding paragraphs should make it more clear what we are setting out to do. It would be an interesting exercise to compare the vision statement above to the final product once we are done with the case study. But, of course, the author will have had ample time to revisit the vision and make any 'corrections', so that the vision and the actual results are properly synchronized.

Functional Requirements

Another one of those necessary project management devices is a well stated Functional Requirements document. Although not necessary, documenting exactly what your application is to do in as much detail as possible is a great way to ensure you deliver the general goals or targets you outlined in the Project Vision.

Typically, functional specs are written in the format of "the product will…" or "the application shall…" declarative statements that leave little room for misinterpretation. In the case of our calendar Web Service application, keep in mind that there are three main groups of services we'll be delivering – working with events, tasks, and reminders.

The functional requirements for this case study can be stated as follows:

Calendar Events Service

For our purposes in this case study, an event is any scheduled calendar item that has a defined start that can be expressed in terms of a date and time and a known or estimated conclusion.

The product will allow users to:

- ❑ retrieve an event list containing individual event details by date and by user ID
- ❑ create new calendar events
- ❑ update existing calendar events
- ❑ remove existing calendar events
- ❑ share calendar events with other users aggregated into groups

Tasks Service

In this case study a task will be a to-do item that can be assigned to particular users and will contain data like a due date, priority, etc.

The product will allow users to:

- ❑ retrieve task lists containing task details by date and user ID
- ❑ create new tasks
- ❑ update existing tasks
- ❑ remove existing tasks
- ❑ share tasks with other users aggregated into groups

Reminders Service

Reminders are time- and date-based notifications of an existing event or task. In our case study, we'll list any reminders only when an application requests them. In many desktop applications, like MS Outlook, reminders are raised to the user automatically.

The product will:

- ❑ retrieve reminders that have fired by date and user ID
- ❑ set reminder dates for any event or task
- ❑ dismiss fired reminders

Sharing Tasks and Events

Many calendar applications allow users to share events and tasks between users to some degree. For instance, Outlook users can see the scheduled events of other Outlook users, assuming proper rights have been granted. We will implement a similar feature. In our application we will have groups of users that allow the sharing of tasks and events (and their associated reminders) between users within that group. So, assuming that groups are merely pre-defined lists of users with whom we'd like to share our calendar, we can state our sharing requirements as follows:

The product will:

- support sharing by assigning groups to individual tasks and events
- maintain a list of valid user groups
- create users
- update existing users
- remove or disable existing users
- create user groups
- update existing user groups
- remove existing user groups

Our requirements are really rather simple, and in a more complex application we could have pages and pages of functional requirements. We could have stated our calendar requirements in a few short paragraphs as well. Admittedly, the format above lends itself to large, more complex applications, but as an example it may be useful to review this particular format.

There is more benefit to stating requirements in such a manner than just making sure developers and users are on the same page. At some point during an application development project, you need to measure whether the product is actually going to deliver what was promised. If your functional requirements are done well, they can be used as a test down the road to determine if you development efforts are paying off. By choosing a consistent, meaningful numbering scheme it is possible to refer to particular requirements or requirement groups through an entire project from this stage through testing and quality assurance activities.

Technical Requirements

There are also technical requirements to be addressed. In many cases, you may be limited in your choice of technology by department or corporate standards. In other cases, you may be required to interface with other applications that require a particular data integration standard like Electronic Data Interchange (EDI). In our case, we are constrained somewhat by the particular technologies this case study is to showcase.

The technical requirements for this case study are that the product will:

- be developed using the Visual Studio .NET
- be written using VB .NET (although we could have chosen any .NET language)
- use IIS as its Web Server
- use a SQL Server 2000 database
- support only SOAP Web Service messages
- provide its client applications with .NET `DataSets` as Web Service return parameters
- support mobile and handheld applications developed using the .NET Mobile Toolkit

Nothing too shocking here. This is a .NET application implementing Web Services so there are some inherent requirements like Visual Studio .NET. The SQL Server 2000 database requirement isn't necessarily a requirement, any ODBC compliant database will work, that just happens to be the database the author is running on his development machine. The code that accompanies this chapter on the Wrox web site will contain SQL scripts for building a SQL Server 2000 database, but you could easily recreate the database in just about any other database with little or no changes to the code.

So, at this point, we have our basic requirements listed. If we wrote them correctly, we should know what our product will do functionally, understand what kind of additional requirements our particular environment or business has placed on us, and have made clear any initial technical requirements that may affect our design or implementation. It may seem like overkill to spend several pages in a technical case study on issues like this, but I've found that writing good software is as much of a technical exercise as it is an analytical exercise. And, if you work in a large organization full or rules and bureaucracy, you know that writing good software is often an administrative task trying to get users and decision makers all in the same room at the same time.

Usage Scenarios

If you follow the Unified Modelling Language, UML, one of the first things you may do is develop use cases. In larger development projects, use cases are an invaluable technique for eliciting what exactly it is users do, or what they will expect their applications to do for them once completed.

Use cases come in different shapes and sizes and I've adopted a consistent format for my own use cases. The common elements are shown in the following table:

Use Case Element	Description
Use Case Number	A number or letter in some consistent scheme for uniquely identifying individual use cases.
Title	A short, description title.
Primary Actor	The main actor, a person or application, who executes the use case.
Secondary Actor	Any other actor who can execute the use case.
Starting Point	The state at which the use case starts. In a UI application the state could be expressed as "The actor is viewing the Invoice Detail form."
Ending Point	The state at which the use case ends. In a database application, the ending point could be expressed as "The Invoice was saved to the Invoice table."
Measurable Result	The result we expect from the use case.
Flow of Events	A running narrative of everything that occurs between the Starting Point and the Ending Point.
Alternative Flow of Events	Any thing that doesn't occur in the Flow of Events, typically error conditions and error handling.

Since the analyst or developer is forced to document who is doing what activity, when a particular activity starts and when it ends, what its outcomes are, and how events flow from the start through to the end of the activity, there is generally little room for misinterpretation in terms of how the application should be built, and how the user should expect to interact with the application. That is, if the use cases are done properly.

One thing we haven't talked about yet that is ominously missing is who exactly might be using our application. If you noticed, a big part of the use case is the `Actor`, and in most cases the `Actor` is actually a human user. It is entirely possible and generally appropriate to include applications as `Actors`, but let's focus on human users for the time being. In fact, as cool as automating the interaction between applications might be, this entire case study will be focused on exposing functionality for human users to manipulate.

User Classes

The particular terms may differ from one source to the next, but users are generally grouped into abstract classes based on the role they play in the context of an application. The user classes for our calendar application are actually rather simple. There are three or four at the most. But, consider an application that supports many security levels with administrators, super users, guests, normal users, etc. Defining what exactly each user class is, why they exist, and what they are allowed to do in certain situations is important.

Our simple calendar service user classes are as follows:

User Class	Description
Administrator	An internal administrator responsible for maintaining the calendar service application. No external users belong to this class.
Calendar User	An internal or external user who is interacting with standard calendar service functionality as defined in the Functional Requirements.
Shared Calendar User	An internal or external user who is working with shared events and tasks that were originally created by another user. (You'll understand this one in a few pages.)

Let's have a look at a use case we could derive from our function requirements. Take the requirement "The product will allow the user to create calendar events". If we assume the user is at the Main Calendar view (for now picture Outlook Today in your mind) when this use case starts, and that saving the event and indicating success or failure to the user is the official end of the use case, our use case could be completed like the following example:

```
Use Case: Create New Calendar Event.

Overview
The purpose of this use case is to save an individual calendar event.

Primary Actor
Any calendar user.

Secondary Actor
Any other calendar service user.

Starting Point
The actor must have been authenticated by a client application and have displayed
the actor's main calendar view [Note: the main calendar view will be defined in
subsequent sections of this chapter].

Ending Point
The calendar event is saved in the database.
```

Measurable Result
The actor is displayed a message indicating the success or failure of the event save.

Flow of Events
This use case starts when the actor is viewing the main calendar view which contains events, tasks, or reminders. The actor will select the New Event button or link, depending on client application. The actor will be shown a Create New Event form containing blank fields for basic Event information. The actor will complete the form and press the Save button or link. The client application will format an appropriate message containing the new Event data and transmit that message to the Calendar Service. The Calendar Service will attempt to create a new Event and respond to the client with either a success or failure message. The client application will display some indication to the client that the Create New Event procedure succeeded or failed.

Alternative Flow of Events
An error will result if the actor's username and password are not properly authenticated when the Calendar Service message is processed.

An error will result if the Event data is not properly validated.

An error will result of the database operation fails.

Typically, every user action possible within an application would be defined by a use case. That's definitely more detail than we want or need for this case study. That having been said, I'd like to point out one note of caution here: if you decide to implement Use Cases in your own projects, don't do it part way and then give up. They are only effective when you, you users and your management fully buy into their value. Anything but a full and proper description of each use case (and every use case) is time that could be better spent elsewhere.

Now that we have spent a lot of time on software project-related issues, let's get to some more tangible stuff. The project issues are as important as the technical issues sometimes. This isn't the forum for a pure software project discussion, but hopefully the little material we've covered as it related to our Web Services case study will be useful in your own work.

For more information on UML and project management, see any of the following books from Wrox Press: *Instant UML*, ISBN 1-861000-87-1; *Visual Basic 6 UML Design and Development*, ISBN 1-861002-51-3; *Visual Basic 6 Project Management*, ISBN 1-861002-93-9.

The next section focuses on high-level design issues. Among other things, we'll see our database contents, the basic interface our Web Service will expose, and the purpose and functional specs of our client software.

Web Service Design

It's time now to jump into how we are going to build the application in terms of the components necessary to meet our functional requirements. That includes discussing the functions exposed by our Web Services, the database that stores our calendar data, the messages our Web Service expects to receive as client requests, and those it will generate and return as responses.

Let's take the major components of our application, including clients, first.

Calendar Service Components

There are several key pieces to the Calendar Service application. We'll cover each in this section in enough detail to ensure that you understand their purpose by the time we get to the code. Hang in there a little bit longer, the code is coming.

Calendar Web Service

This is the main working component of the entire application. For the sake of discussion, both the Web Services themselves and the classes that support the Web Services are included here. The main purpose of this component is to expose the processes necessary to meet our functional requirements. Since we've already listed out functional requirements a few pages ago, listing the methods exposed as Web Services is relatively straightforward (we'll review particular input and output arguments in a few pages):

Web Service Method	Description
GetEvents()	Returns all active events for a particular user, given a start date and an end date.
SaveEvent()	Saves an event.
RemoveEvent()	Removes a particular event from a user's calendar.
GetTasks()	Returns all active tasks for a particular user, given a start date and an end date.
SaveTask()	Saves a task.
RemoveTask()	Removes a task from a user's calendar.
GetReminders()	Gets all the reminders that have a reminder date sometime in the past.
SaveReminder()	Saves an individual reminder. Typically used to turn off the reminder for a task or event. (You'll find that reminders don't have their own database tables, they are characteristics of events and tasks.)
RemoveReminder()	Removes a particular reminder from a user's calendar. Has the same effect as saving a reminder with the ReminderFlag set to false.

Logging Module

The logging module is significant to this Web Service application only because it is useful to discuss how we will monitor the traffic and usage of our Web Services. If you read the previous chapter, *Web Services and SOAP*, you might recall that Web Services will eventually generate revenue for their owners using a pay-for-service model.

Our logging module will help us to track subscriber usage levels. Subscribers can be, among other things, third-party resellers of our Calendar Web Service, business partners we want to share our calendar functionality with, or internal users. Regardless of who is using our Web Services, we want to track them and eventually bill them for the use of our services.

Calendar Service Clients

Although we will deal with clients that consume our calendar Web Service in a later section of this chapter, they are an important component in the entire Web Service application. Remember that we intend to build calendar service consumers on two of the three most common application platforms – a web application and a Windows desktop application. Time and space do not allow us to write a mobile or handheld application.

Calendar Service Database Structure

Logically, the Calendar Service doesn't have that much information to keep track of. We really only have three main lists of data, two of which are represented by a tables. The third is something of a virtual list made up of data from the other two lists:

- ❑ **Events** – any calendar event characterized by an event date, a subject, a location, start and end times if applicable, and some other information. These are what Outlook calls Appointments.

- ❑ **Tasks** – a task list is similar to a To-Do list. Tasks are characterized by a subject, due date, task date, complete date, etc.

- ❑ **Reminders** – a reminder results when the reminder date and time of a task or event is set and the current system date passes that reminder date and time. Again, using Outlook as an example, a reminder is that little form that pops up 15 minutes before a meeting. In our case, we won't be popping up any little windows, but displaying a separate list of reminders. The burden of asking for reminders that have 'fired' will be on each client application.

There is some other information we need to keep on the Calendar Service database, but this is more system level than user or data level. For security purposes, we need a list of Users and a list of Groups to which individual users belong. We'll look at the details of how users and groups are used together in a few pages, but for now just understand that we are going to return events, tasks, and reminders based on an `OwnerUserID` field that relates back to the `Users` table. We will also build the capability to share events and tasks within a group of users. The `Group` table represents all the groups that a particular user belongs to. When it comes to retrieving shared events or tasks, we'll use a combination of the `Users` table and `Group` table.

Another logical group of database tables is found on our logging module. As you will see in a few paragraphs, the physical implementation of the database in this case study includes all tables (or modules) in one SQL Server 2000 database. However, logically, each database group – logging, calendar data, and users and groups can exist in different databases on different machines. In a big-time production environment that makes money selling access to Web Services, logging, and ultimately, billing activities would be a very serious part of the operations. That's how it makes money. We don't take as serious an approach to logging in this case study. We'll leave it to others to offer ideas on how to best monitor Web Service usage.

The physical implementation of our database model is rather straightforward. Our database will contain tables for each of our event and task lists. Remember that reminder data is stored with each individual task and event.

Here are the tables themselves with their constituent fields. The code that accompanies this chapter will also include a SQL Server script to create these tables. The following screenshot on the next page illustrates their relationships:

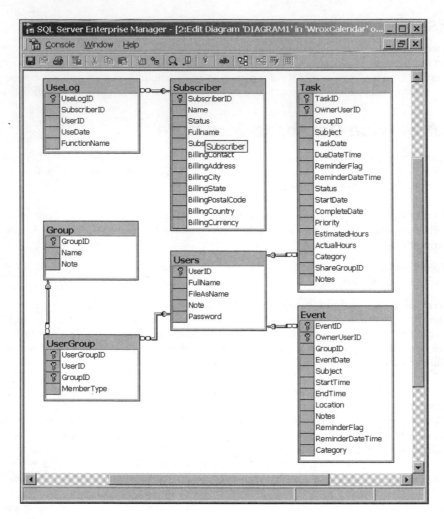

Event Table

Field Name	Data Type	Description
EventID	nchar	A unique, sequential Event ID. The Primary Key for the table.
OwnerUserID	char	The User ID of the user to whom this event belongs. Foreign key relationship to the Users table.
GroupID	nchar	The Group this event is shared with. Can be empty.
EventDate	datetime	The dates on which this event occurs.
Subject	nvarchar	The subject of the event – used mainly for descriptive display purposes.
StartTime	datetime	The date and time on which the event starts or started.

Field Name	Data Type	Description
EndTime	datetime	The date and time on which the event ended or is scheduled to end.
Location	nvarchar	The physical location of the event, if applicable.
Notes	nvarchar	A collection of textual notes.
ReminderFlag	nchar	Indicates whether a reminder has been enabled for this Event.
ReminderDateTime	datetime	The date and time on which the reminder fires if the ReminderFlag is set to true.
Category	nvarchar	A text field containing category information available for future use and/or reporting.

Task Table

Field Name	Data Type	Description
TaskID	nchar	A unique, sequential Task ID. The Primary Key for the table.
OwnerUserID	char	The UserID of the user to whom this Task belongs. Foreign key relationship to the Users table.
GroupID	nchar	The Group this Task is shared with. Can be empty.
TaskDate	datetime	The date on which this Task occur(s).
Subject	nvarchar	The subject of the task – used mainly for descriptive display purposes.
DueDateTime	datetime	The date and time on which a particular task is due.
ReminderFlag	nchar	Indicates whether a reminder has been enabled for this Task.
ReminderDateTime	datetime	The date and time on which the reminder fires if the ReminderFlag is set to true.
Status	nchar	A text-based status of this Task. Values can be Active, Error, etc.
StartDate	datetime	The date and time on which the Task starts or started.
EndDate	datetime	The date and time on which the Task ended or is scheduled to end.
Priority	nvarchar	The priority assigned to this Task.
EstimatedHours	int	An estimate of how long it might take to complete the task.
ActualHours	int	The actual number of hours it took to complete the task.
Category	nvarchar	A text field containing category information available for future use and/or reporting.

The `Event` and `Task` tables are the main working tables of this application. It is a rather simple data model, actually. Notice that both the `Event` and `Task` tables have a reminder capability. As we'll see in a few pages, users have the ability to turn on a Reminder by setting the `ReminderFlag` field to 'Y' and setting the `ReminderDateTime` to some date and time combination. When we ask the Calendar Web Service for reminders it simply finds any Event or Task with a `ReminderFlag='Y'` and a `ReminderDateTime` sometime in the past.

The next group of tables relates to how we apply security and how we share events and tasks between users. Each Event and Task record in the database has a field called `OwnerUserID` that is used whenever a request comes to the Calendar Web Service. Our request messages will contain some security information that includes a `UserID` field. The code we'll write shortly will retrieve Tasks and Events matching the `UserID` field we receive with the `OwnerUserID` stored in the database. Also, we have the ability to share Events and Tasks between users by the use of groups. In a separate table named `Group`, we maintain a list of groups that users can belong to. When a user creates a Task or Event, they have the option to share it with any other groups in the system. At any point in time, a user can be a member of many groups. To maintain that list, we have a third table named `UserGroup` that contains a list of the intersection of a particular `UserID` with one or more `GroupID`s.

Users Table

Field Name	Data Type	Description
UserID	char	A unique, textual user identifier. The Primary Key for the table.
Password	char	The user's password.
FullName	nvarchar	The User's full name.
FileAsName	nvarchar	The `FullName` field expressed as Last, First MI.
Note	nvarchar	A general field for any additional information.

Group Table

Field Name	Data Type	Description
GroupID	nchar	A unique, textual group identifier. The Primary Key for the table.
Name	nvarchar	A relatively short Group name used for display.
Note	nvarchar	A general field for any additional information.

UserGroup Table

Field Name	Data Type	Description
UserGroupID	nchar	A unique, sequential key value. The Primary Key for the table.
UserID	nchar	Foreign key to `Users` table.
GroupID	nchar	Foreign key to `Group` table.
MemberType	nvarchar	The role or type of member a `UserID` fills in the group identified by `GroupID`.

The next group of tables exist mainly for monitoring and logging features. Although we won't be billing any of our users in this case study, it is worthwhile to review how you might go about building such a feature.

In our case, we'll be exposing our services to other companies and organizations. Those companies could be other software companies that want to build calendaring functionality into their own products. In our application, all of those companies are termed Subscribers and each one is assigned a particular `SubscriberID` to identify any of the individual users using our service in their name. Assuming that we capture the total number of individual users connecting to our service by `SubscriberID`, it would be a relatively straightforward process to create an invoice based on some price per user or price per usage rate agreed to ahead of time in a contract.

Subscriber Table

Field Name	Data Type	Description
SubscriberID	char	A unique, sequential subscriber identifier assigned to each subscriber group. The Primary Key for the table.
Name	char	A short display name.
Status	nchar	Status of the Subscriber account.
FullName	nvarchar	Full name of the Subscriber company or organization.
SubscriberType	nvarchar	Type of Subscriber account. Eventually the Calendar Web Service could support different functionality based on premium or standard subscribers.
BillingContact	nvarchar	Contact name for billing purposes.
BillingAddress	nvarchar	Street address for billing purposes.
BillingCity	nvarchar	City name for billing purposes.
BillingState	nvarchar	State name for billing purposes.
BillingPostalCode	nvarchar	Postal Code for billing purposes.
BillingCountry	nvarchar	Country for billing purposes.
BillingCurrency	nvarchar	The currency to be used for any invoices.

We've included some basic billing information to illustrate how the Subscriber concept can be extended to actually make money with Web Services. In this case study, we'll be focusing on the first few fields, however. Every request that comes to our Calendar Web Service will be required to contain a `SubscriberID`. That `SubscriberID` will be validated by a quick lookup in the `Subscriber` table and its `Status` will be set to `Active` if it does.

UseLog Table

Every request the Calendar Web Service receives will be logged in this table. From this data, we can monitor what functions get used the most and what functions don't get used at all. Of course, we could use it to generate billing information as well. Imagine a type of use license that limits the number of total requests per calendar month. Our logging module would be able to tell us how many times a particular `SubscriberID` has been used. When we hit whatever limit was set in the license, we return a message that tell the user to pay us more money.

The `UseLog` table contains the basics required for tracking usage counts by `SubscriberID`. It looks like this:

Field Name	Data Type	Description
UseLogID	char	A unique, sequential key. The Primary Key for the table.
SubscriberID	char	The `SubscriberID` contained in a service request. Foreign key relationship to the `Subscriber` table.
UserID	nchar	The `UserID` contained in the service request.
UseDate	nvarchar	The date of use.
FunctionName	nvarchar	The function requested.

AutoSequence Table

This last table is used to keep track of a unique set of IDs:

Field Name	Data Type	Description
AutoSeqID	int	A unique, sequential key. The Primary Key for the table.
AutoSeqCode	char	A unique value to determine each set of IDs.
AutoSeqValue	char	The next value available.

Functional Specifications

In the previous sections, we discussed the general architecture of the application and reviewed our data model for the Calendar Web Service. In this section, we'll review each Web Service method and what exactly it does. We will also take a look at our client applications and how we expect them to work. On that basis, we'll take on the task of actually building the Calendar Web Service.

Design Considerations

As we move from the logical to the physical design, let's list a number of design considerations we want to keep in mind. It's a good idea to write down items like these to refer to throughout a development project. They are easy to agree to before the coding actually starts, but are often forgotten as soon as the programmers take over:

- ❑ **Expose simple methods**. Our philosophy is to expose simple methods in our Calendar Web Service that perform very specific tasks. As our service matures, we can add more complex methods, but to start with, "keep it simple" is our rule of thumb. There are a few good reasons for this attitude. First, we are giving ourselves a chance to succeed. Second, we are going to put the responsibility for combining simple, distinct services in useful ways on the other software companies who will use our service.

- ❑ **Make the service secure**. We've already talked about security, but it's obviously a design issue. We will be requiring our Calendar Web Service clients to authenticate their users and send us a User ID and Password. Our service will also enforce User ID and Password security.

❑ **Log all activity**. Every request that the Calendar Web Service receives will be logged. It sounds trivial, but we don't want to create bottlenecks and slowdowns in our core service because system-level logging activity is not implemented well.

❑ **Support synchronous and asynchronous operation**. Kind of technical all of a sudden, but this consideration may become more obvious as we get into the code. The idea here is to support clients that want to work either way. In the case of asynchronous operations, we'd like our clients to be able to display results as they are generated for long running operations instead of waiting for the entire operation to complete.

Web Service Methods

In this section, we'll review each of our Calendar Web Service methods in some detail. We'll detail what function each method is responsible for performing. We'll review our input and output parameters and talk about other design issues.

The GetEvents() Method

Since this is a Calendar application, our most import method may be the one responsible for returning our event list for a given day, week, or month. Its only job is to retrieve event records from the database that have `EventDate` values between a `StartDate` and an `EndDate` for the current user.

It has several input parameters and one output parameter, defined in the table below:

Parameter Name	Type	Description
StartDate	In	A date representing the start of the event period
EndDate	In	A date representing the end of the event period
OwnerUserID	In	The owner of events for which an event period is requested
DataSet	Out	A .NET DataSet containing the method results

The activity for this method is decently straight, meaning there are not a lot of custom business rules or other conditional processing that might occur:

1. Validate the `StartDate`, `EndDate`, and `OwnerUserID`.

2. Determine if the `CurrentUserID` is the `OwnerUserID`. If `true` then no sharing is required. Go to Step 5. If `false` then current user is asking to see calendar of another user. Go to Step 3.

3. Retrieve every group that the `CurrentUser` is member of from the database.

4. Build a SQL statement to select every record from the `Event` table where the `OwnerUserID` equals the value passed in, and the `GroupID` of the record is in the set of `GroupID`s that the `CurrentUser` belongs to. Go to Step 6.

5. Build a SQL statement to select every `Event` record where the `OwnerUserID` field value equals the `OwnerUserID` value passed in.

6. Execute the SQL.

7. Build a `DataSet` with the results of Step 6.

8. Return the `DataSet` to the client.

There is also a list of possible error codes or other results we could expect back:

Error Code	Description
ERROR_INVALID_PARAMETER	Invalid input parameter. A date parameter is not valid.
ERROR_INVALID_USERID	Invalid `UserID`.
ERROR_DATABASE_CONNECT	Database error. Unable to connect to Calendar Web Service database.
ERROR_INTERNAL	Internal Error. A critical error has occurred within the Calendar application.

We'd expect a client application to ask for a list of events for a particular user after that user has authenticated themselves somehow in the client application. There is a difference between the `OwnerUserID` and the current `UserID` in this application. In the `GetEvents()` method call, the `OwnerUserID` is the individual to whom the event belongs. Typically, that is the person who created the event. But, the current `UserID` could be someone else's. Remember, we can share events and tasks. So, when we ask for events we have to force the client application to tell us not only what user's events we want, but also who the current user happens to be. You'll see when we discuss groups, users, and security how all of that works.

One question, though; if the current user isn't in the input parameter list (only `OwnerUserID` is), how do we get the `UserID` into our Web Service? Hopefully you noticed that problem. Since I have the luxury of knowing where this case study is going, and how it will be implemented at this stage, I can give a little hint away. Every request message received by our service will require some information in addition to the input parameters in the method call itself. We'll include that information in a specialized portion of the message structure itself called the message header. We'll see the details in a few pages, but this little tidbit needs to be mentioned now to avoid any confusion.

The SaveEvent() Method

Since we are trying to be a moderately useful Calendar Web Service, retrieving events only gets us half way to our goal of being able to 'manage' calendar events. We also have to be able to create new events and update existing events.

The interface exposed by this method is simple as well. We'll expect our clients to pass in a data structure representing a calendar event and we'll return some kind of string indicating success or failure of the save operation. Let's have a look at the parameters:

Parameter Name	Type	Description
Event	In	A data structure representing a event with detail
String	Out	An indication of a successful or unsuccessful save operation

The program flow within this Web Service method is relatively easy and is as follows:

1. Validate input as a proper event structure

2. Ensure required information exists – event date, subject, `OwnerUserID`

3. Determine if this event already exists

4. Save the new event record or update the existing event record

5. Return success or failure notification

The only twist that you may find in this method is the ability to create new database records or update existing records. There are probably quantifiable pros and cons to this approach, as opposed to having a distinct `UpdateEvent` method and a distinct `CreateEvent` method, but I look at it as a style issue. The purpose of combining both features into one Web Service method call is simplicity for the client. They build the event structure and send it to your `SaveEvent()` method regardless of whether it's a new event or not.

If you are thinking ahead and you read the previous chapter on Web Services and SOAP, you'll realize our `Event` parameter that we call a data structure is really a class, and that class will be serialized into a message for us by .NET.

Our possible error codes for this method will be wrapped up in the return parameter that the client receives, and they are in the following table:

Error Code	Description
ERROR_INVALID_PARAMETER	Invalid input parameter. An invalid event was detected.
ERROR_INVALID_USERID	Invalid `UserID`.
ERROR_DATABASE_CONNECT	Database error. Unable to connect to Calendar Web Service database.
ERROR_INTERNAL	Internal Error. A critical error has occurred within the Calendar application.

These error codes are just about identical to the `GetEvents()` error codes. For the sake of saving printed space, let's leave the error code lists out of our discussions from this point forward unless they become important in a particular portion of the code.

The GetTasks() Method

Very similar to `GetEvents()`, the `GetTasks()` method asks for a `StartDate`, `EndDate`, and `UserID`. It will return a list of Task details matching those input criteria. We also have the ability to share tasks – that is ask for someone else's tasks.

The input parameters are identical:

Parameter Name	Type	Description
StartDate	In	A date representing the start of the task period
EndDate	In	A date representing the end of the task period
OwnerUserID	In	The owner of events for which an task period is requested
DataSet	Out	A .NET DataSet containing the method results

The output parameter is still a DataSet type, but it will contain task details and task table information. Our client applications might do something a little different with the task information they receive. Instead of a day or week view that we might expect for a list of calendar events, tasks are less date- and time-oriented. They still have due dates and start and complete dates for progress monitoring, but they do not always have a specific start time and end time in the way that a calendar event might. For this reason, our clients will probably display them as a list of tasks for a particular day or a list of tasks with no time element at all, just any active task in the database for a particular user.

One nice thing about tasks is that they can be assigned to others as long as those individuals have a proper UserID. The OwnerUserID field is an effective way of showing ownership, sharing, and assigning any of the event and task data. Chances are we wouldn't be assigning events to someone else, so the assignment feature is really a task-oriented item. It would be nice to have someone go in your place to a boring meeting sometime so maybe that event assignment idea would be a nice feature for Microsoft to add to Outlook.

The SaveTask() Method

There is no appreciable difference between SaveEvent() and SaveTask(). The only real difference is the data structure we expect as input and the exact error code that could be returned. You'll see the Task class that represents that data soon. I already let the cat out the bag about how we are representing events and tasks.

Parameter Name	Type	Description
Task	In	A data structure representing a task with detail
String	Out	An indication of a successful or unsuccessful save operation

The GetReminders() Method

Retrieving reminders from the database is a little more interesting. Reminders do not exist as entities in and of themselves. Rather, they are properties or attributes of tasks and events. For instance, if I wanted to be warned of a scheduled phone call fifteen or twenty minutes before the actual phone call, I would set a reminder. In this case, the phone call would be an event with a set EventDate and a StartTime. The reminder itself only exists when two other fields are populated – the ReminderFlag and the ReminderDateTime. Both fields exist in the Event table and the Task table.

When we retrieve a list of reminders, we have to query both database tables using the same rules that we've already seen regarding current UserID and OwnerUserID, but we'll be returning a consolidated DataSet to our clients that contains both Event and Task reminder data.

Having applied a little foresight, our input and output parameters are the same as our other `GetTasks()` and `GetEvents()` service methods:

Parameter Name	Type	Description
StartDate	In	A date representing the start of the period
EndDate	In	A date representing the end of the period
OwnerUserID	In	The owner of events for which a period is requested
DataSet	Out	A .NET `DataSet` containing the method results

The program flow of the `GetReminders()` method should be similar to both `GetTasks()` and `GetEvents()`. The only difference is performing two queries on two different tables.

The RemoveReminder() Method

The last service method we'll discuss is designed to make it easy to disable reminders. Users of Microsoft Outlook will be familiar with that application's reminder Dismiss button. This method exists to do the same thing, except via a Web Service.

The `RemoveReminder()` method expects a unique identifier as one input parameter. It also expects another input parameter that qualifies the first. We use this combination to support passing in an `EventID` or a `TaskID` as the first parameter and what type of ID we passed in as the second parameter:

Parameter Name	Type	Description
ReminderID	In	A unique reminder ID – either an `EventID` or `TaskID`
ReminderType	In	A value that indicates if we are working with an Event or Task record
String	Out	An indication of a successful or unsuccessful delete operation

In the case of reminders, we don't really delete a record, we just set the `ReminderFlag` field to 'N' and blank out the `ReminderDateTime`. If we removed a reminder by deleting the record, we'd be removing a potentially needed Event or Task.

Having walked through our list of Web Service methods, let's spend a little time describing the clients we'll build for this case study and some of their characteristics. Immediately following this next section, we'll start building the actual `WroxCalendar` Web Service.

Calendar Service Application Clients

As we build the `WroxCalendar` Web Service application, it may be useful to imagine what our clients will look like and what kind of functionality they'll support. With that impression in our mind, our Web Service will probably be more useful. There is a saying that goes something like "start with the end in mind". It means understand what you are working toward and make decisions along the way based on the particular requirements of your goal, or your 'end'. In our case, the end is not just a good Web Service application, but client applications that can easily implement our Web Service functionality. If, as we've mentioned already, we intend to make any money with our Web Services or build a successful product regardless of revenue, we want to make life easy on the client application developers. If our stuff is hard to use or not intuitive, then it won't get used.

Calendar Service Implementation

We are finally ready to start building the server side of our Calendar Web Service. In this section, we'll be covering most of the details of implementing an ASP.NET Web Service. The actual code will be done in VB .NET. Along the way, we'll encounter some features of Visual Studio .NET that make our development lives a bit easier. We'll point those out as we go along.

Creating the ASP.NET Web Service

Assuming our database has been constructed, the first step in our development project is to create a new ASP.NET Web Service. The preceding Web Services overview covers this topic in some detail, so we will move quickly through some of the basic Visual Studio .NET work and focus instead on coding and implementation.

So, to create a new Web Service, Select Visual Basic Projects and then ASP.NET Web Service. Name your project WroxCalendar. The project name is just so your code and the case study code are similar. Here's what your first dialog box should look like:

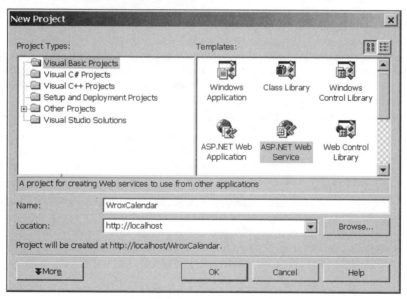

The location field should read http://servername where servername is your machine's name if you are running this locally and the name of your web server if you are using IIS on a different machine. I've personally yet to create a .NET project using Visual Studio .NET anywhere but my local machine, so use localhost. You'll see that machine name in all of our URLs in the upcoming examples and screenshots.

Once you press the OK button, Visual Studio .NET will try to create a new Web Application on your server. There are plenty of setup and configuration issues relative to IIS and actually having this process succeed. It is important to understand at this point that you do need IIS installed and running properly for the code in this case study to work. For this reason, I suggest doing all of your early development on your local machine. Once you get familiar with Visual Studio .NET and any particular quirks, then you could move it to some shared IIS instance. The most common error you might get here occurs when Visual Studio .NET cannot find the web server you named in the location field. If we tried to create a new Web Service project called SampleProject and IIS was disabled or the service was stopped, you'd see this error message:

As of this writing, we are using Visual Studio .NET Beta 2. That explains the **LAME!** button. If you press it, a browser page will open that allows you to send comments to the Visual Studio .NET development team.

If your new project was successfully created, you'll now be looking at the template Visual Studio .NET built for you. In the Solution Explorer find `Service1.asmx`. That's the main Web Service file. **Rename** it `WroxCalendar.asmx`. It is in `WroxCalendar.asmx` that we will create the interface our calendar service will present to client applications.

Open the file in code view. You can right-click and select **View Code** or find the first icon in the Solution Explorer and then press it. If you double-click on the file, you'll be taken to the **Design View** of the form associated with `WroxCalendar.asmx`. If you've worked with ASP.NET before, you'll notice the similarity in the way Visual Studio .NET works with Web Service pages and Web Form pages. As far as Visual Studio .NET is concerned, they are the same types of files just with different file extensions. We won't be using any controls for this case study. We could easily drag the `OleDbConnection` control on the design form, configure it, and use it in this application, but this author has shied away from data controls since their advent in VB 3 or VB 4. Maybe not the best logic in the world, but there you have it.

The strategy at this point is to create the methods in our Calendar Web Service in `WroxCalendar.asmx`, all seven or eight of them. Refer to the design information we listed earlier for a list of them all. Each method will then call a function or subroutine located elsewhere, in another class most likely. That gives us some flexibility for the future because all of our code is not wrapped up in one place. If, for some reason, we want to restructure our application, working with granular pieces of an application is far easier that trying to chop up a large, monolithic application.

Building the GetEvents() Method

So, let's create our first Web Service method. Since we've already said above that `GetEvents()` is probably our most important method, we'll start with it. In our design a few pages ago we specified that the `GetEvents()` method was responsible for returning all events for a particular user between a `StartDate` and an `EndDate`. With that already having been worked out (that's why we spent all those pages on higher-level design), we know that our `GetEvents()` function will look something like this when the coding is done (remember we are using VB .NET so watch the syntax):

```
Public Function GetEvents(dtStateDate as Date, _
                          dtEndDate as Date, _
                          sOwnerUserID as String) as DataSet


End Function
```

There is, of course, some Web Service-specific syntax we need to wrap around the GetEvents() function, so let's take that code snippet above and make it a real Web Service method. In the code view window of WroxCalendar.asmx, find the class definition that reads Public Class Service1. **Rename** the class WroxCalendarWS. Also you can delete the commented sample WebMethod code that Visual Studio .NET automatically puts in there. You should be looking at a relatively simple file now that looks like this (add the line Imports System.Web.Services.Protocols):

```
Imports System.Web.Services
Imports System.Web.Services.Protocols

Public Class WroxCalendarWS
    Inherits System.Web.Services.WebService

End Class
```

You've undoubtedly noticed the generated code. Don't mess with it. You can expand that line to see what that region contains, but the comments you'll find in there make it clear it shouldn't be modified. From this point on, you won't see any generated code in our examples, nor will we pay it much attention.

To create the GetEvents() method, type our code snippet from the last page into the WroxCalendarWS class. The Visual Studio .NET editor generally takes care of formatting, like tabs. The only additional step we have to take to expose this function as a Web Service method is adding one line immediately before our function definition. This is the directive (or keyword) that indicates to Visual Studio .NET that we are building a public function to be exposed as a part of the Calendar Web Service. Its basic syntax is very simple; just add <WebMethod()> before your function definition. We'll take it a little further by building a Description attribute into the WebMethod command. At this point, our GetEvents() function, without implementation code, is starting to take shape as something that Visual Studio .NET will recognize as a Web Service method.

```
<WebMethod(Description:="Returns a populated dataset containing all" & _
                       " Events between dtStartDate and dtEndDate.")> _
Public Function GetEvents(ByVal dtStartDate As Date, _
                          ByVal dtEndDate As Date, _
                          ByVal sOwnerUserId As String) As DataSet

End Function
```

We now have a true WebMethod named GetEvents() that accepts three input parameters – dtStartDate, dtEndDate, and sOwnerUserID.

The Web Service overview chapter showed us in some detail how Visual Studio .NET lets us test a Web Service in different stages of development. As a quick indicator of how successful we've been to this point in creating a real Web Service, save everything in Visual Studio .NET and press the Start button, use the Debug | Start menu, or press the *F5* key. A browser window should appear that looks something like the screenshot on the next page:

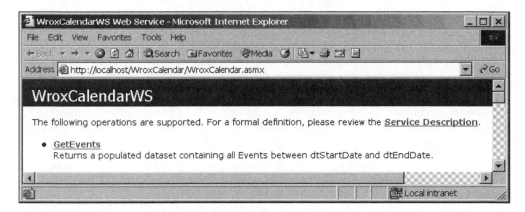

Notice the description underneath the **GetEvents** link, which is generated from the Description attribute we gave to the GetEvents() WebMethod. Click on the **GetEvents** link and you'll see a new window with a form that lists our three input parameters:

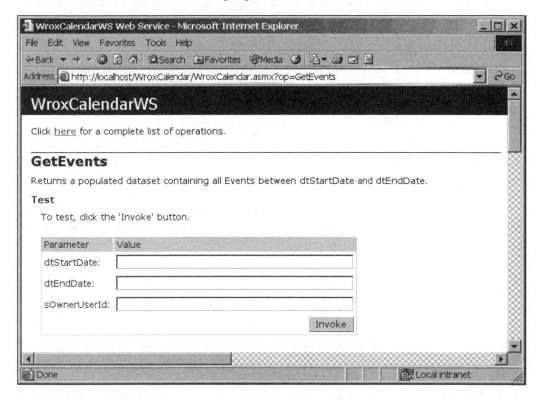

You can press the Invoke button now, but nothing will happen as there is no code for this particular function yet. It is useful to point out that setting a breakpoint in the code on the GetEvents() function definition line and then pressing the Invoke button will actually transfer control back to Visual Studio .NET as the debugger takes over. Keep that in mind as we build more functionality into this case study and your troubleshooting possibilities increase.

We know from the design work we've already done that this function is responsible for returning every event from the database between dtStartDate and dtEndDate for whichever sOwnerUserID is passed in. That's fine, we can meet that responsibility, but what about security? Don't we need to know who the current user is somehow? And what about the SubscriberID we talked about, how does that get input into this method?

If you recall, the design portion of this chapter hinted at delivering UserID, Password, and SubscriberID as a part of the message that our clients build and submit to the Web Service methods. We call that message a request. Server output is correspondingly called a response. Adding the UserID, Password, and SubscriberID to our input messages is easy because of some of the low-level work Visual Studio .NET does for us.

The first step in adding those three pieces of information is telling our Web Service code how and where to expect them. The browser screenshots on the last couple of pages clearly use HTTP-POST to get values into our Web Service method. That's OK, but we decided in our high-level design not to list the UserID, Password, and SubscriberID parameters in our function signatures. Every Web Service method in this application will want to use them so there needs to be a cleaner way of getting the values in.

Whether you've realized it yet or not, we've swerved into using SOAP (Simple Object Access Protocol) messages for our requests and responses. SOAP gives us the ability to require those three pieces of information in the SOAP Header element. That way, every request sent to our calendar service will always contain that information, otherwise an error is raised back to the client.

Enabling this in our simple GetEvents() function requires adding a bit more code to the WebMethod directive and a simple class to our project. First, we need to create a class that represents our three security fields. Let's call it AuthInfo and code it as follows (place this code immediately beneath the Imports statements):

```
Public Class AuthInfo
    Inherits SoapHeader

    Public SubscriberID As String
    Public UserID As String
    Public Password As String
End Class
```

AuthInfo has to be public so that Visual Studio .NET can create a proper proxy class. More on that later. The class also has to inherit SoapHeader. To get the SoapHeader class to work, you have to import System.Web.Services.Protocols. Other than those two items, it is a very simple class consisting of variables for each of our security fields.

Add the AuthInfo class to the WroxCalendar.asmx and create a public instance called authHeader inside the WroxCalendarWS class, as follows:

```
Public authHeader As AuthInfo
```

Now we have to tell the GetEvents() method itself to expect and support our new SOAP Header requirements. Make the following change to the GetEvents() function:

```
<WebMethod(Description:="Returns a populated dataset containing all " & _
                "Events between dtStartDate and dtEndDate."), _
                SoapHeader("authHeader")> _
Public Function GetEvents(ByVal dtStartDate As Date, _
                ByVal dtEndDate As Date, _
                ByVal sOwnerUserId As String) As DataSet

End Function
```

The `SoapHeader` attribute indicates that a `SoapHeader` should be expected for this method and to use the data structure found at `authHeader` to represent it. Our purposes are relatively simple, but you can see how complex data structures can be passed into functions using SOAP Headers. Visual Studio .NET makes all of this relatively easy for us to pull off by doing a lot of low-level, behind the scenes work for us.

In fact, we now know what our request and response messages will look like. Some of the work Visual Studio .NET does is to create the WSDL (Web Services Definition Language, see Chapter 13, *Web Services and SOAP*) that defines, among other things, what our SOAP request and response formats are. In the case of `GetEvents()` the SOAP request is:

```
<?xml version="1.0" encoding="utf-8"?>
<soap:Envelope xmlns:xsi="http://www.w3.org/2001/XMLSchema-instance"
               xmlns:xsd="http://www.w3.org/2001/XMLSchema"
               xmlns:soap="http://schemas.xmlsoap.org/soap/envelope/">
  <soap:Header>
    <AuthInfo xmlns="http://tempuri.org/">
      <SubscriberID>string</SubscriberID>
      <UserID>string</UserID>
      <Password>string</Password>
    </AuthInfo>
  </soap:Header>
  <soap:Body>
    <GetEvents xmlns="http://tempuri.org/">
      <dtStartDate>dateTime</dtStartDate>
      <dtEndDate>dateTime</dtEndDate>
      <sOwnerUserId>string</sOwnerUserId>
    </GetEvents>
  </soap:Body>
</soap:Envelope>
```

Notice the `<AuthInfo>` element in the `<soap:Header>`. As you would expect, it contains our three security properties, all of type string.

The SOAP response is a little simpler:

```
<?xml version="1.0" encoding="utf-8"?>
<soap:Envelope xmlns:xsi="http://www.w3.org/2001/XMLSchema-instance"
               xmlns:xsd="http://www.w3.org/2001/XMLSchema"
               xmlns:soap="http://schemas.xmlsoap.org/soap/envelope/">
  <soap:Body>
    <GetEventsResponse xmlns="http://tempuri.org/">
      <GetEventsResult>
        <xsd:schema>schema</xsd:schema>xml
      </GetEventsResult>
    </GetEventsResponse>
  </soap:Body>
</soap:Envelope>
```

The return is a little more cryptic. But notice the response we receive is called `<GetEventsResponse>` and the actual result, contained in `<GetEventsResult>`, is an XML schema and XML data. That is our `DataSet`. A SOAP Header is not necessary in the `GetEvents()` response.

We now have our Web Service method just about set up and ready to do some work. Our interface is taken care of – we know what should be passed in and what is returned by this function. We also have configured the `GetEvents()` method to require a SOAP Header as a part of the input request, and we've defined exactly what the contents of that header should be. Let's talk about how we are going to execute our code.

Recall from our earlier design conversations that we've decided the business rules and working code in this application will be separated from the Web Service file itself. Although we don't have a true UI, it still holds that separating your business logic from the interface (in our case a Web Service interface) is a proper design technique. The way we'll accomplish this is to create classes that expose the functionality that our Web Service methods require.

So, what we'll do is create another class that holds our database access code, among other things. In fact, we'll create classes for our events, tasks, and reminders. Each class will contain the functionality necessary to deliver the promises we've made with our earlier functional specifications. Let's start by adding another class to our Visual Studio .NET project. Call it `CalendarUtil.vb`.

When you create the new VB .NET class you get an empty class file. Create a new class within the `CalendarUtil.vb` file called `CalendarEvent`. We cannot call it just `Event` because that's a VB .NET reserved word.

It is within this class that all of our work will take place. The `WebMethod` functions we defined in `WroxCalendar.asmx` are merely stubs, or pass-through type functions, that gather parameters from our clients and pass them into the real worker functions in this class. As you might expect, all of the functionality for working with events will be contained within the `CalendarEvent` class. Similarly, we'll have classes for tasks and reminders as well, `CalendarTask` and `CalendarReminder` respectively.

The `CalendarEvent` class will have three functions – `GetEvents()`, `SaveEvent()`, and `RemoveEvent()`. Sounds familiar doesn't it? That's due to the pass-through nature of our `WebMethods`. Once we get this class built, the code we find in `WroxCalendar.asmx` is almost trivial.

Here's what `CalendarUtil.vb` looks like with our event, task, and reminder classes, as well as the necessary `Imports` statements:

```
Imports System.Data.OleDb
Imports System.Web.Services.Protocols

Public Class CalendarEvent
End Class

Public Class CalendarTask
End Class

Public Class CalendarReminder
End Class
```

Now, we'll add the code. Let's have a look at `CalendarEvent.GetEvents()`. Here's the code of an early implementation of this function. Remember to add this within the `CalendarEvent` class.

```
Public Class CalendarEvent

Private Const strConnect As String = _
    "Provider=SQLOLEDB;Data Source=localhost;" & _
    "Initial Catalog=WroxCalendar;Integrated Security=SSPI;"

Public Function GetEvents(ByVal dtStartDate As Date, _
                    ByVal dtEndDate As Date, _
                    ByVal sOwnerUserId As String, _
```

```
                        ByVal sCurrentUserID As String) As DataSet

    Dim strSQL As String
    Dim dsEvents As New DataSet()
    Dim conEvents As New OleDbConnection()
    Dim adpEvents As New OleDbDataAdapter()

    ' Basic input params validation
    If Not (IsDate(dtStartDate) And IsDate(dtEndDate)) Then
        'Error of some sort
    End If

    If sOwnerUserId = sCurrentUserID Or sOwnerUserId = vbNullString Then
        strSQL = "select EventID, OwnerUserID, GroupID, EventDate," & _
                 "Subject, StartTime, EndTime, Location, Notes " & _
                 "ReminderFlag, ReminderDateTime, Category " & _
                 "from Event " & _
                 "where EventDate >= '" & dtStartDate & "' " & _
                 "and EventDate <='" & dtEndDate & "' " & _
                 "and OwnerUserID ='" & sCurrentUserID & "' "
    Else
        ' Implement the Security Groups lookup here.
    End If

    conEvents.ConnectionString = strConnect
    adpEvents.SelectCommand = New OleDbCommand(strSQL, conEvents)
    adpEvents.Fill(dsEvents)

    Debug.Write(dsEvents.GetXml)

    Return dsEvents
End Function

End Class
```

Notice the input parameters are nearly identical to the parameters we require for the public WebMethod GetEvents(). The only difference is the last parameter, sCurrentUserID. If you recall, that value is passed into every WebMethod in the SOAP Header. You'll see how to get the current User ID when we get back to the WebMethod code.

First, we declare a constant called strConnect to hold the information we need to connect to our database. Then the function creates a SQL SELECT statement using the start and end dates, and the user information passed into it. It then uses an OleDbConnection to connect to our Calendar database and fills a DataSet with the results of executing the SELECT statement. The only real twist in the function is determining whether the user for which tasks have been requested, the sOwnerUserID parameter, is the current user, sCurrentUserID. If those two values are equal then we can assume some user has asked for their own calendar. If the two values are different then we have to do some more complicated processing to determine if the user making the request, sCurrentUserID, is actually allowed to see any events belonging to sOwnerUserID. We'll wrap all of this processing into another class called clsSecurityGroups, so let's leave that piece for the moment.

Once our SQL statement is built, three lines in this function do all of the work, the first of which simply sets the connection string of an existing OleDbConnection instance. The next line does several things in one line of code. Let's take a closer look:

```
adpEvents.SelectCommand = New OleDbCommand(strSQL, conEvents)
```

`adpEvents` is an instance of an `OleDBDataAdapter`, which is merely a bridge between an existing data source, like `conEvents`, and a `DataSet`. In the line of code above, the `SelectCommand` statement registers a SQL statement with our data adapter. In this case, the SQL statement is represented by an `OleDbCommand` instance. The `OleDbCommand` is created by `New OleDbCommand(strSQL, conEvents)`. In one line we create a new command that uses our existing connection and the SQL statement our code has already built and register it with our data adapter.

The next line fills our previously created `DataSet`, `dsEvents`, using the data adapter's `Fill()` method:

```
adpEvents.Fill(dsEvents)
```

Assuming the SQL statement actually returns some results, we now have a fully populated `DataSet` to be returned back to our client. Notice the `Debug.Write` statement that prints the contents of our newly created `dsEvents` to the output window. At this stage of development, we don't have a good client application up and running. This is a quick way to evaluate the contents of `dsEvents`. Of course, the debugging features of Visual Studio .NET give us many ways to view the value of variables at run time, but sometimes it is convenient to dump the contents somewhere and see them in a somewhat human-readable form.

This is not something you want to do in a production environment, but since our Web Service code doesn't have a real UI, it is nice to have a simple mechanism to verify results as we develop our `WebMethods`. The XML representation of some sample data in our event table looks like this:

```
<NewDataSet>
  <Table>
    <EventID>100</EventID>
    <OwnerUserID>jslater</OwnerUserID>
    <EventDate>2001-08-10T00:00:00.0000000-04:00</EventDate>
    <Subject>Review Chapter Outline</Subject>
    <StartTime>2001-12-30T13:00:00.0000000-05:00</StartTime>
    <EndTime>2001-12-30T14:00:00.0000000-05:00</EndTime>
    <Location>John's Office</Location>
    <Notes>1</Notes>
  </Table>
  <Table>
    <EventID>101</EventID>
    <OwnerUserID>jslater</OwnerUserID>
    <EventDate>2001-08-10T00:00:00.0000000-04:00</EventDate>
    <Subject>Write Chapter 17</Subject>
    <StartTime>1899-12-30T14:00:00.0000000-05:00</StartTime>
    <EndTime>1899-12-30T15:00:00.0000000-05:00</EndTime>
    <Location>John's Office</Location>
    <Notes>2</Notes>
  </Table>
  <Table>
    <EventID>102</EventID>
    <OwnerUserID>jslater</OwnerUserID>
    <EventDate>2001-08-10T00:00:00.0000000-04:00</EventDate>
    <Subject>Rewrite Chapter 16</Subject>
    <StartTime>1899-12-30T15:00:00.0000000-05:00</StartTime>
    <EndTime>1899-12-30T16:00:00.0000000-05:00</EndTime>
    <Location>John's Office</Location>
    <Notes>3</Notes>
  </Table>
</NewDataSet>
```

That happens to be the XML representation of the calendar events for a user named jslater. The data is bogus, but otherwise, valid. This is what the client can expect to receive from our GetEvents() WebMethod. It will be wrapped in a SOAP request, of course.

At this point we have a functioning business class for our GetEvents() function. It is a very simple function that does little more than find all events for a particular user between particular dates, but that fundamentally is what a calendar application does. Existing calendar apps like Outlook add many more features with a tremendous amount of flexibility, but the basic responsibility that application and others like it have is displaying a particular day's scheduled events. We've just built that feature into our application, now let's make sure our clients can get to it.

Switch back to WroxCalendar.asmx and our WroxCalendarWS class. Let's add the code to our existing WebMethod definition that calls the CalendarEvent class GetEvents() function. Since all of the details of GetEvents() are not totally relevant in CalendarEvent, we only need a few lines of code to pull this off and make it all work.

The first thing to do is create an instance of CalendarEvent and an instance of a DataSet for our return parameter.

```
        Dim oEvent As New CalendarEvent()
        Dim dstResults As New DataSet()
```

Now, set the value of dstResults equal to the value returned by the function CalendarEvent.GetEvents(). The line of code that does it is:

```
    dstResults = oEvent.GetEvents(dtStartDate, dtEndDate, _
                            sOwnerUserId, authHeader.UserID)
```

That's it. Let's assume that it is appropriate to return to our client whatever CalendarEvent.GetEvents() returns to our WebMethod. Depending on what type of errors CalendarEvent.GetEvents() generates, that may be a dangerous assumption. There is a final line of code that actually returns our DataSet, but any function requires the Return statement.

Your entire class, including the AuthInfo definition, now should look something like this:

```
    Imports System.Web.Services
    Imports System.Web.Services.Protocols

    Public Class AuthInfo
        Inherits SoapHeader

        Public SubscriberID As String
        Public UserID As String
        Public Password As String
    End Class

    Public Class WroxCalendarWS
        Inherits System.Web.Services.WebService

        Public authHeader As New AuthInfo

    <WebMethod(Description:="Returns a populated dataset containing all " & _
                    "Events between dtStartDate and dtEndDate."), _
```

```
                            SoapHeader("authHeader")>  _
         Public Function GetEvents(ByVal dtStartDate As Date, _
                                   ByVal dtEndDate As Date, _
                                   ByVal sOwnerUserId As String) As DataSet

             Dim oEvent As New CalendarEvent()
             Dim dstResults As New DataSet()

             dstResults = oEvent.GetEvents(dtStartDate, dtEndDate, _
                                           sOwnerUserId, authHeader.UserID)

             Return dstResults
         End Function
```

GetTasks() is a very similar function implemented within CalendarUtil.vb just like
CalendarEvent, except that, of course, it is contained within the CalendarTask class. The
framework we've built including the Visual Studio .NET project and the WroxCalendarWS class makes
building the task functionality almost a matter of copying CalendarEvent code and the GetEvents()
WebMethod code and making minor modifications to support task functionality.

The only real different between the two functions, GetEvents() and GetTasks(), is the code in the
CalendarTask.GetTasks() function. And even there, we only have one line to change, the SQL
SELECT statement:

```
    strSQL = "select TaskID, OwnerUserID, GroupID, TaskDate, DueDateTime, " & _
             "Subject, StartDate, CompleteDate, Notes, ReminderFlag, " & _
             "ReminderDateTime, Status, Priority, EstimatedHours, " & _
             "ActualHours, Category" & _
             "from Task " & _
             "where TaskDate >= '" & dtStartDate & "' " & _
             "and TaskDate <='" & dtEndDate & "' " & _
             "and OwnerUserID ='" & sCurrentUserID & "' "
```

The SELECT statement gets records from the task table following the same scheme as the GetEvents()
function. It literally retrieves all tasks from the database for a particular user between two given dates.
Just like GetEvents(), GetTasks() generates and returns a DataSet. Since the functions are so
similar, we won't cover GetTasks() in any more detail.

Building the SaveEvent() Method

Now that we have a method for retrieving our calendar events and tasks, we need the ability to save them.
Just like the similarity between the methods to return events and tasks, the methods for saving events and
tasks are very similar. The data, obviously, is different, but the structure of our implementation and how
clients will implement these methods is so similar that we'll cover only one of the two – SaveEvent().

SaveEvent() does one thing, it saves an event, but it can save using one of two methods. In the case of
a new event, SaveEvent() executes a database insert. If SaveEvent() determines than an event
already exists, it executes an update.

We'll use the existing framework that we established with GetEvents() and GetTasks(), so the discussion of SaveEvent() should be relatively straightforward. First, we need a function definition in our Web Service class, WroxCalendarWS. From our design portion of this case study we know that the SaveEvent() method takes one parameter as input – an EventData structure represented by a VB .NET class. We also know that SaveEvent() returns a string as an output parameter.

The SaveEvent() WebMethod will seem similar to GetEvents(), except for the input and output parameters.

```
<WebMethod(Description:="Saves the event described by oEvent."), _
        SoapHeader("authHeader")> _
    Public Function SaveEvent(ByVal oEventData As EventData) As String
        Dim oEvent As New CalendarEvent()
        Dim dstResults As New DataSet()

        oEvent.SaveEvent(oEventData)
    End Function
```

Notice we still include the SoapHeader("authHeader") for this WebMethod. The single input parameter is a class that represents a particular event. It is exclusively used to represent event data - there are no methods in this class - hence the EventData name. It is merely a collection of properties of any event as the following code shows. This class should be defined in the CalendarUtil.vb file.

```
Public Class EventData
    Public EventID As String
    Public OwnerUserID As String
    Public GroupId As String
    Public Subject As String
    Public EventDate As Date
    Public StartTime As Date
    Public EndTime As Date
    Public Location As String
    Public Notes As String
    Public ReminderFlag As Boolean
    Public ReminderDateTime As Date
    Public ReminderType As String
    Public Category As String
    Public DBAction As DBActionTypes
End Class
```

If you read the Web Service overview chapter immediately preceding this case study, you might be able to guess that our client applications will use a Web Service proxy class. Since we have made the assumption that all of our clients will be .NET applications, we can also assume that they will be able to implement proxy classes that will help define and represent items like this class EventData. In other words, our client implementation won't have to worry about the details of formatting a SOAP request that contains an XML representation of EventData. Visual Studio .NET will do all of that for us.

If we want to support clients that are not built using .NET, we can do that too, but it will take a little more work on the client side. For instance, the raw SOAP request for SaveEvent() looks like this:

```
<?xml version="1.0" encoding="utf-8"?>
<soap:Envelope xmlns:xsi="http://www.w3.org/2001/XMLSchema-instance"
              xmlns:xsd="http://www.w3.org/2001/XMLSchema"
              xmlns:soap="http://schemas.xmlsoap.org/soap/envelope/">
  <soap:Header>
```

```
      <AuthInfo xmlns="http://tempuri.org/">
        <SubscriberID>string</SubscriberID>
        <UserID>string</UserID>
        <Password>string</Password>
      </AuthInfo>
    </soap:Header>
    <soap:Body>
      <SaveEvent xmlns="http://tempuri.org/">
        <oEventData>
          <EventID>string</EventID>
          <OwnerUserID>string</OwnerUserID>
          <GroupId>string</GroupId>
          <Subject>string</Subject>
          <EventDate>dateTime</EventDate>
          <StartTime>dateTime</StartTime>
          <EndTime>dateTime</EndTime>
          <Location>string</Location>
          <Notes>string</Notes>
          <ReminderFlag>boolean</ReminderFlag>
          <ReminderDateTime>dateTime</ReminderDateTime>
          <ReminderType>string</ReminderType>
          <Category>string</Category>
          <DBAction>dbaNoChange or dbaInsertRecord or dbaUpdateRecord or
                    dbaDeleteRecord</DBAction>
        </oEventData>
      </SaveEvent>
    </soap:Body>
  </soap:Envelope>
```

A non-.NET developer can easily create the SOAP message programmatically, given the example above. It's still easier to let .NET do the grunt work for us, though. Notice the DBAction element near the end of the request. It can contain one of four different values that have obvious purposes. Those values come from the following enumerator that helps us wrap updates and inserts into the SaveEvent() function. Enter the following Enum at the top of CalendarUtil.vb:

```
Public Enum DBActionTypes
    dbaNoChange = 0
    dbaInsertRecord = 1
    dbaUpdateRecord = 2
    dbaDeleteRecord = 3
End Enum
```

As you might expect, the WebMethod is another pass-through function. The real work for saving event information is conducted in the CalendarEvent.SaveEvent() function in our business class, which actually performs all of our database operations. Add the following code to the CalendarUtil.vb file in the CalendarEvent class:

```
Public Function SaveEvent(ByVal oEvent As EventData) As String
    Dim myConn As New OleDbConnection(strConnect)
    Dim strSQL As String
    Dim intRows As Integer

    Select Case oEvent.DBAction
        Case DBActionTypes.dbaNoChange
            ' do nothing
        Case DBActionTypes.dbaInsertRecord
```

```
                ' insert new record into Event table.
        strSQL = "INSERT INTO Event(EventID, OwnerUserID, GroupID, " & _
                 "EventDate, Subject, StartTime, EndTime, Location, " & _
                 "Notes, ReminderFlag, ReminderDateTime, Category) " & _
                 "Values('" & GetAutoSeqValue("EventID") & "','" & _
                 oEvent.OwnerUserID & "','" & oEvent.GroupId & "','" & _
                 oEvent.EventDate & "','" & oEvent.Subject & "','" & _
                 oEvent.StartTime & "','" & oEvent.EndTime & "','" & _
                 oEvent.Location & "','" & oEvent.Notes & "','" & _
                 IIf(oEvent.ReminderFlag, "Y", "N") & "','" & _
                 oEvent.ReminderDateTime & "','" & oEvent.Category & "')"
    Case DBActionTypes.dbaUpdateRecord
        ' update existing record using oEvent.EventID
        strSQL = "UPDATE Event " & _
                 "set OwnerUserId = '" & oEvent.OwnerUserID & "'," & _
                 "GroupdID = '" & oEvent.GroupId & "'," & _
                 "EventDate = '" & oEvent.EventDate & "'," & _
                 "Subject = '" & oEvent.Subject & "'," & _
                 "StartTime = '" & oEvent.StartTime & "'," & _
                 "EndTime = '" & oEvent.EndTime & "'," & _
                 "Location = '" & oEvent.Location & "'," & _
                 "Notes = '" & oEvent.Notes & "'," & _
                 "ReminderFlag = '" & oEvent.ReminderFlag & "'," & _
                 "ReminderDateTime = '" & oEvent.ReminderDateTime & _
                 "'," & _
                 "Category = '" & oEvent.Category & "'," & _
                 "WHERE EventID = '" & oEvent.EventID & "'"
    Case DBActionTypes.dbaDeleteRecord
        ' delete existing record using oEvent.EventID
        strSQL = "DELETE from Event where EventID = '" & _
                 oEvent.EventID & "'"
End Select

Dim myOleDbCommand As New OleDbCommand(strSQL)
myOleDbCommand.Connection = myConn
myConn.Open()
intRows = myOleDbCommand.ExecuteNonQuery()
myOleDbCommand.Connection.Close()

Return CType(intRows, String)
End Function
```

In the preceding code notice the `Select Case` structure. Using the value of `oEvent.DBAction`, we can determine what type of save operation to perform. Not only are inserts and updates consolidated into one `SaveEvent()` function, but we also have the ability to delete event records. `oEvent.DBAction` gets set on the client side and is passed into our Calendar Web Service as one of the `DBActionTypes` enumerator values we listed previously.

If we detect `dbaInsertRecord` in `DBAction` then our `SaveEvent()` function will build an `INSERT` statement. Similarly, if `SaveEvent()` encounters `dbaUpdateRecord` then an `UPDATE` statement will be generated. The last case in the `Select Case` structure is `dbaDeleteRecord`. It grabs the `EventID` and builds a `DELETE` SQL statement using that unique identifier to remove that event record.

Once our SQL statement is built, the code creates a new `OleDbCommand` instance and executes the query using `ExecuteNonQuery`, which is used to run `UPDATE`, `INSERT`, and `DELETE` SQL statements and returns no rows - perfect for our purposes in `SaveEvent()`. In fact, `ExecuteNonQuery` actually returns a total number of rows the SQL statement affected. It may not be entirely elegant, but we'll return that result from our `SaveEvent()` function as an indication of success or failure.

You may have notice within the `Insert` SQL statement a function called `GetAutoSeqValue()`. This function is used to fetch a new auto sequence number from the `AutoSequence` table in our database. We will not list the function here but it is, of course, available in the code download.

Let's use the same reasoning for `SaveTask()` as we did for `GetTasks()` – the event processing code is so similar it doesn't really make sense to review the `SaveTask()` code in any detail. Its implementation is very similar to `SaveEvent()` with just table and field names changing. The only key difference is the use of a `TaskData` class that contains some task-specific information. Just like `EventData`, the `TaskData` class should be built in our `CalendarUtil.vb` file:

```
Public Class TaskData
    Public TaskID As String
    Public OwnerUserID As String
    Public GroupId As String
    Public Subject As String
    Public TaskDate As Date
    Public DueDateTime As Date
    Public ReminderFlag As Boolean
    Public ReminderDateTime As Date
    Public ReminderType As String
    Public Status As String
    Public StartDate As Date
    Public CompleteDate As Date
    Public Priority As String
    Public EstimatedHours As Integer
    Public ActualHours As Integer
    Public Category As String
    Public DBAction As DBActionTypes
End Class
```

`TaskData` has an identical role to `EventData`. It does, however, result is a slightly different SOAP request:

```xml
<?xml version="1.0" encoding="utf-8"?>
<soap:Envelope xmlns:xsi="http://www.w3.org/2001/XMLSchema-instance"
               xmlns:xsd="http://www.w3.org/2001/XMLSchema"
               xmlns:soap="http://schemas.xmlsoap.org/soap/envelope/">
  <soap:Header>
    <AuthInfo xmlns="http://tempuri.org/">
      <SubscriberID>string</SubscriberID>
      <UserID>string</UserID>
      <Password>string</Password>
    </AuthInfo>
  </soap:Header>
  <soap:Body>
    <SaveTask xmlns="http://tempuri.org/">
      <oTask>
        <TaskID>string</TaskID>
        <OwnerUserID>string</OwnerUserID>
        <GroupId>string</GroupId>
        <Subject>string</Subject>
```

```
              <TaskDate>dateTime</TaskDate>
              <DueDateTime>dateTime</DueDateTime>
              <ReminderFlag>boolean</ReminderFlag>
              <ReminderDateTime>dateTime</ReminderDateTime>
              <ReminderType>string</ReminderType>
              <Status>string</Status>
              <StartDate>dateTime</StartDate>
              <CompleteDate>dateTime</CompleteDate>
              <Priority>string</Priority>
              <EstimatedHours>int</EstimatedHours>
              <ActualHours>int</ActualHours>
              <Category>string</Category>
              <DBAction>dbaNoChange or dbaInsertRecord or dbaUpdateRecord or
                        dbaDeleteRecord</DBAction>
          </oTask>
       </SaveTask>
     </soap:Body>
  </soap:Envelope>
```

Building the RemoveEvent() Method

The RemoveEvent() and RemoveTask() methods are the simplest of all. The SQL statement can be shown on a single line:

```
strSQL = "DELETE from Event where EventID='" & strEventID & "'"
```

Let's move on and have a look at the GetReminders() function, and that will about do it for our core Calendar Web Service code.

Building the GetReminders() Method

Recall that reminders can be associated with either a task or an event and that reminders themselves are merely attributes of those items. To find all reminders that should be raised for a particular user, we are merely going to find all tasks or events that have a ReminderDateTime that is between a StartDate and a StopDate and the ReminderFlag field has a value of 'Y'.

The interesting thing here is returning one DataSet from two different tables. Since our Event and Task table structures are relatively similar, we can pull this off without too much effort. The idea is to return only enough information to make a usable reminder in a client application, but allow the same function, GetReminders(), to generate the returned DataSet.

By executing two different SQL statements and returning only the fields that the task and event tables have in common, we can create a generic DataSet. For instance, to get all of our event reminders for a Start and Stop date range with a particular sOwnerUserID, we'd use the following code to build our SQL:

```
strSQL = "select EventID as ReminderID, OwnerUserID, GroupID, " & _
        "'Event' as ReminderType, Subject, Notes, ReminderFlag," & _
        "ReminderDateTime " & _
        "from Event " & _
        "where ReminderDateTime >= '" & dtStartDate & "' " & _
        "and ReminderDateTime <='" & dtEndDate & "' " & _
        "and OwnerUserID ='" & sCurrentUserID & "' " & _
        "and ReminderFlag = 'Y' "
```

The SQL just grabs any event record with a `ReminderFlag` turned on, equal to `'Y'`, and a `ReminderDateTime` between the standard Start and Stop dates. But look at the field list. There are a couple of tricks buried in there. First notice the `EventID` value is renamed `ReminderID` in the SQL results. By renaming `EventID` (and `TaskID` below) to a generic `ReminderID`, we can use the same `DataSet` to represent both types of reminders. Also notice the `'Event'` as `ReminderType` as the fourth element. That is a quick and dirty method for hard-coding a reminder type value. We know that the particular piece of SQL will always generate event reminders, so something like this is safe, if not elegant.

Similarly our task reminder SQL is almost identical. Literally change the `EventID` field to a `TaskID` and change the table name to read `Task` and you can reuse the SQL.

```
strSQL = "select TaskID as ReminderID, OwnerUserID, GroupID, " & _
         "'Task' as ReminderType, Subject, Notes, ReminderFlag," & _
         "ReminderDateTime " & _
         "from Task " & _
         "where ReminderDateTime >= '" & dtStartDate & "' " & _
         "and ReminderDateTime <='" & dtEndDate & "' " & _
         "and OwnerUserID ='" & sCurrentUserID & "' " & _
         "and ReminderFlag = 'Y' "
```

After each query executes we can use the `Fill()` method to fill the same `DataSet` just as our `GetTasks()` and `GetEvents()` methods work now using this one line of code:

```
adpReminders.Fill(dsReminders)
```

We are taking advantage of the fact that each `Fill()` method call is not destructive to the `DataSet`.

Implementing Event and Task Sharing

One of the features of our Calendar Web Service is the ability to share events and tasks between users. A client application can share by setting the `GroupID` property of an event or a task to some recognized group identifier. When a non-owner asks to see that particular event or task item, the application will realize that they are not the original owner and check their group membership. If the non-owner is a member of a group that matches the `GroupID` of the event or task, then they receive a record with that item's detail. Otherwise, they don't have any indication that the record exists, and remain none the wiser.

There are a couple of extra tables we talked about during the design section in this chapter – `Users`, `Group` and `UserGroup`. If you recall (I'm afraid there are more pages between us now and the original design discussion that I had planned), the `UserGroup` table contained records that indicated a user's membership in a group. The user would be identified by `UserID` and the group would be identified by `GroupID`. There is also a `type` field used to indicate the type or level of membership a particular `UserID` has in a group. We'll leave the implementation of the membership qualifier and maintenance module of our `Users`, `Group`, and `UserGroup` tables to an enterprising reader.

This whole sharing concept is helped out by the implementation of a new class called `SecurityGroups`, which actually gets its own file. It seemed to make sense to put this off on its own since its complexity would grow over time and has application in more places than this particular application.

Let's take a look at the code. In the section of our `GetEvents()` and `GetTasks()` code, we left an `Else` block empty with a comment promising to revisit the sharing issue. The code we'll implement in place of that IOU comment is simply another way to write the `SELECT` SQL statement, but with a bit of a twist to implement our sharing scheme. If we detect the current user is not the owner of the events or tasks being requested, we know we have a sharing situation on our hands and need to turn to our `UserGroup` table. The resulting query we build should, in plain English, read something like "return to me all of the event, task, and reminder records between the start and stop dates that have a `GroupID` in the set of `GroupID`'s belonging to the current user."

Somehow we need to know what `GroupID`'s belong to the current user. No problem, we say, because we have the class `SecurityGroups` and that does the work for us. All we have to do is add a line to the `WHERE` clause of our `SELECT` statement asking that, among other things, we receive in our `DataSet` rows that have a `GroupID` in the set of `GroupID`'s to which our current user belongs. The `If...Then` structure looks like this; notice the last line of the second SQL statement as it is the only one that has changed:

```
If sOwnerUserId = sCurrentUserID Or sOwnerUserId = vbNullString Then
    strSQL = "select EventID, OwnerUserID, GroupID, EventDate," & _
            "Subject, StartTime, EndTime, Location", Notes " & _
            "ReminderFlag, ReminderDateTime, Category " & _
            "from Event " & _
            "where EventDate >= '" & dtStartDate & "' " & _
            "and EventDate <='" & dtEndDate & "' " & _
            "and OwnerUserID ='" & sCurrentUserID & "' "
Else
    ' Implement the Security Groups lookup here.
    Dim oGroups As New SecurityGroups()
    strSQL = "select EventID, OwnerUserID, GroupID, EventDate," & _
            "Subject, StartTime, EndTime, Location, Notes " & _
            "ReminderFlag, ReminderDateTime, Category " & _
            "from Event " & _
            "where EventDate >= '" & dtStartDate & "' " & _
            "and EventDate <='" & dtEndDate & "' " & _
            "and GroupID in(" & oGroups.GetSecurityGroups(sOwnerUserId) & ")"
End If
```

As you can probably guess, `SecurityGroups.GetSecurityGroups` returns a comma-delimited list of `GroupID`'s. By separating this code into another class, we have the ability not only to share the `SecurityGroups` functionality between applications, but we also have the ability to increase its capabilities or complexity as the need arises. When you see the code, you'll notice how simple it really is. I doubt it could survive long in a production environment as it stands now.

The entire `SecurityGroups` class as it stands now contains only the one function we've seen in use, `GetSecurityGroups()`. The code creates the standard `OleDbConnection` and `OleDbCommand` combination to execute a `SELECT` statement. The difference between this bit of database code and the other examples we've seen is the inclusion of an `OleDbReader` to read our stream of `UserGroup` records. `SecurityGroups.vb` should contain the following code:

```
Imports System.Data.OleDb

Public Class SecurityGroups

    Private Const strConnect As String = _
                "Provider=SQLOLEDB;Data Source=localhost;" & _
                "Initial Catalog=WroxCalendar;Integrated Security=SSPI;"
```

```
Public Function GetSecurityGroups(ByVal sUserId As String) As String

    Dim strSQL As String
    Dim sGroups As String = vbNullString

    strSQL = _
        "Select groupid from usergroup where userid = '" & sUserId & "'"

    Dim conUserGroups As New OleDbConnection(strConnect)
    Dim cmdUserGroups As New OleDbCommand(strSQL, conUserGroups)
    conUserGroups.Open()
    Dim rdrUserGroups As OleDbDataReader = cmdUserGroups.ExecuteReader()
    Try
        While rdrUserGroups.Read()
            sGroups = sGroups & rdrUserGroups.GetInt32(0).ToString() & ", "
        End While
    Finally
        rdrUserGroups.Close()
        conUserGroups.Close()
    End Try

End Function

End Class
```

Once the query executes properly, we loop through the resulting set of data using the
`OleDbDataReader.Read()` method, in this case named `rdrUserGroups.Read()`. Once the loop is
complete, the `Finally` section of code executes, cleaning up our reader and connection.

If you run the application now you should be presented with something like the following screenshot:

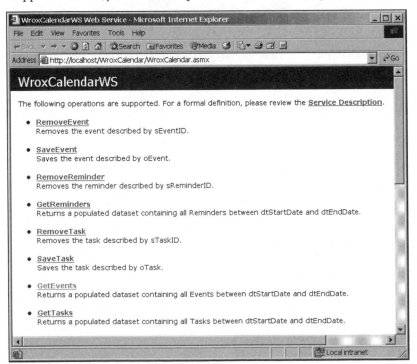

Notice, however, that if you now click on the GetEvents link you will not be presented with the new window you saw earlier that presented the list of the three input parameters. You will be presented with a screen stating that no test form is available as the service does not support the HTTP GET protocol. You should see something like the following screenshot:

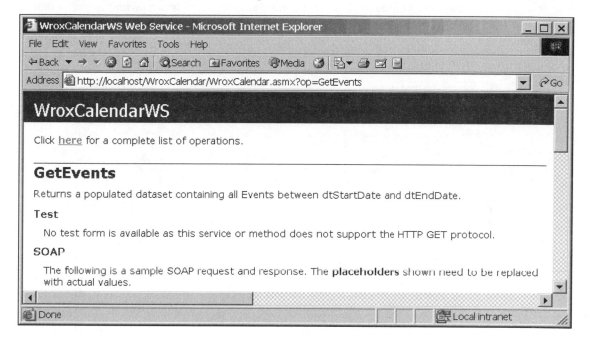

Calendar Service Client Implementation

Well, it looks like we are ready to build a simple client, or two, to test out our Calendar Web Service. We've mentioned before that we need to support web and desktop clients. Let's take the web client first and then the desktop client. Both will be written in VB .NET and you'll find that the core functionality necessary to implement the WroxCalendar Web Service is remarkably similar. In fact, when you get right down to it, the Web Service implementation code isn't the biggest portion of the client development process, in terms of time or complexity. It's all the other things you have to wrap around the Web Service integration that take time and effort.

Building an ASP.NET Web Client

We'll tackle a web application first. Let's play the part of a third-party developer who needs to get a simple calendar application up and running as quickly as possible. We know now that building a simple calendar application isn't too daunting, but put yourself in the shoes of a harried developer. If our application promises just enough features and doesn't cost too much in terms of licensing or integration time, then the Calendar Web Service might seem an attractive solution.

If you can, envision an application that lists for its users all events and tasks for a particular day, week, or month. All three item types are displayed in a browser window encoded in HTML. That's basically what our web application is going to look like. The ASP.NET application will be responsible for sending requests to the WroxCalendar Web Service we just build in the preceding section and formatting its results into something useful to the application's users. Since it's easier to start with the end in mind, here's a screenshot of what our application might look like when we're done:

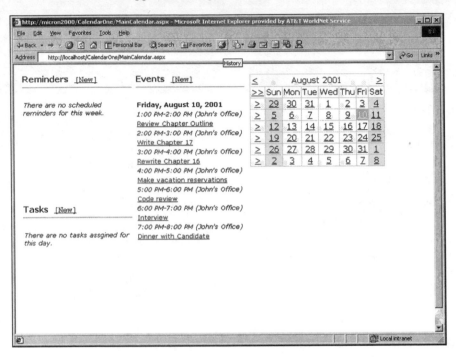

You'll notice simple Events, Tasks, and Reminders lists plus a .NET calendar control to help change the days, weeks, and months. This is what we are working towards for the web application. As we review each section, it might be useful to refer back to this screenshot.

The first thing to do for a client application is to start a new Visual Studio .NET project. Once again we'll select Visual Basic .NET as our development language of choice, but select ASP.NET Web Application this time instead of ASP.NET Web Service. You'll get a very similar looking project created for you to that for the Web Service project. Notice that the main ASP.NET file has an .aspx extension and not the .asmx that stands for Web Services.

In the following sample code, the project is named CalendarOne. The default WebForm1.aspx should be renamed to MainCalendar.aspx. The Calendar Web Service is running on the same machine as the client applications. It's more convenient from a development standpoint to do that because you'll undoubtedly be changing both sides at the same time and having them close to each other and both under your control makes synchronizing code on the server and client easier in the early stages of development.

Creating the Main Calendar View

Our web application will consist of one main page for displaying tasks, events and reminders with a few other pages for editing events and tasks. The main page is simply an `asp:Table` with its `ID` property set to `MainCalendar`. The first `asp:TableRow` consists of three `asp:TableCells`. The first cell contains our Reminders, the next contains our Events, and the third contains a .NET calendar control that makes switching between day, week, and month views easier. The second row contains a single `asp:TableCell` for current tasks.

The ASP.NET design-time code for the HTML Form in the main calendar view is a little different from HTML tables you may be familiar with:

```
<%@ Page Language="vb" AutoEventWireup="false"
        Codebehind="MainCalendar.aspx.vb"
        Inherits="CalendarOne.WroxCalendar"%>
<!DOCTYPE HTML PUBLIC "-//W3C//DTD HTML 4.0 Transitional//EN">
<HTML>
<HEAD>
<title></title>
  <meta name="GENERATOR" content="Microsoft Visual Studio.NET 7.0">
  <meta name="CODE_LANGUAGE" content="Visual Basic 7.0">
  <meta name="vs_defaultClientScript" content="JavaScript">
  <meta name="vs_targetSchema"
        content="http://schemas.microsoft.com/intellisense/ie5">
</HEAD>
<body MS_POSITIONING="GridLayout">
<form id="Form1" method="post" runat="server">
  <asp:Table id="MainCalendar" style="Z-INDEX: 102; LEFT: 13px; TOP: 15px"
          runat="server" Height="532px" Width="90%" CellSpacing="3"
          CellPadding="3">
   <asp:TableRow>
     <asp:TableCell VerticalAlign="Top" Width="25%" ID="Reminders">
       <font face='Verdana'><b>Reminders</b></font><hr size="1">
     </asp:TableCell>
     <asp:TableCell VerticalAlign="Top" RowSpan="2" Width="45%"
               ID="CalendarEvents">
       <font face='Verdana'><b>Events</b></font><hr size="1">
     </asp:TableCell>
     <asp:TableCell VerticalAlign="Top" RowSpan="2" Width="30%"
               HorizontalAlign="Right" ID="CalendarControl">
       <asp:Calendar runat="server" ShowGridLines="True"
               BackColor="WhiteSmoke" Height="117px"
               Font-Names="Verdana" Width="163px"
               ID="DisplayCalendar">
         <WeekendDayStyle BackColor="#C0FFFF"></WeekendDayStyle>
         <TodayDayStyle BorderWidth="1px" BorderStyle="Solid"
                   BorderColor="IndianRed" BackColor="Transparent">
         </TodayDayStyle>
         <TitleStyle BorderStyle="Double" BackColor="Transparent">
         </TitleStyle>
       </asp:Calendar>
     </asp:TableCell>
   </asp:TableRow>
   <asp:TableRow>
     <asp:TableCell VerticalAlign="Top" Width="25%" ID="Tasks">
       <font face='Verdana'><b>Tasks</b></font><hr size="1">
     </asp:TableCell>
   </asp:TableRow>
```

```
        </asp:Table>
    </form>
    </body>
    </HTML>
```

When viewed in a browser, this code gives us a decent framework for building our event, task, and reminder displays. The `asp:Table` is not unlike HTML tables you may be familiar with in terms of laying out our rows and columns. Look closely at the code above and you'll see the table structure. There are two rows – `asp:TableRow`. The first row contains three cells or `asp:TableCell`; one each for our Reminders, Events, and the .NET Calendar control. The last two cells, or columns, have their `RowSpan=2` to force them to scroll over top of the second row, immediately below. That gives the effect you can see in the screenshot above where the Event list scrolls past the Task list.

Notice the ID values of each of the Event, Reminder, and Task `asp:TableCell`'s. This will become important shortly because we will simply set the `Text` attribute of each of the `asp:TableCell`'s to be the results of our Calendar Web Service. We are taking a relatively simple approach to formatting the HTML page served to the client, as you are about to see.

The basic approach here is to fill in the `Text` property of each of our table cells. We'll invoke each Web Service method in turn getting Events, Tasks, and Reminders for a particular user. Our job as a client that consumes the Web Service is to reformat the results we receive however we want. In our case, we'll be building little HTML tables in code and dropping them into the structure we've just built using the `asp:Table`.

With our main Web Form built, our Visual Studio .NET project should look something like the following screenshot. Let's not walk through the steps necessary to get here; that's been covered enough already in other chapters. If you have something close, you're ready to go. I took the liberty of modifying the Calendar control's properties for colors and font because I couldn't help messing with it; yours does not have to be similar, the only functionality we need is the date selection.

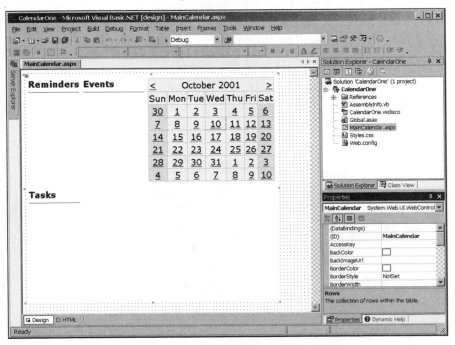

Adding the WroxCalendar Web Reference

We have our UI structure built, now we have to start the process of filling in that structure with data. To talk to our WroxCalendar Web Service we need to create a reference. The process was covered in some detail in Chapter 13, so let's do it quickly here and see what we get. One thing to keep in mind is that you need your Web Service running somewhere you can browse to. For development purposes at this early stage, I like them on the same machine, mainly for debugging.

Right-click on the References node in the solution explorer and select Add Web Reference. Follow the wizard to add a Web Reference. Since you know explicitly where this Web Service is running, you can type the patch in the address field. If you get the address correct, you'll see a wizard dialog like the following (using the Web References on Local Web Server link):

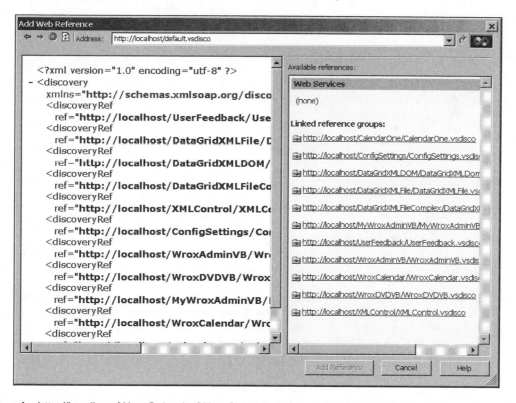

Select the http://localhost/WroxCalendar/WroxCalendar/vsdisco link in the right-hand pane, which displays all the linked reference groups contained in the `default.vsdisco` file on your local web server:

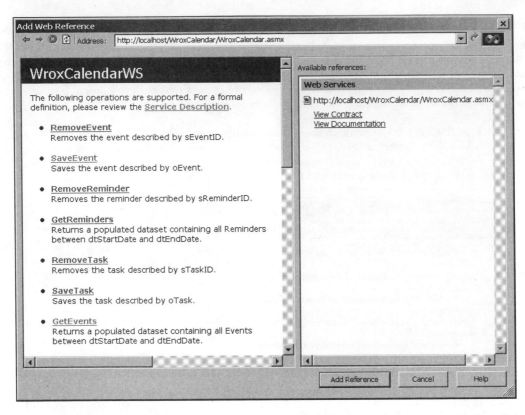

Click the View Documentation link and you will see the same list of methods we saw earlier. Select Add Reference and that's it. Expand your Solution Explorer and you should see a new child node under Web Reference representing our WroxCalendar Web Service.

Behind the scenes, Visual Studio .NET just created a proxy class that represents the WroxCalendar Web Service. If you've read Chapter 13, you'll be familiar with proxy classes and the help they give us. Select the Show All Files button in the Solution Explorer toolbar (it looks like a bunch of files on top of each other), and you'll see a child file appear underneath WroxCalendar.wsdl called WroxCalendar.vb. That's your proxy class. You can look at the code, but modifying it could have unpredictable or unintended consequences. You can always rebuild the Web Reference if you like, so don't be shy about poking around in that code.

When the Web Reference procedure is complete, we can now reference our WroxCalendar Web Service via the proxy class. That enables lines of code like the following:

```
Dim wsWroxCal As New localhost.WroxCalendarWS()
```

WroxCalendarWS is the name of the public class in our Web Service project that contains our Web Service methods.

Populating Events HTML

Recall our intent is to ask for Event, Reminder, or Task data from the Web Service and format it to meet our particular needs in this application. In our case, we'll just build a simple HTML table in code. Since we know the name of the `asp:TableCell` for each of our three main lists, the code that renders our calendar is actually quite simple.

In this section, we'll be populating the Events HTML. We have a `TableCell` already waiting for us in the `MainCalendar` Web Form named `CalendarEvents`, but there is some work that needs done before we can start working with that control. First, we need to prepare the code, or more correctly the class, behind `MainCalendar.aspx`. When you create the `MainCalendar` Web Form with the `asp:Table` control and the Calendar control, you get code generated for you that looks like this:

```
Public Class WroxCalendar
    Inherits System.Web.UI.Page
    Protected WithEvents MainCalendar As System.Web.UI.WebControls.Table
    Protected WithEvents DisplayCalendar As _
                      System.Web.UI.WebControls.Calendar

    Private Sub Page_Load(ByVal sender As System.Object, _
                        ByVal e As System.EventArgs) Handles MyBase.Load
        'Put user code to initialize the page here
    End Sub

End Class
```

That code identifies our calendar control named `DisplayCalendar` and our table named `MainCalendar`. You may find that you have to add the line that defines the `DisplayCalendar` control yourself; for some reason VS .NET doesn't always do it. VS .NET creates the `Page_Load` event for us, assuming that's our most likely place to start coding, which is a correct assumption for this case study. What's missing, though, are our table cells. They exist in the HTML and will be rendered on the client, but we don't have any way to work with them in code. That's taken care of by three lines of code as follows.

```
Protected WithEvents Reminders As System.Web.UI.WebControls.TableCell
Protected WithEvents CalendarEvents As System.Web.UI.WebControls.TableCell
Protected WithEvents Tasks As System.Web.UI.WebControls.TableCell
```

Any code we write within the class `WroxCalendar` in our ASP.NET application can now work with these three controls. This is key to our application design as we are about to see.

Since we can group all of our display-generating code together logically, let's create a new class called `RenderCalendar` for our three rendering methods – `GetEventsHTML()`, `GetTasksHTML()`, and `GetRemindersHTML()`. All three methods are relatively similar, so let's just cover getting events to display properly.

Let's look at a simple version of `GetEventsHTML()` then add code as needed.

```
Public Class RenderCalendar

Public Function GetEventsHTML(ByVal dtStartDate As Date, _
                            ByVal dtEndDate As Date, _
                            ByVal DisplayMode As EventViewType) As String
```

```
    Dim i As Integer
    Dim oRow As DataRow
    Dim sTodayHTML As String
    Dim sOutputHTML As String

    Dim dsEvents As New DataSet()
    Dim wsWroxCal As New localhost.WroxCalendarWS()
    Dim oAuthInfo as New localhost.AuthInfo()

    oAuthInfo.SubscriberID = "Wrox"
    oAuthInfo.UserID = "author"
    oAuthInfo.Password = "easytocrack"

    wsWroxCal.AuthInfoValue = oAuthInfo

    dsEvents = wsWroxCal.GetEvents(dtStartDate, dtEndDate, "jslater")

    Dim drEvents() As DataRow
    Dim filterExp As String = "EventDate = #" & _
                              Format$(dtStartDate, "short date") & "#"
    Dim sortExp As String = "StartTime"

    drEvents = dsEvents.Tables.Item(0).Select(filterExp)

    sOutputHTML = sOutputHTML & _
                "<table cellpadding='1' cellspacing='1'>" & _
                "<font face='Verdana' size='3'><b>Events</b>" & _
                "  <a href='addevent.aspx'>" & _
                "<font face='Courier' size='3'>[New]</a>" & _
                "</font><hr size='1'><br>"

    If dtStartDate = Format(Now, "short date") Then
        sTodayHTML = "<tr><td><font face='Verdana' size='2'><b>TODAY - " & _
                    Format$(Now, "Long Date") & "<b></font></td></tr>"
    Else
        sTodayHTML = "<tr><td><font face='Verdana' size='2'><b>" & _
                    Format$(dtStartDate, "Long Date") & _
                    "<b></font></td></tr>"
    End If

    For i = 0 To (drEvents.Length - 1)
        sTodayHTML = sTodayHTML & _
                    "<tr><td><i><font face='Verdana' size='2'>" & _
                    Format(drEvents(i)("StartTime"), "Short Time") & "-" & _
                    Format(drEvents(i)("EndTime"), "Short Time") & _
                    " (" & drEvents(i)("Location").ToString & _
                    ")</font></i></td>"
        sTodayHTML = sTodayHTML & _
                    "<tr><td><font face='Verdana' size='2'>" & _
                    "<a href='addevent.aspx?eventid=" & _
                    drEvents(i)("EventID").ToString & "'>" & _
                    drEvents(i)("Subject").ToString() & _
                    "</a></font></td></tr>"
    Next

    If drEvents.length = 0 Then
        sTodayHTML = sTodayHTML & _
            "<tr><td><i><font face='Verdana' size='2'>" & _
```

```
                  "There are no scheduled events for this day." & _
                  "</font></i></td></tr>"
        End If

        sOutputHTML = sOutputHTML & sTodayHTML & "</table>"

        Return sOutputHTML

    End Function

End Class
```

Early on we create a `DataSet` representing the return value we expect from our Web Service method, `GetEvents()`. Also, notice the object representing our Web Service proxy class, `wsWroxCal`.

The design of our Web Service says that we have to send some header information in addition to calling the Web Service method itself. Our proxy class takes care of exposing the required header data, making assigning that data very simple:

```
oAuthInfo.SubscriberID = "Wrox"
oAuthInfo.UserID = "author"
oAuthInfo.Password = "easytocrack"

wsWroxCal.AuthInfoValue = oAuthInfo
```

Calling the Web Service for events is isolated in a single line of code at this point. The proxy class is doing more work, of course, but our code in `RenderCalendar` is very clean:

```
dsEvents = wsWroxCal.GetEvents(dtStartDate, dtEndDate, "jslater")
```

That line calls the `GetEvents()` Web Service method, passing required input parameters as well as the `AuthInfoValue` data that we just populated containing Subscriber and User information. If all goes well, we'll receive a populated `DataSet` containing scheduled events between `dtStartDate` and `dtEndDate` for the user `jslater`.

The balance of the code in this function creates an HTML table for displaying our event data. To iterate through the `DataSet` the code creates an array of `DataRows`:

```
drEvents = dsEvents.Tables.Item(0).Select(filterExp)
```

It loops through each row, building appropriate HTML along the way. You are welcome to read through the HTML generation code, but we won't cover it in any detail here. Notice, however, what happens if `drEvents` has a length of zero:

```
If drEvents.length = 0 Then
    sTodayHTML = sTodayHTML & _
        "<tr><td><i><font face='Verdana' size='2'>" & _
        "There are no scheduled events for this day." & _
        "</font></i></td></tr>"
End If
```

The output of this function should be properly formatted HTML representing our events for a given date range. So, when our page loads for the first time, we can assume the user would like to see their events to the current date. The code to do that in the Page_Load event isn't too difficult:

```
CalendarEvents.Text = _
    oCalendarHTML.GetEventsHTML(Format(Now, "Short Date"), _
                                Format(Now, "Short Date"), _
                                RenderCalendar.EventViewType.CalendarDay)
```

oCalendarHTML is an instance of our RenderCalendar class dimensioned as a private class within the WroxCalendar class in our ASP.NET project:

```
Private oCalendarHTML As New RenderCalendar()
```

Astute readers may have noticed the third parameter in the GetEventsHTML() function. It is an enumerator value that gets passed into any of our rendering functions indicating the type of calendar selection the user has asked for. Since the calendar control gives us the ability to select single calendar days, entire weeks, or entire months, this is a nice feature to have.

The enumerator is defined within the RenderCalendar class:

```
Public Enum EventViewType
    CalendarDay = 0
    CalendarWeek = 1
    CalendarMonth = 2
End Enum
```

In the code you can download for this chapter, you'll notice a case statement in the GetEventsHTML() function that uses that third parameter to change the display HTML for events. Since a single day is likely to have few events, we return more information about each particular event. Week and month requests are likely to have more data and therefore each particular event is given less room.

If the calendar web application is run and we pick a date for which data exists in the database, we get a display something like we saw earlier. Definitely not the best looking web application ever to hit the market, but it's a good example of using a Web Service to return our event data.

Building an Desktop Client

Let's quickly review building a Windows desktop application that consumes the Calendar Web Service. The process of building a web application to use our Web Service and the process of building a desktop application are very similar. That's an important point. Implementation of Web Services in terms of sending requests and receiving responses, regardless of platform, is rather simple.

In this example, we'll build a simple Windows form that shows our calendar events and tasks for a particular day. We won't worry about displaying weeks or months at a time like the web application. Like the web application exercise we just finished, let's start with an idea of what our final application looks like. See the a screenshot on the opposite page:

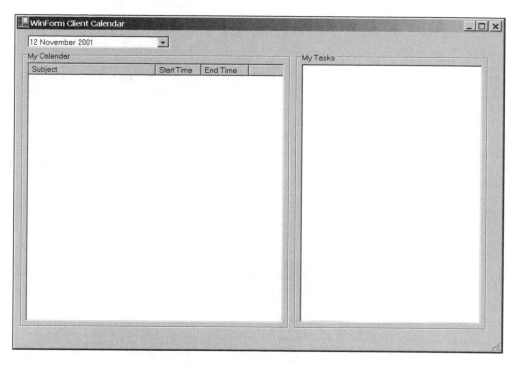

Creating the Event and Task Form

Let's set up our event and task display form first. Notice that we are not building any functionality to create new events or tasks, or even edit them even though the Web Service exposes that functionality. The purpose of this final example is just to illustrate a Web Service implementation in a Windows application and not to recreate the functionality we've already illustrated in our previous web application.

So in Visual Studio .NET create a new project by selecting **Windows Application** and name it DesktopCalendar.

Rename the Form1.vb that is automatically created to frmCalendar.vb. You'll need to modify the code in frmCalendar.vb to reflect that name change as the following code fragment illustrates:

```
Public Class frmCalendar
    Inherits System.Windows.Forms.Form

End Class
```

On frmCalendar there are two list views – lstEvents and lstTasks. You can create your own form if you want and arrange it something like the screenshot above. The code is available for download, though, so you don't have to recreate this entire project. You will also need to add a DateTimePicker control to the form named dtpCurrentDate. That control drives the display of events and tasks just like the ASP.NET Calendar control in our web application example earlier in this chapter. However, since the DateTimePicker only represents one day at a time, this Windows application will only display events and tasks for a single day at a time.

Once the form is built with the appropriate controls, we need to add a reference to our Web Service. We've done this once already in this chapter, so we won't cover the process again. If you'd like to walk through the process again, refer to the section titled *Adding the WroxCalendar Web Reference* above.

So, to this point we have a form with controls for displaying events and tasks that are returned by our Calendar Web Service. Let's build the functions that actually build our list of events and tasks, after a little bit of security housekeeping first.

Recall that the Web Service `GetEvents()` method requires a start date and a stop date and a `OwnerUserID`. We already know that our start and stop dates will come from the `DateTimePicker` control. How will we get the `OwnerUserID`? In the ASP.NET example it was hard-coded, which is OK for an illustration, but not realistic. Let's add a login process for our desktop application.

Create a form named `frmLogin.vb` and place the standard **User Name** and **Password** labels and textboxes. Also add a **Login** button named `cmdLogin` and a **Cancel** button named `cmdCancel` so your form looks like the following:

Behind the `cmdLogin` button add the following code to execute a simple database login. Notice that we are reusing the `Users` table from our previous web application example:

```
Private Sub cmdLogin_Click(ByVal sender As System.Object, _
             ByVal e As System.EventArgs) Handles cmdLogin.Click
    Dim bLogin As Boolean

    Try
        Dim myConn As New OleDbConnection(strConnect)
        Dim myReader As OleDbDataReader
        Dim strSQL As String = "SELECT UserID, Password " & _
                    "FROM Users WHERE UserID='" & txtUserID.Text & "'"
        Dim myOleDbCommand As New OleDbCommand(strSQL)
        myOleDbCommand.Connection = myConn
        myConn.Open()
        myReader = myOleDbCommand.ExecuteReader()

        myReader.Read()
        If myReader("Password") = txtPassword.Text Then
            bLogin = True
        Else
            bLogin = False
        End If

    Catch ex As Exception
        MsgBox("Database error:  " & ex.Message, MsgBoxStyle.Critical, _
                "WinForm Desktop Web Service Client")
        Application.Exit()
```

```
      End Try

      If bLogin Then
         Me.Close()
      Else
         MsgBox("Invalid user name or password", MsgBoxStyle.Critical, _
               "WinForm Desktop Web Service Client")
         txtPassword.Text = vbNullString
         txtUserID.Text = vbNullString
      End If

   End Sub
```

The code behind the button builds an `OleDbCommand` and executes a simple query on the `Users` table attempting to verify if the User ID and Password supplied by the user match the values stored in the database. If they don't match a message is displayed to the user, otherwise the user is authenticated and allowed to continue with the application. Notice the `Try...Catch` structure that wraps the query execution. If a database error occurs, the user will receive a message box and the application will terminate.

The `frmLogin` is created and displayed in the `Page_Load` event of `frmCalendar` as the following code illustrates.

```
   Private Sub frmCalendar_Load(ByVal sender As Object, _
                  ByVal e As System.EventArgs) Handles MyBase.Load

      Dim fLogin As frmLogin
      fLogin = New frmLogin()

      fLogin.ShowDialog()

      m_strUserId = fLogin.txtUserID.Text
      m_strPassword = fLogin.txtPassword.Text

      Call GetEvents(Format(Now, "Short Date"), _
                  Format(Now, "Short Date"), m_strUserId)
      Call GetTasks(Format(Now, "Short Date"),
                  Format(Now, "Short Date"), m_strUserId)

   End Sub
```

If the login process succeeds, the code after the `fLogin.ShowDialog` will execute. If login fails for any reason, `frmLogin` itself calls `Application.Exit`. Immediately after the login form is dismissed by a successful login, the code captures the `UserId` and `Password` supplied by the user. It then calls `GetEvents()` and `GetTasks()`, which contain our Web Service invocations.

Populating the Event and Tasks Lists

`GetEvents()` is very similar to the `GetEventsHTML()` function in our web application example. The difference between the two is merely UI implementation issues. Here's the code for the procedure `GetEvents()` that is found in the `frmCalendar.vb` file:

```
   Private Sub GetEvents(ByVal dtStartDate As Date, ByVal dtEndDate As Date, _
                  ByVal strOwnerUserID As String)
      Dim i As Integer
      Dim wsWroxCal As New localhost.WroxCalendarWS()
```

```
        Dim dsEvents As DataSet
        Dim drEvents() As DataRow
        Dim oAuth As New localhost.AuthInfo()

        oAuth.SubscriberID = "Wrox"
        oAuth.UserID = "author"
        oAuth.Password = "easytocrack"

        wsWroxCal.AuthInfoValue = oAuth

        dsEvents = wsWroxCal.GetEvents(Format(dtStartDate, "short date"), _
                                       Format(dtEndDate, "short date"), _
                                       m_strUserId)

    If dsEvents.Tables.Count = 0 Then
       lstEvents.Items.Clear()
    Else
       Dim filterExp As String = "EventDate = #" & _
                                 Format$(dtStartDate, "short date") & "#"
       Dim sortExp As String = "Priority"

       drEvents = dsEvents.Tables.Item(0).Select(filterExp)

       If drEvents.Length = 0 Then
          lstEvents.Items.Clear()
       Else
          For i = 0 To (drEvents.Length - 1)

             lstEvents.Items.Add(drEvents(i)("Subject"))
             lstEvents.Items(i).SubItems.Add(Format(drEvents(i)("StartTime"), _
                                             "hh:mm tt"))
             lstEvents.Items(i).SubItems.Add(Format(drEvents(i)("EndTime"), _
                                             "hh:mm tt"))

          Next
       End If
    End If
End Sub
```

The code creates a new `WroxCalendarWS` instance and names it `wsWroxCal`. Then the `AuthInfo` instance is populated with our standard `SubscriberID` (standard in that we used it in the web application example) and the `UserId` and `Password` we gathered from the login form.

The actual Web Service call is as simple as the web application:

```
dsEvents = wsWroxCal.GetEvents(Format(dtStartDate, "short date"), _
                               Format(dtEndDate, "short date"), _
                               m_strUserId)
```

The code passes a start date and end date and an `OwnerUserId` to the Web Service. Notice that the start and end dates are the same value for this application since we can only represent one day at a time with the `DateTimePicker` control.

Once we get a `DataSet` back from our Web Service, the code simply populates the `lstEvents` `ListView` control by looping through every `DataRow` in the `DataSet` and adding a `ListViewItem` and accompanying `ListViewSubItems`. The following line of code creates the `ListViewItem` itself:

```
lstEvents.Items.Add(drEvents(i)("Subject"))
```

These two lines create `ListViewSubItems` that are displayed as additional columns in the ListView control.

```
lstEvents.Items(i).SubItems.Add(Format(drEvents(i)("StartTime"), _
                          "hh:mm tt"))
lstEvents.Items(i).SubItems.Add(Format(drEvents(i)("EndTime"), _
                          "hh:mm tt"))
```

The `Subject`, `StartTime`, and `EndTime` columns were configured at design time when the `ListView` was created. See the Columns collection in the properties box.

Our task list is populated almost identically. For completeness, here is the code. Notice that the ListView is populated a little differently – we are not displaying the same level of detail:

```
Private Sub GetTasks(ByVal dtStartDate As Date, ByVal dtEndDate As Date, _
                ByVal strOwnerUserID As String)
  Dim i As Integer
  Dim wsWroxCal As New localhost.WroxCalendarWS()
  Dim dsTasks As DataSet
  Dim drTasks() As DataRow
  Dim oAuth As New localhost.AuthInfo()

  oAuth.SubscriberID = "Wrox"
  oAuth.UserID = "author"
  oAuth.Password = "easytocrack"

  wsWroxCal.AuthInfoValue = oAuth

  dsTasks = wsWroxCal.GetTasks(Format(dtStartDate, "short date"), _
                          Format(dtEndDate, "short date"), _
                          m_strUserId)

  If dsTasks.Tables.Count = 0 Then
    lstTasks.Items.Clear()
  Else
    Dim filterExp As String = "TaskDate = #" & _
                          Format$(dtStartDate, "short date") & "#"
    Dim sortExp As String = "Priority"

    drTasks = dsTasks.Tables.Item(0).Select(filterExp)

    If drTasks.Length = 0 Then
      lstTasks.Items.Clear()
    Else
      For i = 0 To (drTasks.Length - 1)
        lstTasks.Items.Add(drTasks(i)("Subject") & "-" & _
                          drTasks(i)("Status"))
      Next
    End If
  End If
End Sub
```

If any tasks are returned from the Web Service method `GetTasks()`, the list view will be populated.

So, in this simple Windows application, we've illustrated how easy it is to consume Web Services from a desktop application. In fact, the actual invocation code in this example and the previous web application example are literally identical. The only difference between the applications is how we use the data once it is returned from the Calendar Web Services.

Conclusion

In this chapter we created a sample Web Service providing calendar features. We walked through the Web Service conceptual design including use cases and functional requirements. We created and discussed a simple database to support our calendar application. The focus of the case study was coding the Web Service and its constituent methods. After discussing that code, we built simple ASP.Net and Window Forms client applications to consume the Web Service.

15

Remoting Overview

Remoting may be one of the most overlooked technologies in .NET. Hot topics like Web Services and the advent of new languages like VB .NET and C# are getting much more attention. In .NET, remoting is a framework for allowing objects to work together in different applications running in potentially different locations. In a nutshell, .NET remoting allows applications to interact with other applications, regardless of whether those applications are on the same or different machines, which could be connected via LAN/WAN, or across the Internet. The framework of services that ships with .NET provides a set of beneficial functionality that makes writing and deploying a remoting application straightforward.

.NET remoting is functionally similar in many ways to the Distributed Component Object Model (DCOM), Microsoft's technology for distributed objects. DCOM gives developers the ability to interact with objects running on another machine or in another process. Deploying a .NET remoting application is probably easier than a DCOM one because the remoting framework does a lot of work for us, and .NET remoting is a bit less complicated under the covers when all is said and done.

As we'll see in this chapter, remoting applications can be very similar to Web Service applications. In fact, they share some of the same supporting technologies. However, Web Services are generally stateless applications (although it is possible to maintain session state) whereas remote objects made available via the remoting framework are potentially better suited for applications requiring state maintenance. In addition, Web Services rely predominantly on HTTP, and although a significant benefit of Web Services is the use of HTTP, there are times when the potentially faster and more secure TCP is more appropriate. Remoting gives us the choice of either protocol.

When using .NET remoting, developers have the ability to create more complex objects that could respond to multiple method calls for the same business process. Consider a `Customer` object in an order fulfillment application. Using remoting, we could instantiate such an object running on some middle tier somewhere and expect a particular instance of that object to survive multiple method invocations from a single client, all the while maintaining state regarding a particular customer. Our application has the convenience of being able to treat that remote object as if it were instantiated and residing locally. In a Web Service scenario we could have the same functionality, but best-practice Web Service design generally says we create stateless functionality that requires reinitializing remote objects for each method invocation and incur start up costs every time our application needs `Customer` object functions.

The .NET remoting framework is to be the focus of this chapter. We'll take a high level, survey-type look at the framework and its capabilities including remote object activation and object lifetime support, communication channels for moving messages back and forth between remote objects, and the formatters responsible for encoding the messages. Here's how the chapter is laid out and what you should expect to find in each section:

- ❏ **Remoting Basics** – at times remoting can be complicated. It's important that we understand the basics of remoting before we encounter some of the more complex, code-oriented sections of this chapter. In this first section, we'll review some overview concepts, describe remoting with a diagram or two, and generally set the stage for more technical discussion.

- ❏ **Activation and Lifetime Support** – .NET remoting provides for server and client-activation of objects. There are a variety of issues to consider whether remote objects are server- or client-activated including serializing objects and creating proxy classes. Additionally, we need to review the lifetime support services provided by the remoting framework for client-activated remote objects.

- ❏ **Object References and Proxies** – remoting relies heavily on creating local proxy objects used to represent a remote object in client applications. In this section, we'll review how object references are used to create proxy objects and the structure and usage of proxy objects.

- ❏ **Channels and Formatters** – remoting supports sending methods using two types of channels – HTTP and TCP. We'll review the rules for using both types of channels, look at when one channel type is preferable, and see some examples of registering channels with remote objects.

Remoting Basics

Let's think beyond just .NET for a moment. If we wanted two applications on different machines to share objects somehow, we'd need a few things just to get the conversation started. First of all, we'd need a way of knowing where to find some remote application's objects that we want our other applications to use. Then, we would need to know some details on what methods or properties those remote objects contained, and what protocols they use or support. Once we knew how to talk to those objects, we'd want some consistent method of delivering our requests and receiving responses containing notifications of execution, successful or otherwise, or typed data, or whatever. At some point, we'd probably want to secure our conversations with those remote objects, so we'd need some mechanism for doing that.

Well, knowing about remoting features before writing that last paragraph is a little unfair. Everything mentioned in the previous paragraph is done by .NET remoting, and then some. Let's reword that pie-in-the-sky list of needs into something closer to what we are used to dealing with. First, when we say applications can talk to one another, we really mean cross-process (not to be confused with cross-platform, which is something else entirely) communication. Enabling such a thing has been possible for a long time. .NET remoting just adds the latest twist to talking between processes. As a quick aside, we'll occasionally be using the phrase "application domain". That's .NET-speak for process. If we say "across or between application domains" that really means "between .NET processes".

So, we have processes talking to processes regardless of where they are running. OK, there are some obvious technical hurdles here, but getting two processes to trade information is nothing to write home about. Bear with us as this gets incrementally more interesting! In .NET remoting, when one application needs to use objects from another application or process, it has the capability to expose a remote object's methods and data in a couple of ways:

❑   It can create a **copy** of that object and move it over the wire

❑   It can create a **reference** to that object and deliver that to a remote application

The first method works well for relatively small, innocuous objects that have little security impact. The second is preferred because code and data aren't moving around a network, an intranet, or the public Internet.

Using the object reference, a .NET remoting client will create a **proxy** of the remote object to serve the client as if the client was communicating with the remote object itself. Similar to Web Services, the proxy object has some extra built-in functionality that manages creating proper messages and delivering them to the true remote object. In this chapter we won't cover the details of how the proxies are implemented, but proxies are key to the successful implementation of .NET remoting. We will be seeing a lot of them as this chapter unfolds.

Here's what happens when a remote call is made from one application to another using proxies. The client application creates a proxy using the object reference returned by the remoting framework. The proxy looks like the remote object in every way, as far as the client application is concerned. The client calls a method of what it thinks is the remote object, but we know to be the proxy. Remoting takes the method call and routes it to the server process, wherever it happens to be. It runs the server object, creating, and initializing it if necessary, and returns some result back to the client application via the proxy. At least in this regard, remoting works in a manner very similar to COM or DCOM.

The delivery mechanisms for messages sent between proxies in client applications and remote objects or servers are called channels. In the simple example above, the routing of a method invocation from proxy to remote object is done by sending a formatted message over a channel. .NET remoting supports two types of channels – HTTP and TCP. Early on there was talk of a third channel, SMTP, but it isn't supported at the time of writing (in Beta 2).

Channels are seemingly simple, and we'll struggle to keep them that way, but there are some rules as to how and when to use channels in general as well as some specific implementation guidelines for HTTP and TCP channels in particular. Channels can send, listen, or both. The two default channels in .NET send and listen. We can create our own channels to meet any specific application requirements easily using .NET. Any custom channel we create can use just about any network protocol. .NET makes this easy for us by providing an `IChannel` interface.

The mechanisms for managing remote object instantiation, method invocation, channels, and other remoting tasks are often grouped together into one entity called remoting services.

Here's a picture of the remoting conversation to keep in mind as we continue through this chapter. It is deliberately simple. We're going to add enough complexity shortly.

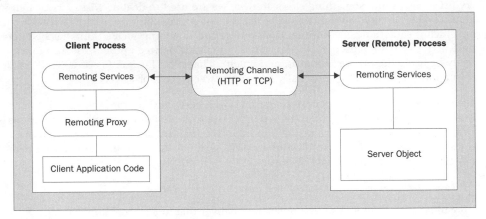

Assuming both sides are working properly, when the client process (on the left), invokes a method on the server (on the right), a proxy is created for the client. Actually the proxy is created before the invocation, as we'll see in a few pages, so how can we invoke something if we don't know it's there? We'll cover that topic in the *Object Activation* section.

Therefore, assuming the proxy exists, a method invocation is made via the proxy, which gets routed through the remoting services at the client side and delivered to the remote host via a predefined channel. On the host or server side, whatever method was requested gets executed and results return to the client the same way the initial request came out – via either the TCP or HTTP channel.

That's an overview of the remoting process including some of the major components – proxies and channels. Let's move to the details of how objects are created, where they run (client or server side), and the issues of managing their lifetimes. In the upcoming sections we'll be building objects that reside on a server and the client applications that invoke methods from those remote objects.

Object Activation

The process of creating and initializing objects is called activation. In a local application, activation is of little concern to most developers. We think about when and how we create the objects we need in our applications, but the details of how that activation works is of little interest most of the time. However, this is not the case with .NET remoting. We do need to pay attention to the details of creating and initializing our remote objects. This section will review issues pertaining to object activation starting with the different types of object activation.

Server or Client Activation

.NET remoting provides a few object activation models to give developers flexibility in their designs. The models available to us can be categorized into client-activated objects and server-activated objects. In this section, we'll review each activation model, discuss implications for designing applications using each model, and present a few examples.

Server-Activated Objects

Server-activated objects are those whose lifetimes are controlled by a server process. Typically, server-activated objects are used when an application requires remote objects that maintain no state information between method calls. In this way, remote objects are not unlike the functionality exposed by Web Services. Another common scenario is the case of multiple clients calling methods from the same object instance that does maintain state between calls. Applications that use server-activated objects, which share state across multiple client method calls are highly scalable because only one object instance exists at any time. This is particularly convenient if our application contains objects with large start up or instantiation processing costs, for example when creating database connections.

Server-activated objects can be useful for all remote applications given their requirement for either being stateless or sharing state information for multiple clients at the same time. Let's take a look at the activation models in more detail.

There are two activation models for server-activated objects:

- ❑   Singleton
- ❑   SingleCall

.NET terms these two states the **object modes**. Singleton objects never have more than one instance active at any time. If an instance of a Singleton remote object exists in a server process, all client method requests are routed through it. Otherwise, a new instance will be created and all new client method requests will be routed through that instance. As long as the object instance is active, any client request will share the same state information with other client requests.

As an illustration, let's say we have a Singleton object activated on a machine on our wide area network (WAN). Let's call the object Customer and give it a method called LoadCustomer() that takes a CustomerID as an input parameter. The LoadCustomer() method will populate the class with a database call – properties and other data will be filled with data and exposed. Now, when our first remote client calls the LoadCustomer() method, the Customer class gets populated. Maybe it goes on to build some type of UI that represents that particular Customer class in a call center application. What happens when the second or third client application tries to use the same remote object? If it doesn't call LoadCustomer() and pass in a new CustomerID it will get the data the first remote client asked for. What happens if the second client does calls LoadCustomer()? The first client instance will have the Customer data it was working with changed.

That having been said, there are times when data should be shared between client requests for applications. For example, when the cost of spinning up new instances of objects is high. The classic example of this type of application object is for providing information that requires processing but doesn't change from client request to client request. Take a weather information site or a business market conditions application. The data exposed by any method in remote objects in those types of applications is not particularly client-specific, therefore sharing that information between clients' requests is entirely reasonable and may even be preferable. Think about the processor time made free by working through the instantiation of a heavy-duty object only once.

The other type of server-activated object, SingleCall, is stateless irrespective of how many instances of the object exist. That is, a SingleCall object cannot maintain state between method calls. When the first method call comes into a SingleCall server object, a new instance is created. When a second method call for the same client comes in, a new object instance is created even if the first still exists.

A Simple Remoting Server

So, what does a server-activated object look like in code? At this point it's rather simple. Even though we still have some material to cover regarding channels and other important topics, let's have a look at a simple remoting server and a client that uses server-activated objects. In this example, which you can download from the Wrox web site, we'll be building a Console Application that registers a server-activated object named `Customer`. It has a very simple method called `GetCustomer()` that returns a string. We are using a Console Application for this example because we need an application that will start and make our objects available to other processes until we stop the application. And since we don't want to get caught up in user interface issues at this point, a Console Application suites our purposes nicely.

Let's start by creating a new project in Visual Studio .NET by selecting **File | New Project**. In the **Project Types** list, select **Visual Basic Projects**. Then select the **Console Application** in the **Templates** list. Finally, name the project `RemotingServerConsole`.

When Visual Studio .NET creates the project, you'll get a default VB .NET module named `Module1.vb`. Rename that file to `modMain.vb`. Notice that Visual Studio .NET created a `Sub Main()` for us. That is where all of our code for this example is going to be placed.

However, before we can actually add the server object code we need to configure the project to support .NET remoting. The first step is to reference the .NET Remoting dll so our application will have access to the `System.Runtime.Remoting` namespace. To create the reference, find the Solution Explorer tree view in the Visual Studio .NET IDE. Right-click on the **References** node. Select **Add Reference**. You'll be presented with a list of possible references. Scroll down and find `System.Runtime.Remoting` as the following screenshot illustrates:

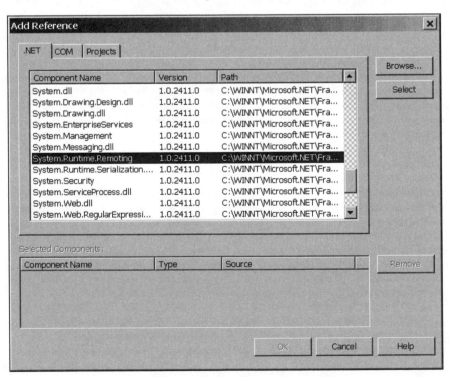

Press the **Select** button to add `System.Runtime.Remoting` to the **Selected Components** list near the bottom of the References form. Finally, press the **OK** button to save the new reference. Now we have access to the `System.Runtime.Remoting` namespace.

Let's start adding code to `modMain.vb`. Open the file by double-clicking on the `modMain.vb` node in the Solution Explorer in Visual Studio .NET. You'll find skeleton code that looks like this:

```
Module modMain

    Sub Main()
    End Sub

End Module
```

To make the remoting object model available to our application, we have to import several namespaces. Each `Imports` statement is important, and we'll cover the details in each of the following sections. For now, just include the following three `Imports` statements in `modMain.vb` above the module `modMain` declaration.

```
Imports System.Runtime.Remoting
Imports System.Runtime.Remoting.Channels
Imports System.Runtime.Remoting.Channels.Tcp
```

Now, add the following code to `Sub Main()`. Remember you can download this code from the Wrox web site.

```
Module modMain

    Sub Main()
        Dim oChannel As TcpChannel

        oChannel = New TcpChannel(8888)
        ChannelServices.RegisterChannel(oChannel)
        Try

            RemotingConfiguration.RegisterWellKnownServiceType _
                    (Type.GetType("Customer"), "Customer.GetCustomer", _
                    WellKnownObjectMode.SingleCall)
        Catch ex As Exception
            MsgBox(ex.Message)
        End Try

        System.Console.WriteLine("--Wrox Simple Remoting Server--")
        System.Console.WriteLine("Press <enter> to exit.")
        System.Console.ReadLine()

    End Sub

End Module

Public Class Customer

    Inherits MarshalByRefObject
```

```
      Public Function GetCustomer(ByVal strCustomerID As String) As String
         Return "Customer.GetCustomer here."
      End Function

   End Class
```

Let's take a moment to talk about those `Imports` statements. All remoting applications will use `System.Runtime.Remoting` and most will use `System.Runtime.Remoting.Channels` for obvious reasons. In this example, we are going to use a TCP channel, hence the `System.Runtime.Remoting.Channels.Tcp` namespace. It contains the `TcpChannel` class.

A Console Application is quite useful for demonstrating remoting concepts, so we'll be relying on them quite a bit in this chapter. They are also very simple. In the case of our `RemotingServerConsole` project, make sure that `modMain` is the start up object so that `Sub Main()` will be executed when the project runs. You can find the Startup Object configuration for each Visual Studio .NET application by right-clicking on the VS .NET project in the Solution Explorer and selecting **Properties**. Make sure that dropdown box reads `Sub Main()`.

In `Sub Main()` there is some code for creating and registering a channel:

```
      Dim oChannel As TcpChannel

      oChannel = New TcpChannel(8888)
      ChannelServices.RegisterChannel(oChannel)
```

Recall from the earlier overview that channels are used for moving method invocation methods from application to remote object and back again. We'll spend some time later in this chapter reviewing types of channels and what it is the code directly above happens to do. For now, just understand that those three lines of code create a new channel using TCP that monitors a port that I selected entirely at random, `8888`, and registers it with the remoting framework.

The next line of code, `ChannelServices.RegisterChannel`, actually registers the remote object. `RegisterWellKnownServiceType` tells the remoting framework the location of the object. Before a client can activate the object, our server Console Application must register the `Customer` object, otherwise the remoting framework won't know where or how to route remote invocation requests. Notice in our example above, the `Customer` object is registered as a `SingleCall` object. The first parameter to the `RegisterWellKnownServiceType()` method is the type of object we're registering, the second parameter is the object's URI, and the third is the now familiar object mode – `SingleCall` or `Singleton`:

```
      RemotingConfiguration.RegisterWellKnownServiceType _
                  (Type.GetType("Customer"), "Customer.GetCustomer",
                  WellKnownObjectMode.SingleCall)
```

It is important to note that registering the object with the remoting framework doesn't actually activate or instantiate the object. That only happens when a client asks for its own instance of the object using the `New` keyword, or something we'll discuss shortly called `Activator.GetObject()`, and then actually invokes an object method.

The remaining code in Sub Main() merely writes a few lines to the Windows console and forces the application to wait for a user to press the *Enter* key. It is a convenient technique for easily starting and stopping a server process that hosts remote server-activated objects.

The class that is being exposed to clients via the remoting framework is called Customer and comes last in the code. Notice that it inherits something called MarshalByRefObject. Any object made available to the remoting framework has to inherit MarshalByRefObject. We will see more on this in an upcoming section. The rest of the code contains a simple method that returns a string indicating that the code was executed.

When we run the application we get a small Console Application window that looks like the following screenshot. Behind the scenes, however, the remoting framework has come to life and registered the Customer object ready to interact with remoting clients on TCP port 8888.

A Simple Remoting Client

Building a client to invoke our Customer object remotely is just as simple as building the server. Take the following example. Its container project type can be just about any Visual Studio .NET project type. In this case, we've chosen a simple Windows application, but we could just as easily be using another Console Application. The core code that activates the server object looks simple, but there's a lot going on in these one or two lines. Let's have a look:

```
Dim oRemoteCustomer as Customer = _
        CType(Activator.GetObject(GetType(Customer), _
        "tcp://computername:8888/Customer.GetCustomer"), Customer)
```

In this code example, we are creating an instance on the server of our Customer object. Technically, the object isn't created until the first method invocation is issued. The code uses Activator.GetObject() to activate our server object and make it available for use within a remote application. The second parameter indicates the location and port at which we can find out remote Customer object.

Client-Activated Objects

Client objects are instances controlled by local application domains. That is, the lifetime of a client-activated object is nearly identical to that of a non-remote, or local, object instance. As we've already mentioned in our remoting overview section that got us started in this chapter, there is a series of steps required for a client-activated object to serve a remote application. In a nutshell, when the client tries to create an instance of a remote server object, an object reference is created. The ObjRef class represents the object reference. A local proxy is created using the ObjRef instance that is streamed back from the remote object.

Let's take a little time to look at the ObjRef class.

The objRef Class

When a remote object is registered with the remoting framework, something called an `ObjRef` is produced. The `ObjRef` is a serialized snapshot of any object that extends `MarshalByRefObject`. Recall that's what our `Customer` object in the earlier example does. The `ObjRef` contains information about the remote object. Enough information, in fact, that a proxy can be created on the remoting client. That information includes:

- Remote object name
- Remote object's class hierarchy
- All interfaces the object supports
- Remote object URI
- Channels available to communicate with the remote object

Using this data, the remoting framework will create a proxy through which the client application communicates with a remote object across application domain boundaries.

There are two ways `ObjRefs` are created:

- Directly by registering any object extending `MarshalByRefObject` with the remoting framework, as in our example above
- Indirectly by passing a `MarshalByRefObject` object as a parameter when calling a remote object

Unsurprisingly, remoting supports multiple methods for passing objects around. All of these should be familiar:

- Input or output parameters in method calls
- Return values of remote Public methods
- Property values of remote objects

Proxy Objects

We've been talking about the proxy objects created by remoting. Let's take a more detailed look. As we've seen, proxy objects are created when a client-activates a remote object. The proxy acts as the remote object, and with the help from the remoting framework ensures that calls made from the client are made to the appropriate instance of the remote object.

When a client-activates a remote object, local instance of the class `TransparentProxy` is created. `TransparentProxy` contains a list of all classes and methods of the remote object. Any calls made by the client at this point are intercepted by the proxy and have their validity quickly determined. A check is also made by the proxy to see if the requested object instance exists within the client application's application domain. If that instance exists, the remoting process is abandoned and a standard, local method invocation is executed. If no local instance is found then parameters and other method information are added to an `IMessage` object instance and the method invocation request is routed to the remote object.

To add a little more detail to the scenario described above, consider that the TransparentProxy class is actually wrapped by an abstract class called RealProxy. RealProxy contains the functionality necessary to forward method invocations to remote objects. TransparentProxy's role in this entire process is to give the illusion of a localized remote object. Ultimately, routing a method invocation using the IMessage object we just mentioned in the last paragraph is accomplished using the RealProxy's Invoke() method. Invoke() transforms the IMessage object into an IMethodCallMessage object and sends it to the remote object for which the RealProxy has required invocation information.

IMessage itself contains one property that is of some interest. IMessage.Properties is an IDictionary that contains name-value pairs that represent everything known about a particular remote object method call.

In simple applications, this whole process is hidden from view. To create a client-activated object instance of our Customer object from previous examples, the code is simple:

```
Public Class RemotingClientSample

    Public Function CallRemoteObject() As String
        Dim oCustomer As Customer

        oCustomer = Activator.CreateInstance("BusObjects", "Customer")
    End Function

End Class
```

Notice the code uses the Activator.CreateInstance() method. CreateInstance() itself is overloaded several times, but in this example the only two parameters necessary to create the instance are the assembly name containing our remote object and the object name itself.

Lifetime Leases

Lifetime is a term used to describe the period of time a particular variable is available for use. A lifetime lease is a collection of properties and other mechanisms for working with the lifetimes of particular variables. The lifetimes of client-activated objects are controlled by the lease manager in the CLR. All local objects are subject to the rules of the lease manager, but it is worthwhile to review this topic in the context of invoking remote objects. Whenever an object is marshaled outside its application domain (that's the process we've previously described using ObjRef) a lease is created in the local application domain subject to the lease manager.

Each application domain has its own lease manager. Each active object has a lease. The lease manager periodically polls all existing leases to determine if each lease has expired. If a particular lease has expired then the lease manager will inform any lease sponsors of that object, assuming they exist. The sponsors then have the chance of renewing the lease for that object. If they choose not to renew the lease, or the sponsors don't exist, the lease manager removes the lease and the object is deleted and the memory is cleaned up via garbage collection. Since we are dealing with remote objects running over a network, it is possible that interruptions or slowdowns could occur when sponsors are asked to renew a lease. For that reason, a sponsor timeout value exists.

Each lease managed by the lease manager implements the ILease interface. ILease contains properties that dictate lease policies and methods used for renewing the lease lifetime. The following table summarizes these:

ILease Property	Description
CurrentLeaseTime	The amount of time remaining on the current lease
CurrentState	One of the list defined by LeaseState: Active, Expired, Initial, Null, or Renewing
InitialLeaseTime	Gets or sets the initial lease time
RenewalOnCallTime	Gets or sets the amount of time the LeaseTime is incremented after each remote object method call
SponsorshipTimeout	Gets or sets the amount of time the lease manager will wait for lease sponsor to respond to a renewal request

ILease also contains several methods for registering and unregistering lease sponsors and for renewing the lease itself.

The lease manager maintains a list of sponsors ordered by decreasing sponsorship time. When a lease is about to expire, the first sponsor in the list is notified. The lease manager will wait for the duration of the SponsorshipTimeout value and remove that particular sponsor if no response is received.

Getting the lease for a particular object instance is simple. By passing our remoting object instance, one that was derived from MarshalByRefObject, into the function InitializeLifeTimeService(), we will get an instance of the object that controls the lifetime for our object, an ILease. For example, if we revisit out Customer object from earlier in this chapter, we can directly control the lease lifetime of our object instances if we so choose:

```
Imports System.Runtime.Remoting.Lifetime

Public Class Customer
    Inherits MarshalByRefObject

    Public Overrides Function InitializeLifetimeService() As Object

        Dim lease As ILease
        lease = InitializeLifetimeService()

        If lease.CurrentState = LeaseState.Initial Then
            lease.InitialLeaseTime = TimeSpan.FromMinutes(2)
            lease.SponsorshipTimeout = TimeSpan.FromMinutes(2)
            lease.RenewOnCallTime = TimeSpan.FromSeconds(2)
        End If


        Return lease
    End Function

End Class
```

Notice the inclusion of a new namespace – System.Runtime.Remoting.Lifetime. This namespace includes all of the classes responsible for managing lease lifetimes including ILease, ISponsor (that represents each lease sponsor), and the class LifetimeServices.

Recall that our `Customer` object still inherits from `MarshalByRefObject`. None of this would be possible with out that extension.

We've added a new public function that overrides `InitializeLifetimeService`. Inside the function, we create a new `ILease` and set it equal to the value of the base `InitializeLifetimeService`. Since we can only set `ILease` properties when the `CurrentState` (refer to the properties list above) equals `Initial`, that check is made. If the `CurrentState` is `Initial`, the code will set the initial lease time, sponsorship timeout, and renewal call time to two minutes. The `ILease` instance itself is returned from the function.

Once an object has been marshaled to a remote client, the `CurrentState` value is set to `Active` and any attempt to set the `ILease` properties will throw an exception.

Lease times can be extended using a combination of the code above to access a particular instance's lease and one of the three techniques below:

❑ Invoking the `Renew()` method by passing a new `RenewalTime` into the `Lease` object. The new lease time will be set to the maximum of the current lease time and the current system time plus the renewal time.

❑ A sponsor responds to a `Renewal` request by the lease manager.

❑ A client invokes a method on the remote object. In this case, the `RenewOnCallTime` property amount is used to refresh the lease.

To this point we've reviewed some of the details of how objects and their references are passed around using the remoting framework. We discussed proxy classes and how they get used to create the illusion of object localization. We also reviewed the impact of lifetime leases on remote objects and how a particular object can influence its own lifetime management. Let's now turn to remoting channels – the mechanism for transporting messages to and from remote objects.

Remoting Channels

Channels are used to carry remote method invocation requests including information about the request and any parameters. Results of the method call are returned to the calling application via the same method. When objects are registered on their server, they have the option of registering one or more channels. In fact, at least one channel is required, but developers have the option of building objects that can serve requests on multiple channels.

Channels can be configured to listen for messages, send messages, or do both. In addition, channels can be extended to support many more protocols than the two that ship with .NET Beta 2, HTTP and TCP. This is possible because all channels implement `IChannel`, which has two properties:

❑ `ChannelName` – the unique name of the channel. The channel name is used to retrieve channels once they have been registered. Non-unique channel names will raise an exception.

❑ `ChannelPriority` – the priority of the channel. Priority is expressed as an integer where higher values have a greater likelihood of being connected first.

`IChannel` also includes a simple public method, `Parse()`, that returns the URI of the object to which the channel is registered as well as the URI of the current channel.

There are rules to keep in mind when working with channels:

❏   At least one channel must be registered for each remote object that can be called. Channels are registered before remote objects are registered with the remoting framework. It is possible, and in many cases a good idea, to register more than one channel for a remote object. With more than one registered channel you have some built-in fault tolerance in case a channel goes down due to network problems. The `IChannel.ChannelPriority` gives developers the ability to prioritize one channel over another.

❏   Channels are registered in the context of an application domain and survive within the lifetime of a process. When a process dies, the channel goes with it. That's why our earlier Console Application example waited for the user to kill the running application with a keystroke. That's the only way the channel would have still been available to clients.

❏   Channels cannot be registered on the same port more than once. This only stands to reason. It is possible to create complicated channel scenarios in which multiple applications are involved registering the same channel on the same port causing run-time errors.

❏   Clients must call `RegisterChannel` before attempting to communicate with a remote object. The fact that a remote object is registered with the remoting service ensures the object's side of the channel configuration has been done properly; otherwise remoting would raise errors.

❏   Any channel that acts as a receiver of messages implements `IChannelReceiver`. Any channel that sends messages must implement `IChannelSender`. .NET Beta 2 ships with two ready made channel classes – `TcpChannel` and `HttpChannel`. Both implement `IChannelSender` and `IChannelReceiver`, in addition to `IChannel`. We will be working with these two classes in this chapter.

Registering Channels

There are a lot of details surrounding channels and their application in the remoting framework, but before we get into those details, let's consider a simple example. Recall our `Customer` object registered on a server in a Console Application. In the server code there were three lines relating to channels. At that time we said we'd be dealing with what exactly that code did, later on. Let's do it:

```
Dim oChannel As TcpChannel

oChannel = New TcpChannel(8888)
ChannelServices.RegisterChannel(oChannel)
```

In this example, we've created a `TcpChannel` instance that is listening on port 8888. The `RegisterChannel()` method actually registers our new channel with channel services. `RegisterChannel()` can throw two exceptions. The first is the standard bad argument exception – `ArgumentNullException`. The other is more important. As we've already mentioned, channels cannot be registered on the same port more than once. If your code registers oChannel on port 8888 twice, a `RemotingException` will be thrown. In multiple channel environments it may be prudent to wrap the channel registration in a `Try ... Catch` structure as follows:

```
oChannel = New TcpChannel(8888)
Try
    ChannelServices.RegisterChannel(oChannel)
Catch ex As Exception
    MsgBox(ex.message)
End Try
```

Let's take a quick look at the standard .NET channels – HttpChannel and TcpChannel.

HTTP Channel

The HttpChannel classes transport messages encoded in SOAP. It is very similar to the way Web Services can be configured in that Web Services expose functionality via HTTP and send and receive SOAP requests and responses. Any outbound messages are passed through a SOAP formatter where they are transformed into XML and serialized. The resulting stream is then sent to the remote object URI using HTTP. Inbound messages reverse the process.

Use the HttpChannel for applications that have to work across the Internet where firewall access is a concern. Since HTTP can be transported on port 80 and most server administrators have to open a port 80 to allow for web access, our applications will still work.

TCP Channel

The TcpChannel object is nearly identical to the HttpChannel object, with two differences. Firstly, any messages transported via the TcpChannel will be encoded in a proprietary binary format by default. Secondly, the TcpChannel is faster because it doesn't require larger XML messages to be encoded then serialized.

The drawback of the TcpChannel is the potential of not surviving trips through firewalls. For this reason, the TcpChannel is ideally suited for LAN and WAN applications.

Summary

In this chapter we've covered the basics of creating a .NET Remoting application. We covered how remote objects are instantiated and activated and our options for controlling that behavior. We also discussed the how .NET accomplishes Remoting using local proxies that represent remote objects.

In the last chapter in the book, we will look a revolutionary new way to document your code in Visual Studio .NET; C# XML Code Documentation.

16

C# Code Documentation

Documenting code has always been one of the most dreaded tasks in a development project. Even more painful is the thought of actually writing the same thing twice, adding comments above our lines of code to explain each variable, function, loop, and so on. It''s also tedious at the project end to create a document to be supplied to our client or employer that explains the functionality of our application. In most cases, we are not even allocated time at project completion to create this documentation. At that time, we generally would not find ourselves being as thorough and detailed in our comments either, so the best time to do this would be during development.

A lack of documentation in our source code is considered by many to be a bug and it can certainly make maintenance of the application very difficult. For example, very often we add a few lines of code to our source in order to handle a condition in our program, and these lines of code may not be very self-explanatory. Many times we have.cracked open a chunk of code for maintenance purposes and scratched our heads while saying to ourselves, "what does that line do?" or "what was I thinking when I wrote that?". A few lines of comment would definitely be a great asset in this situation.

Getting ourselves into the habit of commenting our code as we go along is not an easy task, and getting other programmers to do this can be worse that pulling teeth! In order to sell the idea of commenting to ourselves and other developers, we need to know in advance what the return on investment would be.

The purpose of this chapter is an introduction to the new XML documentation feature of C# and how we can transform this XML into more user-friendly documentation. It is important to note that this feature is currently not available in any other .NET language.

In this chapter, we will examine the following:

❑ Advantages of the XML documentation feature in C#

❑ Each of the predefined XML elements

❑ Compiling code with XML documentation

❑ Practical use in middle-tier components

❑ Examples of transforming XML documentation

❑ Options in Visual Studio .NET

❑ Best practices with comments

Advantages of XML Documentation in C#

Although the XML documentation feature in C# doesn't write comments for us, it does make documenting code much more rewarding by making extraction of the documentation simple. If we take the time to use this feature while we are creating our classes, then at the end of our project development, we will end up with completely documented code. Even better, a document separate from our source code, with all our comments in XML format, will be waiting for us once we've compiled our work.

Note that this feature doesn't replace the traditional single-line and multiple-line style of commenting code that we are used to; traditional commenting is still useful. The difference between traditional comments and XML comments is that the XML comments will be included in the aforementioned separate document, whereas the traditional comments will not.

As stated earlier, the most painful part of development can sometimes be creating documentation for our application source code. Those who have the responsibility for managing a large development project can appreciate the frustration involved with gathering documentation from individual developers into one standard format to be used as the specification for an application. One clear advantage of using the XML documentation feature of C# is that all generated documentation is in one common format, the beloved XML. Developers working on a large project can be instructed to use either the predefined XML documentation elements, which we'll be looking at shortly, or any custom elements required to comment code as it is being generated. They can even go so far as to provide code samples showing how to use the classes being created. It is important to mention that this will only benefit those developers who are coding in C#. Any classes written in languages other than C# will not (at least at the time of writing this book) be able to use this feature.

By adding XML documentation to our application, we gain the advantage of having the documentation included in the source code, which aids us in making future enhancements. At the same time we have a separate XML document with the same information that can be used as a help file for those interfacing with our application. We will take a look at transforming this raw XML into an easily displayable format later in this chapter.

Compilation of XML Documentation

In C#, XML documentation is not generated by default just because we have included XML documentation tags in our source code. The C# compiler must be instructed to do so.

To get familiar with this, let's take a quick look at some sample code that uses XML documentation tags. Open the well-known text editor, Notepad, type in the following lines of code, and save the file as `MyClass.cs` in a new folder named `Samples`:

```
using System;

namespace MyCompany.MyTechnology
{
    /// <summary>
    /// This class does nothing more than serve as a simple example
    /// </summary>
    public class MyClass
    {
    }
}
```

Notice the three lines of code directly beneath the namespace declaration. These lines are all preceded by three forward slashes. This tells the compiler that all characters found after these three forward slashes are to be treated as XML documentation. Even if the comments supplied are not enclosed within XML tags, the compiler will add these comments to the resulting document without any complaint. The `<summary>` element we used here is one of the pre-defined XML elements, which we'll be taking a closer look at later. Again, the existence of these lines alone does not cause the XML document to be generated; we need to instruct the compiler to give us this XML document as an output.

Compiling at Command Line

In order to generate an XML documentation file, we need to include the `/doc:filename` option in the list of compiler switches. If we omit this option, the compiler will simply ignore the XML comments. So let's open a command window, navigate to our `Samples` folder, and execute the following command:

>**csc /out:MyClass.dll /t:library /doc:ApplicationDocs.xml MyClass.cs**

As you know, `csc.exe` is the C# command line compiler and it has many switches for the various options available when compiling a C# application. These include the `/doc:filename` option, which instructs the compiler to create an XML output file in the location specified by `filename`. This location can be a relative path or an absolute path. In the example above, we will get a file `ApplicationDocs.xml` generated in the `Samples` folder, since we compiled from this folder. Also notice the use of a relative path instead of an absolute path like `C:\Samples\ApplicationDocs.xml`, which is certainly another acceptable option.

To see the resulting XML file of this comilation, let's open the `ApplicationDocs.xml` file in Notepad:

```
<?xml version="1.0"?>
<doc>
    <assembly>
        <name>MyClass</name>
    </assembly>
    <members>
        <member name="T:MyCompany.MyTechnology.MyClass">
            <summary>
                This class does nothing more than serve as a simple example
            </summary>
        </member>
    </members>
</doc>
```

Note the XML elements in this document. We included only the `<summary>` element in our code; all the other elements are supplied by the compiler. We'll take a look at these compiler-supplied elements later in the chapter.

What happens if we use the `/doc:` *filename* option without having any XML comments inside our source code? The compiler will still generate an XML file as we have instructed it to. However, the file will simply include a `<doc>` element containing an `<assembly>` child element. The `<assembly>` element will contain a `<name>` element and the text within the `<name>` element will be the value of whatever we have specified in the `/out:` switch. If we haven't specified anything in the `/out:` switch, then the name of the file containing our source code less the file extension will be supplied as the text within the `<name>` element.

For example, consider the case where we remove the three lines having XML comments from our `MyClass` code, and compile it with the same command we used before. The compiler will create the XML documentation file, but spit out a warning:

warning CS1591: Missing XML comment for publicly visible type or member "MyCompany.MyTechnology.MyClass".

The resulting documentation file will be as follows:

```xml
<?xml version="1.0"?>
<doc>
    <assembly>
        <name>MyClass</name>
    </assembly>
    <members>
    </members>
</doc>
```

Each time we compile an assembly and specify that we want an XML documentation file, the XML document will not simply be appended to or modified, but will be completely overwritten. However, as we will see soon, we can override this by using the `/incremental` command option. This is an important note to remember for any of us who decide to do any modification to the generated XML after the assembly is compiled.

Compiler Warnings

The C# compiler is keenly aware of our use of XML tags. In fact, if we create a class with two methods and place a `<summary>` tag before one method and not the other, the compiler will give us a warning similar to 'warning CS1591: Missing XML comment for publicly visible type or member'. This is only a warning and therefore still allows the application to compile if the option to treat warnings as errors is not turned on. This can become a bit of a nuisance when several warnings are output by the compiler. We may find ourselves staring at the results to see if a fatal error occurred or just a bunch of warnings. To stop these warnings from displaying, we can use the `/nowarn` option during compilation. This option can be used in conjunction with specific error numbers. For example, in order to stop the display of the above mentioned error, we would use the option `/nowarn:1591`, and this would put a stop to all 'CS1591' warnings.

A comma-separated list of error numbers can be used to specify more than one error number. The following example will suppress the warning we would get when an XML comment was not supplied for a publicly visible type or member, and the warning we would get for declaring a variable and never using it in our code:

```
>csc /nowarn:1591,168 /out:MyClass.dll /t:library /doc:ApplicationDocs.xml
  MyClass.cs
```

The /incremental Option

As we mentioned above, the C# compiler offers the /incremental option in its long list of options. This option, which can also be specified as /incremental+, enables incremental compilation, meaning that only those methods that have changed since the last compilation are recompiled. The compiler automatically creates .dbg and .incr files which contain the information about the state of previous compilation. Every time we change the compiler option from the previous /incremental option, these two files are fully rebuilt. By default, this option is disabled (/incremental-).

In an incremental build, the compiler will not rebuild the XML documentation file during compilation since the /doc option is ignored. Hence, if any additions were made to the comments within the source code, they would not be seen in the documentation file after compilation.

Since output files created with the /incremental option may be larger than those created with incremental compilation disabled. However, this option is good for those who have manually made changes to the XML documentation file and do not wish for the compiler to rebuild it.

Compiling for Visual Studio .NET

If we choose to create a C# project in Visual Studio .NET, then we will want to know how to instruct the compiler to generate an XML documentation file inside the development environment.

Inside Visual Studio .NET IDE, let's create an empty C# project named **MyClass** under our Samples folder. This will crate a project directory named MyClass under our Samples folder. Right click within the **Solution Explorer** window (on the righthand side of Visual Studio .NET), and select **Add | Add Existing Item** option from the resulting menu. Add our class MyClass to this project.

To generate the XML documentation, right click on the **MyClass** assembly. From the resulting menu, click the **Properties** menu option. This will open the **Property Pages** dialogue box for **MyClass** assembly as shown below:

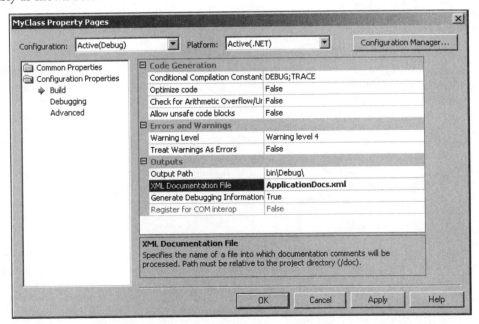

Select the Configuration Properties folder in the left hand window, and then select the Build option. You should then see the options that are displayed above in the right hand window. The XML Documentation File option specifies the name of the file into which documentation comments will be processed.

The documentation file will be created in our project directory, by default. However, we can also give a relative path, which will create the file in the specified directory relative to the project directory. If the specified directory doesn't exist, the project system will create it for us.

Once you enter the file name in the appropriate textbox, click OK. The next time we compile the application within the IDE, an XML document will be generated just as if we had used the /doc:*filename* option at the command line.

The incremental build property can be set to True or False by selecting the Advanced option in the left hand window.

Notepad has long been the favorite text editor of many developers. However, note that the Visual Studio .NET editor will give us intellisense for all the predefined XML documentation tags, even if we are simply using it as our editor and we have not created a project.

Compiler-supplied Elements

Now that we've seen how to compile our code to produce the XML documentation, let's take a look at the elements we see within the documentation file. Except for the <summary> element, these elements are all supplied by the C# compiler.

<doc>

The root element is generated for us and is named <doc>. The compiler will always supply this element as the root element.

<assembly>

Another element that the compiler creates for us is <assembly> and it has the child node <name>. The value supplied for the <name> element is determined by what we supply in the /out: switch during compilation, minus the file extension. In our earlier example, we compiled with /out:MyClass.dll, thus the value of the <name> element is MyClass.

The <assembly> element will always be present as the first child element in our resulting XML document, unless we are compiling a module and not an assembly. A module is a portable executable file of type .dll or .exe consisting of one or more classes and interfaces. One or more modules can be deployed as units to make up an assembly. So, if we were to use /t:module in our compiler options instead of /t:exe, /t:winexe, or /t:library, then we would not get an <assembly> element. Instead, the first child element following <doc> would be <members>. And this, of course, makes perfect sense since a module is not an assembly!

<members>

The <members> element will always have <member> elements as its children, and each of these <member> elements will always have a name attribute. Simply put, for each type in the assembly, a <member> element will be present.

<member>

The `<member>` element is used to describe the various members that can exist in a module or assembly. The members could be a class, interface, delegate, struct, enum, field, property, method, or an event. All XML tags, preceded by three forward slashes, that are placed directly above any one of these members in our source code will be processed by the C# compiler and output to the specified XML file, within the associated `<member>` element. This is illustrated in the earlier example where we have placed a `<summary>` tag above the `MyClass` member. `<summary>` has been appended as a child of the `MyClass` member in the resulting XML document.

The name Attribute

The value of the automatically generated name attribute of the `<member>` element can be broken down into three distinct parts. Let's break down the value `T:MyCompany.MyTechnology.MyClass`, which is the value given for the name attribute of the `<member>` element in our documentaion file.

First, notice the `T` followed by a colon. This is supplied by the compiler to indicate the nature of the member being identified. The table below explains the values that can be supplied as this first character, as well as a description of each one. This is useful later in this chapter when we decide how to transform this XML into a more user-friendly help file:

Character	Description
T	Type – can be a class, interface, delegate, struct, or enum
F	Field (member variable)
P	Property
M	Method (Constructors are considered methods also)
E	Event

The second distinct part of the name attribute's value, `MyCompany.MyTechnology`, is the namespace that this member belongs to. If we weren't using namespaces, then this second portion of the name attribute would simply not exist and our name attribute would consist of only two distinct parts, `T` and `MyClass`.

The third distinct part, `MyClass`, is the name given to the member in the member declaration.

Elements in XML Documentation

The C# compiler will actually process any valid XML elements that are properly placed in the source code. This means that these XML elements must be preceded by three forward slashes and defined directly above a class, delegate, interface, event, property, method, or a member, such as a field. However, several elements have been predefined by the developers of C#, because each of these elements has a function that is commonly used in most documentation. To get familiar with the use of this feature, we should begin by examining each of the predefined elements shown in the table below:

`<c>`	`<include>`	`<paramref>`	`<see>`
`<code>`	`<list>`	`<permission>`	`<seealso>`
`<example>`	`<para>`	`<remarks>`	`<summary>`
`<exception>`	`<param>`	`<returns>`	`<value>`

Though the table above only lists the predefined elements, we are not limited to only these elements. We can create any custom elements we feel necessary.

To illustrate the use of the pre-defined elements, we will create a class that interfaces with a shipping company. This class will have no real implementation; we will just create some types and members for the sake of illustrating the use of each element.

`<summary>` and `<remarks>`

We have already seen the `<summary>` element used in the *Compilation of XML Documentation* section. We used this element to give a brief summary of the class `MyClass`.

This element can be used to describe types, and the compiler will gladly supply our comments as an output in the XML document file. However, it is recommended that this element should be used to describe members of a 'type', such as class, interface, etc., and not the type itself. In comparison, the `<remarks>` element is intended for describing the type itslef.

When using Visual Studio .NET as our editor, we will notice that it will automatically add XML elements for us when we add three forward slashes directly above a type or member. Oddly enough, even though the SDK documentation recommends the use of `<remarks>` to describe a class, when we type three forward slashes above a type the IDE automatically adds the `<summary>` element for us instead of `<remarks>`. (At least this is the behavior in Beta 2 – maybe this will be changed in the final product.) The example below illustrates the proper use of these two elements. Notice that `<remarks>` is used to describe the class and `<summary>` is used to describe the method within the class:

```
using System;

namespace Wrox.Samples.Utility
{
    /// <remarks>
    /// This is the ShippingRates class
    /// It allows HTTP communication with
    /// Speedy Shippers to get shipping rates.
    /// </remarks>
    public class ShippingRates
    {
        /// <summary>
        /// This method is used to get shipping
        /// rates from Speedy Shippers.
        /// </summary>
        public string GetRates(string strXML)
        {
            return "";
        }
    }
}
```

<c>

The <c> element allows us to define the text within it as code. This would be used to mark a snippet of code that fits on one line. The word 'ShippingRates' in our example is the name of the class, and therefore should be distinguished as a word used in code by using the <c> element. The example below illustrates its use:

```
using System;

namespace Wrox.Samples.Utility
{
    /// <remarks>
    /// This is the <c>ShippingRates</c> class
    /// It allows HTTP communication with
    /// Speedy Shippers to get shipping rates.
    /// </remarks>
    public class ShippingRates
    {
    ...
    }
}
```

When transformed to HTML by our transformer application created later in the chapter, the line using the <c> tag would look like this:

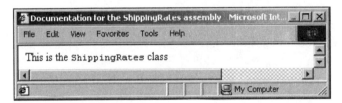

<para>

The <para> element is used to indicate a new paragraph inside other elements such as <summary> or <remarks>. Lengthy and descriptive comments are encouraged while creating our XML documentation, so, at times, we may want to specify a block of comments as a paragraph. The <para> element can be used as follows:

```
using System;

namespace Wrox.Samples.Utility
{
    /// <remarks>
    /// This is the <c>ShippingRates</c> class.
    /// <para>It allows HTTP communication with
    /// Speedy Shippers to get shipping rates.</para>
    /// </remarks>
    public class ShippingRates
    {
      ...
    }
}
```

When transformed it would look like this:

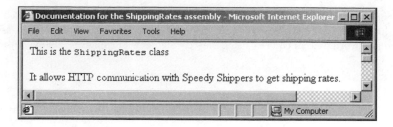

<param> and <returns>

The <param> element is used to describe the parameters of a method. The <returns> element is pretty self-explanatory as it is used to describe the return value of the method. One of the very cool features of the Visual Studio .NET editor is that it will add <summary>, <returns>, and <param> elements for each method in our class as soon as we type three forward slashes directly above a method declaration. However, we have to specify the data type of the return value and all parameters. The compiler doesn't make any distinction as to what data types these are.

name Attribute of <param>

The <param> element has one attribute, name. For each parameter in a method, a <param> element should be supplied. The name attribute would understandably hold the name of the parameter. When the Visual Studio .NET editor adds the <param> element it also supplies a name attribute and the parameter name in quotes for us. An example of their use is as follows:

```
public class ShippingRates
{
    /// <summary>
    /// This method is used to get shipping
    /// rates from Speedy Shippers.
    /// </summary>
    /// <param name="strXML">
    /// This is a string of well formed XML
    /// that describes the packages to be rated. </param>
    /// <returns>A string of well formed XML with all
    /// available shipping rates and options.
    /// </returns>
    public string GetRates(string strXML)
    {
        return "";
    }
}
```

After we transform the resulting XML doc, this is what we will get:

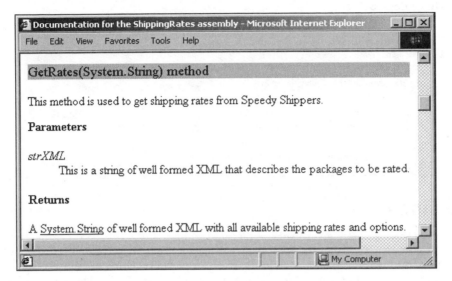

<paramref>

The <paramref> tag is used to mark a word in text as a parameter that is used in a method. This tag serves the purpose of allowing a transformation to highlight this word in some distinct way. It is not intended to be used as a hyperlink to more information on the parameter. The <paramref> tag has one attribute, name. The value of this attribute should be the name of the parameter being referenced. In our example below, we are referring to a parameter used by the GetRates() method inside the ShippingRates class:

```
public class ShippingRates
{
    /// <summary>
    /// This method is used to get shipping
    /// rates from Speedy Shippers. A string
    /// of XML is supplied to the <paramref
    /// name = "strXML"/> parameter of the
    /// GetRates method
    /// </summary>
    /// <param name="strXML"> This is a string of well formed XML
    /// that describes the packages to be rated. </param>
    /// <returns>A string of well formed XML with all
    /// available shipping rates and options.
    /// </returns>
    public string GetRates(string strXML)
    {
        return "";
    }
}
```

We can transform the resulting XML so that it will display the value of the name attribute in a special font as we have done below:

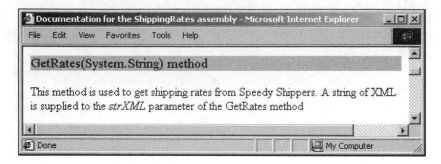

<permission>

The <permission> element gives us the ability to document the access to a member. In the SDK documentation, each class from the .NET framework class library has a 'members' page, which breaks the properties and methods up into sections by their accessibility. Using the <permission> element gives us the ability to do the same when transforming the resulting XML. This element has one attribute, cref. The cref attribute should have its value set to a member that is available in the current compilation environment. The value given to the <permission> element itself should describe its accessibility. Notice its use in the example below:

```
public class ShippingRates
{
    ...
    /// <returns>A string of well formed XML with all available shipping
    /// rates and options.
    /// </returns>
    /// <permission cref="GetRates">
    /// Public Instance Method</permission>
    public string GetRates(string strXML)
    {
        return "";
    }
    /// <summary>
    /// If kilograms is supplied as the UnitOfMeasurement
    /// then we need to convert it to pounds before requesting
    /// rates
    /// </summary>
    /// <param name="packageXML">XML string
    /// describing a package</param>
    /// <returns>Converted XML package</returns>
    /// <permission cref="ConvertKGStoLBS">
    /// Protected Instance Method</permission>
    protected string ConvertKGStoLBS(string packageXML)
    {
        return "";
    }
}
```

The following shows what the documentation for the `ConvertKGStoLBS()` method would look like after being transformed:

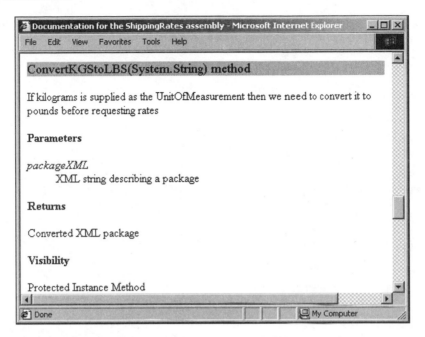

<see> and <seealso>

The `<see>` element can be placed within `<summary>` or `<remarks>` elements and used to specify a hyperlink to any another section in the document. A 'See Also' section is an area that is generally located at the bottom of a member definition and contains hyperlinks to other members that are referenced in the definition of this particular member. The `<seealso>` element can be used to specify a hyperlink to a member to be included in the 'See Also' section of the documentation. Later in the chapter, we'll use this element while creating our help file.

These elements should be used when referring to other classes or members. This provides the transforming application an opportunity to create a hyperlink to the documentation for that particular type or member.

Cref Attribute

Both `<see>` and `<seealso>` elements have one attribute named `cref`. The value of this attribute must be a reference to a member or field that is available to be called from the current compilation environment. The C# compiler will check that the value supplied to the `cref` attribute is a real member that exists.

In the example below, notice the use of the value `String` supplied to the `cref` attribute of the `<see>` element. The compiler will check for the existence of a class named `'String'` in the context of our assembly. Since we have a `'using System;'` directive supplied at the top of our source code, the compiler will output the fully qualified name `T:System.String` as the value for the `cref` attribute in our XML documentation file. If we omit the `'using System;'` directive, then the compiler will issue the warning:

XML comment on "Wrox.Samples.Utility.ShippingRates.GetRates(string)" has cref attribute "String" that could not be found.

This warning will be issued as long as we are not using the /nowarn:1574 option to suppress it. We have also added a `<see>` element with 'XmlDocument' supplied as its cref attribute value. This requires that we include a 'using System.Xml;' directive to avoid the compiler warning. Also notice the use of the two `<seealso>` elements:

```
using System;
using System.Xml;

namespace Wrox.Samples.Utility
{
    ...

    public class ShippingRates
    {
        /// <summary>
        /// This method is used to get shipping
        /// rates from Speedy Shippers. A string
        /// of XML is supplied to the <paramref
        /// name = "strXML"/> parameter of the
        /// GetRates method
        /// </summary>
        /// <param name="strXML"> This is a string of well formed XML
        /// that describes the packages to be rated.</param>
        /// <returns>A <see cref="String"/> of well formed XML with all
        /// available shipping rates and options. This value can be loaded
        ///into a <see cref="XmlDocument"/>
        /// This string of XML should be validated.</returns>
        /// <permission cref="ConvertKGStoLBS">
        /// Protected Instance Method</permission>
        /// <seealso cref="XmlTextReader"/>
        /// <seealso cref="XmlValidatingReader"/>
        public string GetRates(string strXML)
        {
            return "";
        }
    ...
    }
}
```

Below is what this would look like after transforming it with our sample application described later:

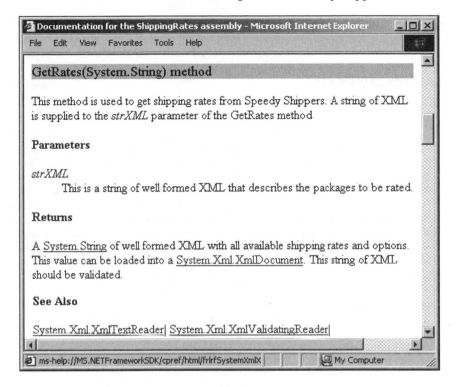

<list>

The <list> element can be used within elements such as <summary> or <remarks> to define a bulleted list, a numbered list, or a definition table. The <list> element has one attribute called type. This element can have one <listheader> element as its first child and one or many <item> elements as its children.

type attribute

The purpose of the type attribute is to describe the type of list being supplied. The value of type can be bullet, number, or table. When bullet is specified, it is expected that when transforming the XML, a bulleted list will be output. Specifying number assumes the transforming application will output a numbered list. Supplying the value as table expects a transformation of list items into a table.

<listheader>

The <listheader> element can be used to supply header information to our list of items. If we were to equate a <list> element to an HTML table, then the <list> element would be the equivalent of the <table> element in HTML and the <listheader> would be the equivalent of the <thead> and <tr> HTML combination in HTML.

<item>

The <item> element allows us to supply each individual item being described in the body of the <list>. The <item> tag could be considered as the equivalent of the <tr> HTML tag within the <table> element.

<term> and <description>

The <term> and <description> elements are supplied as children of both the <listheader> and <item> elements. When used as children of <listheader> they can be equated to <th> tags of a table element in HTML. When transformed, the values supplied to these children of <listheader> should be output in a way that indicates a heading, such as bold text. When these tags are supplied as children of <item>, they can be considered as the equivalent of <td> HTML table element tags.

As we will notice in the following example, this requires quite a bit of extra typing. Using tables and bulleted lists within the documentation is certainly not necessary, but can give a much more professional look when used. It is understandable that the great amount of extra typing would be intimidating to some of us who have a difficult time with just adding single line comments. But notice how the following example shows the use of these elements to create a <list> in table format. Let's decide for ourselves if this is worth the effort. I certainly think so. Our <list> will describe the string of XML that is expected as an input to the GetRates() method:

```
public class ShippingRates
{
    /// <summary>
    /// This method is used to get shipping
    /// rates from Speedy Shippers. A string
    /// of XML is supplied to the <paramref
    /// name = "strXML"/> parameter of the
    /// GetRates method
    /// </summary>
    /// <param name="strXML">This is a string of well formed XML
    /// that describes the packages to be rated.</param>
    /// <returns>A <see cref="String"/> of well formed XML with all
    /// available shipping rates and options. This value can be loaded
    ///into a <see cref="XmlDocument"/>
    /// This string of XML should be validated.</returns>
    /// <remarks>This table describes the XML
    /// string required by this method
    /// <list type="table">
    /// <listheader>
    /// <term>XML Element</term>
    /// <description>Value of Element</description>
    /// </listheader>
    /// <item>
    /// <term>Packages</term>
    /// <description>Root node with only child
    /// elements as content</description>
    /// </item>
    /// <item>
    /// <term>OriginatingPostalCode</term>
    /// <description>Zip code of shipping location</description>
    /// </item>
    /// <item>
```

```
///    <term>DestinationPostalCode</term>
///    <description>Zip code of ship-to location</description>
///    </item>
///    <item>
///    <term>UnitOfMeasurement</term>
///    <description>This value must be either
///    kilograms or pounds</description>
///    </item>
///    <item>
///    <term>Weight</term>
///    <description>This is a number specifying the
///    weight of the package</description>
///    </item>
///    </list>
///    </remarks>
///    <permission cref="ConvertKGStoLBS">
///    Protected Instance Method</permission>
///    <seealso cref="XmlTextReader"/>
///    <seealso cref="XmlValidatingReader"/>
public string GetRates(string strXML)
{
    return "";
}
...
}
```

Here is what it looks after being transformed by the aforementioned application:

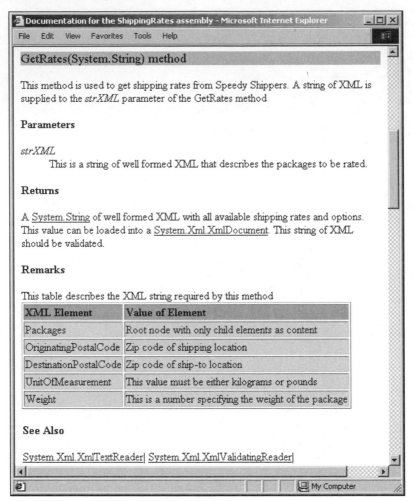

<example> and <code>

The <example> element is used to specify an example of how to use a method or class. This is always used with the <code> element, which is used to mark text as code. We already saw the <c> element, which serves the purpose of marking up single line code fragments, but the <code> element would be more appropriate for large blocks of multiple lines of code. We can apply special formatting to text within a <code> element. I find that replacing the <code> tag with a <pre> tag while transforming the XML to HTML is a great way to display the example code. Supplying examples of how to use classes and their methods adds a great deal of value to our documentation. Notice the use of these two elements in the sample below:

```
public class ShippingRates
{
    ...
```

```
/// <remarks>...
/// </remarks>
/// <example> This example shows how to use the
/// GetRates method of the ShippingRates class
/// <code>
/// ********************************************************
/// using System;
/// using System.Text;
/// using Wrox.Samples.Utility;
///
/// public class Run
/// {
///     public static void Main()
///     {
///         try
///         {
///             ShippingRates shippingRates = new ShippingRates();
///             StringBuilder sbXML = new
///                 StringBuilder("&lt;Packages&gt;");
///             sbXML.Append("&lt;OriginatingPostalCode&gt;" +
///                 "80000&lt;/OriginatingPostalCode&gt;");
///             sbXML.Append("&lt;DestinationPostalCode&gt;" +
///                 "90000&lt;/DestinationPostalCode&gt;");
///             sbXML.Append("&lt;UnitOfMeasurement&gt;" +
///                 "kilograms&lt;/UnitOfMeasurement&gt;");
///             sbXML.Append("&lt;Weight&gt;3.5&lt;/Weight&gt;");
///             sbXML.Append("&lt;/Packages&gt;");
///             string retXML =
///                 shippingRates.GetRates(sbXML.ToString());
///         }
///         catch(Exception e)
///         {
///             Console.WriteLine(e.ToString());
///         }
///     }
/// }
/// </code>
/// </example>
/// <permission cref="ConvertKGStoLBS">
/// Protected Instance Method</permission>
/// <seealso cref="XmlTextReader"/>
/// <seealso cref="XmlValidatingReader"/>
public string GetRates(string strXML)
{
    return "";
}
...
}
```

In the above example, we want to show users of this class how to create a string of well formed XML to be supplied as an input to the GetRates() method. But notice that we are creating the '<' and '>' characters using the '<' and '>' encoding. This is done because our output is XML and these characters, obviously, have special meaning in XML. This is what it would look like when transformed:

Documentation for the ShippingRates assembly - Microsoft Internet Explorer

File   Edit   View   Favorites   Tools   Help

Example

This example shows how to use the GetRates method of the ShippingRates class

```
*****************************************************************
using System;
using System.Text;
using MyCompany.Utility;

public class Run
{
    public static void Main()
    {
        try
        {
            ShippingRates shippingRates = new ShippingRates();
            StringBuilder sbXML = new
                StringBuilder("<Packages>");
            sbXML.Append("<OriginatingPostalCode>" +
                "80000</OriginatingPostalCode>");
            sbXML.Append("<DestinationPostalCode>" +
                "90000</DestinationPostalCode>");
            sbXML.Append("<UnitOfMeasurement>" +
                "kilograms</UnitOfMeasurement>");
            sbXML.Append("<Weight>3.5</Weight>");
            sbXML.Append("</Packages>");
            string retXML =
                shippingRates.GetRates(sbXML.ToString());
        }
        catch(Exception e)
        {
            Console.WriteLine(e.ToString());
        }
    }
}
```

My Computer

<value>

The <value> element is simply used to describe properties that we have defined in our classes. It should be placed directly above that property and used to define a property. The example below illustrates its use:

```
public class ShippingRates
{
    ...
    public string GetRates(string strXML)
    {
        return "";
    }
    ...
    /// <summary>
    /// this is a private field
    /// </summary>
```

```
      private string shippingRatesURL =
      "www.SpeedyShippers.com/SpeedyRates";
      /// <value>This property holds the URL that
      /// we are posting to</value>
      /// <permission cref="ShippingRatesURL">
      /// Public Instance Field</permission>
      public string ShippingRatesURL
      {
         get{return this.shippingRatesURL;}
         set{ShippingRatesURL = this.shippingRatesURL;}
      }
   }
```

After transforming the XML it would look like this:

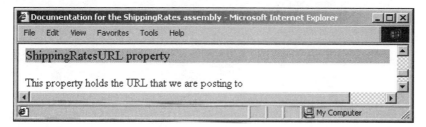

<exception>

The <exception> element is used to supply documentation for our custom exception classes. The <exception> element has one attribute, cref. The value supplied to this attribute must be the name of an exception class that is accessible to the current compilation environment. This value will be checked by the C# compiler to verify that it does exist.

In our example below, we only supply the value ShippingRatesException to the cref attribute; but after compiling, we will notice that the C# compiler has replaced this value with T:Wrox.Samples.Utility.ShippingRatesException. The single letter 'T' followed by a colon is to identify the kind of member, followed by the fully qualified name of the exception class. We will create an exception class below for our ShippingRates class:

```
using System;
using System.Xml;

namespace Wrox.Samples.Utility
{
    public class ShippingRates
    {
    ...
    }
    /// <exception cref="ShippingRatesException">
    /// This exception will be thrown when
    /// an error occurs in the <c>ShippingRates</c>
    /// class</exception>
    public class ShippingRatesException: Exception
    {
```

```
      /// <summary>
      /// The <c>ShippingRatesException</c> class
      /// constructor
      /// </summary>
      /// <param name="message">
      /// This is the error message
      /// </param>
      public ShippingRatesException(string message): base(message)
      {
      }
      /// <summary>
      /// Overloaded constructor for <c>ShippingRatesException</c> class
      /// </summary>
      /// <param name="message">This is the error message</param>
      /// <param name="innerException">This is the innerException</param>
      /// <seealso cref = "Exception"></seealso>
      public ShippingRatesException(string message, Exception
                       innerException)
      : base(message, innerException)
      {
      }
   }
}
```

Here is the transformed output:

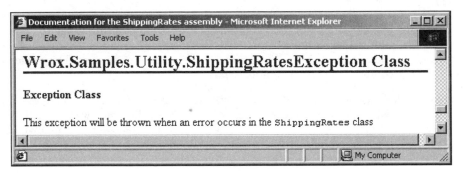

<include>

The <include> element gives an alternative to putting XML comments directly in our source code. This tag is available to us so that we can have better portability and more flexibility in using XML comments. This is a very nice feature to have, since XML comments can become quite lengthy and quickly begin to take up the bulk of characters in our source code files. This wouldn't necessarily be a bad thing, but some developers might like to have the XML comments separate from the source code just because of personal preference.

The <include> element also gives us the ability to include supplemental documents that we would like to include in our documentation without copying all the comments into our source code.

When creating generic helper objects, we may want to have more than one set of XML comments for our classes. We may reuse our objects in several different projects, and while doing so we may find it necessary to customize the documentation accordingly. So the <include> element allows us to point to an external file that will hold our XML comments for that class. The <include> element has `file` and `path` attributes.

file Attribute

The value of the `file` attribute of the <include> element must be set to the name of our external XML documentation file. This can be a qualified path or a relative path. We will take a look at how to create an external file in a moment.

path Attribute

The value of the `path` attribute is an XPath statement that points to the element holding the XML comments for an individual member. To include the element (with name such as `'id'`) holding these comments, XPath syntax would be `rootElement/memberElement[@name = "id"]`. Let's look at an example of using the <include> element. We'll call this file `ShippingRatesWithExternalComments.cs`:

```
using System;
using System.Xml;

namespace Wrox.Samples.Utility
{

    /// <include file="ExternalComments.xml"
    /// path="members/member[@name="ShippingRatesClass"]/*"/>
    public class ShippingRates
    {

        /// <include file="ExternalComments.xml"
        /// path="members/member[@name="GetRatesMethod"]/*"/>
        public string GetRates(string strXML)
        {
            return "";
        }


        /// <include file="ExternalComments.xml"
        /// path="members/member[@name="ConvertKGStoLBSMethod"]/*"/>
        protected string ConvertKGStoLBS(string packageXML)
        {
            return "";
        }

        private string shippingRatesURL;

        /// <include file="ExternalComments.xml"
        /// path="members/member[@name="ShippingRatesURLProperty"]/*"/>
        public string ShippingRatesURL
        {
            get{return this.shippingRatesURL;}
            set{ShippingRatesURL = this.shippingRatesURL;}
```

```
        }
    }

    /// <include file="ExternalComments.xml"
    /// path="members/member[@name="ShippingRatesExceptionClass"]/*"/>
    public class ShippingRatesException: Exception
    {
        public ShippingRatesException(string message): base(message)
        {
        }
    }
}
```

We have placed an `<include>` element above each member we want to have external XML comments generated for. We have chosen to use a single external file named `ExternalComments.xml`, even though we have the flexibility to specify several separate external comment files if we choose to.

External File

The external XML comments file needs to be formatted as a valid XML document. A root node should exist and each child node of the root should describe a member in our source code. The file can be named whatever we choose and can have any extension we choose. For our example we will use the `.xml` extension. The `ExternalComments.xml` file referenced in the `<include>` elements is available for download from http://www.wrox.com.

Keep in mind that each `<member>` element has a name attribute. This name attribute must be unique within the `<members>` element in order to get the proper results.

Now we will compile the `ShippingRatesWithExternalComments.cs` file with the following command:

>csc /out:ShippingRatesWithExternalComments.dll /t:library /nowarn:1591,0649
  /doc:ShippingRatesDocsExternal.xml ShippingRatesWithExternalComments.cs

This will result in a file called `ShippingRatesDocsExternal.xml`.

Extensibility

We have now seen every predefined XML documentation tag supplied for us by the designers of C#. But what if we wish there were some other tags available that would be useful to us? What if you wanted to have a `<developer>` element to identify the name of the developer of a class, or perhaps `<dateCreated>`, `<dateModified>`, or `<email>` elements? Well, keep in mind what was noted earlier, the C# compiler will process any valid XML tags that are placed above a type or member. We can add whatever tags you need in your comments.

These XML comments are unquestionably going to force us to spend more time typing while we write our code, but the end result is well worth it. These comments are very useful when developing in a team environment. When handing over a chunk of code to be used, finished, or changed by another team member, the ability to scan through the comments in a nicely formatted document will certainly make any team member more productive. But what other reasons may we have for using these XML comments? What if we are in the business of creating third party utilities to be included in larger projects? How can XML comments be of benefit to us? Let's see the next topic.

Practical Use in the Middle-tier

Early in this chapter, help files were mentioned a few times. Depending on the type of development we have done, we may think of help files differently. Take for example a small application that only requires a single developer to write it. If this developer was responsible for generating a help file for this application, it would most likely consist of instructions on how to operate the various user screens and controls within them. Therefore, the C# XML documentation would not prove to be very useful in aiding the production of this help file. But one of the biggest benefits of XML comments in C# is the use of them in middle-tier components.

The type of help file being discussed here should be understood as the type of documentation that describes how to use an object or set of objects in a development project. This is very similar to the type of documentation that is used when developing with the .NET libraries.

When developing helper objects, data objects, business objects or any middle-tier component, we always have to keep in mind that we are developing these components for use by other developers. Middle-tier components serve the purpose of doing heavy duty processing many times, but also serve the purpose of creating a layer of abstraction between the developer and the data being processed by the component.

We don't want other developers to waste time trying to understand the inner workings of a component we have created. The component should expose the leanest interface possible to its user, in order to keep its use as simple as possible. Let's face it, when we crank up the digital surround sound in our living room, most of us are content knowing that we can do this with a couple buttons and knobs and we aren't forced to understand digital decoders and all their inner workings to use them. With that thought in mind, what about the 'user's manual' that comes with any sophisticated electronics equipment. Does this manual usually tell us, in detail, exactly how everything inside it works together to produce a certain output? No, but it does tell us how to use it. And compared to the complex inner workings of many devices, the buttons and knobs we learn to use by reading the owners manual seem quite simple to operate.

With middle-tier component development we should be mindful of how to best use the XML comments.

Best Practices with Comments in the Middle-tier

In this section we'll look at some points to keep in mind when using XML comments with middle-tier components.

Detailed Comments for Public Types and Members

When creating classes, we can use the `<remarks>` element to fully explain the practical use of the class. Mentioning some specific business requirements that made the development of this class is useful. The `<example>` and `<code>` elements could be used together to show how this class is instantiated and how to cast it into the various interfaces it may implement.

A class may have several overloaded constructors that are useful in a variety of circumstances. Consider using the `<summary>` element to explain when and why each constructor should be used. Why not use the `<example>` and `<code>` elements to show how these constructors are used? When appropriate, use the `<see>` element to make hyperlinks from the constructor parameters, since these constructor parameters are likely setting a property that is also defined within the class.

s may also have many properties defined within it. The `<value>` element can be used to explain what these properties are used for, because property names aren't always descriptive enough.

We'll consider using `<summary>` elements on public methods explaining the functions performed within them. All parameters would be better understood if a `<param>` element was associated with them and a detailed description of the purpose they serve was provided. Any method that returns a value could have a `<returns>` element defined to describe it. The `<permission>` element can also be used to identify the members' accessibility. This will allow members to be grouped by their accessibility when the resulting XML document is transformed.

It would be a great benefit if all public structs, enums, events, and delegates were thoroughly explained with the `<summary>` tag.

We shouldn't always assume that when referring to another type or member, the reader of the documentation knows how to get more information about it. Why not use the `<see>` element to create hyperlinks to these other types or members within elements such as `<summary>` and `<remarks>`. The `<seealso>` element can also be used to create references to related types that may be used in conjunction with the one you are currently documenting. This allows greater flexibility and a more user-friendly help file when this XML doc is transformed.

Good Enough Comments for Non-Public Types and Members

We will undoubtedly be creating many private and protected fields and methods within our classes. At times we will be creating private inner classes. These members that are not seen at the public interface level, generally do the brunt of the work in our classes. The fact that these members remain inaccessible to the user of the component doesn't necessarily mean that the user shouldn't know of their existence or what they do.

Non-public members generally won't need comments in as great a detail as public ones. For example, we would most likely not need to use the `<example>` and `<code>` tags since these non-public methods don't expose an interface to the user. However, it would be very beneficial to use the `<summary>` elements to explain these members. In many cases, several private methods exist in a class, carrying out very specific functions. Don't leave the user of a component completely in the dark; give a summary of the work done by these methods. This will serve as a great aid in better understanding the functionality of a component. And again, we could use the `<permission>` element to identify the members accessibility`, allowing the members to be grouped by their accessibility when the resulting XML document is transformed.

Transformations

The XML document that is generated by compiling with the `/doc:filename` option is completely full of all the information we need to properly document our application, provided we have used the XML tags properly and in detail.

We have taken a look at each supplied XML tag in detail. Let's take a look at the complete `ShippingRates` class, fully commented, using all predefined tags, and compiled with the `/doc:filename` option. We will then examine a helper application that will take our XML as an input documentation file and transform it into a more user-friendly help file. This is compiled with the following command:

```
>csc /out:ShippingRates.dll /t:library /doc:ShippingRatesDocs.xml ShippingRates.cs
```

The following is a portion of the compiler-generated `ShippingRatesDocs.xml` file:

```xml
<?xml version="1.0"?>
<doc>
  <assembly>
    <name>ShippingRates</name>
  </assembly>
  <members>
    <member name="T:Wrox.Samples.Utility.ShippingRates">
      <remarks>
      This is the <c>ShippingRates</c> class
      <para>It allows HTTP communication with
      Speedy Shippers to get shipping rates.</para>
      </remarks>
      <seealso cref="T:System.Net.HttpWebRequest"/>
      <seealso cref="T:System.Net.HttpWebResponse"/>
    </member>
    <member name="M:Wrox.Samples.Utility.ShippingRates.#ctor">
      <summary>
      This is the default constructor
      </summary>
    </member>

    . . .

  </members>
</doc>
```

Sample Transformation Application

The resulting XML file above is now ready to take on a more friendly presentation. Our goal is to take raw XML and transform it into a more user-friendly help file. The best suitable tool for the job would no doubt be **eXtensible Stylesheet Language Transformations (XSLT)**. Hence, what we will do is create the `HelpFile.xsl` stylesheet file which will transform our `ShippingRatesDocs.xml` file into an HTML help file.

We are also going to create the `XMLTransformer.exe` console application. This application takes three command line arguments – the filename of an XML documentation file, the filename of the `.xsl` file containing our XSLT transformation, and a filename to output the HTML that is generated by our application. So let's get started by first creating a file named `HelpFile.xsl` and defining our transformations. This file will also make use of the `<msxsl:script>` tag and some C# script. The C# script is included in our example so that we can use the `System.String` class supplied in the .NET libraries as well as the reflection capabilities in order to distinguish between types.

The XSLT Stylesheet

Let's begin by creating the base shell for this stylesheet. First we need to add the XML processing instruction. We then create our `<xsl:stylesheet>` element and add the appropriate namespaces. Notice that we have included the `xmlns:msxsl="urn:schemas-microsoft-com:xslt"` namespace, because the `<msxsl:script>` element belongs to this namespace. The `xmlns:user="urn:my-scripts"` namespace is used to identify a script block and we have chosen to use this namespace as our namespace; but this can be whatever we choose.

The `<msxsl:script>` element must include a `language` attribute and have its value set to either `C#`, `VB`, `JScript` or `JavaScript`. The language we specify refers to the language we will use to write our script and has nothing to do with the language used when creating our XML output. The `implements-prefix` attribute is also mandatory. This attribute is used to declare a namespace and associate it with the script block. The value of this attribute is the prefix that represents the namespace which in our case is `xmlns:user="urn:my-scripts"`.

We will be adding C# script as we go along:

```
<?xml version="1.0" ?>
<xsl:stylesheet version="1.0"
    xmlns:xsl="http://www.w3.org/1999/XSL/Transform"
    xmlns:msxsl="urn:schemas-microsoft-com:xslt"
    xmlns:user="urn:my-scripts">
    <msxsl:script language="C#" implements-prefix="user">

    </msxsl:script>
</xsl:stylesheet>
```

Let's take a minute to add a few functions to our script. These functions will be used to determine the kind of member being processed based on the first letter in the name. Let's enter the following functions within our `<msxsl:script>` element. These functions simply return a Boolean value based on the first letter of the member name. Remember, if our member name starts with 'T' then we know it's a type, if it starts with 'M' then we know it's a method, if it starts with a 'P' then it's a property, and if it starts with 'F' it's a field. We will call these functions as we evaluate our members so that we can process them appropriately:

```
bool IsType(string name)
{
    return name.StartsWith("T");
}
bool IsMethod(string name)
{
    return name.StartsWith("M");
}
bool IsProperty(string name)
{
    return name.StartsWith("P");
}
bool IsField(string name)
{
    return name.StartsWith("F");
}
```

Since we are on a roll adding to the script, we continue adding the rest of the functions that will be using in our transformation. We will add the `FullTypeName()` function directly below the previous functions but still within the `<msxsl:script>` element. This function will only be called if the member being processed is a type (class, interface, enum, struct, etc). The `FullTypeName()` function will take two parameters as an input. The first parameter is the name of the type and the second parameter is the name of the assembly that this type belongs to:

```
string FullTypeName(string typeName, string assemblyName)
{
    // Trim off the T:
```

```
            typeName = typeName.Substring(2);
            System.Reflection.Assembly a =
            System.Reflection.Assembly.Load(assemblyName);
            Type t = a.GetType(typeName);
            if(t.IsClass)
            {
                return t.FullName + " Class";
            }
            // use other methods of the Type
            // class to determine if this
            // type is a struct, enum, interface......
            else
            {
                return t.FullName;
            }
        }
```

As we have already discovered, the XML documentation doesn't distinguish between types. Whether the type is a class, interface, enum, or whatever, the member name starts with a 'T'. In order to determine if our type is a class or any other kind, we need to use classes in the `System.Reflection` namespace to discover this. In our `FullTypeName()` function, we are loading the assembly containing the type being evaluated and then creating an instance 't' of the `type` using the `a.GetType()` method where 'a' is our assembly name. We then pass in the type name as a parameter to this method in order to reflect against our type. Now that we have a reference to our type, we can determine if this is a class or some other type. For the sake of brevity, we are only testing to see if this is a class, and if it is then we append the word `'Class'` to its name. However we could use other properties of the `type` to test for other types such as interface, struct, etc.

We'll add the method called `MethodName()` directly below the `FullTypeName()` method but within the `<msxsl:script>` element. This method will be called when the member we are evaluating is a method. Since constructors are methods, we will check to see if we are evaluating a constructor; we can determine that a method is a constructor if the name ends with `'.#ctor'`. And if so, we will remove the `'.#ctor'` from the name and append the word `'constructor'` to the name. If it's not a constructor then we will append the word `'Method'` to the name. The rest of the string manipulation in this method is in place to trim the name down to only the method name and any parameters it may accept:

```
        string MethodName(string name)
        {
            // Check to see if this method is a constructor
            // and if so remove ".#ctor" from the name
            // and append the word "Constructor"
            // or append the word "Method"
            if(name.IndexOf("#ctor") != -1)
            {
                name = name.Replace(".#ctor","");
                name +=" constructor";
            }
            else
            {
                name += " Method";
            }
            // Check for the existence of parameters
```

```
        int i = name.IndexOf("(");
        // If no parameters exist then remove all characters
        // existing before the last "." in the name
        if(i == -1)
        {
            int lastDot = name.LastIndexOf(".") + 1;
            name = name.Substring(lastDot);
        }
        // If parameters exist then remove all the
        // characters in the name except for the
        // characters between the last '.' found
        // existing before the first " ('), and the
        // first ' ('
        else
        {
            int lastDot2 = name.LastIndexOf(".",i,i );
            lastDot2++;
            name = name.Substring(lastDot2);
        }
        return name;
}
```

Let's add two more simple functions immediately after `MethodName()` function to handle property and field names. These two functions simply return the name of the property or field with the word 'Property' or 'Field' appended. The `PropertyName()` function will only be called if a property is being evaluated whereas the `FieldName()` function will only be called if a field is being evaluated:

```
string PropertyName(string name)
{
    return name.Substring
    (name.LastIndexOf(".") + 1) + " Property";
}
string FieldName(string name)
{
    return name.Substring
    (name.LastIndexOf(".") + 1) + " Field";
}
```

Now just two more functions are to be added in our script and we are ready to create our XSL templates. The `MakeHyperlink()` and `Reference()` methods are called when a `<see>` or `<seealso>` element is evaluated. The value of the `cref` attribute is sent as the parameter for both the methods. The purpose of the `MakeHyperlink()` method is to create a path to be used as the value for an `href` attribute in an anchor (`<a>`) tag in HTML. If we have the .NET framework SDK installed then the hyperlink created by this method will direct us to the class in the SDK documentation. The method removes the first two characters of the class name (usually 'T:'), then all periods are stripped from the fully qualified name of the class and used to make up part of the hyperlink. The `Reference()` method is simply used to remove the first two characters from the value sent in. Let's add these two functions next to `FieldName()`:

```
string MakeHyperLink(string reference)
{
    // Remove the first two characters from
    // the cref attribute
```

```
            string strSee = reference.Substring(2);
            // create a link to the SDK docs by using the
            // class name without the periods
            return "ms-help://MS.NETFrameworkSDK" +
            "/cpref/html/frlrf" + strSee.Replace(".", "") +
            "ClassTopic.htm";
        }
        string Reference(string name)
        {
            return name.Substring(2);
        }
```

In the above `MakeHyperLink()` function, we are returning a hyperlink to the .NET framework documents. I used the path `"ms-help://MS.NETFrameworkSDK/cpref/html/frlrf"` with the fully qualified class name minus the periods appended afterward, and then appending `"ClassTopic.htm"`. (The link seems to work fine for me.) All of the `<see>` and `<seealso>` elements used in this example are links to classes found in the .NET SDK. However, we may also consider the cases where we would be creating links to other classes within our own set of documentation.

Now that we have all our script functions done, we can start createing XSL templates. The first thing we need to do is get a match to our root node and add some HTML tags. We'll add a `<style>` tag to help make the resulting HTML a slight bit more appealing to the eyes. We will use the name of the assembly as the title of the document. In the body of the HTML document we will first display the name of the assembly and then proceed to process each member element. Let's add the following code within the `<xsl:stylesheet>` element after the `<msxsl:script>` element:

```
<xsl:template match="/">
    <html>
        <head>
            <style>
                h1{border-bottom-color:Black;
                border-bottom-style:double;
                border-bottom-width:thick}
                h2 {font-weight:700;color:Blue;
                border-bottom:solid 3px blue}
                h3{font-weight:500;background-color:silver}
                i{color:Blue}
            </style>
            <title>
                <xsl:apply-templates select=
                "doc/assembly/name" mode="title" />
            </title>
        </head>
        <body>
            <xsl:apply-templates select=
            "doc/assembly/name" mode="body" />
            <xsl:apply-templates select=
            "doc/members/member" />
        </body>
    </html>
</xsl:template>
<xsl:template match="name" mode="title">
```

```
      <xsl:value-of select="concat
      ("Documentation for the ", ., " assembly")" />
   </xsl:template>
   <xsl:template match="name" mode="body">
      <h1>
         <xsl:value-of select="concat(., " Assembly")" />
      </h1>
   </xsl:template>
   <xsl:template match="member">
   <!--To be filled in later -->
   </xsl:template>
```

Now we'll write code for processing `<member>` elements. The `<xsl:template match="member">` element will include an `<xsl:choose>` element to test for the sort of member we are processing. Almost all of the script functions we created earlier will be called from inside the `<xsl:template match="member">` element. We need an `<xsl:when>` element for each Boolean test. Each `<xsl:when>` element has a nested `<xsl:value-of>` element to call the appropriate function that will return the formatted name of the member. In order to achieve this, we'll now make some amendments to the `<xsl:template match="member">` element as shown below:

```
<xsl:template match="member">
   <xsl:choose>
      <xsl:when test="user:IsType(@name)">
         <h2>
            <xsl:value-of select="user:FullTypeName
            (@name, parent::members/parent::doc/assembly/name)" />
         </h2>
      </xsl:when>
      <xsl:when test="user:IsMethod(@name)">
         <h3>
            <xsl:value-of select="user:MethodName(@name)" />
         </h3>
      </xsl:when>
      <xsl:when test="user:IsProperty(@name)">
         <h3>
            <xsl:value-of select="user:PropertyName(@name)" />
         </h3>
      </xsl:when>
      <xsl:when test="user:IsField(@name)">
         <h3>
            <xsl:value-of select="user:FieldName(@name)" />
         </h3>
      </xsl:when>
   </xsl:choose>
</xsl:template>
```

Our `<xsl:template match="member">` element is not yet finished. We now want to call other `<xsl:template>` elements with an `<xsl:apply-templates>` element to process the XML documentation tags within each member element. For each sort of member we are processing, we will call the appropriate `<xsl:apply-templates select= "elementName"/>` elements. So whatever elements we expect to find within a certain kind of member, we should apply a template for that specific element. We'll notice that some `<xsl:if>` elements are used to determine if one or more `<seealso>` elements exist within a member. When the member is a method, we use an `<xsl:if>` to determine if the method has one or more `<param>` elements. If either of these elements exists then we supply a heading of either 'See Also' or 'Parameters', then we process all `<seealso>` or `<param>` elements under this heading. If no `<seealso>` or `<param>` elements exist, then the heading isn't displayed at all. We would also want to consider any custom XML tags used in on our development and create templates for these as well:

```xsl
<xsl:template match="member">
    <xsl:choose>
        <xsl:when test="user:IsType(@name)">
            <h2>
                <xsl:value-of select="user:FullTypeName
                (@name, parent::members/parent::doc/assembly/name)" />
            </h2>
            <xsl:apply-templates select="returns" />
            <xsl:apply-templates select="remarks" />
            <xsl:apply-templates select="example" />
            <xsl:apply-templates select="permission" />
            <xsl:apply-templates select="exception" />
            <xsl:if test="seealso">
                <h4>See Also</h4>
                <p>
                    <xsl:apply-templates select="seealso" />
                </p>
            </xsl:if>
        </xsl:when>

        <xsl:when test="user:IsMethod(@name)">
            <h3>
                <xsl:value-of select="user:MethodName(@name)" />
            </h3>
            <xsl:apply-templates select="summary" />
            <xsl:if test="param">
                <h4>Parameters</h4>
                <dl>
                    <xsl:apply-templates select="param" />
                </dl>
            </xsl:if>
            <xsl:apply-templates select="returns" />
            <xsl:apply-templates select="remarks" />
            <xsl:apply-templates select="example" />
            <xsl:apply-templates select="permission" />
            <xsl:if test="seealso">
                <h4>See Also</h4>
                <p>
                    <xsl:apply-templates select="seealso" />
                </p>
            </xsl:if>
```

```
        </xsl:when>

        <xsl:when test="user:IsProperty(@name)">
            <h3>
                <xsl:value-of select="user:PropertyName(@name)" />
            </h3>
            <xsl:apply-templates select="value" />
            <xsl:apply-templates select="permission" />
            <xsl:if test="seealso">
                <h4>See Also</h4>
                <p>
                    <xsl:apply-templates select="seealso" />
                </p>
            </xsl:if>
        </xsl:when>

        <xsl:when test="user:IsField(@name)">
            <h3>
                <xsl:value-of select="user:FieldName(@name)" />
            </h3>
            <xsl:apply-templates select="summary" />
            <xsl:apply-templates select="permission" />
            <xsl:if test="seealso">
                <h4>See Also</h4>
                <p>
                    <xsl:apply-templates select="seealso" />
                </p>
            </xsl:if>
        </xsl:when>
    </xsl:choose>
</xsl:template>
```

Within the <xsl:stylesheet> element, we will add few more <xsl:template> elements beneath the <xsl:template match="member"> element, so that we can process some of the other elements that were supplied to our XML documentation. When we process a <summary> or <value> element, we will simply put these values inside a <p> element. When we process a <remarks>, <returns>, <exception>, <permission>, or <example> elements, we will add an appropriate heading:

```
<xsl:template match="summary">
    <p>
        <xsl:apply-templates />
    </p>
</xsl:template>

<xsl:template match="value">
    <p>
        <xsl:apply-templates />
    </p>
</xsl:template>

<xsl:template match="remarks">
    <h4>Remarks</h4>
    <xsl:apply-templates />
```

```
    </xsl:template>

    <xsl:template match="returns">
       <h4>Returns</h4>
       <xsl:apply-templates />
    </xsl:template>

    <xsl:template match="exception">
       <h4>Exception Class</h4>
       <xsl:apply-templates />
    </xsl:template>

    <xsl:template match="permission">
       <h4>Visibility</h4>
       <xsl:apply-templates />
    </xsl:template>

    <xsl:template match="example">
       <h4>Example</h4>
       <xsl:apply-templates />
    </xsl:template>
```

Directly below the last chunk of code we will want to place the following <xsl:template> elements. When we process a <paramref> element we will italicize and display the value of the name attribute. We will change <c> elements to the HTML <code> elements, and <para> elements to the HTML <p> elements. The <param> elements will be put in an HTML definition list and the parameter name will be italicized. All code elements will be wrapped in the HTML <pre> element to keep their formatting, and the background color will be changed to highlight the sample code. Text nodes will be written out as they are encountered:

```
    <xsl:template match="paramref">
       <i>
          <xsl:value-of select="@name" />
       </i>
       <xsl:apply-templates />
    </xsl:template>
    <xsl:template match="c">
       <code>
          <xsl:apply-templates />
       </code>
    </xsl:template>
    <xsl:template match="para">
       <p>
          <xsl:apply-templates />
       </p>
    </xsl:template>
    <xsl:template match="param">
       <dt>
          <i>
             <xsl:value-of select="@name" />
          </i>
       </dt>
       <dd>
          <xsl:apply-templates />
```

```
        </dd>
    </xsl:template>
    <xsl:template match="code">
        <pre style="background-color:wheat">
            <xsl:value-of select="." />
        </pre>
    </xsl:template>
    <xsl:template match="text()">
        <xsl:value-of select="." />
    </xsl:template>
```

Continuing in the same fashion, let's add the following code directly below the above shown code. These two <xsl:template> elements process the <see> and <seealso> elements. Any <see> and <seealso> elements will be written out as a hyperlink to the .NET SDK documentation for that class, but <seealso> elements will all be placed beneath a 'See Also' section found at the bottom of each member definition. Notice that the MakeHyperlink() and Reference() methods are being used from our script created earlier:

```
    <xsl:template match="see">
        <a>
            <xsl:attribute name="href">
                <xsl:value-of select="user:MakeHyperLink(@cref)" />
            </xsl:attribute>
            <xsl:value-of select="user:Reference(@cref)" />
        </a>
    </xsl:template>

    <xsl:template match="seealso">
        <a>
            <xsl:attribute name="href">
                <xsl:value-of select="user:MakeHyperLink(@cref)" />
            </xsl:attribute>
            <xsl:value-of select="user:Reference(@cref)" />
        </a>
    </xsl:template>
```

For the last time we will be adding <xsl:template> elements to process our <list> elements. You may recall that a <list> element can be either a numbered list, a bulleted list, or a table. This is determined by the type attribute of the <list> element. In our example, we have only written code to handle <list> elements of type table. This was done for the sake of simplicity and brevity. It should be noted that we could add the code to handle creating bulleted or numbered lists, if we need to.

In this particular example, when we process a <list> element we simply output an HTML <table> element. A <listheader> element will be output as an HTML <tr> element with a heavy font and unique background color. All <item> elements will also be output as HTML <tr> elements with a lighter background color than the <listheader>. All of the <term> and <description> elements will be output as HTML <td> elements. Let's append the following <xsl:template> elements to the previous snippet of code:

```
    <xsl:template match="list">
        <table border="1">
            <xsl:apply-templates />
        </table>
```

```
    </xsl:template>

    <xsl:template match="listheader">
        <tr style="font-weight:800;background-color:sandybrown">
            <xsl:apply-templates />
        </tr>
    </xsl:template>

    <xsl:template match="item">
        <tr style="background-color:wheat">
            <xsl:apply-templates />
        </tr>
    </xsl:template>

    <xsl:template match="term | description">
        <td>
            <xsl:apply-templates />
        </td>
    </xsl:template>
```

Now we have our XSL stylesheet file, `HelpFile.xsl` ready. Since we have the XML documentaion file and XSL stylesheet ready, let's leap towards creating our user-friendly help file.

The Command Line Application

Now that we have created our stylesheet, the next task at hand is to create the simple command line application to do the transformation for us. This application named `XMLTransformer.exe` will use the stylesheet we just created and apply it to the XML documentation. As a result of this application an HTML file will be generated reflecting all of our transformations.

In order to create this simple application, we need just two classes, `XMLTransformer` and `Run`. The `XMLTransformer` class has just one method called `TransformXML()`, which takes two parameters, one is the path to the XML documentation file and the other is the path to an XSL stylesheet. This method returns a string that represents the transformed document.

Inside this method we create an `XslTransform` object to do our transforming, an `XPathDocument` to hold our XML documentation file, and a `StringBuilder`. We also create a `TextWriter` that we wrap around our `StringBuilder`. We need to do this because the `Transform()` method needs a `TextWriter` as one of its parameters. After calling the `Transform()` method of the `XslTransform` object, we have the transformed XML inside our `StringBuilder`. So we call the `ToString()` method of the `StringBuilder` and this is our return value, which is a string of HTML in our case.

We complete this utility application by creating a `Run` class that has a `Main()` method in it, so we can run it from the command line. We simply need to add this class into the assembly within the same namespace as the `XMLTransformer` class. The `Main()` method of this class takes three arguments; the path to the XML documentation file, the path to the XSL file, and the path to a location where we want the HTML output file created. This class creates an instance of the `XMLTransformer` class and calls the `TransformXML()` method passing in the path to the XML documentation and the XSL file. The resulting string of HTML is then written to disk at the path specified in the third argument:

Here is the complete XMLTransformer.cs file:

```csharp
using System;
using System.Xml;
using System.Text;
using System.Xml.Xsl;
using System.Xml.XPath;
using System.IO;

namespace Wrox.Samples.Utility
{
    public class XMLTransformer
    {
        public string TransformXML(string strXML, string XSLT)
        {
            try
            {
                StringBuilder sbTransformed = new StringBuilder();
                TextWriter tw = (TextWriter)
                new StringWriter(sbTransformed);
                XslTransform xslt = new XslTransform();
                xslt.Load(XSLT);
                XPathDocument xpathdoc = new XPathDocument(strXML);
                xslt.Transform(xpathdoc, null, tw);
                return sbTransformed.ToString();
            }
            catch(Exception e)
            {
                throw e;
            }
        }
    }

    public class Run
    {
        public static void Main(string[] args)
        {
            XMLTransformer t = new XMLTransformer();
            string strHTML = t.TransformXML(args[0], args[1]);
            FileStream fs = new FileStream(args[2],
            FileMode.Create, FileAccess.Write);
            StreamWriter sw = new StreamWriter(fs);
            sw.WriteLine(strHTML);
            sw.Flush();
            fs.Close();
            sw.Close();
        }
    }
}
```

We will compile the application from the command line with the following syntax, which will create the XMLTranformer.exe application for us:

```
>csc /out:XMLTransformer.exe /t:exe XMLTransformer.cs
```

We can now run our `XMLTransformer.exe` application from the command line as shown below. We'll supply the path to our XML documentation file as the first argument, the path to our `HelpFile.xsl` file as second, and the third argument as the file name we would like generated as our output HTML file, TransformedToHTML.html. We are assuming that the first two files supplied as arguments reside in the same path as our application.

>XMLTransformer.exe ShippingRatesDocs.xml HelpFile.xsl TransformedToHTML.html

The resulting HTML file should look like this when opened in a browser such as Internet Explorer:

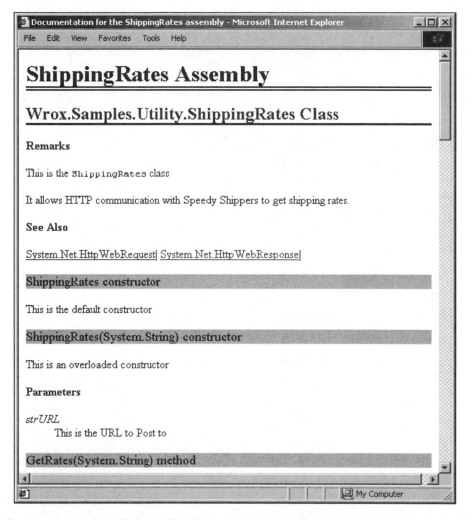

This makes a very user-friendly help file. With some creative designing, a very sophisticated programmer help system could be created. This would prove to be quite an asset to developers using our compiled libraries.

Other Considerations

While creating a large application that requires several developers, it is quite possible that the application will be broken up into several assemblies. Hence a possibility also exists that we will have several XML documentation files to compile into one complete set of application documentation. Our transforming application, XMLTransformer.exe is a very simple application, but think about how it could be built upon to generate richer and more attractive documentation.

We could design a bigger, better version of XMLTransformer.exe that allows for multiple XML documentation files as an input and compiles them into one documentation. You should look carefully at the .NET SDK documentation, and if you like its design, model your implementation accordingly. If there are things that you wish were different, then you can implement them differently in your application. You have full control to transform the XML the way you would like.

Delve deeper into the System.Reflection namespace to produce more details about members. Whatever information is not available via the XML documentation option can likely be extracted using reflection.

Admittedly the presentation layer of an application is a specialized area for many developers and graphic designers, so the example above is intended only as a starter application to give us ideas for our own transformations. If you are a developer of middle-tier components then there is a good chance that you will not be responsible for transforming these XML documents anyway; but by getting the whole picture, from adding XML comments in your classes, to transforming them into a presentable format, you are better able to see how to use them in your source code. And you can clearly see the huge benefit that comes from using them properly. The use of reflection in your transformations can greatly enhance the usefulness of your transformed output. Take a look at the .NET Framework Class Browser that is provided as part of the Quickstart SDK for .NET. It is available at http://localhost/quickstart/aspplus/samples/classbrowser/cs/classbrowser and provides us with a great example of using reflection.

Support for Documentation in VS.NET

Visual Studio .NET also provides us with some web-based documentation based on our use of the XML documentation tags. To see this in action, start up Visual Studio .NET and create a new C# Class Library project. Name the solution and project VSNETDocumentationTest. Rename the default class file, Class1.cs to VSNETDocumentationTest.cs. Copy all of the code in the ShippingRates.cs file we created earlier and overwrite the data in the VSNETDocumentationTest.cs file. You should have something similar to the illustration that follows:

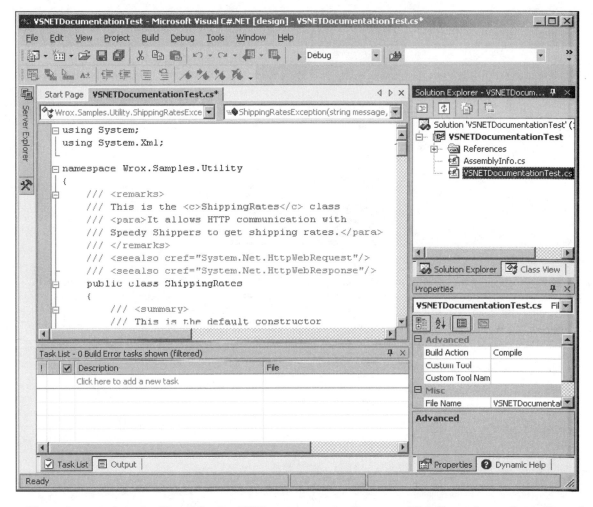

We are now ready to let Visual Studio .NET generate some Comment Web Pages for us. In order to do this we navigate to the Tools menu and choose the Build Comment Web Pages menu option. This should bring up the following dialogue box:

Enter the path to the folder that you would like to have the Comment Web Pages created in and click OK. The designer will produce several web pages for us that make up the complete documentation. After doing this you should be able to navigate to the folder you had the Comment Web Pages created and open the VSNETDocumentationTest.HTM in Microsoft Internet Explorer. You should now see something similar to the following illustration:

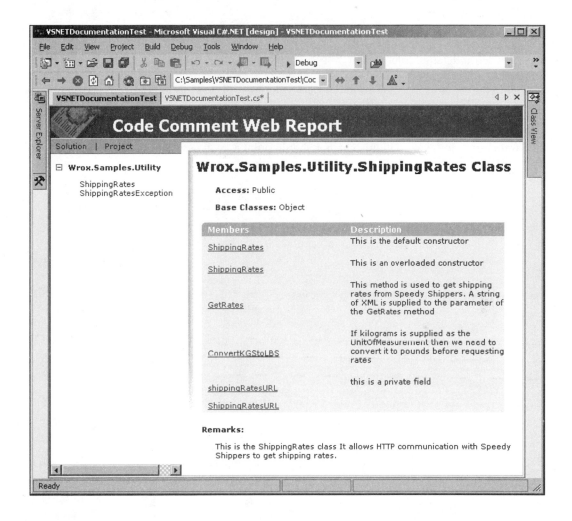

Summary

In our discussion of XML documentation in C#, we covered many things. We looked at the advantages of using this feature in our applications, and how having the documentation included in our source code can be of great benefit to us.

We took a look at how to generate this XML documentation using the `/doc:filename` command line compiler option, and we also saw how to instruct the Visual Studio IDE to generate this file for us when we build our application.

We were able to examine in depth each of the predefined XML tags that can be used in our XML comments. We also learned that we are not limited to only the predefined tags. We can extend the set of XML tags used in our documentation as far as we need to. We saw what a great benefit it is to have all of our documentation in XML format, especially in the middle-tier development. We were able to see the benefits of using these XML comments in the middle-tier especially.

We were able to create a sample XSLT transformation to turn our raw XML into a more readable help file. We took advantage of C# script in an XSL file, using the `System.Reflection` namespace in order to get more detailed information on types.

We also had a look at how Visual studio .net provides us with some web-based documentation based on our use of the XML documentation tags

User interface design is generally very low on the skills meter for many component developers, but the sample transformation we did in this chapter should point a good developer in the right direction.

Professional XML fo
pers Professional XML for .
XML for .NET Developers
Developers Professional XM
essional XML for .NET Devel
.NET Developers Professio
Professional XML for .NET
.NET Developers Pro
Professional XML fo
for .NET Develop
pers Professional
XML for .NET D
velopers Profes
onal XML for
Developers
ofessional XM
r .NET Devel
rs Profession
XML for .NET D
velopers Profess
sional XML for .NE
NET Developers Pro
Professional XML fo
L for .NET Developer
elopers Professional XM
onal XML for .NET Develo
velopers Professiona
al XML for .NET De
Developers Profess
ET Developers Professional XML for .N
ofessional XML for .NET Developers Professional XML
for .NET Developers Professional XML for .NET Develop

System.Xml

An **XML namespace** is a collection of names, identified by a URI reference, which are used in XML documents as element types and attribute names. XML namespaces differ from the "namespaces" conventionally used in computing disciplines in that the XML version has internal structure and is not, mathematically speaking, a set.

You can find more information about namespaces, classes, and related methods and properties, under .Net Framework | Reference | Class Library, *in .Net Framework documentation or Visual Studio .NET documentation.*

In this appendix, we will look at System.Xml Namespace. This namespace, the overall namespace for the XML classes, deals with the functionality of accessing, navigating, and maintaining XML data.

The System.Xml namespace is the root namespace for the XML classes that provide standard-based support for processing XML. System.Xml supports standards like XML 1.0, DTD support, XML Namespaces, XML Schemas, XPath expressions, XSL/T transformations, DOM Level 2 Core, and SOAP 1.1.

Overview of System.Xml Classes

The System.Xml namespace contains the following classes:

Class	Description
NameTable	This class implements a single-threaded XmlNameTable.
XmlAttribute	This class represents an attribute, valid and default values for which are defined in a DTD or Schema.

Table continued on following page

Class	Description
XmlAttributeCollection	This class represents a collection of attributes that can be accessed by name or index.
XmlCDataSection	This class quotes or escapes the block of text to avaoid any misinterpretation of that text as markup language.
XmlCharacterData	This abstact class provides methods for text-manipulation that are used by several classes.
XmlComment	Thic class represents an XML comment.
XmlConvert	This class is used to encode and decode XML names, and convert between XSD types and CLR types.
XmlDataDocument	This class allows storing, retrieving, and manipulating structured XML data, with the use of DOM or a relational dataset like A ADO.NET Dataset. dataset represents an in-memory cache of data.
XmlDeclaration	Consists of data from the XML declaration node. (<?xml version='1.0'...?>).
XmlDocument	This class represents an XML document.
XmlDocumentFragment	This class represents a small object that is used for tree insert operations.
XmlDocumentType	This class represents the document type declaration.
XmlElement	This class represents an element of an XML document.
XmlEntity	This class represents an entity declaration of an XML document (!ENTITY ...).
XmlEntityReference	This class represents an entity reference node of an XML document.
XmlException	This class returns the details of the last exception.
XmlImplementation	This class defines the context for a set of XmlDocument objects.
XmlLinkedNode	This class returns the immediately preceding or following node.
XmlNamedNodeMap	This class represents a collection of nodes accessible by name or index.
XmlNamespaceManager	This class manages the scope of namespaces by resolving them, and adding them to, or removing them from a collection. This class is used by the XsltContext and XmlReader classes.
XmlNameTable	The abstact class, XmlNameTable is a table of atomized string objects that helps an XML parser to use the same string object for repeated elements and attribute names.
XmlNode	This abstact class represents a single node of an XML document.

Class	Description
XmlNodeList	This class is an ordered collection of nodes.
XmlNodeReader	This is a fast reader that provides a non-cached, forward-only access to XML data in an XmlNode.
XmlNotation	This class represents the notation declaration (`<!NOTATION ...>`).
XmlParserContext	This class provides the context information required by XmlText Reader or XmlValidatingReader to parse an XML fragment.
XmlProcessingInstruction	This class represents a processing instruction defined by XML to keep processor-specific information in the document text.
XmlQualifiedName	This class represents an XML qualified name.
XmlReader	This abstract class represents a fast non-cached, forward-only reader for accessing XML data.
XmlResolver	This abstract class is used to resolve external XML resources named by a Uniform Resource Indentifier (URI).
XmlSignificantWhitespace	This represents whitespace between markup in a mixed content node. This is also referred to as significant whitespace. These nodes will be created automatically at load time only if the PreserveWhitespace flag is true.
XmlText	This represents the text content of an element or attribute.
XmlTextReader	This is a fast, non-cached, forward-only reader for accessing XML data.
XmlTextWriter	This represents a writer that provides a fast, non-cached, forward-only way of generating streams or files containing XML data that conforms to the XML specification and the Namespaces in XML specification.
XmlUrlResolver	This class is used to resolve external XML resources named by a URI.
XmlValidatingReader	This class represents a reader for validating DTD, XDR, and XSD Schema.
XmlWhitespace	This class represents whitespace in element content. Only if the PreserveWhitespace flag is true will these nodes get created automatically at load time.
XmlWriter	This abstact class is a fast writer providing a non-cached, forward-only way of generating streams or files containing XML data that conforms to the XML specification and the Namespaces in XML specification.

Table continued on following page

The XmlException Class

The XmlException class holds the detailed information about the last exception that may have been thrown by any of the System.Xml objects. Now, we will have a quick look at some important XmlException methods and properties:

XmlException Methods

Name	Parameters	Description
GetBaseException()		Returns a reference to the original exception object
GetObjectData()	*info:* SerializationInfo *context:* StreamingContext	Used to stream all the exception properties into the SerializationInfo class for the given StreamingContext
ToString()		Returns the fully qualified name of this exception and the error message, the name of the inner exception, and the stack trace.

XmlException Properties

Name	Type	Description
HelpLink	String	Gets or sets the link to the help file associated with this exception.
InnerException	Exception	Gets the reference to the inner exception, if there is any.
LineNumber	Integer	Gets the line number where the error occurred in the sourcecode.
LinePosition	Integer	Gets the line position where the error occurred in the sourcecode.
Message	String	Gets the error message describing the exception.
Source	String	Gets or sets the name of the application or the object that causes the error.
StackTrace	String	Returns the stack trace identifying location in the code where the error occurred.
TargetSite	MethodBase	Returns the method that throws the exception.

The XmlConvert Class

The XmlConvert class encodes and decodes XML names and provides methods for converting between XSD types and CLR types. Let's take a look at some XmlConvert methods:

XmlConvert Methods

Name	Parameters	Description
DecodeName()	name (String)	Used to convert XML names such as "Customer_x0020_Name" into a valid name "Customer Name". It will decode the _xHHHH_(where HHHH stands for a four digit hexadecimal UCS-2 code) into a Unicode 2.1 character.
EncodeLocalName()	name (String)	Used to convert XML names such as "Customer Name" into a valid ADO.NET object name. It works in the same way as the EncodeName() method, but it also encodes the colon character.
EncodeName()	name (String)	Used to convert XML names such as "Customer Name" into a valid ADO.NET object name. If we encode the name "Customer Name" the method will return the string "Customer_x0020_Name". It will not encode the colon character.
EncodeNmToken()	name (String)	The EncodeNmToken() method is used to validate a name to see if it conforms to the XML specification.
ToBoolean()	s (String)	Converts the string to a Boolean.
ToByte()	s (String)	Converts the string to a Byte.
ToChar()	s (String)	Converts the string to a Char.
ToDateTime()	s (String)	Converts the string to a DateTime.
ToDateTime()	s (String) format (String)	Converts the string to a DateTime with a format structure.
ToDateTime()	s (String) format (String())	Converts the string to a DateTime with an array of the format structure.
ToDecimal()	s (String)	Converts the string to a Decimal.
ToDouble()	s (String)	Converts the string to a Double.
ToGuid()	s (String)	Converts the string to a GUID.

Table continued on following page

Name	Parameters	Description
ToInt16()	s (String)	Converts the string to an Int16.
ToInt32()	s (String)	Converts the string to an Int32.
ToInt64()	s (String)	Converts the string to an Int64.
ToSByte()	s (String)	Converts the string to an Sbyte.
ToSingle()	s (String)	Converts the string to a Single.
ToString()	data (Strongly typed data)	Converts data types data to a String.
ToTimeSpan()	s (String)	Converts the string to a TimeSpan.
ToUInt16()	s (String)	Converts the string to a UInt16.
ToUint32()	s (String)	Converts the string to a UInt32.
ToUInt64()	s (String)	Converts the string to a UInt64.

The XmlImplementation Class

The XmlImplementation class defines the context of XmlDocument objects. Some of the XmlImplementation methods are shown below:

XmlImplementation Methods

Name	Parameters	Description
CreateDocument()		Creates a new XmlDocument
HasFeature()	feature (String)	Checks if the DOM implementation implements a specified feature.
	version (String)	

The XmlNamedNodeMap Class

The XmlNamedNodeMap class represents a collection of nodes that can be connected to a name or index. Let's review the XmlNamedNodeMap methods and properties:

XmlNamedNodeMap Methods

Name	Parameters	Description
GetEnumerator()		Used to support the "for-each" iteration statement, over the XML nodes in the XmlNamedNodeMap.
GetNamedItem()	name (String)	Gets the specified XmlNode from the node collection in XmlNamedNodeMap.
GetNamedItem()	name (String) namespaceURI (String)	Gets the XmlNode from the XmlNamedNodeMap collection by a given name and namespace URI.
Item()	index (Integer)	Gets the node from the specified index in XmlNamedNodeMap.
RemoveNamedItem()	name (String)	Removes the specified node from the XmlNamedNodeMap.
RemoveNamedItem()	name (String) namespaceURI (String)	Removes a node from the collection by the given name and namespace URI.
SetNamedItem()	node (XmlNode)	Adds a new XmlNode into the collection by using the Name property.

XmlNamedNodeMap Properties

Name	Type	Description
Count	Integer	Returns the number of nodes in the collection.

The XmlAttributeCollection Class

The XmlAttributeCollection class is a collection of attributes that can be accessed by name or index. It contains all the methods and properties of the XmlNamedNodeMap class, together with the following:

XmlAttributeCollection Methods

Name	Parameters	Description
Append()	node (XmlAttribute)	Adds a node to the end of his collection.
CopyTo()	array (XmlAttribute()) begin (Integer)	Copies attributes to an Array. The begin parameter specifies were in the collection the copy should begin.

Table continued on following page

Name	Parameters	Description
InsertAfter()	node (XmlAttribute) reference (XmlAttribute)	Inserts the node after the given reference node.
InsertBefore()	node (XmlAttribute) reference (XmlAttribute)	Inserts the node before the given reference node.
Prepend()	node (XmlAttribute)	Inserts an attribute as the first node of the collection.
Remove()	node (XmlAttribute)	Removes a node from the collection.
RemoveAll()		Clears the collection from data.
RemoveAt()	index (Integer)	Removes an attribute from the collection by a given index of the collection.

XmlAttributeCollection Properties

Name	Type	Description
ItemOf()	XmlAttribute (Has one name String parameter)	Returns an attribute from the collection by a name.
ItemOf()	XmlAttribute (Has one index Integer parameter)	Returns an attribute from the collection by its index.
ItemOf()	XmlAttribute (Has two parameters, name String, namespaceURI String)	Returns an attribute from the collection by a local name of the attribute and its namesace URI.

The XmlNamespaceManager Class

The XmlNamespaceManager class is used to manage namespaces. Let's see some XmlNameSpaceManager methods and properties:

XmlNamespaceManager Methods

Name	Parameters	Description
AddNamespace()	prefix (String) uri (String)	Used to add the given namespace to the collection of namespaces.
GetEnumerator()		Used to support the "for-each" statement, so we can iteration over the collection of namespaces.
HasNamespace()	prefix (String) namesapceURI (String)	Adds a namespace to the collection.
LookupNamespace()	prefix (String)	Checks if the prefix has a namespace.
LookupPrefix()	namespaceURI (String)	Returns the namespace URI for the prefix.
PopScope()		Removes namespaces from the stack.
PushScope()		Adds namespaces to the stack.
RemoveNamespace()	prefix (String) namespaceURI (String)	Removes a namespace.

XmlNamespaceManager Properties

Name	Type	Description
DefaultNamespace	String	Returns the namespace URI.
NameTable	XmlNameTable	Gets the XmlNameTable for this object.

The XmlNameTable Class

The XmlNameTable class is a table of string objects that use the same objects for all repeated element and attribute names. XmlNameTable is implemented in NameTable class, that is, a single-threaded XmlNameTable. This class is abstract. Some of XmlNameTable methods are:

XmlNameTable Methods

Name	Parameters	Description
Add()	key (String)	Creates new element or attribute names as atomized strings to the NameTable.
Add()	key (Char()) begin (Integer) length (Integer)	Creates new elements or attributes.
Get()	key (String)	Gets a string object.
Get()	key (Char()) begin (Integer) length (Integer)	Gets names from the NameTable

The XmlNode Class

The XmlNode class represents a single node of an XML document. This class is abstract. The following are a few XmlNode methods and properies:

XmlNode Methods

Name	Parameters	Description
AppendChild()	node (XmlNode)	Adds a node to the end of this node.
Clone()		Used to duplicate this node
CloneNode()	subtree (Boolean)	Used to duplicate this node, if subtree is true it will recursively clone the subtree of this node.
CreateNavigator()		Used to create an XmlXPathNavigator.
GetEnumerator()		Used to support the "for-each" statement, so we can iterate over the XML nodes in the node.
GetNamespaceOfPrefix()	prefix (String)	Finds the closest xmlns declaration and returns the namespace URI.

Name	Parameters	Description
GetPrefixOfNamespace()	namespaceURI (String)	Finds the closest xmlns declaration for the given namespace URI and return the prefix of the declaration.
InsertAfter()	node (XmlNode) reference (XmlNode)	Inserts a node after the reference node.
InsertBefore()	node (XmlNode) reference (XmlNode)	Inserts a node before the reference node.
Normalize()		Puts XmlText node into a normal form.
PrependChild()	node (XmlNode)	Adds a node to the beginning of this node's children.
RemoveAll()		Removes all the children and/or attributes.
RemoveChild()	node (XmlNode)	Removes one child from this node.
ReplaceChild()	new (XmlNode) old (XmlNode)	Replaces a child with a new one.
SelectNodes()	xpath (String)	Returns a collection of nodes from the given XPath expression.
SelectNodes()	xpath (String) nsmgr (XmlNamespaceManager)	Returns a collection of nodes from the given XPath expression and the XmlNamespaceManager is used to resolve namespaces for prefixes in the XPath expression.
SelectSingleNode()	xpath (String)	Selects a single node from the given XPath expression.
SelectSingleNode()	xpath (String) nsmgr (XmlNamespaceManager)	Selects a single node from the given XPath expression and the XmlNamespaceManager is used to resolve namespaces for prefixes in the XPath expression.

Table continued on following page

Name	Parameters	Description
Supports()	feature (String) (name of the feature e.g. "XML") version (String) (version of the feature e.g. "1.0")	Checks if the installed DOM supports a given version and feature.
WriteContentTo()	writer (XmlWriter)	Saves all the children to an XmlWriter.
WriteTo()	writer (XmlWriter)	Saves the current node to an XmlWriter.

XmlNode Properties

Name	Type	Description
Attributes	XmlAttributesCollection	Gets a collection of attributes.
BaseURI	String	Gets the Base URI of the node.
ChildNodes	XmlNodeList	Gets all the children of this node.
FirstChild	XmlNode	Gets the first child of this node.
HasChildNodes	Boolean	Checks if this node has any children.
InnerText	String	Returns the concatenated values of this node and its children or sets its value.
InnerXml	String	Returns the markup of this node's children.
IsReadOnly	Boolean	Indicates if this node is read-only.
Item	XmlElement (Has one name String parameter)	This property takes one parameter, which is the name of the child element to return.

Name	Type	Description
Item	XmlElement (Have two parameters, name String and namespaceURI String)	This property takes two parameters: the name of the child and the namespace URI of the child element to return.
LastChild	XmlNode	Returns the last child of this node.
LocalName	String	Returns the name of this node with any prefix removed.
Name	String	Returns the name of the node.
NamespaceURI	String	Returns the namespace URI of this node.
NextSibling	XmlNode	Returns the next node after this node.
NodeType	XmlNodeType	Returns the type of the node.
OuterXml	String	Returns the markup for this node and its children.
OwnerDocument	XmlDocument	Returns the XmlDocument where this node belongs.
ParentNode	XmlNode	This will always return a null reference.
Prefix	String	Returns the namespace prefix of this node or sets a prefix for the node.
PreviousSibling	XmlNode	Returns the previous node.
Value	String	Returns the value of this node or sets a value for the node.

The XmlAttribute Class

The XmlAttribute Class represents an attribute that is defined in a DTD or schema. It has all the properties and methods of XmlNode, as well as:

XmlAttribute Properties

Name	Type	Description
OwnerElement	XmlElement	Returns the element containing this attribute.
Specified	Boolean	Indicate if the attributes value has been explicitly set.

Table continued on following page

The XmlDocument Class

The `XmlDocument` class represents an XML document. This class implements the W3C Document Object Model (DOM). This class has the XML data in memory (like a cache) and we can use it to modify, navigate, and edit the XML document. It has all the properties and methods of `XmlNode`, in addition to the following:

XmlDocument Methods

Name	Parameters	Description
`CreateAttribute()`	name (String)	Creates an `XmlAttribute` with the name.
`CreateAttribute()`	name (String) namespaceURI (String)	Creates an `XmlAttribute` with the name and namespace URI.
`CreateAttribute()`	name (String) namespaceURI (String) prefix (String)	Creates an `XmlAttribute` with the name, namespace URI, and prefix.
`CreateCDataSection()`	data (String)	Creates a CDATA section.
`CreateComment()`	comment (String)	Creates an `XmlComment`.
`CreateDocumentFragment()`		Creates and returns `XmlDocumentFragment` object of the XML document.
`CreateDocumentType()`	name (String) publicId (String) systemId (String) internalSubset (String)	Creates a new `XmlDocumentType`. There can only be one `DocumentType` node in the `XmlDocument` and must be inserted before the root element. A DOCTYPE declaration can contain the name of the document or root element, an internal subset of the DTD declaration and a system and public identifier for the DTD.
`CreateElement()`	name (String)	Creates an `XmlElement` with the name.
`CreateElement()`	name (String) namespaceURI (String)	Creates an `XmlElement` with the name and namespace URI.

Name	Parameters	Description
CreateElement()	name (String) namespaceURI (String) prefix (String)	Creates an XmlElement with the name, namespace URI, and prefix.
CreateEntity Reference()		Is not supported.
CreateNode()	name (String) namespaceURI (String)	Creates an XmlNode with a namespace URI and name.
CreateNode()	nodeType (XmlNodeType) name (String) namespaceURI (String)	Creates an XmlNode with the XmlNodeType object, name, and namespace URI.
CreateNode()	nodeType (XmlNodeType) prefix (String) name (String) namespaceURI (String)	Creates an XmlNode with the XmlNodeType object, prefix, name, and namespace URI.
CreateProcessing Instruction()	name (String) data (String)	Creates an XmlProcessingInstruction with name and data. A processing instruction name is for example "xml-stylesheet type='text/xsl' href='viewbook.xsl'".
CreateSignificant Whitespace()	text (String)	Creates an XmlSignificantWhitespace node. The text string can only contain the following characters &#20;,
, , and 	.
CreateTextNode()	text (String)	Creates an XmlText node.
CreateWhitespace()	text (String)	Creates an XmlWhitespace node. The text string can only contain the following characters &#20;,
, , and 	.

Table continued on following page

641

Name	Parameters	Description
CreateXmlDeclaration()	version (String) encode (String) alone (String)	Creates an XmlDeclaration node (<!xml>) and sets its version, encoding, and standalone attributes.
GetElementById()	ElementID (String)	Gets an XmlElement by ID.
GetElementsByTagName()	name (String)	Gets an XmlNodeList by name.
GetElementsByTagName()	name (String) namespaceURI (String)	Gets an XmlNodeList by a local name and namespace URI.
GetRowFromElement()	element (XmlElement)	Returns the DataRow associated with an XmlElement.
ImportNode()	node (XmlNode) deep (Boolean)	Imports a node from another document.
Load()	source (XmlReader)	Loads an XML document from an XmlReader.
Load()	source (Stream)	Loads an XML document from a Stream.
Load()	source (String)	Loads an XML document from a URL.
Load()	source (TextReader)	Loads an XML document from a TextReader.
LoadXml()	xml (String)	Loads an XML document from a string.
ReadNode()	reader (XmlReader)	Reads one node from the XmlReader. Returns an XmlNode.
Save()	destination (Stream)	Saves the XML document to a Stream.
Save()	destination (String)	Saves the XML document to a file.
Save()	destination (TextWriter)	Saves the XML document to a TextWriter.
Save()	destination (XmlWriter)	Saves the XML document to an XmlWriter.

XmlDocument Properties

Name	Type	Description
DocumentElement	XmlElement	Gets the root element of the XML document.
DocumentType	XmlDocumentType	Gets the DOCTYPE declaration of the XML document.
Implementation	XmlImplementation	The XmlImplementation of the XML document; <u>many documents can be shared with the same implementation</u>.
NameTable	XmlNameTable	Gets the XmlNameTable for the XML document. XmlTable consist of the attribute and element names.
PreserveWhitespace	Boolean	Indicates if the document should preserve whitespace.
XmlResolver	XmlResolver	Used to read DTD or expand entity references

The XmlDataDocument Class

The XmlDataDocument class is used to store, retrieve, and manipulate XML data using the W3C Document Object Model (DOM). This class also has a close affiliation with the ADO.NET DataSet and extends the XmlDocument class. We should use the XmlDataDocument class if we want to work with the XML document like a DataSet. It has all the methods and properties of XmlDocument, as well as:

XmlDataDocument Methods

Name	Parameters	Description
GetElementFromRow()	row (DataRow)	Returns the XmlElement associated with a DataRow.
GetRowFromElement()	element (XmlElement)	Returns the DataRow associated with an XmlElement.

XmlDataDocument Properties

Name	Type	Description
Dataset	Dataset	Gets a DataSet with data from the XmlDataDocument.
Length	Integer	Represents the length of the data.

The XmlDocumentFragment Class

The `XmlDocumentFragment` class is used as a fragment of an XML document. It has the same methods and properties as the `XmlNode` class as well as:

XmlDocumentFragment Methods

Name	Parameters	Description
CloneNode()	subtree (Boolean)	Used to duplicate this node; if subtree is `true` it will recursively clone the subtree of this node.

XmlDocumentFragment Properties

Name	Type	Description
InnerXml	String	Returns the markup of these node children.
LocalName	String	Returns the name of this node with any prefix removed.
Name	String	Returns the name of the node.
NodeType	XmlNodeType	Returns the type of the node.
OwnerDocument	XmlDocument	Returns the `XmlDocument` where this node belongs.
ParanetNode	XmlNode	This will always return a null reference.

The XmlEntity Class

The `XmlEntity` class represents the `<!ENTITY>` declaration node of the XML document. It has all the methods and properties of `XmlNode`, as well as:

XmlEntity Properties

Name	Type	Description
Encoding	String	The encoding level of the XML document.
NotationName	String	Gets the name of the NDATA attribute.
PublicId	String	Gets the value of the public identifier.
SystemId	String	Gets the value of the system identifier.

The XmlLinkedNode Class

The `XmlLinkedNode` Class represents the node preceding or following a node. This calss is abstract. It has all the methods and properties of `XmlNode` except the `NextSibling` and `PreviousSibling` properties.

XmlLinkedNode properties

Name	Type	Description
NextSibling	XmlNode	Returns the next node after this node.
PreviousSibling	XmlNode	Returns the previous node.

The XmlCharacterData Class

The `XmlCharacterData` class provides methods for text manipulation, used by several classes. This class is abstract. It has all the methods and properties of `XmlNode`, as well as:

XmlCharacterData Methods

Name	Parameters	Description
AppendData()	data (String)	Adds the data to the end of this node.
DeleteData()	start (Integer) number (Integer)	Deletes number characters from the start position, in characters and the number of characters to delete.
InsertData()	start (Integer) data (String)	Inserts data at the start positions, in characters, within the existing data.
ReplaceData()	start (Integer) number (Integer) data (String)	Replaces number characters from the start position, in characters, and the number of characters to replace.
Substring()	start (Integer) number (Integer)	Returns a substring from the start position, in characters of length number characters to get.

XmlCharacterData Properties

Name	Type	Description
Data	String	Gets this node's data.
Length	Integer	Represents the length of the data.

The XmlCDataSection Class

The `XmlCDataSection` class is used to keep text from being mixed up with markup language. It has all the methods and properties of `XmlCharacterData`.

The XmlComment Class

The `XmlComment` class represents the XML comment. It has all the methods and properties of `XmlCharacterData`, as well as:

XmlComment Methods

Name	Parameters	Description
DecideXPNodeType ForWhitespace()	node (XmlNode) xnt (XpathNodeType)	Decides if the xnt is an XPath for a whitespace of the node.

The XmlSignificantWhitespace Class

The `XmlSignificantWhitespace` class represents whitespace between markups, also referred to as significant whitespace. It has all the methods and properties of `XmlCharacterData`, as well as:

XmlSignificantWhitespace Methods

Name	Parameters	Description
DecideXPNodeType ForWhitespace()	node (XmlNode) xnt (XpathNodeType)	Decides if the xnt is an XPath for a whitespace of the node.

The XmlText Class

The `XmlText` class manages the text content of an element or attribute. It has all the properties and methods of `XmlCharacterData`, as well as:

XmlText Methods

Name	Parameters	Description
DecideXPNodeType ForWhitespace()	node (XmlNode) xnt (XpathNodeType)	Decides if the xnt is an XPath node type for a whitespace of the node.
SplitText()	start (Integer)	Used to split the node into two nodes at a start location.

The XmlWhitespace Class

The XmlWhitespace Class represents whitespace between markups. It has all the methods and properties of XmlCharacterData, as well as:

XmlWhitespace Methods

Name	Parameters	Description
DecideXPNodeType ForWhitespace()	node (XmlNode) xnt (XpathNodeType)	Decides if the xnt is an XPath for a whitespace of the node.

The XmlDeclaration Class

The XmlDeclaration class represents the XML declaration node <?xml?> of the XML document. It has all the methods and properties of XmlNode, as well as:

XmlDeclaration Properties

Name	Type	Description
Encoding	String	The encoding level of the XML document.
Standalone	String	Indicates if the standalone attribute is "yes" or "no".
Version	String	Gets or sets the version of the XML document.

The XmlDocumentType Class

The XmlDocumentType class represents the document type declaration. It has the properties and methods of XmlLinkedNode, as well as:

XmlDocumentType Properties

Name	Type	Description
Entities	XmlNamedNodeMap	Gets collection of XmlEntity
InternealSubset	String	Gets the DOCTYPE declaration.
IsReadOnly	Boolean	Indicates if the node is read-only.
LocalName	String	Returns the name of this node with any prefix removed.
Name	String	Returns the name of the node.

Table continued on following page

Name	Type	Description
NodeType	XmlNodeType	Returns the type of the node.
Notations	XmlNamedNodeMap	Gets a collection of XMLNotation.
PublicId	String	Gets the value of the public identifier.
SystemId	String	Gets the value of the system identifier.

The XmlElement Class

The XmlElement Class represents an element that is defined in a DTD or schema. It has all the methods and properties of XmlNode, as well as:

XmlElement Methods

Name	Parameters	Description
GetAttribute()	name (String)	Gets the specified attribute's value.
GetAttribute()	name (String) namespaceURI (String)	Gets an attribute's value by name an namespace URI.
GetAttributeNode()	name (String)	Finds an attribute by name, and returns it.
GetAttributeNode()	name (String) namespaceURI (String)	Finds an attribute by name and namespace URI, and returns it.
GetElementsBy TagName()	name (String)	Gets an XmlNodeList by name.
GetElementsBy TagName()	name (String) namespaceURI (String)	Gets an XmlNodeList by a local name and namespace URI.
HasAttribute()	name (String)	Checks if the node has the specified attribute.
HasAttribute()	name (String) namespaceURI (String)	Checks if the node has an attribute with the given name and namsespaceURI.
RemoveAll Attributes()		Removes all attributes.
RemoveAttribute()	name (String)	Remove an attribute by the name.
RemoveAttribute()	name (String) namespaceURI (String)	Removes an attribute by the name and namespace URI.
RemoveAttributeAt()	Index (Integer)	Removes an attribute with the given index from the element.

Name	Type	Description
RemoveAttribute Node()	name (String)	Removes an XmlAttribute by the name.
RemoveAttribute Node()	name (String) namespaceURI (String)	Removes an XmlAttribute by the name and namespace URI.
SetAttribute()	name (String) value (String)	Sets the value of the given attribute.
SetAttribute()	name (String) namespaceURI (String) value (String)	Sets the value of the attribute that matches the name and namespace URI.
SetAttributeNode()	attribute (XmlAttribute)	Creates an XmlAttribute with the given attribute.
SetAttributeNode()	name (String) namespaceURI (String)	Creates an XmlAttribute with the given name and namespace URI.

XmlElement Properties

Name	Type	Description
HasAttributes	Boolean	Indicates if the node has attributes.
IsEmpty	Boolean	Indicates if the element is to be serialized as short: <element/>, or long: <element></element>

The XmlEntityReference Class

The XmlEntityReference class is used to create, modify, and get data from an entity reference node. It has all the methods and properties of XmlNode, as well as:

XmlEntityReference Properties

Name	Type	Description
Encoding	String	The encoding level of the XML document.

The XmlProcessingInstruction Class

The XmlProcessingInstruction class represents a processing instruction. It has all the methods and properties of XmlNode, as well as:

XmlProcessingInstruction Methods

Name	Parameters	Description
ReplaceData()	start (Integer) number (Integer) data (String)	Replaces number characters from the start position, in characters, with data.

XmlProcessingInstruction Properties

Name	Type	Description
Data	String	Indicates the processing instruction.
Target	String	Indicates the target of the processing instruction.

The XmlNotation Class

The XmlNotation class represents the notation declaration. It has all the methods and properties of XmlNode, as well as:

XmlNotation Properties

Name	Type	Description
PublicId	String	Gets the value of the public identifier.
SystemId	String	Gets the value of the system identifier.

The XmlNodeList Class

The XmlNodeList class is a collection of nodes. This class is abstract.

XmlNodeList Methods

Name	Parameters	Description
GetEnumerator()		Used to support the "for-each" statement, so we can iterate over the XML nodes in the XmlNodeList.
Item()	index (Integer)	Returns an XmlNode from the specified index of the collection.

XmlNodeList Properties

Name	Type	Description
Count	Integer	Returns the number of nodes in the collection.
ItemOf	XmlNode (Has one index integer parameter)	Returns a node at the specified index.

The XmlParserContext Class

The XmlParserContext Class provides information required to parse an XML fragment.

XmlParserContext Properties

Name	Type	Description
BaseURI	String	Gets the Base URI of the node.
DocTypeName	String	The DocType name.
InternalSubset	String	Returns the internal DTD subset or sets it value.
NamespaceManager	XmlNamespaceManager	Gets or sets the XmlNamespaceManager.
NameTable	XmlNameTable	Gets the XmlNameTable for the XML document. XmlTable consist of the attribute and element names.
PublicId	String	Gets the value of the public identifier.
SystemId	String	Gets the value of the system identifier.
XmlLang	String	Indicates the language of the node.
XmlSpace	XmlSpace	Returns the xml:space value.

The XmlQualifiedName Class

The XmlQualifiedName class represents an XML qualified name.

XmlQualifiedName Methods

Name	Parameters	Description
Equals()	other (Object)	Checks if the specified object is the same instance object as this object.
GetHashCode()		Returns the hash code for the object.

Table continued on following page

651

Name	Parameters	Description
ToString()		Returns the string value of the object.
ToString()	name (String) namespace (String)	Returns the string value of the object specified by a name and the namespace of the object.

XmlQualifiedName Properties

Name	Type	Description
IsEmpty	Boolean	Indicates if the object is empty.
Name	String	Returns the qualified name of the object.
Namespace	String	Returns the namespace of the object.

The XmlReader Class

The XmlReader class is a fast, non-cached, forward-only reader for accessing XML data. This class is abstract.

XmlReader Methods

Name	Parameters	Description
Close()		Closes the reader.
GetAttribute()	index (Integer)	Gets the specified attribute's value by an index.
GetAttribute()	name`(String)	Gets the specified attribute's value.
GetAttribute()	name (String) namespaceURI (String)	Gets an attribute's value by name and namespace URI.
IsStartElement()		Checks if the node is a start tag or an empty element.
IsStartElement()	name (String)	Checks if the specified node is a start tag or an empty element.
IsStartElement()	name (String) namespaceURI (String)	Checks if the specified node is a start tag or an empty element.
LookupNamespace()	prefix (String)	Looks up the namespace prefix of the element's scope.
MoveToAttribute()	index (Integer)	Moves to an attribute by an index.

Name	Parameters	Description
MoveToAttribute()	name (String)	Moves to an attribute by name.
MoveToAttribute()	name (String) namespaceURI (String)	Moves to an attribute with the name and namespace URI specified.
MoveToContent()		Goes to the first content.
MoveToElement()		Goes to the attributes element.
MoveToFirstAttribute()		Goes to the first attribute.
MoveToNextAttribute()		Goes to the next attribute.
Read()		Reads the next node.
ReadAttributeValue()		Reads the attributes value.
ReadElementString()		Reads the element.
ReadElementString()	name (String)	Reads the specified element.
ReadElementString()	name (String) namespaceURI (String)	Reads the element specified with a name and namespace URI.
ReadEndElement()		Makes the reader to go to the next node if the current node is an end tag.
ReadInnerXml()		Reads all the content and markup.
ReadOuterXml()		Reads all the content and markups of the node and its children.
ReadStartElemenet()		Makes the reader to go to the next node if the current node is an element.
ReadStartElement()	name (String)	Makes the reader to go to the next node if the specified name is an element.
ReadStartElement()	name (String) namespaceURI (String)	Makes the reader to go to the next node if the specified name and namespace URI is an element.
ReadString()		Reads the content of the element.
ResolveEntity()		Returns an entity as an XmlNode.
Skipv		Skips the current element.

XmlReader Properties

Name	Type	Description
AttributeCount	Integer	Returns the current node's attributes.
BaseURI	String	Returns the base URI of the node.

Table continued on following page

Name	Type	Description
CanResolveEntity	Boolean	Checks if the parser can parse and resolve entities.
Depth	Integer	Returns the depth of the node.
EOF	Boolean	Indicates if the reader has reached the end of the stream.
HasAttributes	Boolean	Indicates if the node has attributes.
HasValue	Boolean	Checks if the node can have a value.
IsDefault	Boolean	Checks if the attribute is generated from the default value of the DTD or schema.
IsEmptyElement	Boolean	Indicates if the node has no value.
Item	String (Has an index integer parameter)	Returns the value of the attribute specified by an index.
Item	String (Has a name string parameter)	Returns the value of the attribute specified by a name.
Item	String (Has a name string and namespaceURI string parameter)	Returns the value of the attribute specified by a name and a namespace URI.
LocalName	String	Returns the LocalName of the node.
Name	String	Returns the name of the node.
NamespaceURI	String	Returns the namespace URI of the node.
NameTable	XmlNameTable	Returns the XmlNameTable.
NodeType	XmlNodeType	Returns the type of the node.
Prefix	String	Returns the namespace prefix of the node.
QuoteChar	String	Returns a double quote (") character.
ReadState	ReadState	Indicates the state of the reader.
Value	String	Returns the value of the node.
XmlLang	String	Indicates the language of the node.
XmlSpace	XmlSpace	Returns the xml:space value.

The XmlNodeReader Class

The XmlNodeReader class is a fast reader providing non-cached, forward-only access to an XmlNode. It has all the methods and properties of XmlReader, apart from the IsStartElement() method.

The XmlTextReader Class

The XmlTextReader class is a fast reader for accessing XML data; it will not cache any data and reads forward only. It has all the methods and properties of XmlReader, without the IsStartElement() method, as well as:

XmlTextReader Methods

Name	Parameters	Description
GetRemainder()	TextReader	Gets the remainder of the buffered XML.
ReadBase64()	array (Byte())	Reads data containing Base64 data and returns the number of bytes written to the buffer.
	start (Integer)	
	length (Integer)	
ReadBinHex()	array (Byte())	Reads data containing BinHex data and returns the number of bytes written to the buffer.
	start (Integer)	
	length (Integer)	
ReadChars()	array (Byte())	Reads the text content of an element into the buffer. This method can read large streams of text.
	start (Integer)	
	length (Integer)	

XmlTextReader Properties

Name	Type	Description
Encoding	String	The encoding level of the XML document.
LineNumber	Integer	Returns the line number.
LinePosition	Integer	Returns the line position.
Normalization	Boolean	Indicates whitespace normalization.
WhitespaceHandling	WhitespaceHandling	Indicates how whitespace would be handled.
XmlResolver	XmlResolver	Used to resolve DTD references.

The XmlValidatingReader Class

The XmlValidatingReader class is a reader for validating DTD, XDR, and XSD schemas. It has all the methods and properties of XmlReader, as well as:

XmlValidatingReader Properties

Name	Type	Description
Encoding	String	The encoding level of the XML document.
EntityHandling	EntityHandling	Indicates how the reader handles entities.
Reader	XmlReader	Returns an XmlReader.
Schemas	XmlSchemaCollection	Used to return an XmlSchemaCollection to use for validation.
SchemaType	Object	Returns a schema type object.
ValidationType	ValidationType	Returns the type of validation.
WhitespaceHandling	WhitespaceHandling	Indicates how whitespace would be handled.
XmlResolver	XmlResolver	Used to resolve DTD references.

The XmlResolver Class

The XmlResolver class is used to resolve external XML resources such as a DTD schema location reference. It can also be used to process include and import elements that are found in XSL stylesheets or XSD schemas. This class is abstract.

XmlResolver Methods

Name	Parameters	Description
GetEntity()	absoluteUri (Uri)	Used to map a given URI into an Object containing the resource of the URI.
	role (String)	
	objectToReturn (Type)	
ResolveUri()	baseUri (Uri)	Used to resolve the absolute URI from the base and relative URIs.
	relativeUri (Uri)	

The XmlUrlResolver Class

The XmlUrlResolver class is used to resolve external XML resources named by a URI. This class is abstract. It has all the emthods of XmlResolver, as well as:

XmlUrlResolver Properties

Name	Type	Description
Credentials	ICredentials	Used to authenticate web requests

The XmlWriter Class

The XmlWriter Class generates a stream or file containing XML data.

XmlWriter Methods

Name	Parameters	Description
Close()		Closes the stream.
Flush()		Flushes data from the buffer to a stream.
LookupPrefix()	namespaceURI (String)	Returns the prefix that match closest to the given namespace URI.
WriteAttributes()	reader (XmlReader) defaultattribute (Boolean)	Writes out all the attributes from the given XmlReader. If the defualtattribute is true it will also write out the default attributes from the XmlReader.
WriteAttributeString()	name (String) value (String)	Writes out the attribute given by the name and value.
WriteAttributeString()	name (String) namespceURI (String) value (String)	Writes out the attribute given by the name, namespace URI, and value.
WriteAttributeString()	prefix (String) name (String) namespceURI (String) value (String)	Writes out the attribute given by the prefix, name, namespace URI, and value.
WriteBase64()	buffer (Byte) index (Integer) length (Integer)	Encode, binary data to text and saves it to an XML document.

Table continued on following page

Name	Parameters	Description
WriteBinHex()	buffer (Byte) index (Integer) length (Integer)	Encodes binary data to text and saves it to an XML document.
WriteCData()	data (String)	Writes out a CDATA section with the specified data.
WriteCharEntity()	ch (Char)	Generates a hexadecimal character entity of the specified Unicode character.
WriteChars()	buffer (Char()) index (Integer) length (Integer)	Writes large amount of text.
WriteComment()	data (String)	Writes a comment with the specified data.
WriteDocType()	name (String) pubId (String) sysId (String) subset (String)	Writes the DOCTYPE declaration with the given name, public ID, system ID, and subset.
WriteElementString()	name (String) value (String)	Writes an element with a name and a value.
WriteElementString()	name (String) namespaceURI (String) value (String)	Writes an element with a name, namespace URI, and value.
WriteEndAttribute()		Closes the attribute. Use this after Write StartAttribute() to close the attribute.
WriteEndDocument()		Closes an attribute or element, and moves the writer to the start.
WriteEndElement()		Closes an element.
WriteEntityRef()	name (String)	Writes an entity reference.
WriteFullEndElement()		Closes and writes the end tag of an element.
WriteName()	name (String)	Writes a name.
WriteNmToken()	name (String)	Writes a name that is a valid NmToken.

Name	Parameters	Description
WriteNode()	reader (XmlReader)	Reads a node from the reader and copies it to the writer.
	defaultattribute (String)	
WriteProcessingInstruction()	name (String)	Writes a processing instruction.
	text (String)	
WriteQualifiedName()	name (String)	Writes a namespace-qualified name.
	namespaceURI (String)	
WriteRaw()	xml (String)	Writes XML data.
WriteRaw()	buffer (Char())	Writes XML data from a buffer.
	index (Integer)	
	length (Integer)	
WriteStartAttribute()	name (String)	Writes the beginning of an attribute.
	namespaceURI (String)	
WriteStartAttribute()	prefix (String)	Writes the beginning of an attribute with a prefix and a namespace URI.
	namc (String)	
	namespaceURI (String)	
WriteStartDocument()		Writes the XML declaration.
WriteStartDocument()	standalone (Boolean)	Writes the XML declaration with the standalone attribute.
WriteStartElement()	name (String)	Writes the start tag of an element with a given name.
WriteStartElement()	name (String)	Writes the start tag of an element with a given name and namespace URI.
	namespaceURI (String)	
WriteStartElement()	prefix (String)	Writes the start tag of an element with a given prefix, name, and namespace URI.
	name (String)	
	namespaceURI (String)	
WriteString()	text (String)	Writes the given text.
WriteSurrogateCharEntity()	lowChar (Char)	Writes a surrogate character pair.
	hiChar (Char)	
WriteWhitespace()	ws (String)	Writes whitespace.

XmlWriter Properties

Name	Type	Description
WriteState	WriteState	Indicates the state of the writer.
XmlLang	String	Indicates the language of the node.
XmlSpace	XmlSpace	Returns on of the xml:space value.

The XmlTextWriter Class

The XmlTextWriter class generates streams or files containing XML data. It has all the methods and properties of XmlWriter, as well as:

XmlTextWriter Properties

Name	Type	Description
Formatting	Formatting	Indicates the output format.
Indentation	Integer	Works only if the Formatting property is set to Formatting.Indented, and sets or gets the number of indentChars to write for each level in the XML tree.
IndentChar	Char	Which character to use for indenting when the Formatting property is set to Formatting.Indented.
Namespaces	Boolean	Indicates if namespaces are supported.
QuoteChar	Char	Which character to use to quote attribute values.

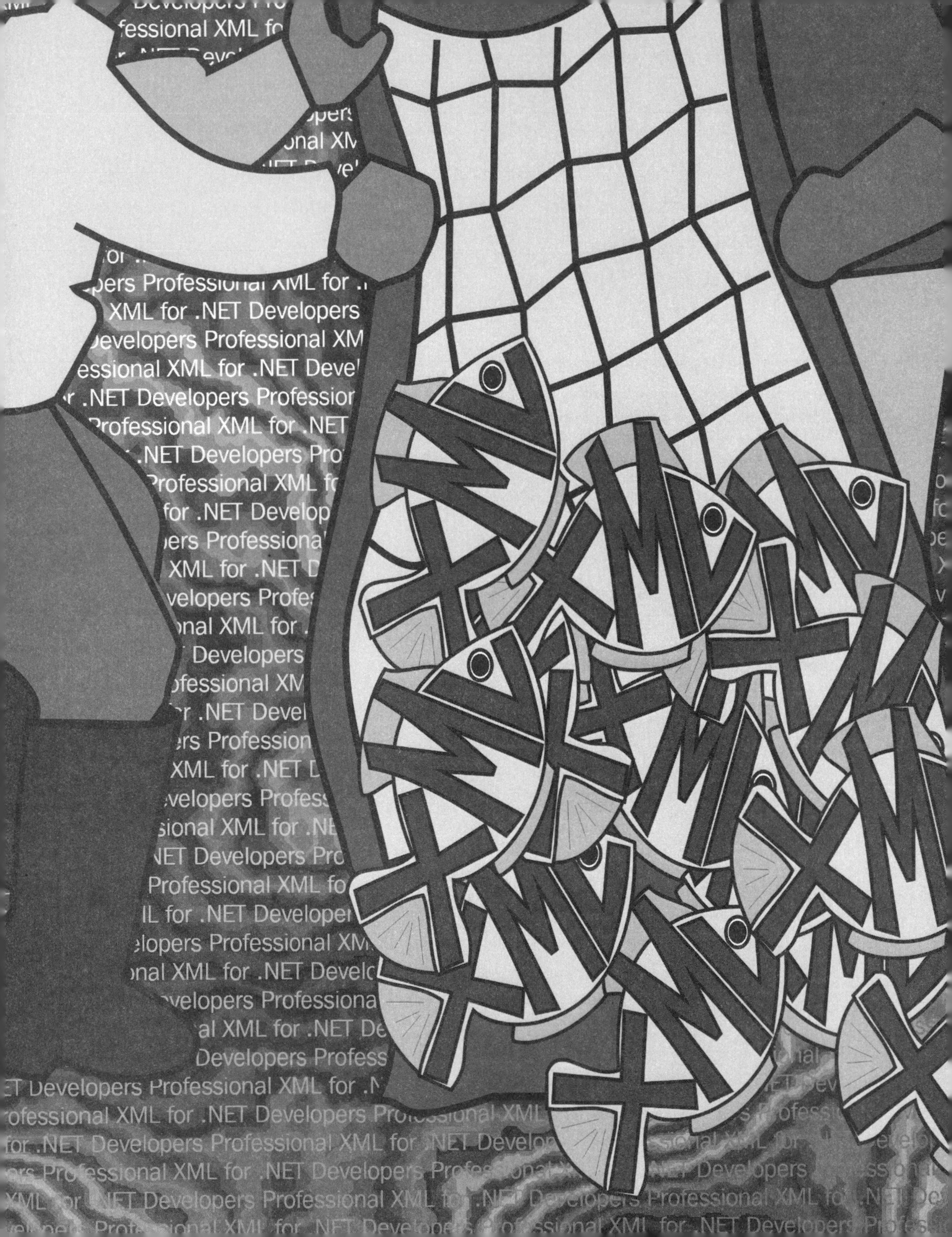
for .NET Developers Professional XML for .NET Developers

B

System.Xml.Xsl and System.Xml.XPath

In this appendix, we will look at the following commonly used namespaces:

❑ **System.Xml.Xsl** – This namespace deals with XSL/T transformations

❑ **System.Xml.XPath** – This namespace contains classes for the XPath parser

You can find more information about namespaces, classes, and related methods and properties, under .Net Framework | Reference | Class Library, *in .Net Framework documentation or Visual Studio .NET documentation.*

System.Xml.Xsl Namespace

The System.Xml.Xsl namespace deals with the XSL/T transformations of an XML document. Let's look at the System.Xml.Xsl classes.

Overview of System.Xml.Xsl Classes

System.Xml.Xsl namespace contains the following classes:

Class	Description
XsltArgumentList	This class contains a list of arguments in the form of XSLT parameters or XSLT extension objects
XsltCompileException	This class is an exception thrown when the processing of XSL transformation fails
XsltContext	This class summarizes the current XSLT execution context allowing XPath to resolve functions, parameters, and namespaces within XPath expressions
XsltException	This class contains information about the last exception thrown while processing an XSL transform
XslTransform	This class is used to transform XML data with an XSLT document

The XsltArgumentList Class

The XsltArgumentList class is a list of arguments containing XSLT parameters or XSLT extension objects.

XsltArgumentList Methods

Name	Parameters	Description
AddExtensionObject()	namespaceUri (String) extension (Object)	Adds a new object to the list with the namespace URI as a key
AddParam()	name (String) namespaceURI (String) parameter (Object)	Adds the specified parameter to the list
Clear()		Removes all objects from the list
GetExtensionObject()	namespaceUri (String)	Gets an object by the given namespace URI
GetParam()	name (String) namespaceUri (String)	Returns the specified parameter
RemoveExtensionObject()	namespaceUri (String)	Removes the object with the specified namespace URI as a key from the list
RemoveParam()	name (String) namespaceUri (String)	Removes the specified parameter from the list

The XsltContext Class

The abstract class `XsltContext` encapsulates the current XSLT execution context.

XsltContext Methods

Name	Parameters	Description
AddNamespace()	prefix (String) namespaceUri(String)	Adds a namespace
GetEnumerator()		Used to support the "for-each" statement, so we can iteration over the collection of namespaces
HasNamespace()	prefix (String)	Checks if the prefix has a namespace
LookupNamespace()	prefix (String)	Lookups the namespace URI for the prefix
LookupPrefix()	namespaceUri (String)	Lookups the prefix for the namespace URI
PopScope()		Removes namespaces from the stack
PreserveWhitespace()	node (XPathNavigator)	Checked if the whitespace should be preserved or stripped for the context
PushScope()		Adds namespaces to the stack
RemoveNamespace()	prefix (String) namespaceUri (String)	Removes the given namespace
ResolveFunction()	prefix (String) name (String) argTypes (XpathResultType())	Resolves the specified function and returns an `IXsltContextFunction()` that can be used at execution time to get the return value of the function
ResolveVariable()	prefix (String) name (String)	Resolves the specified variable and returns an `IXsltContext Variable()` that can be used at execution time to get the value of the variable

XsltContext Properties

Name	Type	Description
DefaultNamespace	String	Returns the namespace URI
NameTable	XmlNameTable	Gets the XmlNameTable for this object
Whitespace	Boolean	Indicates if there is any need to evaluate whitespace nodes

The XsltException Class

The XsltException class contains information about the exception that is thrown when the XSL transformation fails.

XsltException Methods

Name	Parameters	Description
GetBaseException()		Gets the base exception
GetObjectData()	info (SerializationInfo) context (StreamingContext)	Sets the Serialization object with exception information
ToString()		Returns the full error message

XsltException Properties

Name	Type	Description
HelpLink	String	Returns the link to the help file of this exception or set a new link
InnerException	Exception	Returns the inner exception if there is any
LineNumber	Integer	The line number where the error occurred in the document
LinePosition	Integer	The line position where the error occurred in the document
Source	String	Indicates the name of the application that threw an exception
SourceUri	String	Returns the path to the stylesheet document
StackTrace	String	Returns the location of the code where the error occurred
TargetSite	MethodBase	The method that throws the exception

The XsltCompileException Class

The XsltCompileException class is thrown when the processing of XSL transformation fails. It has all the properties and methods of the XsltException class, as well as:

XsltCompileException Properties

Name	Type	Description
Message	String	The error message

The XslTransform Class

The XslTransform class is used to transform XML data with an XSLT document.

XslTransform Methods

Name	Parameters	Description
Load()	stylesheet (IXPathNavigable)	Loads the XSLT document with an XmlNode, XmlDocument, or XPathDocument containing XSLT data
Load()	url (String)	Loads the XSLT document from a given URL.
Load()	stylesheet (XmlReader)	Loads the XSLT document from a given XmlReader
Load()	stylesheet (XPathNavigator)	Loads the XSLT document from a given XPathNavigator
Load()	url (String) resolver (XmlResolver)	Loads the XSLT document from a given URL and use the resolver to load any included document found in the XSLT document
Load()	stylesheet (IXPathNavigable) resolver (XmlResolver)	Loads the XSLT document from the given IXPathNavigable and uses the resolver to load any included document found in the XSLT document
Load()	stylesheet (XmlReader) resolver (XmlResolver)	Loads the XSLT document from a given XmlReader and uses the resolver to load any included document found in the XSLT document
Load()	stylesheet (XPathNavigator) resolver (XmlResolver)	Loads the XSLT document from the given XPathNavigator and uses the resolver to load any included document found in the XSLT document
Transform()	input (IXPathNavigable) args (XsltArgumentList)	Transforms the XML data from the given IXPathNavigable and the args parameter and returns the result with an XmlReader

Table continued on following page

Name	Parameters	Description
Transform()	inputfile (String) outputfile (String)	Transforms the XML data from a given file and saves the result to a given outputfile
Transform()	input (XmlPathNavigator) args (XsltArgumentList)	Transforms the XML data from the given XmlPathNavigator and the args parameter and returns the result with an XmlReader
Transform()	input (IXPathNavigable) args (XsltArgumentList) output (Stream)	Transforms the XML data from the given IXPathNavigable and the args parameter and returns the result to a specified Stream
Transform()	input (IXPathNavigable) args (XsltArgumentList) output (TextWriter)	Transforms the XML data from the given IXPathNavigable and the args parameter and returns the result to a specified TextWriter
Transform()	input (IXPathNavigable) args (XsltArgumentList) output (XmlWriter)	Transforms the XML data from the given IXPathNavigable and the args parameter and returns the result to a specified XmlWriter
Transform()	input (XPathNavigator) args (XsltArgumentList) output (Stream)	Transforms the XML data from the given XPathNavigator and the args parameter and returns the result to a specified Stream
Transform()	input (XPathNavigator) args (XsltArgumentList) output (TextWriter)	Transforms the XML data from the given XPathNavigator and the args parameter and returns the result to a specified TextWriter
Transform()	input (XPathNavigator) args (XsltArgumentList) output (XmlWriter)	Transforms the XML data from the given XPathNavigator and the args parameter and returns the result to a specified XmlWriter

The System.Xml.XPath Namespace

The System.Xml.XPath namespace contains the XPath parser and has classes for reading data with XPath expressions.

Overview of System.Xml.XPath Classes

Class	Description
XPathDocument	This class is like a cache for XML documents. It uses XSLT to processing the XML document.
XPathException	Contains information about the exception that will be thrown when the processing of an XPath expression fails.
XPathExpression	Can be used to encapsulate a compiled XPath expression.
XPathNavigator	Reads data and can be used to create XPath queries.
XPathNodeIterator	Uses to iterate over selected nodes.

The XPathDocument Class

The XPathDocument class is a cache for XML documents. This class use XSLT to process the XML document. The constructor of this class loads the document into the cache.

XPathDocument Methods

Name	Parameters	Description
CreateNavigator()		Returns an XPathNavigator for this document

The XPathException Class

The XPathException class is thrown while the processing of an XPath expression fails.

XPathException Methods

Name	Parameters	Description
GetBaseException()		Gets the base exception
GetObjectData()	info (SerializationInfo)	Sets the Serialization object with exception information
	context (StreamingContext)	
ToString()		Returns the full error message

XPathException Properties

Name	Type	Description
HelpLink	String	Returns the link to the help file of this exception or sets a new link
InnerException	Exception	Returns the inner exception if there is any
Message	String	The error message
Source	String	Indicate the name of the application that thrown an exception
StackTrace	String	Returns the location of the code where the error occurred
TargetSite	MethodBase	The method that throw the exception

The XPathExpression Class

The XPathExpression class is used to encapsulate a compiled XPath expression. This class is abstract.

XPathExpression Methods

Name	Parameters	Description
AddSort()	expression (Object) comparer (IComparer)	Used to sort the selected nodes by the XPath expression
AddSort()	expression (Object) order (XmlSortOrder) caseOrder (XmlCaseOrder) lang (String) dataType (XmlDataType)	Used to sort the selected nodes by the XPath expression after the specified XmlSortOrder, language, upper/lower case letters, data types
Clone()		Used to clone the XPath expression
SetContext()	nsmg (XmlNamespaceManager)	Sets the XmlNamespaceManager for resolving namespaces

XPathExpression Properties

Name	Type	Description
Expression	String	Returns an XPath expression
ReturnType	XPathResultType	Returns the type of the XPath expression's result

The XPathNavigator Class

The abstact class XPathNavigator is used to read data and to create XPath queries. This class is abstract.

XPathNavigator Methods

Name	Parameters	Description
Clone()		Returns and duplicates an XPathNavigator for this node
ComparePosition()	navigator (XPathNavigator)	Compares this nodes position with the given navigators position
Compile()	xpath (String)	Compiles the given XPath into an XPathExpression
Evaluate()	xpath (String)	Evaluates the given XPath
Evaluate()	expression (XPathExpression)	Evaluates the given XPathExpression
Evaluate()	expression (XPathExpression) context (XpathNodeIterator)	Evaluates the given XPathExpression with the given context
GetAttribute()	name (String) namespaceUri (String)	Returns the value of the specified attribute
GetNamespace()	name (String)	Returns the value of the specified namespace node
IsDescendant()	navigator (XPathNavigator)	Checks if the specified navigator is a descendant of the current XPathNavigator
IsSamePosition()	navigator (XPathNavigator)	Checks if the current XPath Navigator is at the same position as the given XPathNavigator
Matches()	xpath (String)	Checks if the specified XPath expression matches the current node

Table continued on following page

Name	Parameters	Description
Matches()	expression (XPathExpression)	Checks if the specified XPathExpression matches the current node.
MoveTo()	navigator (XPathNavigator)	Moves the current navigator to the same position as the specified XPathNavigator.
MoveToAttribute()	name (String) namespaceUri (String)	Moves to the specified attribute.
MoveToFirst()		Moves to the first sibling of the current node.
MoveToFirstAttribute()		Moves to the first attribute.
MoveToFirstChild()		Moves to the first child of this node.
MoveToFirstNamespace()		Moves to the first namespace node of the current element.
MoveToNext()		Moves to the next sibling.
MoveToNextAttribute()		Moves to the next attribute.
MoveToNextNamespace()		Moves to the next namespace.
MoveToParent()		Moves to the parent of this node.
MoveToPrevious()		Moves to the previous sibling.
MoveToRoot()		Moves to the root node of this node.
Select()	xpath (String)	Select a node using the XPath expression.
Select()	expression (XPathExpression)	Select a node using the XPathExpression.
SelectAncestors()	type (XpathNodeType) self (Boolean)	Selects all the ancestor element of this node with the specified type. The self parameter indicates if this node would be included in the selection.
SelectAncestors()	name (String) namespaceUri (String) self (Boolean)	Selects all the ancestor elements of this node with the specified name and namespace URI. The self parameter indicates if this node would be included in the selection.

Name	Parameters	Description
SelectChildren()	node (XPathNodeType)	Selects all the child element nodes of this node that match the specified node type.
SelectChildren()	name (String) namespaceUri (String)	Selects all the child element nodes of this node with the given name and namespace URI.
SelectDescendants()	type (XpathNodeType) self (Boolean)	Selects all the descendant element of this node with the specified type. The self parameter indicates if this node would be included in the selection.
SelectDescendants()	name (String) namespaceUri (String) self (Boolean)	Selects all the descendant element of this node with the specified name and namespace URI. The self parameter indicates if this node would be included in the selection.

XPathNavigator Properties

Name	Type	Description
BaseURI	String	Returns the base URI if this node
HasAttributes	Boolean	Checks if this node has any attributes
HasChildren	Boolean	Checks if this node has any children
IsEmptyElement	Boolean	Checks if the element has no value
LocalName	String	Returns the name of this node without the namespace prefix
Name	String	Returns the name of this node
NamespaceUri	String	Returns the namespace URI of this node
NameTable	XmlNameTable	Returns the associated XmlNameTable
NodeType	XmlPathNodeType	Returns the type of the node
Prefix	String	Returns the prefix of the associated node
Value	String	Returns the value of the node
XmlLang	String	Indicates the language of the node

The XPathNodeIterator Class

The XPathNodeIterator class is used to iterate over selected nodes. This class is abstract.

XPathNodeIterator Methods

Name	Parameters	Description
Clone		Returns a new and duplicated XPathNodeIterator

XPathNodeIterator Properties

Name	Type	Description
Count	Integer	Gets the number of nodes
Current	XPathNavigator	Returns an XPathNavigator for this class
CurrentPosition	Integer	Returns the index of this node's position

C
.NET Glossary

.NET Enterprise Servers: The .NET Enterprise Servers are Microsoft's comprehensive family of server applications designed to help customers build, deploy, and manage scalable, integrated, web-based solutions and services. The core .NET Enterprise Servers include SQL Server 2000, Exchange 2000 Server, BizTalk Server 2000, Commerce Server 2000, Application Center 2000, Mobile Information 2001 Server, Host Integration Server 2000, and Internet Security and Acceleration Server 2000.

.NET Framework: The term .NET Framework refers to the group of technologies that form the development foundation for the Microsoft .NET platform. It has three main components: the Common Language Runtime, the .NET Framework class library, and ASP.NET.

.NET Framework Class Library: The .NET Framework Class Library is a rich set of classes (abstract and concrete), interfaces, and value types useful to perform a huge range of tasks and develop applications ranging from command-line or GUI applications to highly scalable distributed applications or Web Services.

.NET Runtime: The .NET Runtime, also known as the **Common Language Runtime** or **CLR,** is the core component of .NET Framework that actually manages code and provides services like memory management, thread management, security management, code verification and compilation, and other system services.

.NET Serialization: Serialization is the process of taking an object graph, turning it into an XML document, either to persist it or to transmit it. The System.Runtime.Serialization class assumes that the Common Language Runtime (CLR) type system is the dominant type system, and can take any type in the CLR and map in it to the XML Schema type system with full fidelity. Also see *XML Serialization*.

Abstract Base Classes: An abstract base class is a class that declares one or more pure virtual functions and thus cannot be instantiated. Abstract base classes are similar to interfaces, which are also used to describe a set of methods and properties that inherited classes must implement; however, there are two logical differences. Abstract base classes are well suited for describing 'IS-A' specialization, while interfaces are best to express 'CAN-DO'; and interfaces are immutable, once made public, you should not change them, however, you can add methods to classes without breaking derived classes.

Access modifiers: Also known as protection modifiers, these are used to specify how visible, or accessible a given member is, to the code outside its own class. For instance, C# defines four access modifiers that you can use while designing classes of type public, protected, private, and internal.

Accessors: Also known as accessor methods, they are used in class design for defining methods whose job is to retrieve and set class's fields (properties). The get/set accessor methods hide the implementation of the property.

ADO.NET: ADO.NET (formerly called ADO+) is an evolutionary improvement to ADO, designed based on an entirely new programming model for data access, built upon the .NET Framework, and provides highly integrated support for XML, and the model that is best suited for both 2-tier (connected) and n-tier (disconnected) applications.

Application Domains: Application Domains (AppDomains) are an important innovation with .NET that are designed to facilitate a huge scalability and reliability benefit. With Application Domains, multiple components can safely run in a single process. You can run several application domains in a single process with the same level of isolation that would exist in separate processes, but without incurring the additional overhead of making cross-process calls or switching between processes. Application domains prevent code running in one application domain from affecting other domains by preventing types in one domain from seeing and calling types in other domains.

ASP.NET: ASP.NET is an integral part of the .NET Framework. It introduces a whole new way of programming web applications. ASP.NET has been written from the ground up to provide the best possible web development framework.

Assembly: An assembly acts as the smallest distribution unit for component code in the .NET Framework and it is the primary building block of a .NET application. An assembly is a logical collection of one or more `.EXE` or `.DLL` files containing application's code, resources, and metadata.

Assembly Cache: This is the area of disk used for 'side-by-side' storage of assemblies. There are two parts to the cache – the Global Assembly Cache contains assemblies that are explicitly installed to be shared among many applications on the computer; and the Download Cache stores code downloaded from Internet or intranet sites, isolated to the application that triggered the download so that code downloaded on behalf of one application/page does not impact on other applications.

Attributes: An attribute (also known as **Annotation**) is a keyword-like descriptive declaration that can be applied to an item in the code such as a method or class, or even an individual argument to a method, and which supplies extra information about that item. Attributes can be used as complier flags to tell the complier how to handle the compilation of the type. Attributes are saved with the metadata of a .NET Framework file and can be used to describe code to the runtime or to affect application behavior at run time.

Boxing: The conversion of a value type instance to an object. When boxing occurs, the contents of a value type are copied from the stack into memory allocated on the managed heap.

C#: C# (pronounced C Sharp) is the new language for .NET development. It is an evolution of C and C++, and uses many C++ features in the areas of statements, expressions, and operators. C# introduces considerable improvement and innovations in areas such as type safety, versioning, events, and garbage collection, and provides access to the common API styles – .NET Framework, COM, Automation, and C-style APIs. It also supports 'unsafe' mode, where you can use pointers to manipulate memory that is not under the control of the garbage collector.

CCW: COM Callable Wrapper refers to a proxy object generated by the runtime so that existing COM applications can use managed classes, including .NET Framework classes, transparently.

Channels: In .NET Remoting architecture, a channel is used to communicate between a .NET client and a server. The .NET framework ships with channel classes that communicate using TCP or HTTP. We can create custom channels for other protocols.

CLR: The **Common Language Runtime** is a core component of .NET Framework that actually manages code and provides services such as cross-language integration, code access security, object lifetime management, and debugging and profiling support.

CLS: The **Common Language Specification** ensures language interoperability. It is a set of minimum standards laid down, which all compliers targeting .NET must support.

Code Access Security: It is a feature of .NET that the runtime manages code dependent on our trust level on it. If the runtime trusts the code enough to allow it to run, it will begin executing the code. Depending on the permissions provided to the assembly however, it may run within a restricted environment. If the code is not trusted enough to run, or if it runs but then attempts to perform an action for which it does not have the relevant permissions, a security exception is thrown.

Code-behind Programming: This refers to the ability to put the `.aspx` page logic into the external base type, which in turn is derived from `System.Web.UI.Page` object, and also to bind HTML elements on the page to fields in the base type.

COFF: **Common Object File Format** is a format in 32-bit programming for executable (image) and object files that is portable across platforms. The Microsoft implementation is called portable executable (PE) file format.

CTS: **Common Type System** is a specification that determines how the runtime defines, uses, and manages types. Everything in CTS is an object, and all objects derive from a single base class (`System.Object`) defined as part of CTS.

DataSet: The `DataSet` provides the basis for disconnected storage and manipulation of relational data. A `DataSet` is a self-contained in-memory database that consists of tables, relations, and constraints. We can create a `DataSet` from existing data in the database, or fill it directly using code. `DataSet` also has methods to both read and write XML. As opposed to ADO `Recordset`, which can consume and produce a single XML format based on a single schema, the `DataSet` can read and write XML corresponding to any schema.

Delegates: Delegates are .NET Framework's version of callback methods. The delegate indicates the signature of a callback method. In a way, a delegate is very much like a C/C++ *typedef* that represents the address of a function.

DiffGrams: A DiffGram is an XML document that contains the before and after data of an edit session, including any combinations of data changes, additions, and deletions. For instance, a DiffGram can be used as an audit trail or for a commit/rollback process.

Disco: The Discovery Protocol specification defines a process of locating and interrogating Web Service descriptions. The specification defines a discovery document format (based on XML) and a protocol for retrieving the discovery document, enabling developers to discover services at a known URL.

DLL Hell: DLL Hell refers to the most common versioning problem on the Microsoft platforms. In other words, it refers to the set of problems caused when multiple applications attempt to share a common component like a dynamic-link library (DLL) or a Component Object Model (COM) class. In the most typical case, one application will install a new version of the shared component that is not backward-compatible with the version already on the machine. Although the application that has just been installed works fine, existing applications that depended on a previous version of the shared component might no longer work. With .NET, this is no longer an issue; .NET has completely revamped the way that code is shared between applications, introducing the concept of the assembly.

EconoJIT: EconoJIT (Just-in-Time) compiler is targeted at high-speed conversion of Intermediate Language (IL) to managed native code. It allows for caching of the generated native code; however, the output code isn't as optimized as the code produced by the main JIT. The advantage of this fast code generation strategy pays off when memory is constrained. You can fit even large IL programs into this code cache by permanently discarding unused jitted code. Since compiling is fast, execution speed is still rather high.

Enum: An enumeration is a user-defined integer (signed or unsigned) type that inherits from `System.Enum`. When we declare an enumeration, we specify a set of acceptable values that instances of that enumeration can contain. Not only that, but we can give the values user-friendly names. If, somewhere in our code, we attempt to assign a value that is not in the acceptable set of an instance of that enumeration, the complier will flag an error.

Event: An event is an action that you can respond to, or 'handle', in code. In .NET terms, events are actually a special form of delegates.

GC: **Garbage Collection** refers to the means by which the .NET runtime cleans up memory that is no longer needed, freeing applications from having to take responsibility for this. The .NET Framework's garbage collector manages the allocation and release of memory for your application.

IL: When the managed code is complied in the .NET environment, the complier emits **Intermediate Language**, and the .NET runtime (CLR) handles the final stage of compilation just before the code is actually executed. It's important to remember that the Intermediate Language code gets complied, not interpreted, to native machine code.

JIT Compilers: The Just-in-Time complier converts Intermediate Language into machine code at the point when the code is required at run time.

JScript .NET: JScript .NET, the .NET update for today's JScript, is a full .NET language that has been completely rewritten in C#, and is fully complied. It supports types and inheritance.

Managed Code: Any code that is designed to run within the .NET environment is referred to as managed code. Managed code offers several benefits including security (role-based and code-based), memory management (garbage collection), support for application domains, and so on.

Manifest: This is the area of an assembly that contains metadata.

Mobile Internet Toolkit: This is an extension to the controls available in the .NET Framework that adds support for mobile devices. It's a collection of controls that, when placed in ASP.NET pages, will vary the output to HTML or WML depending upon the device accessing the page.

MSIL: Microsoft Intermediate Language. For Intermediate Language, see *IL*.

Namespaces: Namespaces are used mainly for two purposes – to avoid name clashes between classes, and to organize related classes and other types. Namespace is a logical grouping of related types. If a namespace is not explicitly supplied for the types that you define, then they will be added to a nameless global namespace.

Private Assembly: An assembly that is used by only one application. A private assembly is deployed into the directory structure of the application that uses it.

RCW: The term **Runtime Callable Wrappers** refers to the proxy that gets generated when a .NET client accesses a COM component. Its primary function is to marshal calls between a .NET client and a COM object.

Reflection: Reflection is a generic term that covers various .NET base classes that allow you to find out information about the types in your programs or in other assemblies, and also to read other metadata from assembly manifests. You can use reflection to dynamically create an instance of a type, bind the type to an existing object, or get the type from an existing object. You can then invoke the type's methods or access its fields and properties.

Remoting: In simple words, .NET Remoting is a replacement for DCOM. .NET Remoting can be used for accessing objects in another application domain residing in same process, in another process, or on another system.

Satellite Assemblies: Satellite assemblies are used in applications to support language-dependent strings. These assemblies hold only resources and no code.

Shared Assemblies: The assemblies installed in the Global Assembly Cache (GAC) are shared by all applications. Hence, they must have a strong name (signed by the publisher) to uniquely identify the assembly.

Strong Names: In order to avoid risk of name collisions, shared assemblies are given a name that is based on private key cryptography, known as a Strong Name, which is guaranteed to be unique, and must be quoted by applications that wish to reference a shared assembly. The Framework provides a strong name utility (sn) that can be used to create a strong name.

Typed DataSet: A typed `DataSet` is a class that derives from a `DataSet`. As such, it inherits all of the methods, events, and properties of a `DataSet`. Additionally, a typed `DataSet` provides strongly typed methods, events, and properties. In practice, this means you can access tables and columns by name, instead of using collection-based methods. Besides the improved readability of the code, a typed `DataSet` also allows the compiler to automatically complete lines as you type. Additionally, the strongly typed `DataSet` provides access to values as the correct strongly typed value at compile time. With a strongly typed `DataSet`, type mismatch errors are caught when the code is compiled rather than at run time.

UDDI: The UDDI (Universal Description, Discovery, and Integration) specifications define a standard way to publish and discover information about Web Services.

Unboxing: Unboxing is the term used to describe the conversion of an object instance (reference type) to a value type.

Unmanaged code: Code that simply runs on Windows, outside .NET is referred to as unmanaged code and is created without regard for the conventions and requirements of the runtime. Unmanaged code executes in the Common Language Runtime environment with minimal services (for example, no garbage collection, limited debugging, and so on).

User Server Controls: A user-authored server control enables an ASP.NET page to be reused as a server control. An ASP.NET user control is authored declaratively and persisted as a text file with an .ascx extension. The ASP.NET page framework compiles a user control on the fly to a class that derives from System.Web.UI.UserControl. It's also possible to define properties and methods for user server controls.

VB .NET: Visual Basic .NET is a complete revamp of yesterday's Visual Basic, to make it a powerful object-oriented language. Its new features include inheritance, interfaces, and overloading, among others. It supports structured exception handling, and custom attributes. In addition, VB .NET now supports multithreading, the ability to assign individual tasks to separate processing threads.

Web Forms: The ASP.NET page framework, which supports server-side controls that render HTML user interface on Web browsers.

Web Service: A Web Service in it simplest form is a new way to perform a remote method call over HTTP using XML and SOAP. It extends the distributed-application example from the enterprise to the Internet.

WSDL: Web Services Description Language is a W3C Specification, used to describe Web Services. A .wsdl file is an XML document written using WSDL XML vocabulary. It defines how a Web Service behaves and instructs clients as to how to interact with the service.

XCopy Deployment: All you need to deploy an application is to simply copy all of the assemblies that make up the application to a directory on the disk. This is known as XCopy Deployment, since the only tool required to deploy the files to disk is the XCopy Console Command.

XML Serialization: This is the process of taking an object graph, turning it into an XML document, either to persist it or to transmit it. The System.Xml.Serialization class assumes that the XML Schema type system is the dominant type system, and that there is an XSD complex type for each Common Language Runtime struct and class.

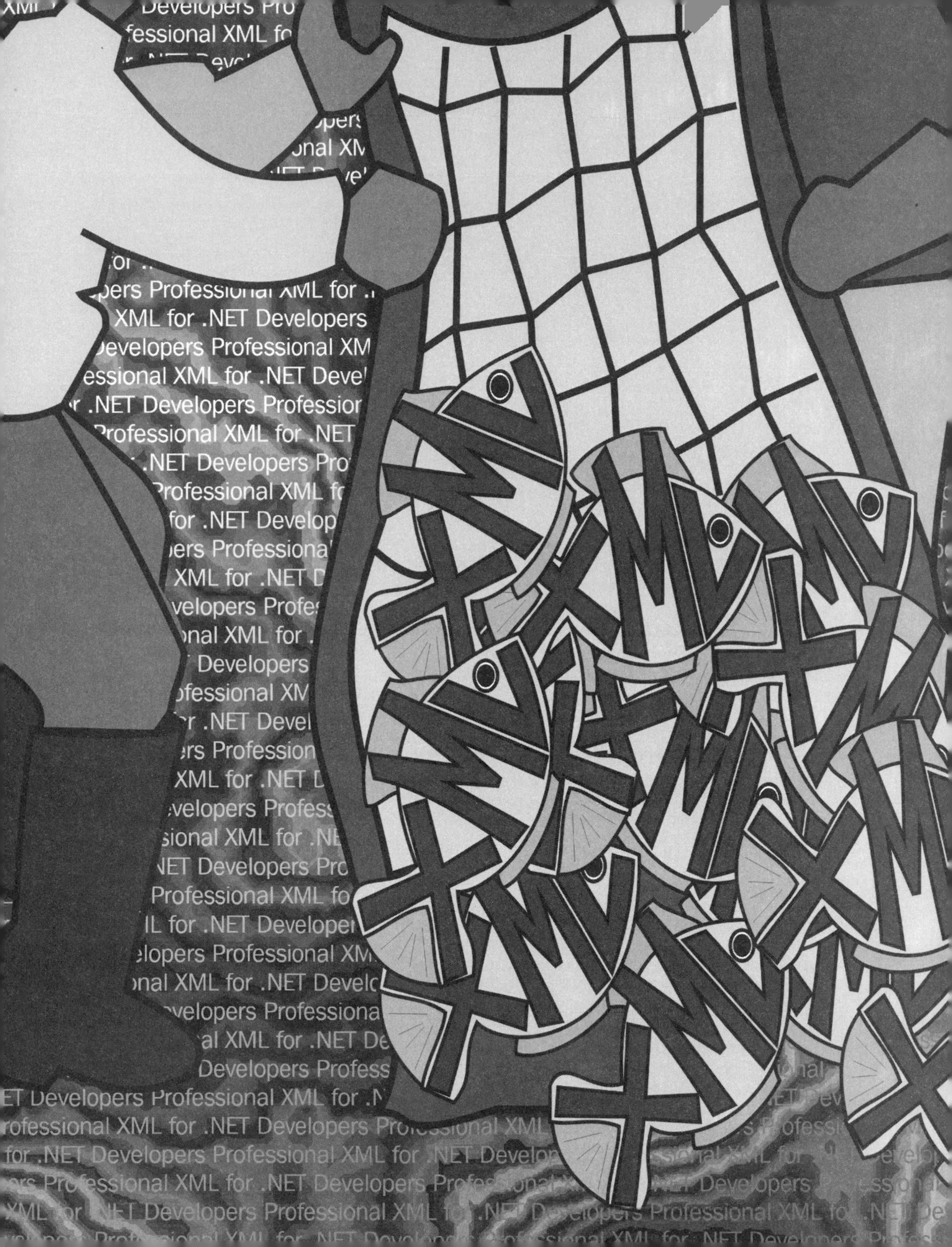
Professional XML for .NET Developers

D

Resources

Web Sites

The examples from this book are available for download from:
http://www.wrox.com

The Programmer's Resource Centre for various technologies:
http://www.p2p.wrox.com

A community web site providing articles and solutions by programmers on ASP and related technologies:
http://www.ASPToday.com

A community web site providing fast, effective solutions and in-depth analysis about C#:
http://www.CSharpToady.com

Books

For further information about the topics covered in this book, we recommend the following books, also published by Wrox Press:

Professional .NET Framework, ISBN 1-861005-56-3

Beginning C#, ISBN 1-861004-98-2

Professional C#, ISBN 1-861004-99-0

Beginning Visual Basic .NET, ISBN 1-861004-96-6

Professional VB .NET, ISBN 1-861004-97-4

Professional ASP.NET, ISBN 1-861004-88-5

ADO.NET Programmer's Reference, ISBN 1-861005-58-X

Professional XML 2nd Edition, ISBN 1-861005-05-9

Professional XML Schemas, ISBN 1-861005-47-4

XSLT Programmer's Reference 2nd Edition, ISBN 1-861005-06-7

Professional XML Web Services, ISBN 1-861005-09-1

Professional SQL Server 2000 XML, ISBN 1-861005-46-6

Professional ASP XML, ISBN 1-861004-02-8

Instant UML, ISBN 1-861000-87-1

VB6 UML Design and Development, ISBN 1-861002-51-3

Professional Visual Basic Project Management, ISBN 1-861002-93-9

Technical Articles and Reports

More information on SOAP can be found at:
http://www.develop.com/soap/

More information on Extensible Markup Language:
http://www.oasis-open.org/cover/xml.html

A nice review of MSXML can be found at:
http://www.perfectxml.com/msxml.asp

Specifications

Simple Object Access Protocol 1.1:
http://www.w3c.org/TR/SOAP/

XML Schemas Part 0: Primer:
http://www.w3.org/TR/xmlschema-0/

XML Schemas Part 1: Structures:
http://www.w3.org/TR/xmlschema-1/

XML Schemas Part 2: Datatypes:
http://www.w3.org/TR/xmlschema-2/

XSL Transformations 1.0:
http://www.w3.org/TR/xslt

Web Services Description Language 1.1:
http://www.w3.org/TR/wsdl

Suitably succinct specification of Minimal XML:
http://www.docuverse.com/smldev/minxml.html

Other Web Sites

W3C XML page:
http://www.w3.org/XML/

Home page for Microsoft .NET:
http://www.microsoft.com/net/default.asp

Home Page for Microsoft Visual Studio .NET:
http://msdn.microsoft.com/vstudio/nextgen/default.asp

Microsoft Visio:
http://www.microsoft.com/office/visio/

Downloads page for Microsoft tools, add-ons, service packs, product updates, and beta and preview releases:
http://msdn.microsoft.com/downloads/

MSXML 4.0 Release: Microsoft XML Core Services component (a.k.a. MSXML Parser) and SDK:
http://www.microsoft.com/downloads/release.asp?ReleaseID=33037

Microsoft Mobile Internet Toolkit for .NET release candidate:
http://msdn.microsoft.com/downloads/default.asp?url=/code/sample.asp?url=/msdn-
files/027/001/516/msdncompositedoc.xml&frame=true

UDDI project:
http://www.uddi.org/

Microsoft SQL Server home page:
http://www.microsoft.com/sql/default.asp

Downloads and trial software for Microsoft SQL Server:
http://www.microsoft.com/sql/downloads/default.asp

Index

A Guide to the Index

The index is arranged hierarchically, in alphabetical order, with symbols preceding the letter A. Most second-level entries and many third-level entries also occur as first-level entries. This is to ensure that users will find the information they require however they choose to search for it.

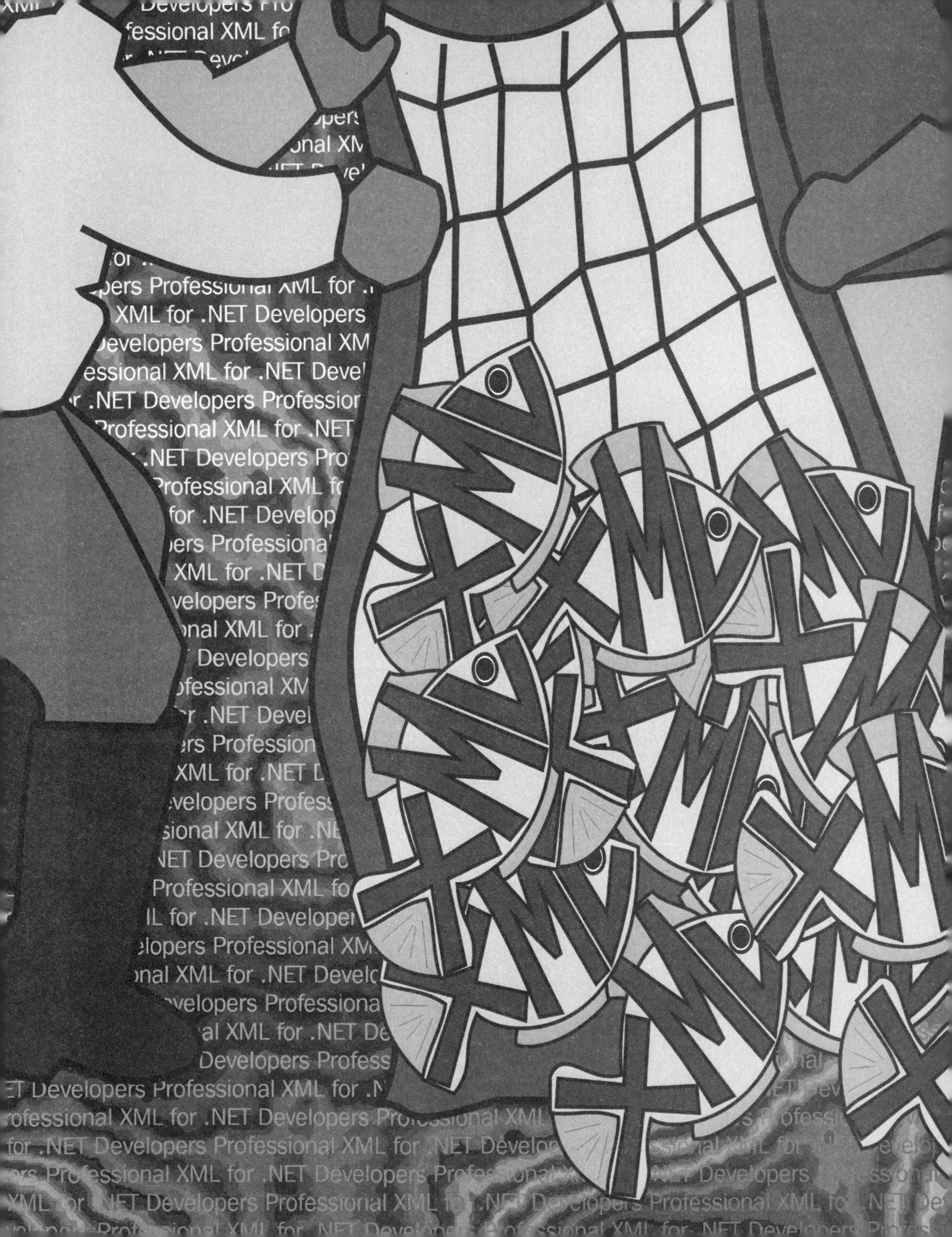

wrox

Programmer to Programmer™

Wrox writes books for you. Any suggestions, or ideas about how you want information given in your ideal book will be studied by our team. Your comments are always valued at Wrox.

Free phone in USA 800-USE-WROX
Fax (312) 893 8001

UK Tel.: (0121) 687 4100   Fax: (0121) 687 4101

Professional XML for .NET Developers – Registration Card

Name _____

Address _____

_____

_____

City _____ State/Region _____

Country _____ Postcode/Zip _____

E-Mail _____

Occupation _____

How did you hear about this book?

☐ Book review (name) _____

☐ Advertisement (name) _____

☐ Recommendation _____

☐ Catalog _____

☐ Other _____

Where did you buy this book?

☐ Bookstore (name) _____ City _____

☐ Computer store (name) _____

☐ Mail order _____

☐ Other _____

What influenced you in the purchase of this book?

☐ Cover Design   ☐ Contents   ☐ Other (please specify):

How did you rate the overall content of this book?

☐ Excellent   ☐ Good   ☐ Average   ☐ Poor

What did you find most useful about this book? _____

_____

What did you find least useful about this book? _____

_____

Please add any additional comments. _____

_____

What other subjects will you buy a computer book on soon?

_____

What is the best computer book you have used this year?

_____

Note: This information will only be used to keep you updated about new Wrox Press titles and will not be used for any other purpose or passed to any other third party.

wrox

Programmer to Programmer™

Note: If you post the bounce back card below in the UK, please send it to:

Wrox Press Limited, Arden House, 1102 Warwick Road,
Acocks Green, Birmingham B27 6HB. UK.

Computer Book Publishers